GLOBAL
MEGATRENDS
AND AVIATION

GLOBAL MEGATRENDS AND AVIATION

THE PATH TO FUTURE-WISE ORGANIZATIONS

To Lewis Harper,
with my compliments!

Aug. 5, 2019

Pierre Coutu, Ed.D., FRAeS
In Collaboration

ASI INSTITUTE
A DIVISION OF AVIATION STRATEGIES INTERNATIONAL

Library and Archives Canada Cataloguing-in-Publication

Title: Global megatrends and aviation: the path to future-wise organizations / Pierre Coutu.

Names: Coutu, Pierre, author.
Description: Includes index.

Identifiers: Canadiana (print) 20190063467 | Canadiana (ebook) 20190063513 |
ISBN 9781999007706 (softcover) | ISBN 9781999007720 (hardcover) | ISBN 9781999007713 (PDF)

ISBN 978-1-9990077-2-0

Subjects: LCSH: Airlines – Forecasting. | LCSH: Aeronautics, Commercial – Forecasting. |
LCSH: Airports – Forecasting. | LCSH: Aircraft industry – Forecasting. |
LCSH: Airlines – Management. | LCSH: Aeronautics, Commercial – Management. |
LCSH: Airports – Management. | LCSH: Aircraft industry – Management. Classification:
LCC HE9780 .C68 2019 | DDC 387.701/12 – dc23

Email: *megatrends@asi-institute.aero*
Web: *megatrends.asi-institute.aero*

ASI Institute
c/o Aviation Strategies International
440 René-Lévesque Blvd West, Suite 1202
Montréal (Québec) H2Z 1V7
Canada

www.aviationstrategies.aero

To our families and friends,
and the next generation of aviation leaders.

ABOUT THE AUTHORS

LEAD AUTHOR

Pierre Coutu, A.A.E., Ed.D., FRAeS

Dr. Coutu is the founding President, Aviation Strategies International (ASI) and Chair, ASI Institute. He is a specialist in Aviation Business Strategy. He has taught in several Aviation MBA programs at: Concordia University (Canada), the Toulouse Business School (France), and the Beijing University of Aeronautics and Astronautics (China). He is an honorary Fellow of the Royal Aeronautical Society (*FRAeS*), a member of the Editorial Board of the Journal of Airport Management, and an Advisor to the Board of the Global Development Learning Network. In 1996, the Minister of Transport of Poland awarded Dr. Coutu a Medal of Achievement for his special contribution to the development of the Polish Air Transportation sector. In 2005, he was appointed to the Transportation Appeal Tribunal of Canada by the Minister of Transport of Canada and, in 2011, he became the first recipient of the Airports Council International (ACI) Paul Genton Medal receiving the award for his leadership in executive-level training. In 2013, he co-authored *Airport Operations* (McGraw-Hill), currently available in available in English, Japanese and Portuguese. He holds a doctorate in Education from Nova Southeastern University, Miami. Dr. Coutu has been the Executive in charge of the Global ACI-ICAO Airport Management Professional Accreditation Programme (AMPAP) since its inception in 2007.

CO-AUTHORS

Ruwantissa Abeyratne, DCL, PhD, LLM, LLB, FRAeS

Dr. Abeyratne has worked in the field of aviation law and management for more than 35 years. He is retired from the International Civil Aviation Organization (ICAO) as Senior Legal Officer. He holds the degrees of Doctor of Civil Laws (DCL) from McGill University, Doctor of Philosophy (Ph.D.) from the University of Colombo, Master of Laws (LL.M) from Monash University, and Bachelor of Laws (LL.B) from the University of Colombo. Dr. Abeyratne has published 32 books and over 400 articles on international law and air law in leading journals, and has presented many papers at conferences. His professional reputation rests largely on work in aerospace law, diplomacy, and economics. He is Senior Associate, Air Law and Policy at Aviation Strategies International and a visiting Professor of Aviation Law and Policy at McGill University.

Peter Adams, M.App.Sc. (OH&S), Grad.Dip. OHM, Dip.App.Sc. (ENVH), IAP

Mr. Adams is a specialist in operational risk management, airport operations, airfield standards, works planning, operations training, and safety management systems. He is Senior Practice Executive, Aviation Safety & Risk Management at Aviation Strategies International. He has worked on various international airport management consultancy projects including training development and delivery. He previously worked at Sydney Airport, and in the financial sector and, before that, was a senior officer in the Royal Australian Air Force. He is an International Airport Professional (IAP) and an Instructor for the Airport Management Professional Accreditation Programme (AMPAP) of the Airports Council International (ACI) and International Civil Aviation Organization (ICAO). He is also an active member of the ACI World Safety & Technical Standards Committee.

Paul Behnke, M.Sc. Economics

Mr. Behnke functioned as course designer in the Global Airport Management Professional Accreditation Programme (AMPAP), jointly owned by Airports Council International (ACI) and International Civil Aviation Organization (ICAO). He is also an AMPAP instructor. Prior to that he worked for ACI World as the director responsible for coordinating economic and security policies with members. That 12year stint at ACI followed a 20-year career at the U.S. Department of State where he served in seven diplomatic postings on five continents, focusing on aero-politics and international trade issues. His graduate degree in Economics is from Purdue University. Mr. Behnke is Senior Associate, Knowledge and Industry Intelligence with Aviation Strategies International.

Christophe Bouchaud, BA, MBA, AMPAP Assoc.

Mr. Bouchaud is Senior Vice President, Business Operations and Information Technology at Aviation Strategies International. He has always been involved in the field of high technology, bridging the gap between technology, management, and operations within highly diversified strategic and international contexts. He has resided in 10 countries and worked for a range of multinational corporations, including the Alfa-Laval Group, United Technologies Corporation and Stanley Black and Decker, as well as financial and educational institutions. Mr. Bouchaud has worked closely with the aviation industry throughout his career, providing expert solutions and turnkey projects in the fields of high-speed industrial automation, information and communications technologies, complex systems integration, video surveillance, analytics and AI, biometrics, and security.

Denis Chagnon, B. Journalism

Mr. Chagnon is a seasoned communications professional, public speaker and writer. He has held senior public relations positions in the financial and aviation fields, including with the International Civil Aviation Organization (ICAO). Notably, he collaborated on the Memoirs of the ICAO President of the Council, Dr. Assad Kotaite, a privileged insight into the evolution of global air transport through an increasingly complex, competitive, and politically and socially challenging environment. Mr. Chagnon remains actively involved in aviation matters, largely as Master of Ceremony for international and national (Canada) conferences and events. He is Senior Associate, Corporate Communications, at Aviation Strategies International.

Gordon Hamilton, B. Eng., M.Sc.

Mr. Hamilton is Executive Vice President at Aviation Strategies International. His experience in airport development and operations spans more than 30 years and includes aeronautical and commercial revenue development, financial advisory services for airport PPP transactions, master planning for existing and Greenfield airports, terminal planning, and airport operations improvements. Gordon led the development of the level of service standards for terminals that are in use worldwide. He is also one of the authors of the 2004 and 2014 International Air Transport Association's *Airport Development Reference Manual*, and of the Airport Cooperative Research Program Report 54 *Resource Manual for In-Terminal Concessions.* He has an extensive list of publications in airport journals and has been a frequent speaker at industry conferences.

Jean-Marc Trottier, AMBA, AVSEC-PM

Mr. Trottier has more than 50 years of experience in almost every area of airline and airport operations. He is Vice-Chairman Aviation Strategies International (ASI) and Executive Director of the ASI Institute. A graduate of Concordia University's MBA Global Aviation Program, he also holds a Certificate in International Terrorism Studies from St. Andrews University. He co-developed and is an instructor for the Aviation Security Professional Management program for ICAO and Concordia University, as well as for the Global ACI-ICAO Airport Management Professional Accreditation Programme (AMPAP). He has given seminars around the world including Concordia University in Montreal, Beijing University of Aeronautics and Astronautics, Danube University in Austria, and Helwan University in Cairo. Mr. Trottier was a co-creator of the World Aviation MBA Association.

David Ze, Ph.D. Communications

Dr. Ze is Vice President, Asia-Pacific, at Aviation Strategies International holds a doctorate in Communications from Simon Fraser University (Vancouver, Canada). Since 1982, he has provided advisory services related to international exchanges between China and various North American and European countries. More recently, his main professional activities have focused on air transportation and education. He has played key roles in the organization of numerous aviation industry events, including a seminar for a Team Canada visit to China led by the Prime Minister of Canada. He has also provided significant contributions to air transportation management training programs.

EDITOR

Shaun Fawcett, MBA

Mr. Fawcett is a Montreal-based writer, business consultant, online entrepreneur, book author, and publisher. He spent the first 25 years of his career working in management positions in the aviation sector, from airport planning, to aviation accident investigation and safety, to management training. During those years, his areas of focus were: systems design and development, project management, and strategic planning and management. The most recent 20 years of his career were spent as: webmaster, online entrepreneur, and author of numerous non-fiction books. In parallel with that, he managed his own editorial services and publishing firm, as well as providing consulting services related to online business and book publishing.

CONTENTS

PREFACE

The idea of creating a book about megatrends and aviation for aviation industry leaders and executives had been on my mind for some time. Even as far back as when the ASI Institute was established several years ago, I knew that it could eventually become the channel for such a book. And because the primary mission driving the ASI Institute is to educate, provide advice on, and promote best practices for effective management in aviation organizations, for me, the development of this book is a natural extension of that mission.

During my decades-long involvement in various aspects of the international aviation industry, I have often taken notice of how many organizations in the business seem pressured to focus their time and their resources on whatever is happening in the immediate moment and rarely prepare for what is coming in a meaningful way. Time and again, I have also observed that organizations in the aviation sector tend to pay lip service to activities such as analyzing megatrends as a way to prepare for the future. Sytematically managing for the future is a serious challenge for all.

Senior managers have acknowledged that global megatrends are important factors, but have done precious little to follow up on that stated belief by way of actually studying the possible impacts of such megatrends on the future of their organizations.

In fact, after working over the years with numerous aviation leaders and executives in strategic planning seminars, training sessions, and other management exercises, I am convinced that many of my colleagues and counterparts have their heads buried deep in the sand, if you will, on this particular subject. Perhaps this is because the challenge of dealing with the complexity of a fast-approaching and seemingly unpredictable future is so daunting that, very simplistically, by ignoring it, there is hope that it might go away. This way of handling things can often result in our being forced into constantly "putting out fires" through crisis management.

It's this sense of ambivalence and lethargy towards megatrend analysis that I have observed among many aviation executives that motivated me, in association with the

ASI Institute, to develop this global megatrends book as a path to creating and stimulating future-wise aviation organizations. I believed from the start that in order to create a meaningful book that would be credible and also resonate with senior aviation executives, it would have to be a collaborative effort involving well-qualified and experienced international aviation professionals who have also been intimately familiar with management perspectives in a wide range of aviation industry activities.

Over time, I was fortunate to be able to assemble such a team of experts as advisors and co-authors throughout the research and several draft phases of this book. Collectively, our team possesses hundreds of years of senior management and operational experience from across the entire spectrum of aviation industries activities, many at the international level.

I also knew from the outset that the final version of this book would have to surpass theorizing and spouting management platitudes about global megatrends. I recognized from my experience working with senior executives from various organizations that the book had to offer practical approaches and guidance that senior managers could use to identify and analyze megatrends and their impacts and enable them to prepare their organizations for the future. Our team wanted to make sure that this book would help them build "future-wise" aviation organizations. For the most part, I believe we have succeeded in doing just that.

Nevertheless, the work to understand global megatrends and predict their impacts on the future of aviation is far from complete. I see this book as an important first step in a process that will eventually make global megatrend analysis an important standard method for preparing aviation organizations to go into the future with a deliberate means to deal with that future.

We realized early on that the structure of this book would be important. We knew that it had to be more than just a compendium of facts and figures—more than just another reference book. We wanted to offer easy accessibility to the important information and background needed to fully understand the megatrends, while also offering practical approaches and tools that senior managers could actually use to guide their organizations into the future with confidence.

Accordingly, the book is made up of one detailed chapter on each of the six global megatrends, followed by a comprehensive chapter on how to use each megatrend's background information to create a future-wise aviation organization.

Because each megatrend chapter is by necessity quite detailed, we decided to provide busy executives with an easy way to access the essence of the detailed discussion without having to wade through all the background data and discussion. We therefore have included at the end of each megatrend chapter a four- to five-page bullet point "management summary". These summaries provide a quick reference guide to the essential observations and conclusions that are discussed in greater detail earlier in the chapter. Readers wanting more background on a subject can easily refer back to the body of the chapter.

After hundreds of hours of readings, research, brainstorming and personal sacrifice from my co-authors/colleagues whom I respect and hold in high esteem, I am deeply grateful for their cohesion and brilliant contributions. I feel particularly indebted to Dr. Ruwantissa Abeyratne for his wise counsel and encouragement about the necessity of pursuing this project and must praise Shaun Fawcett, our editor, a relentless yet extremely gifted taskmaster who remarkably kept us on point and on schedule. Sincere thanks also go to our ASI teammates for their invaluable support, as usual.

Pierre Coutu
Montreal, March, 2019

1

INTRODUCTION

A couple of weeks before the dawning of 2019, Gatwick, the second-busiest airport in Britain and the eighth busiest in Europe, was suddenly closed to aircraft operations due to the unauthorized incursion of unmanned aerial vehicles, or drones, believed to be circulating over the runways and taxiways.[1] The airport was closed to all flights for almost 36 hours because the drones were considered to be a serious safety threat to arriving and departing aircraft. The impact of this incident was significant, directly affecting thousands of travelers and dozens of businesses. The plans of almost 100,000 travelers were seriously interrupted during the peak travel period of the year. Beyond the inconvenience factor, the total financial costs to the airport, the airlines, and the many support services involved ranged well into the millions of dollars.

In September 2018, one of Japan's largest airports, Kansai International Airport, serving Osaka, was closed down for a number of days after Typhoon Jebi caused severe flooding of the runways and taxiways.[2] More than 3,000 travelers were stranded at the offshore airport overnight when the only bridge to the mainland was knocked out of commission by the impact of the storm. Even after the storm had passed, the airport had to remain closed until the water flooding the airfield was drained. Thousands of airline passengers were inconvenienced, and the costs to the airport, airlines, and support services were significant.

In June 2017, during an extreme heat wave across the US southwestern states, dozens of flights had to be canceled by airlines due to excessive temperatures. In Phoenix, Arizona, temperatures rose to 120°F (49°C) making the air too thin for certain types of passenger aircraft to take off safely. One regional airline had to cancel more than 50 flights because its aircraft were not certified to take off at temperatures greater than 118°F (48°C).[3]

Airlines can be expected to encounter such situations ever more frequently as average temperatures continue to rise globally. Experts estimate that the effects of increased temperatures on current passenger aircraft will be significant because during the hottest parts of the day, 10% to 30% of fully loaded planes may have to remove payload to take off safely, causing considerable financial and operational consequences to airlines, including reduced payloads/revenues, canceled and/or delayed flights, disrupted airport operations and air navigation services, and inconvenienced passengers, all causing a ripple effect throughout the global aviation network.

The above are recent examples of the significant impacts that global megatrends can have on international aviation operations, policies, and regulations. The particular megatrends primarily involved in the above examples are Innovative Technological Change and Climate Change. In the past, some people have argued that such incidents are entirely unpredictable and organizations just have to deal with them when they occur. However, these days, many experts will argue convincingly that it is possible to better prepare for the eventuality of such occurrences. Their reasoning is that, by now, we have accumulated sufficient experience, information, and data processing power that we can proactively adopt a posture to better weather the stormy conditions brought about by these kinds of events whenever they will inevitably occur. Essentially, by being as "equipped" as possible to deal with such events, we can maximize rapid response in order to minimize impact and damage. This is why, in recent years there has been increased interest and focus on the study of global megatrends as well as on the development of plausible scenarios of the future.

This book has two main objectives. The first is to define and describe six global megatrends, and their sub-trends, that will be impacting the international aviation industry over the next couple of decades and beyond. The second purpose of this book is to give aviation leaders and executives a practical approach that they can use to analyze and interpret megatrends and sub-trends, as well as to show them how to prepare their organizations most effectively for the future.

WHAT ARE GLOBAL MEGATRENDS?

The term "global megatrend" appears in the media with ever-increasing frequency. It has become the current buzzword for a trend, or for changing conditions. The Oxford Dictionary defines a megatrend as, "an important shift in the progress of a society or of any other particular field or activity; any major movement." A megatrend is not simply a significant trend. It is a global transformative force changing the entire world. A megatrend affects everything: labor, assets and infrastructure, systems and processes, the structure of organizations and political institutions, political stability, and even human existence. Over the past 25 years, numerous books have been written on the subject of global megatrends, some of them general in nature, some industry-specific, and some focused on particular regions of the world.

The six megatrends discussed in this book are: *climate change, the global economic shift from West to East, increasing urbanization, demographic changes, technological innovation, and global connectedness.* Each of these megatrends also involves various sub-trends. For example, the economic power shift to the East includes sub-trends such as political factors, GDP and investment changes, shifting purchasing power, and changing trade dynamics.

Each megatrend creates a challenge for political and business leaders. Identifying the potential impact of a megatrend and preparing an organization, an industry, or even a country to respond effectively is difficult—so difficult that in many cases, the challenge is being ignored. The situation is significantly more complicated because all the megatrends are in play simultaneously.

A fitting analogy would be the interaction of multiple pharmaceuticals ingested simultaneously into the human body—even if we understand the impact of each drug individually, the combined effects may be entirely different. In the same way, the interaction of megatrends, or their systemic effect, can lead to results that are more dramatic than might be anticipated. The risk of one or more tipping points creating breakdowns in entire systems is possible, as one megatrend impact creates a chain of spinoff effects from the other megatrends.

Some of the megatrends may be correlated, others likely not. For example, possible correlations include:

- Rapid Urbanization with increasing environmental concern and political action.

- Rapid Urbanization and Global Connectedness.

- Demographic Changes and Trends and Economic Power Shift.

- Technology Innovations and Global Connectedness.

Not only is the systemic impact of these many variables very difficult to forecast, but even the general direction can be challenging to foresee.

On the one hand:

- Increasing urbanization and growing environmental concern may make it extremely difficult to develop new airports in many countries,

- Technological innovations combined with connectedness may reduce the need for travel with such innovations as virtual reality business meetings and tourist experiences,

Whereas, on the other hand:

- Demographic changes and the economic power shift to the East may dramatically increase tourism for a period of time,

- Growing urbanization and increasing connectedness, combined with the related tendency for higher incomes, may increase business and tourist travel.

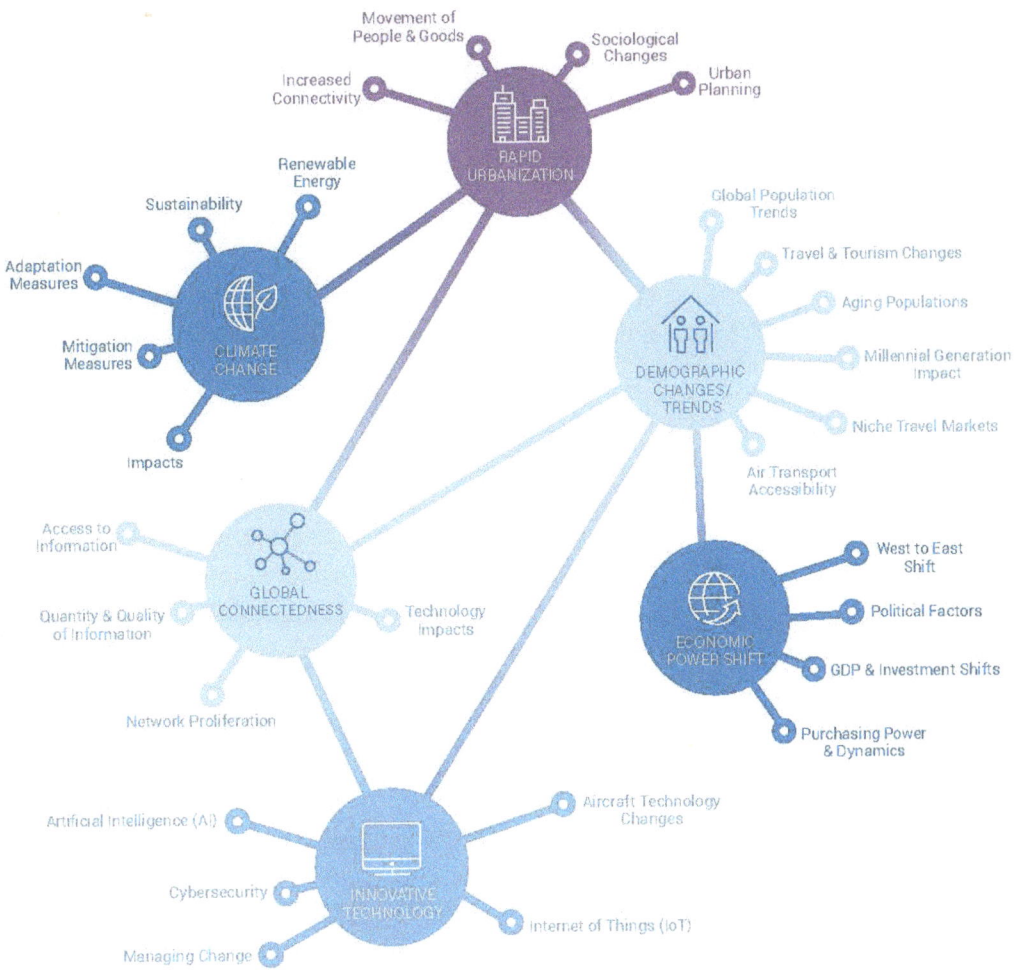

Figure 1-1   Megatrends, sub-trends, and primary linkages (ASI Institute).

Accelerating Pace

The accelerating pace of megatrends and the increasing complexity of dealing with their impacts mean that the time needed to adapt is increasing, whereas the time available to make changes is decreasing.

This acceleration is exemplified primarily by the advent of new technologies. A report prepared by the marketing specialist Comsense for IBM Marketing Cloud in 2017 stated that, "90% of the data in the world today have been created in the last two years alone, at 2.5 quintillion bytes of data a day."[4] The rate of change is obvious in other broad dimensions of the world macro-environment, including the reshaping of world socio-political forces, the swift evolution of global connectedness, and the rapid degradation of the environment, which is made visible as glaciers vanish and natural disasters occur with greater frequency and severity.

Change is happening at an ever-increasing pace on a global scale. Economic and politi-cal transformation materializes more rapidly than ever, and technology is evolving more quickly than most of us can comprehend. For most organizations, their horizon and outlook will also require ongoing rapid change to keep abreast.

Megatrends and Aviation

Air transportation is a global system made up of the air transport industry, the airport industry, the air navigation services (ANS) industry, and the aircraft manufacturing industry. Each interacts with the others and with changing technologies, rules, and procedures. This makes dealing with megatrends and the systemic impact of megatrends even more challenging.

Adding to the complexity that aviation leaders and executives face in dealing with mega-trends is the systemic nature of aviation. A change in one element of the aviation system in one country can affect other elements in numerous other countries. For example, an increase in extreme weather events in Bangkok will not only have an impact on airlines and airports in Thailand, but also on international airlines and even on major airports in Europe, as departures for Thailand are more frequently canceled and aircraft remain on-airport.

Unfolding megatrends have already caused significant disruption in the aviation system. The growth of the middle class in Asia, combined with the growth of low-cost carriers, has created capacity shortfalls, congestion, reduced levels of service, and delays in many countries in the region. The increasing frequency of major weather disruptions (typhoons, hurricanes, etc.) is disrupting worldwide operations more often.

The impact of these megatrends will not be uniform throughout the industry. For example, agile airlines will cope better than those that are more set in their ways. Because of their ability to change fleets and routes, the impact on airlines may be less challenging than the impact on airports, with their long investment cycles and need for land. Technology will impact air navigation services differently than airports or airlines. Even the role of regulators will significantly change with technology.

Rates of technology adoption may also differ, or the pace of regulatory changes may vary. Recent evidence indicates that developing countries adopt technology more readily than some wealthy countries. Similarly, developing countries have proven to be more responsive to regulatory changes.

Impacts of Megatrends on Aviation

For aviation, the changes caused by megatrends will all translate into impacts in three areas—demand, services, and regulation:

- **Demand:** impacts will be changes in levels of passenger traffic, movements, or cargo traffic.
- **Services:** impacts will be changes in demand for types or levels of services provided.
- **Regulation:** impacts will be changes in guidelines, directives, and protocols that affect aviation, including safety, security, land use, and environmental regulations.

The fact that all impacts from all megatrends and their sub-trends result in changes to traffic levels, types and levels of services, and regulations, actually focuses the discussion considerably because these three impacts can be addressed by only four means:

- **People:** Changes to the numbers or competencies of staff in airlines, airports, ANS, and regulatory bodies.
- **Assets:** Changes to the types and/or sizes of assets (aircraft, mobile assets, airport infrastructure, and ANS facilities).
- **Systems and Processes:** Changes to the systems and/or processes used by airlines, airports, ANS providers, and regulators.
- **Structure:** Changes to the governance, organization, and financing of aviation organizations to respond to the changing environment.

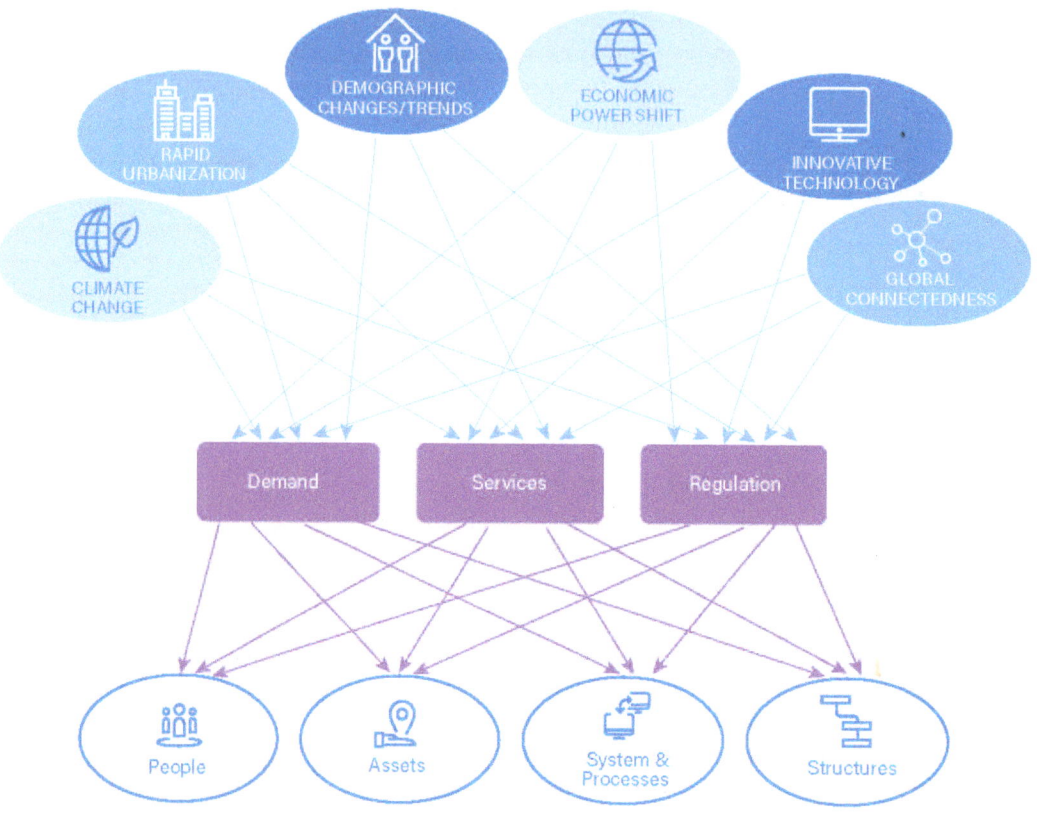

Figure 1-2   Megatrends and their impacts (ASI Institute).

By way of example, the growing middle class in Asia has already resulted in impacts that include:

- Large increases in demand.
- Increased expectations of levels of service.

These will need to be addressed through:

- **People:** Rapid growth in staff levels at airports, airlines, and possibly ANS providers, and regulators, along with changing staff competencies to manage and maintain new assets.
- **Assets:** Significant investments in aircraft, airport infrastructure, and IT systems.
- **Systems & Processes:** Changes to airport and ANS processes and systems to provide additional capacity.

- **Structure:** Changes in airport governance, including ownership models, to enable more rapid responses to megatrend impacts and related investment needs.

WHAT THIS BOOK IS ABOUT

The collaborators who co-authored this book are convinced that in a rapidly changing world, senior managers in all sectors of the global aviation industry need to understand more thoroughly the megatrends that will be impacting their organizations over the next twenty years. The book is designed to provide aviation industry leaders with the following: a comprehensive view of what is coming, a perspective on how to analyze and interpret these evolving trends and factors, and practical guidance on how to proactively adapt developmental and strategic plans to deal with the future. The book contains a chapter on each megatrend, followed by a chapter on steps that organizations can take to become truly future-wise. A brief description of each of these chapters follows.

Chapter 2: Climate Change – Environmental Crisis and Ongoing Challenge

The Climate Change megatrend first became a serious concern to the international community in the 1970s, when the Stockholm Convention recognized that humanity is both a creator and molder of its environment and that a stage has been reached on this planet where humanity has acquired the power to transform its environment in countless ways and on an unprecedented scale. The Convention concluded that the two main aspects of the human environment, the natural and the human-made, are essential to our well-being and to our enjoyment of basic human rights and the right to life itself. The impacts of environmental/climate change and of measures to deal with it will be in the forefront of human activity in the future.

This chapter focuses on five sub-trends, with an emphasis on how they relate to the aviation industry:

1   The state of climate change.

2   Renewable energy and sustainability.

3   Climate change impacts (i.e., impacts of aviation on climate change, impact of climate change on aviation operations, weather impacts and issues, and infrastructure impacts and requirements).

4   Adapting to climate change (i.e., rising temperatures and sea levels, financial impacts, risk assessments, and multi-party collaboration).

5   Mitigation of climate change (i.e., measures required, setting targets, international leadership and governance, mitigation plans, sustainable aviation fuels, and industry recycling efforts).

Chapter 3: Global Economic Power Shift – West to East

This major trend involves the shift in economic power and influence that has been taking place globally over the last four to five decades, as once-developing nations have begun to rival the economic might of the traditional economic powers such as the United States, Russia, Japan, and the European Union. In the past twenty years, economies in Asian countries in particular have begun to flex their muscles, led by China and India.

Sub-trends covered in this chapter, with a focus on how they impact the aviation industry, include:

1   Economic-political factors (i.e., impacts on travel patterns, influence of emerging economies, rise of megalopolises, and globalization versus protectionism).

2   GDP and investment shifts (i.e., movement of capital, impacts on business and tourism, and increased share of emerging economies).

3   Purchasing power i.e., changing dynamics, rising middle class, increasing impact of emerging economies, and industrial output changes (e.g., increased speed of move-ment of goods, impacts on air cargo operators, infrastructure investment needs, and international cooperation).

Chapter 4: Rapid Urbanization

Over the past 40 years, the rate of migration from rural to urban areas has tripled worldwide. The primary drivers of this megatrend have been both increased economic development and industrialization, which are known to compel humans to migrate from rural areas to cities in search of employment and economic prosperity. This has been occurring more in developing countries rather than in established economic powers as the global economic shift continues. This trend is influenced by changing population dynamics and migration patterns and will have wide-reaching impacts in urban planning, including the design, location, and scale of airports.

This chapter highlights four sub-trends in particular and how they relate to the aviation industry:

1   Urban planning (i.e., land availability/scarcity, rise in mega-cities, eco-cities and eco-airports, airport relocations, and impacts on urban transport).

2   Sociological changes (i.e., changing travel behaviors, airport ownership changes, new service requirements, and different passenger profiles).

3   Movements of people, goods, and services (i.e., changing consumer needs, impact of smart technology, decrease in airport car parking, and sustainable development needs).

4   Connectivity among urban centers (i.e., new/modified transport networks, inter-linking of transport networks, and leveraging new technologies).

Chapter 5: Demographic Changes and Trends

World population is forecast to grow from seven billion today to more than nine billion within 20 years. The main reasons for this are continuing advances in medical science and technology, which have resulted in increased life spans and reduced infant mortality rates. The behavior and influence of one particular socio-economic group, the millennial generation, is expected to be a major influencer and key driver of the global economy over the next couple of decades. Impacts of this particular group are expected to have significant repercussions on both travel and employment. By definition, demographic changes of all types have varying degrees of impact on aviation.

Six demographic sub-trends are discussed in this chapter, with a focus on how they are likely to impact the aviation industry:

1   Global population trends.

2   World travel and tourism (i.e., passenger travel increases, growing middle class in emerging economies, airline and airport capacity issues, and workforce deficiencies).

3   The millennial generation (i.e., increased travel frequency, spending patterns, and different needs).

4   Aging populations (i.e., increased life expectancy, economic-social impacts, and requirements for new facilities and services).

5   Niche travel markets (i.e., dual residences, religious pilgrims, international students, and migrant laborers).

6   Air transport accessibility (i.e., need to serve air travelers with physical mobility and mental health issues, gender equality issues in the workforce, and more focus on needs of traditionally under-served groups).

Chapter 6: Innovative Technological Change

The influence of innovative technology on almost all aspects of the world is an incontrovertible fact. The driving force behind the continued development of innovative technology is the desire to extend human intelligence and create digital intelligence as a mental, physical, and social extension of human beings. Use of this technology has already reached the point where both businesses and consumers have become dependent on it for their day-to-day functioning.

Five sub-trends and their specific relationship to the aviation industry are discussed in this chapter:

1   Aircraft technology (i.e., new aircraft designs, point-to-point vs. hub-and-spoke, alternative fuel impacts/issues, air space and ground space issues, and impacts on airports and ANS providers).

2   Automation and human-machine symbiosis (i.e., the impact of Internet of Things (IoT) technology on security, robotics, blockchain, and aviation operations; the lag in implementation of IoT in aviation; and impacts of automation and robotics on increased data collection, air cargo operations, information and communication technology (ICT) security capabilities, remote towers, and centralized airport operations/facilities).

3   The data revolution (i.e., artificial intelligence (AI) and data ubiquity and their impact on airline and airport decision-making, the user experience (UX) approach, optimized airfare systems, enhanced regulatory tools, ATS management modifications, changes to airport management, systems convergence, and ongoing investment needs).

4   Cybersecurity (i.e., privacy and security challenges, data and network security, threat assessment needs, cloud-based applications, standardization needs, data-centric models, and need for AI-based systems).

5   Managing technological change (i.e., radical transformation required, planning needs, IoT and UX teams, and multi-disciplinary approach).

Chapter 7: Global Connectedness

Billions of human minds are already connected through rapid and ongoing advances in various technologies and networks. This trend is dramatically accelerating how individuals and groups of individuals communicate, collaborate, share/exchange information, work collectively, conduct business, socialize, and exchange information in general. The challenge of this megatrend is trying to predict its pace and the degree to which it will impact all aspects of human existence.

Four key sub-trends/issues are discussed in Chapter 7 in terms of their impact on global aviation:

1   Access to information (i.e., data ubiquity, global access, and instant access).

2   Network proliferation (i.e., global interaction, rapid growth, online communities, and benefits for aviation).

3   Quality and quantity of information (i.e., leverage of data/information, the need for management filters, dealing with online communities, impacts on aircraft maintenance, possible global operations, development of highly personalized services, and more and better regulation).

4   Connectedness and technology advances (i.e., unmanned aerial vehicles, ancillary services, and streamlined operations).

Chapter 8: The Future-Wise Organization

This chapter of the book focuses on how aviation organizations can better posture to face the future. It provides an approach to becoming a "future-wise organization". It is all about managing the future of aviation organizations by increasing the odds of successfully leading them through the ongoing rollercoaster of unpredictability and turbulence created by the impact of global megatrends on the international aviation industry. This chapter is not about managing megatrends, which by definition cannot be done. Rather, it is about guiding aviation organizations on how to better strategize on how to weather the impact of megatrends. Leadership needs to be proactive in addressing the uncertainties and complexities associated with the impact of interrelated megatrends. A future-wise organization will ensure continuous high performance by taking advantage of the upside of megatrends while avoiding the negative impacts. The focus needs to be on overall performance, resilience, and agility.

No one knows exactly how things will unfold, so a resilient stance is needed that allows rapid responses to megatrend impacts. The choice is between being a bystander and having the future just happen, or instead preparing people, assets, systems and structures to face the uncertainty and turbulent times ahead; in other words, being future-wise.

It is hoped that senior executives and managers involved in any aspect of the international aviation industry will enjoy reading this book and find the information interesting as well as helpful in propelling their organizations forward into the future.

Chapter 9: Conclusion

This brief concluding chapter summarizes some of the challenges that were faced by the co-authors in defining and developing texts about global megatrends within the specific context of their impacts on the international aviation industry. It emphasizes the fact that this book is a focused starting point only, and that much ongoing research needs to continue that seeks to find innovative and effective ways to create truly future-wise aviation organizations.

BACKGROUND TO THIS BOOK

What Makes This Book Unique

This book is significantly different from other papers and research documents that have looked at certain aspects of the future of the international aviation industry. The few such publications that exist have tended to focus on future trends from the viewpoint of their specific stakeholders or particular segments of the industry (i.e., members, user groups, clients, etc.). The perspective that makes the approach of this book to megatrends and the aviation industry unique is that it is all-encompassing and presents a structured approach and practical guidelines that senior managers from all sectors of the aviation industry can apply when assessing megatrends and making preparations for their future business activities. It is believed to be the first book that specifically addresses the relationships between global megatrends and the worldwide aviation industry in a comprehensive and practical manner.

Methodology

This publication is the product of extensive discussions and brainstorming involving collaboration among a seasoned international team of aviation experts over many months. The team was made up of a multi-disciplinary group of professionals with collectively hundreds of years of experience, education, and knowledge in a wide variety of aviation operations and aviation-related disciplines worldwide. In addition to managing aviation operations, a number of the co-authors possess many years of experience in overall aviation management, including extensive experience in strategic analysis and planning as it applies to this sector.

The development of the content in this book involved a number of steps: extensive research into the information that already exists about megatrends in general; additional research into the relationships between the global megatrends identified and the worldwide aviation industry; discussions and brainstorming to identify the impacts of megatrends on the international aviation industry; additional research into aviation-specific sub-trends under each megatrend with a focus on how they will affect the aviation industry in the future; and identification of measures and development of tools to respond to megatrends and sub-trends appropriately and effectively in the future. Finally, after each megatrend chapter was drafted, it was subjected to rigorous peer reviews and challenges, the results of which were incorporated into the final version of the book.

REFERENCES

1   https://www.nytimes.com/2018/12/27/world/europe/gatwick-airport-drone.html.

2   https://www.businesstimes.com.sg/transport/kansai-airport-flooded-following-typhoon-jebi.

3   https://www.independent.co.uk/travel/news-and-advice/heatwave-arizona-phoenix-ameri-can-airlines-bombardier-cancellation-a7798466.html.

4   "10 Key Marketing Trends For 2017; http://comsense.consulting/wp-content/uploads/2017/03/10_Key_Marketing_Trends_for_2017_and_Ideas_for_Exceeding_Customer_Expectations.pdf.

2

CLIMATE CHANGE
Environmental Crisis and Ongoing Challenge

THE STATE OF CLIMATE CHANGE

At the heart of global warming are greenhouse gases (GHG), which are generated by human activity. A greenhouse gas is any gaseous compound in the atmosphere that is capable of absorbing infrared radiation, thereby trapping and holding heat in the atmosphere. Some greenhouse gases such as carbon dioxide, methane, water vapor, and nitrous oxide occur naturally in the atmosphere. Of these, the primary concern for aircraft is carbon dioxide because aviation is considered to cause 2% of the entirety of the globe's carbon dioxide emissions. Throughout millennia, these GHGs have helped to regulate the temperature on the planet. The emission of greenhouse gases into the atmosphere creates what is called the "greenhouse effect", which in turn causes global warming. It is said that if aircraft emissions go unchecked, this figure could go up to 20% over the next 10 to 20 years.

Climate change is both a present reality and a potential threat that experts believe could lead to a global catastrophe if it is not addressed diligently and with vigor. The most informed scientific findings reveal that unless drastic action is taken globally within the next twenty years, global temperatures will increase by at least 3.6°F, (2°C)where ice caps will melt, and oceans will rise. Adverse effects of this global phenomenon will be seen in drastically uninhabited and abandoned land due to devastated agricultural industries and flooded cities. Yuval Noah Harari in his book *21 Lessons for the 21ˢᵗ Century*[1] is of the view that we are facing a tipping point where any action after that point will not reverse the trend that is progressing now. The Secretary General of the World Meteorological Organization has stated that if rapid cuts in CO_2 and other greenhouse gases are not made, climate change will have increasingly destructive and irreversible impacts on life on Earth and that we have already reached the danger level as the window of opportunity for action is almost closed. Harari suggests that individual States can make a difference by taking sound economic steps that make practical sense: "government can tax carbon emissions; add the cost of externalities to the price of oil and gas, adopt strong environmental regulations, cut subsidies to polluting industries and incentivize the switch to renewable energy". Although these are sensible policies for individual States, the issue has to be stretched beyond national boundaries toward reaching a global solution to a global problem. Key drivers of a global response will be economic measures and the development of alternative energy and renewable energy that will replace fossil fuel energy.

The potentially catastrophic consequences of climate change and global warming loom large in public discourse, from headlines in the news and social media to boardrooms

and living rooms, yet current measures to mitigate the phenomenon and begin revers-
ing its destructive effects seem eerily wanting. In November 2018, a statement issued
by the World Meteorological Organization cautioned that since 1990, there has been a
41% increase in the warming effect by various greenhouse gases on the climate. The 5th
Assessment Report of the Inter-Governmental Panel on Climate Change (IPCC), a body
created by the United Nations Environmental Programme and the World Meteorological
Organization, unequivocally stated in 2013 that, "warming of the climate system is
unequivocal, and since the 1950s, many of the observed changes are unprecedented over
decades to millennia. The atmosphere and ocean have warmed, the amounts of snow
and ice have diminished, sea level has risen, and the concentrations of greenhouse gases
have increased". The Report of the National Climate Assessment of the United States,
prepared by a team of more than 300 experts guided by a 60-member Federal Advisory
Committee and released in November 2018, states that, "Scientists and engineers from
around the world have compiled this evidence using satellites, weather balloons, thermometers at surface stations, and many other types of observing systems that monitor
the Earth's weather and climate. The sum total of this evidence tells an unambiguous
story: the planet is warming", calling for an unavoidable response strategy based on the
fact that the amount of future climate change will largely be determined by choices society makes about emissions. Lower emissions of heat-trapping gases mean less future
warming and less severe impacts. Emissions can be reduced through improved energy
efficiency and switching to low-carbon or non-carbon energy sources.

The cover story of the August 4, 2018 edition of the British magazine *The Economist*
suggests that the summer's historic fires in Europe and North America are indications
that we are "losing the war against climate change".[2] It adds that the world looks poised
to get a lot hotter before things improve if corrective action is not taken.

This global concern is echoed by numerous world leaders and international organizations
in a call to take concerted and urgent action.

United Nations Secretary-General António Guterres warned on September 11, 2018,
that the world is facing "a direct existential threat". He told the UN in New York: "If we
do not change course by 2020, we risk missing the point where we can avoid runaway
climate change, with disastrous consequences for people and all the natural systems that
sustain us," adding that scientists have been warning about global warming for decades,
but "...far too many leaders have refused to listen—far too few have acted with the vision
the science demands".[3]

Christiana Figueres, Executive Secretary of the UN Climate Change body, emphasized that: "There is no task more urgent, more compelling, or more sacred than that of protecting the climate of our planet for our children and grandchildren."[4]

Jim Yong Kim, President of the World Bank, speaks about climate change in these terms: "We have to wake up to the fierce urgency of the now."[5]

Christine Lagarde, Managing Director of the International Monetary Fund, insists that addressing climate change is "a collective endeavor, it's a collective accountability, and it may not be too late."[6]

Indeed, scientific evidence and observable phenomena worldwide relating to climate change demonstrate that humanity is headed in the wrong direction and moving there at an ever-increasing speed.

The Inter-Governmental Panel on Climate Change (IPCC), in its authoritative fifth assessment report of 2013 and further updates, could not have been clearer. "Warming of the climate system is unequivocal, and since the 1950s, many of the observed changes are unprecedented. The atmosphere and ocean have warmed, the amounts of snow and ice have diminished, sea level has risen, and the concentrations of greenhouse gases have increased."[7]

Greenhouse Gases – A Growing Problem

The main human or anthropogenic sources of greenhouse gas emissions are: fossil fuel use, deforestation, intensive livestock farming, use of synthetic fertilizers, and various industrial processes. The generation of carbon dioxide (CO_2) from the burning of fossil fuels is by far the largest single source of human impact on the environment. It is the rapid increase of GHG created by human activity that over the years has strengthened the earth's natural greenhouse process, leading to a steady increase in the mean temperature of the planet – hence the term "global warming".

The centuries-old trend toward the warming of the planet began with the industrial revolution. Since the mid-1700s, sustained improvements in manufacturing processes and, more recently, astounding technological advances have made for exponential progress in the production of an incredible range of goods and services that have arguably made life easier for hundreds of millions of people around the world. Unfortunately, the downside to this remarkable ingenuity has been a significant and consistent growth in GHG emissions.

Figure 2-1 Greenhouse effect (ASI).

As an indication of scale, the Carbon Dioxide Information Analysis Center (CDIAC) reports that: "Since 1751, just over 400 billion metric tons of carbon have been released to the atmosphere from the consumption of fossil fuels and cement production. Half these fossil-fuel CO_2 emissions have occurred since the late 1980s. The 2014 global fossil-fuel carbon emission estimate is an all-time record."[8]

Moreover, the current rapid industrialization taking place in the developing world will significantly boost the demand for energy and thus the consumption of more carbon-based fuels. Although some progress is being made in the development and use of alternative sources of energy in some of those countries (as is also the case in the developed world), the overall result certainly will be an increase in GHG emissions. Some experts suggest that GHG emissions could grow by as much as a further 52% by 2050.

Total and Individual Contributors

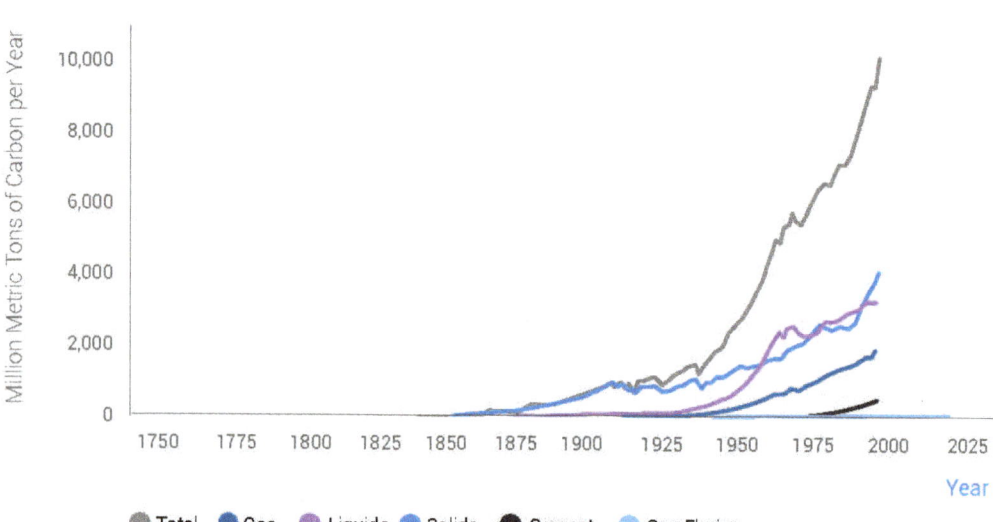

Figure 2-2   Rate and source of CO_2 emissions (CDIAC).

This level of increased emissions, even on a smaller scale, can only mean higher average temperatures. Already, some of the hottest years on record have been witnessed in many parts of the world. As a World Meteorological Organization (WMO) official recently summed up the situation, "The long-term temperature trend is far more important than the ranking of individual years, and that trend is an upward one.... Seventeen of the 18 warmest years on record have all been during this century, and the degree of warming during the past three years has been exceptional."[9]

Most disconcerting is a report published in the *Washington Post* newspaper that stated that, "...by 2027 the climatic tipping point will have started in Manokwari, Indonesia; by 2023 in Kingston, in the Caribbean; by 2029 in Lagos; by 2047 in Washington; by 2066 in Reykjavik; and by 2071 in Anchorage.[9]

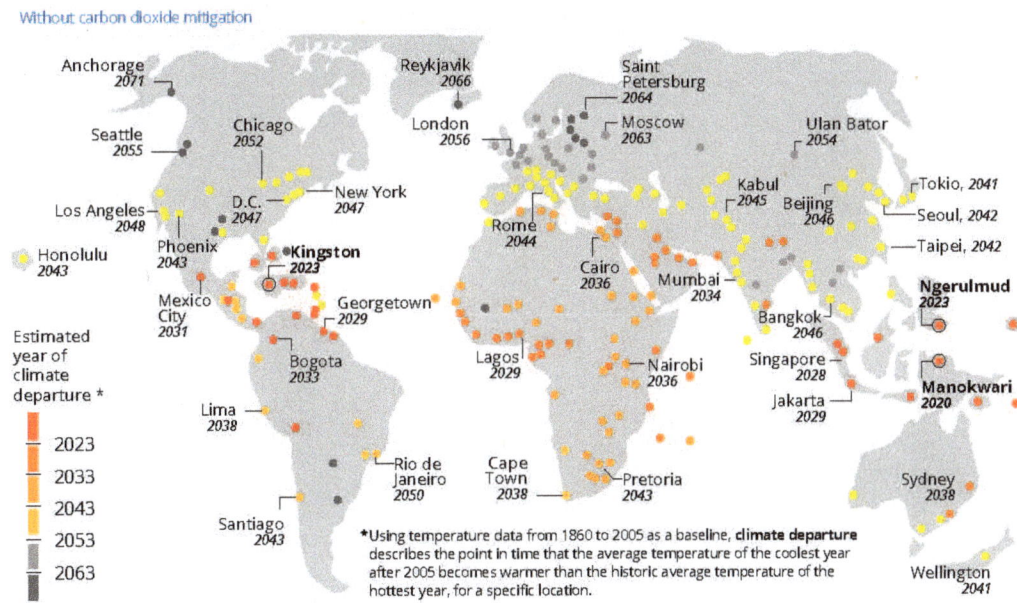

Figure 2-3   Climatic tipping point scenario (Washington Post).

Climate Change Impacts

The bottom line is that humankind has mismanaged the planet's ecosystem and is now facing the daunting consequences brought about by climate change and global warming, many of which are already noticeable. Some of the possible manifestations predicted by experts due to humanity's missteps in this area are listed below:

- A projected rise in sea levels of 1 to 4 feet by 2100. This will be due mostly to two major factors: melting ice sheets in the Arctic, Greenland, and especially Antarctica, as well as thermal expansion of the oceans. This threatens to inundate coastal, low-lying areas and increases the risk of flooding, storm surges, and erosion of coastlines. This would inevitably bring about the displacement of large populations and potentially serious armed conflicts among neighboring states and/or regions.

- Changing precipitation patterns could cause increased rainfall in some regions and water shortages in others, with implications for agriculture and access to safe drinking water. The number of people suffering from absolute water scarcity could increase by at least 40% by 2100.

Figure 2-4   Erosion causing road collapse (stock photo).

Figure 2-5   Drinking water becoming scarce (stock photo).

Figure 2-6   Lower crop yields (stock photo).

Figure 2-7   Climatic change displacement refugees (UNHCR).

- For each 1-degree increase in global temperature, grain yields are forecast to decline by about 5%. This could pose a serious threat to international security as countries and regions compete to maintain their food supplies.

- Severe weather extremes could result in more intense and more frequent tropical cyclones and hurricanes, threatening communities and local infrastructure in areas at risk. Extreme heat, changing disease patterns, and other costly and growing public health impacts could threaten hundreds of thousands, if not millions, of lives every year. These populations could also look for safe haven elsewhere.

An Outdated Economic Model

We cannot have infinite growth on a planet with finite resources. At the moment, the global economy is using up natural resources at a rate that is outstripping the capacity of the planet to renew them. Moreover, should the global population reach 9.6 billion by 2050, as per a United Nations forecast, the equivalent of almost three planet Earths could be required to provide the natural resources needed to sustain current lifestyles.

Statistics published by the UN Sustainable Development Goals program illustrate the current climate nexus in terms of water, food, and energy:[10]

Water

- Less than 3% of the world's water is fresh (drinkable), of which 2.5% is frozen in Antarctica, the Arctic, and glaciers. Humanity must therefore rely on 0.5% for all humanity's ecosystems and fresh water needs.

- Humanity is polluting water faster than nature can recycle and purify water in rivers and lakes.

- More than 1 billion people still do not have access to fresh water.

Food

- Food is wasted at the rate of 1.3 billion tons every year while almost 1 billion people go undernourished and another 1 billion go hungry.

- More than 2 billion people globally are overweight or obese.

- Overconsumption of food is detrimental to human health and the environment.

- Land degradation, declining soil fertility, unsustainable water use, overfishing. and marine environment degradation are all lessening the ability of the natural resource base to supply food.

- The food sector accounts for about 30% of the world's total energy consumption and causes around 22% of total greenhouse gas emissions.

Energy

- Despite technological advances that promote energy efficiency gains, energy use in Organization for Economic Cooperation and Development (OECD) countries will continue to grow another 35% by 2020.

- Commercial and residential energy use is the second most rapidly growing area of global energy use after transport.

- In 2002 the motor vehicle stock in OECD countries was 550 million vehicles (75% of which were personal cars). A 32% increase in vehicle ownership is expected by 2020. At the same time, motor vehicle kilometers are projected to increase by 40%.

- Global air travel is projected to triple during the same period.

Whatever the actual figures turn out to be, it is clear that a prolonged pattern of over-consumption such as the one in which we are currently engaged can only lead to more environmental degradation and the eventual loss of vital natural resource bases. In addition, according to the International Energy Agency (IEA), peak oil – the point at which the rate of global conventional oil production begins to fall – was reached in 2006. Should demand remain at current levels, supply might only last some 40 years beyond that.

An added consideration is that the inhabitants of the developed nations of the world consume resources at a rate almost 32 times greater than those in the developing world, who make up the majority of the current human population of 7.6 billion people. Yet the developing world is a growing market of consumption that is increasing its purchasing power. It is expected to eventually account for 56% of global consumption growth by 2030. This involves consumption rates that will have plateaued for the developed nations and increased more in developing countries.

The end result may well be greater overall exponential growth in consumption, something the planet cannot support indefinitely. The logical conclusion is that the current economic model is globally unsustainable. And what is not sustainable is doomed to slow down or implode.

It seems that humanity has come to a fork in the road. As it ponders the direction it will take, it would be wise to heed the popular wisdom that "...Mother Nature doesn't argue, she doesn't negotiate; if one does not play by her rules, eventually one will suffer the consequences".

RENEWABLE ENERGY AND SUSTAINABILITY

The two key areas that must be focused on when dealing with the impacts of climate change in a constructive and productive manner are the development and use of renewable sources of energy and the utilization of sustainable patterns of production and consumption. The following sections discuss these two areas in more detail.

A Time for Renewal and Regeneration

The World Energy Council (WEC) has reported that fuel demand in the transport sector in the next 40 years will come mainly from developing countries such as China and India, where demand will grow by 200% to 300%. In contrast, the WEC is of the view that the transport fuel demand in the developed countries will drop by up to 20%, mainly due to increased efficiencies. The demand of the developing countries is expected to surpass that of the developed countries by 2025.

The report also forecasts that oil may still fuel more than 80% of the global transport sector for the next 40 years due to strong demand growth from the heavy-duty sector, shipping, and air traffic. WEC projects that by 2050, global fuel demand in all transport modes could increase by 30% to 82% compared with 2010 levels. This indicates the inevitability that fossil fuels, the reserves of which are still being discovered, will retain their heavy influence over the coming years and that therefore global efforts must be concentrated on market-based measures as well as the development of alternative fuel technology.

At the 39th Session of the Assembly of the International Civil Aviation Organization (ICAO), held in September/October 2016, the Council of ICAO (consisting of 36 elected member States) pointed out that a trend analysis had revealed that despite an anticipated increase of 4.2 times in international air traffic by 2040, fuel consumption was projected to increase by only 2.8 to 3.9 times over the same period. It was estimated that up to 2% of this fuel consumption could consist of sustainable alternative fuels in 2020, but that significant uncertainties existed in predicting the contribution of sustainable alternative fuels in the long term. However, the Assembly recognized that the technological feasibility of drop-in sustainable alternative fuels for aviation is proven and that the introduction of appropriate policies and incentives to create a long-term market perspective was required. It was also recognized that there was a need for such fuels to be developed and deployed in an economically feasible and socially and environmentally acceptable manner and for the progress achieved to be in harmony with approaches to sustainability. In accordance with the 7th Sustainable Development Goal of the United Nations - Ensure access to affordable, reliable, sustainable, and modern energy for all – the ICAO Assembly acknowledged the compelling need to explore and facilitate civil aviation sector's access to renewable energy, including through its cooperation with the Sustainable Energy for All (SE4ALL) initiative.

The above discussion leaves no room for doubt that renewable sources of energy represent the true option against non-renewable GHG-producing fossil fuels. The expression 'renewable' refers to natural sources as opposed to 'alternative', a term that is sometimes used in reference to other sources of non-fossil fuels such as nuclear power.

According to the International Energy Agency (IEA), the following are the five most commonly used renewable energy sources, in order of importance.[11]

1   Hydropower remains the world's most important source of renewable energy.

2   Wind turbines are becoming more widespread around the world and are used primarily to generate electricity.

3   Biomass consists of material that comes from plants and animals. It includes wood and wood waste, municipal solid waste, landfill gas and biogas, ethanol, and biodiesel.

4   Solar energy is used increasingly for heating and electricity production, thanks to modern technological developments.

5   Geothermal energy is heat within the Earth. Where available, it can be used to heat or cool buildings and produce electricity.

Figure 2-8   System of integration of renewables (stock photo).

Although the use of renewable energy sources is gaining traction, collectively they provide only about 7% of the world's energy needs. This means that fossil fuels, along with nuclear energy, are still supplying 93% of the world's energy resources, primarily for heating, electricity production, and all forms of transportation.

The amount of energy produced from renewable sources will continue to increase as the technology improves across the sector and as interest grows worldwide. This trend will support efforts by governments to meet the global target of keeping average global temperature levels well below two degrees Celsius above pre-industrial levels. This target was established by the Paris Climate Change Agreement of 2015. It is a UN Sustainability Goal and is also the IEA's own sustainability target. Nevertheless, the IEA has emphasized that the world is not on track to meeting its energy sustainability goals, based on existing and announced policies. Much more has to be done on a number of fronts, including the more widespread integration of renewable energy sources into the overall power grid.

The case for a major shift towards more renewables is strongly encouraged by numerous parties, including various levels of government, non-government organizations, segments of the business community, and millions of concerned citizens around the world. The universally recognized benefits of renewable energy include reduced global warming, improved public health, inexhaustible energy supplies, job creation, general economic benefits, and stable energy prices. It will also result in a more reliable and resilient supply of energy.

However, according to the Union of Concerned Scientists (UCS), a number of barriers remain in the path of full implementation of renewables, including:

- Renewable infrastructure is relatively cheap to operate, but can be expensive to build, particularly wind and solar installations. Nevertheless, renewable energy capital costs keep falling, and the sector remains the least expensive of energy-generating sources over the long term.

- Wind and solar projects are based on a decentralized model, in which smaller generating stations, spread across a large area, work together to provide power. This involves a potentially complex process of securing land for installations and transmission lines, both of which can be expensive.

- Competition with well-established and well-funded utilities is an enormous challenge for new entrants to the renewable industry.

- Whereas solar and wind sources of energy, when paired with complementary generation sources, can be both predictable and reliable, erroneous perceptions to the contrary have to date inhibited their installation.

The UCS believes that the solution involves three key factors: strong government investments, better information and promotional campaigns, and public demand for renewables.[12]

Sustainability: Mantra for a Shrinking Global Village

The great challenge of the 21st Century is for humankind to consume less and, more to the point, to consume in a sustainable manner.

This was recognized early on, at the UN Conference on the Environment held in Rio de Janeiro (Brazil) in 1992. Two statements made there merit highlighting: "...states should reduce and eliminate unsustainable patterns of production and consumption", and "...the major cause of continued deterioration of the global environment is the **unsustainable patterns of consumption and production**..."[13]

According to the UN, sustainable consumption and production involves a number of activities: promoting resource and energy efficiency, building sustainable infrastructure, providing access to basic services, and creating green and decent jobs, all of which are meant to lead to a better quality of life for everyone. Implementation of sustainable consumption and production helps to achieve overall development plans, reduce future economic, environmental, and social costs, strengthen economic competitiveness, and reduce poverty.

In other words, sustainable consumption and production aims at "doing more and better with less". It thus increases net welfare gains from the economic activities involved in producing a product by reducing resource use and minimizing pollution along the lifecycle of a product, while also increasing the quality of life. It involves numerous stakeholders, including business, consumers, policy-makers, researchers, scientists, retailers, media, development cooperation agencies, and others.

Sustainable consumption also requires a systematic approach and cooperation among players operating in the supply chain, from producers to the final consumer. It involves engaging consumers by raising awareness and educating them about sustainable consumption and lifestyles. Standards need to be developed and publicized, and consumers need to be provided with adequate information through informative labels and information campaigns.

In the spirit of the IPCC findings, using a wide array of technological measures and changes in behavior could certainly contribute to limiting the increase in global mean temperature. Prime examples of such measures include a wide range of new developments in renewables, leading-edge technologies for reducing emissions, new production strategies, and major policy decisions encapsulated by the Paris Agreement and the UN Sustainability Development Goals.

Among the promising options is the 'Cradle to Cradle' (C2) approach. It consists of sustainable design methodologies that aim to create things that not only avoid environmental damage altogether, but actually give back to the earth by having a regenerative effect, such as decomposing in the local environment and providing nutrients to the soil. Another alternative to the traditional linear economy, which is based on the "make, use, dispose" model, is the circular economy model in which resources are kept in use for as long as possible and utilized to the maximum while in use. The savings can then be recovered and used to regenerate products and materials at the end of each service life.

Certainly, there are many more avenues and solutions to be explored. Yet time is of the essence. The message heard ever more frequently these days is that humanity must act now before it is too late.

CLIMATE CHANGE AND AVIATION
– AIR TRAVEL ON A HOTTER PLANET

The global air transport system has proven to be extraordinarily progressive and resilient since its inception some 70 years ago. This is exemplified by the creation of such bodies as ICAO in 1944 and+ the International Air Transport Association (IATA) in 1945, followed by the advent of similar global bodies representing all other major components of international civil aviation.

Such organizations have fostered and demonstrated consistent levels of collaboration among all stakeholders in the global aviation industry. Their presence has allowed the industry to overcome numerous economic downturns such as oil crises, regulatory transformations, and some of the most dramatic terrorist attacks of the 20th Century, culminating with the horrific events of September 11, 2001.

Within that context, air traffic has managed to flourish. Passenger traffic increased from a few million passengers annually in the late 1940s to more than 3.8 billion in 2017. In parallel with this practically uninterrupted growth over the past seven decades, air travel has become progressively safer, more secure, and more efficient.

Now comes the biggest challenge so far for the global aviation industry – one of truly planetary proportions: global warming. The following section first considers the potential impact of global warming on the air transport industry, primarily airlines, airports, and air traffic control. It then reviews aviation's two-pronged strategy – adaptation and mitigation – for dealing with this latest, multi-faceted challenge to the operational and financial integrity of the industry.

As with the overall societal impacts of climate change, the scope and reach of all possible consequences are difficult to predict with a high degree of certainty. One obvious reason is the uncertain rate of global warming. Also, impacts on aviation may vary according to geographic location, scale of operations, and degree of connectedness with national or international systems and networks. For example, the flooding of an airport runway will produce a domino effect on flight schedules of any number of airlines operating at that particular airport.

This should not be cause for procrastination or inaction, but rather a time for intelligent and imaginative action. In his delightful and mind-altering book, *How to Think Like Leonardo Da Vinci*, author Michael Gelb suggests that we learn to face the unknown proactively by following the lead of one of the most creative minds that ever lived and cultivating *sfumato*, as Da Vinci called it, which literally means: "a willingness to embrace ambiguity, paradox, uncertainty."[14] As shall be seen later, planning ahead is one of the most powerful strategies for limiting the anticipated impacts of climate change.

Airlines, airports, and air navigation services providers (ANSPs) are adept at dealing with the full range of weather-related situations. Climate change and global warming have considerably expanded the nature and scope of these challenges. The following section deals with a number of weather-related phenomena that are already known to be directly impacting aviation operations and are expected to increasingly do so in the future.

The Heat Is On

In June of 2017, a severe heat wave hit the southern United States. The mercury soared beyond maximum operating temperatures for planes to take off. Dozens of commercial flights had to be delayed, cancelled, or rerouted from affected airports. Some waited countless hours on the tarmac for the required operating conditions.

Figure 2-9   Aircraft waiting on the taxiway (stock photo).

That particular occurrence was all about physics. The amount of lift that an airplane wing generates is affected by the density of the air. Air density, in turn, depends mostly on air temperature and elevation; higher temperatures and higher elevations both reduce density. The lower the air density, the faster an airplane must travel on a runway to generate enough lift to take off. Since it takes more runway to reach a higher speed, depending on the length of the runway, some airplanes might risk running out of room before reaching sufficient speed for takeoff.

One option to deal with this situation is to reduce the aircraft's weight in order to lower its required takeoff speed – by removing passengers, cargo and fuel. Such weight restriction measures are already commonly used in regularly hot locations around the globe. This especially affects long-haul flights that require large amounts of fuel and often take off when near maximum weights.

The foregoing is but one example of the implications of the effect of increased average temperatures on current passenger aircraft technology. As the planet gets progressively warmer, such occurrences may become more frequent in the future. A study of the subject that was published in the journal, *Climatic Change,* found that in the coming decades, during the hottest parts of the day, between 10% and 30% of fully loaded planes may have to remove payload in order to be able to take off. The authors of the study estimate that weight may have to be reduced by up to 4% on the hottest days, roughly equivalent to removing a dozen or so passengers from a 160-seat aircraft or removal of significant cargo for a cargo carrier. This would have a considerable economic impact on both types of carriers, which typically already operate on thin profit margins.

In addition to reduced payloads/revenues for airlines, other financial and operating consequences would include disrupted operations of airport operators and air navigation service providers, inconvenience to affected passengers, and ripple effects throughout the global network. In a systemic industry like air transport, one event can easily snowball and impact stakeholders worldwide, including travel and tourism.

As such heat-related events become chronic in parts of the world, some airlines could consider investing in different aircraft that would allow them to operate regularly in hotter weather. As for designing new and more flexible types of planes, this would be impractical as designing new equipment is extremely expensive and involves a very lengthy development process of usually a decade or more.

An alternative to reducing the weight of aircraft is to shift flights to the evening, when temperatures are cooler and more conducive for takeoff. That is the reason why long-distance flights out of the Middle East are regularly scheduled during the night. The same may eventually apply in the US, Southern Europe, and other regions susceptible to higher temperatures. This practice, however, may be difficult in places where noise curfews are in effect for nighttime operations, whether passenger or cargo.

Another possible solution to the temperature-weight ratio problem would be to opt for extending runways or building new ones, in the case of airports wishing to maintain or increase operational levels. This is an expensive proposition at the best of times, made more difficult for airports located in densely populated urban areas where opposition from communities and local governments could block such initiatives, as has been the case in the past. Industry competition might also be affected. In some markets, airports in hotter areas and with shorter runways or at higher altitudes might be at a disadvantage compared with those with longer runways, milder climates, or those able to operate without the concern of curfews.

Airports have operational and safety concerns as well regarding rising temperatures. Extreme heat could cause serious damage to infrastructure such as cracks or deformation of runways and taxiways. Warmer temperatures would also impact facilities much in the same way as other large public places due to increased demand for air conditioning in terminals and office buildings in the summer and, where applicable, increased heating due to a colder climate. There would also be increased pressure on local power utilities.

Figure 2-10   Pavement cracking due to heat (stock photo).

Paradoxically, higher temperatures could provide benefits in parts of the world normally associated with extreme cold weather, as a relatively warmer climate would have less snowfall and associated ice removal or de-icing costs. On the other hand, airport runways built on permafrost in northern regions would be subject to deterioration in the heat and might have to be strengthened or relocated. For example, Iqaluit Airport in northern Canada is a good case in point. The permafrost on which the runway and taxiway are built had to be resurfaced, and the melting is deepening.

Research into the financial impact of rising temperatures on airline operations is still limited, yet according to a Columbia University study, heat waves will probably become more prevalent, with annual maximum daily temperatures at airports worldwide projected to go up by 4 to 8 degrees C (7.2° to 14.4°F) by 2080. And so will their implications for the global air transport system.

Rain, Rain, Snow, and Ice

While menacing on their own, increasing temperatures and heat waves are also expected to continue to produce extreme weather patterns that will lead to a number of related events that will affect airport and airline operations.

Storm water runoff that exceeds the capacity of collection and drainage systems can cause airport flooding, flight delays and cancellations, and airport closings. Moreover, heavy downpours can affect the structural integrity of airport facilities through flood damage to runways, taxiways, and other infrastructure. There could be water inundation of underground infrastructure such as electrical systems and/or ground transport access for passengers and staff. In all such cases, airport throughput can be seriously affected.

Over the past few years, limitations affecting ground and flight operations have been noticed in various parts of the world where these were not a factor before. They include high wind events, freezing rain, heavy precipitation, and lightning strikes, all of which can also damage buildings, facilities, and aircraft. Similarly, in winter, there are challenges associated with snow prediction and removal, a situation that can be demanding in areas not accustomed to harsh winter conditions.

Runways constructed along the locally prevailing wind direction may experience more crosswinds due to more frequent deviations from that prevailing direction, or an airport may start to experience crosswinds but have no crosswind runway. This may entail the need for changes in procedures and airspace redesigns. Such changes may then in turn produce additional environmental risks due to the redistribution of noise impacts around the airports.

All the above can have implications for normal airport operations, as well as facility maintenance, safety, and emergency evacuations in the case of disasters. For airlines, these same problems can cause flight cancellations, delays, or the re-routing of flights.

Blowing Hard and Wild

A number of studies have suggested that higher temperatures brought about by climate change are creating atmospheric conditions that could lead to increased turbulence in some areas, as well as longer flight times.

The area in and around the high-altitude jet streams will be one of the most affected, primarily on the North Atlantic flight routes. The reason for bumpier (and thus slower) rides is that stronger winds will increase the amount of shear in the jet stream, leading to what is known as clear-air turbulence, or CAT. The term "'clear" is used, because it occurs away from storm clouds, is practically invisible, and therefore is difficult to fly around.

Although normal turbulence is annoying or even frightening to many passengers, it is rarely dangerous. Anyone familiar with aircraft manufacturer testing procedures knows very well that the planes are subjected to severe conditions that they would probably never encounter in real life.

Figure 2-11   Stress test for aircraft (stock photo).

CAT is different in that it is sometimes heavier than normal turbulence and especially unexpected. Passengers today often fly without their seat belts on. This may become less frequent in the future. A study published by the University of Reading (UK) suggests that there will be three times more CAT in future decades and that by 2050 the rate of inflight injuries will have increased proportionally.[15]

Figure 2-12   Heavy turbulence in flight (stock photo).

Such a scenario may never unfold, yet a projected increase in more frequent and heavier turbulence may well lead to additional fuel burn as pilots attempt to counter affected zones, resulting in additional expenses for airlines.

As is often the case, technology is coming to the rescue in a number of ways. The industry is investing in new satellite-based navigation systems that would allow flight crews to more accurately avoid areas of significant turbulence. For its part, Boeing is already preparing to test new laser technology that could allow pilots to detect clear-air turbulence up to 10 miles away, giving them enough time to warn passengers and cabin crew.

High-Altitude Icing

On June 1, 2009, an Air France flight on route from Rio de Janeiro to Paris crashed in the Atlantic Ocean, killing all on board. The aircraft had stalled after the autopilot disconnected when ice crystals disabled its speed sensors located outside the aircraft. This accident was an extreme example of the dangers of high-altitude icing, a condition that may become more frequent as climate change pushes stronger and more frequent thunderstorms into cruising altitudes.

High-level ice is also dangerous when tiny particles of ice infiltrate into turbofan engines. In recent years, more than 100 engine failures have been attributed to this phenomenon. Of concern as well is that modern energy-efficient and lean-burn engines may be more susceptible to high-altitude ice.

Sea-Level Rise – The Perfect Storm

One of the most documented impacts of climate change is sea-level rise, or SLR, which is likely to impact airport and other ground infrastructure located in low-lying and coastal areas.

Airports in coastal cities are often close to rivers, estuaries, or oceans. Airport runways could face flooding where drainage capacity cannot handle higher water levels. Critical installations such as underground electrical equipment may be affected, with serious repercussions. Moreover, these low-lying sites are often in the path of major storms or hurricanes as they hit land from the open seas, causing even greater damage to facilities and equipment on both the airside and landside of airports.

In addition to sea-level rise, regions with strong monsoons, tropical storms, and storm surges linked to more intense cyclones will likely experience more intense precipitation. In cases that involve an entire region or area, the choice of diversionary airports may be reduced, and those that are available may not have sufficient capacity to accommodate the required overflow. Moreover, extreme cases such as hurricanes may become frequent and may have even more severe impacts in the future because of higher sea levels.

At worst, sea-level rise has the potential to cause closures or restricted access to several of a country's busiest airports, affecting service to high-density population centers and connecting passenger and commercial transportation systems. Economies of entire regions would be at risk of severe disruptions.

A dramatic example was the Kansai Airport, which was flooded by Typhoon Jebi on September 4, 2018 (see Figure 2-13). In its reporting of the event at the time, the *New York Times* stated that, according to analysis of data from Airports Council International (ACI) and OpenFlights, a quarter of the world's 100 busiest airports are less than 10 meters, or 32 feet, above sea level. Twelve of these airports — including hubs in Shanghai, Rome, San Francisco, and New York — are less than 5 meters above sea level.[16]

Even an increase of only one meter in sea level, coupled with more intense storms and higher waves, will require robust measures to adapt to the most demanding scenarios. Some climate scientists predict that sea levels may rise by as much as six feet by the end of this century. This would threaten operations at hundreds of aviation hubs around the world. Accordingly, a number of international airports are in the process of implementing measures to deal with rising sea levels and are including them in development plans.

Figure 2-13   Kansai Airport flooded by Typhoon Jebi (stock photo).

For example, Singapore's Changi Airport, one of the world's busiest, is raising its new passenger terminal 5.5m above sea level as a precaution against future storm tides. Hong Kong is constructing a wall, eight miles (13km) long, around a new runway. In Hong Kong, officials say that a project to build a third airport runway on soon-to-be reclaimed land was influenced by climate and sea-level projections made in 2014 by the Inter-Governmental Panel on Climate Change. They say that the $18 billion runway will have a sea wall that stands at least 21 feet above the waterline and can withstand 100-year storms, as well as a drainage system that is designed to handle rare floods.

Perhaps more radical solutions are required. For example, back in the 1990s, Japan built a 1-km-long floating airstrip in Tokyo Bay as a "scale model" for a full-size floating airport that could rise with the tides.

In short, unless effective measures are taken to increase the resilience of airports, many of these projections could indeed become reality and cause increasing harm to the global air transport system. The costs associated with infrastructure damage by future sea-level rise, storm surges, and flooding could be substantial. This situation is perhaps most worrisome for small islands that rely on air travel as a lifeline to the outside world and are particularly vulnerable to the threat posed by SLR.

Air Traffic Growth and Shifting Consumer Preferences

Adapting to the direct impacts of climate change is challenging enough. It becomes even more complex when considering some of the indirect impacts such as growth in air traffic and shifting consumer preferences as they relate to climate change.

With the rise in temperatures, some travel destinations may become simply too hot, causing traffic to divert to more temperate climates, which would then enjoy a surge in clientele. Long-time favorite resorts along coastlines may become severely affected by rising sea levels and thus rendered unattractive to vacationers, or they might have to close down altogether for at least part of the year. With reduced snowfall, ski resorts might suffer a similar fate, with skiers looking for alternate locations or having to adjust their travel plans to a shift in the winter season. This will have major impacts for airlines on scheduling and route configurations. Airports will also need to adjust to either reduced or increased passenger flows, depending on their specific situations.

At the same time, a study performed on behalf of EUROCONTROL titled *Adapting European Airports to a Changing Climate* clearly outlined the linkage between climate change and traffic growth. The main finding is that traffic growth may well place increasing pressure on operations in both emerging and established markets, compounding the risks of climate change at some European airports. As the study stated, "...some of the locations where the highest growth rates are forecast, such as Southeast and Central Europe, are also some of the areas where the greatest potential climate change impacts are predicted".[7] Many of these airports will need to deal at the same time with dual challenges of rapid traffic growth coupled with climate change adaptation. The situation is more demanding at peak travel times, when airport capacity is constrained.

As discussed in the next section, many airports and airlines not already facing new or extreme problems are approaching climate change as a situation that they realize they will need to address before it impacts them directly. This is probably a prudent strategy. Taking stock of the situation and planning ahead is essential before an emergency strikes.

ADAPTING TO CLIMATE CHANGE

In the preceding pages, this chapter looked at some of the most powerful expected impacts of climate change on airports, airlines, and air navigation service providers (ANSPs), alluding as well to the down-line effects on regional, national, and international transportation networks. This section shifts its attention to the first half of the strategy for strengthening resilience: adaptation.

The focus is primarily on airports, as these fixed installations are the most vulnerable to climate change in terms of: potential damage, complexity, and size of operations, linkages to surrounding communities, and the air transport system as a whole. Nevertheless, it must be emphasized that all other stakeholders, particularly airlines and air navigation service providers, must also be prepared to deal with the situation when the time comes.

Interestingly, although climate change and global warming may soon threaten the operational integrity and financial viability of many aviation stakeholders, one would think that most, if not all, of them would be active in developing and implementing robust countermeasures. Surprisingly, this is not the case.

In 2013, EUROCONTROL conducted a survey of European aviation stakeholders as part of its Challenges of Growth initiative. Results indicated that while more than 80% of respondents considered it necessary to adapt to climate change now or in the future, almost half of them indicated that their organization did not yet have an official position on the issue. Also, fewer than half the organizations that responded had begun planning for adaptation to climate change, although a significant number of them nevertheless expected that they would need to take action.[18]

Survey results also revealed two main obstacles to taking adaptation action:

1   Lack of information or guidance, meaning that either an organization did not know if action needed to be taken or it wasn't sure how that action should be carried out.

2   Lack of an official organizational position on the issue, unavailability of resources, or a decision had been made that action was not required at the time.

Meanwhile, a poll conducted in the United States by the National Academy of Sciences came up with a somewhat different reaction. Many airport operators and managers indicated that they indeed felt prepared for climate change because they had already contended with a variety of weather-related issues. Caution might be in order when considering those reactions. As pointed out earlier, many of the impacts attributed to global warming are much stronger and more varied than "typical" weather situations encountered to date in day-to-day operations, and the prognosis is for them to get much more severe in the future.

Nevertheless, the initial lesson learned from both these surveys – which are probably representative of attitudes in other parts of the world – is that providing better information on the potential risks of climate change for the aviation sector, and guidance on how to address those risks, is key to promoting effective climate adaptation action.

The IPCC defines adaptation as "…adjustment in natural or human systems in response to actual or expected climatic stimuli or their effects, which moderates harm or exploits beneficial opportunities".

For its part, ICAO refers to climate adaptation as "…the ability of a system to adjust to climate change to moderate potential consequences or to manage the consequences of those impacts that cannot be avoided". Successful adaptation can reduce vulnerability by strengthening existing strategies. A typical case of adaptation for aviation would be improvements in coastal area airport defenses against sea-level rise, as mentioned earlier in this chapter.

Climate Change Risk Assessments

One approach to identifying and dealing effectively with the consequences associated with climate change is a formal risk assessment and response process. This has many advantages.

First and foremost, a risk assessment helps ascertain whether there are risks or not to an entity. If there are risks, it makes it possible to identify those risks with a high degree of accuracy, keeping in mind that this is often a moving target because of the "changing" nature of climate change itself. A risk assessment also provides a better understanding of the potential "ripple effect" of climate change, beyond conventional operational disruptions and related financial impacts. These might include:

- New and more demanding operating conditions that could stretch the current limits of the experience and expertise of airport personnel, as well as those of the facilities and equipment.
- Health and safety concerns of customers and staff.

- Erosion of capital investments.

- Previously unsuspected systemic repercussions on the air transport network beyond the airport's operations.

- Operational and business risks such as ground transport access or utility supply that may not be entirely within the control of the airport itself.

- Impact on the local economy and community services.

- Other factors unique to the particular airport.

A thorough risk assessment also takes into account local, state, and international legal and/or regulatory requirements. Not considering these may jeopardize an otherwise well thought-out climate change adaptation plan. Management, which is traditionally focused on operational and financial considerations, may have a tendency to sometimes overlook this.

Most important is the ability to properly cost out such a plan, again keeping in mind that flexibility must be built in to account for fluctuations due to shifting climate conditions. This becomes critical in submitting a convincing case to boards or senior executives who must approve the allocation of human and financial resources for preventive measures and programs that may come to fruition well beyond normal budget cycles, sometimes a decade or more into the future.

In their paper titled "*The impact of climate change and weather on transport: An overview of empirical findings*", authors Mark J. Koetse and Piet Rietveld put forth a highly pertinent commentary for those wishing to perform a more detailed and holistic financial reviews of costs associated with climate change impacts, which eventually would involve a number of outside stakeholders.[19]

As Koetse and Rietveld pointed out, "Natural and man-made hazards disturb transportation systems that are essential to the well-being of the society at an increasing rate and severity to cause extensive physical damage. Direct economic losses resulting from physical damages diffuse and expand continually through economic activities between different regions and industries, resulting in enormous indirect losses." They then go on to say, "We find that more than often, networked transportation systems are abstracted from economic analyses. Moreover, despite the advances in hazards science, realistic simulations of locally relevant hazards are not fully integrated into economic studies. These will limit our ability to comprehensively quantify the economic impacts of infrastructure disruptions caused by disasters."

Carrying out this additional analysis of economic costs, where warranted, might be quite demanding, yet it can enhance the comprehensiveness and value of the adaptation process. It also allows for the participation and support of all those involved, many of whom might not previously have been thought to be part of the solution. Among these are local, regional, and national politicians, who have a crucial role to play in determining policies and financial allocations regarding adaptation and eventually mitigation measures related to climate change. Ensuring close ties with the political establishment can also help to keep abreast of current thinking, contribute to a better understanding of issues involved, and help shape more enlightened decisions.

Finally, based on all the elements discussed above, specific goals and objectives can be established, priorities set, and a detailed operational and financial plan of action developed and implemented which will allow an organization to take appropriate measures in a timely and cost-effective manner. Ideally, the climate change adaptation plan should be part of an airport's "Master Operation and Development Plan", making it easier to combine the financial, operational, and human resources requirements into an overall corporate perspective. For example, planned improvements to equipment or facilities might be performed with adaptation features incorporated into them, resulting in a more cost-efficient solution.

In short, as summarized by the National Academy of Sciences, climate change adaptation risk assessment encompasses a number of steps and valuable exercises. These can be easily adapted to aviation scenarios as outlined below:

- Develop an effective advisory team and identify other important contributing stakeholders, both within management and outside the organization such as airlines, tenants, nearby municipalities, and other bodies.

- Gain an understanding of climate change projections and the limitations of the projections affecting adaptation decision-making at their airport.

- Learn how climate impacts pose risks to airport assets and operations.

- Evaluate those risks from a likelihood and vulnerability perspective.

- Generate a climate adaptation plan containing strategies tailored to the mix of assets and operations present at the airport.

- Understand how to integrate adaptation strategies into existing and future airport planning documents and procedures.

- Understand how to qualitatively evaluate specific adaptation options for incorporation into individual project designs.

- Identify external partners (municipalities, utilities, transportation agencies, etc.) whose input and adaptation responses are critical to airport operations.

Organizations contemplating an adaptation risk assessment might wish to kick start the process using the following 15 high-level questions provided by EUROCONTROL to confirm that they should indeed carry one out:

1   Do you know how the climate will change in your area?

2   What will be the financial and carbon impacts of increased diversions to avoid storm events?

3   Will your systems be able to manage capacity during more frequent extreme and disruptive weather?

4   Can changes to the jet stream be harnessed to improve flight times and performance?

5   How will temperature changes impact aircraft performance and demand for cabin air conditioning (on the ground)?

6   Are your runways and taxiways at risk of flooding?

7   Is the wind load factor of your control tower high enough to handle any projected stronger stormy weather?

8   Can your equipment withstand severe storms or flooding?

9   Can your drainage system handle any projected increase in rainfall?

10 Do you know how much it will cost to implement the climate adaptation measures you need?

11 Will climate changes increase or decrease tourism demand in your region?

12 Can your electrical supply and critical systems (e.g., IT) be maintained in more frequent and extreme disruptive weather?

13 Who is responsible for climate change adaptation within your organization?

14 Can ground access to the airport be guaranteed in case of increased precipitation (rain or snow)?

15 Can your cooling system handle any projected increase in temperature?

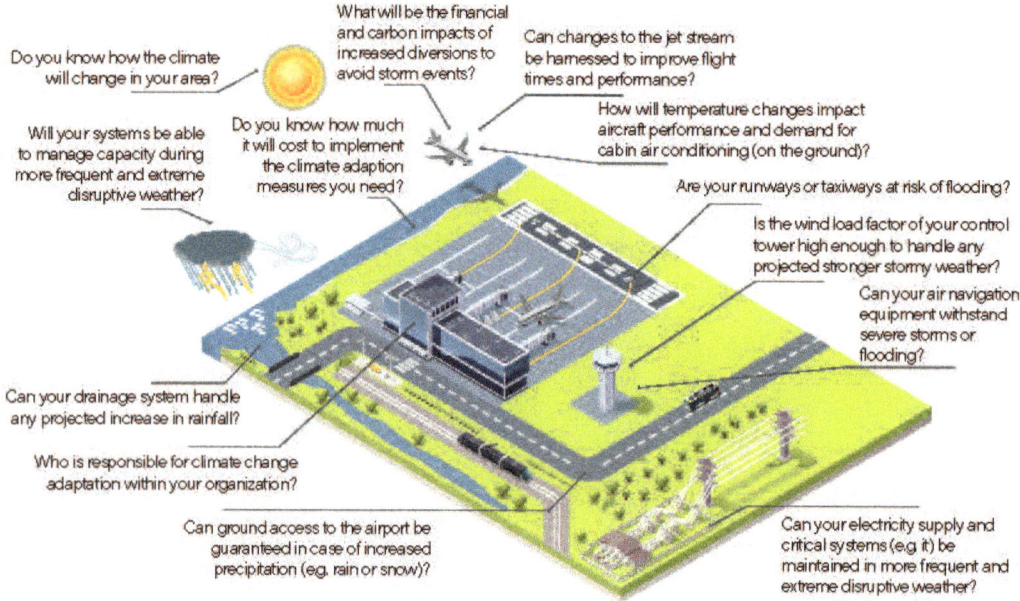

Do you know how the climate will change in your area?

What will be the financial and carbon impacts of increased diversions to avoid storm events?

Can changes to the jet stream be harnessed to improve flight times and performance?

Will your systems be able to manage capacity during more frequent and extreme disruptive weather?

Do you know how much it will cost to implement the climate adaption measures you need?

How will temperature changes impact aircraft performance and demand for cabin air conditioning (on the ground)?

Are your runways or taxiways at risk of flooding?

Is the wind load factor of your control tower high enough to handle any projected stronger stormy weather?

Can your air navigation equipment withstand severe storms or flooding?

Can your drainage system handle any projected increase in rainfall?

Who is responsible for climate change adaptation within your organization?

Can ground access to the airport be guaranteed in case of increased precipitation (eg. rain or snow)?

Can your electricity supply and critical systems (e.g. it) be maintained in more frequent and extreme disruptive weather?

Figure 2-14   Climate change risk assessment adaptation questions (EUROCONTROL).

Obviously, each airport, airline, and ANS provider operates under specific circumstances. Assessments are likewise unique to each situation and must reflect particular realities in terms of geographic location, magnitude and complexity of operations, and legal status (i.e., state-owned or private sector).

The question is, where to begin? Fortunately, practical and user-friendly guidance material is available from a variety of sources, including national governments and industry associations as well as academia and consultancies.

One last point on adaptation: the same spirit of multi-party industry collaboration that has maintained the resilience of the global air transport system over time will prove just as important in ensuring the success of risk assessments. Ongoing communications among airports, airlines, ANSPs, and all other stakeholders mentioned previously will tap vast resources of knowledge and expertise that would otherwise not be available, while also contributing to filling the information gaps in understanding climate change.

Adaptation Case Studies

Following are five case studies of European air transport that illustrate the benefits of risk assessments and follow-up action, courtesy of EUROCONTROL.

Case Study 1: Norwegian Airports – Wetter and Wilder Weather!

Most of Avinor's[20] airports are scattered along the rugged Norwegian coastline, with several having runways less than 4m above sea level. Avinor has been looking systematically into climate adaptation since the turn of the century. However, when new legislation was introduced in 2006, requiring safety areas at the sides and ends of runways at several airports to be expanded, theory had to be turned into practice. The seabed close to the runways in question was very deep in some places. In collaboration with technical experts, this required looking into projections for future sea levels, wind directions, wave directions and – in some instances – underwater topography to calculate the size, shape, and amount of rocks needed to make robust fillings which would be able to withstand future storms. A procedure was developed for dimensioning criteria for safety areas close to the sea, as well as a set of guidelines for low-lying coastal runways and strengthened requirements for potential new runways – they now have to be established at least 7m above sea level.

A comprehensive risk assessment of all Avinor airports, connected navigation systems, and surface access to the airports was undertaken. In general, more extreme weather events, storms, and storm surges are expected. Increased precipitation and freak rains challenge the drainage of runways, aprons, buildings, and other infrastructure. During the planning phase of the terminal expansion at Oslo Airport and the related work on the apron, for example, it was revealed that the new drainage systems were in need of 50% added capacity compared with the drainage systems from the 1990s, when the airport was constructed. Among other things, it was also discovered that the batteries for some of the NAV equipment are placed on the floor at airports and are at risk of flooding. This will now be rectified. Avinor's experience is that minor adaptation investments in already planned and/or ongoing projects can have a positive impact on punctuality and regularity and save on future resources.

Case Study 2: NATS[21] – Preparing for More Extreme Winter Weather

Snowfall where not expected, or which is much heavier than normal, causes the most disruption to operations due to lack of preparedness. As heavy snowfall events are currently relatively rare in the UK, part of NATS' adaptation strategy involved developing a plan to deal with such events should they become more frequent as the climate changes. The strategy was put to the test sooner than expected in winter 2010, when heavy snowfalls and record low temperatures brought travel chaos and disruption to Great Britain and Ireland. This led to severe disruption to the road and rail networks, with several airports being closed, including London Heathrow Airport for a time.

During the period of disruption, NATS managed to maintain full ATC service with no disruptions. In response to the disruptive weather, NATS initiated coordination calls three times a day with airport and airline stakeholders. Standard operating procedures remained unchanged. However, the main challenge in keeping the ATC service available was ensuring that staff could make it to work. This was achieved by providing accommodation for key staff at hotels within walking distance of their workplace (i.e., at the airports) and also by using Land Rovers to shuttle key operational staff between home and work. All key equipment (radar systems and radio communication systems) remained operational throughout the period, despite record-breaking low temperatures. NATS assets are designed to operate independently of the national grid (i.e., they are island sites), and NATS maintains a number of suitable vehicles and access equipment to ensure that continuity of service is delivered. This situation demonstrated that NATS has a suitable strategy in place should such extreme and unexpected snowfall events become more frequent as the climate changes.

Case Study 3: AENA[22] – Preparing for Higher Temperatures

In 2012, a joint initiative between Spain's Ministry of Public Works and Ministry of Agriculture, Food, and Environment was launched to conduct a preliminary analysis of the needs to adapt the core network of Spain's transport infrastructure to climate change. The work identified higher temperatures as one of the key climate change risks to the core infrastructure network. It then went on to determine which adaptation measures could mitigate this risk. Key impacts identified included: new airport infrastructure should account for the rise in energy demand for air-conditioning systems in terminal buildings due to increases in temperature; and longer runways may be needed as higher temperatures mean lower air density, a factor that reduces the thrust produced by aircraft engines and reduces the lift of the wings.

Proposed adaptation measures include assessing what additional restrictions the current runway length may impose on the operation of aircraft in warmer temperatures and what might be the best operating alternatives when a runway requires lengthening and this is not possible. At existing airports, the usual practices aimed at reducing risks associated with high temperatures and heat waves should be continued, e.g., the pruning and removal of dry vegetation in the vicinity of the airport, or campaigns for the prevention of fires. However, the impact of both higher temperatures and other climate change risks on the existing airport infrastructure will depend largely on local conditions and the specific design of each airport. Therefore, it is recommended that an in-depth assessment of the risks posed to airports be launched.

Case Study 4: DGAC/STAC[23] – Developing a Risk Assessment Methodology for French Airports

A national climate change resilience program was launched in France in 2006. It aims to prepare the country to both address and take advantage of the effects of climate change. As a result, the French civil aviation authority (DGAC) is carrying out a three-stage study, known as VULCLIM.

So far, the VULCLIM project has drawn a complete picture of the likely climatic changes that could impact French airports by the end of the 21st Century. Impacts have been identified that could both positively and adversely affect airport infrastructure, construction, and operations. Then, based on the potential climate risks and their impacts, a method to assess the vulnerability of airports to climate change was developed. Taking the characteristics of a specific location, the method combines the probabilities of the occurrence of climate change risks and the intensities of the potential impacts to assess the vulnerability of the location. DGAC applied the assessment methodology to two of France's top five airports, both located on the Mediterranean coast. Both cases have identified sea-level rise and extreme precipitation as the major threats to the locations considered.

Today, DGAC/STAC is working on the development of a tool aimed at helping airport operators to assess the vulnerability of their airport to climate change. The tool, which is based on the assessment method developed, will provide airport operators and aviation organizations with information on the weaknesses and strengths of any location to potential climate risks. It will highlight where an airport needs to take action in order to adapt and build resilience to climate change.

Case Study 5: London Heathrow[24] – Preparing for Changing Winds and Temperatures

As a result of climate change, the UK may experience more extreme summer and winter temperatures, as well as changing wind speeds and direction, which can slow aircraft flow.

One way that Heathrow is mitigating the impact of changes to wind is to introduce time-based separation (TBS) procedures, which were implemented in 2015. TBS brings additional operational benefits in addition to providing future climate resilience to Heathrow. Another measure being considered is vortex separations in crosswind conditions – whereby under certain crosswind conditions the vortex is blown away – opening up the potential to reduce separations a little and sustain the flow of aircraft traffic. Heathrow is undertaking more work and analysis in this area, as wind is a key issue at the airport.

Heathrow's climate change risk assessment also examined how more extreme temperatures might affect the airport pavements. Standards were checked, and the risk from the effects of extreme temperature was determined to be low in the near to medium term. In the longer term, say in 50 years or more, there may be more significant temperature increases. The adaptation response plan is revisited regularly to ensure that it is up to date and that the engineering strategy is responding to the changing risks. The work is also fed into the UK Government's national adaptation program.

MITIGATION OF CLIMATE CHANGE

"Mitigation" is the second prong of the two-pronged strategy to strengthen the resilience of the global air transport system. Whereas the first part, "adaptation", is concerned with responding immediately and directly to the impacts of climate change, mitigation consists of future actions that will stabilize or reduce GHG concentrations in the atmosphere.

Using a medical analogy, "adaptation" aims at treating a disease, whereas "mitigation" strives at prevention. Because of its proactive nature, mitigation reduces risks at an early stage and hopefully lessens the need for adaptation. The sooner the aviation industry fully understands and acts on climate change, the better the position it will be in to reduce and eventually eliminate its contribution to climate change and global warming.

According to the IPCC, aviation produces around 2% of the world's CO_2 emissions. It also produces other GHGs in relatively small quantities. Between 91.5% and 92.5% of aircraft engine exhaust is normal atmospheric oxygen and nitrogen. As aviation grows to meet increasing demand, particularly in fast-growing emerging markets, the IPCC forecasts that the industry's share of global human-created CO_2 emissions will increase to around 3% by 2050. CO_2 emissions therefore remain the main target in reducing emissions altogether, and considerable success has been achieved over the years. For example, in spite of the consistent growth in passenger traffic, which is currently about 5% annually, aviation has kept the growth rate in emissions to around 3% per year.

In today's context, however, this remains unacceptable from the perspective of social responsibility and aviation's own future growth as an essential element of global society. Not only will there be growing public and media pressure for aviation to cut emissions more drastically, financial reasons will become even more critical, with fuel making up roughly 30% of airline operating costs. Aviation must do even more to meet the targets set forth by the international community under the Paris Climate Agreement and in the spirit of the United Nations Agenda 21 Sustainability Development Knowledge Programme.[25]

Under the umbrella of ICAO, and in cooperation with its 192 Member States, all major aviation stakeholders representing airlines, airspace, and airports have committed to policies and actions that promote these universal objectives and those adopted by ICAO. For ICAO, that means 2% annual fuel efficiency improvements through 2050 and carbon-neutral growth from 2020 onwards.

Through IATA (International Air Transport Association), the airline industry similarly has adopted a set of ambitious targets to mitigate CO_2 emissions from air transport, as follows:

- An average improvement in fuel efficiency of 1.5% per year from 2009 to 2020.
- A cap on net aviation CO_2 emissions from 2020 (carbon-neutral growth).
- A reduction in net aviation CO_2 emissions of 50% by 2050, relative to 2005 levels.

For its part, ACI (Airports Council International), IATA's airport equivalent, is dedicated to promoting aviation and airport sustainable development and limiting or reducing environmental impacts, while supporting economic and social benefits. This objective, as ACI points out, is key to community permission to operate and grow at both local and global levels.

For its part, CANSO (Civil Air Navigation Services Organization) looks to encouraging the development of procedures that reduce fuel use and emissions while maintaining operational efficiency. As in the past, efforts to constantly reduce fuel burn, and hence all GHG emissions from aviation, will center on three specific areas: aircraft technology, operational measures, and alternative or sustainable fuels, as well as more recent attention to market-based measures (MBMs).

The following sections of this chapter discuss some of the key mitigation measures that are being taken in a number of operational areas with the involvement of various industry groups and one or more of the abovementioned organizations.

Aircraft Technology Measures

It is a well-known fact in the aviation world that jet aircraft entering the market today are at least 80% more energy-efficient per passenger kilometer than their predecessors of the 1960s. By any measure, this is a remarkable achievement and a promising one.

The ever-increasing speed and scope of technological advances coupled with a wider selection of aircraft types better adapted to route structures are setting the stage for still higher levels of performance in terms of less fuel burn and reduced GHG emissions, thus helping to meet both financial and environmental objectives. Technological innovations address all aspects of design, manufacturing, and regular upgrades to aircraft. Carbon composite materials have considerably reduced the weight of planes, and more aerodynamic fuselages and incremental improvements such as wingtip devices have considerably improved efficiency.

Re-designed engines will also contribute to reduced fuel burn through new designs and technologies. Manufacturers are making significant efforts to support compliance with ICAO's CO_2 emissions standard adopted in 2016 for all new aircraft designs from 2020 onward, and for engines and newly built models of aircraft beginning in 2023.

While progress continues in all these areas, other technologies are appearing on the (albeit distant) horizon. For example, the Airbus Group has been developing an electric aircraft, the E-Fan, powered by a series of batteries contained in the wing's inboard section. The initial use for the aircraft will be for pilot training and general aviation. E-Fan's engines are electric motors that provide all the power needed, from takeoff to landing. The engines are almost noise-free, and their zero emissions capability will contribute to reducing aviation's impact on the environment. NASA has also been busy developing a small electric plane, and its research has stimulated interest in similar projects. Although public or promotional announcements have been made for much larger commercial electric aircraft to come into service in the next decade, time will tell if those initiatives come to fruition in the projected timeframe.

More likely, however, is the introduction of hybrid aircraft, basically using the same principle as hybrid fuel electric cars. A Boeing-backed start-up, Zunum Aero, plans to deliver such hybrid aircraft to the regional carrier, JetSuite, beginning in 2022. As reported in the media, the new plane will be powered by twin electrically powered ducted fans attached to the rear of its frame. This will eliminate the loud noise of combustion-based engines. Battery packs, rather than fuel, will be housed in the aircraft's wings. A conventional fuel-powered motor will serve as a backup system at the outset. Competitors such as Europe's Airbus SE and a partnership that includes EasyJet, the U.S. military, and NASA are pursuing similar concepts.

Solar-powered aircraft are even further in the future as far as commercial passenger flights are concerned. The Solar Impulse 2's extraordinary exploit of flying a plane around the world while relying exclusively on solar energy generated much enthusiasm. However, transferring that concept to passenger aircraft may not be possible. Hybrid, and eventually electric, aircraft are expected to make their way into the airline fleets of the world well before that.

The foregoing section summarizes some of the more noteworthy examples of new aircraft technology that is designed to reduce GHG emissions. Chapter 5, *Innovative Technology Change*, contains a more detailed overview of most of the latest developments in aviation technology in a more general sense.

Streamlined Flight Operational Measures

For many years now, every step in the operation of an airplane flight has been examined in detail in order to find more opportunities to incrementally reduce fuel burn and related GHG emissions. The effect of the "small steps" approach may not be as spectacular as new aircraft technology, but, now and in the future, it represents a mainstay in meeting the industry's environmental goals while helping to shrink an airline's fuel bill.

Improvements begin even before a plane takes off. For example, while still at the gate, aircraft at some larger airports can connect directly to fixed electrical ground power and pre-conditioned air, making it possible to carry out pre-flight preparations without noisy and fuel-consuming APUs. Airports are also looking at, or in some cases using, alternative sources of power such as natural gas or electricity to power ground service equipment, including catering trucks and passenger buses.

A number of technologies and operational approaches are currently being developed that focus on pre-flight activities while an aircraft is on the ground or before it reaches cruising altitude. These include:

- New ways of taxiing aircraft to takeoff position are being looked at. One technology currently in development is a self-driving device that would allow aircraft to reach the runway without using the full power of the engines.

- A "green departures" initiative is being pursued collaboratively by airports, airlines, and air navigation services that would enable aircraft to take off and climb more effectively towards the efficient cruise phase of flight.

- One option being tested is for pilots and flight planners to review wind patterns just before departure and then select the optimal routing that will minimize flight times.

- Along the same lines, "flexible routing" may provide more leeway for pilots to choose optimal flight altitudes and flight paths.

Although all these air navigation procedures are very positive developments, the ICAO Global Air Navigation Plan and Aviation System Block Upgrades is the centerpiece of globally streamlined flight operations. The aim of this 15-year forward vision of the global air traffic management system is to help the industry cope with the pressing challenges of growth and related environmental effects.

Finally, during the arrival phase of a flight, the relatively new "continuous descent operations" technique allows aircraft to almost "glide" into an airport, with engines at a very low setting. In addition to saving fuel, this approach also reduces noise levels for communities located close to airports.

In years to come, new technologies and modified procedures will come to the rescue of the industry in improving aircraft performance in all phases of flight through time-tested cooperation among regulators, aircraft manufacturers, airlines, airports, pilots, and particularly the ANSPs.

Sustainable Alternative Fuels: From CAF to SAF

As discussed above, continuous improvements in aircraft technologies and air navigation operations are expected to continue to help reduce fuel burn and related GHG emissions through 2050 and beyond. That will not be enough, however. The trends assessment performed by ICAO's CAEP Committee indicates that even with the anticipated gain in efficiency from technological and operational measures, aviation CO_2 emissions will increase in the coming decades due to a continuous growth in air traffic.

The urgency to do more stems from estimates that burning 1 kg of conventional aviation fuel (CAF) generates 3.16 kg of CO_2. Therefore, the sooner reductions in CAF can come, the better. This is especially true in light of the global objective of carbon-neutral growth from 2020 onwards, as agreed to by ICAO Member States and industry alike.

One of the most promising options is the development and use of sustainable aviation fuels (SAF), especially drop-in fuels that can be substituted for, or blended with, conventional fuels. These types of fuels hold much promise in the short- and mid-term. A flight completely powered by sustainable fuel has the potential to reduce the carbon emissions of that flight by up to 80%.

ICAO convened the Conference on Aviation and Alternative Fuels (CAAF) at Rio de Janeiro in Brazil in November 2009. The Conference was a major event showcasing the state of the art in aviation alternative fuels and an event at which a Global Framework for Aviation Alternative Fuels (GFAAF) was considered. The GFAAF was designed as a living document that is continually updated on the ICAO website. It provides general information, best practices, and future initiatives by ICAO Member States and the air transport industry.

The Conference adopted a Declaration which recognized the urgent need for measures to facilitate access to financial resources, technology exchanges, and capacity building specific to aviation alternative fuels. It acknowledged that the demand for sustainable fuels extends beyond international aviation, but that aircraft have unique fuel specification requirements. It also recognized the need to encourage supply-chain stakeholders to ensure that sustainable alternative fuels are made available to aviation, and it acknowledged that with sufficient incentives and supply, international aviation could deliver a substantial CO_2 reduction benefit from the use of sustainable alternative fuels for aircraft. It made the point that, due to its small network of fuel distribution points and its predictable demand, international aviation is well suited to become a global first adopter of sustainable alternative fuels.

The Declaration recommended that ICAO and its Member States endorse the use of sustainable alternative fuels for aviation, particularly the use of drop-in fuels in the short- to mid-term, as an important means of reducing aviation emissions; and that ICAO establish a Global Framework for Aviation Alternative Fuels (GFAAF) on aviation and sustainable alternative fuels to communicate what individual and shared efforts expect to achieve with sustainable alternative fuels for aviation in the future for consideration by the 37th Session of the ICAO Assembly. The GFAAF will be continually updated by Member States and stakeholders, who will work together through ICAO and other relevant international bodies to exchange information and best practices.

The use of sustainable fuels on commercial flights began in February 2008 when a Virgin Atlantic Boeing 747 flew from London to Amsterdam with sustainable aviation fuel in one of its engines. That flight confirmed the viability of drop-in biofuels blended with traditional jet fuel while using existing airport infrastructure. Since then, considerable progress has been achieved in this area, as shown in Figure 2-15.

Pathways and processes	Feedstock options	Producers using the path way	Date of approval	Current blending limit
Fischer-Tropsch Synthetic Paraffinic Kerosene (FT-SPK)	Biomass (forestry residues, grasses, municipal solid waste)		2009	up to 50%
Hydroprocessed Esters and Fatty Acids (HEFA-SPK)	Algae, jatropha, camelina	Alt Air	2011	up to 50%
Hydroprocessed Fermented Sugars to Synthetic Isoparaffins (HFS-SIP)	Microbial conversion of sugars to hydrocarbon	Amyris	2014	up to 10%
FT-SPK with aromatics (FTSPK/A)	Renewable biomass such as municipal solid waste, agricultural wastes and forestry residues, wood and energy crops		2015	up to 50%
Alcohol-to-Jet Synthetic Paraffinic Kerosene (ATJ-SPK)	Agricultural waste products (stover, grasses, forestry slash, crop straws)		2016	up to 30%

Figure 2-15   Sustainable aviation fuel can be made through five different processes, all internationally approved. It is expected that more such 'pathways' will be approved in the coming years (ATAG).

On the tenth anniversary of that ground-breaking commercial flight across the English Channel, IATA announced a goal of one billion passengers on flights powered by a CAF/SAF mix by 2025. The threshold of 100,000 such flights was reached in 2017, and expectations are that the one million mark will be attained in 2020.

Reaching the one billion target will depend in part on government policies that support the SAF industry and that will allow it to increase production of truly sustainable sources of alternative fuels, such as:

- Allowing SAF to compete with automotive biofuels through equivalent or magnified incentives.

- Loan guarantees and capital grants for production facilities.

- Supporting SAF demonstration plants and supply-chain research and development.

- Harmonized transport and energy policies coordinated with the involvement of agriculture and military departments.

CORSIA: A Key Global Market-Based Measure

In 2016, ICAO adopted a resolution creating CORSIA – a Carbon Offsetting and Reduction Scheme for International Aviation.[26] This was done in response to the realization that achieving one of ICAO's aspirational goals, carbon-neutral growth by 2020, would not be possible through only the measures taken in the three areas of aircraft technologies, air traffic management, and sustainable aviation fuel improvements.

The objective of this global market-based measure is to be achieved through the acquisition and cancelation of emissions units from the global carbon market by airplane operators. Essentially, operators record annual emissions and then multiply them by a growth factor, which results in CO_2 offset requirements. The growth factor is the percent increase in the amount of emissions from the baseline level to a given future year level and is calculated by ICAO, which maintains a central registry through CORSIA.

The adoption of CORSIA was hailed as the first climate measure of its type for any global industry. One of its main advantages is that it will help airlines avoid a complex patchwork of different schemes while helping to achieve carbon-neutral growth in a cost-effective manner.

In June 2018, the ICAO Council adopted Standards and Recommended Practices (SARPs) that specify mandatory actions by States and airline operators to implement CORSIA.[27] The measures cover the following areas: administration; requirements monitoring, reporting, and verification (MRV); CO_2 offsetting requirements and emissions reductions from sustainable aviation fuels; and emission units. It also provides an agreed basis for emissions baselines and for measuring and reporting emissions reductions.

IATA signaled early its commitment to help achieve the objectives of CORSIA and quickly implemented a system wide sensitization program to ensure full and active participation of all its members in the scheme.

Economic Measures

Carbon Offsetting or Carbon Tax?

The Fifth Assessment Report of the Inter-Governmental Panel on Climate Change (IPCC) advised that in 2010, 14% of all greenhouse gas emissions were from the transport sector. Aviation produces around 2% of the world's human-generated emissions of carbon dioxide (CO_2), which according to the IPCC will rise to 3% by 2050 if not checked. The air transport sector is a rapidly growing force, and measures to mitigate aircraft engine emissions continue to be the main focus of the aviation community. Substantial technological, economic, and infrastructural changes would be needed to attempt to reach the target of the 2015 Paris Agreement of a maximum increase of 2 degrees Celsius (3.6°F) (ideally 1.5°C or 2.7°F) warming compared with pre-industrial levels. In the air transport sector, two mechanisms have been considered under carbon pricing that aim to reach zero carbon growth by 2020. The first is an emissions trading scheme that is advocated by the European Union. The second proposed mechanism is ICAO's Carbon Offsetting and Reduction Scheme for International Aviation (CORSIA), which was summarized above as a market-based measure. In reality, this system is both an emissions trading scheme and a carbon tax.

Compelling arguments have emerged from credible sources and academia supporting a carbon tax on aircraft engine emissions. Two arguments in favor of a carbon tax are: 1) it provides across the board incentives for reducing energy use and shifting to cleaner alternative fuels; 2) carbon taxes increase revenues for finance ministries (up to 1%–2.5% of national GDP), thus enabling governments to reduce other burdensome taxes and facilitate more funding for investments for growth. At the same time, carbon offsetting, which CORSIA advocates, has been discarded on the basis that offsetting does not necessarily result in reduction of emissions, but merely shifts emissions from one source to another.

A carbon tax works on the "polluter pays" principle, where the volume and mass of carbon emitted is calculated and, based on a fixed price on a metric ton of carbon emitted, the polluter is charged accordingly. On the other hand, an offsetting scheme enables a polluter to keep polluting beyond his allocated tonnage of carbon allowable for emission by buying carbon credits from other polluters who are not polluting up to the level of emissions allowed to them. Offsetting operates on a quota system, whereas a carbon tax operates on how much pollution is generated.

The only ICAO pronouncements that address taxes on fuel, although not directly related to the subject at hand, are contained in ICAO Council Resolutions on taxation. These advocate the imposition of charges rather than taxes, making a distinction between a charge and a tax in that charges are levied to defray the costs of providing facilities and services for civil aviation, which in turn are pumped back into aviation, whereas taxes are levied to raise general national and local government revenues that are applied for non-aviation purposes. For example, charges levied for the provision of air navigation services are to be put back into purposes directly or indirectly related to aviation, whereas a departure tax levied on passengers could be pumped into the national treasury of a State and used for non-aviation purposes such as health and education services for the community. The Resolution discourages the imposition of national or local taxes on the acquisition of fuel, lubricants, and consumable technical supplies for use by aircraft in connection with international air transport on the basis that such an imposition may have an adverse economic and competitive impact on international air transport operations.

Implementing ICAO's CORSIA

As already stated, CORSIA is to be implemented through an Annex – Annex 16, Volume IV, Part II – to the Chicago Convention, which prescribes a monitoring, review, and verification (MRV) model. The applicable scope of this is stipulated in Chapter 2 of the Annex, to the effect that the Standards and Recommended Practices (SARPs) of the Annex are applicable to an aircraft operator that produces annual CO_2 emissions greater than 10,000 tons from the use of an aircraft(s). They apply to aircraft with a maximum certified takeoff mass greater than 5,700 kg conducting international flights, on or after 1 January 2019, with the exception of humanitarian, medical, and firefighting flights. The Chapter also recognizes specific aircraft categories that do not fall within the applicability scope and specific requirements associated with new entrants.

CORSIA applies to international flights carried out by civil aircraft to the exclusion of State aircraft. An international flight is defined as the operation of an aircraft from take-off at an aerodrome of a State or its territories and landing at an aerodrome of another State or its territories. Flights within a State, or between a State and one of its territories, or between the territories of a State, are considered as domestic flights and are therefore not within the scope of applicability of Annex 16, Volume IV. Questions have been raised in ICAO by some member States as to why CORSIA is not made applicable to domestic flights since pollution caused by these has no boundaries and could permeate international airspace.

The Annex prescribes CORSIA implementation as follows:

Between 2021 and 2026 – Participation of all international flights between States that decide to voluntarily participate in the scheme.

Between 2027 and 2035 – International flights between States that have an individual share of international aviation activities in revenue ton kilometers (RTKs) in 2018 above 0.5% of total RTKs, or whose cumulative share in the list of States from the highest to the lowest amount of RTKs reaches 90% of total RTKs.

International flights between State pairs which include least developed countries (LDCs), small island developing states (SIDS), and landlocked developing countries (LLDCs) are not within the applicability scope of the offsetting requirements, unless the State decides to voluntarily participate.

A number of valid questions have been raised about the implementation of CORSIA:

- Why wait for another ten years (from 2017) or more for a mandatory system for timely, accurate, and transparent reporting of emissions data and emissions units surrendered to be put in place?

- Who has/have the legal, financial, and human resources needed to hold participants accountable for compliance?

- Is there a suitable venue for resolving disputes over compliance?

- What are the financial penalties that exceed the cost of compliance with the GMBM, including enhancements for false or fraudulent data reporting?

Some have claimed that offsetting is widely considered a false solution because it does not lead to emission reductions, but merely shifts emissions from one sector to another and, at best, is a zero-sum game. CORSIA is founded upon a key concept called MRV (monitoring, reporting, and verification). If the States do the reporting, would they also monitor and verify? What exactly would ICAO's role be? And what specifically would be expected of the airlines?

Arguments Against a Carbon Tax

Environmental taxes are difficult to craft and implement, and, from an international perspective, it would be difficult to design environmental taxes that would be country-specific on a global scale. However, the most difficult obstacle to efficient global environmental taxation is the adverse impact that such a levy would have on various economic factors related to production, such as employment, market competition, economic output, and equity.

The other consideration in environmental taxation – equity – brings to bear the complexity of the problem of legal implementation of an environmental tax. Although in theory it can be easily established that an environmental tax can be calculated based on the marginal internal benefit and marginal social cost of a given source of pollution, whether such a levy could be legally implementable on a global scale is another question. Given the zealously guarded internal fiscal policies of nations and their internal economic factors, it would be a difficult task to seek global accord on an appropriate internationally applicable environmental tax, unless there is certainty in the exact quantity of emissions released, such as the known amount of CO_2 from an aircraft engine. This brings to bear the credibility of the argument for a carbon tax.

Arguments in Favor of a Carbon Tax

The International Monetary Fund (IMF) has suggested that a charge of $30 per ton on carbon dioxide embedded in international transport fuels could have raised $25 billion in 2014. The call for a carbon tax on aviation (and maritime transport) by the IMF is based on the argument that a low starting price would raise valuable revenues that could be used to drive innovation, efficiency, and change where the market is failing to do so. The IMF argues that a carbon tax would be a better, more efficient use of resources than current practices that are costly and add both cost and harm to the rest of human activity. Furthermore, the IMF states: "The revenue potential of ETSs (emission trading schemes) is generally around 20–60 percent that of the carbon tax, primarily because ETSs tend to miss about half the potential revenue base (and the portion they do cover is typically more mobile due to relatively low-cost mitigation opportunities in the power sector)."

One problem with ETS schemes is that they set limits on carbon and allow polluters to buy and sell allowances, which makes way for manipulating the system and using political leverage to gain exemptions. A compelling argument for a straight carbon tax is that it is a direct levy that is not a variable. One commentator says: "A much more straightforward plan is simply to tax carbon directly. It removes the arbitraging games and artful dodges that have helped undermine cap-and-trade schemes in places like Europe, but in return it requires that politicians vote for a tax. A carbon tax can be levied by taxing distribution, sale, or use of fossil fuels based on their carbon content." The Guardian states: "Ideally, there should be a uniform carbon price across the world, reflecting the fact that a ton of carbon dioxide does the same amount of damage over time wherever it is emitted. Uniform pricing would also remove the risk that polluting businesses flee to so-called "pollution havens" – countries where a lack of environmental regulation enables them to continue to pollute unrestrained."

In contrast to a uniform tax, a cap-and-trade system, as advocated by ICAO, will create many uncertainties. As one commentator has said: "In a cap-and-trade system, some-one must decide how to allocate carbon emission allowances. The allowances might be awarded based on existing emissions, but that system would favor those who now have high emissions because they have not acted to reduce their emissions and penalize those who have been working hard to lower emissions. Awarding emissions rights based on evaluation of particular industries and practice is likely to be highly politicized... A carbon tax would avoid many of these issues."[28] A further criticism is that those who advocate cap-and-trade systems themselves doubt their effectiveness in reducing carbon emissions. States would have different capabilities to implement carbon offsetting, and a simple tax on the mining of carbon products could be the solution.

A carbon tax policy published in 2017 states: "Under simple assumptions, a carbon tax is economically equivalent to a cap-and-trade program in which the government sells all the permits at auction."[29] Adding real-world uncertainties suggests, however, that the carbon tax is superior to such a program. Moreover, a carbon tax is far superior to a cap-and-trade program that follows the commonly proposed approach of giving away permits to firms that emitted carbon dioxide in the past. Economists Lucas Chantel and Thomas Piketty have suggested a €180 ($196/£130) levy on business class tickets and €20 on economy class tickets that is calculated to raise the estimated €150bn a year needed for climate adaptation. Piketty, the author of the best-selling book *Capital*, stated that 10% of the world is responsible for 45% of emissions.[30]

Recycling Also to the Rescue

A final promising option for mitigating the impact of aviation on the environment is an exciting concept that has been filtering down through many industrial sectors around the world, namely, recycling.

By 2030, 18,000 currently in-service aircraft are expected to be retired from operations. Recycling aircraft components and materials through environmentally responsible procedures can meaningfully reduce the consumption of natural resources as well as landfill allocations. Compared with the production of new parts and components from source materials, recycling aircraft can also reduce air, water, and soil contamination, as well as energy demand.

Boeing's goal is to achieve 90% to 95% recyclability of its world fleet by taking advantage of industry expertise and new technologies. Meanwhile, Airbus is setting up a special center in southwestern France for its aircraft recycling project called PAMELA, which will test procedures for the environmentally friendly recycling of jetliners that have reached the end of their operational lifetimes.

In 2016, ICAO and the Aircraft Fleet Recycling Association (AFRA) announced a new Memorandum of Understanding aimed at reinforcing cooperation on dismantling and recycling end-of-life aircraft.

CONCLUSION AND SUMMARY

The first part of this closing section is a brief Conclusion that contains some overall general remarks that summarize the essence of the foregoing discussion of the climate change megatrend and offers some general advice to managers about how best to cope with it. The second part of this section is a Management Summary that recaps in point form all the major subjects discussed earlier in the detailed analysis and discussion of the Environmental/Climate Change megatrend. The points are presented with the perspective of aviation professionals and managers in mind. Essentially, each point in the Management Summary represents a key observation or conclusion that was made during the detailed analysis and discussion.

Conclusion

The global climate change challenge is one of the greatest, if not THE greatest, human-made threats to its survival that humanity has ever faced.

The planet itself is not at risk. It has withstood enormous cataclysms, from the ice ages, the bombardment of meteorites, the shifting of its axis, and the breaking up of continents with the movement of tectonic plates. It has survived all this and will continue to survive whatever is thrown at it.

Humanity, however, may not survive – at least not in its present form.

From the UN Secretary General to business leaders, from humanitarian organizations to cultural icons, from news media to local community groups and concerned individuals, a consensus has emerged that concrete action must be taken now to avert or at least minimize a possible worldwide catastrophe.

The global air transport system has been a powerful driver of economic, social, and cultural development for our now very tightly knit global society – our "global village". At the same time, aviation has itself contributed to the warming of the planet. The industry must accelerate efforts even to curb its impact on global warming. It has no choice if it wants to prosper and grow amidst social and political demands for change.

The latter half of the 20th Century was the time for purely mitigation measures to be taken that would reduce and/or slow down climate change. However, not enough was done. The stark reality is that we are now in adaptation mode; we now have to react to and manage the results of our previous inaction while at the same time implementing measures that will lessen the future impacts of climate change on the planet and on the global aviation industry.

In the 2018 AGM issue of IATA's corporate *Airlines* magazine, one article contains a sobering quote: "Best estimates suggest aviation will require liquid fuel – especially for long-haul flights – for another 50 years". This will take us up to 2068 or thereabouts. What will we do then?

As discussed in this chapter, notwithstanding progress in the development of electric and solar power, the world's passenger aircraft will most probably be hybrid models in the foreseeable future – a combination of liquid fuel and electric batteries. Hence, the primary determining factor for reduced GHG emissions will be the degree to which liquid fuel becomes truly sustainable. This will determine the extent to which global aviation will be able to reduce (or ideally eliminate) its carbon footprint. This will be supplemented by mechanisms such as market-based measures, operational improvements, technological breakthroughs, and as of yet unidentified or undiscovered improvements.

Aviation managers around the world, indeed anyone working in aviation, should feel compelled by the urgency of the situation and heed the call to work together in making sure that the global air transport industry continues to grow in an exemplary sustainable manner for the long-term benefit of humanity.

With regard to what the most appropriate economic instrument to counter the deleterious effects of aircraft engine emissions should be, it is relevant to note that both the cap-and-trade scheme and the carbon tax are measures under the broad rubric of carbon pricing. Both have the common advantage of incentivizing industry toward cleaner energy technologies. Both are calculated to result in CO_2 abatement. Both have conceptually the objective of balancing the costs of emission reduction with the attendant benefits of emission reduction. However, as seen in the foregoing discussion, there are pros and cons with regard to both measures. For instance, ICAO's CORSIA tends to be ambivalent in failing to explicitly identify national commitment in the scheme. Added to this disadvantage, the timing is questionable because CORSIA will drag its feet until 2035, when the ravages of global warming will already have brought about observable ramifications. CORSIA has no vision or plan beyond 2035. The most significant weakness of CORSIA is that because it had its genesis in an ICAO Assembly Resolution to which some member states have recorded reservations, and because it is only a political compromise between

States and therefore has no legal legitimacy, CORSIA remains lacking in both foundation and credibility. Furthermore, it remains to be seen how far CORSIA would succeed in reducing carbon emissions. To make matters worse, CORSIA derives its justification from an Annex to the Chicago Convention, which in and of itself is a discretionary document that leaves States the flexibility of choosing to opt out at any time. In other words, the sustained existence of CORSIA would depend on the goodwill of ICAO Member States.

There are also logistical challenges to CORSIA's implementation. How many allowances would be issued? What would the limits of the cap be? What would the cap cover? Would the allowances and cap be determined based on the carbon content of fuels or on the emissions that are monitored? Would allowances be auctioned? Could high allowance prices discourage research and development and innovation with regard to alternative energy sources? Would the costs of implantation exceed benefits?

On the other hand, in addition to the many supporting arguments for a carbon tax, as seen in the discussion above, one could argue that because it is based on a simple calculation, a carbon tax could positively contribute to carbon capture (and not just offsetting and reduction as espoused by CORSIA), which is essential to drastically reduce global warming. However, would States (particularly developing States) sign on to a global carbon tax? Would they be fearful that such a tax would be rigid and therefore unable to adapt to changes in abatement costs over time? Would a carbon tax encourage the polluter, who, untrammeled by an allowance scheme, would feel free to keep polluting, given the exponential growth of demand in the world for air transport?

It is incontrovertible that this issue should be discussed against the backdrop of the future of air transport and the large transformative forces – megatrends – that affect our existential lives. In 2014, the Organization for Economic Cooperation and Development (OECD) released a report on airline competition that said that by 2026, air transport will contribute $1 trillion to the world's GDP. The Report went on to say that at that time, worldwide, aviation and related tourism would generate over 56 million jobs, of which 8.36 million would be directly linked to the aviation sector. Approximately 35% of international tourists traveled by air in 2014. Four years later, these statistics have grown exponentially. ICAO, which has as one of its strategic objectives the Economic Development of Air Transport with a view to fostering the development of a sound and economically viable civil aviation system, states in its Global Air Transport Outlook to 2030 that there will be an average annual growth rate of 4.5% by 2030 in passenger traffic (of both scheduled and unscheduled services). ICAO admits that there is a need for its leadership in harmonizing an air transport framework focused on economic policies and supporting activities. IATA (International Air Transport Association, which is the trade association of the airlines), has stated, in its document *The Shape of Air Travel Markets over the Next 20 Years*, that world air transport will double in the next 20 years.

It is in this context that the issue of carbon offsetting has to be viewed against a carbon tax.

Management Summary

Based on the foregoing discussion, there is no doubt that the Environmental/Climate Change megatrend will have major impacts on the international aviation industry over the next 15 to 20 years and beyond. In many ways, adapting to this megatrend and implementing mitigation measures will have considerable impact on the way in which airlines, airports, and air navigation services will develop and operate their businesses, particularly during the next decade, as they continue to adjust to this new reality. Numerous significant conclusions and observations have been made during the course of the detailed analysis described earlier in this chapter. The following are the important "action points" that aviation managers at all levels will need to take into account when determining how best to deal with the Environmental/Climate Change megatrend when planning for the future.

The State of Climate Change

- Greenhouse gases (GHG) generated mostly by human activity are at the heart of climate change, which is also referred to by some people as global warming. Half the fossil-fuel CO_2 emissions produced by human activity in the last 300 years have occurred since the late 1980s, and the 2014 global fossil-fuel carbon emission estimate was an all-time record.

- The Inter-Governmental Panel on Climate Change (IPCC) has stated that, "warming of the climate system is unequivocal, and since the 1950s, many of the observed changes are unprecedented. The atmosphere and ocean have warmed, the amounts of snow and ice have diminished, sea level has risen, and the concentrations of greenhouse gases have increased".

- Numerous major international organizations have recognized climate change as one of the major challenges of our time. These organizations include the United Nations, the World Bank, the International Monetary Fund, and the International Energy Agency, among others.

- Rapid industrialization in the developing world in the coming decades will significantly boost energy demand and therefore the consumption of more carbon-based fuels. Some experts suggest that GHG emissions could grow by as much as a further 52% by 2050.

- The World Meteorological Organization (WMO) says that "… seventeen of the 18 warmest years on record have all been during this century, and the degree of warming during the past three years has been exceptional."

- Possible manifestations of climate change as predicted by experts include:

  - Rise in sea levels of 1 to 4 feet by 2100, due mostly to melting ice sheets in the Arctic, Greenland, and Antarctica, and to thermal expansion of the oceans. This will cause flood threats in coastal, low-lying areas and increased storm surges; which could result in the displacement of large populations and possible armed conflicts among neighboring states and/or regions.

  - Increased rainfall in some regions and water shortages in others, with implications for agriculture and access to safe drinking water. Up to 40% of the world's population could experience water scarcity by 2100.

  - For each 1-degree increase in global temperature, grain yields are forecast to decline by 5%, which could threaten international security as countries/regions compete to maintain their food supplies.

  - More intense and frequent tropical cyclones and hurricanes, threatening communities and infrastructure in high-risk areas. Extreme heat, changing disease patterns, and other negative public health impacts could threaten millions of people every year, who could seek safe haven elsewhere.

  - Should the global population reach the forecast 9.6 billion by 2050, the equivalent of almost three planet Earths could be required to provide the natural resources needed to sustain current lifestyles.

Renewable Energy and Sustainability

- Renewable sources of energy are the recognized solution to GHG-producing, non-renewable fossil fuels.

- By 2018, renewable resources met only about 7% of the world's energy needs, meaning that fossil fuels, along with nuclear energy, were still supplying 93% of the world's energy, primarily for heating, electricity production, and all forms of transportation.

- The International Energy Agencyasserts that the world is not on track to meeting its energy sustainability goals, based on current policies. IEA says that much more needs to be done, including more widespread integration of renewable energy sources into the overall power grid.

- The shift towards more renewables is strongly encouraged by numerous parties worldwide, including various levels of government, non-government organizations, segments of the business community, and millions of concerned citizens.

- Renewable infrastructure is relatively cheap to operate, but can be expensive to build, particularly wind and solar installations. Nevertheless, renewable energy capital costs keep falling, and the sector remains the least expensive of energy-generating sources over the long-term.

- As far back as the UN Conference on the Environment in Rio de Janeiro (Brazil) in 1992, it was clearly recognized that, "...states should reduce and eliminate unsustainable patterns of production and consumption", and "...the major cause of continued deterioration of the global environment is the unsustainable patterns of consumption and production..."

- Sustainable consumption requires a systematic approach, cooperation, and awareness among players operating in the supply chain, from producers to the final consumer, with a focus on sustainable consumption and lifestyles. Standards need to be developed and publicized, and consumers need to be provided with adequate information.

Climate Change Impacts

- Between 1940 and 2018, global air traffic increased from a few million passengers annually to more than 3.8 billion, while air travel has become safer, more secure, and more efficient than ever before.

- The single biggest challenge to face the aviation industry so far is global warming.

- Increasing temperatures and heat waves are expected to continue to produce extreme weather patterns that will lead to a number of events that will affect airport and airline operations.

- Impacts of a changing global climate change on aviation operations will vary according to geographic location, scale of operations, and degree of connectedness with national/international networks. For example, the flooding of an airport runway will produce a domino effect on flight schedules of any number of airlines, as well as on air traffic control operations and on travel and tourism operators.

- Although airlines, airports, and air navigation service providers are adept at dealing with a wide range of weather-related situations, climate change and global warming have expanded the nature and scope of such challenges that will likely be faced in the upcoming years.

- The effects of increased average temperatures on current passenger aircraft will be significant. As the Earth heats up, during the hottest parts of the day, 10% to 30% of fully loaded planes may have to remove payload to take off, causing considerable financial and operational consequences such as reduced airline payloads/revenues; disrupted airport operations and air navigation services, and inconvenienced passengers, and causing a ripple effect throughout the global network of stakeholders.

- Extreme heat or cold at airports unaccustomed to those conditions could cause serious damage to infrastructure, such as cracks or deformation of runways and taxiways. Warmer temperatures would also increase demand for air conditioning in terminals and office buildings in summer, or increased heating would be needed in colder climates; both putting increased pressure on local power utilities.

- Airports will likely have to deal with more extreme weather events such as heavy downpours of rain that can cause airport flooding, flight delays/cancellations, and airport closings. Flooding can affect the structural integrity of airport facilities through damage to runways, taxiways, and other infrastructure.

- Other expected effects of climate change in the future include high winds, freezing rain, heavy precipitation, and lightning strikes, all of which can damage buildings, facilities, and aircraft. In winter, there will be challenges associated with snow prediction and removal, a situation that can be demanding in areas not used to harsh winter conditions.

- Runways constructed along the locally prevailing wind directions may experience more crosswinds due to more frequent deviations from the prevailing wind direction, or an airport may start to experience crosswinds but have no crosswind runway. This may require changes in airspace procedures that could produce an additional environmental risk due to the redistribution of noise impact around airports.

- High-altitude jet streams will be affected by climate changes, primarily on the North Atlantic flight routes. Stronger winds will increase the amount of shear in the jet stream, leading to more clear air turbulence.

- High-altitude icing may become more frequent as climate change pushes stronger and more frequent thunderstorms into cruising altitudes. It is known to be dangerous when tiny particles of ice infiltrate turbofan engines, and this can also cause problems for modern energy-efficient and lean-burn engines.

- In the future, rising sea levels will affect airports and other ground infrastructure located in coastal, low-lying areas as flooding damages critical installations. Small islands that rely on air travel as a lifeline to the outside world will be particularly vulnerable to the threat posed by this phenomenon.

- Sea-level rise (SLR) has the potential to cause closures or restricted access to many major airports, affecting service to/from high-density populations as well as connecting passengers and commercial transportation systems. According to an OECD report, 64 airports have been identified as likely to be affected by the predicted SLR.

Adapting to Climate Change

- As average temperatures rise, some warm-weather travel destinations may become too hot for tourists, causing traffic to divert to more temperate climates, which would then enjoy a surge in clientele. Long-time favorite resorts along coastlines may be severely affected by rising sea levels and become unattractive to vacationers, or they might have to close down altogether for at least part of the year.

- Reduced snowfall in ski resorts might cause them to suffer a similar fate, with skiers looking for alternate locations or having to adjust their travel plans to a shift in the winter season. This will have major impacts for airlines relative to scheduling and route configurations. Airports will also need to adjust to either reduced or increased passenger flows, depending on their specific situations.

- Increasing traffic growth may put additional pressure on airport operations in both emerging and established markets, compounding the risks of climate change at some airports. As one study stated, "...some of the locations where the highest growth rates are forecast, such as southeastern and central Europe, are also some of the areas where the greatest potential climate change impacts are predicted".

- Although climate change threatens the operational integrity and financial viability of many aviation stakeholders, not all of them are rushing to develop and implement countermeasures. In fact, a EUROCONTROL survey of European aviation stakeholders found that although more than 80% of respondents considered it necessary to adapt to climate change, almost half of their organizations did not have an official position on the issue.

- The proven methodology for identifying and dealing effectively with the impacts associated with climate change is a formal risk assessment and response process. Coupled with an additional analysis of economic costs, it can enhance the comprehensiveness and value of the adaptation process. It also allows for the participation and support of some parties that have not previously been part of the solution, including local, regional, and national politicians, all of whom have a crucial role to play in determining policies and financial allocations for both adaptation and mitigation measures related to climate change.

- Using such a process, specific goals and objectives can be established, priorities set, and a detailed operational and financial plan of action developed and implemented which will allow an organization to take appropriate measures in a timely and cost-effective manner.

- Ideally, a climate change adaptation plan should be part of an airport's "Master Operation and Development Plan", making it easier to combine the financial, operational, and human resource requirements into an overall corporate perspective. For example, planned improvements to equipment or facilities might be performed with adaptation features incorporated into them to produce a more cost-efficient result.

- Multi-party industry collaboration is essential to ensure the success of a risk assessment exercise. Ongoing communications among airports, airlines, ANS providers, and all other stakeholders will tap vast resources of knowledge and expertise that would otherwise not be available, while also contributing to filling the information gaps in understanding and reacting to climate change.

- A number of successful risk assessment adaptation exercises have been completed or are still in progress, involving air transport organizations operating in various countries in Europe, and their progress and results have been tracked and documented by EUROCONTROL.

Mitigation of Climate Change

- According to the IPCC, aviation produces around 2% of the world's CO_2 emissions. As aviation grows to meet increasing demand, particularly in fast-growing emerging markets, the IPCC forecasts that the industry's share of global manmade CO_2 emissions will increase to around 3% by 2050. This is why mitigation measures are required.

- CO_2 emissions remain the main target in reducing emissions altogether, and considerable success has been achieved over the years. For example, in spite of a consistent

5% annual growth rate in passenger traffic, the aviation industry has kept the growth rate in emissions to around 3% per year.

- Nevertheless, this 3% level will be unacceptable in the future from a social responsibility perspective and given aviation's future growth. Financial reasons to reduce emissions will become even more critical for the airlines, with fuel making up roughly 30% of total airline operating costs.

- There will be increasing public and media pressure for aviation to cut emissions even more drastically, and the industry must do even more to meet the targets set forth by the international community under the Paris Climate Agreement and in the spirit of the United Nations Sustainability Goals.

- Through IATA, the airline industry has adopted a set of ambitious targets to mitigate CO_2 emissions from air transport as follows:

  - An average improvement in fuel efficiency of 1.5% per year from 2009 to 2020.

  - A cap on net aviation CO_2 emissions from 2020 (carbon-neutral growth).

  - A reduction in net aviation CO_2 emissions of 50% by 2050, relative to 2005 levels.

- Airports Council International (ACI), IATA's airport equivalent, is dedicated to promoting aviation and sustainable airport development and limiting or reducing environmental impacts, while supporting economic and social benefits. ACI believes that these objectives are key to community permission to operate and grow at both global and local levels.

- Civil Air Navigation Services Organization (CANSO) encourages procedures that reduce fuel use and emissions while maintaining operational efficiency. Ongoing efforts will continue to reduce fuel consumption, and hence all GHG emissions from aviation, and will center on: aircraft technology, operational measures, and alternative or sustainable fuels, as well as market-based measures.

- Aircraft manufacturers continue to make technological advances in designing and re-designing more fuel-efficient aircraft engines and airframes, coupled with a new aircraft types better adapted to route structures that will lead to less fuel burn and reduced GHG emissions. They are making significant efforts to support ICAO's CO_2 emissions standard (2016), which calls for the compliance of all new aircraft designs from 2020 onward, and for engines in newly-built aircraft models beginning in 2023.

- For many years, every step in the operation of an airplane flight has been examined in detail in order to find more opportunities to incrementally reduce fuel burn and related GHG emissions. Although not very spectacular, the "small steps" approach is now and will be in the future a key element in meeting the industry's environmental goals while helping to shrink an airline's fuel bill.

- Various technologies and operational approaches are currently being developed that focus on pre-flight activities while an aircraft is on the ground or before it reaches cruising altitude. As a result, in the coming years, new technologies and modified procedures will further improve aircraft performance in all phases of flight. These advances will be achieved through time-tested cooperation among regulators, aircraft manufacturers, airlines, airports, pilots, and particularly the ANSPs.

- The ICAO Global Air Navigation Plan and Aviation System Block Upgrades is the centerpiece for globally streamlined flight operations. The aim of this 15-year forward vision of the global air traffic management system is to help the industry cope with the challenges of growth and related environmental effects.

- Incremental improvements in aircraft technologies and air navigation operations are expected to continue to help reduce fuel burn and related GHG emissions through 2050 and beyond. Those efforts alone will not be enough, however. ICAO's CAEP Committee has determined that even with the anticipated gains in efficiency from technological and operational measures, aviation CO_2 emissions will increase in the next decades due to continuous growth in air traffic.

- One of the most promising options is the development and use of sustainable aviation fuels (SAF), especially drop-in fuels that can be substituted for, or blended with, conventional fuels. These types of fuels hold much promise in the short- and mid-term. A flight completely powered by sustainable fuel has the potential to reduce the carbon emissions of that flight by up to 80%.

- IATA has set a goal of one billion passengers on flights powered by a CAF/SAF mix by 2025. The threshold of 100,000 such flights was reached in 2017, and expectations are that the one million mark will be reached in 2020. Attaining that one billion target will depend in part on government policies that support the SAF industry and allow it to increase production of sustainable sources of alternative fuels.

- In 2016, ICAO adopted a resolution creating CORSIA (Carbon Offsetting and Reduction Scheme for International Aviation). The objective of this global market-based measure is to offset international CO_2 emissions in order to stabilize those emissions from 2020 onwards. This will be achieved through acquisition and cancelation of emissions units from the global carbon market by airplane operators.

- In June 2018, the ICAO Council adopted Standards and Recommended Practices (SARPs) that specify mandatory actions by States and airline operators to implement CORSIA. IATA signaled early its commitment to help achieve the objectives of CORSIA and quickly implemented a system-wide sensitization program to ensure full and active participation of its members in the scheme.

- By 2030, 18,000 currently in-service aircraft are expected to be retired from operations. Recycling aircraft components and materials through environmentally responsible procedures can reduce the consumption of natural resources as well as landfill allocations. Compared with the production of new parts and components from source materials, recycling aircraft can also reduce air, water, and soil contaminations, as well as energy demand.

- In 2016, ICAO and the Aircraft Fleet Recycling Association (AFRA) announced a new Memorandum of Understanding aimed at reinforcing cooperation on dismantling and recycling end-of-life aircraft.

REFERENCES

1   Harari, Y.N. (2018). 21 Lessons for the *21st Century*. New York: Random House.

2   (2018, August). "Losing the war against climate change", The Economist, Cover.

3   (2018, September 11). *Al Jazeera*, www.aljazeera.com.

4   Climate Action Reserve, www.climateactionreserve.org.

5   World Economic Forum, www.weforum.org.

6   World Economic Forum, www.weforum.org.

7   Climate Change 2013: The Physical Science Basis. IPCC.

8   CDIAC: cdiac.ess-dive.lbl.gov/trends/emis/tre_glob_2014.html

9   WMO: https://public.wmo.int/en/media/press-release/
    wmo-confirms-2017-among-three-warmest-years-record.

10 United Nations, *2030 Agenda for Sustainable Development*.

11 International Energy Agency, www.iea.org.

12 Union of Concerned Scientists USA (UCSUSA) website, www.ucsusa.org.

13 Agenda 21 Action Plan of the United Nations with regard to sustainable development.

14 Gelb, M. (2000). *How to Think like Leonardo da Vinci: Seven Steps to Genius Every Day*. Dell.

15 Williams, P.D. (2017). "Increased light, moderate, and severe clear-air turbulence in response to
    climate change". *Adv. Atmos. Sci. 34*(7): 576–586. https://doi.org/10.1007/s00376-017-6268-2.

16 *New York Times*, September 4, 2018.

17 Burbidge, R. (2016). "Adapting European airports to a changing climate". *Transportation Research
    Procedia 14*, p. 17.

18 Burbidge, R. (2016). "Adapting European airports to a changing climate". *Transportation Research
    Procedia 14*, p. 18.

19 Koetse, M.J., & Rietveld, P. (2008). *"The impact of climate change and weather on transport: An
    overview of empirical findings".* Elsevier.

20 Avinor is a wholly owned state limited company under the Norwegian Ministry of Transport and
    Communications and is responsible for 45 state-owned airports.

21 NATS is the main Air Navigation Service Provider in the United Kingdom.

22 AENA is a state-owned company that manages general-interest airports and heliports in Spain.

23 DGCA/STAC is the *Service technique de l'Aviation civile, Service à compétence nationale de la
    Direction générale de l'aviation civile.*

24 London Heathrow is the second busiest airport in the world by international passenger traffic, as
    well as the busiest airport in Europe by passenger traffic.

25 https://sustainabledevelopment.un.org/outcomedocuments/agenda21.

26 https://www.icao.int/environmental-protection/Pages/A39_CORSIA_FAQ2.aspx/.

27   The measures are part of the First Edition of Annex 16, Volume IV to the Convention on International Civil Aviation (Chicago Convention) that was adopted as one of the core components of CORSIA.

28   Corkery, J. (2009). A carbon tax – Onwards. *Revenue Law Journal, 19*(1), Article 7, Editorial.

29   "Carbon tax policy: A conservative dialogue on pro-growth opportunities". In A.M. Brill (Ed.), *Alliance for market solutions: 2017 at 40*. See https://allianceformarketsolutions.org/wp-content/uploads/2017/04/Carbon-Tax-Policy-A-Conservative-Dialogue-on-Pro-Growth-Opportunities.pdf.

30   "Thomas Piketty proposes flight tax to raise climate funds". *The Guardian*. https://www.theguardian.com/environment/2015/nov/05/thomas-piketty-proposes-flight-tax-to-raise-climate-funds.

3

GLOBAL ECONOMIC
POWER SHIFT
West to East

INTRODUCTION

The theme of economic (and political) power shift from Western nations to those in the East is a megatrend that has been explored in numerous studies and papers over the years. In today's aviation industry, the economic aspect of this shift is obvious and has brought about many changes in the industry in the past thirty years. However, before exploring the drivers of that shift and how it exerts impact on the future aviation industry, it is important to clarify exactly what is meant when discussing this West to East power shift.

Does the economic power shift from West to East mean that the East is getting stronger and the West is getting weaker? This is a difficult question, because any answer to it may be deemed as a continuation of the Cold War mentality, splitting the world into two opposing political regimes or dividing it into North and South with the idea that the North was exploiting the South. This confrontational approach represents the mindset of a zero-sum game, meaning "what I win is based on your loss", and its validity is "based on who you are and where you are in the world."[1] This mindset is reflected by Gideon Rachman in his 2017 book *Easternization*, in which he blames emerging economies, especially China, for all the world's problems: cyber theft and attack, climate change, global warming, water shortage, and nuclear proliferation. He argues that "... the West's centuries-long domination of world affairs is now coming to a close. The root cause of this change is Asia's extraordinary economic development over the last fifty years. Western political power was founded on technological, military, and economic dominance, but these advantages are fast eroding. And the consequences are now defining global politics."[2] This zero-sum mentality is harmful to the continuing growth of the global economy and of cooperation.

This chapter will present the opposite case. It will focus primarily on the economic aspects by examining growing trends in the aviation industry, from which a win-win scenario will emerge: one in which both emerging economies and advanced economies are becoming stronger. The political aspects of this shift are much more difficult to identify and define and will therefore not be discussed in detail in this chapter. Changes in passenger volumes are a good indicator that demonstrates this phenomenon. For example, based on 2017 data, 10 of the top 20 airports worldwide, by passenger traffic, are located in emerging economies, and they are all in Asia. It should be noted that New Delhi International Airport was not on this list in 2016, but has risen rapidly since 2017.

Table 3-1   Total Passenger Traffic – Top 20 Airports, 2017 (ACI)[3].

RANK 2017	RANK 2016	AIRPORT CITY / COUNTRY / CODE	PASSENGERS	
			Enplaning & Deplaning	Percent Change
1	1	ATLANTA GA, US (ATL)	103 902 992	-0.3
2	2	BEIJING, CN (PEK)	95 786 442	1.5
3	3	DUBAI, AE (DXB)	88 242 099	5.5
4	5	TOKYO, JP (HND)	85 408 975	6.5
5	4	LOS ANGELES CA, US (LAX)	84 557 968	4.5
6	6	CHICAGO IL, US (ORD)	79 828 183	2.4
7	7	LONDON, GB (LHR)	78 014 598	3.0
8	8	HONG KONG, HK (HKG)	72 663 955	3.4
9	9	SHANGHAI, CN (PVG)	70 001 237	6.1
10	10	PARIS, FR (CDG)	69 471 442	5.4
11	12	AMSTERDAM, NL (AMS)	68 515 425	7.7
12	11	DALLAS/FORT WORTH TX, US (DFW)	67 092 194	2.3
13	15	GUANGZHOU, CN (CAN)	65 887 473	10.3
14	13	FRANKFURT, DE (FRA)	64 500 386	6.1
15	14	ISTANBUL, TR (IST)	63 872 283	6.0
16	22	NEW DELHI, IN (DEL)	63 451 503	14.1
17	19	JAKARTA, ID (CGK)	63 015 620	8.3
18	17	SINGAPORE, SG (SIN)	62 220 000	6.0
19	20	INCHEON, KR (ICN)	62 157 834	7.5
20	18	DENVER CO, US (DEN)	61 379 396	5.3
TOP 20 FOR 2017			1 469 970 005	5.2

The power shift from West to East can also be seen from an increase of passenger traffic in the Asia-Pacific Region (+10%) and the Middle East (+8.1%). The Asia-Pacific, Middle East, Latin American, and African regions combined now account for about 50% of total global air passenger traffic.

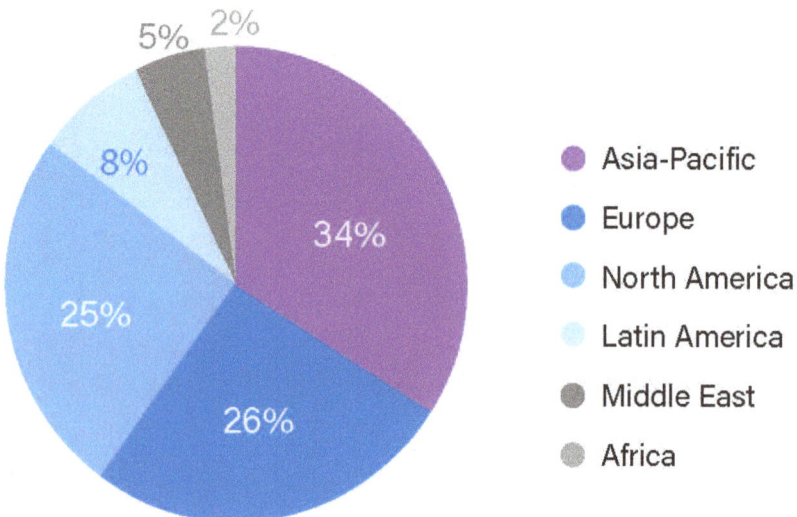

Figure 3-1   Regional distribution of worldwide passenger traffic, 2015 (IATA)[4].

On the other hand, although Asia-Pacific countries are forecast to attract passengers at a stronger rate, which will increase their individual market shares, advanced economies are not static. Europe will continue to be the market leader in overall international visitor arrivals[5], and about 70% of the hub airports with the highest share of connecting passengers remain in the US and Europe. In terms of the size of airline fleets, advanced economies continue to be in the forefront largely due to the volume of their domestic traffic.[6]

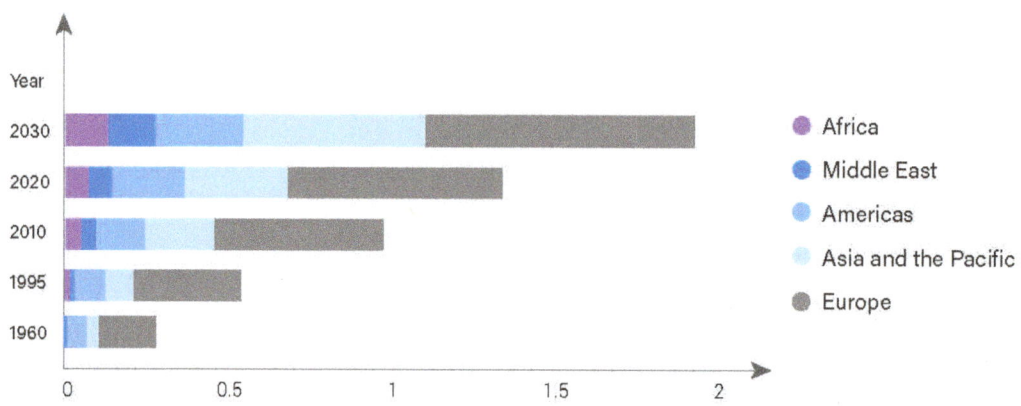

Figure 3-2   International tourist arrivals history and projections by region of destination (UNWTO, 2016).

Table 3-2   World's largest airlines by aircraft fleet size, 2016 (worldatlas.com).

Rank	Airline	Country	Fleet (June 2016)
1	American Airlines	United States	1,789
2	Delta Air Lines	United States	1,330
3	United Airlines	United States	1,229
4	Southwest Airlines	United States	720
5	FedEx Express	United States	688
6	China Southern Airlines	China	515
7	China Eastern Airlines	China	429
8	Air Canada	Canada	404
9	Air China	China	384
10	Ryanair	Ireland	349

In fact, with the economic power shift to the East, the strength of advanced economies is further enriched, and win-win situations are achieved through collaboration among emerging and advanced economies. Nonetheless, not everyone views the power shift in this way. For example, Donald Trump's election campaign slogan "make America great again" promotes moving American offshore production bases back to the US in the belief that developing countries are taking away American jobs, a policy that fails to recognize the benefits to the US of offshore production, such as lower production costs. As both a beneficiary and a driving force behind the global economy, the aviation industry cannot avoid getting caught in the confrontation between the new protectionism and the new globalization. By examining this megatrend from various perspectives, such as how the aviation industry has been impacted by GDP, the changing wealth of nations, and the rise of megalopolises and industrialization, we can conclude that the global aviation industry will expand rapidly in the next 30 years and that this will be enabled by sharing resources and creating social connections on a global basis.

THE ECONOMIC SHIFT — THE DRIVERS

The satellite image of Earth at night taken by *NASA's Earth Observatory* in 2016[7] (Figure 3-3) shows what are often referred to as "night lights". Not only is it a broad and beautiful picture that shows how humans have shaped the planet and lit up the darkness, it also reveals the concentrations of human activities (and light pollution) across the globe.

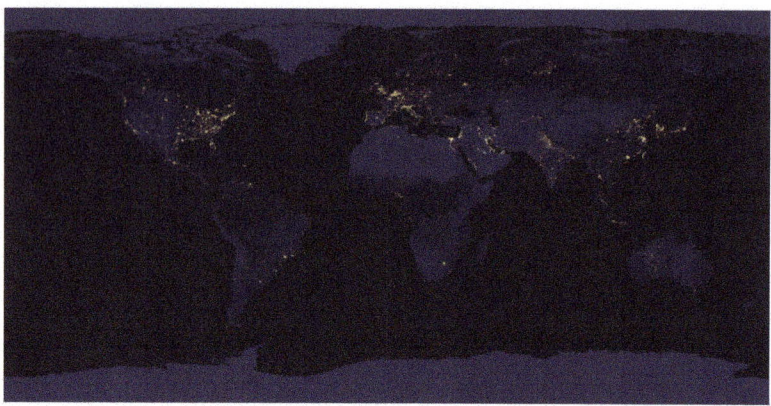

Figure 3-3   Earth Night Lights from Space (NASA, 2016).

The positions of the most lighted locations are almost identical to the concentrations of global air traffic, as depicted in Figure 3-4[8]. The concentrations of lights and of air traffic in advanced and emerging economies are similar, and the air routes between them are dense. Each one of these dense, highly populated areas is referred to as a "megalopolis".

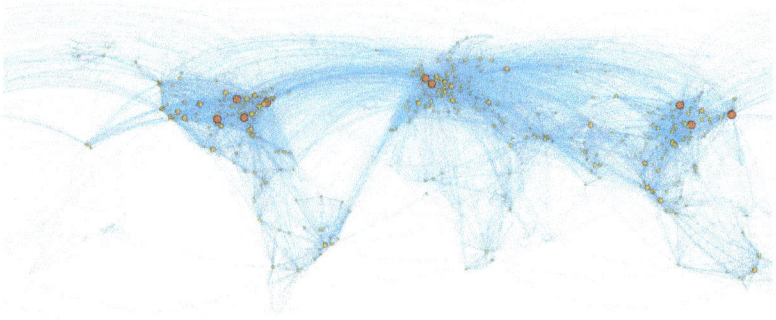

Figure 3-4   Global air traffic nodes (ICAO).

Impact of Megalopolises

A megalopolis is generally defined as a group or series of adjacent metropolitan areas, which may be somewhat separated or may merge into a continuous urban region. In short, it is a very large, heavily populated urban complex of cities. The spread of megalopolis locations in recent decades can be regarded as a symbol of the global economic power shift.

The megalopolis concept was first described in 1961 when the first megalopolis in the world was defined as the area ranging from Washington DC to Boston, with New York City as its center[9]. The total population of a megalopolis is a minimum of 10 million, with visible annual growth. However, this term is often confused with "megacity", which also means a city with a minimum 10 million population. What differentiates a megalopolis is that it is not solely defined by its population. Rather, it is a cluster of neighboring cities with significant industrial productivity and potential. For ease of discussion, this chapter uses the term "megacity" as a synonym for megalopolis unless specified otherwise.

A megalopolis is a product of industrialization and by definition cannot exist in an agricultural economy. The size and extent of a megalopolis signifies the level of industrialization of a country or region. By 2030, there will be about 50 megalopolises in the world, and they will generate over 70% of global GDP. By that time, as Khanna says, "...countries can be suburbs of cities."[10] Despite the fact that the megalopolis first started from advanced economies, in the past twenty years, new megalopolises have developed in emerging economies, and their proportion of the global economy has started to catch up with the megalopolises in the West.

In both the West and the East, all megalopolises share the same features:

Consist of two or more existing metropolitan areas with strong industrial bases: Some megalopolises may contain dozens of cities on a transnational basis, such as the Great Lakes megalopolis in North America that covers Hamilton, London, Montreal, Niagara Falls, Oshawa, Ottawa, Quebec City, Toronto, Vaughan, and Windsor in Canada and Akron, Ann Arbor, Buffalo, Chicago, Cincinnati, Cleveland, Columbus, Dayton, Des Moines, Detroit, Duluth, Erie, Flint, Fort Wayne, Green Bay, Grand Rapids, Indianapolis, Kalamazoo, Kansas City, Lansing, Louisville, Madison, Milwaukee, Minneapolis, Omaha, Pittsburgh, Quad Cities, Rochester (NY), Rochester (MN), Rockford, Traverse City, Saginaw, St. Louis, Saint Paul, South Bend, and Toledo in the USA.[11]

Are neighbors to one another with historical and social links: For example, although the Great Lakes megalopolis extends to two nation states (i.e., the USA and Canada) and covers both Anglophone and francophone regions, the cities carry the same traditions from the colonial age and share the same experiences in their process of industrialization. Because of the historical background, a megalopolis possesses its own "organic" culture with a distinct history and identity.

Maintain efficient inter-connecting transportation networks: These have usually been built over time as a result of and necessity for industrialization, and they are still expanding. These include freeways, railways, regional airlines, bus networks, and, nowadays high-speed trains. Facilitated by the transportation networks, massive and intensive flows of goods and services between the cities of the megalopolis are the norm.

All megalopolises are centers of industrialization and are the economic backbones of the nations involved. Although their original formation as an urban complex might not have been by design, they grew and evolved to support and facilitate trade and manufacturing. As hubs for industrialization, all megalopolises exert considerable impacts on the aviation industry that serves them, as follows:

High levels of urbanization: With their massive population densities, megalopolises attract skilled workers and professionals from both the surrounding areas and from all parts of the world. Immigrants and visible minorities can be found in almost all sectors, even in mono-ethnical megalopolises like the Pearl River Delta (Hong Kong and Guangzhou, China) and Maharashtra (Mumbai, India). As a consequence, the demand for air services is increasing rapidly.

Concentrated money markets: Megalopolises usually host the largest financial institutions, security exchanges, and insurance companies of the nation or region and hold a dominating position over national money markets. As a pattern throughout human history, trading centers see constant and intensified flows of visitors by air.

Expansion of job markets and trade: Workers in megalopolises are also consumers. A high population density means substantial expansion of the consumer market for all kinds of goods and services. By building factories and warehouses inside the megalopolises, manufacturers enjoy easier access to the market for both staff hiring and product sales, thus increasing demands to transport people and freight by air.

Fluid transportation between areas: Because the cities of a megalopolis are more integrated and interdependent on one another than other cities, freeway, railroad, boat, and airplane infrastructure are usually fully developed. All megalopolises have built efficient public transit systems, such as subways, buses, inter-city trains, highway coach lines, and regional airlines. Massive bridges are built to facilitate transportation and resource sharing, such as the newly completed Hong Kong – Macau – Zhuhai Bridge in the Pearl River Delta megalopolis. These networks substantially expand the catchment areas of the mega airports: large airports with around 100 million passenger capacity per year, such as the Hong Kong International Airport, Bao'an International Airport and Baiyun International Airport in the Pearl River Delta, and the new Istanbul Airport.

Centers of tourism: A megalopolis generates its own culture and is usually the center and icon of a nation for the visual and performing arts and other such activities. By their very nature, megalopolises draw attention both nationwide and worldwide and tend to attract air tourists from all over the world.

Land use issues: Megalopolises naturally generate intensified push-pull relationships between rural and urban areas for land use. This often makes mega airport expansions difficult.

Enhanced sense of environmental protection: Rightly or wrongly, aviation is often regarded as a major source of pollution and has to face various criticisms for its development projects. The experience of the past twenty years has shown that environmental awareness and measures for environmental protection are more intense in megalopolises than in other places due to the concentrated attention of media and public opinion as well as more strict control mechanisms at the government level.

Megalopolises in the West have been formed and developed through the history of industrialization over the past two hundred years. Significant ones include the Blue Banana and Golden Banana megalopolises in Europe, the Northeast, Northern California, and Southern California megalopolises in the US, and the Taiheiyō Belt megalopolis in Japan; all of which are centers of technology development and production. Air service to and from these megalopolises has reached a mature level, with steady and slow growth each year. At the same time, the proliferation of newly-developed megalopolises in the East is bringing substantial demands for aviation services, which is consistent with the changes in global GDP and wealth structures resulting from industrialization. Some examples of megalopolises in emerging economies in the East include:

China: the Pearl River Delta megalopolis covering Hong Kong, Shenzhen, Dongguan, Guangzhou, Foshan, Jiangmen, Zhongshan, Zhuhai, Macau, Huizhou (55,000,000 population); the Yangtze River Delta megalopolis covering Shanghai, Nanjing, Hangzhou,

Ningbo, Suzhou, Jingjiang, Wuxi, Changzhou, Zhenjiang, Yangzhou, Taizhou, Nantong, Huzhou, Jiaxing, Shaoxing, Jiangyin, Haimen, Zhangjiagang, Zhoushan and Ma'anshan (pop. 88 million).

India: the Maharashtra megalopolis covering Mumbai (including Thane), Navi Mumbai (including Panvel), Kalyan-Dombivali, Ulhasnagar, Vasai-Virar, Ambernath, and Badlapur, and the Pune megalopolis (including Pimpri-Chinchwad) covering Aurangabad, Solapur, Nashik, Ahmednagar, and Alibag (pop. 39.5 million).

Indonesia: the Java megalopolis covering Jakarta, Bandung, Surabaya, Yogyakarta, Bekasi, Bogor, Depok, Malang, Semarang, Tasikmalaya, Tangerang, and Cirebon (pop. 145 million).

Philippines: the Mega Manila megalopolis covering Manila, Calamba, Angeles, Baguio, Batangas, Dagupan, Olongapo, and Bacoor (pop. 40 million).

Thailand: the Bay of Bangkok Economic Rim covering Bangkok–Ayutthaya–Pattaya (pop. 16 million).

The Green Banana megalopolis covers Gdańsk, Warsaw, Kraków, and Katowice in Poland; Ostrava, Prague, Olomouc, and Brno in the Czech Republic; Vienna in Austria; Bratislava and Žilina in Slovakia; Budapest and Győr in Hungary; Ljubljana and Koper in Slovenia; Zagreb in Croatia; and Trieste in Italy (pop. 40 million).

Megalopolises and Mega-Hub Airports

As a result of this growth in megalopolises across all continents, major hub airports have been built to facilitate the transport of air passengers and cargo. In the 1950s, less than 30% of the world's population lived in cities, and the majority of these were in advanced economies. Currently, that proportion has risen to 50%, and by 2050 the world urban population is expected to increase to 72% of total population. In 2015, the United Nations (UN) estimated that there would be 22 megacities in the world (i.e., with populations of 10 million or more), and 17 of these would be located in emerging economies. By 2050, the world's urban population will have increased by some 44%[12]. Megalopolises have led to aviation megacities (i.e., megalopolises with mega airports), which have become an important component of the world's aviation network today and will be more important in the future. It is no surprise therefore that Euromonitor data show that all the top ten cities in 2015, by visitor numbers, were either aviation megacities today or would be one in the future.[13]

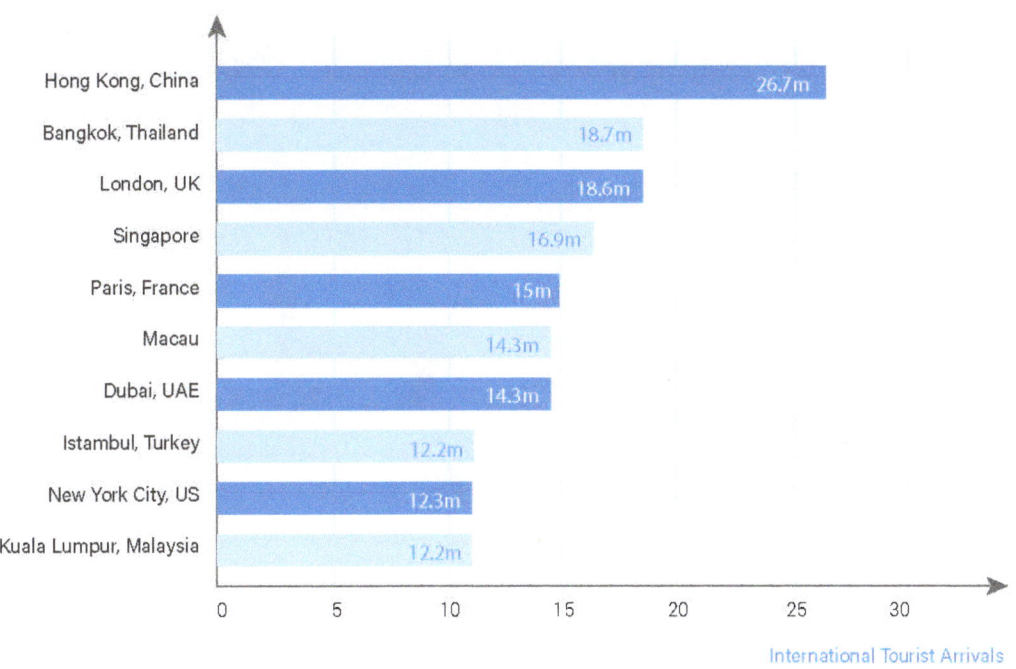

Figure 3-5   Ten most visited cities, 2015 (Euromonitor).

As a result, mega-hub airport development projects have become a trend. Some mega-hubs have been announced to come into service over the next few years, such as the Al Maktoum International Airport (UAE), Beijing Daxing International Airport, Hong Kong International Airport's Three-Runway System, and Singapore's Changi's East extension. When finished, each of these mega-hubs is planned to have a capacity of more than 100 million passengers per annum.

Airports provide the essential connectivity and access required for modern economies. They enable businesses to quickly embrace overseas opportunities and facilitate the coming and going of business people and tourists – all of which fuel economic growth. New transport infrastructure acts as a facilitator of growth, unlocking latent demand. Moreover, the enhancement of transport infrastructure, combined with the development of extensive networks, can decrease general travel costs for passengers and goods and generate more seamless connections. Asia already has the largest share of the world's urban population in its cities (see Figure 3-6). People migrate to the centers of population where they can earn higher wages, and they can do so because of the availability of efficient transportation systems, including airport infrastructure in proximity to such cities. Furthermore, as Asia moves rapidly towards becoming a higher-income region, a rise in global tourism originating from Asia will be seen. As a result, a massive wave of new air travel will be unleashed, and this will be the driver for the development of aviation megacities in Asia.

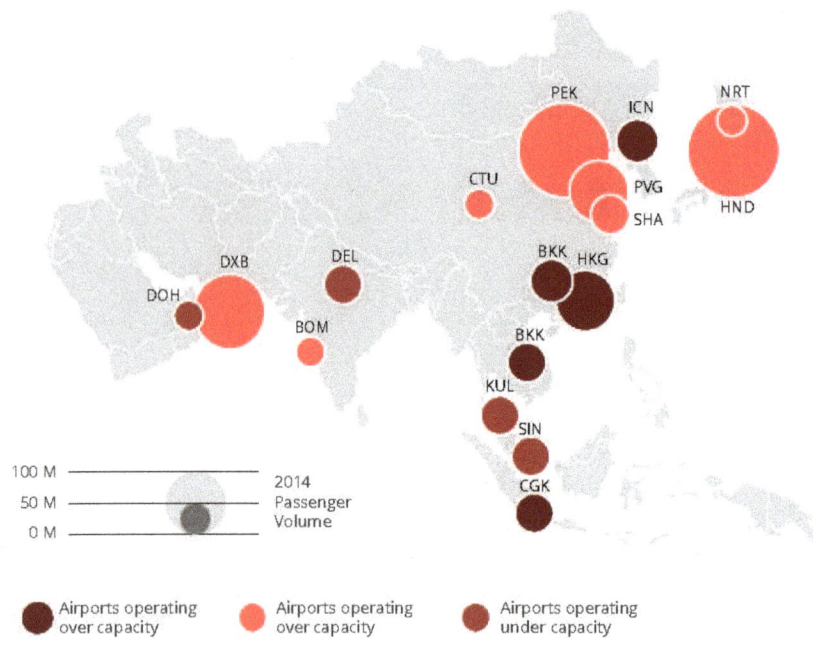

Figure 3-6   Major hub airports in Asia (IATA).

As a ripple effect, the rise of aviation megacities is changing airplane type/size requirements. Historically, airlines, especially those in Asia, have had a pattern of operating large aircraft with relatively lower flight frequencies between major cities. Figure 3-7 shows a 20-year forecast of the demand for aircraft from 2014 to 2033. Out of 31,358 new aircraft, almost 70% will be single-aisle, indicating a shift towards smaller narrow-body airplane flights to meet the increasing demand in both advanced and emerging economies for increased flight frequency between growing megalopolises. Airbus estimates that the need for single-aisle aircraft is expected to be consistent over all the regions of the world.

20-year new deliveries of passenger and freight aircraft

22,071 single-aisle aircraft

7,786 twin-aisle aircraft

Market Value
-
$4.6
trillion

1,501 very large aircraft

31,358 new aircraft

Passenger aircraft (≥ 100 seats)
Jet freight aircraft (>10 tons)

Figure 3-7   Global market forecast – New aircraft, 2014–2033 (Airbus).[14]

The Rise of Protectionism

The economic power shift to the East is never going to be a smooth process. Having started in the context of the "global village" and "globalization" some thirty years ago, this West-East power shift is encountering the rise of a "new protectionism" movement as symbolized by Donald Trump's administration in the USA. The protectionist stance taken by the USA in 2018 was designed to protect and maintain that nation's dominant position in the global economy, as well as to discourage the emerging trend of new globalization. This new globalization trend is best symbolized by China's Belt and Road Initiative, which advocates a new structure for the global economy not dominated by the powers of the West, as was the case in the past. The direct conflict between these two trends will no doubt have significant impacts on the international aviation industry.

Protectionism is based on the creation of trade barriers in order to achieve positive trade balances and protect local markets. The United States was "the mother country and bastion of modern protectionism" since the end of the 18th Century and until the post-World War II period[15]. Although history has proven that protectionism produces more harm than benefits to local markets, it is still a mechanism regularly adopted by many governments. Often, when a country finds another country using a mechanism to stimulate exports, it will retaliate by using a counter-mechanism to protect its local market.

As the International Air Transport Association (IATA) points out in its study of the future of the airline industry, "Monetary and trade protectionism dominate foreign policies. The world has splintered into resource trading blocs, with nations striking deals in the hope of achieving some kind of stability in a zero-sum world."[16] Tariffs, new local procurement rules, and other protectionist barriers are increasing the costs of cross-border trade. A rise in import tariffs increases the price of imported goods; with fewer purchases of imported goods, local producers are favored. National governments use various forms of protectionism to constrain imports or to stimulate exports, and all of them may have both direct and indirect impacts on the business of aviation. Some examples of these types of protectionist measures include:

- Government favoring domestic firms by establishing public procurement policies and forbidding government agencies from purchasing imported goods, especially in the military and medical areas.

- Export subsidies to encourage exports, such as the EU with its Airbus development support program and the USA with its support for Boeing Aircraft, or the longstanding agricultural subsidies and proposed "Buy American" provisions in the United States.[17]

- Health and safety regulations to prevent selected goods from being imported.

- Quality standards that a government may impose to make imports more difficult.

- Bureaucracy that aims to make import procedures complicated and time-consuming, a phenomenon often seen at international airports.

- Manipulating the currency exchange rate to stimulate exports and deter imports.

The growth of monthly airline passenger seat volumes between the USA and China from 45,000 in 2012 to 107,000 in 2018 is currently threatened by a possible massive trade war between the two countries in early 2018.[18]

"New protectionism" is a continuation of traditional protectionism in an environment where Western domination over the global economy is being weakened. It is an attempt by some nations to turn back the clock by overturning various global mechanisms that have emerged over the years to encourage free trade and market liberalization. Protectionism creates uncertainties instead of opportunities for the global economy. As one author points out, the time is disappearing when "the political effects of the rise of Asia have been slowed by the continuing strength of the Western alliance".[19] There are currently voices in some Western nations to adopt stronger measures to rebuild the traditional domination, such as the suggestion that, "a resolute American stance in the

Pacific might then buy time for the internal changes in China that would make Beijing's power seem less threatening to Asian countries."[20]

Figure 3-8   US-China weekly one-way seats – January 2012 to September 2018 (CAPA).

There are opposing voices as well. In April 2009, heads of the G20 meeting in London pledged "...we will not repeat the historic mistakes of protectionism of previous eras". Adherence to this pledge is monitored by the Global Trade Alert, providing up-to-date information and informed commentary to help ensure that the G20 pledge is met by maintaining confidence in the world trading system. However, in November 2017, the World Bank reported that 17 of those G20 countries had imposed restrictive trade measures since 2009. In its report, the World Bank states that most of the world's major economies are resorting to protectionist measures as the global economic slowdown begins to bite. Economists who have examined the impact of new trade-restrictive measures using detailed trade statistics estimate that new measures taken through late 2009 were distorting global merchandise trade by 0.25% to 0.5% (about $50 billion a year).[21]

It is fair to say that the new protectionism is not only found in advanced economies, but in emerging economies as well. For example, China protects domestic automotive manufacturers with 25% import duties on foreign-made automobiles and requires foreign companies to transfer technology to domestic manufacturers. Non-tariff trade barriers are also used by many countries. For example, Nigeria has a requirement that at least half the value of all information and communication technology hardware purchased in the country be generated domestically.

Another type of non-tariff trade barrier has been the rise of "state capitalism" in many countries, which has enabled state-owned enterprises to account for 23% of the world's 500 largest companies, compared with 9% in 2005. State capitalism is manifested through direct subsidies of domestic industries, the growing power of sovereign wealth funds in mergers and acquisitions, and procurement policies that favor local companies in awarding government contracts. As Figure 3-9 demonstrates, a variety of non-tariff trade barriers are seen almost everywhere in the world.[22] This rising economic nationalism has forced global businesses to reconsider their physical presence and the way they operate in various countries.[23]

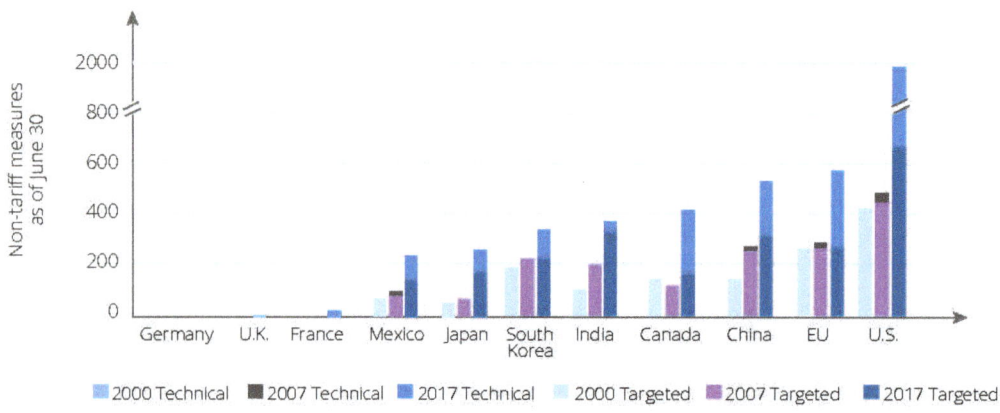

Note: Targeted barriers include anti-dumping, countervailing, safeguards and special safeguards, tariff-rate quotas, export subsidies, quantitative restrictions and state trading enterprises.
Souce: World Trade Organization, RBC GAM

Figure 3-9   Non-tariff trade measures, selected countries – 2000, 2007, 2017 (Royal Bank of Canada).

The New Globalization

The type of state-sponsored protectionism discussed above was not anticipated by Alvin Toffler in his seminal book *The Third Wave* (1980), in which he foresaw that the power of the nation-state would be diminished by the rise of non-national entities such as intergovernmental organizations (IGOs), multinational corporations, religions with global reach, and even terrorist organizations and cartels. Toffler predicted that national economies would gradually merge into a growing network of super-national organizations and affiliations, such as the European Union, the North American Union, the newly formed African Union, and organizations such as the WTO, NAFTA, or the International Criminal Court. However, thirty-five years later, in a global environment with the establishment of numerous super-national organizations, we have seen the Trump administration in the USA threaten massive trade wars in its attempt to rebuild the dominance of nation-states over the global economy. This trend is connected with the decline of globalization and the rise of the new globalization, which are also shaping the future of the aviation industry.

Traditionally, the term "globalization" means a trend that groups all nation-states into one single regime called "the global village". In this context, questions arise as to who pushes whom, to where, and for what. Various forms of globalization have existed since the rise of trading among nation-states, going back to the ancient Greek culture, the Roman Empire, the Chinese Han Dynasty, the Mongol Empire, and the Portuguese and Spanish empires. The first emergence of globalization in its modern sense was after the Industrial Revolution in the 19th Century, which enabled cheap and massive production of household items to meet the increasing demand for commodities from rapidly growing populations. When China was forced to open up its doors due to the first and second Opium Wars, and when India was colonized with the establishment of the East India Company, the vast populations of these regions became ready consumers of European exports. Meanwhile, valuable natural resources such as rubber, diamonds, and coal flowed from sub-Saharan Africa and the Pacific Islands to Europe at a cheap price. Colonial rule was the major feature of globalization during this period leading up to the First World War in 1914, when the European-dominated networks were increasingly challenged by newcomers in the world marketplace, especially the United States. After the war, the role of the world's guardian of universal law and morality changed hands from Europe to North America.

Figure 3-10 illustrates the extent of globalization by 1935. By that time, Great Britain's Imperial Airways already had a route network extending from the UK to Australia and South Africa.

The Second World War saw the dominance of the United States as the leader of a new version of globalization aimed at breaking down borders that were hampering trade at the time. The first landmark was the Bretton Woods Conference, an agreement by the world's leading economies to draft a set of specific rules for the conduct of international commerce and finance. Newcomers who wanted to join in on that globalization wave were required to follow these rules. International institutions were founded to oversee the implementation of the rules, and multinational corporations based in the United States and Europe were established and expanded for worldwide exchange of new developments in science, technology, and products.

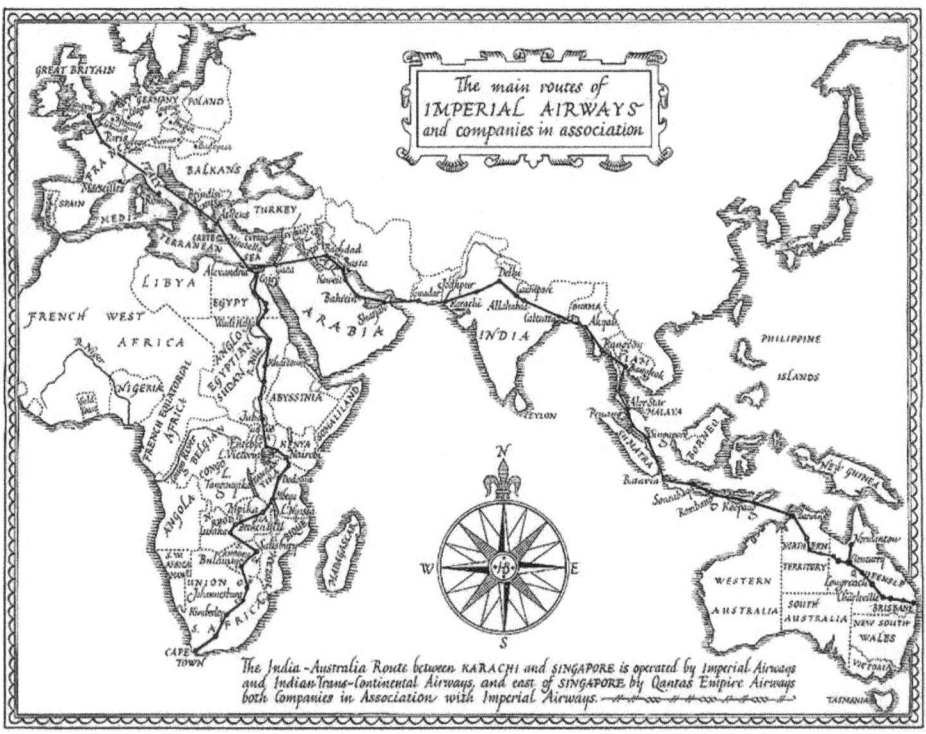

Figure 3-10   Imperial Airways route map, 1935 (Wikipedia).

The pattern of this globalization process involved nations with dominant economic and military power globalizing those nations without. After the Second World War came the spread of Western culture, with Americanization at the core. The ideologies of democracy and liberalism were central, along with the lifestyle of commercialism and consumerism. The "American Dream" loomed large. Unlike colonial times when mass communications were limited to paper, the worldwide export of Western culture has exploded in the last 65 years through new mass media: film, radio and television, recorded music, and nowadays, the Internet. The development of international transportation and telecommunication systems, including the aviation industry, played a significant role in the modern globalization process.

Figure 3-11   Airports gaining competitive advantage and building business confidence
for the local economy[24] (ICAO).

The globalizers advocated free trade to the globalized nation-states on a scale much
larger than at the time of the Opium Wars, including elimination of tariffs, establishment
of free trade zones, reduction of transportation costs through introducing jumbo jets and
containerization, reduction or elimination of capital controls and government subsidies,
and harmonization and enforcement of intellectual property laws across all nation-states.
The outcome has been a continuing flow from West to East of commodities, including
goods, services, and high-technology and intellectual properties, to enhance the latter's
modernization and industrialization processes. In the opposite direction, East-to-West
flows of natural resources and labor-intensive products have reduced the living costs of
Westerners. Almost all trades were conducted in US dollars as most currencies of Eastern
nations were not valid on the global market.

This imbalance has been lessened in recent years by the economic power shift to the
East. With the increase of their national wealth and production capacities, emerging
economies have started to turn their gaze from the West to their neighboring nations to
explore whether they can do trades among themselves without going through the West
and always using US dollars. Thus, a foundation has been built for a new type of globalization, as reflected by China's Belt and Road (B&R) Initiative. The Belt and Road refers

to the ancient routes of trade from China to Europe that passed through the Middle East and northwest Africa, when the main exports were tea and silk. Although the original intention of the B&R Initiative was to export labor and skills from China to the developing regions on the routes, it is now becoming a platform for investment and cooperation among regions. Furthermore, in addition to the ancient land and ocean routes to Europe, the B&R Initiative has expanded to Africa and South America. By March 2017, more than 100 nations had joined the B&R Initiative, and more than 60 countries had signed cooperation agreements with China. In June 2016, the trade volume between China and the B&R countries reached US$1 trillion, or about 25% of China's total foreign trade volume. The total population of the B&R countries has reached 4.4 billion, or about 63% of the world's population, with a combined GDP of US$21 trillion, accounting for about 30% of the world's total GDP.[25]

The new globalization provides a platform on which emerging economies can maintain their own culture, religion, and belief systems while accepting foreign investment and accomplishing their own industrialization initiatives. The B&R Initiative has been welcomed and embraced quickly by emerging economies, not just because China promises to invest, but because it presents a significant difference from traditional globalization and a new pathway towards modernization. As Doris Naisbitt points out, "Many countries of the Global Southern Belt are discontented with Washington lecturing and interfering in their internal affairs without a deft knowledge of the cultural, ethnic, regional, or tribal intricacies and innuendos used in daily communication and the social fabric, which underlies the economic community and politics."[26]

It should be noted, however, that the new globalization trend does not make the West and East enemies. Many countries in the West see the growth of the new globalization as an opportunity to break away from the established controls of the past regime and as an opportunity to build their own global trading systems. For example, the new protectionism that is spearheaded by the USA's Trump administration to counteract the new globalization has been partially offset by Brexit. According to Daniel Hannan, a British Conservative member of the European Parliament and leading intellectual architect of the Brexit movement, the purpose of Brexit is not to form a "little England" and close it off from the rest of the world, but rather it is to escape from the constraints of the EU and uncover more opportunities. As Mr. Hannan stated, "There is a huge difference between Trump and Brexit. Trump is a protectionist. A big part of his campaign was that he didn't want free trade with China. A big part of our campaign was that we *do* want free trade with China. We saw leaving the EU as an opportunity to re-engage with the world."[27]

Unlike other modes of transport, the international aviation industry has been paying for the vast majority of its own infrastructure costs.[28] According to the International Civil Aviation Organization (ICAO), as shown in Figure 3-12, government funding accounts for only 4.19% of total aviation requirements with the industry funding the balance. Meanwhile, rail and road transport are heavily government-funded, at 23% and 54% respectively.

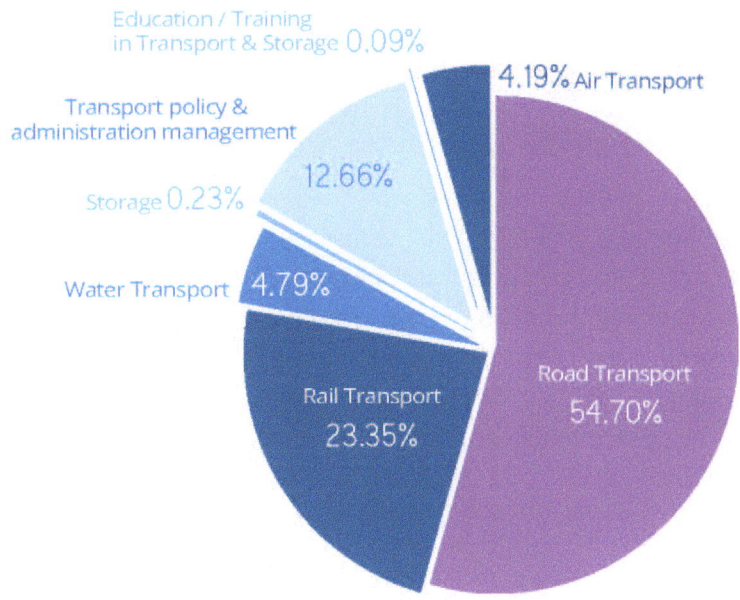

Figure 3-12 Government share of infrastructure funding by mode (ICAO).[29]

Because of its active direct participation in the world economy, the aviation industry is situated right in the middle of many global economic policy conflicts and is therefore sensitive to any moves in global trade. Accordingly, the industry must be careful not to judge the correctness of either the new protectionism or the new globalization. Rather, it needs to become an active participant in whatever form of new globalization becomes manifest so that it may benefit from it. The international aviation industry needs to become the "air bridge" between continents and between the traditional and newly-developed megalopolises.

GDP AND INVESTMENT SHIFTS

Through worldwide networking, aviation plays a unique role in empowering nations and peoples regardless of where they are located. To provide aviation services and infrastructure worldwide requires massive financial investments by both the private and public sectors. This allows the industry to provide people with efficient access to whatever they need: improved livelihoods, food, healthcare, education, business, R&D, family and friends, communities, leisure activities, tourism, etc. Within a region, air transport services act as a lifeline for vulnerable groups and migrant communities and allow people in remote and low-density rural areas to enhance their social inclusion.

Global Aviation Activity

At the global level, aviation brings the advanced and emerging economies of all continents closer together, with over 1,400 scheduled airlines, 26,000 aircraft in service, 3,900 airports, and 173 air navigation services providers. International aviation operates an unmatched global network that serves travelers and businesses in every corner of the world. When international airlines land at the airports of another country, they not only bring passengers and goods, but they also account for numerous socio-economic spinoffs. ICAO estimated that in 2016 the aviation industry supported $2.7 trillion (3.6%) of the world's GDP.

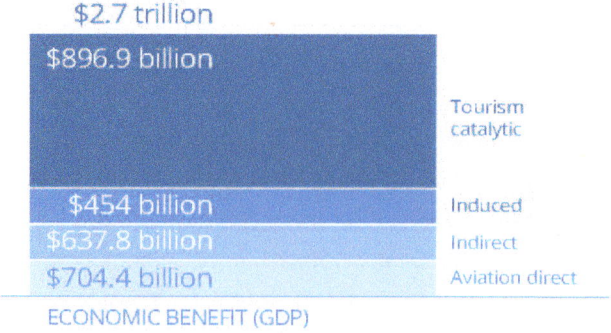

Figure 3-13 Value of the aviation industry to the economy.

With the economic power shift to the East, aviation benefits to emerging economies are increasing. The shift of economic power is most often measured in terms of gross domestic product (GDP). For the aviation industry, the relationship between GDP and air traffic volume has been widely used for forecasting future air travel flows. This is based on the fact that increases in GDP usually lead directly to increases in passenger traffic. Conversely, a decrease in GDP usually triggers a reduction in traffic volume. Accordingly, the rapid increase of GDP growth in emerging economies in recent years has been driving the economic power shift from West to East in the aviation industry. This GDP-aviation relationship has been embraced globally by all sectors of the industry, including government agencies for policy-making, researchers for forecasting, airlines for determining their fleet expansions, airport authorities for making decisions on airport expansions, and airplane manufacturers when planning the number of new aircraft to be built. This chapter also uses GDP as one of the important indicators that illustrates the impact of the economic power shift from West to East. Nonetheless, it is worth pointing out that in addition to GDP, other factors are also important to the aviation industry, as listed below:

- The hub status of an airport changes the pattern and volume of air traffic. Hubs such as Singapore and Dubai offer air connectivity far out of proportion to their sizes because of the availability of their air services and their geographical locations.

- The level of air fares is an important driver of the growth of passenger traffic. The past two decades have seen the rise of low-cost carriers (LCCs) and corresponding decreases in air fares, which have encouraged more air travel and increased preference for flying as a cost-competitive alternative to other transportation modes.

- Demography is another driver of aviation activity. An increase in population in an airport catchment area usually generates more trips.

- Market maturity is a factor related to the total volume of air travel because with a higher level of maturity, a market tends to reach a saturation point in terms of trips per capita. Nonetheless, generally speaking, markets that are more open are more responsive to changes in per capita income because airlines are freer to add routes, increase frequencies, and add seats to capture demand. In a more regulated environment, demand may increase with GDP per capita, but lower service quality and higher pricing may restrain travel growth.

- The geographical features of a country can also play a key role. For example, a region with islands or poorly connected land masses will necessitate more air travel. The need for air travel is also higher in countries with limited land transport.

- A decrease in economic activity does not necessarily mean a decrease in air traffic. Over the past 30 years, the aviation industry has experienced recessions, oil-price shocks, near-pandemics, wars, and security threats, yet traffic has continued to grow at about 5% annually. The demand for air travel is resilient because of discretionary trips for vacations or family events that may take place even during economic downturns (see Figure 3-14).

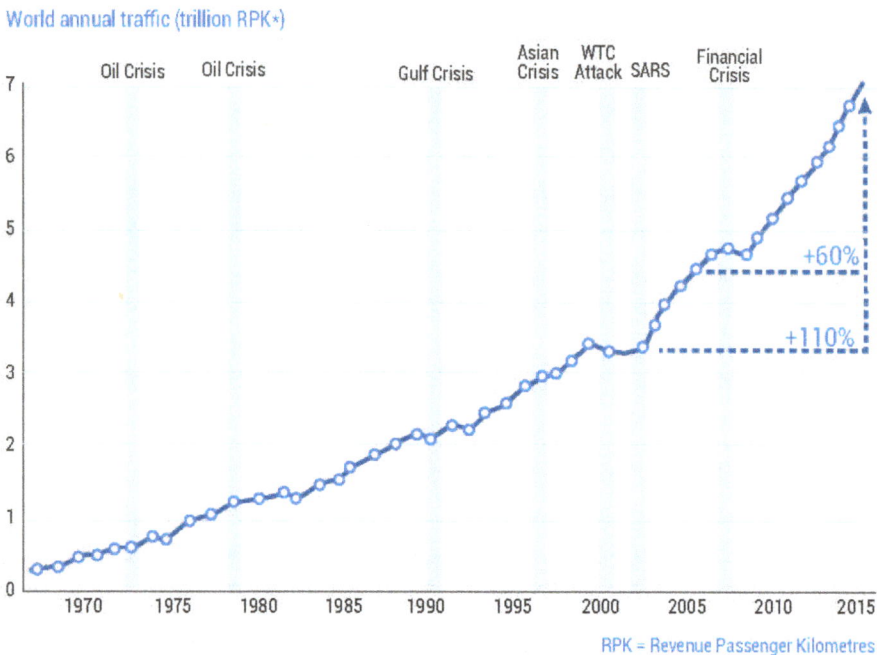

Figure 3-14 Worldwide air passenger travel and external shocks, 1970 to 2015 (ICAO).

In fact, Figure 3-15 shows that in the 70 years since the Second World War, global aviation has seen continuing growth in both passenger volume and freight volume despite various crises.[30]

GDP — The Main Driver of Aviation Activity

Figure 3-15 illustrates that despite major crises, the global GDP growth rate continues to be the most important influencer of worldwide air traffic. According to Boeing's *2014 Current Market Outlook*, the various influences on a region's air-travel growth can be grouped into three categories: economic activity, ease of travel, and local market factors.[31] Among these, economic activity is the most easily understood, and, as already discussed, GDP growth rate is the key metric directly related to air traffic rates. Figure 3-16 highlights the key metrics included in this category.

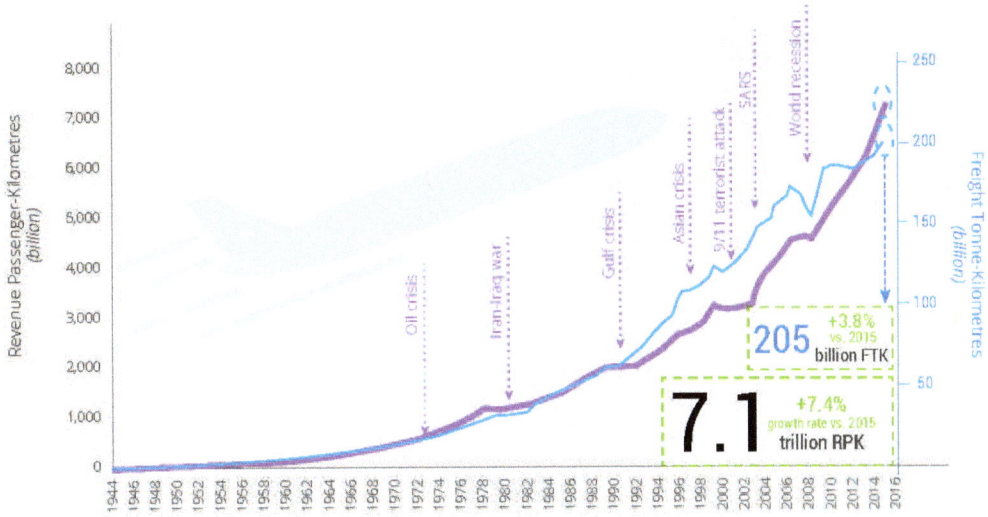

Figure 3-15   Worldwide air passenger travel and major crises, 1944 to 2016 (ICAO).

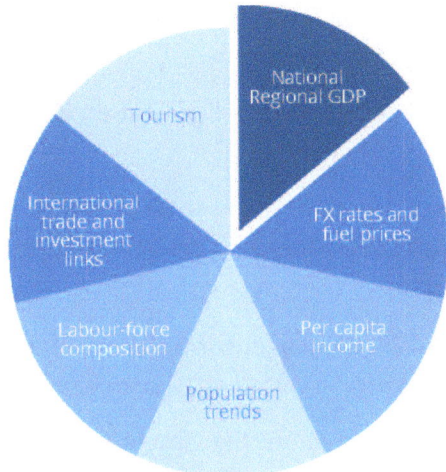

Figure 3-16   Economic activity components that affect air travel demand (Mott MacDonald).

Although GDP and air traffic growth rates are often in step with each other, past performance has shown that air traffic growth can be more rapid. The correlation between GDP and air traffic growth is shown in Figure 3-17 in terms of available seat kilometers (ASKs) flown. The outcome is that the volume of air travel has grown significantly more rapidly than GDP.

Figure 3-17   Relationship between real GDP and air travel (IMF and SRS, 2016).

In order to determine its future airplane production, Boeing Aircraft Company has made the following demand forecasts of future GDP growth and related air travel growth:

- Global GDP will grow at 3.2% per annum over the next 20 years.

- Emerging economies are expected to grow at 5.2% per year, outpacing established economies, which will average 2.2% growth.

- Emerging and developing economies will grow from 27% of total world GDP in 2013 to 40% by 2032.

- The fastest-growing economies are those in the Asia-Pacific region, with a projected growth of 4.4% per year; Latin America is projected to grow at 3.9% per annum and Africa at 4.7% annually.

- Based on the expected 3.2% annual growth in GDP, airline passenger traffic will grow at 5.0% annually and air cargo traffic at 4.7% per year.

- Passenger traffic within China will be the largest travel market, expected to grow at 6.6% annually.

- Travel within North America and Europe will form the second and third largest markets respectively, with annual growth rates of 2.3% and 3.4%.

- Traffic to and from the Middle East and Asia-Pacific, within Asia-Pacific (excluding China), and within Latin America will be among the fastest to grow.[32]

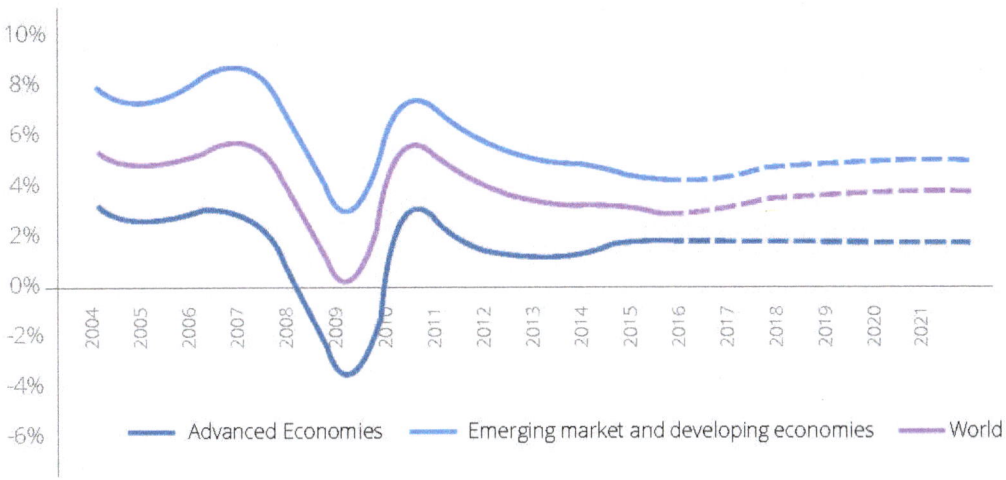

Figure 3-18 Real GDP growth of emerging and advanced economies (IMF, 2016).

Emerging economies have demonstrated a much higher growth potential than established economies, notably in China and India, and their share of global GDP has increased
consistently since 2009. Although their growth rates have slowed, their share of global
GDP has continued to increase, and the importance of these countries to the pace of
global growth has also increased. Figure 3-19 shows a comparison of projected GDP
growth between the leading countries of advanced and emerging economies relative to
the nominal GDP of G7 and BRIC economies. [33]

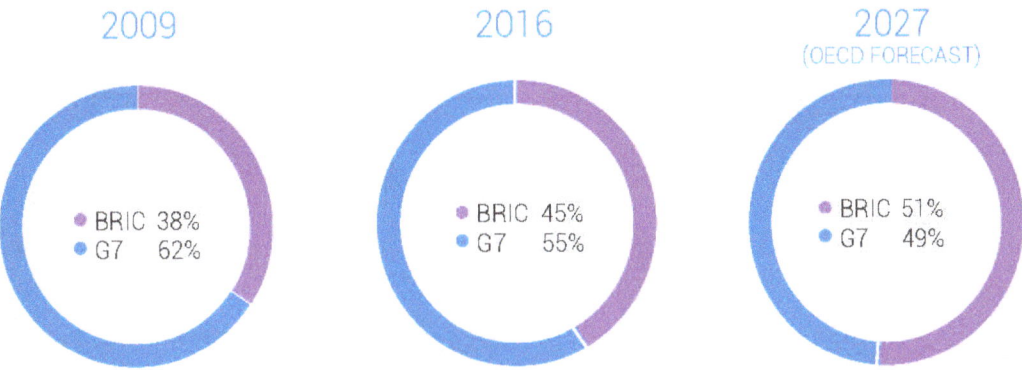

Figure 3-19 Projected GDP growth, G7 vs. BRIC countries in 2009, 2016, and 2027 (OECD).

Global Investment Shifts

The change in global GDP structure is based on the shift of global investment markets over the past twenty years. Since the turn of the 20th Century, the pattern of global investment, measured as gross capital formation, has changed significantly. Between 1965 and 1999, investment in developing countries held a relatively constant global share—averaging 18.5% —but this share increased dramatically in the first decade of the 21st Century, reaching about 40% by 2009. The change is even starker when one adjusts for differences in purchasing power.

Moreover, this convergence in global investment shares was hastened by the global financial crisis of 2008. Since 2007, investment has fallen more sharply in high-income countries than in the developing world. Figure 3-20 shows that the growing influence of developing countries in the global investment picture has clearly paralleled the emergence of developing countries on the world economic stage. As a result, gross investment in developing countries has increased both in absolute terms (a), and as a share of global investment (b).[34] Developing countries will account for a greater share of gross capital inflows and outflows in the future.[35]

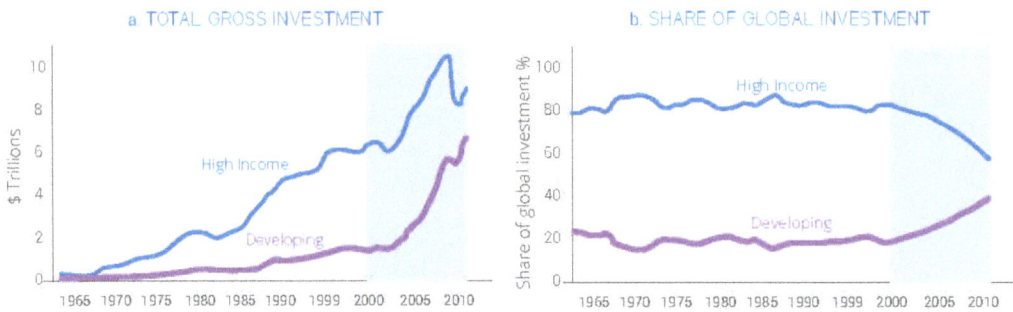

Figure 3-20 Investment comparisons, high-income vs. developing countries (World Bank).

As shown in Figure 3-21, by 2030, nearly half or more of gross capital inflows will likely go to developing countries.[36] Emerging-economy countries will represent more than half of global capital stocks by 2030 in the gradual convergence scenario, compared with about one-third in 2010.[37]

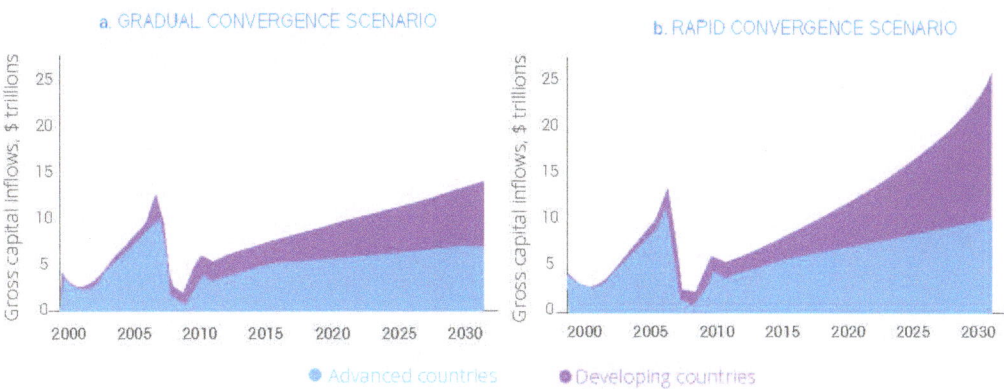

Figure 3-21 Capital inflow comparison, advanced vs. developing countries:
Two scenarios (World Bank).

As volumes of gross inflows and outflows to/from emerging economies expand in the future, the potential benefits to these countries will be significant. These benefits will include diversification of idiosyncratic national risks, the imposition of greater market discipline on policy-making, and the opportunity to supplement domestic saving in ramping up fixed investment and growth.[38] China and India will account for the majority of global investment, and investment will shift toward the services sector, especially in infrastructure. Strong economic growth will underpin China's leadership in global gross capital formation over the next two decades. In the gradual convergence scenario, China will account for 30% of global investment by 2030. China's emphasis on consumption over government investment and India's ongoing structural reform efforts may create conditions for continued economic and corporate earnings growth over both the short and longer terms.[39] Nonetheless, as Figure 3-22 illustrates, the rising share of investment by developing countries in global output is due to more than just changes in China and India.[40] Elsewhere in the developing world, robust growth will be associated with high investment rates as well. Brazil, India, and Russia will together account for more than 13% of global investment in 2030, which is more than the United States.[41]

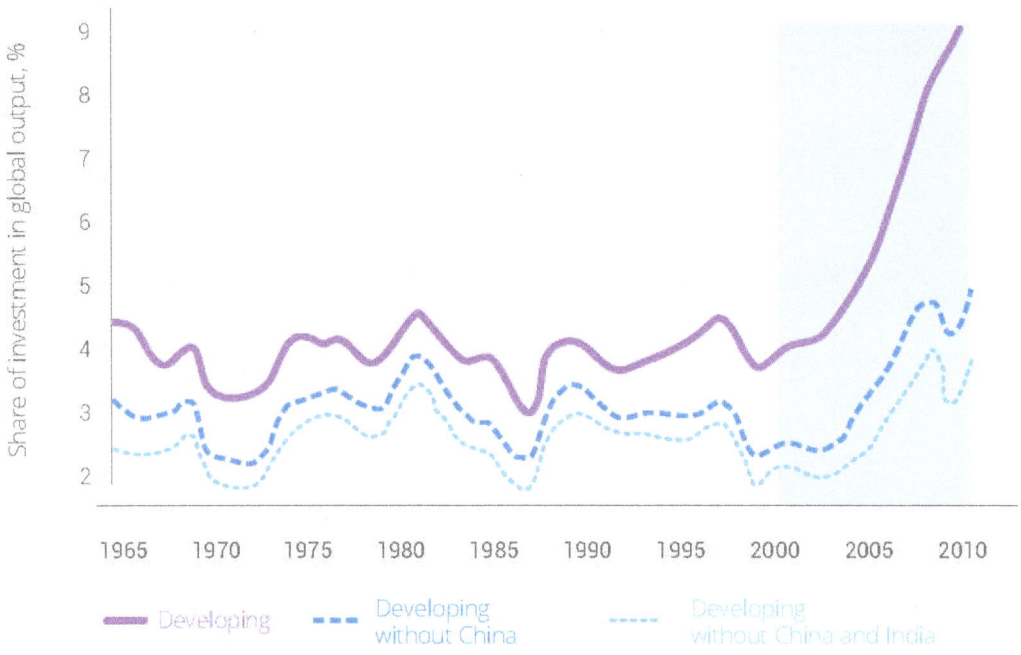

Figure 3-22 Share of global output, developing countries vs. with/without China, India (World Bank).

The significant shift in global investment will continue to boost GDP growth and prosperity in emerging economies, as estimated by the Economist Intelligence Unit of the EU in 2015:

- Economic prosperity across the Asia-Pacific region will continue and is expected to account for over 50% of global GDP by 2050.

- Further growth is also projected in Africa, almost reaching a 10% share of global GDP by 2050.

- In light of this expansion, the relative shares of Europe and America will decline.

- Worldwide GDP is projected to grow at an average annual rate of around 2.5% between 2020 and 2030.[42]

Figures 3-23 and 3-24 illustrate relative GDP growth rates and percentage shares among the various world regions, both historically and as far forward as 2050.

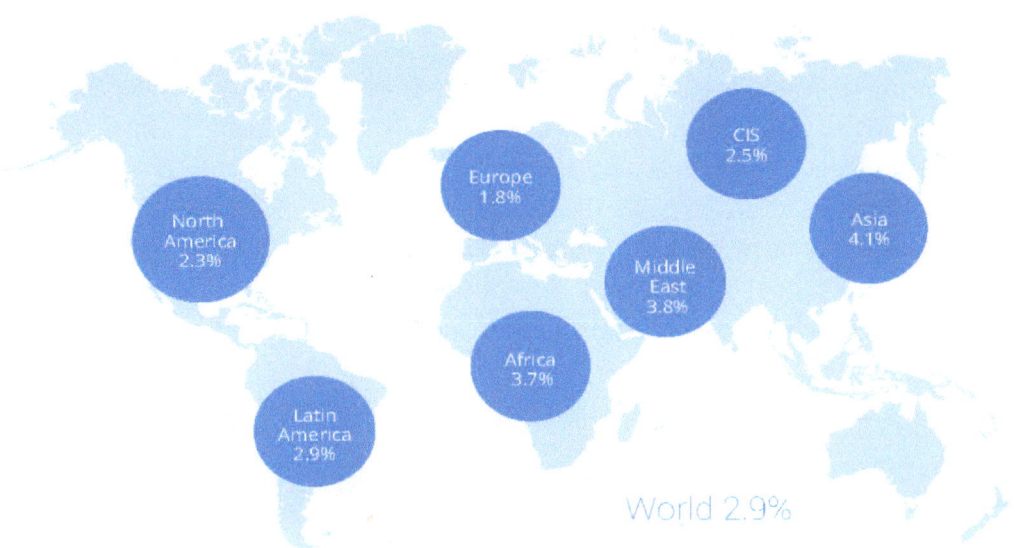

Figure 3-23 Projections of real GDP annual growth by region, 2016-35 (HIS, Boeing).

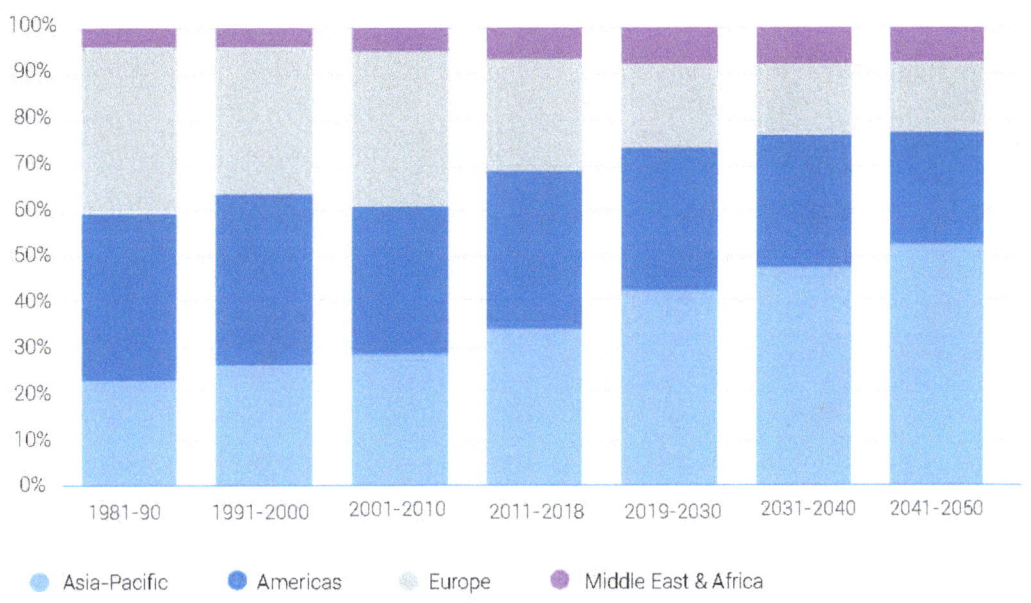

Figure 3-24 Regional share of global GDP, 1981–2050 (EU Economist Intelligence Unit, 2016).

Impacts on the Aviation Industry

As shown in Figure 3-25, Airbus estimates that the fastest growth in air traffic flows will be in emerging economies, including domestic India (5.4% growth rate), domestic China (3.6%), and domestic Asia emerging economies (3.7%). However, this does not mean that traffic flows in advanced economies will decrease. Although domestic traffic flows in advanced economies will continue to increase, they will attract more traffic flows from emerging economies. Their dominant position in the global aviation industry will remain about the same by developing and expanding their connectivity with emerging economies.

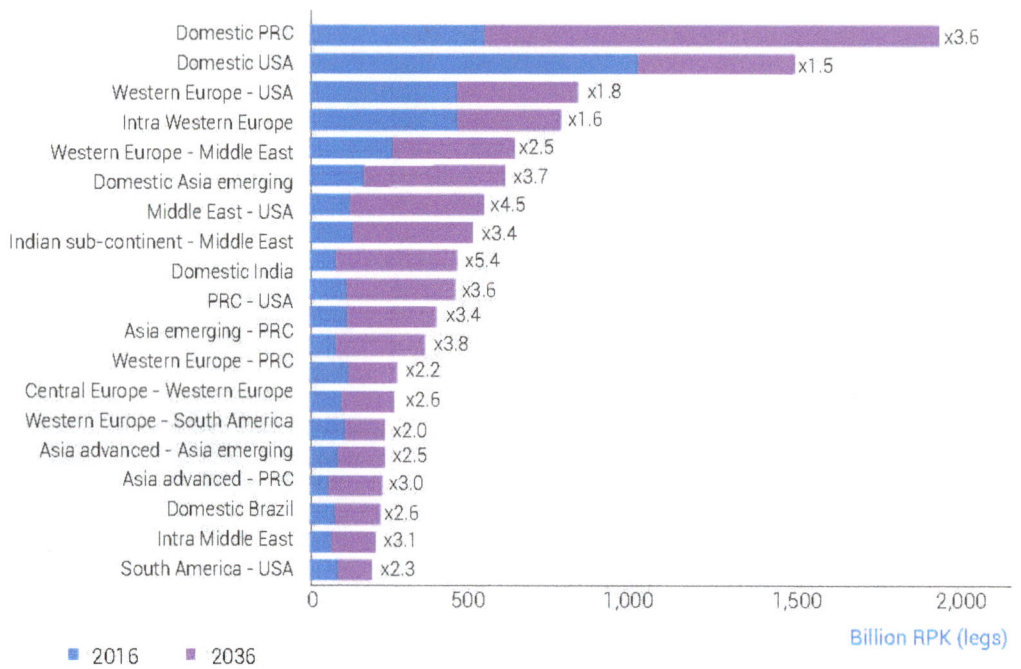

Figure 3-25 Top 20 aviation traffic flows, 2016-2036 (Airbus GMF, 2017).

Figure 3-26 shows more explicitly the future growth points in air traffic among emerging economies. It is interesting to note that with the B&R initiative, traffic flows between China and Africa will grow substantially, but traffic flows with the USA will not expand as much. This is a reflection of the conflict between the new protectionism and the new globalization.

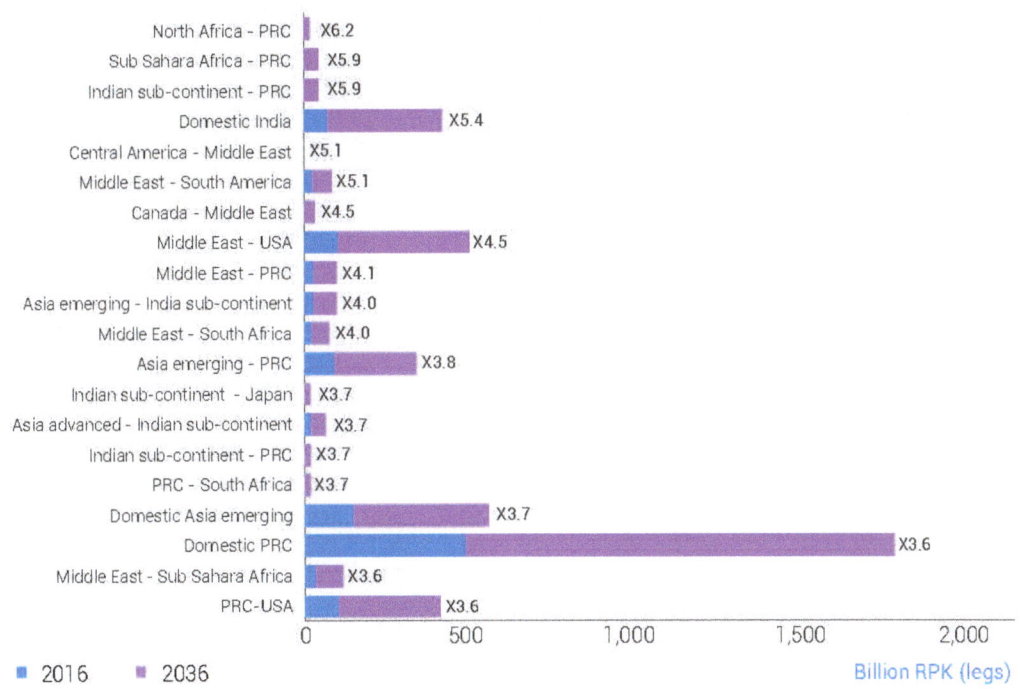

Figure 3-26 Top 20 fastest-growing aviation traffic flows, 2016-2036 (Airbus GMF, 2017).

The increase in traffic flows will be mostly passenger flows, that is, people traveling for business or leisure. It should be noted that the growth points will be regional flights either inside a country or between neighboring countries. This is the basis that aircraft manufacturers have used to determine that their focus should now be on the production of single-aisle airplanes. For emerging economies, this means a significant shift from traditional land transport to modern air transport that will result from their social and economic development.

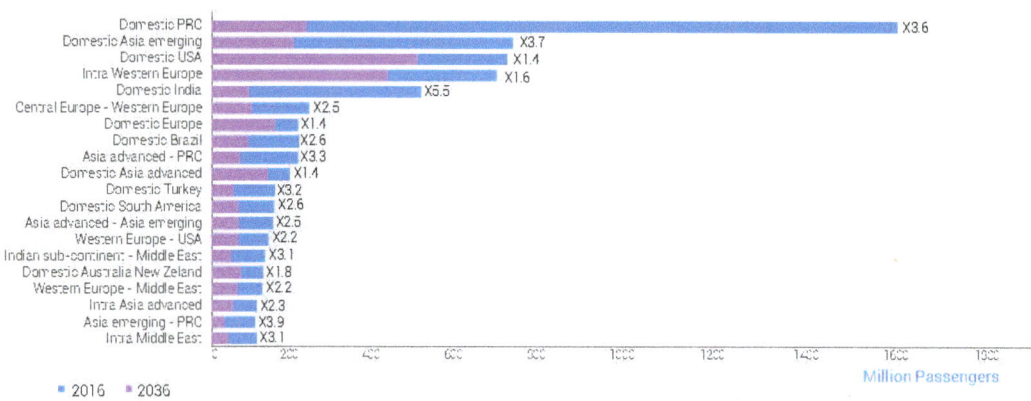

Figure 3-27 Top 20 aviation passenger origin/destination flows, 2016–2036 (Airbus GMF, 2017).

Based on its forecasts (see Table 3-3), Boeing estimates that the global aviation market will need 36,770 new airplanes valued at $5.2 trillion by 2033. Of these, 15,500, or 42%, will replace older and less efficient airplanes. The remaining 21,270 new airplanes will support fleet growth, which will stimulate expansion in emerging markets and is likely to lead to development of innovative airline business models.

Table 3-3   Airplane requirement forecasts by region, 2012–2033 (Boeing Current Market Outlook).

Passenger and freighter airplanes
Market value and demand by region

Region	$B	Airplanes
Asia Pacific	$2,020	13,460
Europe	$1,040	7,450
North America	$870	7,550
Latin America	$340	2,950
Middle East	$640	2,950
CIS	$150	1,330
Africa	$140	1,080
World	$5,200	36,770

Airbus has made similar forecasts, as shown in Table 3-4. According to their estimates, air traffic (RPK) will double every 15 years. They estimate a demand for 34,900 new aircraft by 2036: 34,170 passenger aircraft and 730 freighters. About 40% of the new passenger aircraft will be needed for replacement and 60% for new growth. Airbus estimates that Asia-Pacific will account for 41% of demand, with the US and Europe together representing 36%.[43] By 2036, about two-thirds of their aircraft will be flying in the skies of emerging economies.

Table 3-4   Global demand for new aircraft, 2017–2036 (Airbus GMF, 2017).

	2017 2026	2027 2036	**2017 2036**	SHARE OF 2017-2036 NEW DELIVERIES
AFRICA	350	700	1,050	3%
ASIA-PACIFIC	6,140	8,140	14,280	41%
CIS	340	860	1,200	3%
EUROPE	2,640	4,180	6,820	20%
LATIN AMERICA	940	1,730	2,670	8%
MIDDLE EAST	1,260	1,270	2,530	7%
NORTH AMERICA	2,360	3,260	5,620	16%
FREIGHTERS	410	320	730	2%
WORLD	14,440	20,460	34,900	100%

In the past decade, while global GDP has grown by 28% in real terms, global air passenger traffic has grown substantially, at 70%.[44] An increasingly higher proportion of global GDP growth is being driven by emerging economies, and consequently we will see a substantial shift from the West to the East in air service demand. In fact, emerging markets, led by China, India, and the Middle East, are growing faster than the global average, with double-digit traffic growth. With emerging markets and new business models continuing to expand, there will be increasing geographical diversity in the customer profile. In 1993, more than 73% of all traffic was carried by airlines in Europe and North America; it is estimated that this proportion will shrink substantially in the next twenty years due to the changing structure of global GDP, as shown in Figure 3-28[45].

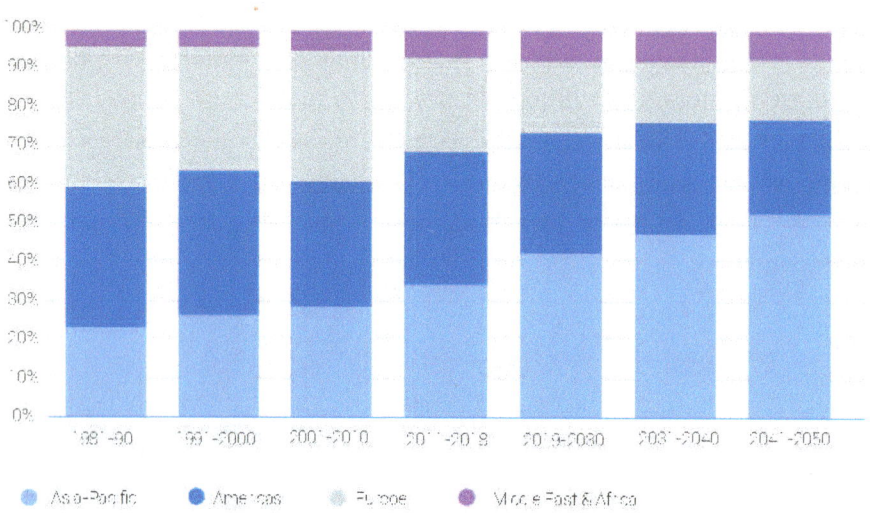

Figure 3-28 World regions' share of global GDP, 1981–2050 (Economist Intelligence Unit, 2018).

According to EU predictions, the Asia-Pacific region will enjoy the highest GDP growth rate in the next twenty years. This means substantial business opportunities for global aviation. Nonetheless, it does not mean that aviation business in advanced economies will be superseded because GDP growth in many emerging markets will outpace growth in advanced economies. As stated earlier, although significant, GDP is only one factor for predicting the future of the aviation industry. The relative wealth of nations and general purchasing power are other important factors that explain why and how the aviation industry of advanced economies will continue to be in the mainstream.

CHANGING DYNAMICS OF PURCHASING POWER

Figure 3-29 shows the most recent forecast of global GDP growth rate by the International Monetary Fund (IMF), in which the most advanced economies are depicted in light blue.

This GDP forecast tends to contradict the discussion in the previous section that expounded on the parallel growth of GDP and air traffic. Despite their lower GDP growth rates, North America and Europe continue to have a bigger share of the global aviation market, indicating that a higher GDP growth rate is not the only influencer of aviation volume. To understand the implications of this, we need to consider the perspective raised by the World Bank about the changing wealth and purchasing dynamics of nations. Our examination of this will show that with the existing and growing wealth of nations on a global scale, the air traffic in advanced economies will not decrease, but that of emerging countries will grow. In fact, the expansion of global wealth will provide more business opportunities for the West.

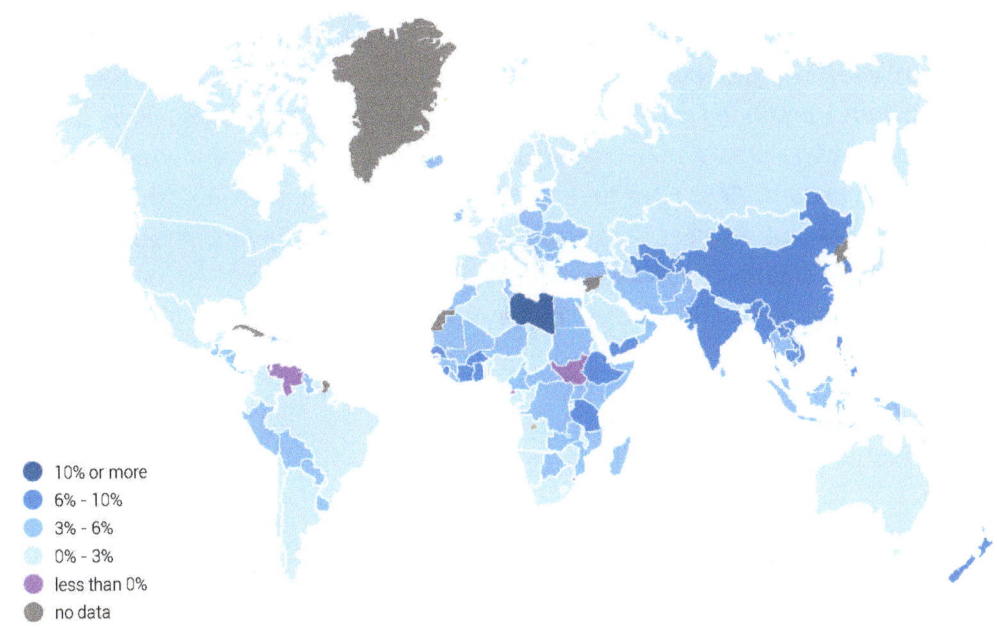

Figure 3-29 Global GDP growth rate forecast (IMF, 2018).

Wealth and GDP are not the same. Whereas GDP is like the annual income statement of a company, wealth is like the balance sheet that lists both its existing debts and assets. The annual income statement of a country, as summarized by its GDP, provides only a partial picture of the country's economic health and potential for future growth. To fully assess a country's economic health, measures of annual economic activity such as GDP per capita need to be complemented by measures of the country's asset base or wealth. This is important because it is the asset base of a country that enables it to generate future income. In other words, GDP indicates whether a country's income is growing, whereas wealth level indicates the prospects for maintaining that income and its growth over the longer term. For example, rapid GDP growth in resource-rich countries was achieved through liquidation of natural capital, causing a temporary boost in consumption, which was a transient situation that created no basis for sustained growth in wealth and human well-being. In the same way that it is impossible for a commercial company to obtain a bank loan by showing only its annual revenue without revealing its asset/liability situation; the economic performance of a nation is best evaluated by monitoring the growth of both GDP and wealth.[46]

Changing Distribution of Wealth

The distribution of global wealth shown in Figure 3-30 demonstrates that advanced economies possess the largest portion of global wealth. According to the World Bank, global wealth includes produced capital (i.e., buildings and infrastructure such as airports), natural capital (e.g., forests, minerals, etc.), human capital, and net foreign assets. Total global wealth grew by 66% from 1995 to reach $1,143 trillion in 2014, with a real rate of growth of 1.3 percent per year. This was accompanied by a significant reduction in the concentration of wealth among high-income countries as it spread among a larger set of countries in the middle and the top of the ranking list.

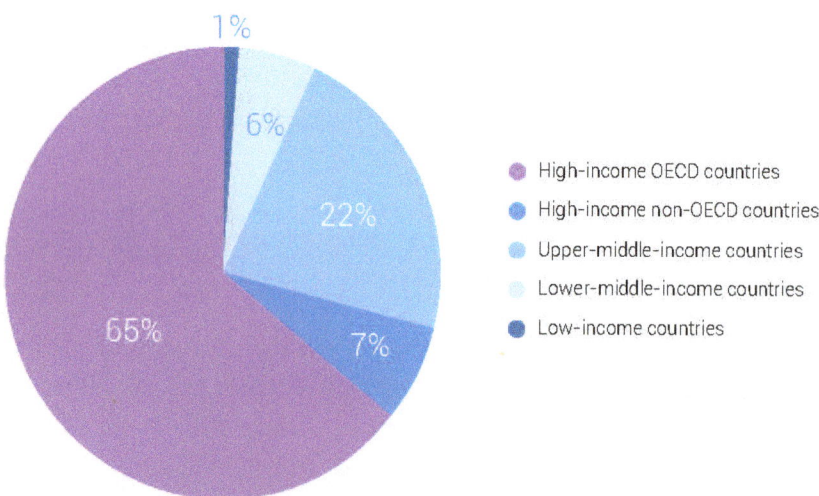

Figure 3-30 Distribution of global wealth by income group, 2014 (World Bank, OECD).

As reflected in Table 3-5, an overwhelming majority of countries increased their per capita wealth between 1995 and 2014, with the fastest growth among middle-income countries. Much of the convergence in wealth is due to the accumulation of human capital, which has resulted from massive investments to improve education and health outcomes.[47]

Table 3-5   Global wealth by type of asset, 1995 and 2014 (World Bank).

	1995		2014	
	Billion US$	Percent	Billion US$	Percent
Produced capital	164,781	24	303,548	27
Natural capital	52,457	8	107,427	9
Forest and protected areas	14,515	2	18,290	2
Agricultural land	25,859	4	39,890	3
Energy resources (fossil fuels)	11,087	2	39,094	3
Metals and minerals	997	<1	10,154	1
Human capital	475,594	69	736,854	64
Net foreign assets	-2,890	<1	-4581	<1
TOTAL WEALTH	689,942	100	1,143,249	100

According to the World Bank, the most important component of national wealth is not a country's natural resources, because they will be eventually exhausted, but rather its human capital. This explains why advanced economies remain at the top of the global wealth list on a continuing basis. According to the World Bank's definition, the concept of human capital is based on the following factors:

- Present value of the expected earnings of the labor force.

- Amount of lifelong earnings as determined by the years of schooling of the population.

- Actual learning taking place in schools (and after leaving school for various skills and experience).

- Health investments that account for health conditions.

- Life expectancy of the labor force.

- Likelihood of labor force participation at various ages.

The human capital derived from education includes investments in early childhood development, basic education which carries high benefit-to-cost ratios, and continuing education and training during the transition to adulthood, which brings higher earnings in adulthood. Labor gender is another issue. Globally, women account for just 38% of human capital wealth, versus 62% for men. Consequently, the level of participation by women in the labor force has a substantial impact on the wealth of a nation. As more women enter the labor force, as expected in the future, total wealth will increase.

The level of industrialization is definitely a factor that impacts wealth level (see Figure 3-31). Globally, self-employed workers, such as handymen and small-shop owners, account for only 9% of human capital wealth, whereas employed workers account for 91% of that wealth. In per capita terms, globally, human capital wealth stood at $108,654 per person in 2014 versus $88,874 in 1995, accounting for roughly two-thirds of global wealth. The growth rates in human capital wealth per capita were 65% for advanced economies, 22% for upper-middle-income emerging economies, and 13% for the rest of the world.[48]

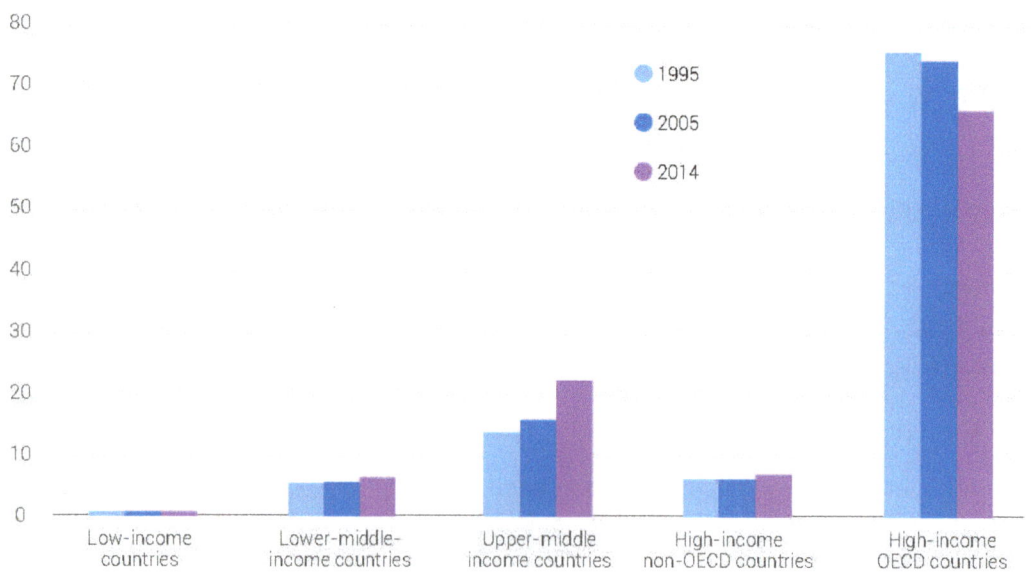

Figure 3-31   Share of global wealth by income group, 1995, 2005, and 2014 (World Bank).

The depository of human capital in advanced economies has enabled them to see continued growth of air traffic. Taking the London-New York route as an example, origin and destination traffic grew by 25% between 2014 and 2017.[49] The trans-Atlantic market has grown by 50% over the last 15 years, and many of those routes have their origins at the start of the air transportation era. Human capital accounts for 70% of advanced economies and natural capital for only 3%. This situation has been achieved, not by reducing the amount of natural capital, but by adding more produced capital and human capital.

The difference in levels of human capital between advanced and emerging economies is largely determined by the amount of investment. Figure 3-32 shows the investment in human capital relative to physical capital in advanced and emerging economies covering the periods 1990–99 and 2000–10.[50]

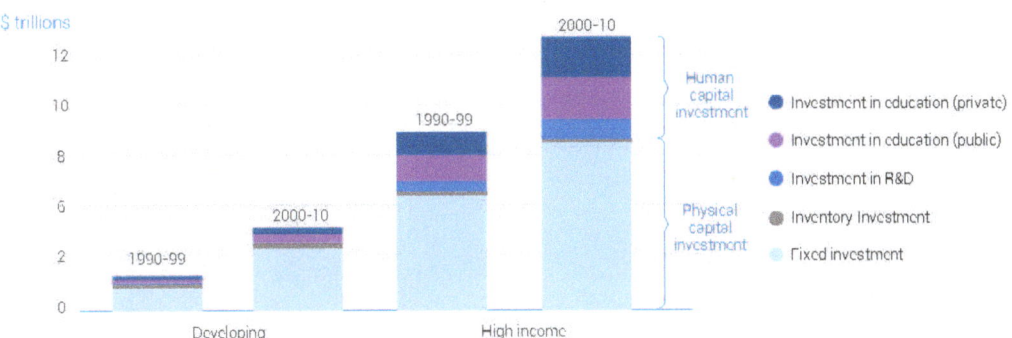

Figure 3-32 Investment in human and physical capital, developing vs. high-income nations: 1990–99 to 2000–10 (World Bank).

Nonetheless, the share of natural capital gradually declines as countries graduate from low–to middle–and then to high-income status and become classified as emerging economies. According to the World Bank, more than two dozen low-income countries, where natural capital dominates the composition of wealth, have moved to middle-income status. This has been achieved in large part by investing resource revenues into infrastructure, education, and health, which has resulted in increased human capital.[51]

As observed by Franklin Templeton Investments, when resource exports are no longer the primary drivers of growth and of the equity markets, as in the case in many emerging economies, "…technology companies now make up a sizable portion of emerging-market stock markets, and these companies have the opportunity to drastically improve economic productivity through things like mobile banking that are hard to replicate in developed economies". The rising middle classes in those economies also tend to encourage these trends. Emerging-market consumers are not only demanding goods, but also require services such as banking, health care, and entertainment.[52] Consequently, air traffic between emerging countries is forecast to grow at 6.2% per annum and will represent a growing share of air traffic, from 29% of world traffic in 2016 up to 40% by 2036.[53]

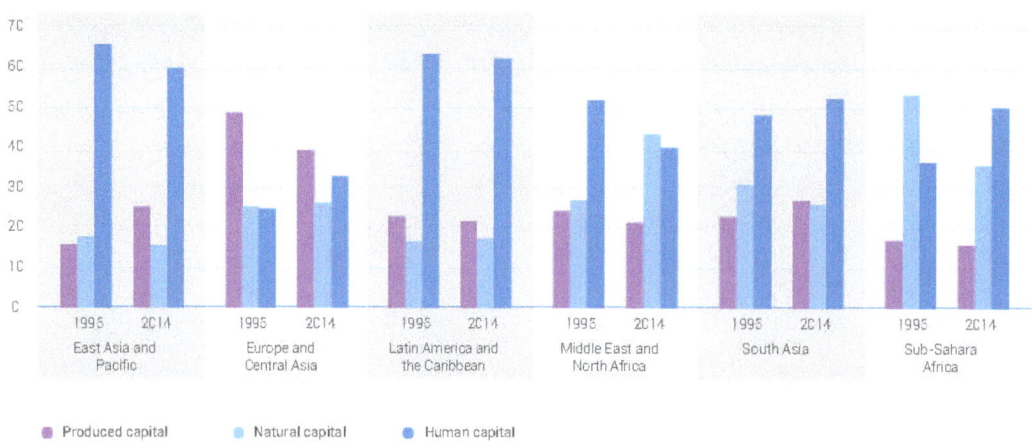

Figure 3-33 Regional composition of wealth, 1995 and 2014 (World Bank).

It needs to be pointed out that advanced economies as a group are seeing a relative decline in their share of global human capital; this has caused an incremental increase in the relative share of global wealth held by emerging economies. The World Bank estimates that the share of human capital global wealth held by advanced countries declined over the past two decades from 69% in 1995 to 64% in 2014. This decline is observed only for the comparatively wealthiest countries because aging and stagnant wages are reducing their portion of human capital as a part of total capital. At the same time, the participation of wage earners in the labor force in emerging economies is growing rapidly, thus boosting their relative human capital level. According to the World Bank, by 2020, growth in the world's working-age population will be exclusively dominated by developing countries.[54]

According to the World Bank, it is the young people in the working age portion of a population that boost wealth, whereas older people consume wealth. People in wealthy countries tend to live longer than in poorer countries, and therefore the national wealth decreases in those countries due to the higher costs of maintaining the health and welfare of seniors.

In most developing countries, the human capital portion of total wealth is rising. In low-income countries, this share increased from 32% to 43% over two decades; in lower-middle-income countries, it rose from 44% to 52%. Many of these countries are experiencing a demographic transition and are reaping the benefits of the demographic dividend as population growth rates are being reduced and the population is becoming better educated. This rising trend is expected to continue.[55] The rise of human capital results in increases in national wealth after adjustments for reductions in population.

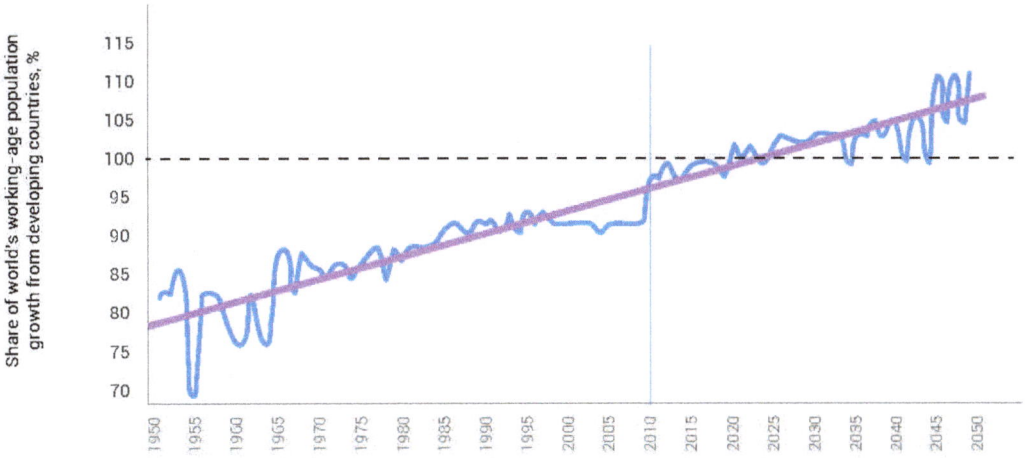

Figure 3-34 Share of working-age population, developing countries, 1950 to 2050 (World Bank).

Table 3-6   Trends in wealth per capita in low- and middle-income countries by region, 1995–2014 (World Bank).

	1995	2000	2005	2010	2014	ANNUAL GROWTH (%)
East Asia and Pacific	31,261	37,507	44,097	71,423	91,581	5.8
Europe and Central Asia	51,967	42,276	56,494	66,066	70,530	1.6
Latin America and the Caribbean	108,167	108,250	116,989	128,859	133,614	1.1
Middle East and North Africa	24,973	27,263	34,790	46,548	48,495	3.6
South Asia	9,251	15,523	12,511	15,710	18,400	3.7
Sub-Saharan Africa	26,403	21,964	22,669	25,362	25,562	-0.2
All low-and middle-income countries	32,198	34,085	38,512	51,515	59,783	3.3

Note: Includes 97 of 141 low- and middle-income countries. Constant 2014 US dollars.

Growth of Aviation Tourism

The growth of the aviation industry largely depends on the continuing growth of human capital. This is because the increase in human capital enables more people to afford flying and to make various purchases during their flights. These non-aeronautical purchases are becoming increasingly important. For example, while airport revenues grew by 8.2% in 2014, non-aeronautical revenues now account for 46% of total income.[56]

Middle-income countries are catching up to high-income countries in terms of propensity to fly (see Figure 3-35). Although the size and growth of national wealth determines air traffic flows in those countries, the dynamics in emerging economies are different. In developed markets, where the demand for essential travel has been met, growth mainly comes from discretionary travel, especially tourism and VFR (Visit Friends and Relatives). Factors that influence traveler decision-making include availability of financing to fund vacations, consumer confidence in tourist products, service pricing, service quality (e.g., availability of nonstop flights), and vacation entitlements. On the other hand, emerging markets have shown that although air travel is a discretionary expenditure, it is one of the first discretionary items to be added to the agenda by consumers when they join the global middle class. Often, in emerging-economy markets, air services start with cheaper charter flights to leisure destinations, gradually migrate to scheduled services offered by low-fare carriers, and then eventually there is a shift to mainstream network airlines.

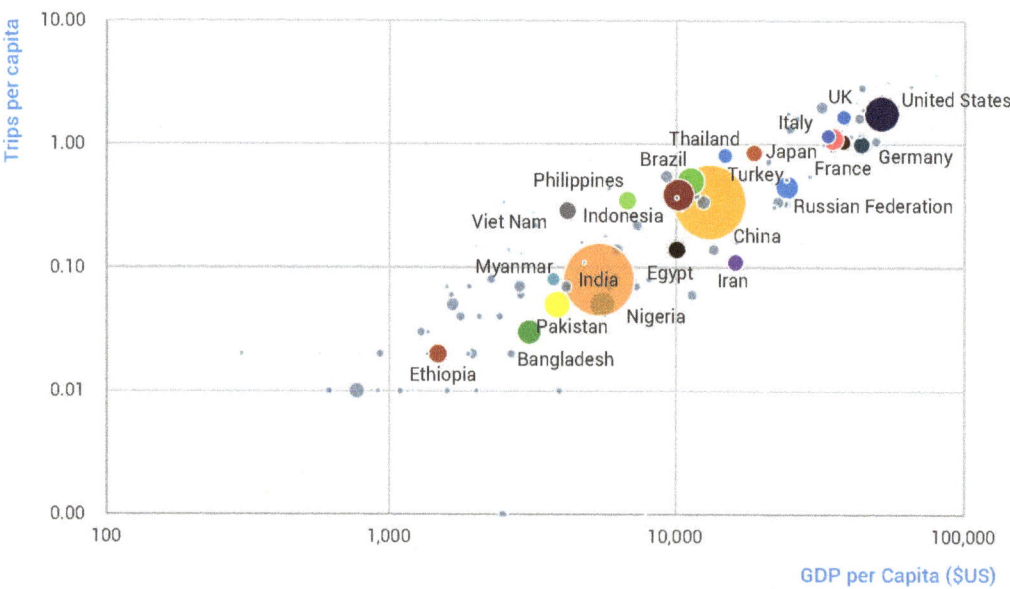

Figure 3-35 Propensity to fly in 2015 (logarithmic scale)[57](Sabre, WBG, HIS, Airbus, 2016).

The change in the global savings structure (i.e., savings in high-income countries and developing countries), forms the basis for the growth in the number of passengers from emerging economies. According to the World Bank, the world will see a gradual convergence scenario in the relative shares of savings in developing and high-income countries.[58] By 2030, developing countries will account for two-thirds of global savings.[59]

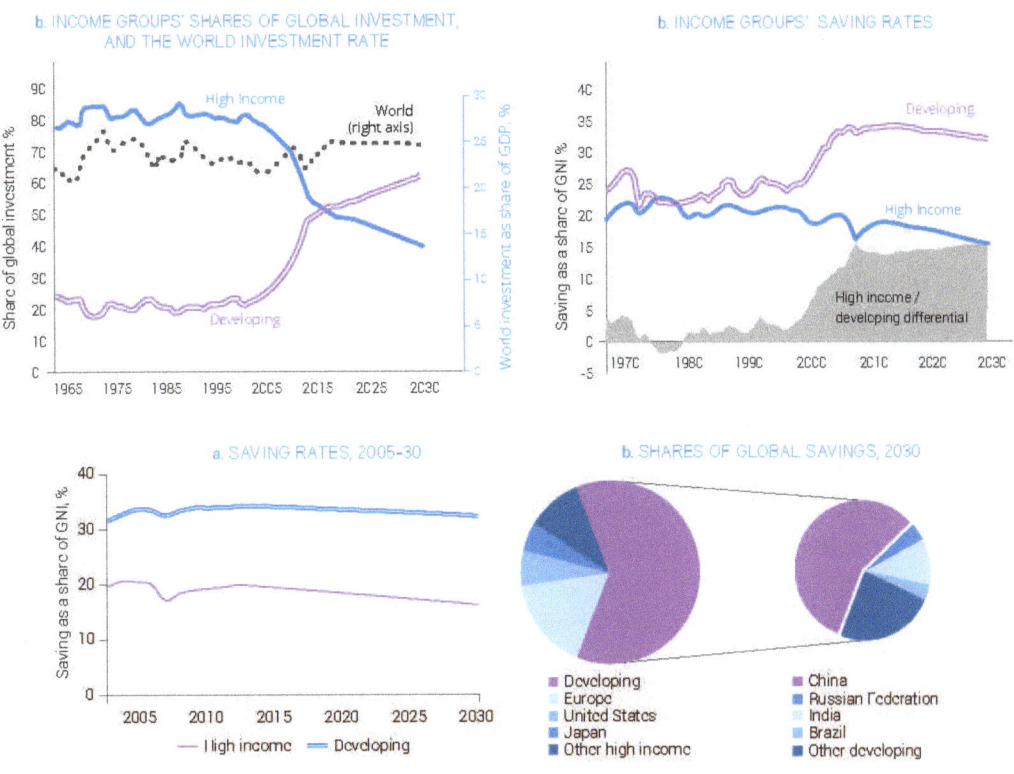

Figure 3-36 Share of global investment and savings rates, 1965–2030[60](World Bank).

The large flows of consumers from emerging economies are changing the profile, behavior, habits, and practices of global air passenger travel. Twenty years ago, airline passengers were most likely to originate in Europe or North America. Over the next 20 years, passengers will see greater diversity in flight origins, with 62% of traffic being carried by airlines outside North America or Europe. Trends in passenger traffic growth are similar to the growth of human capital. Emerging markets will grow faster than established markets. Regions growing above trend are Asia Pacific (6.3%), Middle East (6.4%), and Latin America (6.2%), whereas European (3.9%) and North American markets (2.9%) will be below trend.[61] With the share of global wealth held by advanced economies declining from 75% to 65%,[62] this change is largely reflected by the phenomenal rise of wealth in Asia, which has gone from mostly low- and middle-income status to middle- and high-income status in one generation.

Adding new destinations to an airline's network provides access to new revenue streams and often accelerates economic development in the newly connected markets. The development of new routes in emerging aviation markets stimulates economic growth as a result of the commerce that the increased passenger traffic generates. Air connectivity is essential to tourism development, providing substantial economic benefits for all those involved in the tourism value chain. With over 50% of 1.2 billion global tourists traveling by air,[63] revenues from the spending of international tourists, classified as "visitor exports", account for over 5% of world trade. Tourism in many countries is a main source of foreign exchange earnings, especially the least developed countries (LDCs), the landlocked developing countries (LLDCs), and the small island developing states (SIDS), where exceptional natural and cultural resources are their strong competitive advantage.[64] Therefore, any mishandling of social issues may bring disastrous results not only to the operating companies, but also to these regional economies.

The United Nations World Tourism Organization (UNTWO) has shown how travel for tourism purposes has expanded globally. In the 1950's, the top 15 country destinations absorbed 98% of all international tourist arrivals; in the 1970's, that proportion decreased to 75%. In the new millennium, this has fallen to less than 60%. Many of the new travel destinations are in developing countries. Emerging economies are developing large new middle-class populations through their increased wealth. This means that more people in these regions are reaching the threshold of wealth where discretionary air travel becomes possible. For example, the number of domestic Indian passengers is expected to grow almost six-fold over the next 20 years, reaching the same level as domestic travel in the USA today. Chinese domestic traffic has quadrupled in the last 10 years, with international traffic more than doubling. China will continue to lead global outbound travel after registering double-digit growth in tourism expenditures every year since 2004, which has benefitted Asian destinations such as Japan and Thailand as well as the United States and various European destinations. The outbound China market is predicted to double to over 200 million travelers annually by 2020, along with almost 1.6 billion passengers expected to travel within China in 2036, which is about four times the number of passengers that traveled by air in 2016.[65]

Over half the world's tourists who travel across international borders each year are transported by air, as shown in Figure 3-37.[66] Therefore, any rise in tourism from emerging economies creates huge revenue potential for the global aviation industry. According to the publication *Tourism Highlights - 2016 Edition*, the United Nations World Trade Organization (UNWTO) predicts that international tourist arrivals will grow at an annual rate of 3.3% between 2010 and 2030, reaching an annual total of 1.8 billion tourists. As Figure 3-38 shows, the majority of growth is expected to occur in emerging economies, which are estimated to record a 2.2% annual growth rate in international tourist arrivals between 2010 and 2030, reaching an annual total of 1 billion tourists, or 57% of global international tourist arrivals. According to ICAO, revenue passenger kilometers (RPKs) grew by 6.3% from 2015 to 2016, which represents an impressive 3.7 billion passengers carried by air in 2016.

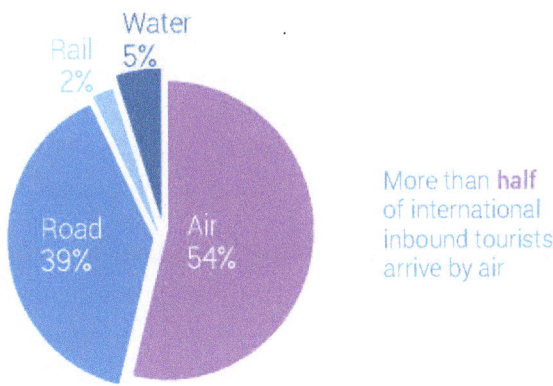

Figure 3-37 International tourist travel by mode (ICAO).

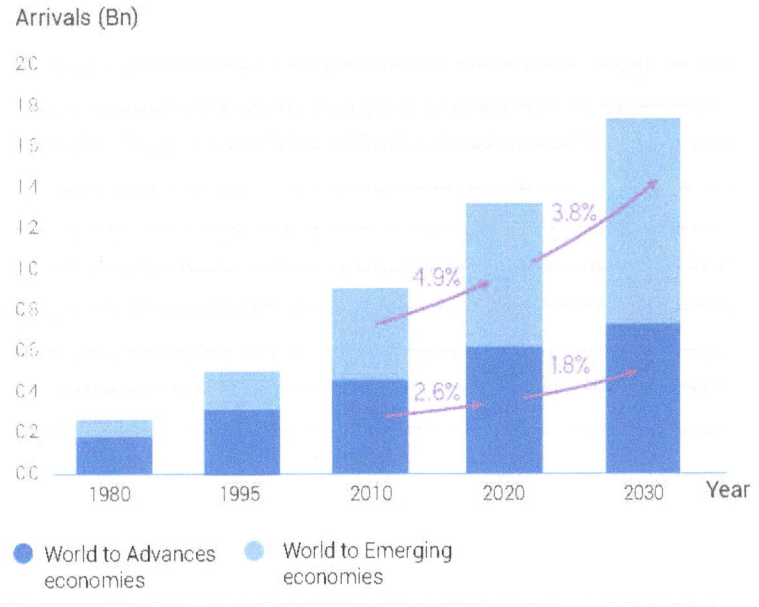

Figure 3-38 History and projections, international tourist arrivals to advanced and emerging economies[67] (UNWTO).

Air connectivity is essential to tourism development, providing substantial economic benefits for all those involved in the tourism value chain. Increased tourism calls for new destinations in airline route networks, which will lead to new revenue streams and acceleration of economic development in newly connected markets. The development of new routes in emerging aviation markets stimulates economic growth as a result of the commerce that the increased passenger traffic generates. With over 50% of 1.2 billion tourists traveling by air,[68] revenues from the spending of international tourists, classified as "visitor exports", account for over 5% of world trade. Tourism in many countries is a main source of foreign exchange earnings, especially in the least developed countries (LDCs), the landlocked developing countries (LLDCs), and the small island developing states (SIDS), destinations where the exceptional natural and cultural resources are their strong competitive advantage.[69]

Nevertheless, the increase in international travelers, which largely results from the rise of purchasing power in emerging economies, does not mean more of the same type of passengers, traveling to the same destinations, with the same purpose. Actually, the changing demographics of air travelers are changing the purposes and patterns of air travel, and therefore consideration needs to be given to possible shifts in consumer needs. The first major change is the decrease in business travelers, traditionally the biggest proportion of air travelers. This is now giving way to leisure passengers and those visiting family/friends. Business travelers are not usually price-sensitive, but rather are time-sensitive, and they look for the flexibility and convenience of services that offer easy rescheduling of trips and changing flights with ease. These travelers appreciate factors such as frequency of service, convenience of schedule, minimum travel times, choice and variety of direct routes, and proximity to city centers. The needs of business travelers used to be the main focus of airlines because the revenue per passenger has been traditionally higher for them than for other types of travelers. Nonetheless, when new market trends result in profile changes to the majority of passengers, more attention will need to be focused on non-business travelers.

Leisure travelers, including tourists and VFR passengers, care more about air fares. Cost-effectiveness is often the most important factor in their decisions, whereas air connectivity is negotiable. In high-income countries like Europe and North America, the number of VFR passengers is increasing rapidly. There are differences between leisure and VRF passengers. Whereas leisure travelers may change their mind about their destinations for the sake of a cheaper airfare, VFR passengers do not have the option of changing their travel destinations, but they can choose how frequently they travel. Figure 3-39 shows the different needs and priorities of business and leisure travelers, as well as some common factors that impact their traffic volume.[70]

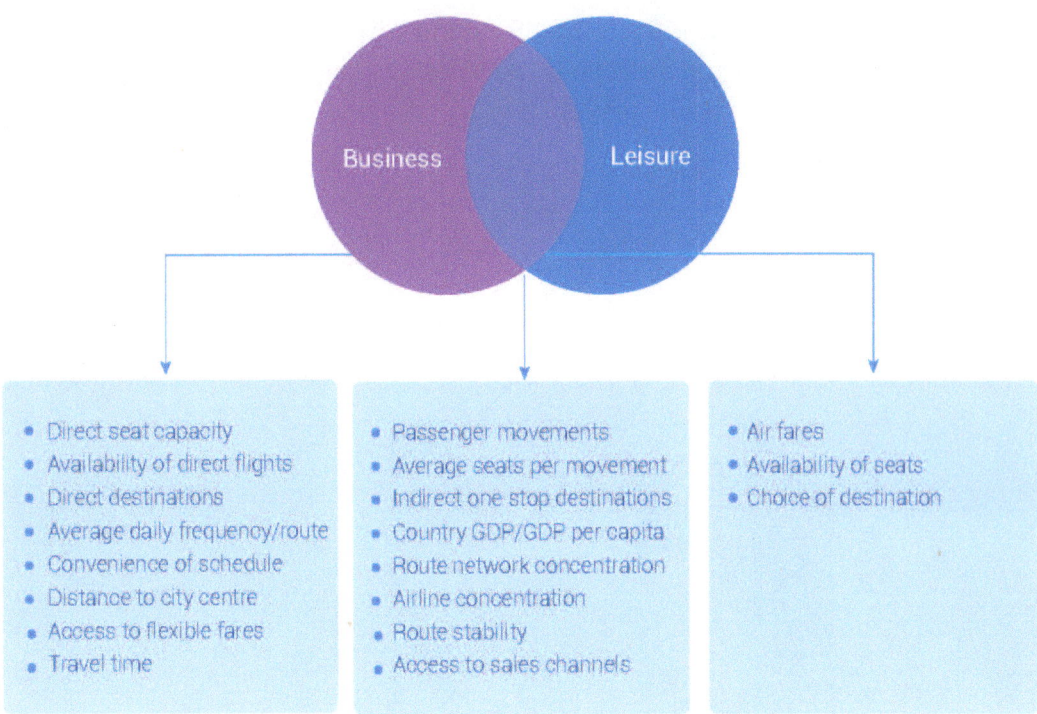

Figure 3-39 Business and leisure air travelers: Needs and priorities (PWC).

Aviation market growth on different continents will vary because such factors as the possession of wealth, growth rates of wealth, travel needs, and market situations will differ from region to region. From the perspective of global wealth growth, there is some consistency about future aviation market characteristics when one looks at three different income region classifications separately: high-income regions, high- or middle-Income regions, and middle- or low-income regions:

High-Income Regions: Europe and North America

These regions possess a deep repository of human capital that they have accumulated since the first and second Industrial Revolutions. Because of that, the aviation business in high-income regions will continue to enjoy stable growth. Some 90% of European travelers and 70% of North American travelers state that their purpose of air travel is personal. Often, when employed outside of their home countries, home states, or home provinces, they have the financial means and the time flexibility to take short air trips to a variety of tourist destinations for short vacations, or to have brief visits with their friends and relatives.[71] European air traffic flows accounted for about 23%

of growth in global capacity in 2016, and this trend is expected to continue, resulting in a proliferation of many origin-destination routes by low-cost carriers (LCCs). Since the European population is forecast to become wealthier, passenger traffic will see continuing growth.

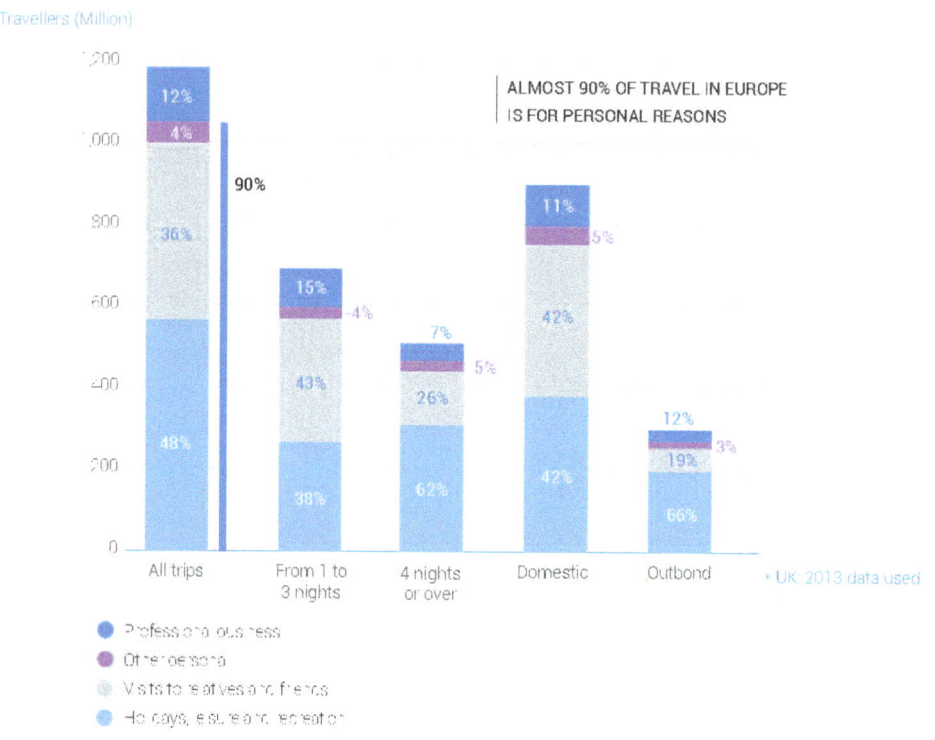

Figure 3-40 Air trips by EU-28 residents: Purpose, duration, destination, 2014
(Eurostat, Airbus GMF, 2017).

Like Europe, North America will continue to be at the forefront of profitability in global aviation (see Figure 3-41). Passenger aircraft load factors in the US and Canadian domestic markets average over 85%, whereas the average for international flights is 82%. US airlines were responsible for 61% of global airline profitability in 2015.[72] In the eyes of both Boeing and Airbus, continuing stable growth in their aviation markets will be the norm because of the wealth and stability of those markets.

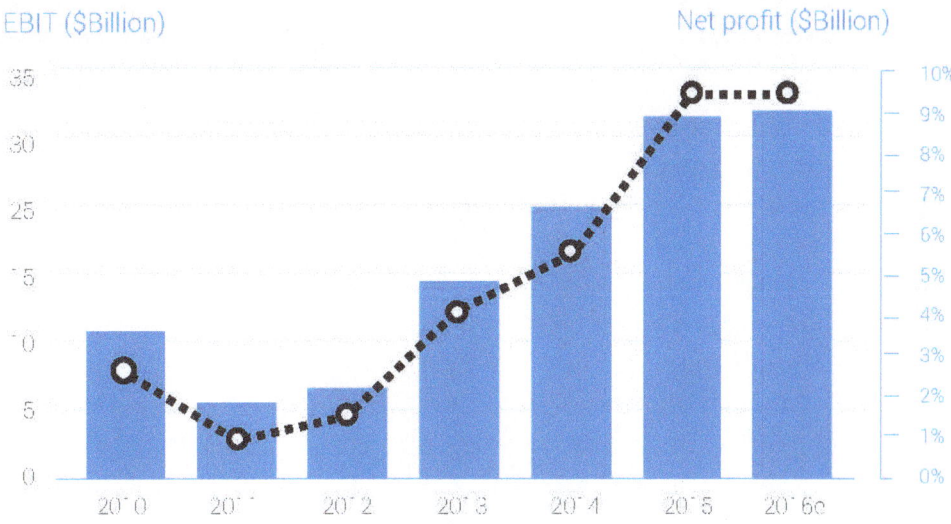

EBIT ($Billion)   Net profit ($Billion)

Figure 3-41   North American airline profitability, 2010 to 2016 (ICAO, IATA, Airbus GMF, 2017).

High – or Middle-Income Regions: Asia-Pacific and the Middle East

As mentioned earlier, Asia's surge in demand for air service is largely based on the rapid increase of its wealth, especially human capital, through the growth of the middle class. Increased opening up of international markets to Asian markets as a result of its widespread industrialization is another factor. Meanwhile, a lack of alternative modes of transport in many of these countries enhances the relative importance of aviation. Unlike in Europe and North America where large contiguous landmasses allow intercity highways and railways, large parts of Asia can only be reached by air. Geographical barriers include mountainous regions, the island nature of much of Southeast Asia (i.e., Philippines, Indonesia, Malaysia, Brunei, and Singapore), and the sheer distances between many major Asian cities. Although high-speed rail is now well developed in parts of North Asia, air travel still remains the best option from a cost and time perspective. At the same time, the extreme density of Asia's population centers is an indicator of the great potential for air markets of the future. With the economic performance of the Asia-Pacific region rising towards the levels of Europe and North America, travelers in Asia-Pacific are reaching the wealth levels where they can afford to fly on a frequent basis, and they tend to take more trips than Europeans and North Americans.

The Middle East is not yet very strong in the development of human capital. However, it does benefit from the growth of global wealth by facilitating the exchange of human capital at the geographic crossroads of trade and transportation between the East and the West. Most of the growth in air routes has been on routes to/from Asia-Pacific and Europe. The number of routes connecting to/from Africa has doubled as well. The Middle East's large world-class airports leverage the advantage of the region's geographical position by offering connections to destinations around the globe. Local origin-destination traffic has also grown. In Dubai, for example, 46% of passenger traffic is local origin-destination traffic, with intra-regional connecting passengers accounting for 17% of traffic (i.e., the start and end of the journey is in the Middle East).[73] Connectivity to and from the region has grown dramatically, with the number of city pairs more than tripling from nearly 200 in 1990 to more than 700 by 2016. Furthermore, regional economic growth is a driver for air traffic in some countries. Iran, for example, had forecast GDP growth from 2015 to 2036 at +3.3% per annum, but this had already risen to +4.1% per annum by early 2017. As a result, 40 new air routes were started by 2016.[74] Although the wealth of the Middle East region still largely depends on its natural capital as defined by the World Bank, its strategic geographic location presents great potential for the global aviation industry.

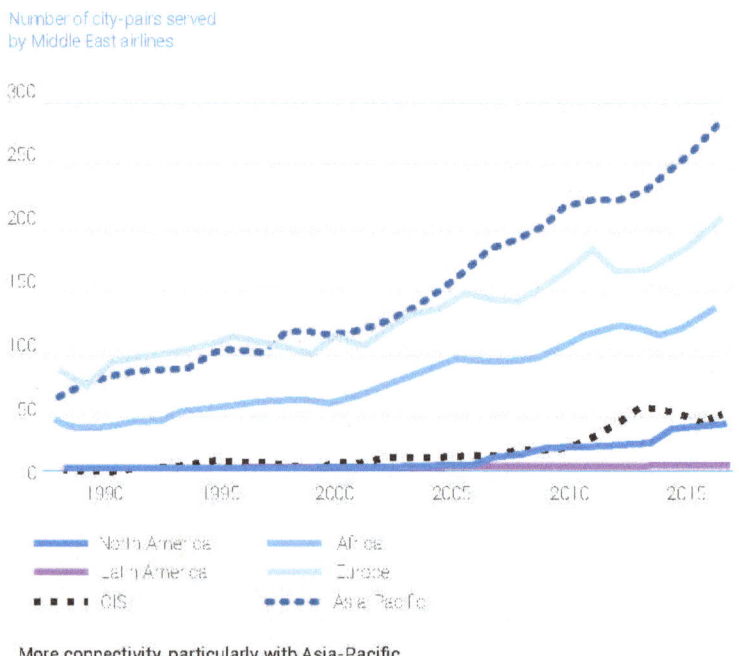

More connectivity, particularly with Asia-Pacific

Figure 3-42 Growing number of city pairs served by Middle East airlines (OAG, Airbus GMF, 2017).

Middle-or Low-Income Regions:
Latin America, Africa, and Independent States

Most countries in these regions are categorized by the World Bank as middle- or low-income countries due to their substantial reliance on natural capital as their national wealth. Nonetheless, many of them have succeeded in using resource wealth to develop human capital, including education, technical training, and health services, which forms the foundation for industrialization and the growth of produced capital. Because many of these countries are agricultural, the rapid increase in the value of their agricultural land is pushing up their national wealth as well. At the same time, these countries have seen a rapid increase in areas protected for environmental reasons, and many of these have become the basis for valuable nature-based tourism.

Aviation market growth in each country is different. For example, Brazil continues to be the largest domestic aviation market in Latin America, and its air traffic is double that of the next biggest market, Mexico. Mexican international traffic continues to lead the region, with about three million monthly seats. The Russian economy is stabilizing after a severe recession that was triggered by a number of factors, but its domestic and intra-regional traffic, especially traffic to and from Asia-Pacific, has been strong. The African economy is being revived, and its real GDP is expected to grow at +3.6% per year over the next 20 years. Africa is the largest region on Earth in terms of land area, but the poorest in terms of its road network density (see Figure 3-45). With industrialization and the concomitant increase in human capital, the demand for air service will rise quickly.[75] Although the demand for air service in these countries is still low in comparison with advanced economies, its rate of increase has been impressive and is expected to speed up.

In summary, the changing wealth of nations in different regions of the world and the impact of this on the future of the aviation industry denies the validity of the zero-sum mentality with respect to the global economy. In the context of the megatrend of economic power shift from West to East, advanced economies will continue to be in the driver's seat in global aviation due to their riches in national wealth and human capital. Meanwhile, as emerging economies are experiencing the fastest growth rate ever in their wealth—especially some nations in Asia—new markets are emerging that require significant growth in air services. In fact, the growth in need for air services is outstripping the growth of wealth. Aviation is not limited by the availability of an individual's disposable income because it is both an outcome of the growth of the wealth of the local economy and a driver for the economic development of the locality. As ICAO points out, "Aviation provides the only rapid worldwide transportation network, which makes it essential for global business. It generates economic growth, creates jobs, and facilitates international trade and tourism."[76] Accordingly, when we predict the future of the global aviation industry in the context of the economic power shift from West to East, it is important that we examine it from the business side as well.

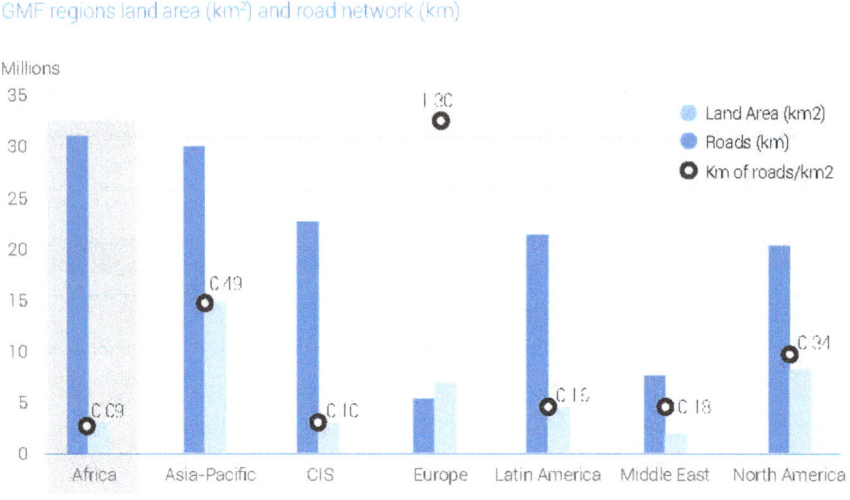

GMF regions land area (km²) and road network (km)

African geography and existing infrastructure makes aviation essential for the regions further development

Figure 3-43 Ratio between land area and length of roads (IRF, World Bank, Airbus GMF, 2017).

INDUSTRIAL OUTPUT CHANGES

All significant success stories in economic development in developing countries since 1950 have been driven by industrialization. Although each country has its own industrialization history, depending on its initial conditions and when it entered the race, the pathway from agriculture to a manufacturing economy has been remarkably similar. In 1950, 41% of GDP generated by developing countries originated in the agricultural sector, but that declined dramatically to 16% by 2005. In 1950, manufacturing in developing countries accounted for only 11% of GDP compared with 31% in the advanced economies. Both developing and high-income countries will see a rise in the share of investment devoted to the services sector. Meanwhile, it is worth noting that the proportion of services in high-income countries is still substantially higher than in developing countries, whereas the shares of agriculture and manufacturing are obviously lower.[77] The changes in industrial outputs in advanced and emerging economies are creating new demands on the aviation industry. Not only is there demand for more physical capacity, such as air cargo facilities and general infrastructure investment, but there is also need for more capacity on the social and cultural side of things, including strengthening international cooperation and developing more social enterprises.

Table 3-7 Economic performance: Developing countries vs. high-income countries (World Bank).

	Agriculture		Manufacturing		Services	
	Share (%)	Growth (%)	Share (%)	Growth (%)	Share (%)	Growth (%)
Developing countries						
East Asia and Pacific	11	6.4	34	7.1	56	8.0
China	10	7.4	35	7.7	56	8.6
Indonesia	22	4.5	24	5.1	54	6.2
Eastern Europe and Central Asia	12	1.8	18	2.8	70	3.8
Russian Federation	17	1.7	11	3.1	73	3.9
Latin America and the Caribbean	10	3.0	19	3.0	71	4.1
Brazil	11	3.4	16	2.9	74	4.3
Mexico	4	2.8	20	2.1	76	3.4
Middle East and North Africa	39	3.1	16	3.9	46	5.0
South Asia	14	5.1	17	6.5	69	8.1
India	13	5.4	17	7.0	70	8.6
Sub-Saharan Africa	26	5.4	17	4.6	57	5.8
South Africa	4	1.6	21	2.1	75	3.3
Hi-income countries						
Europe	3	-0.9	16	0.9	82	1.8
Japan	1	-1.2	15	-0.1	84	1.1
United States	3	-0.8	13	1.1	84	2.3

Since 1980, the share of manufacturing has continued to increase in many emerging economies, whereas it has declined substantially in advanced economies.[78]

Air Cargo as a Proxy

The variables representing industrial growth in developing regions include their level of industrialization, the rate of expansion of their megalopolises, and in terms of aviation, air cargo traffic growth rate. It is well known that the demand for air freight is limited by cost, which is typically four to five times that of road transport and twelve to sixteen times that of sea transport. Nevertheless, as a result of the development of high technology, the need to move high-value-per-unit commodities has been increasing rapidly, and these are shipped mostly by air. The speed and reliability of aviation cargo transportation have contributed to the market for "same-day" or "next-day" delivery services and transportation of urgent or time-sensitive goods, giving it an important advantage over other modes of transport. High-value electrical components and perishable products such as food and flowers are transported all over the world using the services of cargo integrators, which provide steady employment and economic growth to regions benefiting from such trade. For example, 87% of B2C (business-to-consumer) e-commerce parcels are currently carried by air. The e-commerce share of scheduled international mail ton-kilometers (MTKs) grew from 16% to 74% between 2010 and 2015 and is estimated to grow to 91% by 2025.[79]

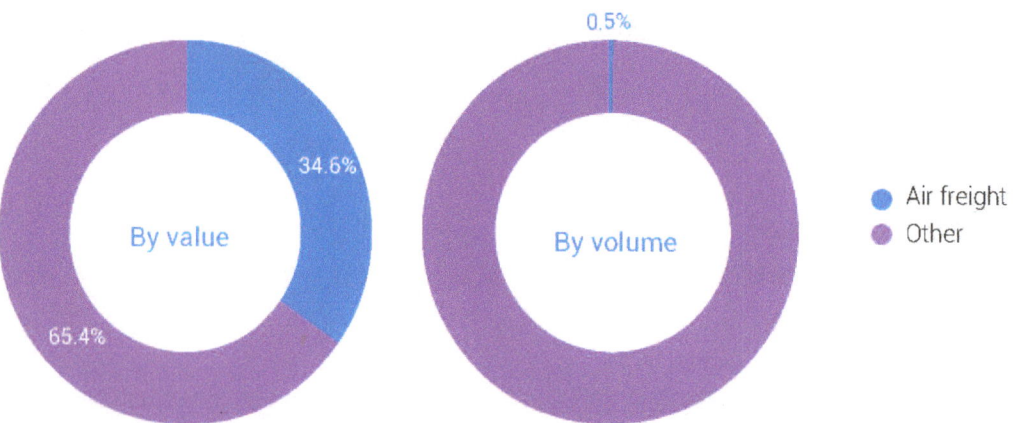

Figure 3-44 Air freight as a proportion of global trade by value and volume, 2014 (ICAO).

With the continuing growth of industrial outputs, air cargo traffic, measured in revenue ton-kilometers (RTK), is projected to grow by an average 4.2% per year over the next 20 years. In turn, the sustained growth of air-cargo traffic will lead to further enhancement of the global economy.[80] Carrying freight and mail gives airlines revenue opportunities beyond transporting passengers. Many airlines carry cargo in the lower hold of passenger jets. Some operate dedicated freighters in addition to passenger airplanes. A handful of airlines, including express carriers that provide fully integrated logistics services for businesses and consumers, focus exclusively on air cargo. The air cargo business differs in many respects from the passenger business. In particular, air cargo flows are more unidirectional than passenger flows; passengers generally travel round trip, but air cargo does not. Therefore, network strategies for cargo operations differ significantly from those for passenger services.

Table 3-8 gives a list of the top 20 airports in terms of air cargo in 2017. North American and Asian airports dominate the ranking due to the large domestic markets of these countries. Meanwhile, the major hubs of Europe and Middle East, such as Frankfurt and Paris, or Dubai and Doha respectively, appear in the ranking as well, as they provide access to a large market of end-point customers for goods flown by air freight.

Table 3-8   Top 20 cargo airports worldwide, 2017 (ACI).[81]

RANK 2017	RANK 2016	AIRPORT CITY / COUNTRY / CODE	CARGO (Metric tonnes)	
			(Loaded and unloaded)	Percent change
1	1	HONG KONG, HK (HKG)	5 049 898	9.4
2	2	MEMPHIS TN, US (MEM)	4 336 752	0.3
3	3	SHANGHAI, CN (PVG)	3 824 280	11.2
4	4	INCHEON, KR (ICN)	2 921 691	7.6
5	6	ANCHORAGE AK, US (ANC)*	2 713 230	6.7
6	5	DUBAI, AE (DXB)	2 654 494	2.4
7	7	LOUISVILLE KY, US (SDF)	2 602 695	6.8
8	8	TOKYO, JP (NRT)	2 336 427	7.9
9	11	TAIPEI, TW (TPE)	2 269 585	8.2
10	9	PARIS, FR (CDG)	2 195 229	2.8
11	10	FRANKFURT, DE (FRA)	2 194 056	3.8
12	13	SINGAPORE, SG (SIN)	2 164 700	7.9
13	14	LOS ANGELES CA, US (LAX)	2 158 324	8.1
14	12	MIAMI FL, US (MIA)	2 071 722	2.9
15	15	BEIJING, CN (PEK)	2 029 584	4.5
16	16	DOHA, QA (DOH)	2 020 942	15.0
17	19	LONDON, GB (LHR)	1 794 276	9.4
18	18	GUANGZHOU, CN (CAN)	1 780 423	7.8
19	17	AMSTERDAM, NL (AMS)	1 778 382	4.9
20	20	CHICAGO IL, US (ORD)	1 721 807	12.6
TOP 20 FOR 2017			**50 618 497**	**6.8**

* Includes transig freight

According to Airbus forecasts, emerging market countries will drive the growth of international cargo traffic as a result of their growing industrial outputs. The "emerging to advanced" flow of air cargo is expected to represent about 30% of total world international freight ton-kilometers (FTK) by 2036. Over the next twenty years, dedicated freighter FTKs will grow at 2.6% per year, and the dedicated freight aircraft fleet in service is expected to increase by 50% during the same period. There will be a demand for about 1,950 freighter aircraft by 2036. Of that total, 730 will be new-build freighter aircraft. Of those, 55% will be mid-size and 45% large. In that same time frame, there will be a need for 350 new-build air freighters in North America (mostly for replacement) and about 200 new-build freighters in Asia-Pacific (mostly for growth).[82]

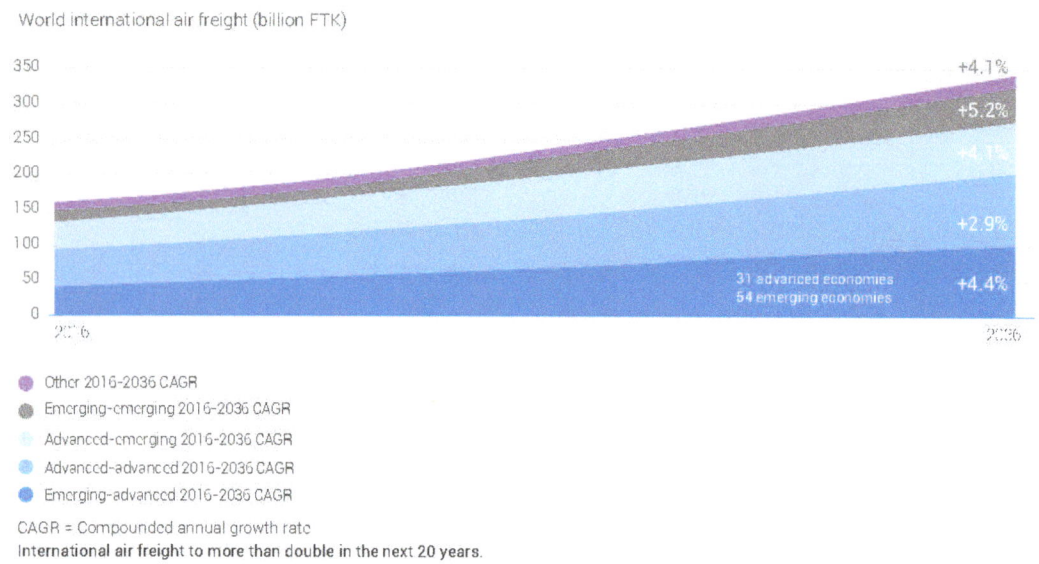

World international air freight (billion FTK)

- Other 2016-2036 CAGR
- Emerging-emerging 2016-2036 CAGR
- Advanced-emerging 2016-2036 CAGR
- Advanced-advanced 2016-2036 CAGR
- Emerging-advanced 2016-2036 CAGR

CAGR = Compounded annual growth rate
International air freight to more than double in the next 20 years.

Figure 3-45 World international air freight (billion FTK) for 2016–2036 (Airbus GMF, 2017).

Airport Infrastructure Investment

Nonetheless, severe challenges are facing emerging economies along with the growing demand for transporting their industrial outputs. Their aviation infrastructure as the "produced capital" is not keeping pace with the fast-growing need for air services. For example, the development of Asia's airport infrastructure has lagged well behind travel growth. Traffic at most major Asian hubs is already exceeding planned capacity, resulting in a rapid escalation of delays, while even secondary hubs are starting to experience capacity strains. Despite the large surge in Asian airport developments since the 1990s, infrastructure has rarely been built ahead of demand. This is a cause for concern because of Asia's predicted high rate of growth and given that runway and terminal projects typically require 5–10 years from need recognition to implementation. As a consequence, congestion-related delays are rapidly increasing at most Asian hubs. Passengers increasingly experience flight delays on a regular basis, long queues for take-off are routine, and aircraft circling in stacks awaiting landing is common. Suitable landing and takeoff slots are suddenly becoming scarce, leaving airports unable to cope with any further growth and airlines with nowhere to operate their newly delivered airplanes.

Accordingly, it is not surprising that in 2013, only 55% of departures from Asian airports were on time. This is considerably lower than airports in North America and Europe, with 72% and 67% of departures on time respectively. As shown in Figure 3-46, the World Bank predicts that annual infrastructure investment needs in developing countries will be substantial for the next two decades (panel a), with the greatest needs arising in East and South Asia (panel b), and that a major focus will be transportation.[83]

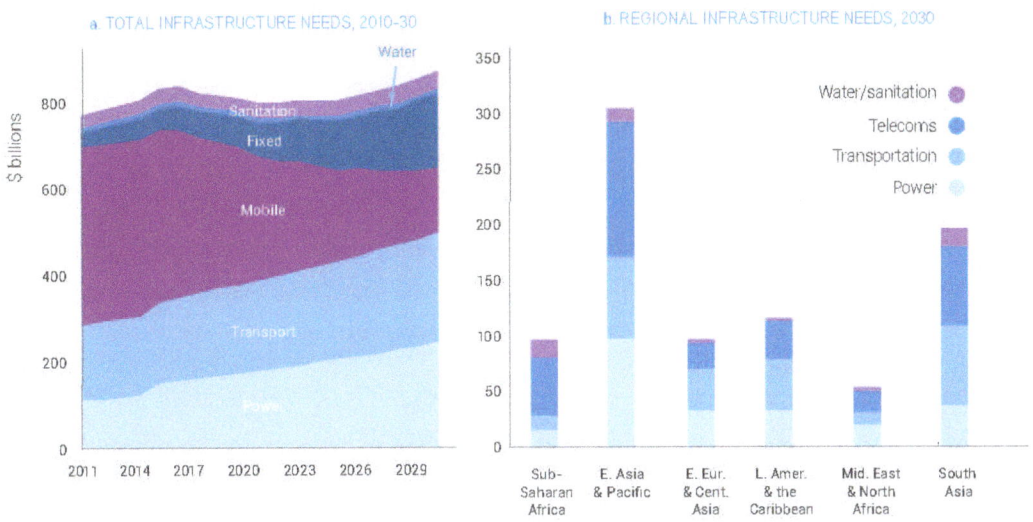

Figure 3-46 Infrastructure needs in developing countries, 2010–2030 (World Bank).

Heavy investments in the airport infrastructure of emerging economies are needed in order to attract airlines and strengthen the linkages between the new megalopolises and the rest of the world. According to Price Waterhouse, the coming decade will bring a vast amount of capital investment in airport-related infrastructure in developing countries, with global growth in airport investment estimated at 2.6% per annum. This amounts to a cumulative investment of US$750 billion between 2015 and 2025. The Asia-Pacific region is expected to see the highest level of investment in airport infrastructure in the coming decade, with an estimated cumulative investment of US$275 billion. It is anticipated that China will account for over half of this, with expectations that it will invest over US$150 billion from 2015 to 2025. Indonesia, a country where airport infrastructure expenditures have picked up strongly in the last few years, is expecting to see around US$25 billion invested over the next decade. Central and Eastern Europe and the Commonwealth of Independent States are primed to burst with infrastructure investment over the coming decade, at levels similar to what was seen in China in the previous decade. Those regions are expecting annual growth of 8.1% in infrastructure investment during 2015–2025, amounting to a cumulative spend of US$30 billion. The level of airport infrastructure investment in the Middle East is estimated at US$94 billion over the next decade compared with US$84 billion in the past decade.[84]

Other Investment Factors

Investment by itself is not enough to ensure the effective transport of people and goods. Because each megalopolis contains a number of centers that produce industrial outputs, effective coordination among the airports within a megalopolis becomes an issue. Most megalopolises in advanced economies are already served by more than one major airport (e.g., London, Paris, Tokyo, New York, and Chicago). Multi-airport systems are also seen in emerging economies, such as Kuala Lumpur, Bangkok, the Pearl River Delta, and the Yangtze River Delta. Multi-airport systems may cause inconvenience to connecting passengers who have to travel between airports by ground transportation; hence, close coordination and cooperation are needed between neighboring airports for the sake of efficient passenger connections.

Operating several smaller airports is very different from operating a mega-hub with capacities exceeding 100 million passengers per annum, both in magnitude of costs and in ease of achieving operational efficiency. The notion of having multiple airports serving one city calls for additional efforts to coordinate and plan these facilities in order to avoid or minimize passengers having to move between airports. An existing case in point is Shanghai, which has two airports 60km apart. Another is Beijing, where a new mega airport is to be completed by 2020 67km away from the current Beijing Capital International Airport. Often, multiple airports in one city are planned so that a single airline or alliance can be accommodated in a single airport with the expectation that transfers between non-alliance airlines will be rare. For example, among the four airports serving Moscow, Sheremetyevo serves primarily SkyTeam, whereas Domodedovo serves Star Alliance. Even for megalopolises with adequate land resources, such as Singapore and Hong Kong, it is still extremely hard to find space in a city for more than one airport. Careful strategic thinking is needed to resolve these types of land use issues. Airports in neighboring territories should be considered for use as alternatives to one another, such as Johor Bahru for Singapore and Shenzhen, Macao, and Zhuhai for Hong Kong. Often, solutions to these issues cannot be found solely within the aviation industry;

clear coordination and policies on the part of all levels of regional governments and the participation of all stakeholders are essential.

This does not mean that the availability of investments and effective coordination can solve all the challenges. National regulations and lack of regional coordination continue to create difficulties for international investors. Although there is an increasing need for aviation infrastructure investment, some key investment markets remain reluctant to open up opportunities to international investors and operators. Some of the biggest investment markets, such as China, Indonesia, and the Philippines, still have stringent ownership regulations, limiting the scope for foreign investment. Emerging economies need time to develop regulatory and economic frameworks that, while reflecting the characteristics and needs of their countries, will at the same time foster effective ways to maintain their air transport growth during their process of industrialization and developing megalopolises.

The Importance of Connectivity

One of the core issues and challenges in emerging economies is how to build their air connectivity in a "seamless" manner. As ICAO points out, the level of air connectivity is an indicator of a network's concentration and its ability to move passengers from their origin to their destination seamlessly.[85] Improved air connectivity, i.e., an effective network of air services, plays an important role in creating economic value by reducing air travel time and providing businesses with access to a wider marketplace. Connectivity is at the heart of what makes airlines successful in profit growth and cost control – finding new routes either directly or via an efficient hub-and-spoke network operation. In doing so, an airline can strengthen the economy of both the origin and destination country, enable investment and human capital to flow more freely across borders, and improve return on investment. This presents new opportunities for advanced economies. The issue for advanced economies is not only how to sustain existing air connectivity through maintaining their current aviation infrastructure such as airports and navigation services, but also how to encourage their airlines to continue to find new routes, especially in emerging markets, and how to address the need for additional aviation capacity expansion in order to avoid loss of air connectivity to competitors.

With new megalopolises being developed around the world, particularly in Asia, many new route development opportunities are presenting themselves. For example, although the number of routes in Europe has substantially increased since 2004 because of the increased penetration of low-cost carriers for point-to-point services, the Middle East and Asia are seeing larger growth in global passenger demand and a significant increase in the number of direct international routes with a higher level of air connectivity. Aggressive expansion of both direct and connecting passenger numbers is found in the air hubs of the Middle East, Asia, Latin America, and Africa.

The importance of air connectivity to a region's economic prosperity calls for stakeholders to work together to ensure that the right steps are taken to improve or maintain the global position of a region or megalopolis within the global air network. As a result, the aviation industry has found that sharing resources and cooperating with competitors are effective ways for expansion. In fact, this trend has been highly visible in the EU market. From 2008, the year of the global financial crisis, to 2016, air connectivity between EU and the rest of the world has substantially increased. According to the ACI Europe Airport Connectivity Report (2016), that growth mainly relied on indirect and airport connectivity because of limited direct connectivity. Indirect connectivity is achieved largely through the strategies of airline alliances and codeshare. In other words, the industrial output of aviation can be achieved not only by investing in infrastructure and airplanes, but also by cooperating with one another in win-win situations.

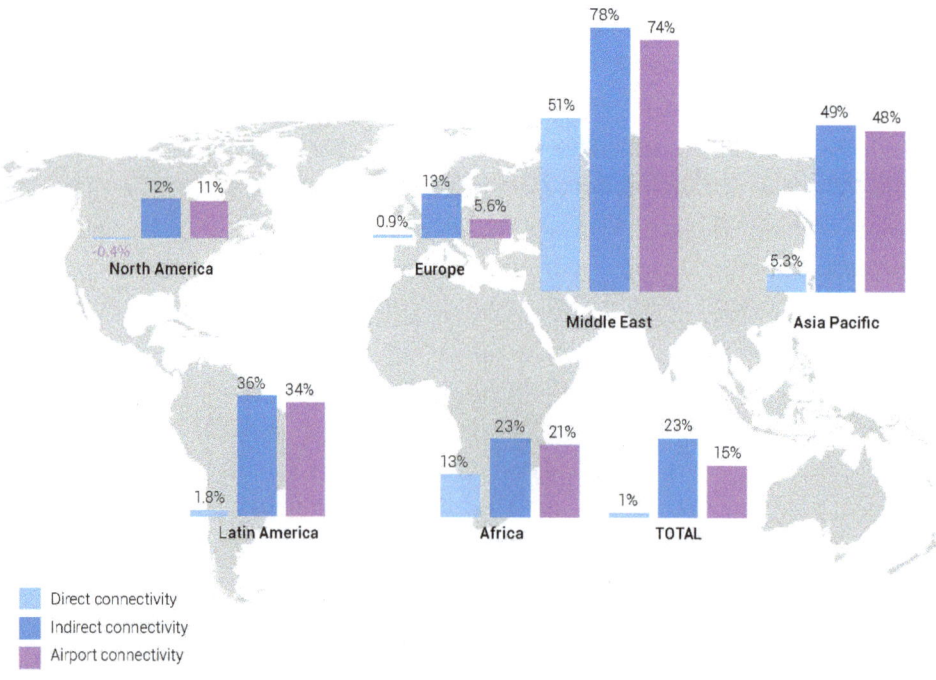

Figure 3-47   Direct, indirect, and airport connectivity from EU airports by world region, 2016 vs. 2008 (ACI).

International Cooperation – Key to Global Aviation Output

The following sections outline the major forms of international cooperation that exist in the aviation industry, namely airline partnerships and alliances, codeshare, city pairs, fifth-freedom air routes, and other forms of cooperation. Due to the continuing growth of industrial outputs in emerging economies, which will result in increasing needs for effective air services, these types of cooperation will increase in the long-term.

Airline Alliances

Global airline alliances, which now account for two-thirds of the world's international air traffic, enable member airlines to augment their profits, both by increasing the customer's willingness to pay and by reducing overall operational costs. These alliances have thus become an important component of the strategies of a growing number of international airlines. Initially regarded as an interim solution to widespread industry consolidation, long-term, ongoing international airline alliances have now been formed throughout the aviation industry. They are preferred because they allow airlines to gain access to other countries without the complication of foreign ownership restrictions on cross-border mergers between airlines and possible changes of key management positions by foreign governments. They also provide opportunities for new members, many of whom are new to the global air travel market, to operate more efficiently. These increased efficiency opportunities include:

- **Improving pricing through the removal of double marginalization.** Airlines within alliances may adopt cooperative pricing mechanisms that result in sharing of revenue arising from interline traffic. The carriers may work together to set interline fare levels that maximize their joint profits while still offering competitive fares to their customers.

- **Reducing costs through economies of scale.** Pooling of resources and facilities, such as sharing check-in services, luggage services, special customer services, and airport lounges.

- **Increasing customer loyalty and engagement.** Can be achieved by offering extra benefits such as enhanced connecting services, premium check-in, better schedule coordination, more convenient connections, and accumulation of award points.

- **Reducing industry competition and increasing customer leverage.** When airlines of the same alliance cooperate on routes with joint businesses and aligned flight schedules, the inconvenience and cost of not flying within the same alliance will increase for travelers. In fact, this was a main reason why distinct competitors in the industry converted into three dominant alliance entities: Star Alliance, SkyTeam, and Oneworld.

- **Reacting effectively to competitive challenges of other transportation modes.** Short-haul airline networks in some regions, including China and Europe, are facing pressure from high-speed rail alternatives. In those markets, frequency of flights is a key driver of network growth, particularly in the competition for business travelers. Through the network of alliances and the advantage of connecting with global hubs, airline alliances can generate incremental market share by increasing frequencies and providing convenience. For example, it is believed that increasing flight frequencies in existing markets has driven 60% of the domestic market growth in China over the past decade.

- **Improving management efficiency.** Airlines from emerging economies often face various challenges such as service quality not up to the standards of advanced economies, obstacles in marketing and distribution, inadequate yield of management systems, and limited networks. By joining alliances and using already-proven support systems, emerging airlines will often find ways to quickly upgrade their management and services, thus improving their services while reducing their costs.

Table 3-9   Major airline alliances of the world (Wikipedia).

	Star Alliance	SkyTeam	Oneworld	Value Alliance	U-FLY Alliance	Vanilla Alliance	Industry
Airlines	28	20	13	8	5	5	1,402
Passengers (million/yr)	642.1	665.4	557.4	92	44	2.3	3,570
Countries	192	177	161	30	18	-	206
Destinations	1,330	1,062	1,016	183	149	-	3,883
Fleet size	4,657	3,937	3,560	201	129	-	26,065
Employees	432,603	481,691	382,913	-	-	-	2,669,000
Revenue Billion US$	179.05	140.98	130.92	-	-	-	664.4
Daily departures	18,500	17,343	13,814	341	339	-	-
billions RPK	23% (1536)	20.4% (1362)	17.8% (1189)	1.6% (107)	0.6% (40)	-	6,678.694

It is worth noting that in addition to the three major airline alliances, new alliances have been formed, and various new approaches have been adopted (see Table 3-9). In 2015, Qantas received authorization from the Australian Competition and Consumer Commission for its planned joint venture with China Eastern Airlines. In Southeast Asia, where airlines were struggling to find profitability in long-haul markets, Singapore Airlines undertook a joint venture with Lufthansa, while Malaysia Airlines took a similar approach with Emirates Airline. Another development was the U-FLY Alliance in Asia, an alliance of independent low-cost carriers founded in 2016 by HK Express, Lucky Air, Urumqi Air, and West Air with the vision of stabilizing a low-cost network and delivering flexible, affordable services to passengers. U-FLY is the world's first LCC alliance. All four founding airlines are affiliated with HNA Group (Hainan Airline).

Codeshare

Codeshare is an aviation business arrangement in which two or more airlines share the same flight. Each airline in the arrangement uses its own airline designator and flight number in its timetable or schedule as if it were its own flight (the "marketing carrier"), but in fact only one airline operates it as the "operating carrier" or "administrating carrier". Most of the major airlines have code-sharing partnerships with other airlines; codeshare routes have grown by nearly 8% annually worldwide during the past decade. Codeshare is a key feature of the major airline alliances, but its application is well beyond alliances. In fact, it happens more and more frequently between airlines of different alliances or airlines not belonging to any alliances, such as new airlines in emerging economies.

The practice of codeshare started in the US in the 1970s following deregulation, after which major airlines forged code-sharing alliances to facilitate expansion. For example, American Airlines and Japan Airlines allied to sell each other's seats and expand the number of destinations for each partner. These alliances have become essential competitive tools for legacy airlines against the new, low-cost airlines that offer simpler fare structures and more direct routes. A good example is the codeshare arrangement between Air China and Air Macau for flights between Beijing and Macau. In effect, codeshare allows an airline to provide their customers with access to cities without having to offer extra flights. Although codeshare does not require alliance membership, global alliances play a significant role in driving airline interline and codeshare partnerships in order to keep passengers within "the family". With more airlines joining global alliances, more opportunities are created for increased codeshare cooperation within the alliances, while reducing the opportunity for airlines outside particular alliances to partner with the alliance airlines.

Codeshare has become a good way for airlines to gain exposure in a market that they do not actually serve directly, while their operations and frequency of service appear to be increasing. Moreover, by giving its capacity to other airlines as codeshare partners, an airline can substantially reduce its operational costs.[86] Airlines not only look at the revenue/profit for a given flight, but they also look at the amount the flight generates for the network as a whole. Sometimes a route can be barely breaking even, but it can bring in substantial traffic for connections on other flights of that same airline. This brings convenience to connecting passengers, who would otherwise have to face problems such as luggage loss/miss or delays. In codeshare situations, the second airline would help passengers with their connecting arrangements.

City Pairs

Traditionally, city pairs refer to the city of origin and the city of destination for flights to and from two cities. On the technical level, city-pair metrics are a useful tool for air traffic controllers, airports, and airlines to plan schedules and anticipate traffic levels, especially between two cities with frequent flights, such as between Toronto and Montreal. Also, city-pair performance is the most direct way for airline operators to connect two markets. Through analysis of flight performance between a city pair, such as the average time between the scheduled departure gate and the actual arrival gate at the destination and the elapsed time from takeoff to landing for a selected city pair, predictability and efficiency can be enhanced. Understanding and tracking the time variation for city-pair operations can lead to improved traffic flow management and flight scheduling, as well as reduced fuel consumption and aircraft exhaust emissions.

The growth of megalopolises is giving a new meaning to city pairs beyond the technical level, and they now act as drivers for the growth of mega-cities. Close cooperation between city pairs on a global level helps bring a megalopolis together. For example, with a new open-skies agreement, China is Australia's fastest-growing and highest-spending international visitor market (see Figure 3-48). More than 1 million Chinese tourists visited Australia in 2015–16 (up by 22.3% from the year before), and they spent almost US$7 billion during their stays. These tourists and other travelers to and from Australia and China have also benefited from increased connectivity, with the number of city pairs having doubled since 2014. The story is similar between China and the US, where the number of city pairs has doubled since 2013. The Middle East has also seen a rapid increase in city pairs.

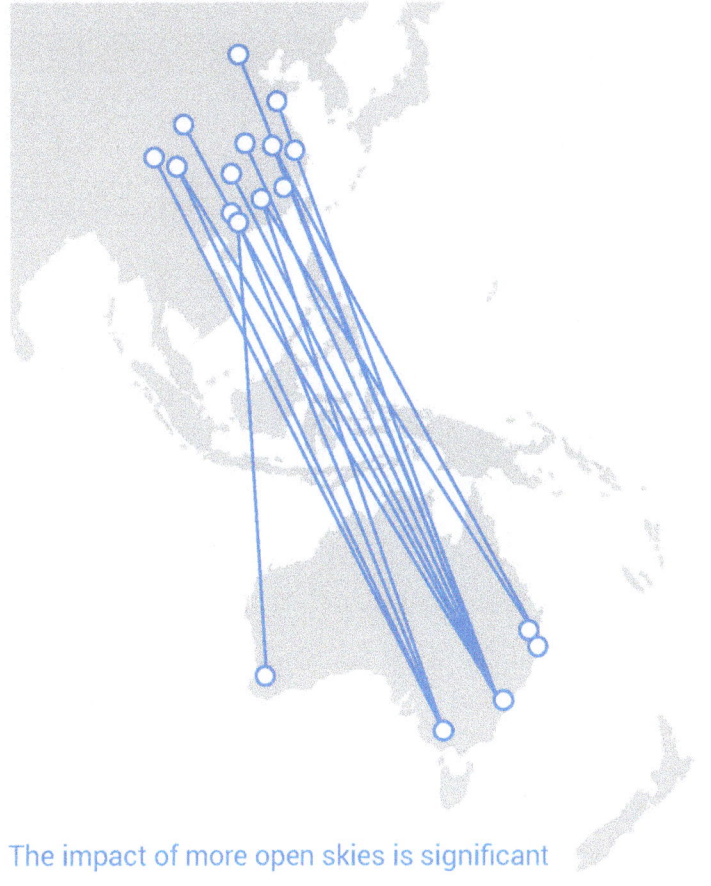

The impact of more open skies is significant

Figure 3-48 City pairs between Australia and China, 2016 (OAG, Airbus GMF, 2017).

Fifth-freedom Air Routes

The global aviation market is fragmented by national and regional airlines for geograph-ical and/or economic reasons. This impedes efficiency, generates friction, and hinders growth.[87] Some nation states are making efforts to remove these barriers in order to improve air connectivity. One approach is to share a nation state's own airspace and passenger market with another nation state by means of "fifth-freedom routes". These fifth-freedom routes are usually operated by foreign carriers flying premium aircraft.[88] For example, Delta operates flights from Minneapolis (MSP) to Tokyo (NRT), and the same aircraft continues on from Tokyo to Singapore (SIN). In effect, the flight between Tokyo and Singapore is operated between two foreign countries by Delta, an American carrier.

Following are some examples of fifth-freedom routes. It is worth noting that some airlines from emerging economies are flying in advanced economies, benefitting from the latter's open-sky policies:

- Cathay Pacific flying between New York (JFK) and Vancouver (YVR).

- Singapore Airlines flying between Houston (IAH) and Manchester (MAN).

- Air China flying between Montreal (YUL) and Havana (HAV).

- Air France flying between Los Angeles (LAX) and Papeete (PPT).

- Air New Zealand flying between Los Angeles (LAX) and to London (LHR).

- Emirates Airline flying between New York (JFK) and Milan (MXP).

- Air Tahiti flying between Los Angeles (LAX) and Paris (CDG).

- Ethiopian Airline flying between Los Angeles (LAX) and Dublin (DUB).

- Ethiopian Airline flying between Newark (EWR) and to Lomé (LFW).

- South African Airways flying between Washington (IAD), Dakar (DKR), and Accra (ACC).

- Fiji Airways flying between Honolulu (HNL), Christmas Island (CXI), and Apia (APW).

- India's Jet Airways flying between Toronto (YYZ) and Brussels (BRU).

Other freedoms are being developed as well. Air Canada's strategy in leveraging "sixth-freedom" traffic is to target passengers in markets such as Boston, Pittsburgh, or Nashville to make one stop in Canada en route to trans-Atlantic and trans-Pacific destinations. KLM already carries sixth-freedom traffic between New York (A) and Cairo (C) with passengers traveling from New York (A) to Amsterdam (B) and on to Cairo (C). Lufthansa operates between New York and Mexico City without serving Germany (seventh freedom); Singapore Airlines enplanes passengers at Wellington, New Zealand, and deplanes them in Auckland as part of its service between New Zealand and Singapore (eighth freedom). With the expansion of open skies, more such flights will improve global air connectivity.

The fifth-freedom routes make airfares competitive among airlines, which benefits air travelers. Table 3-10 lists sample business fares between Australia and Europe in March 2012.

Table 3-10   Sample Australia-Europe business airfares, 2012 (CAPA Center for Aviation).

	Melbourne-Amsterdam Fare – USD	Sydney-Paris Fare – USD
Air China	n/a	6360
China Eastern	n/a	5090
China Southern	5120	5130
Emirates	7690	7780
Finnair	7120	7170
Korean Air	6300	n/a
MAS	8990	6580

For example, as Table 3-10 shows, China Southern flies Melbourne-Amsterdam with a stop-over at Guangzhou, so that its fare is less expensive than Finnair and MAS who fly direct. China Eastern flies Sydney-Paris with a stopover at Shanghai, and its price is cheaper.

Chinese carriers are also undercutting prices on Australia-North America routes, considering that a routing from Australia to North America through China is 50% longer, with associated higher fuel costs, than flying direct.

Table 3-11   Sample Australia-North America business airfares, 2012 (CAPA Center for Aviation).

	Sydney-Vancouver Fare – USD	Sydney-Los Angeles Fare – USD
Air Canada	2150	n/a
Air China	n/a	1460
Air New Zeland	1780	1520
China Eastern	1380	1390
China Southern	n/a	1310
Qantas	1782	1510
Virgin Australia	n/a	1410

As Table 3-11 indicates, on the Sydney-Los Angeles route, Air New Zealand and Qantas do not have stopovers, but their prices are higher than those with stopovers in a third country.

The development of fifth-freedom and sixth-freedom routes with price cuts by Chinese carriers from Australia to Europe and North America may mean that structural competitive and pricing shifts can occur in other markets as well, especially the Middle East, Southeast Asia, and Africa. For the time being, a shortage of network destinations and frequencies may limit their market expansion, but the establishment of their fifth-freedom and sixth-freedom operations over the years may empower them to enlarge their catchment areas.

Other Forms of International Cooperation

Aviation and its infrastructure, including airlines and airports, are often regarded as symbols of nation states rather than as commercial enterprises. Because of this, the state controls ownership of major flag carriers in many countries. However, under market liberalization, some of these airlines have started to take equity shares in other airlines as a growth strategy. Their methods include partial acquisitions, full mergers, and co-branded subsidiaries. These strategies are effective for opening new markets, obtaining new traffic, and rationalizing costs. Creative strategies have been implemented, such as establishing subsidiaries, which allow airlines to expand their brands to foreign countries within the limits of foreign-ownership regulations.

In July 2016, Qatar Airways confirmed a 10% stake acquisition in LATAM Airlines for US$613million. Despite regional difficulties with policy and financing, some non-Latin American airlines see this as the ideal time to gain a foothold in this market. The same year, Virgin Australia announced board approval of a US$159 million investment by HNA Group (parent of China-based Hainan Airlines) for a 19% stake of the Australian airline. HNA Group has also invested US$450 million for a 23.7% stake in Azul Brazilian Airlines. Also, in early 2018, United Airlines increased its share in Azul from 3.7% to 8%. Delta expanded its investment in GOL in July 2015, and in November 2015 it expressed its intention to increase its holdings in Aeroméxico to as much as 49%.[89]

Becoming a Social Enterprise

These days, the international aviation industry is not merely about flying machines. Airlines now face new challenges and opportunities as they move to operate in emerging markets that involve profound social and cultural traditions. As a result, players in the aviation industry need to deal with a series of non-aviation considerations in their strategic planning. Some issues are on the technical level, but social factors are often behind them, and simple technical approaches may fail if they don't address all the social/ cultural issues. As James Canton points out in his book *Future Smart*, "Every business in the future must embrace a Higher Purpose or else they will not be able to compete given customers' changing attitudes and values."[90] In order to achieve this higher calling going forward, airlines will need to deal with a number of significant issues to which they might have only paid lip service in the past.

The first major issue is a possible shift of leadership roles in the process of airline alliance expansion. With the centers of demand for air service shifting from West to East, and with a focus currently on Asia, boundaries are being tested all the time. The three major airline alliances (see Table 3-9), which already cover most of the global aviation map, are facing continuing needs for additional partners to reach new territories. As a result, airlines that have been on the fringe of the market may start to get more involved under the new globalization. For example, the hub airports of newly developed megalopolises may become regional or even global centers for air connections. Through industry-wide consolidation on a regional, continental, and global scale, new classes of industry leaders may emerge on the global aviation stage.

The second big issue is the change in passenger attitudes and values related to flying. Facing a large and increasing array of flight options to more destinations with favorable pricing, consumer focus is shifting from the traditional cost and convenience issues to other more complex concerns like sustainability, the environment, social stability, customer service, industry practices, social norms, cultural values, and even economic nationalism. Such issues are easily politicized and open to media hype and may increasingly affect how consumers perceive and choose their airlines and connecting airports.

Finally, the aviation industry workforce will change from a monoculture to one of diversity. The global aviation industry employs over 450,000 people directly in jobs working for airport operators and over 5.5 million working for other in-airport businesses (e.g., retail outlets, car rental agencies, freight services, etc.). Worldwide, close to 2.7 million people are employed by airlines, and over 1.1 million are working in civil aviation support for air navigation service providers.[91]

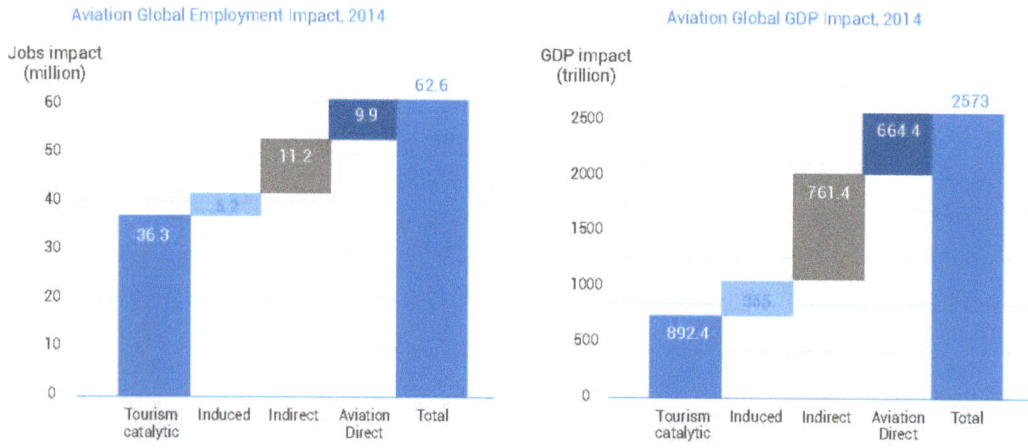

Figure 3-49 Global aviation impact: Employment and GDP, 2014 (ATAG).

The traditional composition of the workforce in the aviation industry is mono-cultural, which means generally home-grown, male, and strongly aviation-industry experienced. However, today's fast-moving global context is challenging the status quo. Diversity in terms of gender, geographic origin, cultural background, and cross-industry experience is becoming the norm for employees in the aviation industry.

These challenges, among others, are pushing the aviation industry into the position of becoming a social enterprise. In this era of new market development, it is naïve to assume that passengers and tourists will automatically fill up an airplane just because it is available. Today's customers are substantially more discerning than ever before, and Canton describes them as the "Empowered Customer".[92] Any serious mishandling of social issues could bring disastrous results, not only to the operating companies, but also to the regional economies.

For example, advertising slogans such as "family reunion" or "take yourself home" are widely used by airlines in their commercials and express social values that have become widely acknowledged and accepted worldwide. British Airway has used this approach for years, and its definition of "family" goes all the way to India, celebrating blessings from Great Britain since 1924.[93] Such an approach, although successful in the past when most airlines in emerging economies were from the West, needs to be re-examined for its social and cultural significance in an industrial context with multiple local airlines flying the same route from their countries to the West. According to Canton, the empowered customer is now less sensitive to commercial deals and bargains and more concerned about the treatment of social values and morals. Nowadays, airline customers are concerned that:

- The company that services me must care about my concerns for social issues and the environment.

- The company must be working to make the world a better place through committed social actions that I agree with.

- The company must believe as I do that business should lead in making the world a better place.

- The company must care about what I care about – the environment, social issues, equality, diversity, and so forth.

- The company must be fair and equitable about their people practices.[94]

Some social issues can be harmful to the image of the aviation industry if not dealt with in a prudent way. Issues like patriotism, economic nationalism, feelings of cultural superiority, ethnic pride, religion, cultural habits and customs, and political correctness are all possible minefields for newcomers to a market. In the current complex operating environment, aviation companies may encounter constant barriers on both technical and policy levels. Such issues can come up whenever they do such things as expanding into new territories, forming partnerships with local airlines, establishing a maintenance, repair, and overhaul center (MRO) at a local airport, discussing the possible opening of a fifth-freedom air route, or negotiating for cooperation on codeshare and city pairs.

As a result, companies are increasingly discussing issues and options and accounting for political risks as an important element of profitability. As stated earlier, Canton believes that such barriers cannot be fully removed unless a "higher purpose" is pursued by companies in order to demonstrate their preparedness for sustainable and socially responsible developments in new markets. He goes on to state that, "Every business must become a social enterprise and embrace a higher purpose in order to conduct business, compete, and relate to the changing customer. Companies that care about what their customers care about will have a competitive advantage."[95] As political and socio-cultural considerations increasingly affect the presence and value proposition of companies in new markets, the need for robust strategies that account for these non-market forces becomes ever more important. Such strategies may involve implementing measures such as working visibly to address local and national priorities, adapting operations and internal processes to local workforce needs, making job-creating investments, and "deepening their identity and footprint in specific countries to comply with norms for higher local content requirements and address heavier government influence."[96]

A symbol of a company's active participation in local culture and society is the establishment of a strong local identity. This can be achieved through such actions as conducting customized local training at the operational level and delivery of strategic consulting services at the executive level.

Aviation Staffing Needs for the Future

In many parts of the world, emerging markets stand to gain greatly from international expertise in running and managing aviation assets effectively, especially airports. Meanwhile, as the world aircraft fleet grows, the demand for more pilots and technicians will increase in parallel to meet the needs of airlines and passengers. Airbus forecasts that over the next 20 years, more than a million such professionals will be trained to the highest levels.

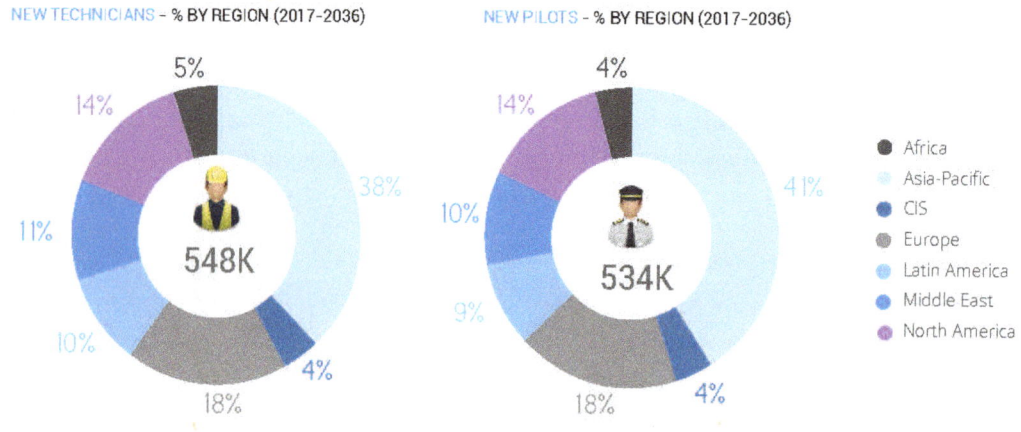

Figure 3-50 Demand for new technicians and pilots in the global aviation industry, 2017 to 2036 (Airbus GMF, 2017).

IATA has predicted a shortage of aviation professionals during the expansion to emerging economies. "Aviation depends on high-skilled employees, whether pilots, engineers, air traffic controllers, or safety inspectors. In the medium term there may be skill supply issues due to the increased demand from emerging markets."[97] Urgent needs for professionals in aircraft maintenance, repair, and overhaul centers (MROs) are an example. Looking at the MRO global market share by region, North America claims the largest share in MRO activity at 29%, with Asia-Pacific at 28% and Europe following close behind at 26%. Based on current and projected aircraft orders, the Asia-Pacific share of the global MRO market is expected to increase and potentially to become the largest global region for MRO activity in the coming years.[98] Global civil MRO spending in 2015 was $64.3 billion, up by 3.5% from the $62.1 billion spent in 2014.

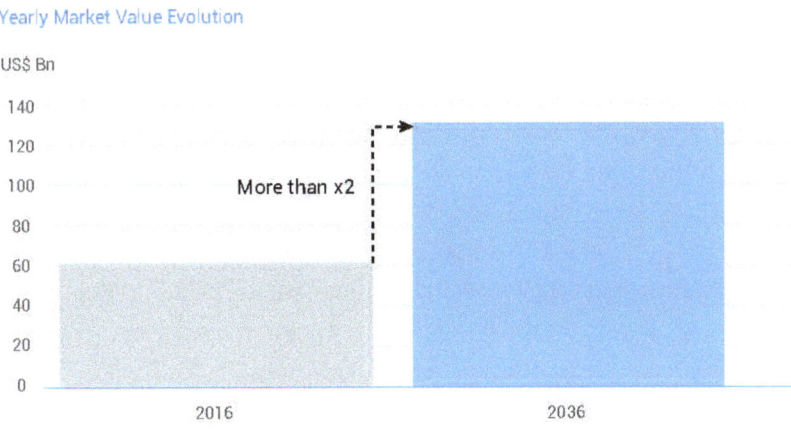

Yearly Market Value Evolution

US$ Bn

More than x2

MRO yearly demand will more than double over the next 20 years

Figure 3-51   Demand for maintenance, repair, and overhaul (MRO) services to 2036 (Airbus GMF, 2017).

In the future, the growth of air routes and fleets will expand the MRO business not only by the size of staff, but by the number of locations as well. Airbus expects that this business will double from US$60 billion to more than US$120 billion a year by 2036, or a cumulative US$1.85 trillion over the same period, with Asia-Pacific handling 36% of the overall MRO business at a value of US$660 billion over the next 20 years.[99] This leads to a growing need for hiring and training, including the establishment of training centers in emerging markets to train local staff. Between 2014 and 2016, Airbus increased its number of training centers from 5 to 15, most of them in emerging megalopolises such as New Delhi, Bangalore, Jakarta, Ho Chi-Minh City, Tunis, and Bangkok.[100] The unique demands for training in emerging market countries cannot be underestimated—English may not be the first language for the local staff, and their educational background may not be fully consistent with that of advanced economies. Another example is the growing size of airline service staff, including flight attendants, as fleets expand. Historically, airlines enjoyed an image of prestige and a cosmopolitan flair that could attract and retain talent, but nowadays they are increasingly considered to be ordinary employers. This shift in perception brings challenges for hiring, training, and retention.

A Paradigm Shift is Coming

The efforts of aviation companies to build social capital are highly commendable and worthwhile. As explained at the beginning of this chapter, just as human capital and produced capital are the most important part of a nation's wealth, social capital forms a genuine part of a company's wealth and competitiveness. As Canton points out, "social capital is a values-based asset that is as important as human capital or money."[101] According to him, in a corporate environment with multicultural origins and multi-social backgrounds, the management philosophy for a successful social enterprise should shift from top-down power to distributed power, from compliance culture to innovation culture, from silos of operation to integrated operations, and from customer service to customer engagement. He believes that the companies of the future will focus on achieving a Higher Purpose on their way to making profits.[102] Under such circumstances, CEOs in the aviation industry need to consider re-examining the current corporate culture, which was founded on the basis of the traditional industrialization model. They need to foster the development and implementation of a new type of culture that will be conducive to socio-cultural integration.

The effect of developing social capital will have two main impacts. At the market level, through emotionalizing airline brands, a new culture will help build and enhance customer loyalty and engagement in new markets. Internally, social capital development will help attract and retain local talent and build teams on the basis of pursuing a higher purpose. As Christoph Wahl put it, it will "infuse senior ranks with people who bring skills and ideas from other industries".[103] In the future, these softer, "non-aviation" factors will loom large in determining the success of international cooperation and growth.

CONCLUSION AND SUMMARY

The first part of this closing section is a brief conclusion that contains some overall general remarks that summarize the essence of the foregoing discussion of the Economic Power Shift—West to East megatrend and offers some general advice to managers about how best to cope with it. The second part of this section is a management summary that recaps in point form all the major subjects discussed earlier during the detailed analysis and discussion of the Economic Power Shift—West to East megatrend. The points are presented with the perspective of aviation professionals and managers in mind. Essentially, each point in the management summary represents a key observation or conclusion that was made during the detailed analysis and discussion.

Conclusion

As can be seen from the foregoing chapter, over the past thirty years, a major economic power shift from the West to the East has been occurring on a global scale. More than one billion people in emerging economies, particularly in the Asian region, have shifted from being poor to occupying a place in the middle class of their societies and are now experiencing a way of life that their ancestors could not have dreamed of. Unlike thirty years ago when large amounts of Western capital were invested in Eastern economies, nowadays the opposite is occurring, and investment capital is flowing rapidly in large amounts from emerging economies to the West. Not only has this shift in wealth led to a more stable and wealthy lifestyle in the East, it has financially empowered millions of people from former "have-not" economies in the East and emboldened them to invest in the West. For example, since the 1990s, thousands of immigrants from China, South Korea, Hong Kong, and Taiwan have purchased properties in Canada, the US, and Australia. Luxuries like Canadian king crabs and Australian lobsters have become "frequent passengers" to almost every city in China.

Major shifts in this economic megatrend have been driven by numerous structural changes in factors that influence the global economic and political equilibrium. These significant changes include structural changes in global GDP, major investment shifts, the growth of megalopolises, shifts in purchasing power, and changes in industrial output dynamics. A significant development that affects the economic megatrend has been the clash that has arisen between the new protectionism and the new globalization. The protectionism forces seek to maintain their traditional dominance over the world economy, whereas the new globalization advocates are determined to establish a new economic-political order in the world.

The changes that drive this megatrend have already had significant impacts on the aviation industry, and that trend is expected to continue well into the future. The unprecedented rise in income levels in emerging economies in the East has moved people's focus from the essentials of life to the desire for a lifestyle similar to their counterparts in the West. Once an unattainable luxury for most people in the East, aviation travel is now financially accessible to millions more people than it was 30 years ago, and this trend is not expected to abate as the emerging economies in the East continue to develop. Aviation is always near the top of the list when people's financial fortunes improve because the type of travel that aviation allows improves their quality of life and makes lives more meaningful. Just as the power company sells warmth and light and the carpet company sells softness and cleaner air, aviation is not merely selling air travel; it is also selling stories and dreams that can contribute to a passenger's authentic experience. Over the years, the aviation industry has managed to successfully build an authentic Westernized experience during the age of globalization. Nevertheless, changes in the economic-political megatrend are now calling for a new approach.

Commercial aviation as we know it today is primarily a high-end representation of technology that originated in the West, built by Western engineers and operated for the use of Western passengers, including those from the East who could afford to adapt to the Western model. Hence, Western culture has always been at the heart of the international aviation industry, even as it transformed from the industrialization period to post-industrialization. During these phases, the global aviation industry went from providing basic transport to providing services and from pursuing basic customer satisfaction to earning customer engagement.

However, in the era of the economic power shift from West to East, this megatrend is rapidly manifesting in the world's emerging economies without a transition period. Compared with the gradual dawning of the old globalization in the West, when air passengers were mainly from advanced economies and the choices of airlines and air routes were limited, the new globalization involves many more passengers from diverse cultural and social backgrounds, with multiple options for destinations and air services. The commercial aviation experience today carries a variety of social meanings. Having the financial resources and access to be able to fly is often regarded as a symbol of affluence, comfortable lifestyle, social prestige, and global connection.

Under the new approach to international aviation, each passenger has his/her own stories; aviation groups them together, gives them a feel for the aviation community, welcomes them with multicultural presentations in the cabin, and provides them with an authentic experience with which to build new stories. These changes to the commercial aviation experience in recent years raise some questions for the aviation industry. These questions include what social meaning should the contemporary commercial aviation experience involve and how can the industry make it happen. The way things have evolved over the past few decades, it is now safe to assume that the future success stories in the aviation industry may not be those with the largest capital holdings, or the latest airplanes and technologies, but those who can best strengthen ties of cooperation on a global basis and provide an ongoing authentic experience for all their newly empowered customers from new and emerging markets.

Management Summary

Based on the foregoing discussion, there is no doubt that the Economic Power Shift—West to East megatrend will have major impacts on the international aviation industry over the next 15 to 20 years and beyond. In many ways, adapting to this megatrend and implementing mitigation measures will have considerable impacts on the way in which airlines, airports, and air navigation services will develop and operate their businesses, particularly during the next decade, as they continue to adjust to this new reality. Numerous significant conclusions and observations have been made during the course of the detailed analysis earlier in this chapter. The following are the important facts and trends that aviation managers at all levels will need to take into account when determining how best to deal with the Economic Power Shift—West to East megatrend when preparing for the future.

Economic Shift – The drivers

- The economic power shift from Western nations to those in the East is not new and has brought about many changes to the aviation industry over the past thirty years.

- Changes in passenger volumes are the most obvious indicator that demonstrates this phenomenon. For example, based on the latest 2017 data, 10 of the top 20 airports worldwide by passenger traffic are located in emerging economies, and they are all in Asia.

- With the economic power shift to the East, the strength of advanced economies is further enriched, and win-win situations will be achieved through collaboration among both emerging and advanced economies.

- The spread of megalopolises is a clear symbol of the economic power shift from West to East. In the past twenty years, new megalopolises have developed as industrial hubs in emerging economies and their proportion of the global economy have started to catch up with those in the West, and they are exerting considerable impacts on the aviation industry that serves them.

GDP and Investment Shifts

- The economic power shift to the East is changing every aspect of the global economy, with significant impacts on the aviation industry. Across all continents, major hub airports have been built to facilitate the transport of air passengers and cargo.

- As Asia moves rapidly towards becoming a higher-income region, a rise in global tourism originating from Asia will be seen. As a result, a massive wave of new air travel will be unleashed, and this will be the driver for the development of aviation mega-cities in Asia.

- The West-East power shift is encountering turbulence with the rise of the new protectionism movement as symbolized by recent US trade policies designed to protect and maintain that nation's dominant position in the global economy, as well as to discourage the emerging trend of "new globalization".

- According to many experts, protectionism creates uncertainties instead of opportunities for the global economy. Protectionist policies are most likely to be active in advanced economies, but they also exist in some emerging countries such as China.

- A new type of globalization that is less driven by the West than in the past is now spreading throughout the emerging economies of the world. This new platform is one in which emerging economies can maintain their own culture, religion, and belief systems while accepting foreign investments and accomplishing their own industrialization initiatives.

- The trend toward new globalization does not put the West and East at odds. Many countries in the West see the growth of the new globalization as an opportunity to break free from the established control of past practices and as an opening to build their own global trading systems.

- International aviation already plays a unique role in empowering nations and peoples regardless of where they are located, providing them with efficient access to improved livelihoods, food, healthcare, education, business, R&D, family and friends, communities, leisure activities, tourism, etc. With the economic power shift to the East, aviation benefits to emerging economies are increasing.

- In the past 20 years, there has been a rapid increase of GDP growth in emerging economies that has been driving the economic power shift from West to East, with significant direct impacts on aviation. The global GDP growth rate continues to be the most important influencer of worldwide air traffic.

- The direct GDP-aviation relationship has been adopted globally by governments and all sectors of the industry for policy-making, forecasting, determining fleet expansions, and decisions about the expansion of airport infrastructure.

- Since 2009, emerging economies have consistently increased their overall share of global GDP growth, particularly China and India, and the importance of these countries to the pace of global growth has also increased.

- The change in global GDP structure is based on the shift of global investment markets over the past twenty years. Between 1965 and 1999, investment in developing countries was relatively constant—averaging 18.5% — but this share increased dramatically in the first decade of the 21st Century, reaching about 40%.

- By 2030, nearly half of gross capital inflows will likely go to developing countries, and emerging-economy countries will represent more than half of global capital stocks, compared with about one-third in 2010.

- The rising share of investment by developing countries in global output is due to more than just changes in China and India. Elsewhere in the developing world, robust growth will be associated with high investment rates as well. Brazil, India, and Russia together will account for more than 13% of global investment in 2030, more than the United States.

- Economic prosperity across the Asia-Pacific region will continue and is expected to account for over 50% of global GDP by 2050; further growth is also projected in Africa, almost reaching a 10% share of global GDP by 2050, but the relative shares of Europe and America will decline.

- It is estimated that by 2050, the fastest growth in air traffic flows will be in emerging economies, including domestic India (5.4% growth rate), domestic China (3.6%), and other domestic Asia economies (3.7%). However, overall traffic flows in advanced economies will not decrease because they will attract more traffic flows from emerging economies.

- The increase in traffic flows will consist mostly of passengers traveling for business or leisure. Growth points will be regional flights, either inside a country or between neighboring countries. For emerging economies, this means a significant shift from traditional land transport to modern air transport that will result from their social and economic development. This is the basis that aircraft manufacturers used to determine that their focus should now be on the production of single-aisle airplanes.

- In the past decade, while global GDP has grown by 28% in real terms, global air passenger traffic has grown substantially more, by 70%. An increasingly higher proportion of global GDP growth is being driven by emerging economies, and consequently there will be a substantial shift from West to East in air service demand. Emerging markets, led by China, India, and the Middle East, are growing faster than the global average, with double-digit traffic growth.

- In 1993, more than 73% of all traffic was carried by airlines in Europe and North America. It is estimated that this proportion will shrink substantially in the next twenty years due to the changing structure of global GDP.

- The Asia-Pacific region will enjoy the highest GDP growth rate in the next twenty years, although this does not mean that the aviation business in advanced economies will be superseded because GDP growth in many emerging markets will outpace growth in advanced economies.

Changing Dynamics of Purchasing Power

- Total global wealth grew by 66% from 1995 to $1,143 trillion in 2014, with a real rate of growth of 1.3% per year. This was accompanied by a major decrease in the concentration of wealth among high-income countries as it spread among a larger set of countries in the middle and the top of the emerging economies list. An overwhelming majority of countries increased per capita wealth between 1995 and 2014, with fastest growth among middle-income countries.

- The trans-Atlantic air travel market has grown by 50% over the last 15 years.

- Human capital (people) accounts for 70% of advanced economies and natural capital (natural resources) for only 3%. This situation has been achieved by adding more produced capital (products) and human capital.

- In recent years, more than two dozen low-income countries, where natural capital dominates the composition of wealth, have moved to middle-income status. This has been achieved in large part by investing resource revenues in infrastructure, education, and health, which have resulted in increased human capital.

- The rising middle classes in emerging economies are not only demanding goods, but also services such as tourism, health services, and entertainment. Consequently, air traffic between emerging countries is forecast to grow at 6.2% per annum and will represent a growing share of air traffic, from 29% of world traffic in 2016 to 40% by 2036.

- The share of human capital global wealth held by advanced countries has declined over the past two decades from 69% in 1995 to 64% in 2014.

- The participation of wage earners in the labor force in emerging economies is growing rapidly, thus boosting their relative human capital level. In most developing countries, the human capital portion of total wealth is rising. In low-income countries, this share increased from 32% to 43% over two decades; in lower-middle-income countries, it rose from 44% to 52%.

- The growth of the aviation industry largely depends on the continuing growth of human capital because it enables more people to afford flying and to make purchases during their flights. In 2014, non-aeronautical purchases accounted for more than 45% of total airport revenues, whereas overall airport revenues increased by 8.2%.

- The large flows of consumers from emerging economies are changing the profile, behavior, habits, and practices of global air passenger travel. Twenty years ago, air passengers were most likely originating from Europe or North America.

- Over the next 20 years, there will be more diversity in flight origins, with 62% of traffic carried by airlines outsides of North America or Europe. Trends in passenger traffic growth are similar to the growth of human capital. Emerging markets will grow faster than established markets. Regions growing above trend are Asia-Pacific (6.3%), Middle East (6.4%), and Latin America (6.2%), but European (3.9%) and North American markets (2.9%) will be below trend.

- Emerging economies are developing large new middle-class populations, and more people in these regions are able to afford discretionary air travel. The number of domestic Indian passengers is expected to grow by almost six times in the next 20 years, reaching the same level as domestic travel in the USA today. Chinese domestic traffic has quadrupled in the last 10 years, with international traffic more than doubling.

- China will continue to lead global outbound travel after recording double-digit growth in tourism expenditures every year since 2004. This has benefitted Asian destinations such as Japan and Thailand as well as the USA and various European destinations. Spending by Chinese travelers increased by 26% in 2015. The outbound China market is predicted to double to over 200 million travelers annually by 2020, with almost 1.6 billion passengers expected to travel within China in 2036, about four times the number that traveled by air in 2016.

- Because over half of the world's tourists who travel across international borders each year are transported by air, any rise in tourism from emerging economies creates huge revenue potential for the global aviation industry.

- International tourist arrivals will grow at an annual rate of 3.3% between 2010 and 2030, reaching an annual total of 1.8 billion tourists. The majority of growth is expected to occur in emerging economies, which are estimated to record a 2.2% annual growth rate in international tourist arrivals between 2010 and 2030, reaching an annual total of 1 billion tourists, or 57% of total global international tourist arrivals.

- The evolving demographics of air travelers are changing the purposes and patterns for air travel. The first major change is the relative decrease in business travelers—traditionally the biggest proportion of air travelers in terms of revenue—now giving way to leisure passengers and VFR.

- North America will continue to be at the forefront of profitability in global aviation, with passenger aircraft load factors in the US and Canadian domestic markets averaging over 85%, whereas the average for international flights is 82%. US airlines were responsible for 61% of global airline profitability in 2015.

- With the economic performance of the Asia-Pacific region rising towards the levels of Europe and North America, travelers in Asia-Pacific are reaching wealth levels where they can afford to fly more frequently, tending to take more trips than Europeans and North Americans.

- Connectivity to and from the Middle East has grown dramatically, with the number of city pairs more than tripling from nearly 200 in 1990 to more than 700 by 2016. The robust regional economic growth is an important driver of air traffic in some countries in the region.

- Advanced economies will continue to be in the driver's seat in global aviation due to their riches in national wealth and human capital. Meanwhile, as emerging economies experience their fastest growth rate ever in wealth creation—especially some nations in Asia—new markets are emerging that require significant growth in air services.

Industrial Output Changes

- Because of the high-technology industry's need to move high-value-per-unit commodities quickly, air cargo has become the mode of choice. The speed and reliability of aviation cargo transportation have contributed to the market for "same-day" or "next-day" delivery services and transportation of urgent or time-sensitive goods, giving air an important advantage over other modes of transport.

- More than 85% of business-to-consumer e-commerce parcels are currently carried by air. The e-commerce share of scheduled international mail ton kilometers (MTKs) grew from 16% to 74% between 2010 and 2015, and is estimated to grow to 91% by 2025.

- Air cargo traffic is projected to grow at an average 4.2% per year over the next 20 years, and this sustained growth in traffic will lead to further enhancement of the global economy.

- The flow of air cargo from countries moving from "emerging to advanced" is expected to represent about 30% of total world international freight ton-kilometers by 2036.

- Over the next twenty years, dedicated air freighter traffic will grow at 2.6% per year, and the dedicated freight aircraft fleet in service is expected to increase by 50% during the same period. There will be a demand for about 1,950 freighter aircraft by 2036. Of that total, 730 will be new-build freighter aircraft, about 55% mid-size and 45% large.

- Despite the large surge in Asian airport development since the 1990s, infrastructure has rarely been built ahead of demand. As a result, congestion-related delays are rapidly increasing at most Asian hubs, with regular flight delays. Long takeoff queues are routine, as are aircraft circling in stacks awaiting landing. Suitable landing and takeoff slots are quickly becoming scarce.

- In 2013, only 55% of departures from Asian airports were on time; this is considerably lower than airports in North America and Europe, with 72% and 67% of departures on time respectively.

- The World Bank predicts that annual infrastructure investment needs in developing countries will be substantial for the next two decades, with the greatest needs arising in East and South Asia, and a major focus will be transportation.

- In the next decade, there will be a vast amount of capital investment in airport-related infrastructure in developing countries, with global growth in airport investment estimated at 2.6% per annum, amounting to US$750 billion between 2015 and 2025.

- The Asia-Pacific region is expected to see the highest level of investment in airport infrastructure in the coming decade, with an estimated cumulative investment of US$275 billion. China will account for over half of this, with expected investment of over US$150 billion from 2015 to 2025.

- One of the core issues and challenges in emerging economies is how to build their air connectivity in a "seamless" manner. As ICAO points out, the level of air connectivity is a key indicator of a network's concentration and its ability to move passengers from their origin to their destination seamlessly.

- With new megalopolises being developed around the world, particularly in Asia, many new route development opportunities are arising. The Middle East and Asia are seeing significant growth in global passenger demand and matching increases in the number of direct international routes with better air connectivity. Aggressive expansion of both direct and connecting passenger numbers is occurring in the hubs of the Middle East, Asia, Latin America, and Africa.

- The aviation industry has found resource sharing and cooperation to be effective ways of expanding and improving connectivity. This has been highly visible in the EU market since the global financial crisis of 2008, where air connectivity between the EU and the rest of the world has increased substantially. Indirect connectivity is achieved largely through such strategies as airline alliances and codeshare. Hence, the industrial output of aviation can be increased not only by investing in infrastructure and airplanes, but also by cooperating with one another in win-win situations.

- The major forms of international cooperation that exist in the aviation industry are airline partnerships and alliances, codeshare, city pairs, fifth-freedom air routes, and other forms of cooperation. Due to the continuing growth of industrial output in emerging economies, which will result in increasing needs for effective air services, these forms of cooperation will continue to develop in the long term.

- Airlines are facing new challenges and opportunities as they move into emerging markets that have deep social and cultural traditions, compelling them to deal with numerous non-aviation considerations in their strategic planning. Some issues are technical, but social aspects are often a factor, and simple technical approaches may fail if they fail to address all the social/cultural issues. In the coming years, airlines will need to deal with numerous issues to which they might have only paid lip service to in the past.

- Three big issues that will be facing the international aviation industry over the next decade and more are shifts in industry leadership and strategic alliances as networks expand to cover emerging-economy markets; changes in passenger attitudes and values related to flying; and the transition of the aviation industry workforce from a monoculture to one of diversity.

- In the future, the international aviation industry will be increasingly pushed to become a true social enterprise. Today's empowered customers are much more discerning than ever before, and any serious mishandling of social issues could bring disastrous results, not only to the operating companies, but also to the affected regional economies. Companies are increasingly discussing social and political issues and options and accounting for political risks as an important element of profitability.

- As the world aircraft fleet grows, the demand for more pilots and technicians will increase in parallel to meet the needs of airlines and passengers. It is forecast that over the next 20 years, more than a million such professionals will need to be trained to the highest levels. IATA has predicted a shortage of aviation professionals as emerging economies expand.

- CEOs in the aviation industry need to consider re-examining their current corporate culture that was founded on the basis of the traditional Industrialization model. They need to foster the development and implementation of a new type of culture that will be conducive to socio-cultural integration and will focus more on building social capital.

- The effect of developing social capital in the global airline industry will have two main impacts. At the market level, through emotionalizing airline brands, a new culture will help build and enhance customer loyalty and engagement in new markets. Internally, social capital development will help attract and retain local talent and build teams focused on pursuing a higher business purpose.

REFERENCES

[1]   Canton, J. (2015). Future smart: *Managing the game-changing trends that will transform your world.* Boston: Da Carpo Press.

[2]   Rachman, G. (2017). *Easternization: Asia's rise and America's decline from Obama to Trump and Beyond,* Kindle Edition.

[3]   https://aci.aero/news/2018/09/20/aci-world-publishes-annual-world-airport-traffic-report/.

[4]   http://www.aci.aero/News/Releases/Most-Recent/2018/04/09/ACI-World-releases-preliminary-2017-world-airport-traffic-rankings--Passenger-traffic-Indian-and-Chinese-airports-major-contributors-to-growth---Air-cargo-volumes-surge-at-major-hubs-as-trade-wars-threaten-.

[5]   European Commission (2016, 2017). *Annual Analysis related to the EU air transport market,* p. 31.

[6]   *"World's largest airlines by fleet size".* Retrieved from https://www.worldatlas.com/articles/worlds-largest-airlines-by-fleet-size.html.

[7]   https://www.nasa.gov/feature/goddard/2017/new-night-lights-maps-open-up-possible-real-time-applications.

[8]   ICAO: *Aviation benefits* 2017, p. 16.

[9]   Wikipedia: *Megalopolis,* 2018.

[10] Khanna, P. (2016). "How megacities are changing the map of the world", Ted Talk, Vancouver, Canada.

[11] Wikipedia: Megalopolis, 2018.

[12] PWC (2016). *Five megatrends and their implications for global defense & security.* p. 12.

[13] Airbus. *Global market forecast: Growing horizons 2017–2036.* p. 18.

[14] Airbus (2014). *Flying on demand: Global market forecast 2014–2033.*

[15] Chang, H.-J., Gershman, J. (2017). *"Kicking away the ladder: The 'real' history of free trade".* Retrieved from http://ips-dc.org. Institute for Policy Studies.

[16] IATA. *Future of the airline industry 2035.* p. 25.

[17] *"Brussels warns US on protectionism"* (2009). Dw-world.de, 2009-01-30. Retrieved 16 October 2017.

[18] CAPA Centre for Aviation (2018). *"Aviation open skies: Protectionism, conflicts of interest, and out-dated ideas"*

[19] Rachman, G. (2017). *Easternization: Asia's rise and America's decline from Obama to Trump and Beyond,* Kindle Edition: Location 329.

[20] Rachman, G. (2017). *Easternization: Asia's rise and America's decline from Obama to Trump and Beyond,* Kindle Edition: Location 4393.

[21] *"Trade and the crisis: Protect or recover".* www.imf.org. Retrieved 16 October 2017.

[22] RBC GAM Investment Strategy Committee (2018). *The global investment outlook,* p. 23.

[23] *"New business models for a new global landscape",* https://www.bcg.com/en-ca/publications/2017/globalization-new-business-models-global-landscape.aspx.

[24] ICAO (2017). *Aviation benefits,* p. 40.

[25]   Naisbitt, D., Naisbitt, J., Brahm, L. (2017). *Creating megatrends: The Belt and Road.* China Industry & Commerce Association Press.

[26]   Naisbitt, D., Naisbitt, J. Brahm, L., p. 13.

[27]   (Autumn 2017). *"Life after Brexit: Global Britain, free trade, and the new protectionism—Tom Switzer talks to Daniel Hannan",* Policy 33(1).

[28]   ICAO (2017). *Aviation benefits* 2017, pp. 39–40.

[29]   https://aviationbenefits.org/economic-growth/value-to-the-economy/.

[30]   ICAO (2017). *Aviation benefits* 2017, p. 14.

[31]   Boeing. *Current Market Outlook* 2014–2033, p. 3.

[32]   Boeing. *Current Market Outlook* 2014–2033, p. 15.

[33]   Franklin Templeton Investments (2017); *"2018 global investment outlook: Reflections on growing economies and fading stimulus".* Franklin Resources, Inc., p. 14.

[34]   World Bank (2013). *Capital for the future: Saving and investment in an interdependent world,* p. 20.

[35]   World Bank (2013). *Capital for the future,* p. 6.

[36]   World Bank (2013). *Capital for the future,* p. 7.

[37]   World Bank (2013). *Capital for the future,* p. 4.

[38]   World Bank (2013); *Capital for the future,* p. 6.

[39]   Franklin Templeton Investments (2017). *"2018 global investment outlook: Reflections on growing economies and fading stimulus".* Franklin Resources, Inc., p. 9.

[40]   World Bank (2013). *Capital for the future,* p. 22.

[41]   World Bank (2013). *Capital for the future,* p. 5.

[42]   European Commission (2016, 2017). *Annual Analysis related to the EU air transport market,* p. 25.

[43]   Airbus. *Global market forecast: Growing horizons 2017–2036,* p. 7.

[44]   Lee, E., Copeland, A., and Morphet, H. (2015). *"Is GDP growth still a reliable indicator for future air travel demand?"* Connectivity and Growth: Issues and Challenges for Airport Investment, PWC, p. 11.

[45]   European Commission (2016, 2017). *Annual analysis related to the EU air transport market,* p. 26.

[46]   World Bank (2018). *The changing wealth of nations 2018: Building a sustainable future,* pp. 38–40.

[47]   World Bank (2018). *The changing wealth of nations 2018: Building a sustainable future,* p. 43.

[48]   World Bank (2018). *The changing wealth of nations 2018: Building a sustainable future,* pp. 15–16.

[49]   Airbus. *Global market forecast: Growing horizons 2017–2036,* p. 15.

[50]   World Bank (2013). *Capital for the future,* p. 30.

[51]   World Bank (2018). *The changing wealth of nations 2018,* p. xiii.

[52]   Franklin Templeton Investments (2017). *"2018 global investment outlook: Reflections on growing economies and fading stimulus",* p. 9.

[53]   Airbus. *Global market forecast: Growing horizons 2017–2036,* p. 24.

[54]   World Bank (2013). *Capital for the future,* p. 73.

[55]   World Bank (2018. *The changing wealth of nations 2018,* p. 14.

[56]   European Commission (2016, 2017). *Annual analysis related to the EU air transport market,* p. 8.

57 European Commission (2016, 2017). *Annual analysis related to the EU air transport market*, p. 27.

58 World Bank (2013). *Capital for the future*, p. 3.

59 World Bank (2013). *Capital for the future*, p. 79.

60 European Commission (2016, 2017). *Annual analysis related to the EU air transport market*, p. 27.

61 Boeing. *Current Market Outlook 2014–2033*, p. 16.

62 World Bank (2018). *The changing wealth of nations 2018*, p. 5.

63 ICAO. *Aviation benefits 2017*, pp. 20–22.

64 ICAO. *Aviation benefits 2017*, p. 22.

65 Airbus. *Global market forecast: Growing horizons 2017–2036*, p. 29

66 ICAO. *Aviation benefits 2017*, p. 21.

67 European Commission, (2016, 2017). *Annual analysis related to the EU air transport market*, p. 31.

68 ICAO. *Aviation benefits 2017*, pp. 20–22.

69 ICAO. *Aviation benefits 2017*, p. 22.

70 Bottini, C., and Morphet, H. (2015). *"Air connectivity: Why it matters and how to support growth"*, Connectivity and Growth: Issues and Challenges for Airport Investment, www.pwc.com/capital-projectsandinfrastructure, p. 21.

71 Airbus. *Global market forecast: Growing horizons 2017–2036*, p. 54.

72 Airbus. *Global market forecast: Growing horizons 2017–2036*, p. 60.

73 Airbus. *Global market forecast: Growing horizons 2017–2036*, p. 68.

74 Airbus. *Global market forecast: Growing horizons 2017–2036*, p. 70.

75 Airbus. *Global market forecast: Growing horizons 2017–2036*, pp. 75–97.

76 ICAO. *Aviation benefits 2017*, p. 6.

77 World Bank (2018). *Capital for the future*, p. 46.

78 Szirmai, A. (2012). *"Industrialisation as an engine of growth in developing countries, 1950–2005"*, Structural Change and Economic Dynamics 23: 406–420.

79 ICAO. *Aviation benefits 2017*, pp. 23–24.

80 European Commission (2016, 2017). *Annual analysis related to the EU air transport market*, p. 76.

81 http://www.airport-world.com/news/aci-news/6601-aci-figures-reveal-the-world-s-busiest-passenger-and-cargo-airports.html.

82 Airbus. *Global market forecast: Growing horizons 2017–2036*, p. 101.

83 World Bank (2013). *Capital for the future*, p. 49.

84 Morphet, H., and Copeland, A. (2015). *"Converting emerging market growth into investment opportunities"*, Connectivity and Growth: Issues and Challenges for Airport Investment, www.pwc.com/capitalprojectsandinfrastructure.

85 ICAO (2013). *Worldwide Air Transport Conference*, ATConf/6-WP/20.

86 http://blog.flydealfare.com/code-share-agreements-meaning-types-benefits/.

87 ICAO: *Aviation benefits 2017*, p. 46.

88 Spelfogel, M. (2016). *"The best fifth-freedom routes from North America to book with points"*, https://thepointsguy.com/2016/09/best-fifth-freedom-routes-from-north-america/.

89 European Commission (2016, 2017). *Annual analysis related to the EU air transport market*, p. 90.

90 Canton, J. (2015). *Future smart: Managing the game-changing trends that will transform your world.* Boston: Da Carpo Press, p. 50.

91 European Commission (2016, 2017). *Annual analysis related to the EU air transport market*, p. 16.

92 Canton, J. (2015). *Future smart: Managing the game-changing trends that will transform your world.* Boston: Da Carpo Press, p. 53.

93 https://www.youtube.com/watch?v=ZFb01yTR9bA&feature=share.

94 Canton, J. (2015). *Future smart: Managing the game-changing trends that will transform your world.* Boston: Da Carpo Press, p. 54.

95 Canton, J. (2015). *Future smart: Managing the game-changing trends that will transform your world.* Boston: Da Carpo Press, p. 49.

96 *"New business models for a new global landscape"*, https://www.bcg.com/en-ca/publications/2017/globalization-new-business-models-global-landscape.aspx.

97 IATA. *Future of the airline industry 2036*, p. 36.

98 European Commission. (2016, 2017). *Annual analysis related to the EU air transport market*, p. 16.

99 Airbus. *Global market forecast: Growing horizons 2017–2036*, p. 113.

100 Airbus. *Global market forecast: Growing horizons 2017–2036*, p. 113.

101 Canton, J. (2015). *Future smart: Managing the game-changing trends that will transform your world.* Boston: Da Carpo Press, p. 50.

102 Canton, J. (2015). *Future smart: Managing the game-changing trends that will transform your world.* Boston: Da Carpo Press, pp. 55-56.

103 Wahl, C. (2011). *Global passenger airline market: Five megatrends and their implications for talent management*, Egon Zehnder International.

4
RAPID URBANIZATION

INTRODUCTION

Over the past 40 years, the rate of migration from rural to urban areas has tripled world-wide. The primary drivers of this megatrend have been increased economic development and industrialization, which are known to compel humans to migrate from rural areas to cities in search of employment and economic prosperity. This phenomenon has been occurring more in developing countries, as opposed to the established economic powers, as the global economic power shift from West to East continues. This trend is influenced by changing population dynamics and migration patterns and will have wide-reaching impacts on urban planning, including the design, location, and scale of airports. There are four areas in particular where rapid urbanization will be in play:

- Urban planning (e.g., land availability/scarcity).
- Sociological changes (e.g., education, crime).
- Mobility of people, goods and services (e.g., changing transport needs).
- Connectivity among urban centers (e.g., new/ modified transport networks).

The above four sub-trends are each expected to have significant direct and indirect impacts on global aviation over the next two decades. This chapter will address each one of these sub-trends separately, both in a general sense and also in the way that it is expected to impact the global aviation industry.

The rapid urbanization in many developing countries over the past half-century seems to have been accompanied by excessively high population concentrations in very large cities. This continues to bring about exponential growth in connectedness, and this chapter will tie in aviation as well as the systemic cohesion of a number of the megatrends discussed in other sections of this book, including climate change, changing demographics, innovative technology, West to East economic power shift, and global connectedness, all of which are linked to urbanization.

In a sense, increased urbanization could be seen as a great thing for aviation by bringing more people closer to airports and cities and becoming the socio-economic driver for people wanting to travel by air (both domestically and internationally) for leisure and/or business purposes. However, other modes of transport, particularly high-speed rail, may create unforeseen competition in this market as point-to-point travel and accessibility becomes even more critical. Driverless vehicles and an increased focus on environmental responsibility and change could pose additional challenges for the aviation industry in the context of urbanization. The need for change in fuel sources will undoubtedly play a key role in aviation sustainability and continued ease of connectivity.

Urban and Rural – What They Really Mean

Before delving into this megatrend in detail, it is important to have a clear understanding of the terms "urban", "rural", and "urbanization". "Urbanization" commonly refers to the population shift from rural to urban areas, or "the gradual increase in the proportion of people living in urban areas", and the ways in which each society adapts to the change.[1] It is the predominant process by which towns and cities are formed and become larger as more people begin living and working in central areas.[2] It is predicted that by 2050, about 64% of the developing world and 86% of the developed world will be urbanized.[3] This is equivalent to approximately 3 billion urban dwellers by 2050, the vast majority of whom will live in Africa and Asia.[4] Notably, the United Nations has also recently projected that nearly all global population growth from 2017 to 2030 will be absorbed by cities, meaning about 1.1 billion new urban dwellers over those 13 years.[5]

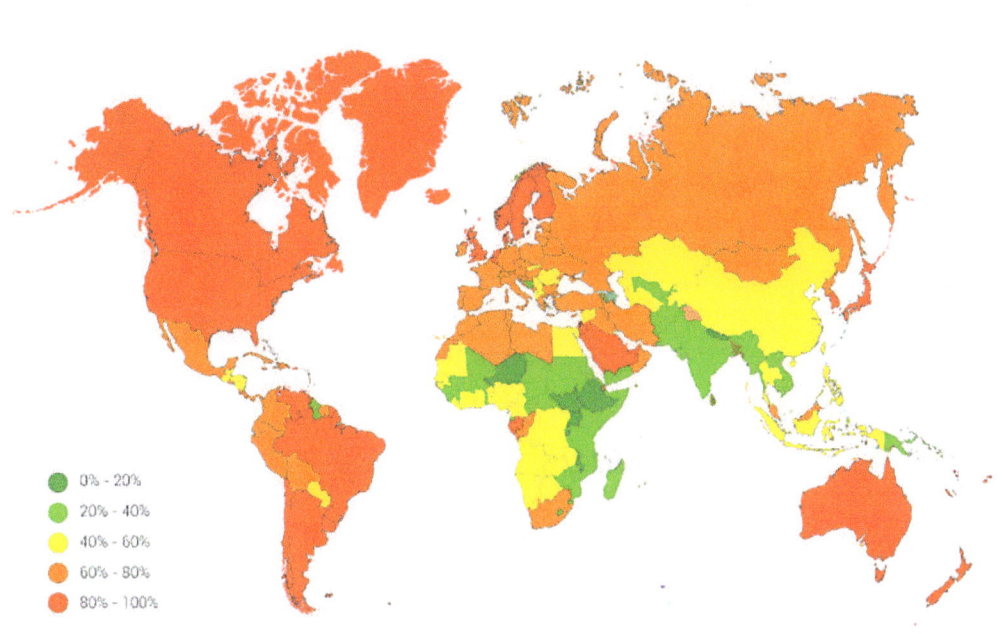

Figure 4-1   Extent of global urbanization, 2014.[6]

Although somewhat dated, Figure 4-1 displays the level of global urbanization in 2014. However, this should be considered as indicative only, given that huge parts of countries or continents (e.g., Australia and North America) are not urbanized at all because they are relatively sparsely populated. The intent is presumably to indicate that even for some countries or continents which are vast, most people in these countries or continents live in urban areas. Today, the most urbanized regions include North America (with 82% of its population living in urban areas in 2018), Latin America and the Caribbean (81%), Europe (74%), and Oceania (68%). This is hardly a major revelation in particular for North America and Australia, given their geographical landscapes. The meaning and implications of this and related factors will be addressed throughout this chapter.

To better understand this concept (or indeed reality) there is a need to further define "urban" versus "rural". An entry in Wikipedia defines an *urban area* as "...an *area* where many people live and work close together". The *population density* is higher than in the surrounding area, and *buildings* are close together. Urban is the *opposite* of *rural*, where *farms* and *nature* co-exist. Urban areas are usually *cities* and *towns*. Most of the work available in urban areas is *factory* and *office* work. *Agricultural* work is rare in urban settings because buildings are close together and there is no space for farmland.

In the future, it is expected that urban areas will be redefined into spaces where people will congregate more than ever before; these areas will increasingly become "eco-cities" in themselves, almost entirely internally sustainable, with little outside influence. Connectivity, mobility, and accessibility will be the key principles of this new urban life. People from many races and religions will mix and enjoy parklands, walking trails, and waterway scenery. The need to focus more on environmental initiatives will transform some cities to some extent into "green spaces". People will be able to work but also to enjoy the surroundings of a more peaceful and less stressful setting than in traditional urban cities. Singapore and some other cities are already leading the way in this respect.

Shopping will continue to evolve, with a strong online market (particularly for supermarket goods), but this will never take away the joys of face-to-face shopping in bricks-and-mortar stores, particularly for hard goods and products. Hospitality will continue to thrive as cities become areas of interest for visitors, with many traditional landmarks expected to be restored to their former glory days. There may also be different urban area definitions for each country. The definitions mostly depend on how populated a country is and whether the definition shows the true degree of *urbanization in* the country. For example, in Poland, an urban area is defined as any place that has the status of a town, whereas in China it is any district, city, or town with a population density higher than 1,500 people per square kilometer. The urban population definition for *Canadian* and *Scandinavian* countries depends on population density. In other words, if there is a house every 200 meters, the area is classified as urban.

In the end, the specific definition of "urban" is not that important when one looks at the possible implications for aviation. Clearly, a larger and denser population is likely to create more demand for air travel. However, numbers alone are not the only factor. People want good connectivity between urban centers within the region/country as well as for international travel. For example, instead of flying from one country into Bangkok to get to Koh Samui in Thailand (for a vacation), the demand in the future is going to be, "I really want to go there directly and not through another airport". This is already beginning to happen right now, but will become much more important for the air transport system in the future. The introduction of long-range aircraft will also lead to "hub busting", where places like Dubai will be bypassed to some extent unless they can maintain the attraction to stop there.

The term "rural" is defined in Wikipedia as "... areas which are not *towns* or *cities*". They are often *farming* or agricultural areas. These areas are sometimes called "the country" or "the countryside". People who live "in the country" often live in small *villages*, but they might also live somewhere with no other houses nearby.

For the aviation industry as a whole, it can be reasonably assumed that people in urban areas will travel by air more than those residing in rural areas. The actual numbers of people as a target group, together with business conducted specifically within cities, will greatly contribute to this need. The demographic and modality changes in these areas provide the aviation industry with opportunities, particularly when blended with spending habit information that could be used at airports.

One of the problems with sparsely populated rural areas is the difficulty for people to find jobs because industry tends to locate in or around urban areas where it has better and less expensive access to both suppliers and customers. This partially explains why there has been a global trend for people (i.e., workers) to move from rural to urban areas. Along with better access to employment, higher salaries and benefits are normally available in urban areas. Other reasons include opportunities for more social contact, better network connectivity, more accessible transportation options, better housing, and access to a broader range of cultural and recreational activities.

The reality is that large cities (particularly in developing countries) are growing, and more people are moving to these areas and making them home. There are a number of reasons for this, which are predominantly based on the *needs* and *wants* of individuals. Many people living in cities (i.e., urban areas) like to go to rural areas to relax. They go there for *recreation*, often for their *holidays*, or just to smell clean air. As long as they can get there and back in a reasonable time frame, without traffic congestion or other such delays, they are content.

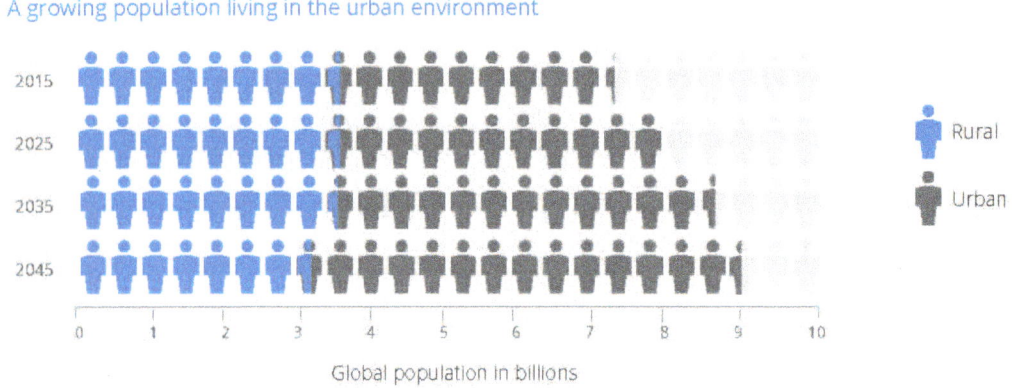

A growing population living in the urban environment

Global population in billions

Figure 4-2   Global urban population growth forecast: 2015–2045 (UN).

Urbanization is directly related to a range of disciplines, including *geography, sociology, economics, urban planning,* and *public health*. The process and meaning of urbanization have also been closely linked to a number of phenomena: *modernization, industrialization,* and the sociological process of *rationalization*. The following paragraphs briefly explain the meaning of these terms in the context of urbanization.

Modernization can be defined as the process of adapting something to modern needs or habits (i.e., keeping up with the times).[7]

Industrialization is the development of industries in a country or region on a wide scale.[8] It marks a change to the marketplace and the ways in which goods and services are provided in a newer world. Having a true understanding of where things come from seems to be a new frontier for the millennials of today (See Chapter 5, *Demographic Changes and Trends* for a detailed discussion about the impact of millennials.)

Rationalization **(in a sociological context)** is defined as the action of attempting to explain or justify behavior or an attitude with logical reasons, even if these are not appropriate.[9] In other words, rationalization is a way to make something seem acceptable or tolerable. It is a way of saying that the methods used to attain a goal are justified by the goal itself (i.e., the end justifies the means).

In short, urbanization is all about the various dynamics of change that come into play when large numbers of people across the globe decide to move from rural to urban areas.

Figure 4-3   Urbanization in action (stock photo).

There is no doubt that the rapid urbanization that has been taking place and is expected to accelerate over the next couple of decades will have a significant impact on the need for, and location of, aviation facilities and services over the next 15 to 20 years. Various aspects of this phenomenon of population shift and its continuing impact on global aviation are discussed in some detail in Chapter 3 – *Global Economic Power Shift - West to East* and Chapter 5 – *Demographic Changes and Trends*.

URBAN PLANNING

Traditionally, cities were founded based on their geographical location and their potential to enable the trade of goods. Being located near waterways (i.e., seaports and rivers) was a key consideration, particularly to provide regional and then global trade of products where practicable. Cities were configured as a base with a central business district where activities such as trading in goods, factory work, and office work (i.e., banking and finance) were conducted. People who could afford to would live outside of cities in order to enjoy the more open spaces and fresh air of suburban life. Many inner cities housed poorer communities where people lived close to their workplace, mostly in high-density communal settings.

The Mega-City

The trend of the future in urban planning is the development of "cities within cities", known as mega-cities or megalopolises (See Chapter 3 on the *Global Economic Power Shift -West to East* for a detailed discussion of megalopolises). Countries such as China, India, and a number of countries in Africa are considered growth regions for the construction of mega-cities. The populations of the first two countries are growing at such a rate that a more sophisticated urban planning approach is now needed to replace traditional planning approaches.

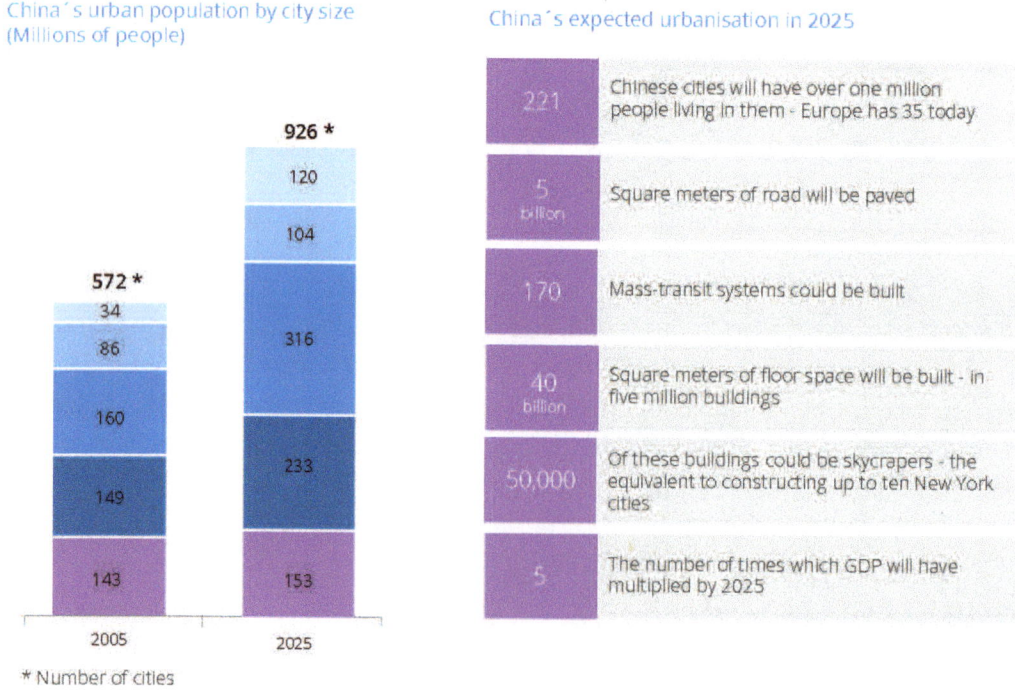

China´s urban population by city size
(Millions of people)

	2005	2025
	572 *	926 *
	34	120
	86	104
	160	316
	149	233
	143	153

* Number of cities

China´s expected urbanisation in 2025

221	Chinese cities will have over one million people living in them - Europe has 35 today
5 billion	Square meters of road will be paved
170	Mass-transit systems could be built
40 billion	Square meters of floor space will be built - in five million buildings
50,000	Of these buildings could be skycrapers - the equivalent to constructing up to ten New York cities
5	The number of times which GDP will have multiplied by 2025

Figure 4-4   Forecast urban growth in China, 2005 to 2025 (McKinsey Global Institute).

These new "cities within cities" are more likely to take the form of replicating each other in terms of services provided rather than a clear division of business functionality. In other words, rather than complementing each other, each one will likely duplicate such functional districts as finance, government, and information technology, although this may vary. The "true" hub of these new megalopolises is likely to revolve around the hospitality and entertainment industries, but could also include parks, gardens, walkways, and waterways. An environmental focus of rest, relaxation, and recreation will likely replace the hustle and bustle of the traditional central business district.

These new cities will most likely involve an inter-connected hub-and-spoke system. Eco-cities will be created outside of the existing city environment and will replicate what already exists in those larger cities. An eco-city is a city built based on the principles of living within its means, environmentally speaking. The ultimate goal of many eco-cities is to eliminate all carbon waste, to produce energy entirely through renewable resources, and to merge the city harmoniously with the natural environment. In addition, eco-cities are intended to stimulate economic growth, reduce poverty, and foster higher population densities, thereby obtaining higher efficiency and improving health.[10] As urban sprawl occurs, the need for efficient access to all services, including airports, will arise.

Figure 4-5   An eco-city of the future (stock photo).

The mega-city concept is likely to localize employment, education, and essential services while providing for work-life balance. For example, the need to visit a more traditional city center will be less because more people will work closer to home. The impact of climate change and the reliance on alternative energy sources will also become more critical. These will include advanced, environmentally friendly solar power systems and/or the clean energy of nuclear power. The possible impacts of climate change on cities and airports are discussed in detail in Chapter 2 on *Climate Change*.

Concerns about how to deal with the rising sea levels that will affect cities located near seas and oceans will need to be addressed in future urban planning exercises. For the same reason, airports that abut the sea will also be at a higher risk than now, and airport development plans will need to reflect this. For example, Sydney Airport in Australia is exposed to rising sea levels, and not just the airport itself could be at risk, but also the associated connecting services to the airport. The connecting services are notably critical and must be considered given the need for accessibility to and from the airport precinct. New York City area airports, as well as many other airports where land has been reclaimed, will also be subject to greater threats from rising sea levels.

The traditional air transport system model may need to be re-adjusted to move future airports away from coastal areas to minimize risks. This may indeed become a key future development consideration, together with connectivity within the hub-and-spoke system of mega-cities.

The 30-Minute City

According to some urban planners, new approaches to city planning will mean that by the middle of this century, citizens should be able to reach their place of work within 30 minutes using public transport or "active" options such as walking or bicycling. For example, in Sydney, Australia, this is the current goal for the future. The New South Wales (NSW) government (in 2018) released its *Future Transport Strategy 2056* report, which suggests that investment will increasingly be focused on "three cities" built around the Western Sydney Airport (currently under construction), Greater Parramatta (to the west of Sydney), and the existing Sydney Central Business District (CBD). The strategy report states that, "Customers will be able to travel to one of these cities or to their nearest center within 30 minutes of where they live by public or active transport. This will give people better access to jobs, education, and essential services."[11]

The report suggests that getting people out of their cars and using sustainable transport will reduce congestion and emissions and improve air quality and well-being. "Well-planned centers and cities will enable a shift from private cars to public transport and active transport modes such as walking and cycling", the strategy says. "In Sydney, the key to this will be the delivery of three 30-minute cities, supported by reliable 'turn up and go' mass transit services." Active transport for short trips will be encouraged by providing safe and accessible footpaths with seating and shade. There will also be better pedestrian crossings, lower traffic speeds, separated cycling paths, and secure bicycle storage. The report notes that by 2056, New South Wales (NSW) will have more than 12 million residents. Sydney (5.07 million in 2017) will be a global city similar in size to London or New York.

This transport strategy was released alongside the *State Infrastructure Strategy* and the *Greater Sydney Region Plan*. The connection between all three strategies and plans is well understood and acknowledged throughout the various government departments. Of course, the current Sydney Airport and the second Sydney Airport are also considered in these plans. This represents a clear vision for the State of NSW for the next 10, 20, 30, and 40 years. The strategy strives to ensure that communities can expect to have jobs in their local area, shorter travel times, and a better environment that ensures ample open and green spaces. It is the stated government policy to improve public transport and roads so that, by 2056, 70% of people live within 30 minutes of where they work or study.

As for airports in general, they need to work much more closely with government sectors responsible for transport, infrastructure, and the city (or cities) within a region as a whole. Up until now, many airports have taken a more local community focus and have only broadly connected with the tourism and travel sectors. Taking a broader community network perspective on airports will put more focus on connecting regions to cities. In the future, a "hub-and-spoke" or even a "spider's web" network of services in regional areas will provide better connections among communities and improved access to regional cities and centers. This will capitalize on the key role that regional cities will play as centers for employment and services such as retail, health, education, and cultural activities.

The megalopolis of the future will consist of a number of mini-cities very closely located to a traditional main city, where people can access the jobs, education, and services they need within 30 minutes by public or active transport. According to urban planning experts, this is expected to become the norm. This may take time to evolve in some countries, but there is evidence that this is already happening in countries like South Korea and in the city of Hong Kong to a lesser extent.

The Aerotropolis

When considering urban planning, one also needs to take into account the "aerotropolis" concept. The term "aerotropolis" was coined fairly recently by John Kasarda, a professor of business at the University of North Carolina in the U.S., but the concept has been around for a while.[12]

The aerotropolis is an urban environment that is anchored by an airport. Over the past few years, the concept has been rapidly gaining popularity around the globe. Although most cities have historically been planned around a river, a port, or an intersection of trade, the aerotropolis is a city designed around an airport. Traditional planners are still grappling with exactly how (and whether) this concept will work in a practical sense. The issue centers on whether a city really can be planned around an airport, or whether airports will always be predominantly designed around a city, as in the past. A key factor is to ensure that the economy within the aerotropolis is truly sustainable. Indeed, this may be a case of ensuring that the model is somehow tested locally before being planned, i.e., it may work in some countries but not in others. It may also depend on the "products" of the airport and their significance, for example, cargo services.

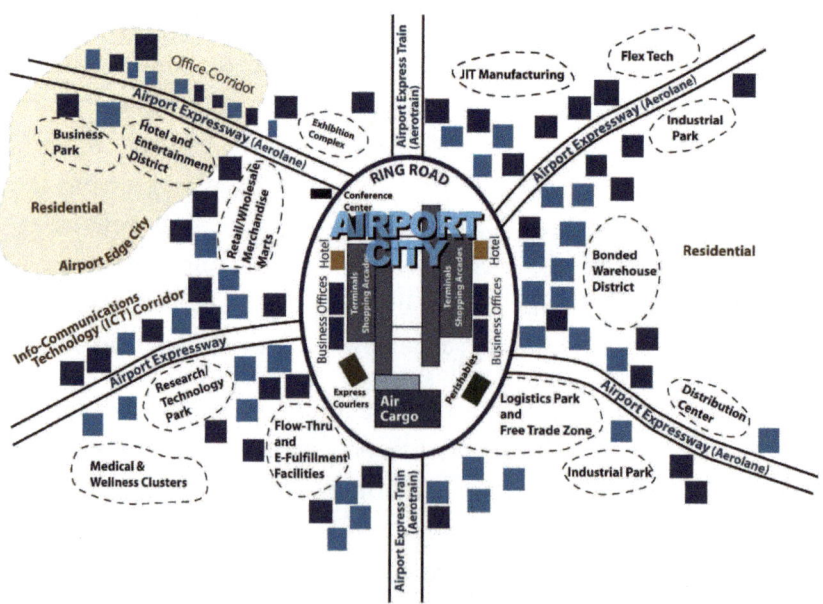

Figure 4-6   The aerotropolis concept (John D. Kasarda, aerotropolis.com).

An example of a functioning aerotropolis has been the development of Dubai since the mid-1980s. That city was built in parallel with the launch of the airline carrier *Emirates* when it took over *Gulf Air*'s routes. That development of Dubai and *Emirates* epitomizes the growth of an aerotropolis, whereby an air carrier and an airport have anchored the entire city's push toward prosperity and global recognition.[13]

Beyond the Middle East, *Malaysia Airports Holdings Berhad* recently released its *Indulge Till You Fly* campaign, which locates *Kuala Lumpur International Airport* at the core of an entire lifestyle, both physically and metaphorically. The campaign depicts an entire lifestyle precinct consisting of leisure facilities and community amenities that are centered on the airport as the keystone piece of infrastructure. However, this is not considered the same as a full-fledged "aerotropolis".

Many other cities have also been advancing towards aerotropolis status, including Amsterdam-Schiphol, Paris-Charles de Gaulle, Incheon, Memphis, and Zhengzhou airports, all of which have received considerable media attention.[14] The model is likewise generating growing interest among airport operators and local governments in how to better leverage their airports to attract business investment, generate revenues, boost trade, and create well-paying jobs.

According to a senior director at the consulting firm *Woods Bagot*, "Global cities are becoming increasingly multi-nodal as they experience continued population growth. For example, most cities have a financial district, a legal district, and a government district. It is becoming increasingly common for cities to also develop a precinct that aggregates IT industry organizations. For example, San Francisco's SoMa (South of Market area, which is a relatively large neighborhood located just south of Market Street), or London's Tech City, or New York's Silicon Alley in recent years." It is natural and expected that the airport can also become a nodal point to an existing city environment, especially considering its critical role as a domestic and international transport interchange.[15] Indeed, sociologist Mark Gottdiener, author of *Life in the Air: Surviving the New Culture of Air Travel*, states that, "...airports have taken over some of the important functions of historic downtowns as new urban centers".[16]

Airports of the future are unlikely to be able to exist as isolated entities. Instead, they will increasingly need to rely on the investment and support of non-aeronautical activities to augment their core aeronautical enterprises. Airports, unlike cities, exploit their unique position as a transport hub to generate growth, attract venture capital investment, target equity investors, stimulate further infrastructure development, and promote shopping, trading, business, leisure, recreation, and entertainment activities.

Yet this does not mean that airports are unable to sustain their own healthy set of support services such as hotels and other concessionaires. It simply means that airports will not replace the cities that they service as a destination. As such, airports need to offer services that augment and complement the city, instead of duplicating the city's existing services. For example, *China Southern Airport City* in the city of Guangzhou uses the airport to stimulate other urban functions, but does not presume to replace the city itself.

The trend for decades was to isolate airports from communities because of environmental issues such as noise and fuel exposure from aircraft. The idea was to keep people away from them and introduce safety buffer zones in terms of land use in the vicinity of airports. However, a shift is occurring in making airports more accessible to the public, even to the extent of creating livable and sustainable communities around them.

Figure 4-7   The community airport concept (Beijing New Airport Terminal. Rendering by Methanoia © Zaha Hadid Architects).

Instead of anchoring a city on the airport, a strong argument exists to locate the airport as an ancillary function to the city. The airport would continue to serve its primary function as the regional and international gateway to the city in which it exists. In this way, the airport can manifest itself as the major transport node of the city.

A key aspect of this for airports to consider is how they can gain positive leverage off such initiatives. For many existing airports, this is almost a process of reverse engineering. For example, the airport owner may be able to control only what falls within the airport boundaries. The land adjacent to the airport is likely to be government-owned or privately held by other entities. Historically, governments (in the main) have attempted to preserve land in the vicinity of airports for environmental reasons. However, over the years, such factors as: opportunities for revenue generation, urban creep, and land re-zoning have meant that communities have been drawn closer to airports because the land has generally been cheaper to acquire.

More recently, other opportunities have arisen through beneficial commercial use of the land surrounding airports. This strategy is based on providing goods and services that directly benefit the airport stakeholders and working community, travelers, and the broader public. They can also indirectly benefit airport stakeholders by providing localized and accessible goods and/or services. The traditional airport master plan approach, which is normally boundary-constrained, needs to be broadened to take into account the bigger picture. It needs to recognize the economic value of the airport as part of a larger transport system, rather than as a mere travel port to get from one location to another.

Private ownership of airports, as opposed to government ownership, also creates an interesting dynamic. It is considered far easier for a fully government-controlled airport to look beyond just the physical legal boundary of the airport and plan accordingly. The private airport operator will generally do all in its power to create non-aeronautical revenue opportunities within its area of control. However, outside this area, the airport operator needs to actively lobby the government to identify joint opportunities that will provide benefits to the broader public and the community as a whole.

Circular Runways

Another interesting planning concept goes back to the early 1960's. This idea was originally depicted as having a circular runway within a city. Also referred to as "endless runways", variations of this concept still exist today.

In the 1990s, the US Navy tested the idea of implementing circular runways, using an automobile test track as an analog for their concept airport. Tests documented by *Popular Science* even earlier, in 1966, reveal that the Navy conducted trials in 1964 and 1965 using an 8,400-foot-wide banked track.[17] Although pilots at first said they felt like they were "flying into a hole," they soon became enthusiasts for the design. Several successful landings and takeoffs were made during the tests, with claims that it would work for both civilian and military purposes. However, the idea never materialized.

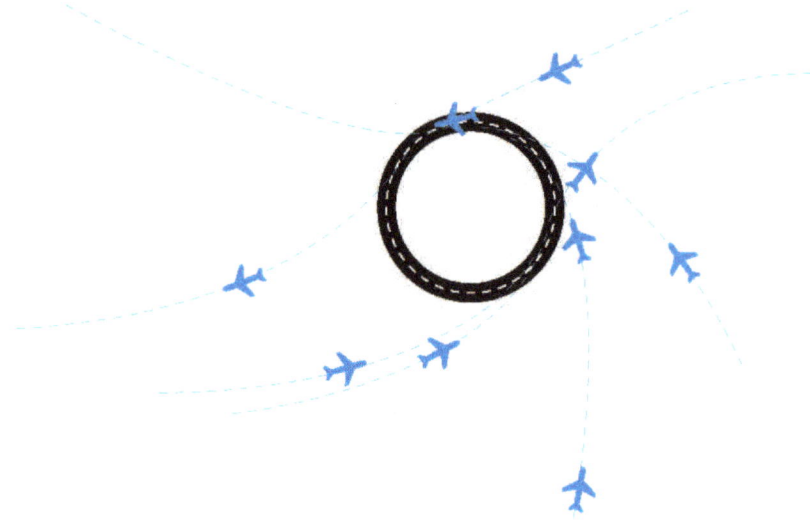

Figure 4-8 The circular runway concept (ASI schematic, 2019).

More recently, the Endless Runway Project, funded by the European Commission, has used simulations to test this radical plan. The project is currently led by a team of Dutch scientists from the *Netherlands Aerospace Centre (NLR)*. Despite its promise for efficiency, there has been little testing of this type of design. However, it could one day offer a way to stay a step ahead of booming travel demands.

The reason why there is continued interest in the endless runway concept is that it could significantly increase airport capacity. The capacity of an airport with an Endless Runway is at least similar to that of a conventional airport with four runways, whereas the length of the circular runway is comparable to three standard runways. This makes it possible to use the runway with several aircraft simultaneously. According to the Endless Runway team, the system works independently of wind direction, unlike a straight runway. This means that planes could take off and land from any direction.

Skeptics about this type of model believe that aviation safety could be compromised and that there are also issues relating to air navigation and airspace management, together with international and regulatory standards for aerodrome design and layout. Nevertheless, although this concept might have seemed like pure science fiction a few years ago, with the rapid pace of technological advances in all areas, it is quite possible that a system like this could be developed and in use somewhere within the next 15 to 20 years.

SOCIOLOGICAL CHANGES

Urban sociology is the sociological study of life and human interaction in metropolitan areas. It is a normative discipline of sociology seeking to study the structures, environmental processes, changes, and problems of an urban area and by doing so, to provide inputs for urban planning and policy-making. In other words, it is the sociological study of cities and their role in the development of society. Like most areas of sociology, urban sociologists use statistical analysis, observation, social theory, interviews, and other methods to study a range of topics, including migration and demographic trends, economics, poverty, race relations, and economic trends.[18]

Urban Transportation and Commuting

With high population growth rates in large cities forecast for both developed and developing countries, there are concerns that unless proactive strategies are implemented, these same cities could be "choked" out of practical existence. For example, road transportation systems, such as those present in Jakarta, Indonesia and Bangkok, Thailand, are currently unable to cope adequately with the huge numbers of vehicles operating there. This phenomenon has worsened in these cities over the past 10 years, and it appears that reactive measures relating to expanded rail systems have come too late. The same could be stated for parts of India and Pakistan and among other emerging countries.

Basically, more people want to live closer to where they work. They want more time to do the things that give them a balanced life, and commuting long hours to and from work is not one of them. High-rise apartment living, on various socio-economic scales, has become the norm. Infrastructure is changing to support this type of high-density population growth in areas where land is scarce. Transport nodes are increasingly being situated at community facilities such as shopping centers, entertainment centers, sporting fields, parks, and gardens as a way to connect better with people living in high-density accommodation.

In Australia, for example, Melbourne (declared the World's Most Livable City 2011 to 2017)[19] is still a car-dependent city, with three of four commuters traveling by private vehicle. That works out to about 1.5 million people on the roads every day. Census data reveals that just 19.6% of commuters in Melbourne travel by public transport, while only 5.5% cycle or walk to work.[20] The city is so spread out that for some commuters, the car is their only realistic option. The Australian Bureau of Statistics analysis of commutes from all suburbs, including the booming outer west and outer southeast areas of Melbourne, found that, on average, workers in northern and western satellite communities traveled the farthest (i.e., daily one-way journeys of more than 30 km). Not surprisingly, central Melbourne residents had the shortest commute, traveling an average 5.13 km to their place of work. Given growth within the city and urban sprawl, there is a need for the government to keep investing in roads, public transport, and bike paths to give commuters optimal choices as to how they travel. The main reason for emphasizing these points is to highlight the need to analyze why people do what they do early on and not fall into the same trap as other cities like Jakarta and Bangkok, where they are now trying to dig their way out of the problems of horrendous traffic congestion. It is not so much the distance traveled as the time spent traveling which is made progressively worse by increased traffic on the roads. Unless the basic transport infrastructure of cities is well planned and then implemented successfully, the congestion burden on airports may only increase, and lack of efficient accessibility will continue to exacerbate the situation unless adequately addressed.

Figure 4-9　Urban transportation congestion in the developing world (stock photo).

When commuting and travel habits are better understood, particularly in relation to urban habits and social needs/ behaviors, then a clearer picture can evolve, which can then translate into possible best-fit remedies. It is important for the aviation industry to understand the environmental realities and dependencies of urban transportation on the product of air travel.

Environmental and Social Issues

As previously mentioned regarding eco-cities, there is expected to be more emphasis on retaining the beauty of the natural environment within highly populated urban areas, or at least replicating that beauty in some form. For example, Singapore (promoted as the "City in a Garden") has transformed itself, with the inner city now described as a green heart that has grown in the center of the city, spreading into the minds of its people and up the walls of its buildings. Part of the ongoing changes related to this approach involves educating students from an early age on the importance of environmental awareness, protection, and advocacy.

Singapore's mission is to preserve the achievements it has made while ensuring the future of its vision as an environmental champion. It believes that its citizens are entrusted with a stewardship that makes caring for common spaces second nature. Other ongoing projects include urban planning and zoning, as well as policy changes and public awareness campaigns focused on a smaller carbon footprint and zero waste, among other goals.[21]

Figure 4-10   Singapore "City in a Garden" (stock photo).

This approach will become more commonplace in the future and will no doubt extend into other areas like airports. For example, Singapore Changi Airport's Butterfly Garden is designed as a tropical butterfly habitat with a profusion of flowering plants, lush greenery, and a 6-meter grotto-waterfall. The garden contains approximately 1,000 tropical butter-flies from as many as 40 species during the different seasons of the year.

Over the years, air travel has gone through dramatic changes, from innovative technolog-ical advancements to advanced security requirements. Aviation is associated with several environmental, economic, and social benefits, but it also has its detrimental effects. Flying is known to be a contributor to air pollution, greenhouse gas emissions, climate change, and noise pollution. The result has been increasing pressure on the aviation industry (among many other industries) to play its part in reducing carbon emissions and other environmen-tal pollutants (See Chapter 2 on *Climate Change* for a detailed discussion of these issues).

The basic environmental, economic, and social impacts of air travel need to be looked at. One initiative relating to aircraft is the transition to fuel-efficient systems. More fuel-efficient aircraft will decrease greenhouse gas emissions and reduce costs for both airlines and customers in the long run. This transition to fuel-efficient aviation can be achieved success-fully in the next 50 years if implemented through conscientious planning and execution.

Airports have an important role to play in this transition. Leading the way is Dallas-Fort Worth (DFW) International Airport, which is the first carbon-neutral airport in the Americas. Using the slogan, "Balance", it is committed to harmony between aviation and the environment. By switching to renewable energy and implementing programs to use less carbon-based fuel, DFW has dramatically reduced its carbon footprint and its energy costs. DFW also goes to the extent of publishing an annual Environmental, Social, and Governance Report. For example, in 2017, DFW transitioned its bus fleet to renewable natural gas captured from local landfills, implemented dynamic glass technology in the terminals, and recycled nearly 279,000 tons of construction material.[22]

The social benefits of air travel are many. Air travel has given all nations the freedom to travel. It connects people, countries, and cultures, providing access to global markets. Air travel connects developing countries to developed countries and serves as a means of inclusion for remote areas in which air travel is the only means of transportation.

Extensive global travel also stimulates economies around the world. According to the International Air Transport Association (IATA), tourism using air transport creates some 34.5 million direct and indirect jobs worldwide. In addition, the aviation industry supports 56.6 million jobs globally. The international food and hospitality industries are substan-tially impacted by the level of tourism. From employment as a pilot, to the owner of a store whose livelihood is contingent on the level of tourism, the aviation industry is a major contributor to economic activity in many locations.

The UK Ministry of Defense issued a report in 2014 that, among other things, detailed the many sociological impacts of transportation in general and aviation in particular. The following paragraphs draw from the findings of that research.[23]

Various other aspects of Environmental and Social Issues are discussed in more detail both in Chapter 2, on *Climate Change*, and Chapter 3, on the *Economic Power Shift – West to East*.

Population Growth Impacts

With 70% of the global population likely to live in cities by 2045, urbanization will be a particularly important theme in developing countries. Urbanization is likely to enhance economic and social development, but without mitigation measures, may also lead to pressure on infrastructure (and the environment) that could contribute to social tensions within the urban population. Urbanization and the effects of climate change are likely to result in an increase in the magnitude of humanitarian crises, particularly since the majority of urban areas will almost certainly be either on, or near, the seacoast, making these cities vulnerable to flooding.

Demand for resources of all kinds is likely to increase as the world's population rises to around nine billion by 2050. While the demand for food is expected to grow, some countries are likely to experience significant declines in agricultural productivity. Water shortages are likely to be particularly acute in many areas, exacerbated by increasing demand and climate change. In the foreseeable future, coal and hydrocarbons are likely to remain the most important sources of energy, with renewable and nuclear energy likely to make an increasing contribution.

A growing population will demand more food and water, increasing the strain on the environment. As centers of population cluster in vulnerable areas such as coastal regions, the consequences of adverse weather are highly likely to be felt more keenly. By 2050, climate change is likely to have more noticeable effects. Without mitigation, rising sea levels will increase the risk of coastal flooding, particularly in regions affected by tropical cyclones. Droughts and heatwaves are also likely to increase in intensity, duration, and frequency. Some of these events could precipitate natural disasters that, because of the interdependencies enabled by globalization, may have consequences far beyond the site where the disaster occurs.

The *2018 Revision of World Urbanization Prospects* produced by the Population Division of the UN Department of Economic and Social Affairs (UN DESA) notes that future increases in the size of the world's urban population are expected to be highly concentrated in just a few countries. Together, India, China, and Nigeria will account for 35% of the projected growth of the world's urban population between 2018 and 2050. By 2050, it is projected that India will have added 416 million urban dwellers, China 255 million, and Nigeria 189 million. The urban population of the world has grown rapidly, from 751 million in 1950 to 4.2 billion in 2018. Asia, despite its relatively lower level of urbanization, is home to 54% of the world's urban population, followed by Europe and Africa with 13% each.[24]

Today, the most urbanized regions include North America (with 82% of its population living in urban areas in 2018), Latin America and the Caribbean (81%), Europe (74%), and Oceania (68%). The level of urbanization in Asia is now approaching 50%. In contrast, Africa remains mostly rural, with 43% of its population living in urban areas.

Chapter 3, *Global Economic Power Shift – West to East*, and Chapter 5, *Demographic Changes and Trends*, both contain more detailed discussion and analysis related to population growth.

Impacts of Technology

New materials, manufacturing techniques, and power systems, as well as advances in information technology, are likely to open up new opportunities for automated transport and generate step changes in speed and efficiency. Driverless transport is likely to be widespread by 2045, providing greater independence for the elderly and impaired. Unmanned systems could play a key role in the mass delivery of people and goods. New developments in supersonic flight could make sub-orbital space transport a commercial reality in the next 30 years.

Developments in technology are also likely to lead to significant improvements in medicine and health, such as the potential for developing cures for some cancers. Advances in diagnostic techniques and the development of artificial organs and mind-controlled prosthetic limbs mean that we are highly likely to live longer and have more productive lives. However, new challenges to good health will almost certainly emerge. Rising physical inactivity and unhealthy diets are likely to contribute to an obesity epidemic and a rise in non-communicable diseases. Anti-microbial-resistant pathogens could become more widespread, making post-operative infections potentially lethal.

Revolutionary advances in how we acquire, store, and analyze information, together with dramatic increases in computer processing power, are likely to give us the ability to predict accurately a wide range of phenomena, from crime hot-spots to the effects of climate change. The advancement of "Smart Cities" will also come to the fore in terms of law and order and energy efficiency. As everyday objects become increasingly connected to the Internet, this vast network of sensors is likely to gather data on more aspects of our lives and the environment, making it hard for anyone to go "off the grid".

Increasing computing power, growing access to the Internet and "Big Data" (i.e., voluminous and complex) are also likely to have a transformative effect on education, with an increasing blurring between online and offline learning. Education levels will almost certainly continue to rise across the globe, for both sexes. At the same time, educational institutions could face a series of major challenges, including facilitating smoother transitions from education to work and encouraging lifelong learning to ensure that the workforce can adapt to a changing job market. These pressures may force educational institutions to provide more informal, distance, and personalized learning. There is likely to be growing emphasis on transferability and constant upgrading of qualifications, as well as a shift towards more personalized forms of assessment that use a range of technologies to trace the paths of individual learners.

Robots or "unmanned systems"—machines capable of carrying out complex tasks without directly involving a human operator—are likely to be as commonplace as computers are today. Unmanned systems are increasingly likely to replace people in the workplace, carrying out tasks with increased effectiveness and efficiency, while reducing risk to humans. As robots become more lifelike, perhaps capable of appearing to express emotion, interactions with people are likely to become more complicated.

Chapter 6, on *Innovative Technological Change*, and Chapter 7, on *Global Connectedness*, both look at the various impacts of technology in more detail.

Figure 4-11   Information robot at Munich Airport (stock photo).

Demographic and Social Shifts

The proportion of older workers in the global labor force is likely to increase over the next 30 or so years, with a possible corresponding decrease in opportunities for younger people. Flexible working practices are likely to become more widespread, with people employed on shorter-term contracts and an increase in the number working remotely. Workers will probably have less predictable income and increasing economic insecurity. By 2040, there is likely to be greater equality between men and women in the job market, particularly in developed countries. In part, this may be driven by a global shift away from manual labor towards a more knowledge-based economy.

Livable communities promote social inclusion and the health and well-being of the people who live in them. Transport is vital to mobility. It can transform the public domain, activate centers, and unlock new commercial and housing developments, renewing existing neighborhoods and spaces. Aviation has a role to play and cannot afford to be left behind given the increasing reliance on air travel.

The best places to live take time and strong partnerships to develop and flourish. Integrated land use and transport planning can activate public spaces, corridors, and networks and positively impact the delivery of health, education, and local government services. Transport can improve the livability and character of places across each state, achieve wider benefits from investment, and encourage more desirable patterns of development.

The sociological aspect of migration is another key area of change given that the world has become smaller in terms of global accessibility. Many non-Asian countries have experienced significantly increased levels of Asian migration, a trend that is expected to continue at a great rate. China in particular is extending itself to all parts of the world and is investing more heavily in major infrastructure projects on a global scale.

It is expected that traditional Western ways will go through a stage of adaptation and that many previous barriers to acceptance of a diversity of races and religions will generally be diminished. Asians in particular have a history of successfully developing higher-density living models, which are now increasingly taking into account alternative energy generation sources and environmental sustainability. However, the area that some Asian countries have historically been struggling with is that of effective and efficient transportation.

It is also important to consider that, with sociological change, some cities have experienced population decline in recent years. Most of these are located in the low birth-rate countries of Asia and Europe, where overall population sizes are stagnant or declining. Economic contraction and natural disasters have also contributed to population losses in some cities. A few cities in Japan and the Republic of Korea (for example, Nagasaki and Busan respectively) experienced population declines between 2000 and 2018. Several cities in the countries of Eastern Europe, such as Poland, Romania, the Russian Federation, and Ukraine, have lost population since 2000 as well. In addition to low birth rates, outward emigration has contributed to lower population size in some of these cities. Globally, fewer cities are projected to see their populations decline between now and 2030, compared with what occurred during the first two decades of this century.

The rural population of the world has grown slowly since 1950 and is expected to reach its peak in a few years. The global rural population is now close to 3.4 billion and is expected to rise slightly and then decline to 3.1 billion by 2050. Africa and Asia are home to nearly 90% of the world's rural population in 2018. India has the largest rural population (893 million), followed by China (578 million).

Tokyo is the world's largest city with an agglomeration of 37 million inhabitants, followed by New Delhi with 29 million, Shanghai with 26 million, and Mexico City and São Paulo, each with around 22 million inhabitants. Today, Cairo, Mumbai, Beijing, and Dhaka all have close to 20 million inhabitants. By 2020, Tokyo's population is projected to begin to decline, but Delhi is projected to continue growing and to become the most populous city in the world around 2028.

By 2030, the world is projected to have 43 mega-cities with more than 10 million inhabitants each, most of them in developing regions. However, some of the fastest-growing urban agglomerations are cities with fewer than 1 million inhabitants, many of them located in Asia and Africa. While one in eight people currently live in 33 mega-cities worldwide, close to half the world's urban dwellers reside in much smaller settlements with fewer than 500,000 inhabitants.

As the world continues to urbanize, sustainable development depends increasingly on the successful management of urban growth, especially in low-income and lower-middle-income countries where the pace of urbanization is projected to be the fastest. Many countries will face challenges in meeting the needs of their growing urban populations, including housing, transportation, energy systems, and other infrastructure, as well as employment and basic services such as education and health care. Integrated policies to improve the lives of both urban and rural dwellers are needed that build on the existing economic, social, and environmental ties between urban and rural areas.

Chapter 3, *Global Economic Power Shift – West to East,* and Chapter 5, *Demographic Changes and Trends,* both contain more detailed discussion and analysis related to sociological changes brought about by population growth and economic and demographic shifts.

Impacts on Aviation

The aviation industry needs to keep abreast of changes brought about by sociological changes stemming from rapid urbanization. These could range from various forms of airport ownership to the vast array of related aviation services that will be required by a growing and changing society.

Max Hirsh, a professor at the University of Hong Kong and a leading expert on airports and urban infrastructure, has conducted research over a number of years and has noticed that airports have been getting bigger and busier and are filled with a wider range of travelers.[25] These observations led to the two main questions that define his work to this day. First, how does the "other half" (or non-elite passengers) fly, and how can airports be redesigned for them? Second, with the number of passengers projected to double in the next two decades, how can we coordinate airport expansion plans with the broader development goals of the cities they serve?

Some insights that come out of Hirsh's research include his point that the needs and desires of air passengers are changing quickly, but that the designs of airports have remained pretty much the same. Over the last decade, travelers have become much more diverse in age, income, cultural background, and trip purpose. Along with that diversity, different types of passengers are emerging, each of which has highly specialized transport needs, taste preferences, and spending habits. As an example, just three of these passenger-types would be: middle-class travelers from China, retirees traveling for pleasure, and business travelers who fly on budget airlines; three very unique groups, each with very different expectations and requirements.

Cultural differences also account for unique practices and expectations that impact aviation facilities and services. For example, many Chinese passengers travel with their tea and are frustrated when they cannot find any boiling water. Asian tourists assume that airports will offer small, packaged gifts—usually food—that they can purchase at the last minute for their friends and relatives. Travelers from a wide variety of countries in the Middle East, Africa, and the Caribbean are often greeted by very large welcoming parties who gather at the airport ahead of time. Awareness of such different expectations is crucial for planning a friendly and efficient terminal. These insights are also an excellent way to identify new sources of revenue.

Chapter 3, *Global Economic Power Shift – West to East*, contains a more detailed discussion of the growing need for the aviation industry to create more specialized products and services that cater specifically to an increasingly diverse and sophisticated traveling population.

Other Impacts

If unchallenged, corruption is likely to continue to exacerbate global inequality and conflict. Consistent attempts to curtail corrupt practices are likely to be made by national governments, international governing institutions, the private sector, and non-state actors. Technology is highly likely to play a significant role in both enabling and combatting corruption.

State-backed currencies will almost certainly still be the dominant form of money, although alternative crypto-currencies are likely to expand, constituting the main shift in the financial landscape. Criminal transactions may increasingly be made using alternative currencies, with a possible growth in the anonymous raising and transferring of funds by terrorist groups. Governments could have less influence over alternative currencies and, as a result, may be less able to shape the global financial system or raise revenues through taxation.

A single international currency is improbable, with the US dollar likely to remain the most important global currency into the future. China is likely to allow greater financial liberalization, contributing to its possible overtaking of the US in terms of gross domestic product (GDP) in the foreseeable future. This is likely to contribute to some erosion of the pre-eminence of the US dollar as the dominant global reserve currency. Increased globalization could also make transmission of financial shocks more widespread.

To make sure that the benefits of urbanization are fully shared and inclusive, policies to manage urban growth need to ensure access to infrastructure and social services for all. The focus needs to be on the urban poor and other vulnerable groups to ensure them housing, education, health care, job creation, and a safe environment.

MOBILITY OF PEOPLE, GOODS, AND SERVICES

As the urban population shifts worldwide, and as technology connects more and more people around the globe, the way in which people access goods and services is rapidly changing. This section looks at the main dynamics of this new mobility of people, goods, and services.

The sense of mobility can mean a number of things, including how easy, efficient, or effective it is to move things including people and goods, and mobility in the way that people conduct themselves in terms of using technology to access goods and services.

Leveraging Mobile Technology

The concept of "Mobility as a Service" (MaaS) is relatively new. MaaS describes a shift away from personally owned modes of transportation and towards mobility solutions that are consumed as a service. This is enabled by combining transportation services from public and private transportation providers through a unified gateway that creates and manages the trip, which users can pay for with a single account. Users can pay per trip or through a monthly fee for a limited distance. The key concept behind MaaS is to offer travelers mobility solutions based on their travel needs.

MaaS is a service model that enables customers to plan and pay for their journeys using a range of services using a single customer interface. It has the potential to enable customers to access integrated, easy-to-understand journeys in a broad market of transport services. In a fully operational service model, the MaaS provider would sell seamless multimodal journeys, offer convenient payment methods such as subscription services, and communicate directly with customers.[26] In the future, mobility will be customer-focused, data-enabled, and dynamic. Personal mobility packages will bundle traditional "modes" with technology platforms and new service offerings like on-demand car share, rideshare, and smart parking. In Australia, for example, the NSW Government is already testing an early form of this technology on the Northern Beaches, where carparks at some bus stops are activated by Opal travel cards.

In the not too distant future, personal smartphones will be the gateway for each journey. Customers will make travel choices based on factors that matter most to them—service frequency, cost, comfort, and/or travel time.

"Big Data" relative to the transport network will continue to be analyzed to reveal travel patterns and trends. This information, in addition to new technologies, will enable service providers to connect with customers, know their preferences, and tailor service offerings in real time. Investments in network information management systems will enable real-time, innovative regional service responses that better use networks. For example, customers will access innovative, on-demand services that aggregate similar trips quickly for more efficient travel, connecting them with a range of public, private, and community transport providers that offer a mix of services. Seamless experiences will also connect customers to facilities for active transport such as walking routes, bike paths, and bike rental services.

When fully implemented, MaaS will decrease costs to the user, improve the utilization of MaaS transit providers, reduce city congestion as more users adopt MaaS as a main source of transit, and reduce emissions as more users rely on public transit components or electric, autonomous vehicles in a MaaS network.[27] MaaS is also known as "Transportation as a Service" (TaaS), and vice versa.

Airports are now progressively moving to connect with the TaaS system as point-to-point service provision becomes more important to the consumer in terms of the total journey experience. A person traveling by air is not only interested in the air travel component (and related airport/airline information), but the whole journey, from one location (be it home, leisure, or business) to another specific location, to complete that particular travel event. In the past, many of the transportation sectors (e.g., rail and bus) have been working in isolation and only dealing with scheduled information under their direct control, without realizing the broader benefits to the traveling public of a more connected and efficiently run multi-modal network.

Figure 4-12 Transportation-as-a-Service: TaaS posters (ASI rendering from TaaS graphic).

Metropolitan and Regional Centers

Metropolitan and regional centers are the places where the majority of jobs and services are located, as well as attractions like shops, restaurants and parks. Roads through and around these centers serve an important purpose by enabling people to travel to and from the center and move around easily within it. They also help to make places attractive to visit and frequent, thus allowing local economies to develop and thrive.

Successful centers include attractive spaces where people can meet and enjoy their leisure time, such as town squares, libraries and community centers, parks, sportsgrounds, and waterways. Being able to access these spaces easily by active or public transport encourages people to be more physically active and increases social interactions in communities.

Changing Airport Business Models

Parking fees are a very important component of the airport business model. For example, in North America, they typically account for at least one-quarter of total operating revenues. In recent years, that model has been undermined by a major shift in how passengers travel to and from an airport. As ride-hailing apps like Uber increase in popularity and as self-driving vehicles become a reality, fewer and fewer people are paying to park (or rent) a car at the airport, a fact that will have significant impact on airport revenues over the next decade or two until adjustments to the model are made. Although the concept of changes to car parking is a global issue, the potential impact at airports is more localized in North America and Europe at present.

As car parking declines, some airports will begin to transform into intermodal transport centers, integrated with long-distance railway networks. That concept is well established at European hubs like *Amsterdam, Paris*, and *Frankfurt*, as well as *Shanghai* and Japan in Asia. Thinking ahead, some airports are even evaluating the potential synergy effects that could be derived by linking air terminals with high-speed bullet trains or even hyperloops. A hyperloop[28] is a proposed mode of *passenger* and/or *freight transportation*. The term was first used to describe an open-source *vactrain* design released by a joint team from *Tesla* and *SpaceX*. Drawing heavily from *Robert Goddard*'s vactrain, a hyperloop is a sealed tube or system of tubes through which a pod may travel free of air resistance or friction, conveying people or objects at high speed while being very efficient.

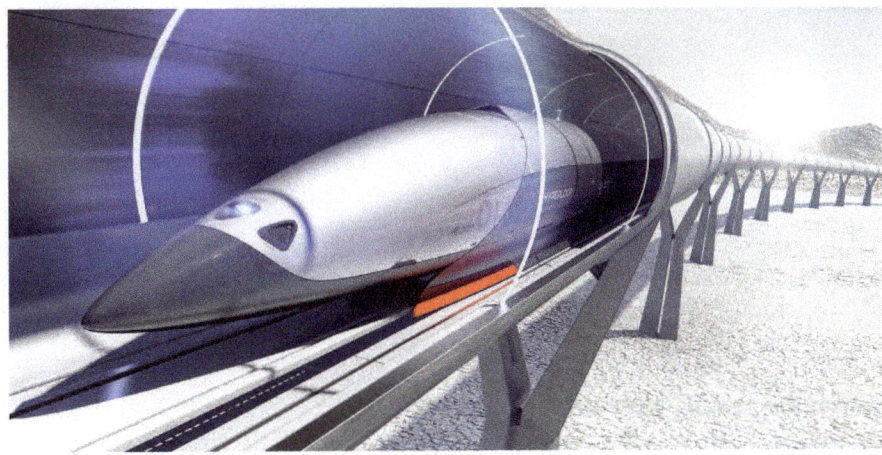

Figure 4-13 The hyperloop concept (stock image).

Overall, this transition to integrated intermodal systems will be good for airports, which can grow their catchment areas through high-speed connections on the ground. However, opposition from airlines, along with poor coordination between air and land transport ministries, will likely create hurdles. The solution may lie in new forms of cooperative governance, cross-investment, and profit-sharing across various transport sectors.

Whether they like it or not, airport operators will need to identify new types of non-aeronautical activities to compensate for the resulting decline in parking revenues. They will also need to redevelop existing parking lots, garages, and car rental facilities for alternative, income-generating purposes. This paradigm shift in ground access is a daunting thought for many airport executives, and understandably so. Nevertheless, it also presents a tremendous opportunity to rethink the types of facilities and services that airports offer to their customers on the landside. It will give them a chance to redesign the airport access roads and internal road networks. It will be interesting to see how airport planners and architects will engage with that challenge.

Aviation Investment and Financing Issues

To help address investment concerns and optimize airport benefits for cities and regions, UN Habitat and International Civil Aviation Organization (ICAO) have embarked on a new partnership. The United Nations Human Settlements Program *(UN Habitat)* works towards socially, economically, and environmentally sustainable human settlements at both urban and rural levels. ICAO, on the other hand, works with Member States to promote, support, and achieve safe, efficient, secure, economically sustainable, and environmentally responsible civil aviation operations through requisite policies and regulations.

The purpose of the ICAO UN Habitat Sustainable Airport Project is to visually examine, identify, and promote synergistic relations between airport development and urban development. The aim is to identify global good practices and principles in urban and regional planning and management around air transport infrastructure that can be applied to help sustainably develop air transport infrastructure and services.[29] The project will achieve this by assessing and documenting the trends and impacts of airports and air traffic on land use around the airport and along the airport-city corridor by tracking land use changes and conformity to urban planning regulations, and their related socio-economic and ecological impacts on sustainable urban development.

UN Habitat and ICAO, together with diverse partnerships among stakeholders, will develop conceptual, methodological, and operational spatial and visualization frameworks that will highlight the role of airport systems (infrastructure and services). They will look at urban development beyond the city, along the airport-city axis, and on the airport-rural area trajectory and study the synergistic relations that could support sustainable development.

Some aviation industry facts (ICAO, 2016):

- Aviation today contributes 2.7 trillion dollars annually to global GDP.

- The industry supports the employment of 62 million people worldwide.

- Aircraft carry over 10 million people to their global destinations on over 100,000 flights per day.

- Aviation worldwide transports more than one-third of global cargo and freight by value.

Despite these significant contributions to socio-economic development globally, only 2.6% of worldwide funding for infrastructure and services is channeled for aviation and/or airport development needs. This situation exists in spite of the fact that airports function as the integral and essential access point gateways to aviation's global network of societies and economies. They represent a city or region's stepping stone to the world's cultures, ideas, and markets. This critical role of airports will be greatly undermined unless they are designed with full consideration of the needs of local citizens, businesses, and governments. A poorly designed and managed airport that is not compliant with international standards adopted by ICAO can both pose safety risks and be a barrier to the economic development of a State.

UN Habitat works towards achieving socially, economically, and environmentally sustainable human settlements. The initiative targeted four African cities: Addis Ababa, Ekurhuleni, Johannesburg, and Nairobi, where a total of five airports are located. The intent was to promote the important interconnections and interrelationships between airports and urban development under the common framework provided by the UN's Agenda 2030. The principle was, "Isn't it time your State considered maximizing how your airports serve your citizens and businesses?"

ICAO has stated that the socio-economic benefits of air connectivity can be maximized only when the many natural synergies between urbanization and aviation infrastructure development are fully leveraged. Sustainable development depends more and more on the successful management of urban growth, especially in low-income and lower-middle-income countries where the pace of urbanization is projected to be the fastest. Aviation is directly implicated in this.

Interestingly, on the theme of aviation infrastructure development, the 2018 ICAO World Aviation Forum (IWAF) in Brazil was focused on *Promoting Investment for Aviation Development*. Topics discussed included:

- The existing and potential future challenges in the aviation industry.

- The financing of quality aviation infrastructure and enhanced connectivity through integrated transport and urban planning.

- Aligning the priorities of the aviation sector in the global, regional, and national agendas in support of the ICAO *No Country Left Behind* initiative.

- Necessary resources for sustainable aviation development to drive economic growth.

Clearly, the future financing of aviation infrastructure will be a top priority in the coming years. The public and private sectors need to explore new approaches to investment and work together in partnership to provide the aviation infrastructure, support networks, and services that will be needed in the coming decades.

CONNECTIVITY OF URBAN CENTERS

In the future, more than ever, there will be a need to connect people to jobs, goods, and services in cities and regions around the world. For example, in Australia, the future vision for Greater Sydney as a metropolis of three cities will guide planning and investment decisions and will deliver to citizens such outcomes as fast, convenient, and reliable travel times to one of the three cities or to the nearest strategic center. As discussed earlier, the 30-minute city will be one where people can conveniently access jobs and services by public or active transport, seven days a week. This vision is based on research that indicates that if people are required to commute more than 90 minutes a day, their quality of life and the livability of their city is impacted negatively (See the *Urban Planning* section earlier in this chapter).

Figure 4-14   The future of urban connectivity (stock image).

Regional cities and centers will be connected to outlying towns and centers by a "hub-and-spoke" network. They will be centers for health, education, and justice services as well as access to employment opportunities and air transport connections. Towns and villages will offer employment and housing and will continue to be important in attracting domestic and international visitors and bringing job opportunities and economic benefits to rural communities.

Toronto Pearson Airport – A Case Study

An excellent example of how ground connectivity will be increasingly important over the next couple of decades and how it is being handled is the case of Pearson International Airport in Toronto, Canada.[30] Against the backdrop of a growing Ontario economy, a booming Greater Toronto Area population, and rising air passenger numbers, Toronto Pearson's Regional Transit and Passenger Processing Center is the key to unlocking the next era of growth for the airport and the region.

Situated in the most densely populated area of Canada's largest province, Ontario, Toronto Pearson is Canada's largest airport in terms of total passenger traffic and North America's second-largest airport in terms of international traffic. The airport is a vital engine of Canada's economy, helping facilitate international business, create jobs, and grow tourism. Passenger traffic at Toronto Pearson is forecast to nearly double over the next 20 years, and with this growth the airport's contribution to Canada's economy will only increase in parallel.

This level of growth also brings its share of challenges, and for the Greater Toronto Area (GTA), ground congestion has reached critical levels. To better connect travelers and residents on the ground and to help unlock the next stage of growth for the airport and for Southern Ontario, Toronto Pearson is working with world-class architects and planners, governments, and other stakeholders to build a Regional Transit and Passenger Processing Center. The Center will include rail, light rail transit, and bus service that will represent a significant leap forward in the way that people connect to the airport, to jobs, to each other, and to the world.

Drive times to Toronto Pearson are expected to rise by an average of 30% over the next 20 years, and hence there is a strong emphasis on better connecting the region on the ground. Toronto Pearson's Regional Transit and Passenger Processing Center will take advantage of the high concentration of travel demand generated by the airport and surrounding zone; provide an economically critical missing link in the regional transit system; connect people to economic opportunities in the Airport Economic Zone (AEZ); and provide a networked transit service to many of the region's most disadvantaged communities.

The concept is to better connect the region to itself and to the world, in the process further driving prosperity across the Greater Toronto Area, Ontario, and Canada at large. The Greater Toronto Airport Authority, along with stakeholder partners that span the aviation industry, governments, and the private sector, is committed to turning the challenges associated with growth into opportunities for a better-connected region. The general belief behind this project is that an airport can do more than simply see Canadians off on a journey or welcome them home. It is about providing people with better connections and ease of movement, whether on the ground or in the air.

Single-Hub Airports vs. Multi-Airports

Many of the world's largest cities have two or more major airports. Paris has four, Los Angeles five, London has six, and Tokyo three. There are also some densely populated urban regions, such as Germany's Ruhr and Japan's Kansai, that are served by several airports.

As mentioned by Max Hirsh, there are conflicting views about whether it makes sense to concentrate a city's air traffic at one hub, or to distribute it to airports located throughout the region.[31] Single-hub advocates argue that this concept keeps costs down for airlines, increases the number of possible flight connections, and limits aviation's adverse effects such as noise and air pollution to one location. Supporters of a multi-airport approach contend that it is a more equitable way to distribute both the positive and negative effects of aerial connectivity throughout a city. It also allows each airport to focus on what it does best. In advanced multiple-airport regions (MARs), airports concentrate on particular passenger types, such as people who are transferring between flights, business travelers who value time more than money, and budget tourists who do the opposite.

Elsewhere, individual airports may serve specific parts of a city or focus on a particular airline alliance. The world's largest airline by fleet size and revenue, American Airlines has been an industry staple since its formation in 1930. The company is headquartered in Fort Worth, Texas, and since its merger with US Airways in 2013, American Airlines operates nine domestic hub airports. Like American, Delta Airlines has been present in the U.S. airline industry for decades. It began carrying passengers in 1929 and has grown rapidly since then due to many airline mergers. Headquartered in Atlanta, Georgia, Delta operates 10 domestic hubs.

Whether with single-hub airports or multi-airports, it seems that the connectivity of air travel will follow an even more aligned path than that of rail, where what were simple connections in the past have become much more advanced and complex over time. As Figure 4-15 illustrates, it is the linking of the whole transportation network within countries that will increase in significance as the population grows, as the economy changes (and in most cases advances), and as people become more accessible to the world.

Figure 4-15 Example of a complex urban ground transportation network: Paris (stock image).

The Luton Direct Air-to-Rail Transit (DART) Project

As already mentioned, Hirsh is a noted fan of the multi-airports in one region approach. The main argument against it is that it reduces the number of flight connections, which is a valid point. On the other hand, if it were easy to transfer between airports, say, via a dedicated high-speed ground connection, then having to change airports would be less of an issue. Widespread implementation of this multi-airport concept connected by high-speed rail links is still far away, but it could start to happen in the next decade or two.

An example of this concept in action is developing in the United Kingdom. Work has already begun on a state-of-the-art 225 million UK pound automated shuttle between London Luton Airport and Luton Airport Parkway railway station. On track to be operational by 2021, the project will provide a journey time of less than four minutes from Luton Airport Parkway to the airport terminal, enabling access from central London to the departure terminal of the UK's fifth largest airport in 30 minutes by the fastest train.[32]

The Luton DART (as it has been called) will be a double-shuttle, fully automated people mover, capable of operating 24 hours a day, seven days a week. The 2.1 kilometer route will run between two purpose-built stations at Bartlett Square and the airport terminal, crossing a new gateway bridge over Airport Way. The DART system will not only benefit airport passengers, but will also support the city's ambitions to secure long-term economic growth and ensure that local people have access to high-quality employment opportunities. It is part of the ongoing transformation of the town under the 1.5 billion UK pound Luton Investment Framework.

The Luton DART will support ongoing growth to 18 million passengers per year by 2021 and is sure to provide a significantly enhanced passenger experience for years to come.

The Xiongan Project

This project in China is an example of how something may start with good intentions and then never seem to come to useful fruition. It is a cautionary tale of what can go wrong if a project is not carefully and logically planned. It is presented here, not to advocate such an approach, but rather to learn from it and ensure that such projects are not repeated.

The Xiongan project is located just outside a dusty village, a two-hour drive south of Beijing. Right now there is an empty lot there that supposedly will one day be one of Asia's largest railway stations. President Xi Jinping stated in 2017 that Xiongan will be a glittering new high-tech city teeming with leading-edge companies, research institutes, and world-class transportation. It was seen as becoming a connectivity model for China's future urban development—an alternative to congested streets, chronic air pollution and sprawl.[33] After Xi rolled out his vision for the new city, textile and plastics factories were closed by local authorities to make way for grand new avenues and state enterprise offices.

Investors who flocked there to buy property—an activity that was quickly banned—or open restaurants and shops to turn a dime on the president's pet project soon learned that not all developments in China move at warp speed. That has now left the local economy in a state of limbo and its inhabitants waiting for planners in Beijing to act.

What is happening in Xiongan may be a sign of things to come as the world's second-biggest economy moves toward its goal of becoming a technological leader. For that to happen, the government decided that local industry, such as the workshops of Guanlimahu Village near the planned station, must give way to more advanced industries like biotechnology and information technology.

"It should be no surprise if the Xiongan project harms the locals", says Derek Scissors, chief economist at the China Beige Book in Washington. "It was never intended to benefit them".

Construction of a high-speed rail line connecting Xiongan to Beijing started this year, and it should be operational by the end of 2020. That will cut the commute to Beijing to about 30 minutes. By 2035, Xiongan is seen as developing into a modern city that is green and intelligent, ending China's "big city malaise", according to its master plan. Whether that will happen as conceived still remains to be seen.

China's top-down development strategy has lifted hundreds of millions out of poverty over the past four decades, but it has often brushed aside the concerns of ordinary people. From the more than one million resettled to build the Three Gorges dam, to the citizens of Beijing or Shanghai evicted from their traditional neighborhoods to modernize those cities, national development has always been the priority.

The key aspect here is that urban development needs to be well conceived and planned, not just based on visionary concepts or whims. Connectivity, which comes with development on the ground, should not be built on the seemingly sole principle of "build it and they will come".

Examples of other urban developments that have seemingly gone wrong could include Astana in Kazakhstan and Naypyidaw in Myanmar. The flashy buildings of Astana rise up implausibly from the flat plains of oil-rich Kazakhstan to form a city stuck between a Soviet past and an aspirational future. The purpose-built city of Naypyidaw in Myanmar boasts 20-lane highways, golf courses, fast Wi-Fi, and reliable electricity. The only thing it does not seem to have is people. If a city is not well planned in the first place, then connectivity seems almost meaningless.

The New Experience in Travel and Technologies (NEXTT) Project

In 2017, global aviation bodies, the Airports Council International (ACI), and the International Air Transport Association (IATA) announced a joint vision initiative called New Experience in Travel and Technologies (NEXTT).[34] They made this move in light of the projected doubling of air travel demand by 2036 and the recognized need for new on-ground connectivity concepts to optimize the use of emerging technologies, processes, and design developments. NEXTT aims to help deliver this future by developing a common vision to enhance the on-ground transport experience, guide industry investments, and help governments improve the regulatory framework.

Specifically, NEXTT will investigate how passengers, cargo, baggage, and aircraft move through the complete travel journey, with a focus on change in three areas:

Off-airport activities: Explore the possibilities of transferring on-site processes off-site, such as security processing and baggage check and drop-off, to streamline the airport experience.

Advanced processing technology: Investigate how advanced processing technology, such as tracking and identification technology, automation, and robotics, can improve safety, security, the customer experience, and operational efficiency.

Interactive decision-making: Promote the better use of data, predictive modeling, and artificial intelligence to facilitate real-time decision-making, which is a key element in improving the passenger experience and optimizing operational efficiency.

IATA and ACI will work with their respective members and other associations, service providers, engineering firms, and manufacturers. Through a collaborative approach, NEXTT aims to align various visions for the future passenger and cargo journey. A number of key airports including Amsterdam Airport Schiphol, Bangalore International Airport, Dubai International, Heathrow Airport, and Shenzhen Airport (Group) Co., Ltd. are already actively involved in a number of projects that explore NEXTT concepts.

Air Connectivity

The International Civil Aviation Organization (ICAO) defines air connectivity as an indicator of a network's concentration and its ability to move passengers from their origin to their destination seamlessly.[35] Air connectivity is key to unlocking a country's economic growth potential, in part because it enables the country to attract business investment and human capital. An increase in air connectivity also spurs tourism, which is vital to the economic prosperity of many countries.

As stated by Morphet and Bottini,[36] by understanding how air connectivity is measured, how it has changed, how it relates to economic growth, and what drives it, key aviation stakeholders (i.e., states, airports, and airlines) can make strategic decisions on how to enable and unlock the air connectivity potential of a country.

Four main factors enable air connectivity: geography, airport infrastructure, airline models, and a country's regulatory and economic frameworks. These enablers all play an important role in ensuring that a country can cement or expand its global air network to enhance air connectivity.

Air connectivity is especially important to countries with isolated air-travel markets (such as islands and large geographical areas) where passengers have few viable alternatives to air travel. In addition, a country's geographical location can enhance its ability to develop a well-connected network. Examples include Singapore, Hong Kong, Incheon, the Middle Eastern hubs of Dubai, Abu Dhabi, and Doha, as well as the emerging Turkish hub of Istanbul, all of which have exploited their favorable position in the global air-travel network to build strong hubs with far-reaching spokes.

Airports provide the connectivity and access required for a modern economy, enabling businesses to capture overseas opportunities and facilitating the coming and going of tourists, all of which fuel economic growth. Transport infrastructure acts as a facilitator of growth by unlocking latent demand. Moreover, enhancement of transport infrastructure, combined with development of an extensive network, can decrease general travel costs for passengers and goods due to lower fares, shorter travel times, and more seamless connections.

A more detailed analysis of what is happening in emerging countries could also shed light on the importance of airport infrastructure for improving air connectivity and fostering economic growth. For instance, some countries, such as Indonesia, India, Brazil, and Turkey, have registered brisk growth in recent years (driven by increases in population and economic wealth). However, inadequacies in their current airport infrastructure are preventing them from fully capitalizing on their growth.

CONCLUSION AND SUMMARY

The first part of this closing section is a brief conclusion that contains some overall general remarks summarizing the essence of the foregoing discussion of the Rapid Urbanization megatrend and offering some general advice to managers about how best to cope with it. The second part of this section is a management summary that recaps in point form all the major subjects discussed earlier during the detailed analysis and discussion of the Rapid Urbanization megatrend. The points are presented with the perspective of aviation professionals and managers in mind. Essentially, each point in the Management Summary represents a key observation or conclusion that was made during the detailed analysis and discussion.

Conclusion

Part of the challenge facing policy-makers today is how to project and plan for the rapid changes occurring globally in terms of urbanization, particularly in relation to its effect on the air transport system. There is a significant role for governments to play (and perhaps they need to be the initiators), but invariably, one party in government may only have a short-term vision and plan. Given that their tenure may not be permanent, government leaders may show reluctance to spend money planning for the future when they may not necessarily be part of that future in a political sense.

In the same way, airports and airlines can be trapped in short- to medium-term strategic thinking that does not necessarily take into account longer-term projections well beyond just the immediate operation of the airport or airline itself. It is a matter of not only being business-aware, but also being socially and environmentally aware of the significant role that aviation and air transport play in connecting people to places.

Management Summary

Based on the foregoing discussion, there is no doubt that the Rapid Urbanization megatrend will have major impacts on the international aviation industry over the next 15 to 20 years and beyond. In many ways, adapting to this megatrend and implementing mitigation measures will have considerable impact on the way in which airlines, airports, and air navigation services will develop and operate their businesses, particularly during the next decade, as they continue to adjust to this new reality. Numerous significant conclusions and observations have been made during the course of the detailed analysis presented earlier in this chapter. The following are the important highlights that aviation managers at all levels will need to take into account when determining how best to deal with the Rapid Urbanization megatrend when preparing for the future.

General

- There is no doubt that the rapid urbanization that has been taking place and is expected to accelerate over the next couple of decades will have a significant impact on the need for, and location of, aviation facilities and services over the next 15 to 20 years and beyond.

- The United Nations has projected that by 2050, about 64% of the developing world and 86% of the developed world will be urbanized. That is equivalent to approximately 3 billion urban dwellers by 2050, many of whom will live in Africa and Asia.

- The United Nations has projected that nearly all global population growth from 2017 to 2030 will be absorbed by cities, resulting in about 1.1 billion new urban dwellers during that period.

- In the future, it is expected that urban areas will be redefined into spaces where people will congregate more than ever before; these areas will increasingly become "eco-cities" in themselves, almost entirely internally sustainable with little outside influence. Connectivity, mobility, and accessibility will be the key principles of this new urban life.

- The urban population of the world has grown rapidly, from 751 million in 1950 to 4.2 billion in 2018. Asia, despite its relatively lower level of urbanization, is home to 54% of the world's urban population, followed by Europe and Africa with 13% each.

- Today, the most urbanized regions include North America (with 82% of its population living in urban areas in 2018), Latin America and the Caribbean (81%), Europe (74%), and Oceania (68%).

- In 2018, one in eight people lived in 33 mega-cities worldwide, whereas another half of the world's urban dwellers resided in much smaller settlements with fewer than 500,000 inhabitants.

- The rural population of the world has grown slowly since 1950 and is expected to reach its peak in a few years. Africa and Asia were home to nearly 90% of the world's rural population in 2018. India had the largest rural population (893 million), followed by China (578 million).

Urban Planning Trends

- A more sophisticated urban planning approach is needed now to replace traditional planning approaches. As urban sprawl occurs, so will the need for efficient access to all services, including airports.

- The trend of the future in urban planning will be the development of "cities within cities", known as mega-cities or megalopolises. These will most likely involve an inter-connected hub-and-spoke transportation network system. They will consist of a number of mini-cities located near a traditional main city, where people can access the jobs, education, and services they need within 30 minutes by public or active transport.

- Eco-cities will be created outside the existing city environment and will replicate what already exists in those larger cities. An eco-city is one that is built and operated on the principles of living sustainably within its means in an environmental sense.

- Eco-airports will be created. The impact of climate change and reliance on alternative energy sources will also become more critical, together with aircraft fuel-efficiency systems and alternative fuel options.

- The traditional air transport system model may need to be re-adjusted to move future airports away from coastal areas to minimize the risks of rising sea levels. This may indeed become a key development consideration in the next 15 to 20 years.

- According to some urban planners, the new "30-minute city" approaches to city planning will mean that by the middle of this century, citizens should be able to reach their place of work within 30 minutes using public transport or "active" options such as walking or biking.

- There will be a need to better leverage airports to attract business investment, generate revenues, boost trade, and create well-paying jobs by optimizing commercial use of the land surrounding airports.

- Airports will need to work more closely with government sectors responsible for transport and infrastructure and with cities within a region. Until now, many airports have taken a more local community focus and have only broadly connected with the tourism and travel sectors. A broader community network perspective for airports will put more focus on connecting regions to cities.

- Airports of the future are unlikely to be able to exist as isolated entities. Instead, they will need to rely on continued investment and support to increase the level of non-aeronautical activities (and associated revenue) to augment their core aero-nautical enterprises.

- A shift is occurring that will result in making airports more accessible to the public, even to the extent of creating livable and sustainable communities around them.

- In the next 20 or more years, a number of urban planning concepts directly related to airports and their functional relationships to cities will come to the fore, including such concepts as the aerotropolis as a city designed around an airport and circular/ endless runways.

Sociological Factors

- The aviation industry needs to understand the environmental realities and dependencies of urban transportation on the product of air travel. When commuting and travel habits are better understood, particularly in relation to urban habits and social needs/ behaviors, then a clearer picture can evolve, which can then translate into possible best-fit remedies for the future.

- The aviation industry (among many other industries) is under increasing pressure to play its part in reducing carbon emissions and other environmental pollutants.

- According to IATA, tourism using air transport creates some 34.5 million direct and indirect jobs worldwide. In addition, the aviation industry supports 56.6 million jobs globally.

- Future increases in the size of the world's urban population are expected to be highly concentrated in just a few countries. Together, India, China, and Nigeria will account for 35% of the projected growth of the world's urban population between 2018 and 2050. By 2050, it is projected that India will have added 416 million urban dwellers, China 255 million, and Nigeria 189 million.

- The level of urbanization in Asia is now approaching 50%. In contrast, Africa remains mostly rural, with 43% of its population living in urban areas. The global rural population is expected to decline from 3.4 billion in 2018 to 3.1 billion by 2050.

- By 2030, the world is projected to have 43 mega-cities with more than 10 million inhabitants each, most of them in developing regions. However, some of the fastest-growing urban agglomerations are cities with fewer than 1 million inhabitants, many of them located in Asia and Africa.

- The aviation industry needs to keep abreast of changes brought about by sociological shifts stemming from rapid urbanization. These could range from various forms of airport ownership to the vast array of different aviation services that will be required by a growing and changing society.

- Flexible working practices are likely to become more widespread, with people employed on shorter-term contracts and more working remotely.

- Passenger profiles are changing quickly, but the designs of airports have remained largely the same. Over the last decade, travelers have become much more diverse in age, income, cultural background, and trip purpose. Along with that diversity, different types of passengers are emerging, each with highly specialized transport needs, taste preferences, and spending habits.

- Cultural differences also account for unique practices and expectations that are increasingly impacting the requirements for aviation facilities and services, a trend which will accelerate over the next couple of decades.

Mobility – People, Goods, Services

- Airports need to take action to connect within the "Transportation as a Service" (TaaS or MaaS) system as the point-to-point service becomes more important to the consumer in terms of the total journey experience.

- In the near future, personal smartphones will be the gateway for each traveler's journey. People will make their travel choices based on the factors that matter most to them, such as service frequency, cost, comfort, and/or travel time. They will expect to have access to innovative, on-demand services that aggregate similar trips quickly for more efficient travel, connecting them with a range of public, private, and community transport providers that offer a mix of services.

- More metropolitan and regional centers will be created as central places where the majority of jobs and services will be located, as well as attractions like shops, restaurants, and parks. A prime consideration in developing these centers will be to provide easy access to and from these spaces, as well as the ability to move around easily within them.

- Car parking (and related fees) at airports are forecast to continue to decrease over the next 15 to 20 years as travelers opt for other ways to get to/from airports. Airport operators, in North America and Europe in particular, will need to identify and implement new types of non-aeronautical revenue-generating activities to compensate for the expected decline in parking revenues.

- As car parking declines, some airports will begin to transform into intermodal transport centers, integrated with long-distance railway networks. Alternative technologies for integrated intermodal systems such as hyperloops and vactrains will continue to be researched and developed.

- Only 2.6% of worldwide funding for infrastructure and services is channeled for aviation and/or airport development needs. The future financing of global aviation infrastructure will need to become a top priority. Public and private sectors need to explore new approaches to investment and work together in partnership to provide the aviation infrastructure, support networks, and services that will be needed in the coming decades.

- Continuing efforts will need to be made by the UN and other stakeholders to address investment concerns by emphasizing airport benefits for cities and regions in the future. Global best practices and principles will need to be identified in urban and regional planning and management and used to sustainably develop air transport infrastructure and services.

- The critical role of airports as integral and essential access point gateways to aviation's global network needs to be better communicated and promoted over the next decade or more. Citizens, businesses, investors, and governments need to be made fully aware that a city or a region's airports are the key stepping stone to the world's cultures, ideas, and markets.

Connectivity of Urban Centers

- There is a requirement to better connect travelers and residents on the ground and to help unlock the next stage of growth for airports. The need to link the entire transportation network within countries will increase in significance as the population grows.

- In the future, more than ever, there will be a need to connect people to jobs, goods, and services in cities and regions around the world. Airports, in particular, will be a crucial part of the solution because they provide the connectivity and access required for a modern economy, enabling businesses to capture overseas opportunities and facilitate the coming and going of tourists, all of which fuel economic growth.

- Over the next couple of decades, Airports Council International (ACI) and the International Air Transport Association (IATA) will need to continue to work with aviation industry partners in pursuing their New Experience in Travel and Technologies (NEXTT) initiative. This project is designed to optimize the use of emerging technologies, processes, and designs, develop a common vision to enhance the on-ground transport experience, guide industry investments, and help governments improve the regulatory framework.

REFERENCES

[1] *"Urbanization". MeSH browser. National Library of Medicine. Retrieved 5 November 2014. The process whereby a society changes from a rural to an urban way of life. It refers also to the gradual increase in the proportion of people living in urban areas.*

[2] *"Urbanization in 2013". Demographic partitions. Retrieved 8 July 2015.*

[3] *"Urban life: Open-air computers". The Economist. 27 October 2012. Retrieved 20 March 2013.*

[4] *Urbanization.* UNFPA – United Nations Population Fund.

[5] Cohen, B. (2015). "Urbanization, city growth, and the New United Nations Development Agenda". *Cornerstone, the Official Journal of the World Coal Industry.* 3(2): pp. 4–7.

[6] Akantamn (2014). World urbanization prospects: The 2014 revision. Own work, based on United Nations, Department of Economic and Social Affairs, Population Division (2014). CD-ROM Edition.

[7] *Oxford Dictionary.*

[8] *Oxford Dictionary.*

[9] *Oxford Dictionary.*

[10] Wikipedia, the free encyclopedia.

[11] New South Wales (NSW) Government. *Future transport strategy 2056.*

[12] Kasarda, J.D., & Lindsay, G. (2012). *Aerotropolis: The way we'll live next.* Farrar, Straus, & Giroux.

[13] Lynch, M. (2016). *Aerotropolis: City airport or airport city?* Retrieved from https://www.woodsbagot.com/ideas/aerotropolis-city-airport-or-airport-city.

[14] Kasarda, J.D. (2017, December 6). "Welcome to Aerotropolis, the city of the future". *The Huffington Post.* Retrieved from https://www.huffingtonpost.com/john-d-kasarda/aerotropolis-city-future_b_7269152.html.

[15] Lynch, M. (2016). *Aerotropolis: City airport or airport city?* Retrieved from https://www.woodsbagot.com/ideas/aerotropolis-city-airport-or-airport-city.

[16] Gottdiener, M. (2000). *Life in the air: Surviving the new culture of air travel.* Rowman and Littlefield.

[17] dailymail.com 18 March 2017.

[18] Wikipedia, the free encyclopedia.

[19] Wikipedia, the free encyclopedia.

[20] Royall, I. (2018, May 23), "Is this Melbourne's most glaring problem?" Herald Sun, Melbourne, Australia.

[21] Sourced from inhabitat.com.

[22] Dallas-Fort Worth International Airport (2018). *2017 environmental, social, and governance report.*

[23] UK Ministry of Defense Strategic Trends Programme (2014). *Global strategic trends out to 2045* (Fifth Ed.).

24   United Nations (UN) (2018). *World urbanization prospects: The 2018 revision.*

25   Hirsh, M. (2017, 13 December) *Virgin Hyperloop One: How airports can keep up with the future of travel.*

26   Wikipedia, the free encyclopedia.

27   Union of Concerned Scientists (2016, 29 February). *Car emissions and global warming.* https://www.ucsusa.org/clean-vehicles/car-emissions-and-global-warming#.XF23r1VKios.

28   Wikipedia, the free encyclopedia.

29   www.icao.int/ESAF/aviation-urbanism.

30   ACI World Report (2018). *Toronto Pearson: Making the connections that matter.*

31   Hirsh, M. (2017, 13 December). *Virgin Hyperloop One: How airports can keep up with the future of travel.*

32   (2018, April). *The International Airport Review, 22*(2).

33   Bloomberg News on 8 June 2018 (with assistance from Kevin Hamlin and Xiaoqing Pi).

34   ACI World Report (2018, June). *New Experience in Travel and Technologies (NEXTT).*

35   ICAO (2013). *Worldwide Air Transport Conference* (ATConf/6-WP/20).

36   Morphet, H., and Bottini, C. (2018). *Air connectivity: Why it matters and how to support growth.*

5

DEMOGRAPHIC
CHANGES AND TRENDS

INTRODUCTION

"The battle to feed all of humanity is over. In the 1970's, hundreds of millions of people will starve to death...". This was the grim introduction to *The Population Bomb,* 1968's best-selling book by Paul and Anne Ehrlich of Stanford University, which alarmed policymakers and citizens worldwide with its dire predictions of mass starvation and social unrest. The chief cause of the impending catastrophe, according to the authors, was unchecked population growth, and the authors recommended draconian policy interventions to bring about stability.[1] The outcomes predicted in the book were of course largely averted. This was achieved by significant increases in agricultural production worldwide, due in large part to breakthroughs in creating new drought- and pest-resistant "hybrid" varieties of staple crops, which brought food supply closer to global demand levels. (It must be noted, however, that famine has indeed devastated a number of nations, particularly in sub-Saharan Africa, since the Ehrlich book was published).

By 2018, global demographics had shifted in ways that few would have predicted, even just twenty years before. Indeed, many nations are now facing declining populations. The UN Population Division listed 83 countries in 2015 that had birth rates below the 2.1-child benchmark "replacement rate" (although longer life expectancies have forestalled the actual move to negative population growth, as discussed below)[2]. These cases of persistent low birth rates, which are occurring mostly in developed and middle-income countries, will be more than offset, however, by continued high rates of population growth in developing countries as well as a select few emerging middle-income nations.

Against this backdrop of demographic flux, major shifts are occurring in the way some groups in the population will access and utilize air transport. This will place heavy demands on the industry to become more efficient and to manage scarce airport and airspace capacity wisely to avoid degrading the travel experience. Recent studies have shown that an alarming number of the world's busiest airports are at or near their saturation point in terms of capacity. If the air transport sector fails to accommodate the anticipated high demand for air travel, travelers could be diverted to other transport modes or choose to take "staycations" closer to home. Various demographic groups in the population approach air travel and tourism with very different goals and expectations. A rapidly growing middle class, particularly in emerging economies, has vast implications for consumption patterns that will affect global aviation significantly.

This chapter examines the underlying sub-trends in demographics that must be understood and factored into long-term decision-making and strategies by air transport leaders to ensure that the system can meet the diverse demands of the flying public. The six main areas of focus are: shifts in the global population and the impact of a growing middle class; a snapshot of the vast economic impact of global transport tourism; the elderly population and increased life expectancy; the behavior and impact of millennials; niche markets contributing to aviation growth; and issues of accessibility to air transport by disadvantaged persons and the various gender groups.

GLOBAL POPULATION TRENDS

Due to the decline in birth rates mentioned above, the UN Population Division projects that the rate of global population growth will taper off somewhat in the decades ahead. The current world population of 7.6 billion is expected to grow to 8.6 billion by 2030 and to reach just over 11 billion in 2050. The continuing decline in birth rates in most regions will occur along with an increase in life expectancy due primarily to advances in medical science. The cohort of the global population over 65 years of age will reach 1 billion persons in 2030 and will account for over 30% of the total population by 2050. Within that group, nearly 6% will be over 80 years old (some 28 nations already have an average life expectancy of over 80 years).[3] That translates to a threefold increase in the number of people older than 80 in just 30 years. Moreover, better health in the elderly population should lead to lifestyle improvements, with the elderly staying active, in many cases retiring later, and enjoying leisure travel well into their "golden years".

In developing nations, life expectancies are also rising, as advances in fighting infectious disease including HIV/AIDS are taking hold. The disparity between average life expectancies in the developed and developing world is shrinking. In 2015, this gap was estimated at 8 years, down from 11 years in 2005. The UN predicts that this trend will continue as the "health gap" between developed and developing countries narrows, in large part due to more equitable dispersal of advances in medicine.

The UN estimates that in the coming decades, over one-half of global population growth through 2050 will be driven by nine countries. They are listed below, ranked by the UN in order of net increase in population (not rate of growth) between 2017 and 2050.

1   India

2   Nigeria

3   Democratic Republic of the Congo

4   Pakistan

5   Ethiopia

6   Tanzania

7   United States*

8   Uganda

9   Indonesia

In addition, another 21 countries in Africa are expected to double in population over the next 30 years. The nine nations listed above, plus 27 countries in Africa, along with India, Pakistan and Indonesia, will be the main drivers of global population growth over the next 30 years. (*The population growth in the USA is based on the assumption of considerable immigration, not on a high birth rate).[4]

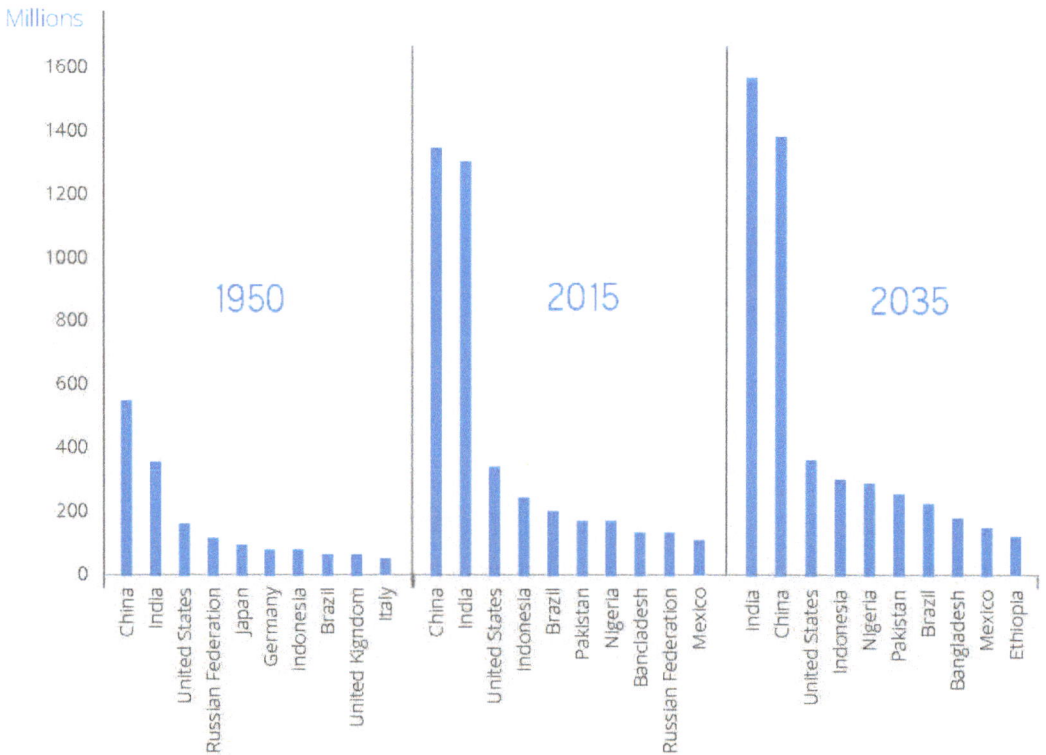

Figure 5-1   Population of ten largest countries, 1950 to 2035 (UN Population Division).

The World Bank has collaborated with the UN to publish statistics on what they term the "age-dependency ratio", a key concept used in analyzing global demographics. This statistic is defined as the proportion of a society that is made up of people either too young or too old to be active in the workforce. When that ratio exceeds 50 percent, continued economic growth becomes very challenging because fewer workers must struggle to keep pace with social outlays in support of the elderly and very young. Many developed countries have already exceeded this point. Somewhat surprisingly, China, despite the expected scrapping of its decades-old policy of limiting family size, is also moving in that direction.[5]

An article published by Bloomberg in 2018 described the current situation in China as follows: "When birth rates fall sharply from high levels, a country can for decades enjoy what has come to be called a *demographic dividend*", with the ratio of those too old or too young to work to the working-age population dropping below 50 percent and (economic) growth accelerating. China's great growth spurt of the past four decades has in fact coincided with a steep drop in its age-dependency ratio. Those days are over; China hit peak demographic dividend in 2010, and its age-dependency ratio is expected to cross 50 percent in 2032." However, this major change in Chinese demography will not alter its status as the world's largest economy (a status it achieved in 2014, when it passed the USA according to PricewaterhouseCoopers (PwC) in a recent study).

The same PwC study forecast that by 2050, India's economy will also have surpassed the United States, which will then fall to third position, measured in terms of GDP. However, the gap between the third-ranked economy and number four will be considerable. By 2050, the U.S. GDP is forecast to be over three times that of the next largest economy (which is projected to be Indonesia, currently ranked eighth). Later in this chapter, we will see a tight correlation between GDP rankings and the largest air traffic markets.

One intriguing aspect of the forecast demographic changes is that these trends emerge from the sum of literally billions of independent decisions on the part of billions of individuals and households. These decisions are about issues such as ideal family size, path to economic well-being of the family unit, where the family should be located (increasingly families are opting to live in urban areas across the globe), and where the family might take a holiday. Attempts by governments to influence demographics with legal restrictions on family size (e.g., China) or government-mandated relocation of families (e.g., Tanzania shortly after independence) tended to have only short-term impacts and did not always achieve the intended results.

The impact of this "demographic dividend" in China and throughout Asia has been carefully documented over the past decade by Homi Kharas of the Brookings Institution, a respected scholar and frequent presenter at the annual World Economic Forum in Davos, Switzerland. The thrust of Dr. Kharas' argument is that the growth of an economically powerful middle class throughout Asia has been driving much of the global economy and is a blend of three megatrends: urbanization, the shift in economic power from West to East, and the leveraging of information technology for greater productivity. It is useful to paraphrase Kharas' key points in the 2017 edition of his paper for the Forum[6].

Kharas estimates that there were some 3.2 billion people in the middle class globally at the end of 2016, "...500 million more than I had previously estimated" only several years before. His assessment of the future is that a 'tipping point' will be reached by as early as 2020, at which point, for the very first time, "...a majority of the world's population will live in middle-class or rich households." Kharas' conclusions include the following:

- The rate of increase of the middle class is currently calculated at an additional 140 million persons achieving middle class status each year.

- An overwhelming majority of new entrants into the middle class—88% of the next billion—will live in Asia.

- The absolute market size of global middle-class spending was about $35 trillion in 2015 and now accounts for one-third of the global economy.

- The global middle-class market is now clearly divided into two distinct groups: a slow-growing developed-country middle class, and a fast-growing emerging-economy middle class.

The pace of growth of the middle class has exceeded many predictions made by the academic community and has tremendous ramifications for the air transport sector. With increased disposable income, many newcomers to the middle class will have the means to travel to both domestic and international destinations for the first time. Increased leisure travel across the Asia-Pacific region is likely to be one of the first results of a burgeoning middle class, creating pressure on both airport and airspace infrastructure to meet demands. Only by maintaining a high level of capital investment to improve and expand existing infrastructure, and through innovative use of technology to process transport flows more efficiently, will the aviation sector be able to deliver a consistently excellent experience for the air traveler of the future.

WORLD TRAVEL AND TOURISM
– GLOBAL ECONOMIC POWERHOUSE

This section describes the nature and tremendous impact of the global travel and tourism industry and its aviation sub-sector. The demographic trends described in the previous section should provide a considerable stimulus to this already-vibrant industry.

The Air Transport Action Group (ATAG), an independent coalition of organizations and companies that represents all sectors of the air transport industry, has published a wealth of data on the economic impact of aviation. To sum up their findings, they use one short phrase: "If aviation were a country, it would rank 21st in size, about the same as Switzerland and Sweden."[7] As impressive as this economic impact is, the broader travel and tourism sector, which includes aviation as a subset, is actually much larger in economic terms. The highly respected World Travel and Tourism Council has quantified the economic impact of this sector across a number of economic parameters. As a starting point, air transport over the past 50 years has consistently maintained a significantly higher rate of growth than global GDP (roughly by a factor of two) and considerably higher than global population growth. That growth trend continues unabated. History has shown that shocks to the air transport system (e.g., 9/11, SARS, global recession, etc.) are absorbed with only a temporary dip in traffic—often less than two years—before the sector fully recovers and resumes its pattern of high growth.

Overall aviation activity is most often measured in terms of passenger traffic and air cargo flows. Recent forecasts from Airports Council International (ACI) project a global rate of passenger growth of just over 4.5% per year through 2030 to reach over 15 billion passengers. Air freight is expected to grow even more rapidly, although its growth tends to be more cyclical than that of passenger traffic. These forecasts are in line with IATA, ICAO, Airbus, and Boeing forecasts for the same period and are used in this chapter because they are considered to be more meaningful and straightforward for assessing actual passenger numbers and freight tonnage. Other forecasters use revenue-passenger and freight-ton kilometers as metrics, but these statistics require assumptions about the length of flight stages as well as passenger numbers. Both passenger and freight traffic forecasts are shown in Figures 5-2 and 5-3.[8]

Passenger Traffic

ACI's year-end traffic statistics for 2017 suggest that the forecasts depicted in Figure 5-2 may have to be adjusted upward. According to year-end totals, passenger traffic increased by 8.4% in 2017, with solid growth measured in all six ACI regions. Air freight was up 9.8% for the year.[9] The high growth rates in emerging markets were not really surprising, but continued robust growth in mature aviation markets in North America and Europe exceeded expectations. This growth was driven by a number of factors: a strong economy, new low-cost services linking under-utilized airports and creating new city pairs, and a return to financial health of the legacy carriers. Long-haul low-cost carriers are also beginning to drive international traffic growth. These carriers have been creative in using the liberalized market access provisions of "open-skies" agreements to inaugurate services between new city pairs. This has particularly been the case with the USA-EU open skies agreement.

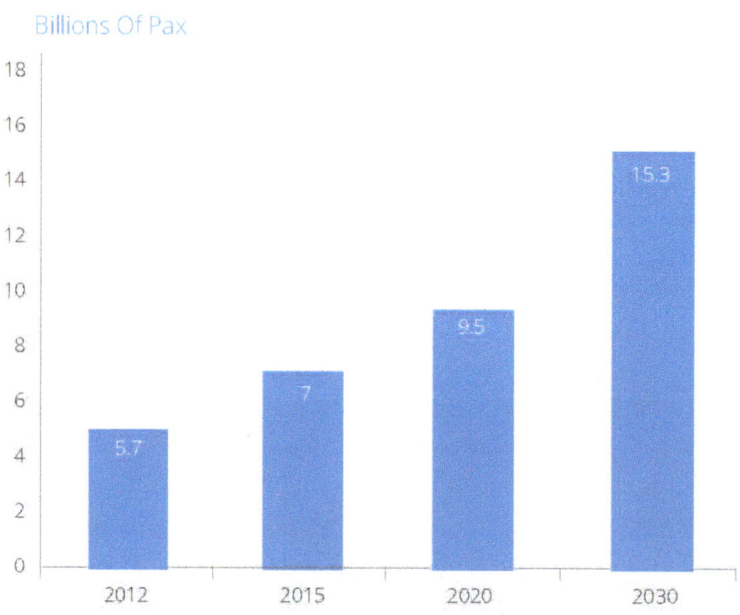

Figure 5-2   World air traffic forecasts – Passenger growth to 2030 (ACI, ICAO).

Air Cargo Traffic

The regional forecasts for freight volumes shown in Figure 5-3 clearly illustrate the dramatic differences in regional performance and show the pattern of world economic growth and trade flows in an ever-eastward direction. Air freight is both enabled and driven by economic growth. In its efforts to improve the efficiency of the interdependent global supply chain, the air freight industry has managed to create huge cost savings.

With same-day and next-day delivery services by air now widely available, companies that ship/receive their materials no longer need to maintain large inventories, and production can be more precisely matched to their end-user demands. The Asia-Pacific region, already the largest market for freight, is forecast by ACI to nearly triple its volume by 2031. Although a high rate of growth will be experienced in all regions, Asia-Pacific is expected to double the volume of air freight over the next-highest-growth region, North America, over the forecast period.

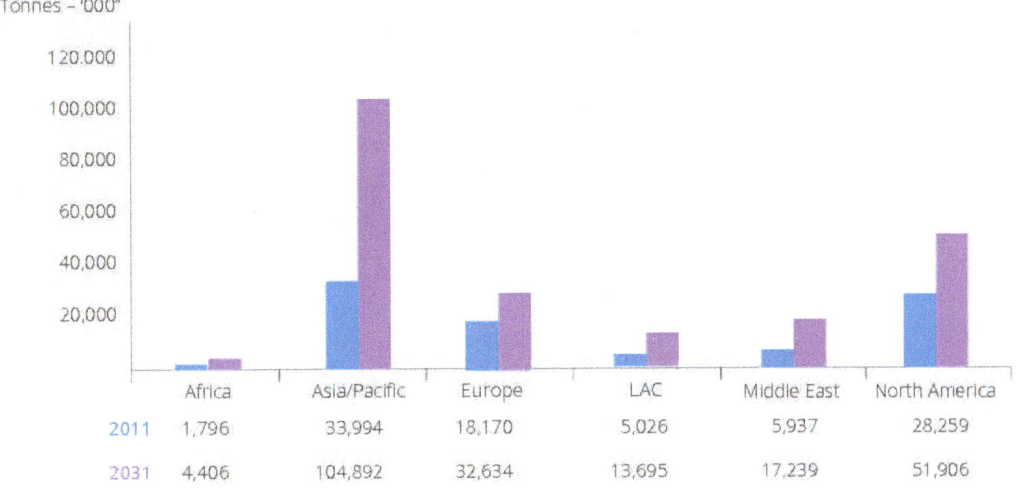

Forecast Cargo Volumes by World Regions

	Africa	Asia/Pacific	Europe	LAC	Middle East	North America
2011	1,796	33,994	18,170	5,026	5,937	28,259
2031	4,406	104,892	32,634	13,695	17,239	51,906

Figure 5-3   Global air cargo volumes to 2031 (ACI, ICAO).

There are two important "wild cards" when forecasting freight flows: fuel prices and world trade flows. When fuel prices rise sharply, there tends to be considerable "modal diversion" of air freight to other transport modes, namely maritime, rail, or trucking. When fuel prices rise, all but the most valuable, time-sensitive, and/or perishable goods can often be shipped by a less expensive method. The second unpredictable factor is that freight volumes are closely linked to world trade flows. Any reduction in trade due to economic malaise or protectionism can cause a sharp decline in traffic. Interestingly, express air freight has proven less prone to suffer from these two often unpredictable and sometimes volatile phenomena. Historically, even when air freight was in the doldrums, the air express carriers normally saw narrow profit margins, whereas all-cargo carriers were in deep negative territory.

Employment – Travel and Tourism

A breakdown of projected employment in travel and tourism in 2026 is shown in Figure 5-4. The statistics again confirm the West-to-East economic power shift that is discussed in detail in Chapter 3 of this book.

Country	Total Jobs in Travel / Tourism
China	94.0 million
India	46.4 million
United States	18.5 million
Indonesia	12.8 million
Mexico	9.8 million
Thailand	9.4 million
Brazil	8.9 million
Vietnam	7.6 million
Germany	6.2 million
Philippines	5.3 million

Figure 5-4   Projected travel and tourism employment, major markets, 2026 (WTTC).

Six of the top ten countries for employment are in the Asia-Pacific region, and the figure for China is fully double that of the second largest country, India. The growth in jobs in China is influenced by several factors related to air tourism:

- Although international air tourist arrivals will continue to grow, the number of Chinese taking holidays in their own nation will also increase dramatically as the middle class grows over time.

- China has taken bold steps in committing to building new airports in provincial areas and also commencing construction of a fast rail network between cities, thus improving accessibility to both modes of transport.

- Chinese air carriers have begun to embrace the low-cost model that has been so successful in other nations.

Travel and tourism is the world's fourth largest sector in terms of revenues and employees. It creates jobs, drives exports, generates global investment, and increases prosperity. The World Travel and Tourism Council (WTTC) has for many years provided statistics on the industry's economic impact. Some of their key findings for 2017 include:

- The travel and tourism sector accounts for 10.4% of global GDP.

- That sector generated some $2.3 trillion in direct economic impact in 2017.

- The sector generated a total of $7.6 trillion in direct, indirect, and induced economic impact in 2017.

- The travel and tourism sector employs some 310 million people, or 9.9% of the world's salaried workers.

Supplementing these impressive figures from the WTTC, ATAG calculates that jobs in aviation are 3.8 times more productive than jobs in other sectors. This is largely due to the assertion by some experts that each employee in aviation tends to leverage multiple infrastructural assets and enabling technologies as part of his/her daily routine. In addition, sectoral growth of 4.6% in 2017 outpaced the global economy for the seventh consecutive year. The WTTC notes that, "Over the past ten years, one in five of all jobs created across the world has been in travel and tourism, and with the right regulatory conditions and government support, nearly 100 million new jobs could be created over the decade ahead"[10].

Meeting the Challenges of Rapid Growth – Airline Specifics

Figure 5-5, produced by IATA's chief economist in 2018, shows that investing in airlines before 2015 would have been a losing proposition. It vividly underscores the fact that until the past few years, airlines in the aggregate were simply a poor investment.

The metric used is unusual, but it makes a good point: an investor evaluating opportunities between 1993 and 2014 would have been much better off investing in equities in other sectors; the airlines simply were not creating value for shareholders. This does not mean that there were not years of aggregate profitability, but those profits tended to be razor-thin (often just 2% to 3%) and except for the strongest performers, not high enough to attract many investors. However, over the past four years, profits have reached respectable levels, often in the order of 5% to 6% across the industry, and the share prices of many of the world's largest carriers have shown even higher rates of growth.

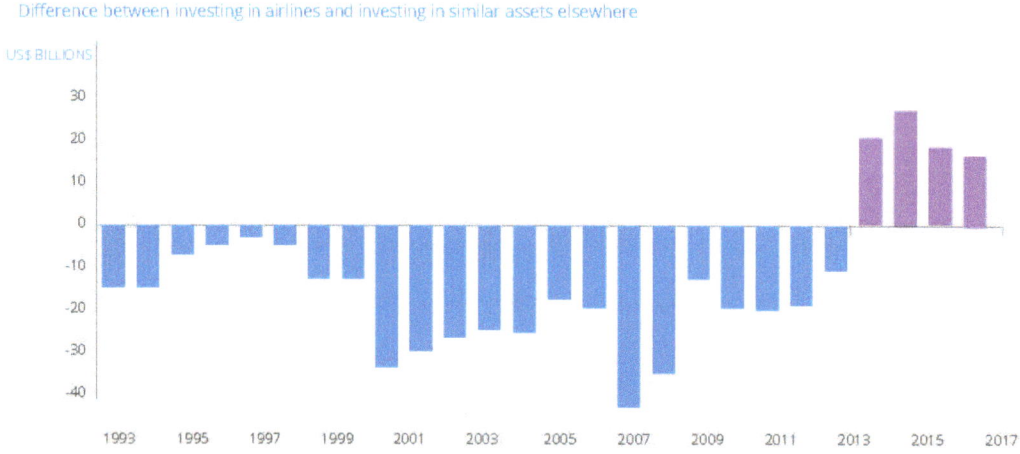

Figure 5-5   Difference between investing in airlines and similar assets elsewhere, 1993-2017 (IATA).

The global airline industry has a long history of financial woes. Indeed, even in the best years since 1980, the global industry in the aggregate was never able to exceed its average cost of capital until 2014. Certainly there were some carriers outperforming the field, but many more were plagued with high cost structures and considerable debt. Bankruptcies were common. State-owned flag carriers were particularly uncompetitive. These operations, which were run more like utilities than businesses, tended to have bloated payrolls and lacked entrepreneurial spirit, but because they were a symbol of national pride, governments worldwide subsidized these airlines, both directly and indirectly, for decades.

There were few incentives for innovation or economic efficiency in the early decades of air transport. In fact, IATA was founded in the 1920s primarily as a price-fixing cartel. Fares were set in meetings of the world's carriers and based on the premise that air travel was strictly a privilege for members of the elite upper class, who were not interested in quibbling over air fares. All that changed in the 1960s and 1970s as carriers began to cut fares. As de-regulation spread in the late 1970s, the aviation market became chaotic, with new low-fare entrants challenging the flag carriers and price wars becoming endemic. By the mid-1990s, IATA would identify the industry's greatest problem as "self-inflicted wounds" caused by this cycle of airline price-cutting behavior. IATA's role moved over time from that of a "cartel" to a more traditional member-based trade association. The decline in airfares meant that air travel was no longer provided only for the elite, but over time would become commodified and much more accessible to middle-income individuals and their families.

Beginning in the 1990s, many carriers simply shut down as ticket prices and operating costs were totally out of balance. In fact, during that period, one large U.S. carrier actually calculated its break-even load factor as greater than 100%! Good customer service and a prestigious brand name were no guarantee of success. Swissair is a prime example of that. With public and private ownership, it was consistently rated as one of the world's finest carriers and had operated for 71 years. However, cash flow problems over one weekend in 2002 (over an inability to pay fuel bills) caused creditors to shut down Swissair for good (with the added ignominy of stranding thousands of passengers at airports around the world.)

The move toward profitability in the airline sector was instigated by a number of changes in the industry business model. Strict controls on costs were implemented by most legacy carriers worldwide, and additional income streams were found by charging for "ancillary services", including checked baggage, specified seating, and in-flight meals. In 2013, as airlines returned to a low level of profitability in the aggregate, IATA credited these ancillary fees with providing the entire profit margin. Passengers were dismayed by the fees, but had little choice as most carriers throughout the industry adopted these new pricing structures across the globe (starting in North America), thus making it difficult to avoid the extra fees.[11]

While the airlines were re-inventing their business model, a megatrend was operating in the background: the movement of aviation's "center of gravity" from Western countries eastward. As illustrated in Figure 5-6, this shift mirrored the same trend as the world economy. (See Chapter 3 of this book for a detailed discussion of the West-to-East economic power shift).

Figure 5-6 shows IATA's calculation of the historic and future "center of gravity" for the airlines and is based on total global inventory of departing seats. To be precise, the center of gravity shown in this chart is a weighted average latitude and longitude for departing seats at an airport level.

As can be seen in Figure 5-6, commercial aviation, at its inception in 1914, was largely focused on North America, but over the century, the center moved inexorably eastward. This West-to-East shift is predicted to continue unabated through 2036 along with parallel shifts in the global economy and in travel and tourism, as noted previously in this chapter.

Figure 5-7 shows changes in the IATA ranking of national markets for aviation through 2036. The demographic trends noted in the global population discussion in the introduction of this chapter are clearly reflected in the realignment of national markets through 2036.

Figure 5-6   Aviation industry shift from west to east over time (IATA).

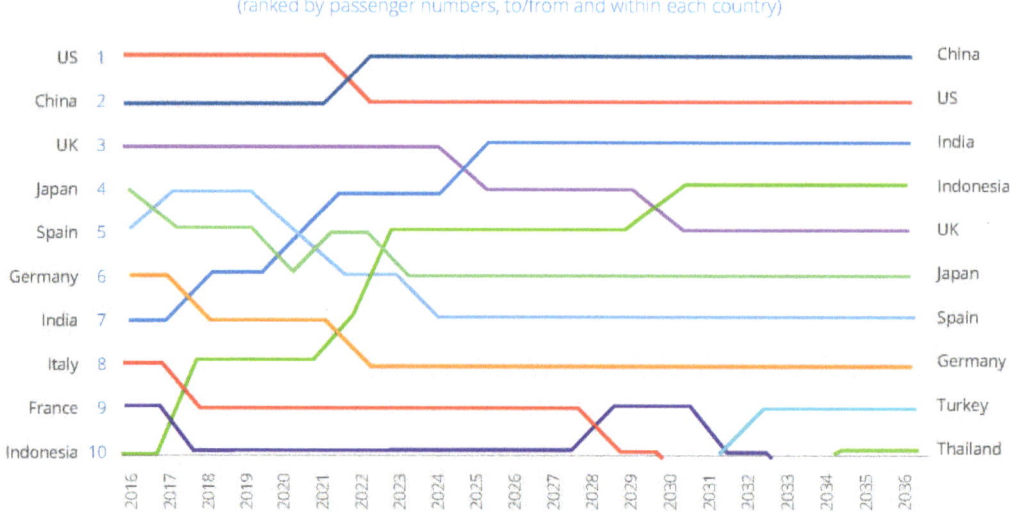

Figure 5-7   Top 10 air passenger travel markets through 2036 (IATA).

Figure 5-7 shows China moving into the top spot by around 2021, replacing the United States. Other significant dynamics are that Italy and France depart from the top 10, replaced by Turkey and Thailand by the end of the period. The two largest net gainers are India, moving from seventh to third place, and Indonesia, from tenth to fourth.

The final graphic in this series, Figure 5-8, illustrates the possible impact of three different economic and geopolitical growth scenarios for the future, depending on the global political, regulatory, and trade environment.

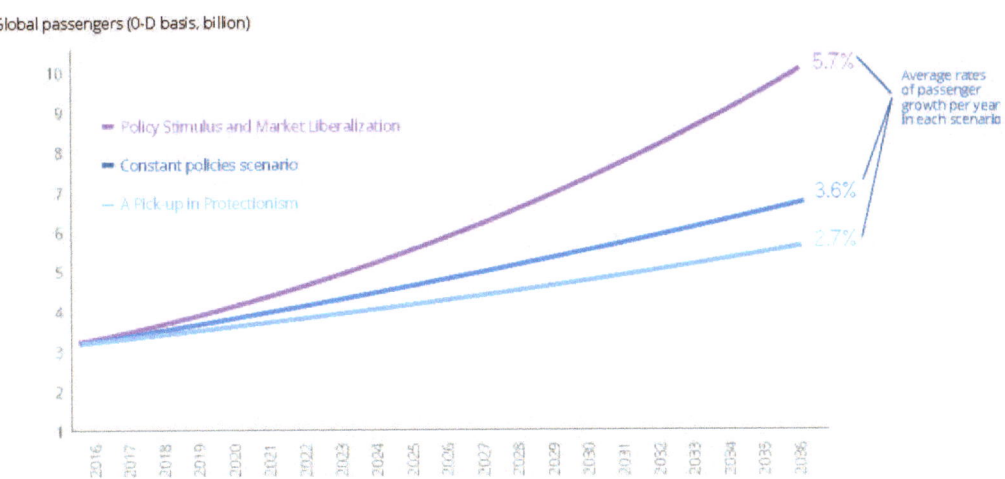

Figure 5-8   Passenger travel outlook under three different economic growth scenarios, 2016-2036 (IATA).

As mentioned previously in the discussion of air freight and its vulnerability to downturns in global trade flows, passenger traffic is likewise not immune to this factor. IATA has calculated outcomes in passenger traffic (measured in enplaned passengers) through 2036 under three assumptions, as shown in Figure 5-8. The first is that governments will liberalize trade through improved market access and lowering of tariffs (much of this could be achieved in bilateral or regional free-trade areas or in multilateral agreements through the World Trade Organization). This scenario (shown by the green line) projects a 5.7% annual increase in passenger traffic through 2036, compared with a 3.6% increase under the current regulatory environment (red line). The third scenario assumes that protectionist measures become widespread, depressing the growth rate to 2.7% (blue line). Because these statistics are compounded over the 18-year period, the actual difference between the high and low options in terms of enplaned passengers is more than 4.2 billion persons. This significant difference drives home the importance of maintaining a free and fair global trade regime, a task that requires considerable international good will and cooperation on the part of all governments involved.

In conclusion, when analyzing the financial condition of the airlines, they have never been in a better position to accommodate the anticipated growth in traffic. Orders for new aircraft, both wide-body and narrow-body, are at their highest point in history. According to the latest forecasts released by Airbus, the world's airlines will need more than 37,000 new aircraft, worth nearly $6 trillion, over the next 20 years to keep pace with demand. However, as the next section explains, the other key element in meeting demand is the financial health of the world's airports and their ability to increase their capacity over the next two decades, which presents a major challenge.

Meeting the Growth: Airport and Airspace Specifics

Unlike their airline partners, airports have had a long-standing record of excellent financial profitability since the early 1990s, when many airports were commercialized under autonomous authorities or privatized outright. As airports diversified their revenue streams by tapping into non-aeronautical sources of income, they came to be seen as sound long-term investments with high credit ratings, often attracting such conservative investors as pension funds and insurance companies. Indeed, the top 100 airports in the world have consistently maintained double-digit profitability over the past two decades.

Airports have become vital catalysts for economic growth and prosperity and arguably one of a community's most valuable assets. It is hard to imagine a thriving economic region without good air connectivity. Below are some key facts compiled by ACI about the world's airports at the end of 2016:

- Nearly 500,000 employees work directly for airport operators worldwide.

- There are some 2,000 commercial airports in service around the globe.

- Approximately 6 million persons work on airport premises (including airline personnel and the staff that operate concessions such as retail, auto parking, duty-free operations, etc.).

- Global airport gross revenues in 2016 were over $152 billion.

- Net profit margins for airports worldwide averaged approximately 17% in 2016 (this could be a bit low because most of ACI's members are airports with low traffic volumes—under two million passengers per year—and airports of that size normally operate at a loss).12

ACI forecasts also show that almost 6 billion additional passengers will need to be accommodated in the decade beginning in 2030. This will require a strong commitment by all parties involved to build new infrastructure. An example of the scope of this challenge is the mid-2018 approval by the British Parliament of a new runway for London's Heathrow International Airport. The cost of that runway alone is estimated at $23 billion, with additional access improvements to run approximately another $8 billion. It is worth noting, however, that Heathrow is something of a special case due to its unique geographical, ecological, and topographical obstacles to overcome, as well as the high property values in the London area. To provide some perspective, St. Louis Lambert International Airport, MO, USA, commissioned a new 9,000-foot runway in 2018 at a price tag of $1.1 billion.

Building new airport capacity has been a key goal of ACI since the organization was formed in 1992. However, as recently as June 2018, there were a number of troubling signs that the challenge is still daunting. *The Challenges of Growth* study recently released by Eurocontrol (the European organization that oversees air traffic control in the European Union and adjacent countries) looked at the problem of congestion from now to 2040. The study draws renewed attention to this thorny issue. As ACI stated when the study was released, "This latest edition (of the study) is very clear—people cannot continue to presume that air traffic growth, and the economic benefits that come with it, can happen without a corresponding increase in airport capacity on the ground. As we stand (today), the lack of airport capacity will result in €88.1 billion in foregone economic activity in Europe by 2040 due to unmet demand for air travel and reduced air connectivity. This isn't something that should just be of concern to the industry—air transport is a vital component of many people's lives. This should be of concern to everyone who values the unparalleled connectivity, mobility, and prosperity that airports bring to their communities." (It is worth noting that in a few countries, building new infrastructure is driven more by the desire to create greater efficiency on the ground, not necessarily directly to high growth in number of passengers).

Echoing these concerns, ACI World recently published a policy brief on "airport privatization and funding". This was a timely release since critical investment decisions are being taken by airports around the world in response to growing demands for air services. This document, published jointly in June 2018 by ACI and InterVISTAS, provides guidance and key principles for governments, policy-makers, and regulators looking to adopt privatization as policy.[13]

To paraphrase key elements of the report, privatization has been shown to be a successful way to fund infrastructure development. ACI World estimates that airports with private-sector participation invested 14% more in capital expenditures (CAPEX) in the last five years compared with their public counterparts. (It is important to note, however, that privatized airports attracted private investors in the first place because they were large and busy, and frequently in need of more CAPEX than their smaller counterparts.)

As the Director General of ACI World stated recently, "ACI has a neutral position on airport ownership and does not suggest that airport privatization is the only suitable policy choice. There is, however, a global need to finance new airport infrastructure to meet future demand, and if government spending cannot be relied upon as it has been in the past, then there is ample evidence of the value created by private investment in airports around the world." ACI went on to point out that "proportionate" oversight of privatized airports by governments—meaning the absence of heavy-handed regulation—can create an environment where private investors can participate to bring operational efficiency and sustainable airport infrastructure enhancements to a project, thus adding value for the airport enterprise and its investors as well as delivering greater connectivity and wider economic benefits.[14] ACI-North America has also called for greater investment in airport infrastructure—some $100 billion over the next five years—in recent appeals to the U.S. Congress.

Figure 5-9   Two extremes – Top: international routes at Atlanta. Bottom: Regional airport in Hungary (stock photos).

The visuals in Figure 5-9 drive home a point made earlier, that the global network of airports does indeed currently have enough capacity, but that capacity is not always in the right places. In addition to the possibility of bringing more private or public sector investment to airports, there are several proven ways to enhance existing airport infrastructure, including:

- More intensive use of under-utilized airports can spread capacity more evenly and effectively. Low-cost carriers are particularly creative in opening up new city pairs serving secondary (non-hub) airports. Until recently, most of these services were regional in nature, but over the past several years, long-haul LCC (low-cost carrier) operations have begun between secondary airports as well, particularly in services between Europe and North America and within the vast Asia-Pacific and Middle East regions.

- "Hub-busting" aircraft such as the Boeing 787 and Airbus A-350 have a range and an on-board configuration that is ideal for overflying traditional hubs. Due to the market access liberalization achieved by open skies agreements, these services are a promising way to relieve pressure on congested hubs. Recent examples include the opening of non-stop routes from London to Perth, Singapore to Newark, and Doha to Auckland.

- Efficiencies in operations on the ground and in the air that take advantage of advances in technology have been shown to "squeeze" more capacity out of even the most congested airports. London Gatwick is perhaps the best example in this regard, now serving some 46 million passengers annually with just a single runway (despite having a night-time curfew as well).

An obvious way to increase capacity is to have larger aircraft in the mix at hubs. However, this approach is only a viable solution if terminals can handle the demands of aircraft holding over 500 passengers.

A Brief Word about Airspace Capacity

In a June 2018 speech, the Director General of Eurocontrol addressed the capacity challenges faced by European aviation in 2018 and into the future. His remarks highlighted the following points:

- The first five months of 2018 had seen many more delays than in recent years, and traffic had increased by 3.4% over the previous year, while on-route air traffic flow management delays had risen dramatically. For example, this is a problem in the Maldives, where they are struggling to manage all the en route air traffic. Some States across the globe may look to outsource ANSP services to other States, which would in turn act on their behalf, creating some level of efficiency, economics, and safety.

- Europe is already struggling to cope with traffic levels, and the most likely scenario predicts a growth rate of 1.9% per year, or 16.2 million flights per year, between 2018 and 2040. However, the increase could be as much as 19.5 million flights per year under Eurocontrol's highest-growth scenario. Under the most likely scenario, there will not be enough capacity for approximately 1.5 million flights, or 160 million passengers, by 2040.

- Many airports will become much busier, with increased delays. The study estimates that by 2040, 16 airports in the region will be highly congested, operating at close to capacity for much of the day, up from six airports today. As a result of this congestion, the number of passengers delayed by one to two hours will grow from around 50,000 per day right now to around 470,000 per day by 2040.[15]

To put these points into perspective, Europe, with its efforts to achieve a "Single European Sky" (SESAR), perhaps faces the most severe challenges of any region. Part of the problem is due to labor issues with air traffic controller unions in several countries, as well as the fact that European airspace operates in a much more confined geographic space than other regions. (Indeed, the German Air Force trains in Arizona in the U.S. to avoid performing exercises in the crowded skies over Europe).

ICAO has put together a comprehensive global plan called the Global Air Navigation Plan (GANP). The GANP represents a rolling, 15-year strategic methodology that leverages existing technologies and anticipates future developments based on State- and Industry-agreed operational objectives. Its structured approach is organized in blocks of upgrades in non-overlapping six-year time increments, starting in 2013 and continuing through 2031 and beyond. It provides a basis for sound investment strategies and will generate commitment from ICAO Member States, equipment manufacturers, operators, and service providers. The key is that the technology to create a seamless global navigation system is already in place (i.e., most of it is satellite-based). However, one issue slowing adoption of the GANP is the huge cost for airlines to install the on-board avionics required for airplanes to interface fully with the latest technology. Still, there is reason for optimism in this regard because as air carriers add new aircraft to their fleets, the more sophisticated on-board systems will be included.

MILLENNIALS
– THE FOREVER-CONNECTED GENERATION

After the foregoing sobering assessment of constraints in meeting the demand for air transport in the future, this section examines several important demographic drivers of air transport growth, in addition to the growing middle class that was already discussed earlier. It is useful to begin with the generation that is changing the way we access and utilize aviation, namely, the millennials.

Millennials Defined

The term "millennial" is widely used but perhaps poorly understood. It has replaced two other synonymous terms: "Generation Y" and "echo boomers", the latter meaning the children of post-World War II baby boomers. (The "baby boom" was largely a North American phenomenon, and this chapter will focus on international trends concerning millennials whenever possible, although some of the best data available on this topic are from the North American region.)

There is total agreement among researchers that the generation classified as "millennial" is enormously influential in the global economy and has had, and will continue to have, a major impact on travel and tourism. However, according to Wikipedia at the time of this writing, it seems that there is considerable disagreement about the precise definition of the term "millennial", as illustrated below:

- Researchers Strauss and Millen, who coined the term "millennial", initially used 1982 to 2004 as the relevant birthdate window in their seminal study of this generation.

- The prestigious Pew Research organization uses the dates 1981 to 1996.

- Nielsen Research (which has done extensive studies on millennials in 23 nations) uses 1977 to 1996.

- In separate articles, the *New York Times* has pegged the millennial "bookends" at 1976–1990 and 1978–1998.

- Goldman Sachs placed the millennials in the period 1980–2000.

- The shortest span found was 1983 to 1994, the period Deloitte-Touche used in its research.

Demographers Strauss and Howe even hedge on their own end date for millennials, noting, "...you can't be sure where history will someday draw a cohort dividing line (in this case with Generation Z) until a generation fully comes of age."[16] That might seem a convenient escape, but it makes sense; it is too simplistic to lock in a set timeframe for a complex demographic trend. A number of other factors, apart from age, also bind a generation together. In the case of millennials, the key drivers of commonality are growing up in an interdependent global economy; being introduced to sophisticated technology at an early age; living with the reality of non-state terrorism and the uncertainty and chaos it has brought; and coping with the Great Recession and its aftermath. The same factors were observed more or less across all developed and emerging economies, thus cementing the place of millennials as a global cohort.

For the purposes of this discussion, examining an extended period is more useful, and therefore this chapter will adhere to the original Howe-Strauss range of 1982 to 2004. That means that the millennials being studied were between 14 and 36 years of age when this was written. For analyzing the research predicated on a similar time window, this is an excellent fit. For comparisons with those researchers opting for narrower timeframes, the data will not be invalidated; indeed, they should represent a useful and complementary subset. In addition, the longer period is close to the UN Population Division's definition for research on millennials, which has been carried out by the firm IRIS-Market Research Worldwide.

In the literature on millennials, there is consensus that their impact on travel and tourism is profound. The Boston Consulting Group *reports that* the millennial generation is more interested than older generations in traveling abroad by a 23-percentage-point margin.[17] (Their definition includes those between the ages of 16 and 34, just two years short of the definition used in this chapter). The United Nations *estimates* that 20% of all international tourists, or nearly 200 million travelers, are millennials. This demographic cohort generates more than $180 billion in annual tourism revenue, an increase of nearly 30% since 2007. The UN attributes that growth both to rising incomes in emerging markets and a commitment by youth in advanced economies to "continue traveling despite economic uncertainty." Millennials are now the *fastest-growing age segment* in terms of money spent on travel, according to the magazine *American Express Business Insights*.

Three Millennial Profiles

There is an overwhelming flood of statistical information on millennials, much of it somewhat contradictory (i.e., are they typically backpackers, or business class travelers, or both?) and steeped in generalities and stereotypes. The approach used in this chapter is to illustrate this group using three short vignettes or profiles, before attempting to list or quantify anything precise concerning millennials.

The day tripper: A senior executive at an airport in Southern California, when entering the parking area near his airport office, recently noticed people on bicycles arriving at the airport. They locked up their bikes and backpacks at the rack marked for "baggage". After investigating, he realized that they were passengers destined for the Silicon Valley area, where their firm was headquartered (they were based in a satellite office near Los Angeles). After a full day of working up north, they had returned in the evening by air and taken the reverse ground route, biking home. This journey has most of the elements usually attributed to millennials: complete and seamless multi-modal mobility, a low carbon footprint (except for the flight), sustainability, efficiency, economy (no hotel night), and finally a contribution to physical fitness.[18]

Finding purpose on an international journey: A young American woman, now an editor, described her experience as follows. "In the summer of 2012, at age 24, I left home to travel the world. In just over a year, I backpacked through South America, South Asia, Western Europe, and the western United States. I hiked the Inca Trail, skied the Alps, hitchhiked through Patagonia, and trekked in the Himalayas. I worked at hostels, stayed in a beautiful Buddhist monastery, and gardened at an English women's relief center in exchange for meals and a place to sleep. And while I learned many things on the trip, what was most surprising was how many people my age were traveling just like me". Indeed, the "gap year", normally considered to be a year between university and a job, is becoming a common occurrence for millennials and a year that frequently involves international travel.[19]

A Chinese millennial's story of upward mobility: "My friend, Xiao Huan, was born in Sichuan Province in 1990. His parents remember how, as kids, the community used to crowd into their neighbors' broken-down house because they had a 12-month calendar tacked to the mud wall of their house. Those 12 pictures—"Fields of Europe" —were the locals' only view of the outside world. For most, the West was reduced to a series of drumbeat slogans pumped out by the Communist Party, giving marching orders for the Cultural Revolution. "Surpass Britain and catch up with America!" they were instructed. Xiao Huan and his peers had a decade or so of mandatory English classes, and although the Chinese Internet was curtailed, he still grew up watching American movies and TV shows, tracking Western fashion, and studying Western politics. (Many of my friends in China can quote Martin Luther King, Jr.) Like my friend, China's young millennials have grown up observing the outside world. They are digital natives, and 90 percent own a smartphone. They aren't just learning about the world from afar. Young Chinese are literally seeing the world for themselves and sending seismic waves through the global travel industry in the process. Two-thirds of all passport holders in China are under the age of

36. "Despite only roughly 6 percent of the population *having a passport, China represents the largest outbound travel market in the world,* driven in large part by these millennials."[20] A *New York Post* portrait of Chinese millennials estimated them at about 400 million strong, which is borne out in the statistics from the UN World Tourism Organization. For all ages of traveler, China's international tourism expenditure was $261 billion, which is more than double that of the U.S.

A recent University of Wisconsin study titled, *"How are Millennials Changing the Workplace",*[21] found that, in North America, millennials are the largest generation currently employed and that by 2025 nearly three out of every four workers will be millennials. Additionally, the average job tenure for a millennial was found to be just two years, compared with five years for Gen X and seven years for Baby Boomers. Millennials change jobs more frequently than any other generation in history.

The same study concludes that the "...relationship between workers and employers has also changed drastically. Alternative employment, such as freelancing, contract work, temporary, and on-call arrangements, is increasing...." Millennials in North America are considered to be the most highly educated generation in history, with some 63% holding a university degree. Nevertheless, as noted in a study by *Forbes Magazine* about the Great Recession and its aftershocks, incomes have been held down to about the same level in real terms as those of the parents of millennials at the same age.

The above-mentioned University of Wisconsin study identified some typical traits of millennials:

- Value flexibility

- Seek opportunities to grow professionally

- Prefer texting over emailing

- Consume more media than any other generation.

These general traits are a useful backdrop to the way millennials travel, both for leisure and for pleasure. Some of the best work in this area is by the firm AC Nielsen, which has done extensive research on millennials from 23 nations.

Nielsen on Millennials:

"In addition to being hyper-connected and digitally driven, millennials are focused on personal experiences. And for many, those experiences happen away from home. Notably,

millennials are very interested in travel. In fact, they travel more than any other generation, including Baby Boomers, and they'll likely travel more as their incomes and financial standings grow. But millennials don't simply represent another generation of travelers. Their preferences and lack of predictability make them different from their older counterparts. At the same time, this uniqueness means that the travel industry will need to adjust in order to meet their specific needs and desires—particularly when it comes to retail. That's because while the retail travel industry has evolved over time, it hasn't faced major consumption shifts. In fact, traveler shopping habits have been somewhat predictable over the last few decades. That predictability ended with this new generation of consumers."

Nielsen also observed that the distinct approach of millennials to their travel stems mainly from them wanting to control their experiences themselves. This represents a major departure from older generations, which were far more likely to embrace brands that designed their travel experiences for them. As Nielsen characterized millennials while traveling, "...it's tough to keep in step with a path that's being cut as it's being traversed."

Nielsen went on to provide some useful quantifying data as well, which are summarized below:[22]

- There are about 1.8 billion millennials in total worldwide, and they tend to travel far more frequently than did their parents.

- The world is more accessible than in the past, with more destinations to choose from and fares lower than they were decades ago.

- China alone is home to 400 million millennials (see previous section on China millennials).

- Goldman Sachs says that some 75 million students will graduate from Chinese universities in the next decade, many of them "travel-ready".

- Many millennials tend to seek out low-cost flights and peer-to-peer accommodation sharing options such as Airbnb instead of booking a hotel. (Hostels are making a huge comeback in filling this market niche, according to Internet Marketing, Inc.).

Another observer of millennials wrote in *Forbes Magazine* that the spontaneity of many of their purchasing decisions could be characterized as "selective splurging", which is a tendency that is very difficult for providers of travel services and facilities to access regularly in a travel context.

The travel industry is still trying to come to terms with the unique way that millennials choose their destinations and make other travel decisions. According to Nielsen, the entire industry (including airlines and airports) needs to "embrace the power of user-generated content" (i.e., material generated by individuals, including posts and photos on Facebook, Twitter, Snapchat, and the like) over more traditional advertising channels to really connect with millennials, bearing in mind that:

- 85% of millennials check multiple websites before booking their travel to get the best deal possible.

- 46% book travel through a smartphone or tablet.

- 60% will upgrade their travel experience by purchasing in-flight Wi-Fi.

- 97% will post their experiences on social media while traveling, while 75% will post once a day.

- 68% will remain loyal to a program that offers them the most rewards.

The bottom line here for providers of travel services can be characterized by the question: "How's your app doing?" Millennials have high expectations in terms of connectivity and convenience and will quickly realign their brand loyalties from brands that are under-performing in IT terms to those that connect them more reliably and rapidly.

In terms of airport shopping, Nielsen's survey found that only a "select handful" of airports are fully exploiting the frequent impulse purchase urges of millennials. These are Dubai, Seoul Incheon, and London Heathrow, with only Singapore Changi and Hong Kong earning an honorable mention. At these five airports, about 70% of millennials were enticed to make a purchase, compared with just 42% at New York JFK and Rome Fiumicino. In comparison, at San Francisco International Airport, some 41% made retail purchases and 53% used airport food and beverage outlets.[23] Often, the most successful airport retail concessions in this regard feature high-end merchandise, which breaks the stereotype of the frugal millennial. A major international fashion designer has opened a "mega-store" in Seoul's Incheon Airport in response to this demand.

The firm Resonance Consulting did extensive surveys of millennial travel habits as well, and although it focused primarily on North America, some of the observations hold true for the worldwide cohort, and they dovetail well with Nielsen's observations. This source revealed two additional findings:

- Although millennials are often seen as solitary figures, in actuality some 58% of American millennials have children, and 44% reported traveling with their kids, at least occasionally.

- Perhaps more than any previous generation, millennials engage in "bleisure" travel, that is, combining a business trip with sightseeing or other leisure activities.

From the unpredictable and mercurial behavior of the millennials, this section will now move to the other extreme, the aging population and the elderly traveler, a cohort of the population that presents both opportunities and challenges to the industry.

AN AGING GLOBAL POPULATION - TRAVELING IN THE GOLDEN YEARS

The reality of an aging population is already here. The UN calculates that over 25% of Europe's population is currently over 60 years old, so many of the future shifts in global demographics can be deduced by viewing the population dynamics in that region as a "sneak preview" of what is likely to come elsewhere. Globally, seniors are healthier and longer-living than ever before. Many of them are now pursuing their personal travel "bucket lists" well into their 70's and 80's. This has tremendous ramifications for every phase of air transport. Although this demographic trend is yet another driver of aviation growth, the elderly passenger places unique demands on both airports and airlines.

The World Health Organization (WHO) released statistics in 2015[24] that calculated the average life expectancy for citizens of 183 countries as 70.5 years—72.7 years for females and 68.3 years for males. The breakdown by country, however, is perhaps more enlightening than these averages. There are 28 countries with an average age of over 80 years, and these people tend to be from developed nations where the propensity to travel is already quite high. Add to that an additional 39 countries where the average life expectancy is over 75 years. As noted above, the general health of senior citizens has improved significantly over the past few decades, helping many to continue to pursue an active lifestyle that includes travel.

The Airport Experience for Seniors

The U.S. Federal Aviation Administration (FAA) published a detailed report on the challenges posed by the elderly air traveler.[25] The preamble of the report is particularly compelling and one to which an air traveler of any age can relate, as follows:

"Where are the restrooms? Where is the baggage claim? How do I locate my rental car? How do I access Wi-Fi? These are questions most travelers ask when navigating an unfamiliar airport. Even experienced air travelers have moments when locating a service or facility within an airport becomes a challenge. Imagine how much more challenging these issues become if the traveler is dealing with musculoskeletal problems that may limit the ability to walk through an airport terminal. Or deteriorating sight and hearing that limit the ability to read terminal signage or understand recorded announcements. Or the psychological challenges of anxiety if running late for a flight..."

Anyone who has traveled by air is familiar with the stressful nature of air travel. Even the best-managed airports can be noisy and somewhat chaotic during peak periods. Security procedures, while increasingly attempting to take on a customer service guise, are unpredictable at best and intimidating at worst. Although both airports and airlines attempt to deliver a "seamless" travel experience, travel involves many unpredictable factors beyond anyone's control. Severe weather, aircraft mechanical problems, IT system malfunctions, congestion on the ramp, and airspace congestion, among other issues, are just some of the factors that can disrupt one's journey.

The FAA report goes on to provide many useful recommendations to enhance the airport experience for the elderly. Without specifically using the word "compassion", that is indeed the mindset that it implies should prevail when considering airport facilitation issues for the growing aging segment of the traveling population.

An interesting example of an airport exhibiting this "compassion" factor is Southwest Florida International Airport (RSW), located in Fort Myers, Florida. The director of operations at RSW summarized the airport's approach as: "A large number of the passengers who travel through Southwest Florida International Airport are more than 65 years of age. Consequently, we have worked to make the terminal experience easier, safer, and compliant with the Airport Cooperative Research Program (ACRP) recommendations of March 2015." Based on that philosophy and approach, during the past five years, management and staff at Southwest Florida International Airport (RSW) have implemented a wide variety of facility and service improvements designed with the older traveler in mind, including:

- Signs were added to direct passengers away from escalators and toward elevators to help create a safer environment for aging travelers.

- Shuttle buses pick up and drop off customers of the long-term surface parking lot and position right at the automobile, and bus drivers assist passengers with luggage.

- Parking lot users are given a parking spot location note so they can tell the shuttle bus driver their car's location upon their return.

- Customers are provided transportation from the long-term surface parking lot to the terminal door closest to a passenger's departure gate to minimize walking distances.

- Passengers who make advance reservations for commercial transportation can be picked up at the front curb closest to their bag carousel, and an on-demand taxi service is allowed to approach the front curb upon the customer's request.

- In the terminal, visual paging integrated into the new Flight Information Display System (FIDS) is used to accommodate passengers with hearing challenges.

- Electronic digital signage was added in the ticketing lobby to more efficiently guide passengers to the airline check-in area.

- Aisle widths were increased to accommodate wheel chairs, walkers, and other mobility devices.

- Wheelchair storage was added.

- Specially marked seats are provided for handicapped and wheelchair travelers in airline gate areas.

- Flat-plate baggage claim carousels were installed to assist the elderly in retrieving their checked bags.

The RSW strategy and measures for dealing with elderly passengers certainly seem to deserve a "best practices" label. However, all airports that have a demographic profile much like the general population will also need a plan for an increasing number of elderly passengers. As explained earlier, there will simply be more of them traveling in the future. Many of the improvements at RSW are not that costly to implement, except possibly for retrofitting the baggage carousels to allow better access.

The On-Board Experience for Seniors

IATA has taken a particular interest in caring for the elderly passenger and has published a document for its member airlines which is paraphrased in the following paragraphs.

The aging demographic of many countries translates for the airlines into many more elderly and infirm (or both) people wanting to travel by air. Airlines will benefit in terms of customer satisfaction by making the on-board experience safe and comfortable. Many international passengers traveling long distances will not have a good level of English or another commonly used language, and when they reach their destination they will require support from ground staff. (In the air, many airlines have their cabin crews wear badges that include the languages they speak on their name badge, a small detail which can be quite comforting to the passenger who is fluent in only one language.)

Health care may need to be provided in airport boarding areas and onboard as well. Robotics may prove to be an efficient and safe way to cater to some of these needs. As demand for travel increases, it may be increasingly difficult to turn planes around rapidly between flights. For example, as the percentage of people needing wheelchairs or enplaning (or deplaning) assistance increases, boarding and/or turnaround times will also increase. IATA has speculated about the need to have doctors or other medical staff on board flights that are carrying a large proportion of elderly passengers. There are also implications for the physical design of airplanes and airports. For example, in the short-term, planes may need to carry more medical devices, supplies, and trained staff. It may be possible to use "traveling health-care professionals" and advances in health-care robotics, as well as therapeutic devices. Airports may also need to be radically redesigned to facilitate accessibility. The document ends with a strong recommendation that, "IATA should establish core principles on facilitating the travel of older passengers and those with reduced mobility. An increasingly active aging population and changing attitudes to disability are likely to result in a greater need for the industry to support passengers with special requirements, for example on account of age, medical need, or disability."[26]

The U.S. Travel Association notes that currently older travelers (defined as over 65 years of age) account for 21% of all leisure travelers and 14% of all business passengers. It is expected that the proportion of older travelers choosing to fly will increase as a result of greater affluence and higher education levels. Although healthier in some respects than earlier generations, today's older traveler is still subject to a variety of chronic illnesses that could negatively impact their ability to navigate airport terminals confidently and safely. The challenge for airports and airlines going forward is how best to respond to the physical and psychological needs of the increasing number of aging and elderly travelers.

NICHE MARKETS CONTRIBUTING TO GROWTH

In recent years, a number of newer types of specialty niche market travelers have emerged that contribute to the growth in international air travel. These main specialty groups are residential tourists, religious tourists, international students, and migrant/

guest workers. Travelers in these groups are expected to grow in numbers over the next decade or more. The following paragraphs describe the characteristics of these groups and how they impact international travel statistics.

Homeowners without Borders – The Second Home Market

One subset of the aging population is the large number of retirees who literally "commute" between two homes. A prime example of this is the Algarve region of Portugal, which is heavily dependent on this type of traveler. In this region, thousands of Northern Europeans maintain second homes and travel back and forth frequently from their primary residences. The Algarve is particularly attractive to UK citizens, who own the majority of second homes in the region, but along with the Mediterranean coast of Spain, the Algarve also attracts home-owners from Germany, Scandinavia, the Benelux countries, and France.

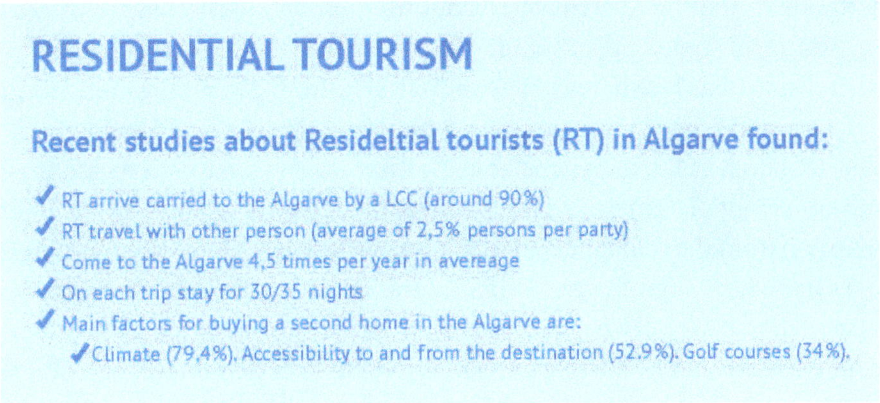

RESIDENTIAL TOURISM

Recent studies about Resideltial tourists (RT) in Algarve found:

✓ RT arrive carried to the Algarve by a LCC (around 90%)
✓ RT travel with other person (average of 2,5% persons per party)
✓ Come to the Algarve 4,5 times per year in avereage
✓ On each trip stay for 30/35 nights
✓ Main factors for buying a second home in the Algarve are:
   ✓ Climate (79,4%). Accessibility to and from the destination (52.9%). Golf courses (34%).

Figure 5-10   Residential tourist statistics, Algarve region, Portugal.[27]

One of the most surprising findings listed in Figure 5-10 is how much time residential tourists spend in their second homes in Portugal. With four to five trips per year, averaging 30 to 35 nights per trip, it turns out that about 40% of the year is spent in the second home. Another interesting point is that 90% of residential tourists arrive on low-cost carriers. The services of these LCCs have been expanded as the housing market has expanded in order to accommodate the demand from Northern Europe's aging population. It is clear that the LCCs are both enabling and benefitting from the second home market. Other major beneficiaries of the second-home boom are Faro airport in the Algarve, which has seen its traffic more than double since 2000, and the

LCCs themselves, which have realized steady growth and have developed a strong partnership with the airport.

Residential tourism is not unique to Portugal and Spain. For many years, Florida has been a second-home destination for retirees from Europe, particularly Germany and the U.K., as well as Canada and some Latin American nations. However, only recently have scheduled long-haul LCC services been available from Europe (mostly via Norwegian Airlines and WOW of Iceland), and the Florida market has been served mainly by seasonal charter operations in the winter months. The longer distance from Europe to the U.S. dictates less frequent visits to second homes than those with homes in Portugal and Spain because these latter destinations are only two to three hours away from Northern Europe by air, compared with the 10-hour flight to Florida. In addition, some 3.5 million Canadians visited Florida in 2017 according to the Orlando Sentinel; almost all these tourists, referred to as "snowbirds", travel during the winter months.

In Asia, there is another variant of residential tourism, something that Max Hirsh of Hong Kong University calls "circular migration". In this scenario, elderly retirees, primarily from Korea, Japan, and Taiwan, but also from Singapore and Hong Kong, maintain a second home in less expensive nations. Malaysia and Thailand are typical examples, and both of those nations actively promote the part-time residency of retirees. These residential tourists are not necessarily the most affluent in their societies. They are often from the middle class. Hirsh has noted that these circular travelers are often persons who "...can increase their standard of living with affordable housing, at the cost of being far from friends and relatives." Again, as in the case of residential tourists in Portugal and Spain, these retired people take advantage of LCCs to make their travel economical and they benefit particularly from the long-haul services provided by carriers such as AirAsiaX, where a large number of passengers have learned to "self-connect" on LCC routes through Kuala Lumpur International Airport, which just recently constructed a $1 billion LCC terminal adjacent to the existing terminals.[28]

Religious Tourism Driving Travel Growth – Pilgrims

The most famous of pilgrim journeys are perhaps the Hajj to Mecca for Muslims and trips to Israel for Christians, Jews, and Muslims. In India, where tourism accounts for about 7.5% of GDP, there is a well-established and growing market for Buddhists to follow the eight most important steps in the journey of Buddha.

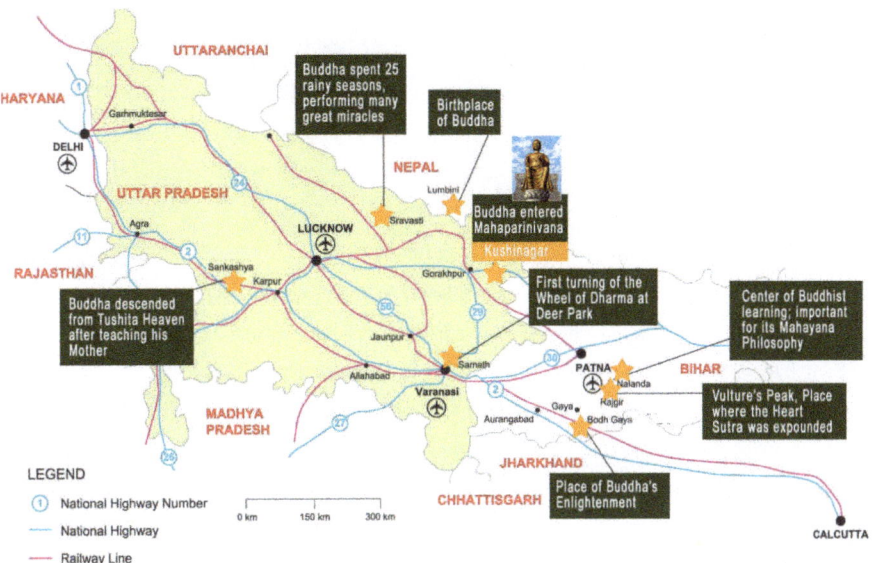

Figure 5-11   Religious tourism example: Buddhist journey through India.[29]

As an example, the map shown in Figure 5-11 depicts the eight stages of the Buddhist journey. Over two million tourists from abroad make this journey each year, arriving primarily from Japan, Thailand, Myanmar, Vietnam, and Cambodia. The Indian government has proposed building a new "gateway" airport at Kushinagar to facilitate entry to the pilgrimage circuit. New highways are also being built to create a more seamless travel experience. India has identified 13 different "circuits" for tourists, involving not only religiously or spiritually motived travelers, but also those focused on Indian ecology, heritage sites, wildlife, and beaches/ocean destinations. By keeping tourists "moving" on the circuit, they are exposed to a wide variety of local experiences and are also more likely to stay for prolonged periods as they complete a circuit.

International Travel by University Students

Recent statistics from the Organization for Economic Cooperation and Development (OECD) show that the global international student population has increased almost threefold since 2000, with an annual growth rate of over 10%, for an estimated total of about 5 million students. The U.S. hosts some one million students on its own, and about one-third of these are from China. According to the OECD, the trend towards international study is expected to rise sharply, and it forecasts that about 8 million students will be studying away from their home countries by 2025.

A key indicator of the globalization of the world economy is the presence of international students as a core portion of the student bodies at the world's leading universities. After remaining fairly stable over the past decade, the composition of host countries for foreign students is beginning to change. Currently, the USA remains the most popular country for international students, followed by the UK, Germany, France and Australia, with half of all international students pursuing degrees in these five countries. However, the traditional share of the USA and UK is declining, with Australia and Canada increasing in popularity as a result of intra-regional mobility (i.e., those who choose to study abroad, but within their home region). For the last few years, the most mobile students remain those from Asia, with China, India, and South Korea the leading sources of international students. Almost one in six international students is Chinese, and Asian students account for 53% of all students studying abroad. Not all these students travel long distances. Japan and Korea host large numbers of international students from neighboring countries, with 81% of international students in Japan and 75% in Korea coming from other East Asian countries.

As already mentioned, international student mobility is shifting geographically. At present, India is the UK's second largest source of international post-graduates (after China), but a recent British Council report indicates that demographic changes and increasing demand means that the percentage of international students from Nigeria is likely to overtake the percentage from India by 2024. The report predicts that Indian post-graduates, in particular, will form only 9% of the UK's growth in international student numbers to 2024—around 24,000 students—compared with 29,000 post-graduates from Nigeria. The number of students from China studying in UK universities is large and growing, with a 44% increase predicted over the next decade by the British Council.

Although very few data is available on the propensity of these students to travel, they are obviously a fertile and growing market for air travel. Most international students are from either middle- or upper-class families, and they tend to travel back to their native countries occasionally during their university tenure. In addition, many of these students tend to celebrate their graduations with family members who travel from abroad to congratulate the student on his or her achievement.

Migrant and 'Guest' Workers

Recent figures from the International Labor Organization (ILO)[30] show that there were about 150 million migrants in the world who were economically active in 2017. (This cohort does not include those immigrating for political or family reasons, or the movement of refugees—only those working short-term abroad are included). The Asia-Pacific region hosts 17.2% of all migrant workers worldwide (25.8 million persons). The Arab Gulf states host the highest proportion of migrant workers compared with indigenous workers (35.6%) and host 11.7% of migrant workers worldwide, most of them from Asia. Construction of the stadiums for the 2022 World Cup in Doha, which relies heavily on foreign labor, drew international attention to the sometimes difficult working conditions that such migrants face.

One of the best ways to quantify the actual number of migrants is to track financial remittances to their home countries because these statistics are revealed in national GDP accounts as economic inflows. There were five Asian countries among the top 10 remittance-receiving countries, according to the World Bank. Migrant workers make an enormous development contribution to regional economies, providing skills, labor, services, and competitiveness to their destination countries. To their countries of origin, migrant workers provide financial remittances, and at the end of their foreign assignment, they bring new skills and knowledge back to their home countries. As mentioned earlier, in destination countries, many migrant workers fill labor market niches by doing jobs that are difficult to fill locally.

Migrant labor provides yet another large cohort that demands aviation services. Most travel arrangements are made for the laborers at the most economical fares possible, in either the lowest fare class on legacy carriers, or when possible, on an LCC. One airport in particular—Cochin International Airport in India—is a good illustration of the market power of the migrant worker cohort (Figure 5-12). That airport was actually conceived and built around the notion that it would be used extensively by migrant laborers from southern India traveling to work in the UAE and other destinations in the Persian Gulf region. As an airport, Cochin International Airport has achieved considerable success. It is a primary base for Air India Express operations and is a focus city for Air Asia India, Air India, Indigo, Jet Airways and SpiceJet, the latter three being LCCs.

When it opened in 1999, Cochin Airport was the first public-private partnership (PPP) in India (and one of the first worldwide). Built for functionality and efficiency, without many architectural frills or elaborate concessions, Cochin cost just over $50 million to construct, far less than the average new airport terminal. Indeed, it had quite likely the lowest construction cost of any comparable airport terminal anywhere in recent decades. (It also was innovative in energy use, becoming India's only 100 percent solar-powered airport.) The airport crossed the 10 million mark for passengers in 2017 and is now the fourth largest airport for international passengers in the country. The backbone of its passenger base continues to be migrant labor travelers. The population of the Kochi metropolitan area was around 2.5 million in 2016. It is quite extraordinary therefore that the airport would have four times that number of passengers. This high ratio is largely due to the fact that it has a large catchment area that serves as a "collection point" for migrant labor moving back and forth from southern India, mostly to the Gulf. Cochin also handles many religious pilgrims and is a major point of departure for flights to Mecca for the Hajj. Two new terminals have been added over the past two decades, and the airport has now moved far beyond its initial niche of providing service for migrants to become a full-service airport with a considerable number of business-class travelers, who have increased in number as the region has prospered.

Figure 5-12   Cochin International Airport in India (stock photo).

AIR TRANSPORT ACCESSIBILITY FOR ALL

In addition to the specialty travel niches discussed above, there are a few other non-traditional travel groups that are increasingly traveling by air. Due to their special circumstances and/or needs, accommodating these groups is already having a direct impact on air service providers, and that trend is expected to increase in the coming years. These groups include persons with disabilities and reduced mobility and traditionally under-represented groups. The following paragraphs describe the characteristics of and needs of these groups and how they impact the services and facilities of all types of travel service providers.

Accommodating Persons of Reduced Mobility and with Developmental Disorders

The UN Convention on the Rights of Persons with Disabilities is based on the premise that persons with disabilities and/or reduced mobility have the same international rights as other citizens, including freedom of movement. Accommodating the special needs of these persons as passengers means that both airports and airlines need to adopt policies and practical measures to ensure that these passengers have a seamless travel experience.

ACI provides extensive guidance for its airport members, both in its Policy Handbook and in the document *Airports and Persons with Disabilities*.[31] In its policy, ACI uses ICAO's definition of such passengers, who are defined as: "...any person whose mobility is reduced due to a physical incapacity (sensory or locomotor), an intellectual deficiency, age, illness or any other cause of disability when using transport, and whose situation needs special attention and the adaptation to the person's needs of the services made available to all passengers". ACI's policy underscores the point that the needs of persons with disabilities and/or reduced mobility should be, "...borne in mind by architects and engineers responsible for designing new structures or modifying existing ones, and by those responsible for operating the airport in question, with a view to the provision of suitable means to ensure easy and comfortable access to all facilities by passengers with disabilities, at a suitable level of quality of service. All procedures forming part of the journey of air travel, including check-in, immigration and customs, security clearance, embarkation and debarkation, departure, air carriage, and arrival should be adapted to the needs of persons with disabilities and/or reduced mobility in order to facilitate clearance and air transportation of such persons in a dignified manner."

Airports and airlines have for many years facilitated the travel of passengers with physical disabilities as a part of their mandate to accommodate the needs of the public. However, some disabilities are "hidden" from view, and they present a real challenge for the industry. This section will focus on two case studies that show a unique approach to these types of passengers, one case from San Francisco International Airport and the other from the UK. Just before looking at the two examples, a brief explanation of autism disorders is given to provide a typical example of a special-needs disability that increasingly needs to be accommodated by air transport providers.

Autism is often described as one of a number of "hidden disabilities". Passengers with autism present unique challenges for airports and airlines because these passengers require a high degree of sensitivity, empathy, and compassion during their journey on the part of both airport and airline staff. The "spectrum" of autistic disorders ranges from extreme (sometimes accompanied by an inability to communicate and/or even violent behavior) to "high-functioning", where the condition is often barely noticeable to outsiders. It is the latter category that represents a fairly large cohort of travelers, although no precise data is available on actual numbers. Even persons at the high-functioning end of the spectrum can be prone to feelings of paranoia and insecurity in situations which are crowded, noisy, or chaotic, conditions that are likely to occur at some point in almost any airport scenario. These passengers can often possess heightened sensitivity to touch and to sound and sometimes recoil from being touched or bumped. In the security process, for example, a "pat-down" could be excruciating to endure for an autistic person. Often, the high-functioning autistic traveler is accompanied by someone who can explain the nature of the condition to airport and airline staff. Many autistic travelers are children traveling with their parents. There are also cases where older autistic individuals travel on their own, and hence the acuity level of the airport and airline staff must be very high. They therefore need to be educated and informed as to how to interact with these individuals.

In 2016, San Francisco International Airport (SFO) inaugurated a program to bring autistic travelers and their families to the airport to interact with airport and airline staff in a simulation of an actual pre-flight and boarding experience. Called *"Ready, Set, Fly"*, the simulation had the stated intention: "...to provide a real-world experience of air travel to individuals and families with autism and developmental disabilities." Their goal was to be an exceptional airport in service to the communities served. After running the *Ready, Set, Fly* simulation for a few years, SFO staff members have seen an ever-growing interest in this type of realistic experience. To host such a simulation requires the co-operation and assistance of numerous parties, including airport staff and participating airlines as well as advocacy groups for people with intellectual and developmental disabilities. According to the parties involved, the onboard experience helps participants achieve a better understanding of how to prepare and gives them a real feel for what a trip by air is like. The simulation gives them all a chance to assess a child's tolerances and triggers before the real flight. SFO and its partners believe that all families deserve the opportunity to fly and that those that understand airport rules, regulations, and support services in advance will be better prepared and will have a much more relaxing and comfortable trip.

The UK Civil Aviation Authority (CAA) recently took decisive action to address the autistic traveler issue with guidance for all UK airports that was published in late 2016. The UK's action came after several high-profile passenger experiences were highlighted in the press, one involving a woman who requested special assistance and was told by airline staff that she was "wasting their time".

The four main elements of the CAA guidance for airports are to:

- Give passengers the option to wear a lanyard or wristband (or other discreet identifier) to make airport staff aware that they might need extra help during security procedures or elsewhere in the airport.

- Provide enhanced disability awareness training to all staff that may interface with the passenger, including those at security search areas, as well as those who provide direct assistance to disabled people.

- Introduce dedicated lanes for families with young children and those requiring assistance. Passengers with hidden disabilities can use these lanes, which provide a less stressful and hurried experience.

- Publish clear information for people with hidden disabilities, including pictorial guides, videos, and other online guides on what to expect at the airport, especially at the security screening stage.

The above cases are just a couple of examples of how airports, airlines, and civil authorities are paying more attention than ever before to special-needs travelers. As travel continues to diversify and open up to all members of society globally, development of such programs will need to become widespread throughout the international aviation industry.

Toward Gender Equality

Another area where increased societal sensitivity will have impacts in the future on the provision of services by air transport services providers will be the increased need to both accommodate and serve traditionally under-represented demographic groups, including women. (Sidebar: Our research found that the traveling needs and behaviors of LGTBQ tourists and business travelers were almost exactly the same as the population at large.)

On January 1, 2018, Iceland became the first country in the world to make pay inequality illegal. Icelandic companies that cannot prove pay equality will be fined *daily* until the gap is erased. That should have been a really big deal, and yes, in Iceland it was. As the Icelandic Women's Rights Association *noted at the time,* however, equal pay for equal work had been mandated by Icelandic law since 1961. However, the law is nonetheless welcomed and unprecedented for any nation. The Association pointed out that: "What is remarkable about the new law in Iceland is how it enforces equal-pay standards. It does not rely on an employee to prove she was discriminated against. Instead, the burden is on companies to prove that their pay practices are fair."

Another highly-publicized legal action occurred in June 2018, when Saudi women were accorded the right to drive an automobile for the first time. Although this represents another uplifting story in the battle for gender equality, it is a minor bright spot against a backdrop of very slow progress. True equality seems a long way off, as noted by the British Ministry of Defense, in its publication *Global Strategic Trends – to 2045*.

With specific reference to the aviation sector, after reviewing the statistics, it was concluded that the gender gap is even wider than in other industries in terms of the proportion of female executive-level employees and flight crew members. As the following section highlights in detail, this is an area where the aviation industry has a lot of work to do to catch up with other industries and society in general.

The Air Transport Workplace: A Pronounced Gender Gap

Speaking to the IATA Annual General Meeting in Sydney, Australia in June 2018, ICAO Secretary General Dr. Fang Liu emphasized that while "air transport connects people, cultures, and businesses across the globe, and strengthens socio-economic development worldwide, at the same time, it has not been very successful at providing an open, inclusive working environment for women." She went on to underscore, "In China, for instance there is a proverb which states that *women hold up half the sky,* but in aviation today, whether we are talking pilots or airline CEOs, women are only making up one-twentieth of these positions." Dr. Liu called on airline CEOs worldwide to make gender parity a personal priority, stressing that it must be driven from the top in any organization, something that he planned to emphasize at ICAO's 2018 Gender Equality Programming Summit on the topic.[32]

The statistics on gender parity in aviation reflect the reality of an "old boys' network" that is perhaps not found in any other sector of the global economy. For example:

- Only six of IATA's 280 member airlines have female CEOs.

- Just two of IATA's 31 board members are female.

- Only a couple of women are CEOs of major international airports in ACI's Asia-Pacific region.

In North America, there are over one dozen women running airports, but basically, in the executive boardrooms, the gender gap is clearly significant. On the flight deck, the news there is a bit more upbeat, but still decades away from parity. The *Airman's Database* website, which maintains records on 650,000 pilots worldwide, ranks Finland as having the highest percentage of female pilots (12.1%). Next on the list is Sweden at 8.2%, then

France at 7.6%, and the U.S. at 5.1%. The global average has been calculated at about 5.4% of all pilots being women. So indeed, Dr. Liu's reference to "one in twenty" was quite accurate in terms of the global community of pilots, but it was overly optimistic in terms of executive positions in aviation. Going forward, the *Airman's Database* notes that over 12% of persons in training to be pilots are female, which would portend that a somewhat higher proportion of females will be in the cockpit in the years ahead.

As highlighted in the above-mentioned *Airman's Database*, a number of initiatives are underway to showcase opportunities for women in aviation, including:[33]

- Alaska Airlines took a unique approach in encouraging male leaders to share a candid dialogue with women about what men can do to support and advance women in the workplace.

- The *International Aviation Women's Association* has for 30 years promoted air transport as a career choice for women and supports their advancement in the industry.

- GE Aviation has a specific program of action called *"Cultivate"* to develop and retain women engineers in the business. The parent company announced in 2017 an objective to hire 20,000 female engineers across the company (a level that would bring gender parity by 2020).

- Airlines such as *British Airways* are ensuring that gender equality is one of their central aims in promoting diversity in the workforce, particularly in leadership positions.

- The easyJet company has *set a target* for 20% of its new pilot cadets to be female by 2020, which would be a significant increase over the current figure of 6%.

- Airbus promotes *gender equality* through a number of programs aimed at inspiring women and young girls to become involved with aviation.

- ICAO has been supporting the *"Dreams Soar"* project, in which the first-ever Afghan-American female pilot, Shaesta Waiz, has been conducting an around-the-world flight to encourage more young women to become pilots.

Programs such as these all contribute to the goal of opening up more career opportunities in aviation for women. In looking at the current international aviation industry and its under-represented proportion of females, there is simply no way to go but up.

CONCLUSION AND SUMMARY

The first part of this closing section is a brief Conclusion containing some overall general remarks that summarize the essence of the foregoing discussion of the Demographic Changes and Trends megatrend and offering some general advice to managers about how best to cope with it. The second part of this section is a Management Summary that recaps in point form all the major subjects discussed earlier during the detailed analysis and discussion of the Demographic Changes and Trends megatrend. The points are presented with the perspective of aviation professionals and managers in mind. Essentially, each point in the Management Summary represents a key observation or conclusion that was made during the detailed analysis and discussion.

Conclusion

The degree to which the aviation industry contributes to global economic growth makes it powerful and essential to the world economy. At the individual level, there are millions of personal air travel stories about connecting with friends, families, and business colleagues. One need only spend some time in the arrivals area of any airport to see the way that aviation brings people together, uniting families, enabling students to study abroad, cementing personal and business relationships, and providing access to tourist and cultural destinations, all of which enable people to gain an international perspective and a respect for the diversity of humanity. Indeed, IATA's CEO recently described the aviation industry as being "in the business of freedom". It's an idealistic and uplifting image that most people working in the industry would willingly embrace, but maintaining that state will be a challenge for all sectors of the international aviation industry.

Perhaps the best way to conclude this chapter on global demographic changes and trends is to go back to the simplicity of supply and demand economics. The demographic trends described herein all point in the same direction, with an increased demand for air travel services above and beyond what is happening today. On the supply side, the scenarios going forward are less clear. Even though the airlines are healthier financially than ever before, with ambitious order books aiming to grow the global fleet, their counterparts in airports and air navigation services are facing serious challenges as to how to provide sufficient airport infrastructure and airspace capacity in the coming decades.

It will take enormous financial outlays as well as political will to expand airports so that they can meet demand. Many airports already face congestion as existing capacity is tested. Even in North America, which has the advantage of having dozens of multiple-runway airports, ACI is calling for $100 billion in necessary new infrastructure spending through 2021. Other regions of the world have calculated similar capital needs. The only possible exception to this trend may be in Africa and Latin America, which, except for a few airports, are expected to be able to accommodate the forecast growth over the coming decades. Constraints on airspace capacity are also troubling, but are less vexing because the technology for more efficient use of airspace is already in place, although there will be some problems in Europe. Other regions do have occasional problems; for example, the U.S. East Coast and China, where the military's control of large sections of airspace often disrupts commercial aviation. Nevertheless, on balance, the global air navigation system can meet future demand.

The ultimate danger on the supply side is that eventually airport congestion could become so annoying that it will discourage air travel altogether for a high proportion of travelers. Even now it is difficult to find a frequent traveler who does not have his or her version of the "travel experience from hell", be it an airport or an airline situation. At what point will passengers—particularly leisure passengers who are looking forward to a relaxing holiday—say "no more"? They might choose alternative means of transport or the ultimate option of foregoing their holiday abroad altogether.

Perhaps the most encouraging factor for the aviation industry as it faces this capacity challenge is that this issue is not slowly creeping into view. Indeed, industry leaders have for many years seen the crunch coming and have adopted strategies designed to cope. There is not a major hub airport anywhere that does not put a premium on customer service, knowing that passengers will gravitate to hubs that produce the most seamless (and perhaps even enjoyable) journey. By leveraging technology to squeeze the most out of existing assets and by simultaneously building services and infrastructure for the future, the industry should continue to play its distinctive role in the "freedom business".

Management Summary

Based on the foregoing discussion, there is no doubt that the Demographic Changes and Trends megatrend will have major impacts on the international aviation industry over the next 15 to 20 years and beyond. In many ways, adapting to this megatrend and implementing mitigation measures will have considerable impact on the way in which airlines, airports, and air navigation services will develop and operate their businesses, particularly during the next decade, as they continue to adjust to this new reality. Numerous significant conclusions and observations have been made during the course of the detailed analysis contained earlier in this chapter. Accordingly, the following section highlights the important challenges that aviation managers at all levels will need to take into account when determining how best to deal with the Demographic Changes and Trends megatrend when planning for the future.

Global Population Trends

- Global population growth has tapered off in recent years, defying the gloomy predictions of scholars back in the 1960s, some of whom were predicting widespread starvation as a burgeoning global population outpaced food production. Although there will continue to be areas of high population growth, mostly in Africa and Asia, they will be largely offset by slow/negative growth in as many as 80 nations, with birthrates too low to produce a net population increase.

World Travel and Tourism

- Total global aviation activity in terms of passengers and air freight is expected to increase in the coming decades. Passenger travel is forecast to grow at an average annual rate of about 4.5% to reach 15 billion passengers by 2030, and air freight traffic is expected to increase even more rapidly.

- The main driver of demand for air transport services and facilities will be a rapidly growing middle class, especially in Asia. Higher disposable incomes will make air travel affordable for many for the first time, and middle-class newcomers will have the means to travel to both domestic and international destinations, including increased leisure travel.

- Travel and tourism represent the fourth largest global economic sector and have consistently maintained a higher rate of economic growth than global GDP. As a catalyst for employment and economic prosperity, the aviation sub-sector is among the most vibrant in both enabling and creating growth.

- Airlines have never been in a better financial position to accommodate the anticipated growth in traffic, with revenues up and orders for new for aircraft, both wide-body and narrow-body, at their highest point ever.

- Although the global network of airports currently has enough capacity on paper, this capacity is not always in the right places. Because of the displaced capacity situation, many airports will become much busier, with significant delays by 2040. More private or public sector investment is needed to enhance and optimize the infrastructure of the existing airport network.

- Jobs in aviation tend to be well-paid and offer a high degree of satisfaction in most instances. Until recently, the industry had few problems attracting talented recruits, although for a time the dynamic economic growth in both India and Malaysia caused shortages in aviation positions.

Millennials – The Connected Generation

- Millennials are expected to be the most influential generation ever in defining the travel experience. The behavior of tech-savvy, always-connected millennials needs to be understood and approached in an entirely different way than that of previous generations.

Aging Global Population

- At the other end of the age spectrum, an aging population, with longer life expectancies due to advances in health care, will continue to travel well into its golden years, creating numerous challenges for the industry in terms of both the airport and on-board experience.

Niche Market Growth

- A number of other "niche" markets will continue to put demands on air transport, including owners of residences in two different countries, pilgrims traveling to/from holy religious sites, migrant laborers working far from their home countries, and international university students.

Air Transport Accessibility

- Passengers with reduced physical mobility and those with behavioral disorders (or unseen disabilities) will grow in number and will require special attention and sensitivity throughout their air journey. Accommodations will have to be made for them by all parties in the aviation industry.

- The gender gap in aviation is very large compared with other sectors of the economy. The proportion of females in executive positions at airports and airlines is estimated at only about 2%, whereas on the flight deck, the proportion is between 5% and 6%. Efforts to achieve male-female parity in both compensation and in numbers in the international aviation industry are still in their infancy.

REFERENCES

1   Ehrlich, P. (1968). *The Population Bomb*. Ballantine Books.

2   https://www.un.org/development/DESA/Publications/2017/06/2017/World Population Prospects: The 2017 Revision.

3   United Nations, Population Division (2017). *World Mortality 2017 – Data Booklet*.

4   United Nations Population Division (2017). *World Population Prospects: The 2017 Revision, Volume 1: Comprehensive Tables*.

5   World Bank, data.worldbank.org/indicators /SP.POP.DPND (2017).

6   Kharas, H., Senior Fellow, Brookings Institution: www.weforum.org/agenda/authors/homi-kharas./

7   https://www.atag.org/component/factfigures (2017).

8   http://www.aci.aero/World_Air Traffic Forecasts (2016)._

9   ACI World Press release/15/06/2018/Strong first-quarter traffic growth continues.

10   http://wttc.org (2018)/economic-impact/.

11   IATA documentation for Annual General Meetings (2013–2018).

12   ACI World/Airport Economics/2018 Report.

13   www.aci.aero/publications/policy-briefs/creating-fertile-ground-for-private-investment-in-airports/2018.

14   Remarks to ACI World General Assembly, June 2018.

15   Eurocontrol (2018, June). *The Challenges to Growth* and remarks by Eurocontrol's Director General upon the release of the report.

16   Strauss, W., and Howe, N. (2000). *Millennials rising*. Random House.

17   Barton, C., Koslow, L., and Beauchamp, C. (2014). *How millennials are changing the face of marketing forever*. Boston Consulting Group.

18   Personal account related by a senior executive at Burbank Bob Hope Airport, March 2018.

19   Clark, S. (2017). "Four ways millennials are changing the face of travel". *Atlantic Monthly*.

20   Dychtwald, Z. (2018, February 17). "Chinese millennials are about to kick U.S. millennials' butts". *New York Post*.

21   University of Wisconsin (epd.wisc.edu), Department of Engineering Professional Development (2018). *How are millennials changing the workplace*.

22   The AC Nielsen Company (2017). *Millennial traveler study report*.

23   Information from SFO surveys, 2017.

24   http://www.who.int/gho/mortality_burden_disease/life_tables/en/.

25   (2014). *Impacts of aging travelers on airports*. Sponsored by US FAA; conducted by the Transportation Research Board.

26   www.iata.org/passenger/passengerfacilitation.

27   Presentation by Professor Claudia Ribeiro at Passenger Terminal Expo-Amsterdam/March 14, 2017.

28   Hirsh, M. (2016). *Airport urbanism: Infrastructure and mobility in Asia*. University of Minnesota Press.

29   Bhatt, N., presentation at Passenger Terminal Expo/Amsterdam/March 14, 2017.

30   www.ilo.org/global/topics/labour-migration/policy-areas/2017/.

31   https://www.aci-na.org/static/conferences/images/13%20-Davis.%20Briggs--ADA.pdf.

32   www.icao.int/2018/SG-speech-IATA-agm.

33   www.aviationdb.com/Aviation/AirmanQuery.shtm.

6

INNOVATIVE
TECHNOLOGICAL
CHANGE

INTRODUCTION

Innovative technology, or more precisely the accelerated development and implementation of new technologies, is probably the most visible and ubiquitous of the megatrends because it affects our daily lives and the way in which we carry out even the most mundane of tasks. Indeed, taking the example of aviation itself, its first 50 years have largely contributed to the transformation, or one might even say disruption, of the world as we knew it and fostered transformative dynamics such as globalization of trade, international movements, and the acceleration of exchanges at all levels.

Technological change by its nature is far from being a smooth process, and its effects have had both positive and negative impacts. For instance, the rise of faster transport, led by the aviation industry, has both shrunk the planet and fostered a more integrated world, creating a truly global economy that has fueled the growth of many economies. On the other hand, it has also accelerated the global spread of diseases such as SARS or Ebola and enabled the rapid growth of the illicit narcotics industry.

Whether one's view of technological change is positive or negative, two premises are critical and will lead the discussion throughout this chapter. First, change is inevitable, and the pace of change is accelerating as new technologies foster and create whole new fields of economic activity. Second, the outcomes are far from certain and difficult to predict. Indeed, technology is simply a tool at the service of societies, economies, and governments, and its application and downstream effects are largely dictated by the level of cooperation and planning, or lack thereof, among various stakeholders.

Another key aspect of technological innovation is that it can have a push or pull effect on the industries that it serves and the problems that it solves. As shall be shown later in this chapter, in some cases, technological advances such as the Internet of Things (IoT) or artificial intelligence (AI) create entire new fields and move industries in new directions.

Technology enthusiasts foresee bright futures where transactions will be facilitated by removing friction points and barriers, trade will be open and transparent, new business models will transform the world, and trust will be at the center of human activity. However, current news reports tell a different story. Media coverage often focuses on negative reports such as invasion of personal privacy, massive cyber-attacks that can bring down entire companies or even governments, and highly disruptive patterns that are at the heart of everything from entire new economic activities such as social media or the so-called sharing economy to the manipulation of democracy and the rise of terrorism. Conspiracy theorists have never been as numerous, widespread, or influential as they are today.

As always, reality is far more complex and nuanced than either of these extremes suggests. In this light, technology is a tool that is used to achieve desired or planned goals, but because of the growing complexity of our societies, it requires far more coordination and collaboration than in the past to become truly successful at a macro or societal level.

Contrary to popular myth, technological change doesn't emerge "out of the blue" from a single person's imagination. As Pablo Picasso commented about computers and their usefulness, "But they are useless. They can only give you answers". In his view, all innovation is the result of a planning and investigation process that seeks answers to questions. Furthermore, innovation is typically built upon a series of existing solutions that are assembled in a new and original combination.

The aviation industry, especially compared with other economic sectors, is quite adept at planning and puts great emphasis on long-range thinking. It should therefore be a fertile environment for disciplined innovation. Reasoned and well-researched planning has made air transport into the safest mode of transportation thanks to the careful integration of new technologies to ensure an ever-greater level of reliability and safety. This, however, has been achieved by imposing regulations, most of which take years to develop and are, most of the time, lagging behind commercial and technical realities. This dichotomy between innovation and cautious regulation profoundly marks the aviation industry and often leads to unforeseen or intended consequences, in spite of the best intentions.

As Clayton Christensen argues in *The Innovator's Dilemma*[1], innovation comes in two flavors, sustaining technologies and disruptive technologies. Sustaining technologies are built progressively upon the previous generation's solutions and technologies. In other words, they improve upon an existing model. The discussion throughout this chapter will make the point that the aviation industry has always been based on sustaining technologies, with the possible exception of the Wright brothers' first flight. It will be shown that this approach also drives and shapes the highly constraining regulatory mechanisms that are a fixture of the aviation industry worldwide. These sustaining changes are one of the main drivers behind aviation's remarkable growth performance, averaging 5% per year since 1950, as illustrated in Figure 6-1.

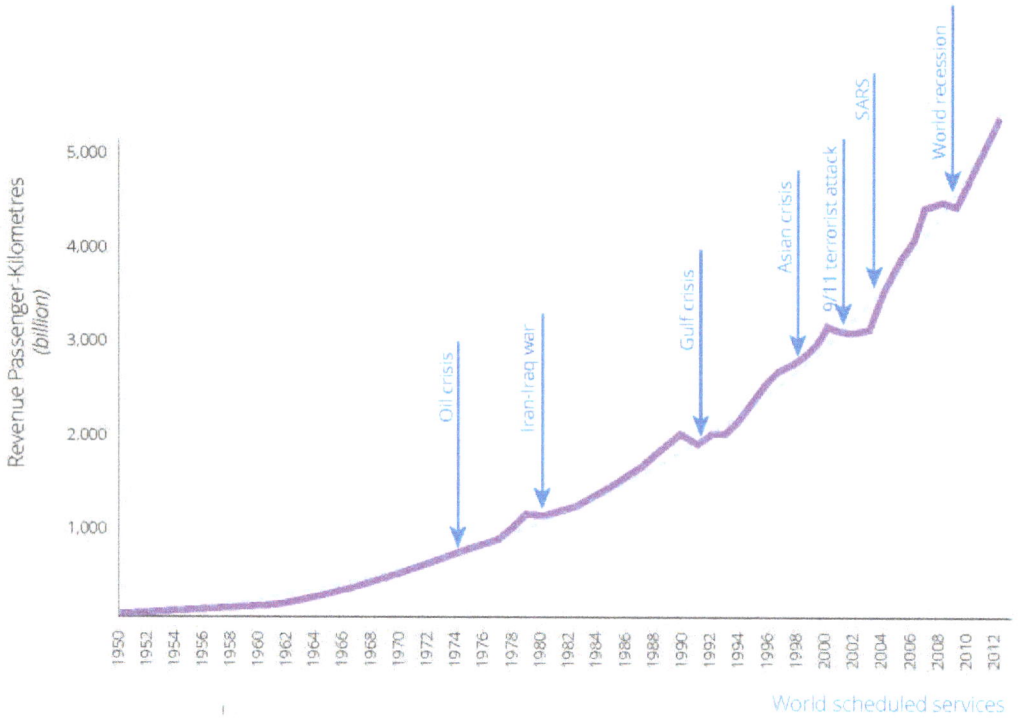

Figure 6-1   Commercial aviation growth (ICAO Facts & Figures, 2017).

Maintaining the growth rate shown in Figure 6-1 is a key challenge for the industry and will require new thinking as aviation, and airports in particular, begin to approach breaking points as they become unable to provide services at the levels of quality, comfort, and reliability that travelers have come to expect. Sustaining technologies are no longer delivering benefits or gains fast enough to cope with growth.

Disruptive technologies, on the other hand, are new solutions, and these solutions might answer existing requirements or fulfill needs that did not even exist before the disruption. The advent of social media and the sharing economy over the past decade are prime examples of disruptive thinking, yet many executives are convinced that the aviation industry will not be disrupted by them. It is their belief that humanity has always had the desire to travel and that the sustained growth of the industry for the last 60 years proves that it is providing the right services. As this chapter will point out, aviation is indeed now ripe for disruption, and it will happen through a combination of things, including new and better data, improved analytical tools, aeronautical technology advances, changes in human behaviors powered by social media, more transparent information, and new business models.

These disruptive innovations are not coming through technological changes from within, but originate from the application of outside innovations that invade the aviation space. Travelers, as well as cargo, will be treated very differently over the next decade or more, and these changes will require major transformations by carriers, airports, regulators, and other service providers to the industry.

Even with the best planning tools, change always brings with it a large degree of uncertainty. This leads to outcomes, positive or negative, that were not foreseen, and this discussion would not be complete without looking at these risks and shedding some light on how they can be better understood and controlled.

All these changes, which can be loosely referred to as the "new economy" or the "industrial Internet", are transforming the world, but they themselves will also be subject to perpetual transformation. This discussion will look at how the disruptors go about conceptualizing, developing, and implementing their radical new ideas. The power of ideas is just as important as the technologies that they have spawned, and this chapter will examine such transformative concepts and methodologies as: disruption theory, agile engineering, and value chain analysis. A basic grasp of these concepts is important to help us understand possible future scenarios.

Finally, before embarking on an examination of innovative technology and its effects, one needs to be aware that the acceleration of innovative technology development itself generates a greater degree of uncertainty and unpredictability. As a result, it is becoming more and more difficult to distinguish between truly meaningful innovations that will affect us in the long run and hyped innovations that sizzle out and disappear as fast as they rise to prominence.

Joe Betts-Lacroix, a noted American biophysicist and entrepreneur[2], captured this effect by comparing the adoption cycle of an innovation with its perception, or visibility, cycle, as illustrated in Figure 6-2.

The model depicted in Figure 6-2 will be used throughout this discussion to assist in gauging where a particular innovation is located on the Betts-Lacroix curve because this will provide clarity regarding how mature the innovation is and whether it will have a meaningful impact in the next couple of decades. Although somewhat arbitrary, this is a very useful tool to filter and select the plethora of innovations that appear every day.

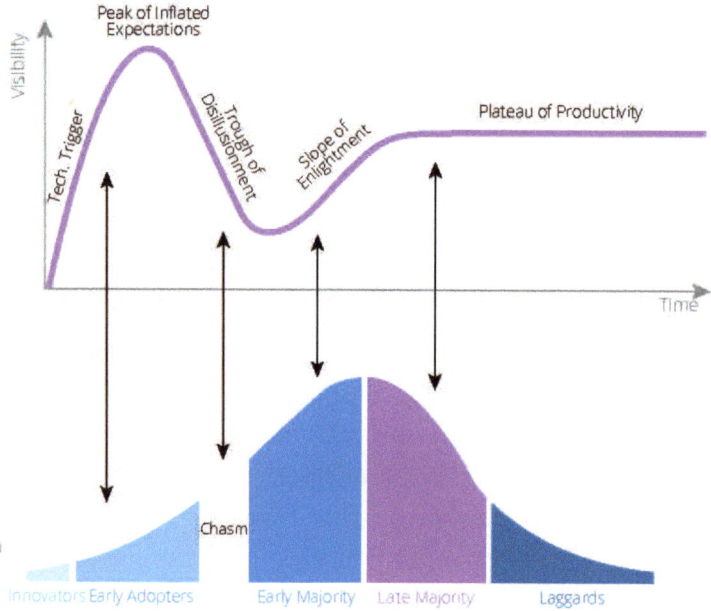

Figure 6-2   Perception vs. adoption (adapted from Joe Betts-Lacroix, Foundersresearch.com, 2010).

In this light, and using the tools described above, this chapter will be looking at technological transformation, both sustaining and disruptive, in four main areas: aircraft technology, automation and human-machine symbiosis, Big Data and artificial intelligence, and convergence and security.

AIRCRAFT TECHNOLOGY

Even though the civil aviation industry has changed enormously over the last 100 years, the workhorse of the industry, the commercial airliner, has hardly changed since World War II. It still uses the basic tube-and-wings design that the Douglas Corporation pioneered with its DC-3 model, launched in 1936. In the same vein, the world's most flown jet plane, the Boeing B-737, also uses the same fundamental design today that it sported when it was launched in 1967.

This is not to say that avionics, as well as propulsion plants, have not changed. Today's engine and avionics technologies are radically different from those used in 1936 and 1967. However, the tube-and-wings design is still here because it is very well understood and reasonably efficient, but this design paradigm is nearing its maximum level of efficiency because engineers have squeezed out almost all the performance and safety improvements that they could out of this venerable configuration. The future will see radical new designs emerge, such as flying wings, and possibly the return of supersonic commercial flights.

However, the design of new airframes is an extremely expensive business, fraught with great risks, an onerous burden of technical and safety tests and regulatory compliance requirements, and a large degree of political interference because all aircraft manufacturers in the world rely to a large extent on various types of subsidies to mitigate their risks and finance their long-term development cycles.

It is therefore safe to say that the industry will not see a radical departure from the tube-and-wings model over the next 20 or so years. What will occur during this period are significant changes in the types of propulsion plants and aircraft types that will be flown, as well as how, and by whom, these aircraft will be flown. These changes will be driven by two main categories of factors; external factors, such as environmental pressures and human resources shortages, and incremental sustaining technological changes in propulsion-plant performance in terms of range and reliability.

In the first category, the International Civil Aviation Organization (ICAO) has recently committed to a reduction in the international aviation industry's carbon footprint, and this will be achieved only by looking at new fuel types. (Chapter 2 of this book discusses this and other subjects related to climate change and environmental issues.) Similarly, the growth of the aviation industry, fueled by other megatrends such as economic prosperity and demographic changes and trends, means that the industry is already facing serious challenges, including a shortage of professional pilots. (Chapters 3, 4, and 5 of this book discuss economic and demographic issues and considerations in detail). Technology will step in to address many of these issues, albeit sometimes in controversial ways.

In the second category, tomorrow's airlines and their business models are being transformed by new aircraft designs that will extend the range and performance of airliners. Long and thin routes, direct point-to-point flights, and aircraft right-sizing are already transforming business models and the airports that they serve.

Environmental Pressures: Biofuels and Electric Propulsion

As discussed in more detail in Chapter 2 on the *Climate Change* megatrend, environmental requirements are putting pressure on the technical community to develop new technologies.

Up to now, each new generation of aircraft engines has yielded energy savings, and the latest generation has produced savings of 5% to 15% over its predecessor. However, the law of diminishing returns works against the engine manufacturers in the long run, and it is clear that, although substantial progress has been made using carbon-based fuels, future generations of engines may not be able to achieve the modest targets set by ICAO, as is clearly illustrated in Figure 6-3.

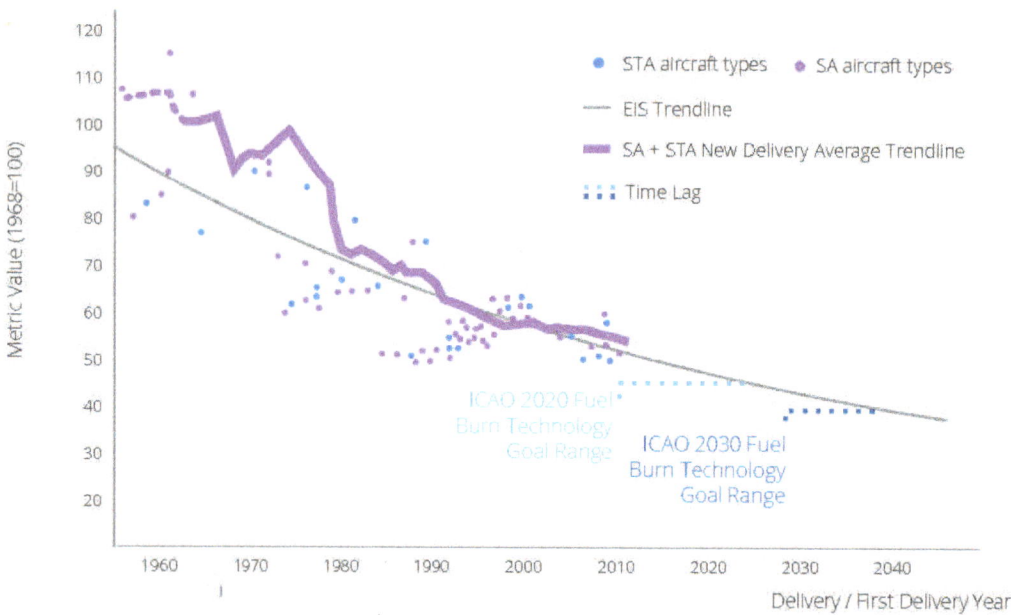

Figure 6-3   New aircraft efficiency gains (ICCT White Paper, 2015).

Although carbon-based fuels are an efficient and energy-dense source of energy compared with all other alternatives, they produce considerable CO_2 emissions, and hence alternative fuel sources are needed. Currently, there are two viable technologies that can diminish carbon emissions in the aviation industry: biofuels and electricity.

Bio-fuels for Aviation

Biofuels have been around for over a century, but it is only fairly recently that they have started competing with carbon-based fuels due to their lower carbon emissions. Various airlines have used plant or algae-based fuels successfully in commercial flights on a trial basis. The three main hurdles to their adoption, however, are energy density, cost, and availability.

A quick comparison shows that Jet A-1 carbon fuel produces 43 MJ/kg (mega joules per kilogram) of energy, as opposed to 16 MJ/kg for wood and 0.16 MJ/kg for lithium batteries. Density is an important factor because aircraft burn a significant amount of fuel just to be able to carry fuel. Biofuels produce about 30 MJ/kg on average, which means that they are less efficient and will require larger fuel tanks and new engines to attain the same ranges as current kerosene-fueled aircraft achieve today. They also have different physical and chemical properties, which will require new on-board control, heating, and storage systems.

Biofuel cost and availability go hand in hand for two reasons. First of all, cost is driven by the production cycle. Biofuels are more expensive to produce because the biomass from which they are derived only allows only about 30% at best to be transformed into fuel. Furthermore, many higher-yield plant-based alternatives cannot be used because they occupy valuable arable land used for food crops. Second, biofuels have to be processed, transported, and stored at airports. Currently, only four airports worldwide are regularly supplied with biofuels.[3]

Hence, on the face of it, there is no real economic incentive for the industry to move away from Jet A-1 fuel. However, biofuels produce between 60% and 75% fewer CO_2 emissions than kerosene-based jet fuel. This reduction, if implemented widely, would help achieve ICAO's targets and will likely be the best solution for the coming years. Unfortunately, as stated earlier, these emissions targets are quite modest, and as other industries reach their carbon reduction objectives, aviation's emissions will become more prominent, leading to increased pressure for the aviation industry to reduce emissions even further.

There are other energy-dense fuels available that produce minimal emissions. For example, hydrogen is very energy-dense, producing energy at 142 MJ/kg, whereas uranium produces 80 million MJ/kg and methane 56 MJ/kg. However, it is easy to understand why regulators would never let nuclear-powered or highly explosive gas-powered aircraft fly over populated areas.

Electric Power for Aviation

Hence, along with biofuels, electrification of aircraft is regarded as another promising solution. The main obstacle to electrically powered passenger aircraft at this stage is the sheer weight of the batteries, but aircraft manufacturers and many other companies have research programs in place studying electrically powered flight.

Electric motors are actually highly attractive from an engineering point of view because they are small and light. Aircraft designers can move away from the large engine design imposed by modern jet engines and can place dozens of small, lightweight motors in numerous locations throughout the airplane. This, in turn, allows designers to come up with more efficient designs for wings. Large wings are currently necessary to support conventional planes at low altitude and low speeds during takeoff and landing and to support the large engines, but they are currently the most inefficient component during flight at cruising speeds and altitudes.

For example, if dozens of electric motors were placed on the leading edges of wings, not only could wing size be reduced, but the motors could be tilted to reduce takeoff and landing distances. Shorter runways would be of enormous benefit to airport operators because land use is one of the most difficult aspects of airport growth management and planning. Shorter wings would also have a major impact on airports because aircraft could be parked in denser formations on terminal aprons.

Maintenance requirements are also extremely low for electric motors and batteries, not only because they are relatively simple mechanisms, but also because they do not require heavy and complex systems to serve them such as hydraulic pumps and air cooling (which causes large amounts of drag). Reliability is also far greater with electric motors because the likelihood of multiple motors out of 60 failing at the same time is far smaller than that of two engines out of two failing, as is possible with today's aircraft. Furthermore, electric-powered airplanes would require fewer heavy redundant systems compared with today's aircraft. All in all, estimates for weight reductions using electric motors compared with jet engines range between 30% and 70%. (Nevertheless, there remains a problem with the significant weight of the batteries that would be necessary to drive those lightweight electric motors).

There is no doubt that in the future, environmental concerns and the resulting solutions will have an impact on the design of both aircraft and airports. Although electric motors and biofuels are well known and already in the plateau of the productivity zone of the Betts-Lacroix model (see Figure 6-2), this is not the case for the other zero-emission alternatives such as hydrogen or electrically powered flight. Given the pace of current electric storage technology development and the even slower pace of the regulatory process, only small incremental gains and changes are expected in this area over the next 15 to 20 years. The aviation industry needs to prepare for change, but in the area of alternative fuels, it should have plenty of time to adapt.

Pilot Shortages and Technological Solutions

Pilots have always been key players in the aviation industry, ranging from the risk-it-all pioneers in the early days, to the glamorous jet-setters in the early days of jet travel, to the hard-working professionals of today. In spite of their important and high-profile role over the years, pilots are now heading towards a "perfect storm" as several trends converge as a result of the megatrends this book is discussing.

Traditionally, many pilots started their careers in the military, where they learned to fly at minimal financial cost to themselves and then moved on to piloting commercial jetliners after they retired from active military duty. Although this path is still open today, the military can produce only so many pilots, and the growth of the industry has far outstripped the supply of ex-military pilots. This means that most pilots today go through civilian for-profit aviation academies, where they accumulate debts of $124K on average to get their training and accumulate the flying hours required by the airlines for an entry-level pilot position.

This means that fledgling pilots need good remuneration packages to be able to absorb and repay their debts. However, the emergence of low-cost carriers (LCCs) has put a lot of pressure on salaries, with starting salaries for freshmen pilots ranging in the low range of $22K to $47K per year. Even after a few years, regional jet services, which constitute the majority of these positions, offer pilot pay packages at around $55K per annum, which is not enough to simultaneously finance student debt and pay basic living expenses such as a home mortgage. As a result of these dire economics, the global supply of new pilots has not changed much in the last 20 years. Since most pilots graduate in North America and Europe, these cohorts barely manage to replace the retiring pilots in these regions, never mind supplying pilots for growth areas such as Asia and the Middle East.

Many airlines have started internal training programs to ease the pressure generated by the global pilot shortage, but they too face problems because they themselves need pilot instructors to train their new recruits.

At the same time, many current pilots have effectively used this shortage to negotiate better pay and benefit packages for themselves, which has further dried up the funds available for beginner pilots at the start of their careers. As a consequence, the major airlines reduced new hires in the 2000s, which effectively increased the median age of pilots, which in turn will lead to a large cohort of airline pilots retiring in the near future.

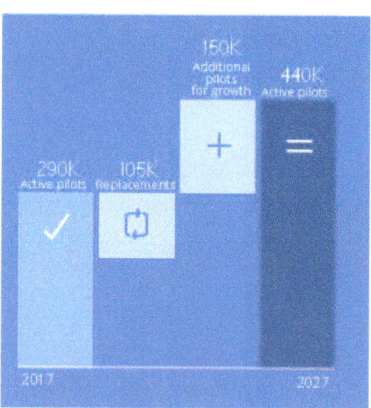

Figure 6-4   Pilot demand to 2034 (CNN Money, 2015; CAE Airline Pilot Demand Outlook, 2017).

Another major headwind comes as a result of the shift of the entire aviation market from the Western countries to Eastern countries as a result of the economic and demographic changes that are now occurring. (See Chapter 3, *Global Economic Power Shift - West to East*, and Chapter 5, *Demographic Changes and Trends*, for a more detailed discussion of these phenomena). This means that most of the new demand is now in Asia, and that market alone will require more pilots than the combination of today's largest markets in Europe and North America. However, Asia produces very few new pilots, and it will take a number of years for the new pilot training academies to start producing significant numbers of new graduates.

Although many different projections have been made, the general consensus is that over the next decade or more, the developed markets (i.e., North America and Europe) will face a slight shortage of pilots, but the Asian markets will require a very large number of new pilots. Although this should be good news for the aviation academies, the new salary economics will make it difficult for aspiring cadets to justify the personal investment, and supply will clearly fall short of demand over the next decade or two.

The technical solution to this dilemma already exists and will present a major disruption regarding who will be in the cockpit in the future. Indeed, as of 2017, the United States Air Force employs more drone pilots than fighter pilots, with over 1,000 remote pilot operators versus 803 F-16 fighter jet pilots.[4]

The US military has perfected remote pilotless technology and runs large-scale remote-control centers such as the one located at Creech Base in Nevada. Remotely piloted aircraft (RPA) pilots work in shifts around the clock in an environment that closely mimics an office environment. The systems have been designed so that RPA pilots can fly different types of drones interchangeably. Similarly, based on the USAF's experience in running RPAs, reliability and safety issues have been mastered and do not pose significant issues. In other words, these facilities prove that airlines could potentially operate a large fleet of aircraft without humans in the cockpit.

In this area, the technology is quickly moving up the slope of enlightenment on the Betts-Lacroix curve (see Figure 6-2). However, there will be significant regulatory, business, and human hurdles to overcome to make this a reality in the civil aviation realm. Nevertheless, the writing is already on the wall, especially since the initial investment in the technology has already been made, with a number of suppliers ready to expand their markets.

Removing pilots from the aircraft, although technically feasible, will generate other significant challenges. Besides passenger trust and confidence, the main issues will come from the regulatory and legal fields. Captains have very specific responsibilities while in the cockpit, inherited from maritime law. In case of incidents on board due to unlawful conduct, panic, or other reasons, cabin crew staff will need to take over, and regulations and laws will need to follow, a process that will be fraught with obstacles and will surely be slow.

Moving further into the future, and beyond remote piloting, there will eventually be pilotless aircraft. This technology is being hyped in large part because of the rapid progress of driverless cars and improved artificial intelligence (AI) software for making autonomous decisions. Even though driverless land vehicles may become a widespread reality over the next 15 to 20 years, adapting this technology to the skies and implementing it in passenger aircraft will be a major challenge on a number of non-technical fronts. This is not to say that it will not happen, but it will likely only come to fruition well past the next two decades.

Matching Passengers with Airplanes Instead of Airplanes with Passengers

In the future, the size of aircraft that airlines require, manufacturers produce, and passengers fly in will be largely determined by the nature of the routes that those aircraft fly. This relationship is explored in the following paragraphs.

A large obstacle to future growth in commercial aviation traffic is already materializing in the form of the lack of available physical air and ground space as aircraft and routes multiply. This is already being felt at most major airports around the world. Istanbul, Beijing, and Dubai are currently building new mega-airports (100M annual passengers and more) to supplement their already very large airports because of space restrictions at their current locations. Similarly, London, Paris, and other major centers are expanding rapidly because they too are running out of space. This trend is fueled by the fact that these cities are both significant final origination-destination locations and transfer hubs for on-going transit passengers.

The hub-and-spoke air route model emerged in the early 1980s in the US as a result of the deregulation of the industry in 1978. Newly deregulated mainline carriers established this system because it is the most efficient and economical way to maximize the number of connections between city pairs across a geographical area. Small airports are connected to hubs through smaller regional hubs and feed larger aircraft flying between the hubs. This increases the frequency of flights available to passengers, especially high-paying business passengers, and also increases the number of passengers boarding aircraft between large hubs. High load factors in turn yield better revenues and maximize aircraft utilization. (Chapter 4, *Rapid Urbanization*, contains additional discussion of the implications of hub-and-spoke operations).

The downside to this trend is that there are fewer direct point-to-point flights because most passengers must now transfer through hubs. This results in longer overall journeys and increased delays as aircraft rotate from hub to hub and accumulate delays as they fly around their circuits. Any disruption due to weather or technical issues immediately has a ripple effect on traffic as a whole.

This model has also divided routes into two main categories: short- and medium-haul routes for regional markets, and long-haul routes for continental and intercontinental travel. This is reflected in Figure 6-5, which shows how aircraft manufacturers offer different types of aircraft for different types of routes/markets. As shown, the smaller airplanes listed in the bottom group are shorter-range aircraft that primarily serve local and regional short-haul routes, whereas the long-haul routes are served using the larger long-range airplanes in the top group.

This means that the vast majority of regional and continental aircraft carry between 150 and 200 passengers and are single-aisle, whereas intercontinental aircraft are double to triple the size and feature two aisles. Since the seat offer is fairly rigid in each segment, this phenomenon further reinforces the existing hub-and-spoke model of the main carriers.

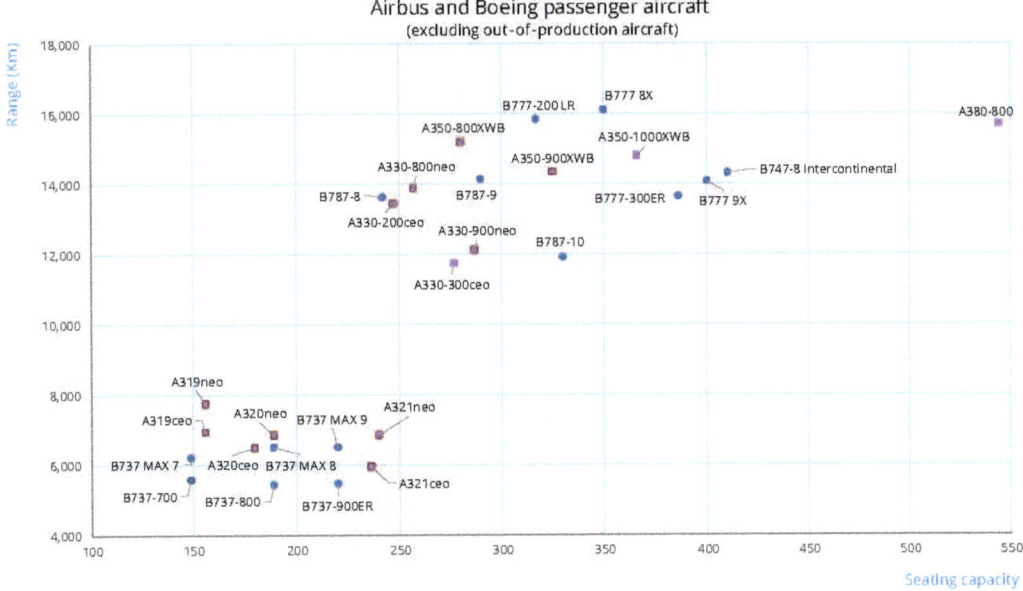

Figure 6-5 Range and passenger capacity (ALAFCO, March 2016).

As a result of this trend, passengers have grown more and more dissatisfied with the airlines as total journey times have increased. One source of longer journey times is, of course, the hub-and-spoke networks themselves, since passengers rarely have direct flights unless they live next to a hub. This problem is compounded by inefficient connection processes because many older airports (and some newer ones) were not built with a seamless sterile security configuration, forcing many connecting passengers to undergo multiple long security checks at the hubs. Add weather and congestion to this mix, and it is easy to see that all these factors significantly impact on-time performance at airports (see Figure 6-6), even at newer airports in Asia.

This situation has been disrupted by new sustaining technological changes, starting with the long-haul segment. As engine reliability has increased thanks to better materials and computerized controls, the airline industry has pushed for and obtained a relaxation of the safety rules, which has allowed for longer flights. These advances have resulted in changes to the regulations governing long-haul flights that have benefitted air carriers. One of the main technical rules governing long-haul flight distances is known as ETOPS (Extended Range Operation with Two-Engine Airplanes)[5], which regulates twin-engine aircraft flying more than a certain distance away from emergency diversion airports. Effectively, before the range was increased beyond the initial 60-minute rule, twin-engine jets were not allowed to fly over large oceans such as the Atlantic Ocean. This meant that airlines had to use fuel-hungry three- and four-engine aircraft on these routes.

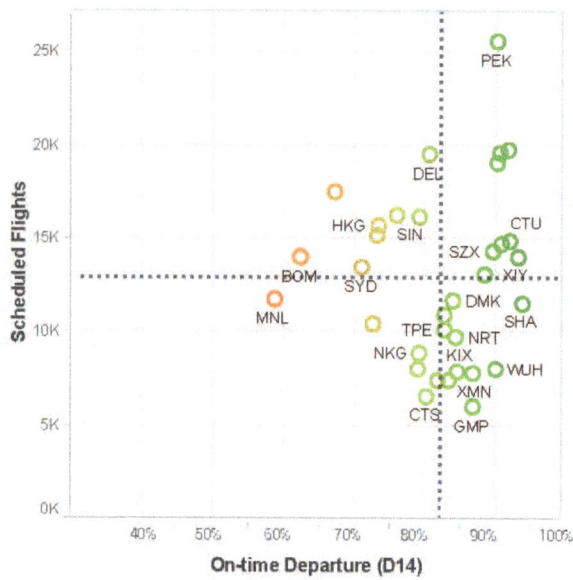

On-time Departure: Flight departs gate less than 15 minutes after the scheduled departure time (D14).

Figure 6-6   On-time performance for airports (adapted from FlightStats, December 2018).

When ETOPS standards were relaxed in 1985, 1998, and again in 2007, the new rules allowed new and more economical twin-engine planes, such as the Boeing B-767 and Airbus A-300, to ply these very busy routes, which greatly increased traffic (and profitability) for the airlines. This logic has been extended with the help of new aircraft such as the Boeing B-777 and Airbus A-330, and more recently the Boeing B-787 and the Airbus A-350, as ETOPS ranges have been expanded, allowing these aircraft to fly even further with even more fuel-efficient engines. The latest development in this market is the appearance of ultra-long-haul routes of 16 hours or more, which now make it possible to fly directly across several continents, such as from Australia to Europe. Thanks to these new aircraft, the airlines are right-sizing their planes to accommodate actual passenger demand between two points, rather than right-sizing the passenger numbers to accommodate their larger planes servicing their hubs.

The new routes that these aircraft fly, known as thin point-to-point routes, are revolutionizing the long-haul segment because they attract many new passengers to direct flights from smaller airports and non-stop routes that offer a significantly better passenger experience. New markets are emerging every day as the new economics of these aircraft allow airlines to bypass the traditional intercontinental hubs. Even more interesting, long-haul travel is the last bastion of full-service airlines, but this monopoly is now being challenged as low-cost carriers such as Norwegian Air Shuttle are now offering transcontinental flights.

Long-haul flights, however, represent only one segment of world air traffic. Intra-regional (short- and medium-haul) flights represent the majority of flights, and this is where the next business model shift is occurring. Here again, the hub-and-spoke model is forcing passengers onto larger planes on routes that connect hubs. A new fleet of regional jets such as the E2 series from Embraer and the A220 from Airbus now enable direct intra-regional flights on longer routes. This is already impacting the growth requirements at smaller regional airports and will help decongest the larger hubs.

In yet another twist made possible by better engine technology, some of the smaller aircraft are now capable of intercontinental flights. For example, British Airways offers a direct London to New York route using an A-318 and the new A-321LR. Due to the improved technology, these two smaller jets are now capable of flying 6,500 km between refueling stops, which is more than enough to fly from any country in Europe to the East Coast of North America.

Airline Networks and Airport Business Models Revisited

These new developments that match aircraft types/sizes with air routes are already having a big impact on competition in the aircraft manufacturing segment. When this chapter was drafted, news had just broken about Airbus's acquisition of Bombardier's C-Series jet program, followed by the announcement of Boeing's purchase of Embraer's E-jet program. These moves were made in conjunction with an ongoing aviation trade war and anti-subsidy legal dispute between the two owner companies.[6]

More importantly, the adjustments due to route changes and aircraft right-sizing described in the previous section will have a significant impact on the current business models of both the airlines and the airports. The biggest upheaval in the modern airline industry was the emergence of the low-cost carrier (LCC) model, which was introduced by Southwest Airlines in the US in the 1980s, following deregulation. The main driver of the LCC value proposition is low air fares, which are made possible mostly by improved aircraft efficiency technologies coupled with cost-cutting measures at every stage of the value chain. The LCC model can be summarized as follows:

- Fares: Unrestricted and low-margin prices.

- Network: Point-to-point high-frequency routes.

- Distribution: Websites, no tickets, no intermediaries.

- Fleet: High utilization, same type of aircraft across the fleet.

- Airports: Secondary airports with short turnaround times.

- Sector lengths: Short (around 400 Nautical Miles).

- Staff: High productivity with competitive wages and profit sharing.

As a result, LCCs have gained market share rapidly at the expense of the FSCs (full-service carriers), especially in Europe (see Figure 6-7), and now in Asia as well.

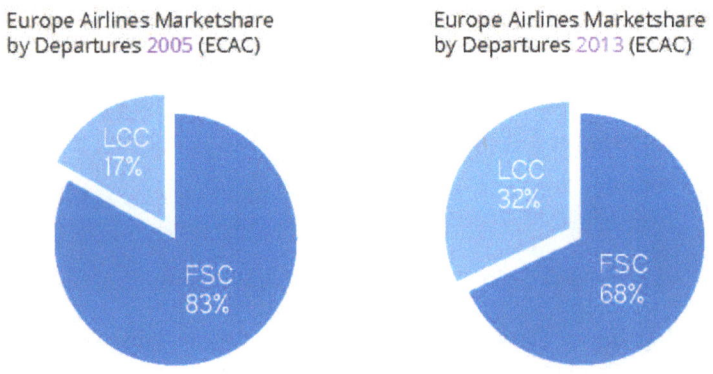

Figure 6-7   LCC market share in Europe, 2005 & 2013 (Airline Profiler, 2017).

FSCs are reacting to these competitive pressures by setting up their own low-cost subsidiaries and by applying the same cost-saving techniques to their own networks. However, they are still dependent on their hub-and-spoke networks, and this is where the new aircraft will blur the lines between regional and intercontinental, forcing them to rethink the structure of their operations.

It is clear that over the next 15 to 20 years, the airline industry will become much more diversified in terms of its approach to business models, and travelers will get a far richer and more diversified service offering than the one they are getting today.

The biggest impact of the paradigm shifts described above will be felt by airports. Indeed, until now, airports have benefited from their natural local monopoly position, especially if they are located in large urban areas. The hub-and-spoke networks preferred by the FSCs over the years reinforced the positions of these larger airports and concentrated their monopolies even further, in turn making small and medium airports less viable. However, as these airports got bigger, their operation and maintenance costs escalated, creating scale disincentives. At the same time, the rise of the LCCs has put a cap on, or driven down, aeronautical charges (such as landing fees), which have remained stable at roughly 4% of airline operating costs over the last 25 years. This scissors effect has made it increasingly difficult for the large airports to remain competitive and has further opened the door to competition from the smaller operators.

With the emergence of the new regional and long-range jets, the small and medium airports find themselves in a much stronger position to attract traffic. As an example, the map in Figure 6-8 shows the route network of airBaltic, an upstart airline based in Latvia. Ten years ago, no one in Riga would have dreamed that they would have the option to fly directly to Barcelona, Heraklion, or Tashkent. Moreover, airBaltic has been able to achieve this with a fleet composed of turboprops and small regional jets.

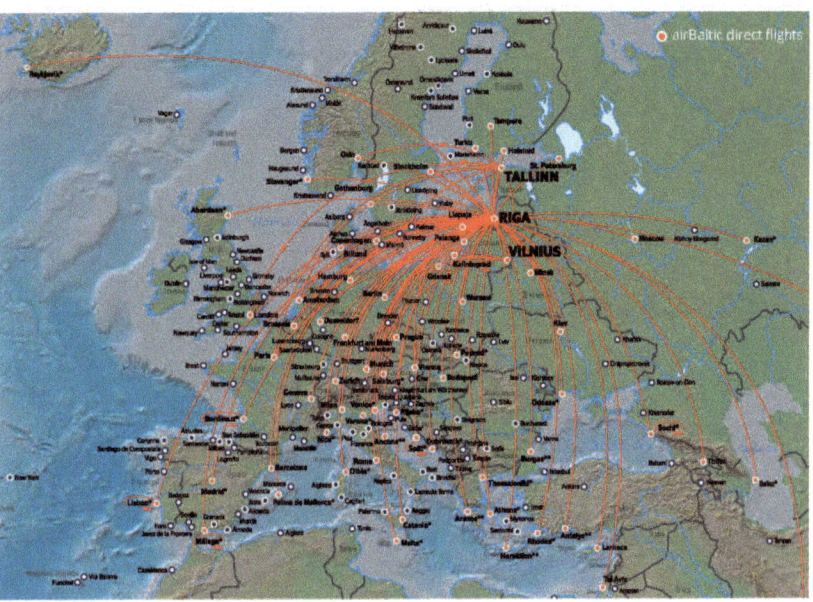

Figure 6-8   airBaltic route network (airBaltic website, 2018).

Although none of the technologies used is new, the combination of innovations makes these changes possible, and they can be classified into the "slope of enlightenment" category (see Figure 6-2) because the major aircraft manufacturers will shift their intense competition into new market segments, which in turn will prompt new agile players to appear. This in turn will fuel further growth in traffic.

AUTOMATION AND HUMAN-MACHINE SYMBIOSIS

Although this observation may at first seem counterintuitive due to aviation's high-tech image, the aviation industry as a whole has actually been a laggard when it comes to implementing or embracing new technologies beyond the actual aircraft. As an example, if a time traveler from 1960 were to look at the operations taking place on an average airport apron today, they would be quite familiar with what is going on today because things have not changed much, as the photos in Figure 6-9 illustrate.

Figure 6-9   Comparison of apron operations: 1950s and 2018 (stock photos).

Contrast that scene with the same scenario at a warehouse or postal operation in the same years, and all one would see today is a highly automated environment with almost no humans in sight, compared with large numbers of workers back in 1960. Similarly, our 1960s time traveler would be familiar with the radios and walkie-talkies that are still extensively used by airlines and airports in their operations, but would be bewildered by the mobile wireless terminals and autonomous robots commonly used in other industries.

Figure 6-10   Comparison of package sorting operations in 1960 and 2018 (stock photos).

Part of this slowness to adapt and change in the aviation industry is due to a highly regulated environment that moves slowly. However, the root causes lie elsewhere. Even though the industry as a whole has to work in a coordinated way to ensure smooth traffic flow, it is actually fragmented into many different players, each with very different and often competing interests.

Over the next 15 to 20 years, scenes such as those shown in Figure 6-10, as well as the technologies involved, will be utterly transformed because three main technological trends are coming of age and are already shaping other less regulated, but similar, activities: transportation, logistics, and telecommunications. The three transformative technologies that have emerged are the Internet of Things, robotics and actuators, and ultrafast communications. These technologies are all well past the "chasm area" in the Betts-Lacroix model and are quickly ascending the "slope of enlightenment" (see Figure 6-2).

To start with, the Internet of Things, or IoT, is advancing very quickly and will transform many aviation functions both on the ground and in the air, such as baggage processing and tracking, maintenance management/operations, passenger processing, and the passenger experience, just to name a few. Rapid strides are currently being made in robotics and actuators, which are empowered by "intelligence on the edge" devices and rendered possible by the increasing sophistication of controllers and autonomous machines. Finally, reliable, ultrafast communications are revolutionizing airport management by enabling remote and virtual operations. The combination of these three technologies will foster new economic efficiencies that will transform the way in which airport operations are structured and managed. Each one of these transformative technologies is discussed separately in the following sections of this chapter.

Internet of Things (IoT)

The Internet of Things is a catch-all expression that covers a vast array of technologies that are already transforming many different and seemingly unrelated industries. Because of its potential, IoT has also garnered a lot of hyperbole and is credited with many things, from delivering packages by air to potentially invading human bodies using nanobots. Because IoT can mean many different things, the following paragraphs look at the five defining characteristics that describe this collection of technologies. The discussion then focuses on how IoT is going to impact the aviation industry, and airports in particular.

The five defining characteristics of IoT technologies are:

1 **IoT devices are concerned with sensing and generating data.** This can cover a wide array of environments and targets, both physical and virtual. For instance, physical data can relate to such characteristics as temperature, friction or texture/smoothness of surfaces, presence or absence of objects, lighting levels, and many other conditions present on a daily basis in various activities. Virtual data can consist of patterns such as coordinated or uncoordinated movements of people or traffic flows. What makes IoT different from previous sensors is its miniaturization, which has allowed the cost-effective packing of detection instruments into ever smaller packages. The best examples of this are the smartphones that people carry in their pockets every day, which combine numerous functions including video and sound sensors, thermometers, accelerometers, gyroscopes, GPS and satellite receivers, radio and near-field communicators such as Bluetooth and NFC, and FM and other analog radio receivers, just to name a few. To put this into perspective, the average personal smartphone of today carries more sensors than were available to NASA's average ground station during the 1960s space exploration age.

2 **IoT devices will soon become ubiquitous.** Thanks to miniaturization and low cost, IoT devices are relatively cheap and easy to deploy in large quantities. Even though they may not be as accurate as larger, more sophisticated devices, their sheer numbers make the data coming from them much more reliable because there are many more data points to compare. They are also more reliable in the sense that the loss of a single device can be easily compensated for by the other devices that still work.

3 **IoT devices are connected to networks.** This means that they can continuously send and receive data. This is possible thanks to the enormous strides in low-power radio communications, brought about, among other developments, by the rapid

deployment and adoption of mobile telecommunications. The original purpose of these networks, the transmission of human voice communications, has long been dwarfed by the volume of data communications that they carry. Today, less than 0.1% of communications traffic volume involves voice traffic.

4   **IoT devices can become (almost) autonomous.** Mostly due to miniaturization, these small devices consume very little power, and the vast majority of them can function for many years on a single battery, simplifying installation and maintenance. The same reasoning applies to data transmission using radio communications. Some sensors are now so efficient in their energy consumption that their useful life is only limited by the longevity of their electronic circuitry, not their power supply.

5   **IoT technology is always closely linked to computers.** This means that data collected by IoTs can be quickly analyzed, sorted, sifted through, interpreted, and presented for further analysis and action. This allows entire functions to be automated, dispensing with human intervention altogether, something which is discussed later in this chapter under the *Artificial Intelligence* heading.

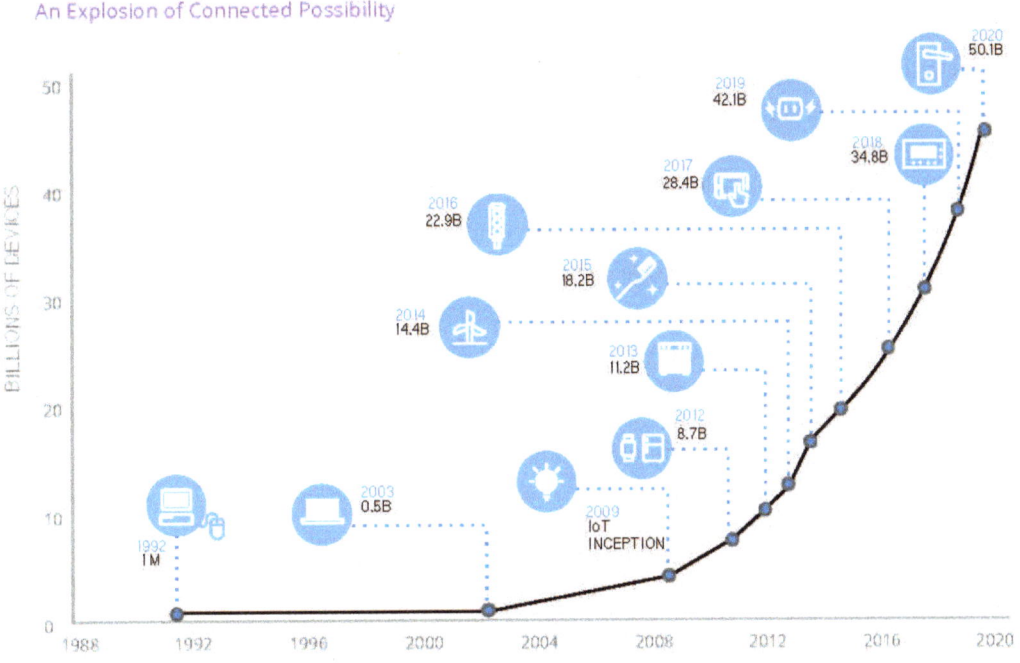

Figure 6-11   The Internet of Things (IoT): Growth from 1992 to 2020 (NCTA, 2017).

The best way to measure the proliferation of IoT is to look at the number of objects that are currently connected. Figure 6-11 illustrates this widespread and growing propagation and is remarkable for two reasons. First, the amount of data generated by these devices is staggering. Today, IoT devices produce more data every single day than what all of humanity produced during the previous 10,000 years, and the pace is accelerating. Second, the aviation industry produces less than a fraction of 1% of the IoT data produced by all other sectors. This is not due to a lack of adoption, but rather because the pace of adoption by the aviation industry is much slower than in other sectors. The good news is that because other sectors have massively adopted IoT, when the new technology does come to the aviation industry, it will be more capable, robust, and cost-effective than ever before.

IoT and Aviation

IoT is already revolutionizing how data is collected and processed by airlines. The most obvious examples concern the operation and maintenance of propulsion units for airplanes. A single modern turbofan engine generates more data during a single hour's flight than the entire airline industry collected from its worldwide fleet in 1990. This means that the industry now has an extremely clear picture of actual engine performance and how it is affected by such factors as wear and tear on parts, the types of fuel used, and weather conditions. From a maintenance perspective, it is now possible to tailor the maintenance of an engine based on actual data, rather than on the rigidly scheduled, sometimes arbitrary preventative maintenance programs of the past, which often resulted in throwing away serviceable parts unnecessarily. As a result, costs will be significantly reduced and safety greatly enhanced as specialized software analytics predict when a component is likely to fail. In fact, due to IoT technology, maintenance of aircraft engines is becoming a more dynamic discipline, a process that will greatly reduce costs because repairs or replacements will be made only on an as-needed basis.

Furthermore, safety will be greatly enhanced because potential failures can now be predicted more accurately using IoT-generated data. Naturally, as aircraft get used more intensively to generate revenue, part failures will occur more often as aircraft flight cycles are increased. Traditional periodic preventative maintenance tasks such as fan blade inspections require specialized tools and are costly to perform because they require immobilizing the aircraft and hence interrupting its ability to generate revenue. In the past, this situation has put airlines in an unavoidable conflict-of-interest position since they were constantly forced to make tradeoffs between maintenance schedules and revenue-generating operational time for their aircraft. IoT sensors provide high volumes of real-time data that will, to a large degree, eliminate these conflict-of-interest situations and the temptation for operators to push their machines to the limits to improve their bottom line.

Extrapolating to airports what is already happening in the field of aircraft engine monitoring and maintenance, as described above, it is easy to see that many of today's routine tasks at airports, such as runway inspections, foreign object detection (FOD), and physical plant repairs will be radically changed. This will impact many departments because they will be able to free up their personnel and reassign them to more value-added tasks.

Another key benefit of IoT is that regulation and enforcement will be much more effective and far less costly because the digitization of data means that it can be shared and supervised by external regulatory bodies in real time. The IoT world is fully transparent.

IoT will also have a huge impact on airport terminal operations. Today's airports employ large numbers of people whose tasks are to collect data and/or ensure compliance. Here again, IoT will greatly enhance the quantity and quality of the data collected, which in turn will help airport operators manage their facilities much more dynamically and proactively than they can today.

What this means from a human perspective is that IoT technologies will greatly reduce the staff required at airports to perform many routine tasks. However, the new insights provided will generate additional new tasks because these systems will require new skill sets to program and manage them. IoT will also require more front-line or customer-facing staff to implement the programs. For instance, people-counting sensors already generate information that helps passengers avoid long lineups at security checkpoints. Customer service staff can now redirect travelers to other checkpoints and provide up-to-the-second information that will greatly enhance the passenger experience.

Pushing this paradigm even further, IoT will make checkpoints a thing of the past because sensors can be placed in many locations and will monitor travelers throughout the curb-to-aircraft-door journey. Both facilitation and security will be improved because IoT data will be able to better handle the unpredictable nature of multiple unique passenger circumstances. Of course, this will streamline and reduce travel costs significantly because security inspection costs have escalated considerably in the last few years, not to mention the stress and poor passenger experiences that these checks often generate.

IoT technologies are poised to transform how baggage and cargo are processed and traced. Baggage handling is becoming ever more complex because of traffic growth, the multiplication of destinations and connections, and added security requirements. Tracing and sorting baggage is a thankless and low-level task that, at best, generates a neutral reaction from passengers, but when it goes wrong, it generates immediate highly negative reactions and costly remedial solutions. More intelligent tags and ubiquitous sensors are already transforming operations in other fields such as manufacturing and logistics. The implementation of these solutions for air passenger baggage handling is one of the lowest-hanging fruits that can be reaped to increase customer satisfaction and decrease airline costs.

Similarly, security inspections will be greatly improved as large, costly, and physical space-hungry inline inspection machines can be replaced with much smaller and more numerous IoT devices. This multiplication of sensors and data will also help resolve one of the toughest security challenges in baggage handling—the possible collusion and criminal activities of some staff that handle and process baggage in the first place.

When it comes to handling cargo, IoT has already transformed the logistics industry as companies such as Amazon, UPS, DHL, and others are able to track and locate any package in their chain within very short timeframes. This transformation has not yet found its way into air cargo handling companies for two main reasons. First, the likes of Amazon were able to implement tracking systems relatively quickly and easily since they control the entire logistical chain, from pick-up to drop-off. On the other hand, air cargo companies are usually only an intermediary among numerous delivery, collection, and handling agencies over which they have no direct control. The second, and bigger, barrier concerns the administrative flow of goods. Current cargo handling and tracking logistics are far from 100% digitized. In reality, most transactions are still paper-bound, and handling costs easily gobble up 10% to 30% of the entire cost of a package journey.

A technology that was much hyped for the aviation industry, RFID (radio frequency ID) tags, quickly fizzled out at the peak of disillusionment and fell into the chasm because it did not support the range and functionality required by its users. Instead of relying on external devices and passive reading of items being processed—as in the RFID model—IoT will allow the items that are being processed to do their own processing, very much as a passenger determines which gate to use and which aircraft they will have to board. By the same token, an IoT device can also carry all the administrative information about its contents and then interact with various inspection stations and/or checkpoints whenever required.

IoT Security Concerns

Of course, none of this will work unless people trust IoT, which is probably the biggest challenge facing the technology. To put it mildly, security and trustworthy ICT (information and communications technology) devices do not spring to anyone's mind in today's context. Every day, another story emerges in the media about yet another massive security breach, or how some virus is affecting millions of users for various criminal or state-sponsored purposes.

However, with a bit of perspective, the main reasons for these vulnerabilities are easy to trace back to the fundamental drivers of modern technology development, namely, acceleration and disruption. Indeed, new technologies are being developed so quickly that even large and organized corporations struggle to keep up with them, and some have even disappeared. Disruptive technologies are disruptive because they are iterated and produced quickly. In order to shorten the development cycle, upstart engineers have replaced the traditional approach that had characterized the industrial world for a long time to what is now known as the progressive method.

From the point of view of IoT developers, security concerns are a significant hindrance to what they are trying to develop, much in the same way that safety was a hindrance to the early aviation pioneers who paid with their lives for ignoring it. Therefore, current ICT systems, including IoT, are plagued with security issues and vulnerabilities that lead to large-scale security breaches. This is because IoT devices were not designed for security, but rather security features were added as an afterthought. Likewise, the networks we use, including the Internet, were designed for speed, ubiquity, and ease of exchange. Here again, security protection features and capabilities are only being added now and are very difficult to implement because of the fundamental open nature of the exchange protocols.

Fortunately, the acceleration spawned by ICT development has also produced solutions to these issues because security concerns have now become critical for the development and deployment of the next phases of IoT. Blockchain, or its newer sibling, hashgraph, technologies are set to transform the way that we exchange data, and they are expected to have a profound impact on the international aviation industry.

Blockchain Technology

In a nutshell, blockchain technology functions like a passport. It can be imagined as a small, portable container that has been verified and validated by its issuing authority. It contains both public and confidential data about its bearer, and it also provides information relating to when and where it was used in the form of stamps and visas. When a traveler presents his or her passport to an immigration officer, the officer will know who this person is, can verify the authenticity of their document, and will also know where the person has traveled previously. Another interesting and often overlooked feature of passports is the fact that they are portable. However, before networks existed, travelers did not have to worry about the invasion of their privacy by external entities because they alone controlled the data contained in their personal travel document.

Fast forward to today, and the notions of data security and protection have become an everyday concern. New legislation such as Europe's GDPR (General Data Protection Regulation)[7] are paving the way in organizing the wild free-for-all that has led private and public entities to use personal data very loosely up to now. Social media may use our data for monetary reasons, but many governments have also been caught as they use, abuse, and share data for different purposes. No matter what the motivations, the end result is impacting the trust of travelers and companies with respect to international travel.

Just like passports, blockchain records are portable and can be contained in many devices. Unlike passports, they are protected by sophisticated algorithms that make them extremely difficult to read or alter without the right permissions. Furthermore, their data is also completely distributed and reside in a series of different and impossible-to-locate servers. This means that if one tried to alter an existing blockchain record for whatever purpose, one would have to synchronize all the other blockchain copies that are all over the world. This would be equivalent to trying to present a forged passport and getting caught: as soon as one presents it, it is compared with all the other copies, and the forgery is immediately evident. It is the combination of all these measures that make blockchain technology practically invulnerable.

The global aviation industry is a rare example of international trust in which international regulations, led by ICAO and other global players, are actually largely similar and compatible worldwide. Because of the conservative nature of the industry, it has an exceptional safety track record, largely because it only uses tried and true secure systems. Because of the nature of the data and functionality offered by IoT and the level of security promised by blockchain technologies, the next 15 to 20 years are expected to be transformational for the international aviation industry. These new technologies are providing the level of trust that the aviation industry requires before it embraces major change.

Robotics, Actuators, and Intelligence on the Edge

Another key aspect of aviation, as illustrated by the earlier comparison of an apron in 1960 and one of today (see Figure 6-9), is that it is a labor-intensive activity. For example, labor costs represent a significant portion of airport costs, ranging from 15% to 25%. More importantly, airport operations offer few economies of scale, meaning that there are few savings to be made as airports grow in size.

The traditional response of historical full-service carriers (FSCs) to this problem was to simply pass on those increasing costs to travelers. Therefore, when analyzing various regions where the commercial aviation industry was deregulated, such as the United States in the 1980s or Europe in the 1990s, airfare prices initially fell significantly and then started creeping up again as the markets got more organized and the airlines started consolidating through mergers and acquisitions, as well as through international alliances.

However, this business model was upset by the emergence of low-cost carriers (LCCs), which led the way in forcing airports to reduce costs. They did this by simply choosing to operate into and out of the airports with the lowest aeronautical fees and charges. This approach has enabled carriers such as Ryanair and easyJet to provide services to destinations that were unheard of even 10 years ago, such as Girona, Rzeszow, or Chania. Faced with the increased bargaining power of their users, airports now have to compete for the business of these airlines, and this has led to increased competition and price cutting by airports. This is a desirable outcome for passengers and airlines alike and fosters further growth in the industry.

As discussed earlier, to cope with growth, airports have simply channeled more resources, such as personnel, machinery, and space, to handle the extra passengers, cargo, and aircraft, while doing little to optimize their operations. As a result, when space limitations are factored in, such as in historical airports with little room to expand, growth often leads to disincentives of scale. In such situations, an increase in size is actually marginally more expensive for every unit added.

New technological developments in other industries, such as IoT and blockchain solutions, will, have a huge impact on how airports deal with these capacity and cost issues. The obvious answer to cutting costs is to utilize existing assets more intensively. One way to do this, which was initiated by the LCCs, is to process and turn around aircraft more quickly at the gates. For this to work, coordination and collaboration across functions has to be optimized because ground handlers, airport personnel, ATC, and others all have to work together.

As explained in the previous section about IoT technology, IoT collects large amounts of real-time data and can therefore provide all the airport-based services just listed with a clearer picture of what is going on. As airports embrace these new technologies, they will also move towards better control structures such as comprehensive AOCCs (Airport Operations Control Centers), which foster a greater level of collaboration.

Over the last 25 years, robots and actuators have taken over the manufacturing industry, particularly in the automotive field. Thanks to design improvements and miniaturization, these robots and actuators have become much more economical and reliable and are invading other industry sectors as well, particularly in the logistics area, as exemplified by Amazon's automated warehouses[8].

There is no doubt that robots and actuators will make major inroads into the aviation industry, starting with cargo handling and then moving to the apron area, where many ground handling tasks will be transformed. This is especially attractive to airlines, especially the LCCs, because short turnaround times are critical to their business model and robots are a perfect tool to achieve this goal.

However, robots and actuators are inherently dumb. They are programmed to do a very specific task and nothing else, which makes them very susceptible to stoppages if they encounter a misaligned part or an unexpected obstacle.

This phenomenon is defined as Moravec's paradox[9], which states that machines and computers are capable of handling massive amounts of data and of performing extremely complex repetitive tasks far beyond a human's capabilities. On the other hand, they are stumped by seemingly mundane tasks that humans perform without even thinking, such as realigning a misaligned part or sidestepping an obstacle. Moravec's paradox explains why many tasks are still done manually, because the investment in automating these processes would be far greater than having humans continue to do them. In many cases, such tasks are impossible to perform by machine.

These machines are dumb because they lack two key elements that humans have: environmental awareness and intelligence. Environmental awareness refers to the fact that, lacking senses or perception, machines have no idea about their surroundings. Intelligence, in this case, refers to the ability to link the task at hand, say, aligning a bridge with an airplane door, with environmental awareness to detect interferences such as moving vehicles or humans, weather conditions, or the presence of objects on the gangway.

As discussed earlier, IoT is revolutionizing many fields because it enables machines to gain environmental awareness thanks to small and cost-efficient sensors that constantly send real-time data. When these are combined with ever smaller and more powerful computers, we can now create intelligent robots that use this data to factor in their environment with the task at hand.

This combination of massive amounts of real-time data and powerful computers is referred to as "intelligence on the edge", where machines can now become autonomous without relying on a connection to a large central computer or device, as exemplified by autonomous vehicles that can navigate roads without driver input. Intelligence on the edge is already present in surveillance cameras that can generate alarms based on video analytics that tell them when intrusions take place or when suspicious objects are left behind.

Such advances will allow many vehicles or specialized devices to carry out tasks with little or no human intervention. This technology will be applied to many processes, particularly in logistical fields such as ground handling or baggage handling, which are expected to be transformed in the near future.

Furthermore, intelligent machines can also work in much tighter spaces than humans. This will allow airports to reduce the amount of physical space they need on the apron to process incoming and outgoing aircraft and will bring back the economies of scale lost as a result of having to constantly expand their footprint. These economies will be driven by a combination of fewer personnel needed for operations with a far more efficient and intensive use of available space.

Remote and Virtual Management: Impact on Airports and Airlines

As discussed in the previous section, IoT and intelligence on the edge will make existing and future airports much more efficient. These technologies will also have a big impact on smaller airports, which in turn will benefit airlines by providing a greater variety of less-expensive places in which to operate.

Airports are currently very labor-intensive operations. This issue is further amplified at smaller airports where labor costs at operations below a certain size are incompressible. This is due mainly to regulatory constraints, mostly in the name of safety and security. For example, the smallest of airports must have a minimum capability in core essential functions such as firefighting, air navigation services, and security. In this light, the smaller airports, especially those under one million passengers per year that constitute the vast majority of airports around the world, tend to under-utilize their human resources.

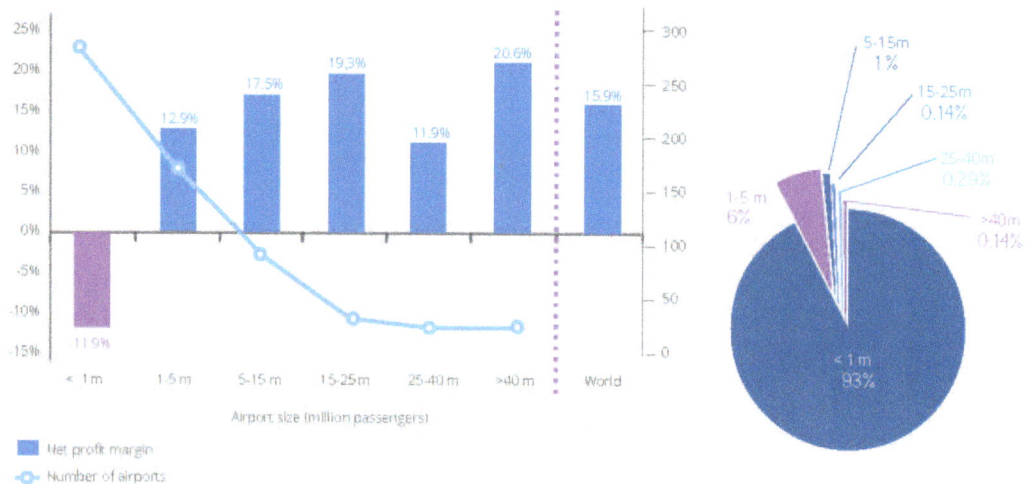

Figure 6-12   Airport profitability by size and distribution of airports with a net loss (ACI Airport Economics survey, 2014, and OAC simulation 2013).

A further complication is that many airports, especially those with tourism-driven local economies, have highly cyclical operations that concentrate most passenger movements during a particular season such as summer or winter in destinations like ski lodges, sea-side resorts, or tropical island venues. This means that these airports have to adjust to large fluctuations in personnel levels and struggle to provide year-round employment.

This is the reason why most small airports can function only if they are subsidized in one form or another. There are obviously compelling reasons for doing this because airports are usually tied to a community for which they fulfill economic, political, and health roles that exceed the cost of running them. In this sense, they are considered to be an essential public service provider.

As fiscal rigor and other budgetary imperatives have become commonplace in modern governments, less funding is available these days to subsidize smaller airports, and many of them are disappearing as a result. For instance, the US registered a 7% decline in the number of operating airports between 1990 and 2015, in spite of traffic growth of over 50% during the same period. When this phenomenon occurs despite the constant growth of, and higher demand for, air travel, it leads to the paradoxical outcome that travelers must travel further to board planes in spite of growing demand.

As stated earlier, airlines have started to respond to this concern by using new aircraft technology to fly more point-to-point flights and by better-sizing their aircraft to suit passenger needs. The missing factor in the equation, though, is to make airports less expensive to operate so that their aeronautical service fees can be lowered to attract airlines.

Just as the technologies examined earlier are transforming local operations, they can also remove the need for local operations. Using medicine as an example, a combination of IoT, robots, and fast and reliable data networks now enables surgeons to conduct complex operations at great distances and provide essential services in remote locations that could not justify other approaches. In aviation, these same technologies have been used to create RTCs (remote tower controls), which currently operate in a number of countries. For instance, the Sundsvall control center in Sweden remotely controls airports more than 150 km away[10]. The cost efficiencies are driven not only by the absence of human operators locally, but also because, without humans, there is no need for an expensive tower to be built, along with all its ancillary infrastructure. LFV, the privatized Swedish air traffic control company that is responsible for the project, estimates that running a local traffic control system represents 30% to 40% of a small airport's total operating costs.[11]

Figure 6-13 Örnsköldsvik airport virtual control tower (Saab Group).

Similarly, certain functions are highly specialized at airports and require specially trained experts to operate them. Using the same idea as remote surgeons, smaller airports can hire a smaller number of generalist personnel and back them up with specialists based in central locations that can cater remotely to several locations through technology. This eliminates the need for an expensive systems technician or avionics expert if their services are immediately required.

This remote operation model is particularly attractive for airport groups because it allows for the centralization and efficient use of expensive resources and reduces the number of local personnel. Indeed, deregulation of the aviation industry was also accompanied by a gradual process of governments divesting themselves from owning and running airports. A recent trend has been the emergence of large multinational groups that develop, manage, and operate networks of airports across the globe, such as VINCI (based in France) or Fraport (based in Germany). These groups are driven by a disciplined management approach that allows them to standardize their operations and reap the benefits in the form of cost savings. Until now, because of the incompressible cost base at low-volume airports, such groups have concentrated their efforts on medium-sized and larger airports. Remote management technologies such as those discussed above are ideally suited for these types of groups since they have both the financial base to set up the remote systems and the capability to then use their network of smaller airports to negotiate with airlines, particularly with the expanding LCCs, to propose new destinations at attractive and stable costs.

THE DATA REVOLUTION

As Charles Dickens stated succinctly, "change begets change." Nowhere is this truer than in modern times as disruptive business and technology models have transformed, killed off, or created entire industries. This next section explains how many new models will emerge that will change some of the dynamics and fundamental premises of the aviation industry. This will occur mostly thanks to the combination of accelerating technological development and mature technologies coming from other industries.

Airlines and airports are two of the principal players in the aviation industry, but they are not the only ones. Passengers and other stakeholders such as air navigation service providers and governments are also important, and the whole balance of power and their relative roles and influences are being transformed by new technologies in the short and medium term.

The first issue is data ubiquity and transparency and how these will affect travel decisions and regulations as a whole. Secondly, the ubiquity of data will facilitate the extensive use of artificial intelligence, and this in turn will impact decision-making at both the operational and strategic levels of the aviation industry. Thirdly, airports in particular will see their role redefined as they become the focal point for most of the technological changes already examined in this chapter. In this context, airports will become crucial data and decision-making nodes, and this transformation will impact the entire air transport system.

Data Ubiquity and Transparency: The Shift to UX Models

One of the most obvious consequences of ICT technology is that nearly everyone now has instant access to information and data. It is impossible to turn back the clock, or even imagine life before the age of the Internet. Just booking a flight 15 years ago was an entirely different experience from what it is today. Not only can travelers, from the comfort of their home, choose the most convenient and price-appropriate flight to suit their needs, but they can also make those choices based on qualitative information that was previously unavailable to travelers. For example, websites like SeatGuru provide information and reviews about such details as where to sit in the aircraft and even which specific aircraft to avoid based on reviews and user feedback. YouTube reviews show in graphic detail what the seat actually looks like, what meal one is likely to get, and so on.

The constant availability of data is referred to in the information industry as data ubiquity and transparency. Data ubiquity refers to the notion that information is available everywhere, all the time. What's important to note here is the real-time aspect, which means that more and more information is made available close to when, or exactly when, the actual event takes place. This means that consumers will make decisions based on near-live conditions, which will make operations management much faster and more complex for service industries like travel. Data transparency refers to the fact that information reflects actual or real conditions more closely. For instance, data about a flight or delays is no longer controlled by a single entity, but rather multiple sources such as airlines, airports, travel sites, mapping applications, and even fellow travelers are now reporting on what is going on. Here again, this means that service providers have to ensure that they put systems in place to get accurate and timely data, lest they be outpaced by their own users.

In this light, data ubiquity and transparency are transforming the very experience of travel by shifting the balance of power towards travelers. This transformative change is being reinforced by the emergence of the millennial generation that places user experience (UX) at the top of their priorities list, ahead of material possessions such as cars or houses. The good news for the aviation industry is that travel is at the top of their to-do list. The flip side is that, unlike previous generations, millennials are very exacting about how they want to travel and will not accept packaged one-size-fits-all or poor service offers. They are also the largest single demographic group in most countries today, and they have the highest purchasing power of any generation so far. (See Chapter 5, *Demographic Changes and Trends*, for a more in-depth discussion of the impact of millennials).

In order for aviation service companies to thrive in the future, they will need to revisit and redesign their entire value chain to provide the right experience for their customers. Research shows that customers will be looking for unique service experiences at different price points. This will be driven by marketing departments whose primary function will be to better understand the new consumers and how to most effectively cater to the complex dynamics of their needs and desires. To understand this model better, a useful starting point can be found in how software and services developers, particularly those in disruptive fields, approach new products based on the UX (user experience) approach. Over the last 10 years, UX design has become a standalone discipline in the ICT and services industry and has spawned many new products that did not exist previously.

UX design looks at the entire value chain for a particular service, rather than its individual components, and its main focus is on facilitation and simplification of the entire experience. Using the Uber car service as an example, the user experience is not just about taking a taxi, but rather about getting from A to B as quickly and smoothly as possible. In this light, taxis are just one element or link in Uber's transportation value chain. Once a person has decided to go from A to B, their first question is, what transportation means should they use? At this stage, they have numerous options: take their own vehicle, rent a car, take public transit, use a bikeshare service, or take a taxi. In all cases, there will be a delay before actually starting the journey because one will need to get to the chosen option. In other words, the car may not be parked close by, or one will need to go to the car rental agency, or there will be a wait for the train, subway, or bus at the station, or one will need to find an available taxi.

There are a number of specific ways that the Uber service disrupted the conventional taxi-trip model when it was introduced:

- The customer already knows before leaving home (via smartphone or computer) where and when the driver will pick them up. They can even track the car in real time to determine when to go down to the door to catch their ride.

- The passenger does not have to worry about navigation or finding their own way. Since Uber is map-based, the drivers will always take the best route, and the price is set in advance, regardless of conditions. No need for the customer to navigate or pay attention to directions.

- Payment is built into the platform, so that no physical payment exchange has to take place because the fare is automatically deducted from the passenger's preferred payment platform.

- Quality assurance is built into the system because both drivers and riders assess and evaluate each other, keeping everyone honest and ensuring the best service possible.

This has obviously forced taxi companies to up their game considerably because some have abused their monopolistic position to offer poor service and substandard vehicles, not providing choice in payment methods, and in many cities, they are just difficult to find. Even public transit has had to improve service by telling travelers when to expect their next train or bus, simplifying or automating payment, and so on.

One might argue that the aviation services industry is different because the value chain is made up of many disparate actors and elements. After all, the curb-to-aircraft-door journey involves some form of transit method, an airline service counter or bag drop-off, a security check, an immigration or ID check, and then a boarding process. None of these services is controlled by a single entity, least of all the airport, and therefore some would argue that UX design will be extremely difficult to apply in the aviation industry.

However, this is not actually the case because, as mentioned previously, the two key components of this technology are data ubiquity and transparency. In the past, it was impossible for these multiple actors to anticipate what demands there would be for their services, or to evaluate what happened in the chain before or after a particular event. Today, however, it is possible to anticipate and manage data in real time and share it transparently across the entire chain to coordinate all the services. This provides an enhanced user experience for travelers and also results in more efficient use of resources by the various players, as well as less stressful working conditions.

To harness this capability in the future, airports in particular will have to take a much more proactive role in controlling the chain of events and will need to collaborate closely with government entities, airlines, and other service providers. Airports will need to invest in real-time data systems to be in a position to make these changes work. This discussion is reviewed and developed further in Chapter 7 of this book on *Global Connectedness.*

The UX model has other implications that go beyond mere facilitation. As mentioned earlier, thanks to services like SeatGuru and YouTube, travelers now know exactly what to anticipate when planning and booking an air trip. They can therefore also decide whether certain features or services are useful to them or not. UX is not about providing a single experience, but rather about providing differentiated experiences. UX designers are as concerned about the flow of an experience as they are concerned about the individual options within it.

Here again, data ubiquity will be able to drive many of these changes to offer value-added services to enhance the experience. Airlines already know that over 50% of millennials are willing to pay additional fees to upgrade parts of their journey experience. UX designs will capitalize on this notion to facilitate the purchasing experience itself. However, airlines have not fully embraced the UX model yet and continue to push complex purchasing experiences onto their customers. For example, buying an airplane ticket today requires one to opt into or out of a multiplicity of options such as seat selection, luggage allowances, and meal service. This has created negative perceptions and reviews from travelers because they feel that airlines or airports do not really care about them.

Artificial Intelligence

As business models move towards greater differentiation, the biggest impact on managing a travel business is the rapid increase in complexity as companies try to provide the right bundle of services. Fortunately, artificial intelligence (AI) technologies are advancing rapidly and will allow users to build these new bundles more easily. In a nutshell, AI uses newly available computers and algorithms to go beyond the simple order software interfaces of the past and perform relatively sophisticated autonomous cognitive thinking, something that was not generally possible until recently. Typically, AI systems are given guidance regarding desirable outcome parameters, and they then ingest the data on a given topic to come up with creative solutions on their own.

AI, just like IoT, is a vast domain that encompasses many different technologies and does many different things. As already discussed, one type of AI is being used at airports to manage and operate ground handling tasks. In the aviation industry, AI systems will gradually penetrate three main areas: air traffic control, airline operations, and the user experience of travelers.

As pointed out earlier, some tasks are far better managed by ICT systems than by humans. Air traffic control is one of these areas, where a large portion of airspace is managed today using the same tools and techniques as 25 years ago. This is further complicated by territorial sovereignty rules and a bevy of other complex regulations. This results in a highly complex system with disparate and incompatible components, which in turn leads to an apparent saturation of airspace in certain areas, particularly in Europe. This saturation will get worse as traffic grows and as more point-to-point (thin) routes are flown to more and more regional airports. The obvious answer will involve unifying these systems because current technologies are already more than capable of managing and running far more complex systems than ATCs. This trend will be reinforced with the implementation of remote control towers and services or autonomous ground handling capabilities, both of which will extend the reach of AI at all operational levels. There is no doubt that as this transformation takes place, the next 15 to 20 years will be fraught with conflicts and negotiations regarding who controls the skies and how.

In a similar vein, airline operations are already using AI to enhance and optimize their flight and technical operations. At this stage, "islands" of AI exist within the airlines, analyzing everything from fuel consumption and staff allocations to aircraft routing. There is, however, no single larger umbrella AI system that spans all the functions of an airline, but there is no doubt that this will happen during the next 15 to 20 years. The real revolution will occur when the AI's primary mission becomes enhancing the passenger user experience, rather than optimizing operations as is currently the case.

AI will also have a deep impact on the passenger UX because that will need to be extended beyond a single airline to create a global experience. This extension is most likely to be based on current airline alliance systems, which will be greatly reinforced as a result of AI technologies. Different airlines will be able to create true end-to-end journey experiences simply by sharing their data and coordinating with each other what those services should be like.

The biggest change brought about by full implementation of AI will occur on the ground at the airport. This is where the air travel experience starts and ends, and it is also where the more difficult interactions take place. AI is particularly good at spotting patterns, and this ability will be greatly enhanced if it understands with whom it is dealing.

For example, for travelers with bags, new IoT technologies will make it possible to eliminate the baggage drop-off area completely because this function will no longer need to be located at the departures level. For example, cruise ships and resorts already do this in a rudimentary way as they pre-register passenger luggage at the hotel before departure, at various terminals, or at the curb. The separation of passengers and their bags will create new security challenges at airports, but these can be easily resolved by decentralizing screening thanks to IoT technologies based on smaller sensors spread around in many locations. The data coming back from the luggage tracers will create flow patterns that can be easily matched with the passenger's own movements. AI algorithms will identify suspicious patterns, such as no-shows or delayed passengers, and will provide the intelligence needed to proactively manage these situations. Moving on to the airline check-in areas, most passengers already choose to bypass them completely by going directly to the security checkpoint. This trend is expected to continue as passengers will be able to manage 100% of their journey before they leave their homes.

Passenger security checks of the future are expected to morph into a multiplicity of random checks as passengers make their way from the curb to the aircraft cabin door. Here again, AI will be able to analyze risk profiles based on the data that it has about a specific traveler and will then be able to analyze his or her behavior within the terminal building. Specific travelers can then be targeted for extra scrutiny or questioning.

This use of AI will allow airports to open up their terminal areas and provide new experiences because spare time will be freed up, and the stress level of the travelers will be reduced by eliminating choke points. Among these experiences, well-wishers and families will find new and gratifying facilities as their journey inside the airport will become much more predictable and enjoyable. Immigration and boarding checks will be facilitated because all information about passengers will be known in advance, and the only real test will be to ensure that passengers are really who they claim to be by matching them with their biometric data. These systems already exist in New Zealand, for example, where biometric information is verified at check-in and then automatically matched again all the way to the boarding gate, using facial recognition.

AI will also bring about major changes to the passenger experience in the sky as airlines will move towards ever more customized experiences that will be designed around the users' known interests. Most LCC operators, and increasingly their FSC competitors, are shifting and blurring their service offerings.

This approach has resulted in a rapid rise of so-called ancillary revenue, which covers anything from fees to reserve a seat, to purchasing extra legroom, to carrying an extra bag. In the global airline industry in 2015, these fees amounted to US$26 billion, up from US$8 billion in 2008 (see Table 6-1). Clearly, consumers are adapting to the LCC extra-fees approach and are becoming more conditioned to the idea of an à-la-carte experience.

Table 6-12   Growth of ancillary fees (adapted from tnooz.com, 2016).

TOP 10 AIRLINES - ANCILLARY REVENUE AS A % OF TOTAL REVENUE				
ANNUAL RESULTS - 2015		ANCILLARY SOURCE	ANNUAL RESULTS - 2008	
43.4%	Spirit	Various	22.7%	Allegiant
37.6%	Allegiant	Various	19.3%	Ryanair
36.4%	Wizz Air	Various	15.5%	easyJet
29.4%	Jet2.com	Various	14.8%	Jet2.com
24.0%	Ryanair	Various	14.1%	Vueling
22.3%	Volaris	Various	13.0%	Germanwings
21.3%	Jetstar	Various	11.0%	Aer Lingus
21.2%	Flybe *	Various	10.3%	JetBlue
20.8%	Tigerair	Various	9.3%	American
19.5%	Alaska Air Group	Various	8.9%	AirAsia Group

2015 and 2008 carrier results were based upon recent 12-month financial period disclosures.
* IdeaWorksCompany estimate based upon updated past disclosure and other sources.

Full-service carriers, on the other hand, used to include all these services, for which the LCCs bill extra, as a package in the overall ticket price, and they have struggled to match and catch up to the LCCs in this area. AI will bring about a major change here as airlines, both LCCs and FSCs, experiment with experience-bundle pricing. Based on data analytics of passenger behavior and purchasing habits, AI algorithms are churning out bundled all-inclusive prices for various market segments, from the bare-fare passenger (basically, just a seat with no bags or services) to ultra-premium packages with everything included, with a range of other service options in between.

The new fare models use AI to integrate and merge customer preferences with yield management theory in order to maximize airline revenues. Yield management software and algorithms were developed in the 1980s by the then newly deregulated airline industry to calculate fares, and their use explains why no two passengers pay the same price for the same seat on a given flight. This approach is based on the mathematical maximization of marginal revenue opportunities, meaning that the seat price is driven by the number of tickets sold in a given section of an aircraft, when they were bought, and how fast new seats are booked. Although very profitable for the FSCs, this model makes pricing opaque and expensive, a characteristic that the LCCs have exploited to promote the transparency of their lower fares. Combining the two approaches, airlines will be able to offer thousands of bundles based on specific combinations of services and experiences, both on the ground and in the air. These tools will allow them to provide differentiated services, a major issue for airlines as travel has become commodified over the past 20 years.

This customized fare approach will translate into significant logistical changes and hurdles based on just-in-time logistical management concepts. For example, as passengers book their experiences, variable numbers and qualities of meals will be required, demand for lounge space will increase or decrease, priority clearance and boarding will vary, and so on. This will require both airlines and airports to provide better and more differentiated services, as well as changing the physical layout of airports because each passenger's curb-to aircraft-door journey will be different.

To make this happen, the various players in the industry, from airlines to airports, as well as other service providers and ground-handlers will need to cooperate and work much more closely than they have in the past, which leads into the next discussion about the new role of airports.

The New Role of the Airport as a Data Node

AI and the other technologies examined earlier are enablers that will make all these new products and services possible. However, for this model to work, all the data must be shared and pooled in real time. Possibly one of the biggest changes that will come about in the next 15 years will be the convergence of all these systems into a new data-centric model.

As the Uber example demonstrated, the reason that Uber is successfully changing the local transportation business model is that it has managed to control the entire data chain related to its customers, from ordering, to fulfillment, to payment. For airports to do this, they will need to move towards a new data-centric model, one that will be the only common link between the passenger, the airline, security, customs, immigration, and the other stakeholders within their geographic limits. These types of models have already taken other industries by storm and are moving up quickly on the "slope of enlightenment" in the Betts-Lacroix model (see Figure 6-2). In fact, the air travel industry as a whole is quite late in its adoption of the data-centric model.

Today, airports are landlords that lease real estate and provide various services to their many tenants. The new data-centric model simply extends this offering to include networks and data services in addition to physical space and terminal services. In essence, airports will become virtual landlords as well as physical ones.

As mentioned earlier, one of the key aspects of IoT and AI is data ubiquity. This is achieved through inter-compatibility between the various systems that provide the data so that they can all share their data across different platforms. By becoming data nodes, airports will be able to provide the different services for which airlines, passengers, and cargo handlers are willing to pay in order to enhance their experiences and business offerings.

Expect the next 15 to 20 years to be marked by significant investments by airports or their DSPs (data service providers) in ICT and communications backbones to enable them to provide their clients with all the services described earlier. Airport operators will be well placed to reap the benefits of this development because they will be able to pool expertise across many locations and minimize costs as they roll out these platforms across various locations. Airlines, especially LCCs, will be particularly attracted to this model because airport groups will be able to propose identical and predictable services across many locations.

This means that airports of the future, much more so than today, will need to shift their focus towards a high-quality service level model in order to attract and retain their customers. High-quality data services will become tomorrow's commercial battlefield where airports will be able to differentiate themselves.

CYBERSECURITY

As discussed in previous sections, technological innovation will have momentous implications for many individual aspects of the aviation industry. It will create many new challenges such as infrastructure requirements and ICT systems development; more importantly, the shift in the human resources skill set requirements will come to the fore. One of the biggest challenges will be protecting individuals and corporations alike from the inherent risks of all these changes and innovations, mostly through enhanced cybersecurity measures.

The pace of change is accelerating because today's innovations originate mostly in cognitive disciplines, such as data and computers, where there are few physical barriers or constraints that inhibit rapid development. This acceleration is compounded by a new approach to systems development in which rapid prototyping, quick failures, and relentless iterations have taken over from yesterday's approach of careful planning and rigorous testing before release. This dichotomy has fueled positive disruption in many fields and activities. However, it does come at a price; what is gained in speed and innovation is sometimes lost in reliability and security.

The picture that emerges from combining all these trends is what makes the subject of "technological innovation" a megatrend in a rapidly shifting world fraught with enormous rewards and highly risky pitfalls. The biggest pitfall is threats to cybersecurity. It is therefore imperative to examine why these threats have emerged and how they can be dealt with using the industry's traditional regulatory approach, as well as what practical solutions can be put in place.

Data and Network Security

In the early 21st Century, data and networks have become a battlefield for malicious attacks, as attested by the numerous news headlines detailing the latest cyber-attacks perpetrated by a number of different actors. Beyond the headlines, it is imperative that cybersecurity experts be able to plan for cyber-attacks in advance so that they can shine a light on who is behind these attacks and what is motivating them. Cyber-attacks can have devastating impacts on various elements of the aviation industry, and it is therefore important to be aware of the tools that are (or are not) at the disposal of airlines, airports, and other aviation players to stop or minimize these attacks when they occur.

Data and networks are vulnerable for two main reasons. As discussed earlier in this chapter, data, and the networks that serve them, were not initially designed with security in mind, but rather with speed and simplicity of information exchange as the priorities. The early Internet, as designed by the US government research institution DARPA[12], was built to facilitate the exchange of information between academic partners who inherently trusted each other. Their concerns focused on exchange and compatibility of information because their biggest issue was to ensure that the files they exchanged were legible by different, and hitherto incompatible, systems. Security concerns were not considered as an issue at the time because their network was completely closed and secure.

Fast forward to today, and many of the protocols and technologies invented by DARPA back in the late 1960s and 1970s are still in use today. These include TCP/IP (the protocol that governs all internet exchanges), various exchange mechanisms such as DNS (domain name servers), and authentication tools. In addition, even though we have technically run out of IP addresses, IPv4, the Internet's current, highly vulnerable addressing system, has not yet been replaced by IPv6, which is far safer and more resilient. The official transition to IPv6 was announced as far back as 1998 and is only now progressing slowly, including a false start in 2012[13].

Cyber Terrorism

This status quo situation on the technology side greatly benefits all manner of hackers out there and has enabled them to wreak havoc and extract precious data to their benefit, much to the detriment of individuals, corporations, and governments. In this context, there is very little difference between a commercially motivated hacker (i.e., one seeking personal monetary gain), a cyber terrorist, or a state-backed hacker who is looking at influencing or distorting another country's online or political activities.

In this context, the notion of "cyber terrorism" first started to come to public attention as early as the 1980s, when Barry Collins coined the term.[14] It is a loaded term in the sense that it tends to conjure up images of dark and sinister hidden worlds, and it feeds conspiracy theorists everywhere. Reality, as usual, is more prosaic and pedestrian, and cyber terrorism should be dealt with within the wider context of ICT security.

Cyber terrorism is a nebulous concept and catch-all term that encompasses everything from random individual attacks to large-scale organized attacks and global viruses. Many such attacks have happened in recent years, including the highly publicized Estonian attacks of 2007 and the Ukrainian incidents of 2017. Both cases were large external attacks based on various technologies that successfully shut down entire networks, either partially or totally, seriously affecting or even paralyzing each country's economic and administrative activities for anywhere between a few hours and a few days.

There are many other examples. Only some attacks have been publicized, and these have further reinforced the notion of a vulnerable world that is at the mercy of powerful and hidden forces, especially since it is almost impossible to pinpoint the originators of such attacks other than through circumstantial evidence.

This being said, it is helpful to break down attacks into three main types and to link them to the main motivating factors to help us understand what countermeasures are needed. There are three main types of cyber-attacks, as defined by the Monterey group[15]:

- Simple-Unstructured: The capability to conduct basic hacks against individual systems using tools created by someone else. The organization possesses little target analysis, command and control, or learning capability.

- Advanced-Structured: The capability to conduct more sophisticated attacks against multiple systems or networks and possibly to modify or create basic hacking tools. The organization possesses an elementary target analysis, command and control, and learning capability.

- Complex-Coordinated: The capability for coordinated attacks that can cause mass disruption against integrated, heterogeneous defenses (including cryptography). Ability to create sophisticated hacking tools. Highly capable target analysis, command and control, and organizational learning capability.

The main motivating factors behind cyberterrorism differ widely, but can be grouped into three main categories:

- Gratuitous or malicious attacks: perpetrated by individual hackers or small teams with no clear goals other than to penetrate or wreak havoc in corporate and government systems.

- Economically motivated attacks: driven by financial rewards. These constitute by far the majority of attacks and range from financial fraud to ransomware and everything in between.

- Ideological and religiously motivated attacks, which can range from State-sponsored attacks, as may have been the case in the Estonian and Ukrainian attacks, to religious or terrorist-group-sponsored attacks, or even undefined collectives.

The very connectivity and the same global networks that enable and propel these attacks are also shaping and intensifying the public's *perception* of an ever more dangerous and fragile world that is teetering on the edge of collapse. This perception is accelerated and fueled by unverified or unfounded news and social media posts, which all contribute to clouding the big picture. In reality, ICT systems are becoming much safer, and negative reports are becoming less frequent overall.

No matter which types of attack occur, or what are the motivations behind them, the simple answer is that we should treat attacks as what they actually are, namely, technical problems that can be dealt with. What matters, then, is to apply regulations, safeguards, mechanisms, and tools that are equivalent to those used in other fields such as aviation operations safety or physical security.

In this light, the perceived dire state of affairs is by no means out of control, at least not yet. It prevails because most of the parties in the value chain do not coordinate their policies and systems for various reasons. For instance, airlines jealously guard their data and only integrate with the systems of others when they absolutely have to because they consider their reservation systems, and rightfully so, as their most precious asset. When compelled to do so, airlines share these databases with government entities such as customs and immigration departments and taxation authorities. These types of exchanges are normally done using simple and often vulnerable tools so as to minimize cost and to be compatible with a wide range of disparate systems. Subsequently, such databases and systems are easily open to cyber-attacks, as exemplified by the numerous attacks on the reservation systems of all major airlines[16].

Technologies are available today that can be implemented to successfully block or minimize external attacks, but this will require a much higher level of cooperation and joint planning by all players involved in the value chain. As briefly mentioned before, at airports, all these data and networks converge in one location, which is the only entity that is nominally responsible for passenger and cargo operations. These responsibilities, and their central role as convergence points, mean that airports will need to transform themselves into data-centric entities. As the key player in the value chain, airports are uniquely placed to become the guarantors and protectors of data and operations. This will undoubtedly provide those airports that embrace this shift with enormous opportunities, which they will be able to monetize and use to their advantage. Needless to say, this is an enormous challenge because the vast majority of airports are not ready for this shift, and they will face opposition from many different angles when implementing this new model. This will require the acquisition of new skill sets and tools, as well as new investments, beginning in the near future.

Cybersecurity Regulations

As convergence and integration accelerate, airlines, airports, and other stakeholders will become more intertwined and therefore much more susceptible to cyber-attacks. A successful and well-directed ICT attack could bring the international aeronautical flow to a halt for days or even weeks, causing maximum harm and the sought-after publicity that many attackers crave. One clear offshoot of this situation is that aviation regulators will need to step in and assume their duties as guardians and custodians of the international aviation industry. After all, bringing down an entire air traffic control system during a busy period is likely to cause much more damage than, say, an old-fashioned bomb detonating on an airliner. Unfortunately, cyber-attack technologies are well understood by the attackers and are already moving onto the "plateau of productivity" (see Figure 6-2), to the chagrin of the rest of humanity.

Regulation in the ICT field will therefore become a major trend over the next 15 to 20 years and will no doubt pose many fundamental challenges because regulators are currently poorly equipped and may even be unaware of what lies ahead of them. Looking at examples from other industries, such as Uber or Airbnb, it is clear that technology-based companies are the ones shaping, bending, and twisting (or ignoring) existing regulations and pushing the regulators to act. Major twists and turns in the regulation of cybersecurity are inevitable in the coming years.

IT industry regulators are starting to come to grips with these new realities, as exemplified by the GDPR (General Data Protection Regulation) issued by the EU[17], which has forced all the large social media firms such as Facebook and Google to change their data privacy rights protection and settings worldwide, not just in Europe.

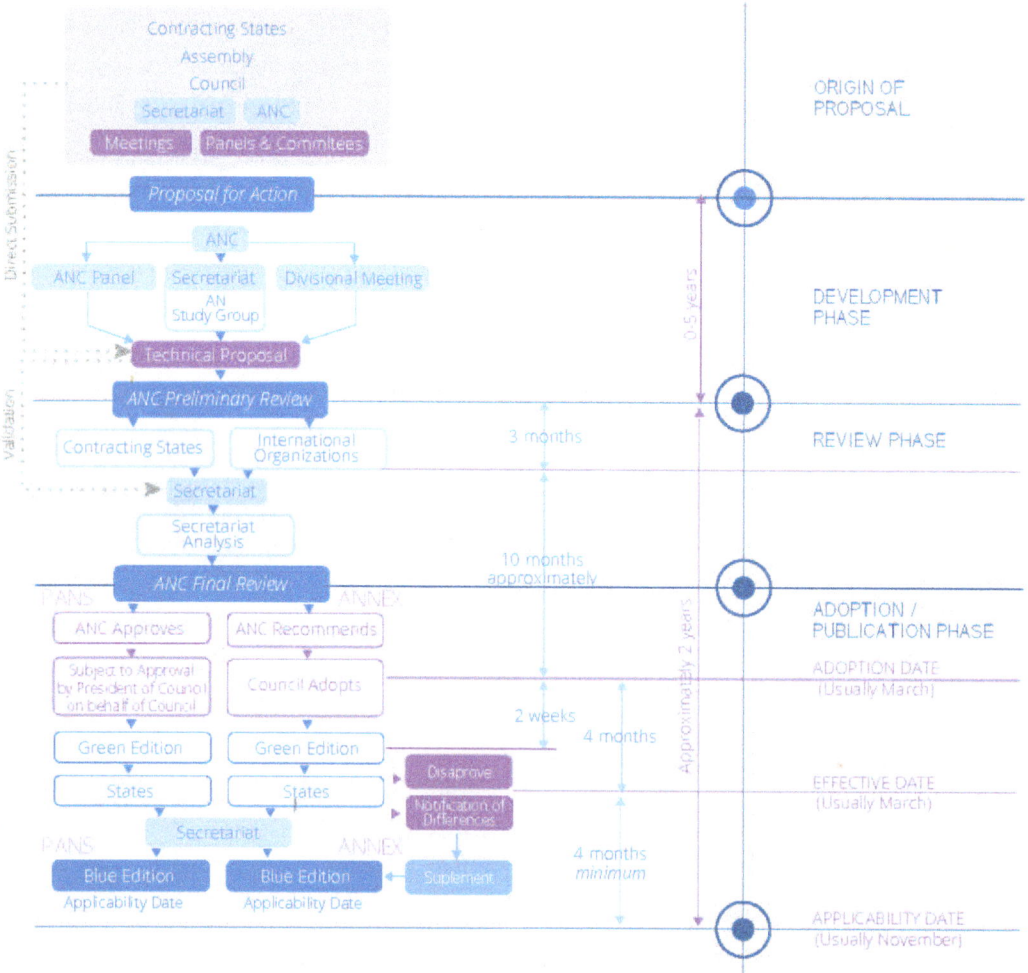

Figure 6-14 Typical ICAO new regulation adoption timeline (ICAO, 2004).

Developing and implementing new regulations in the aeronautical field will take time under the best of circumstances. Figure 6-14 maps out the typical regulation development-to-adoption cycle at ICAO; the timelines given relate to conventional technological topics. It is obvious that a two- to six-year adoption cycle does not match the current and accelerating pace of technological change and innovation. To make matters worse, this timeline relates to conventional technical topics, which do not include information technology, networking, or artificial intelligence. There is currently a worldwide paucity of technical expertise in ICTs (information and communications technologies), and it will take years before ICAO and the national regulatory bodies of ICAO Member States will be able to recruit the right type of experts to deal with this issue.

Under these circumstances, and given the degree of vulnerability and potential damage, time will be of the essence when it comes to developing and adopting new cybersecurity regulations, and the aeronautical industry will need to take a different approach from that it has used in the past.

Cybersolutions

Because regulation is often an after-the-fact solution, industry players must seize the initiative themselves, come up with their own solutions, and adapt to the new reality of possible cyber-attacks that can occur anytime, anywhere, 24/7, worldwide. These solutions include, in many cases, getting out in front of the regulatory debate to shape the future.

As a start, a greater degree of collaboration between the various players is necessary to protect their systems and data exchanges. To achieve this, the major components of an IT system, commonly referred to as the IT stack, must be considered. This is usually visualized as a pile or pyramid made of superimposed layers (hence the term "stack"), where each layer relies on the one below it to deliver its services[18]. The whole stack is referred to as an IT platform.

At this stage, the civil aviation ICT stack is characterized by the lack of standards or dominant technologies.

As the schema shown in Figure 6-15 illustrates, there are five main layers in the ICT stack, each one of which is examined below.

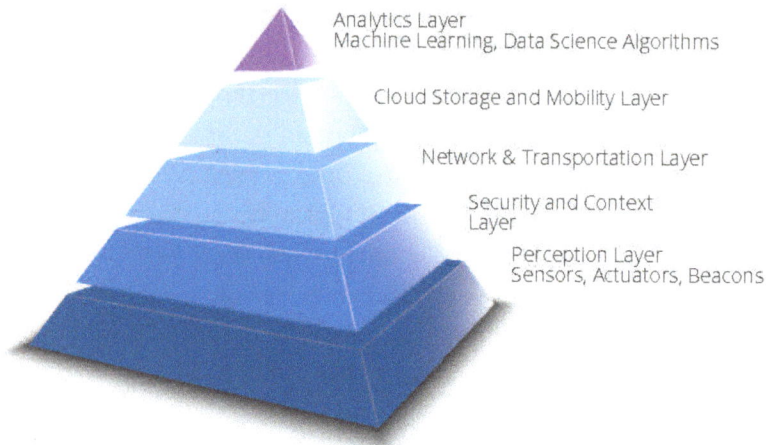

Figure 6-15   ICT/IoT stack (Rob Gravelle, Top 10 IoT Technologies, 2017).

Although well developed in other industries, the "perception layer" at the base of the stack is still developing in the aviation industry and will likely benefit from the progress made elsewhere. This layer is the easiest to regulate through technical specifications and quality standards and will bring about enormous benefits to the entire aviation industry.

The next two layers of the stack, "security and content" and "network & transportation", are quite problematic for the aviation sector. Because of the already discussed fragmented nature of ICT systems in the aviation industry, many technologies and standards and protocols coexist, with a significant portion being obsolete due to outdated regulations or technologies. For example, aircraft navigational systems such as ILS glide path systems have no protection whatsoever and can be easily intercepted and hacked. At the data level, the vast majority of AODBs (airport operation data bases) integrate data feeds that are obsolete and highly vulnerable. For instance, in November 2015, Paris-Charles de Gaulle Airport's ICT system was completely shut down because a 23-year old weather data system stopped working because it was based on the antiquated MS-Windows 3.1 operating system[19]. This reliance on outdated systems is actually quite common, with several analysts stating that it is common for technical data systems to be between 10 and 20 years old.

The root cause of this issue lies in the disparity and sheer volume of systems and entities working together to run a complex operation like an airport, ranging from air traffic control and gate management systems to weather information, flight assignment, and scheduling systems. Many of these systems have been boot-strapped together over the years, often in an ad-hoc fashion, just to make them functional in the short-term. To make matters worse, the network and transportation layers are equally old and diverse. The aviation industry still routinely uses obsolete technologies such as telex and DOS text-based messaging that are highly vulnerable and were phased out long ago elsewhere. Likewise, obsolete network and exchange protocols such as X-25, frame relay, and FTP are still commonly used.

The best way to deal with this is to promote and foster greater voluntary collaboration at a technical level among the various entities. Some work has already been done within airline strategic partnerships, such as Star Alliance and **one**world, but it is not nearly enough. Beyond the airlines, greater collaboration needs to take place among the various other stakeholders such as government entities and weather and traffic services, rather than just in one group like the airlines. In this context, agreements on minimal standards need to be developed, such as plans that would gradually eradicate text-based technologies and obsolete protocols.

After that, airports need to be looked at as the natural convergence point for most of the data involved in their operations because they are the locations where all operations take place. Yet most airport administrations run their ICT systems and make technological choices with little regard for external players, even at the airport, let alone at other airports. These decisions were perfectly logical in the past because each airport operated independently of all others and there has been no universal governance, management, or ownership model across the air transportation system. However, airports are becoming ever more dependent on external influences. For example, a storm in a faraway region will affect the routing of a number of aircraft, which will impact flight arrivals and departures across many airports outside the storm area. Moreover, as skies get busier due to faster growth and higher volumes, greater coordination will be required, as exemplified by the creation of Eurocontrol in Europe.

Therefore, to enhance security and accelerate change, airports will need to move toward a more data-centric model in which they will become the provider of services and data for all their stakeholders. The practical consequences of this will be that airports will not only need to provide ICT services and become data hubs, but they will also need to align themselves with the ICT systems of their main customers, namely, the airlines. This alignment also needs to take into account other players such as air navigation service providers, national administrations, and logistics and cargo firms. In turn, greater alignment and compatibility will lead to better systemic data security measures.

Moving to the fourth layer in Figure 6-15, "cloud storage and mobility", cloud technologies are by far the biggest driver of economies of scale in the ICT field. They allow their users to save up to 80% of their operational costs by drastically reducing the amount of hardware and software they need to own and run, as well as allowing them to scale up and down with little or no additional cost. This equipment and software virtualization also fosters standardization, resulting in even more economies, and it also greatly enhances and facilitates cybersecurity because the number of vulnerable systems and gateways is reduced, creating what is known as a virtuous circle.

For instance, moving to the cloud means that data such as flight movements or passenger lists can be formatted and standardized. Once this is done, the data can be exchanged, which means that the next application in the chain, say, air traffic control or airlines, no longer needs to reformat them. As these applications process and modify the data, they can exchange the updated version with the first application, as well as with other applications such as airport operations databases. Because all the data now conforms to a single standard, they are now easy to encrypt as well, enhancing security. This also means that processing can be simplified and automated for all participants. This all translates to more efficient processing, real-time operations, enhanced security, and lower costs because software can now be unified. This virtuous circle will then propagate further up and down the ICT chain and will also provide a solid base for the application of AI tools.

However, the aviation industry has been slow to move its operations to cloud-based technologies, mostly because there would be few immediate benefits given the disparity of platforms and players. It is difficult to move services and applications to the virtual layers when there is little standardization in the base layers or data exchanges. The cost of redesigning and standardizing long-running applications to run more effectively in a cloud environment would also be prohibitive. Moreover, strict territorial and jurisdictional regulations will also inhibit cloud adoption by aviation as a whole. The very definition of cloud technologies is that data can be processed and stored anywhere, which goes against national regulations in the international aviation industry regarding sovereignty, data privacy, and jurisdiction.

Technical solutions are available to establish local, national, or even regional clouds, but the current fragmentation and lack of cooperation in the international aviation industry leads the cloud vendors and solutions providers to look elsewhere for easier business opportunities. A more unified and collaborative approach needs to be developed by both the aviation industry and the cloud solution providers.

The top layer in the stack depicted in Figure 6-15, the "analytics layer", has the greatest potential to deliver economies of scale and enhanced services to the aviation industry. This is where the true business solution for aviation, and particularly airports, resides. Harnessing artificial intelligence would result in truly smart airports and systems and therefore a fully integrated air transportation system worldwide.

All in all, the aviation industry, like many other industries, needs to take a long hard look at its overall ICT architecture to tailor it to service its growing needs, and more importantly, those of its customers. The bad news is that, given their current state, aviation ICT systems are vulnerable and will be difficult to update. The good news, however, is that new technologies plus market growth and demand are forcing major changes in architecture and service delivery. Through improved cooperation among its various stakeholders, the aviation industry's ICT architects will be able to benefit from tools developed in other sectors, which will allow them to build better and more robust platforms. Unlike previous generations, as these platforms are being developed, ICT teams will be able to build-in cybersecurity from the ground up, thereby creating a virtuous circle that will foster more trust, which will lead to even more business.

MANAGING CHANGE

Up to this point, this chapter has dealt extensively with technologies and innovations, but its overall purpose is to deal with innovative technological change, with the emphasis on "change". In this light, how one goes about implementing change is as important as the technologies or innovations used to bring it about. The following section will suggest how aviation managers can use change management techniques to bring about successful transformations that will change the industry.

Regardless of which change management theory one might subscribe to, whether Lewin's or Kotter's model or the McKinsey 7S approach[20], all models require four main elements: planning, competent teams, methodology, and technology. Each one of these elements will be addressed separately, with respect to the future, in the following paragraphs.

Planning

Fortunately, both major players in the international aviation industry, airlines and airports, are already very good at the first discipline, planning. However, knowledgeable resources and clear strategies that integrate innovation are often lacking. Securing talent is obviously the most difficult part because competition is fierce and the aeronautical field is not particularly enticing to many ICT professionals. Clearly, considerable investment in competent technology professionals will be essential in the future.

Planning in the industry as a whole needs to incorporate a wider array of disciplines and must follow and learn from the progress and transformation of other related sectors such as ground transport. Analytical models such as Betts-Lacroix (see Figure 6-2), and near-industry analyses will go a long way to enlighten and transform the planning approach. A clear understanding and roadmap of what lies ahead is also crucial. Accenture's Four Phase model, shown in Figure 6-16, can provide useful guidance to evaluate and time each stage to be considered.

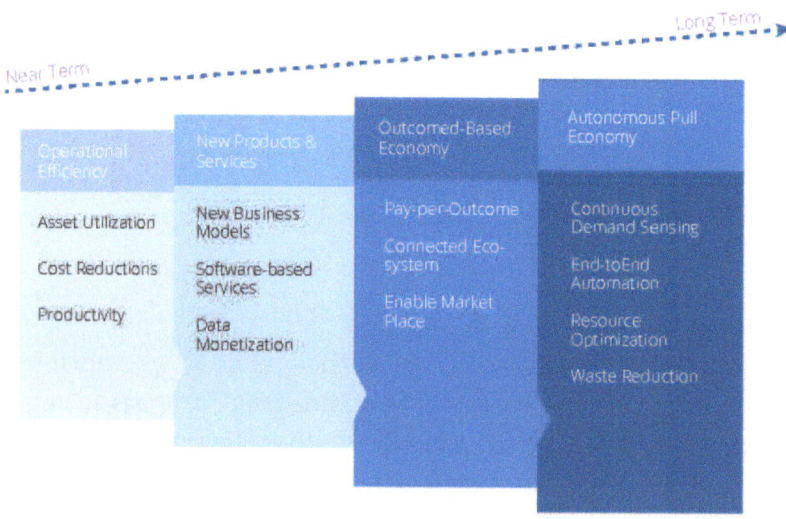

Figure 6-16 Four stages of the industrial Internet (Smart Production, Accenture, 2015).

Effective technology planning also requires a far greater level of cooperation and integration with regulators, clients, and stakeholders. Here again, all the mechanisms are in place, but they just need to be broadened and empowered.

Competent Teams

The second element, assembling competent teams, resides wholly in the quality and diversity of the people who are recruited to work in the aeronautical industry. Airlines, airports, ground handlers, and other stakeholders already have highly professional, competent, and specialized teams. They must now add ICT specialists to this mix and ensure that they are part of the solution, not just a support department.

As discussed, many of the changes implemented elsewhere, such as user experience design, data ubiquity, and data transparency, are in fact based on a change in the approach and culture surrounding a particular task or service. This culture change can only be led by people and teams, from managers to technicians to operators, and from main players to service providers. It is incumbent on the main players in the industry, airlines and airports, to nurture and promote open meritocratic cultures that will make their workplaces attractive to millennials, who are also the largest generation impacting the workplaces of today and tomorrow.

Methodology

The third McKinsey element, methodology, is also a well-honed practice in the aeronautical field. The entire industry culture is based on ICAO Standards and Recommended Practices (SARPs) and guiding principles such as safety, security, and facilitation. Here again, with the right change management skills and planning, aviation is ahead of most other industries in the approaches and experience required to develop and perfect the methodologies leading to transformation.

Technology

The final element necessary for successful change management deals directly with technology. This review of technological innovations that affect the global aviation industry has highlighted many upcoming trends and innovations. The implementation of the new technologies themselves should not pose any major technical challenges for two reasons. One, the aeronautical field has always been characterized by a high level of technical competence, and therefore it is only a matter of developing the right competencies and skills through resourcing and training. Two, many other industries have already gone through these changes, and the aviation industry will be able to reap the benefits of their experiences.

CONCLUSION AND SUMMARY

The first part of this closing section is a brief Conclusion that contains some overall general remarks that summarize the essence of the foregoing discussion of the Innovative Technological Change megatrend and offer some general advice to managers about how best to cope with it. The second part of this section is a Management Summary that recaps in point form all the major subjects discussed earlier during the detailed analysis and discussion of the Innovative Technological Change megatrend. The points are presented with the perspective of aviation professionals and managers in mind. Essentially, each point in the Management Summary represents a key observation or conclusion that was made during the detailed analysis and discussion.

Conclusion

As a megatrend, technological innovation is set to radically transform the way in which many service industries are run, and the airline industry is no exception because it will have to rethink how it is operated, regulated, and monetized. These changes can be categorized into the two main areas they affect, namely operational and efficiency changes and business model changes.

In the first category, this chapter has reviewed how advances in aircraft and propulsion technologies will lead to more fuel-efficient and environmentally friendly airplanes. Similarly, a looming shortage of pilots has spawned new solutions such as remotely controlled aircraft, a solution that the military has deployed on a large scale. New aircraft models are also enabling new modes of flight operations such as direct long and thin routes or longer and smaller direct regional routes. These developments are already affecting the traditional hub-and-spoke operations of larger carriers and will no doubt fuel new competitors to emerge.

Likewise, IoT, robotics, automation, and intelligence on-the-edge are already making inroads into how the industry runs its operations and offers significant saving compared with the existing modus operandi. These technologies will also change the economics of running small, hitherto unprofitable airports. This last trend will be further reinforced by the growth of remote management technologies such as virtual control towers.

Aviation managers need to understand and deploy these technologies, bearing in mind that it is the combination, or symbiosis, of human and machine collaboration that will generate the desired improvements. Yet, as was argued in the Introduction, these are all sustaining technologies that will merely make aviation industry operations run better and more efficiently. The data revolution, on the other hand, is starting to disrupt some of the very foundations upon which the industry is built and monetized.

The shift to user experience-based business models (UX) is already forcing all the players in the industry to work more closely together. This is made possible by the availability of better, more accurate, and more timely data as IoT devices are deployed by airlines, airports, support and service entities, and cargo operators. As discussed earlier, these shifts are already happening in other industries, from which the aviation industry can learn, and it will be able to use these lessons learned to deploy solutions more quickly and with fewer mistakes.

However, there is also a darker side in the form of cybersecurity threats that can potentially derail and threaten this transformation process by creating vulnerabilities and potentially catastrophic outcomes, both in human and financial terms. The good news is that the very changes needed to implement the new UX-driven business models will also help the aviation industry install and rationalize the networks and applications that it uses, thereby tightening the logical security of industry ICT platforms. The creation of this virtuous circle is another incentive to accelerate the transformation of the industry.

However, the aviation industry is also characterized by its prudence, conservatism, and high reliance and compliance with exacting and constraining regulations. This will become an important challenge as the industry itself needs to push for new common standards, and regulators will need time to adjust and to issue appropriate and verifiable rules. The next 15 years will put significant pressure on regulators to acknowledge change and equip themselves in terms of expertise and human resources to face all these changes. Clearly, regulators that are quick off the mark will have a golden opportunity to promote solutions and see their civil aviation industry thrive and grow. The challenge facing regulators will be to attract and retain talented people because they will be competing not only with the other actors in the industry, but also with other technical industries outside the world of aviation.

Airlines, airports, and cargo companies will also need to recruit and hire talented people because these changes will compel all players to widen their planning and forecasting departments, as well as their skill sets. All players need to embrace not only the new technologies, but also the methods that they use, such as agile iteration, UX design, and/or data convergence, or risk being seriously disrupted by outsiders. Indeed, as has happened in other industries, and although it is very hard to predict, it is quite possible that an as yet unknown "disruptor" will emerge that will break up the models used currently.

There are many opportunities and risks facing the aviation industry, but the future is bright. Technological innovation will very likely cause many changes and disruptions among the various stakeholders in the industry, but one thing is already clear: the biggest winners will be passengers and cargo. Thanks to innovation, passengers and shippers will get more choice and control in terms of destinations, services, schedules, pricing, and experiences than ever before. At the end of the day, they are the true raison d'être of the industry.

So, as industry practitioners and stakeholders, where can aviation managers and professionals start in preparing for the future of aviation? Like any transformational management project, adapting to new technologies and new economic models will require an equal mix of human and technology involvement, as was examined in the last section.

Technological innovation was at the very heart of a new aviation industry over one hundred years ago that disrupted the way that humankind moved about and saw its planet. Today, sustaining and disruptive innovations are set, once again, to radically transform the aviation industry and the way people travel. This transformation will no doubt fuel another century of growth to which the global aviation industry can look forward.

Management Summary

Based on the foregoing discussion, there is no doubt that the megatrend Innovative Technological Change will have major impacts on the international aviation industry over the next 15 to 20 years. In many ways, these massive changes will transform the way in which airlines and airports will develop and operate their businesses over the next couple of decades at least. A number of significant conclusions and observations can be made based on the detailed analysis contained earlier in this chapter. Accordingly, the following section highlights the important challenges that aviation managers at all levels will need to take into account when dealing with how the Innovative Technological Change megatrend will impact their operations.

Aircraft Technology

- The design of new airframes is an extremely expensive business, fraught with large risks and an onerous burden of technical, safety, and regulatory issues, and it is therefore unlikely that the industry will see a radical departure from the tube-and-wings model over the next 20 or so years.

- Tomorrow's airlines and their business models are being transformed by next-generation aircraft models such as the A350/B787 and A220/E195 E2. Aircraft right-sizing, long and thin routes, and direct point-to-point flights will make new routes possible and will have an impact on the hub-and-spoke system.

- Due to the high CO_2 emission levels of carbon-based fuels, alternative fuel sources are being researched and tested, with biofuels and electricity currently considered the two most likely technologies to replace carbon fuels in the future. Numerous technical and economic hurdles remain before either of these alternatives will be a viable alternative to jet fuel in the next 20 years.

- Over the next decade or more, the developed markets (i.e., North America and Europe) will face a shortage of pilots, whereas Asian markets will require a very large number of new pilots. For various reasons, the global supply of pilots will clearly fall short of demand over the next 15 to 20 years.

- Although the military has perfected remote pilotless technology, removing pilots from commercial aircraft, although technically feasible, will generate other significant challenges such as passenger trust and regulatory and legal issues and is therefore not expected to happen on a widespread basis within the next 20 years.

- A major obstacle to growth in commercial aviation traffic is the shortage of air and ground space as aircraft and routes multiply. The traditional hub-and-spoke air route model that involves fewer direct point-to-point flights is becoming less efficient and results in increased delays and longer journeys for increasingly dissatisfied passengers.

- Due to better materials and computerized controls, the airline industry has obtained a relaxation of the safety rules, which has allowed for longer flights, which in turn has resulted in changes to the regulations governing long-haul flights that have benefitted air carriers and are expected to carry forward into the future.

- Revised ETOPS rules have allowed new and more economical twin-engine planes to fly busy routes, which has greatly increased traffic and profitability for the airlines. New ultra-long-haul routes of 16 hours or more now make it possible to fly directly across several continents, a trend that is expected to continue.

- New thin point-to-point routes are revolutionizing the long-haul segment because they attract many new passengers to direct flights from smaller airports offering non-stop routes. New markets are constantly emerging as the new economics of these aircraft allow airlines to bypass the traditional intercontinental hubs.

- Due to improved technology, long-range smaller passenger jets are now capable of intercontinental flights of 6,500 km or more, which is more than enough to fly from any country in Europe to the East Coast of North America. This trend is expected to continue into the next decade and beyond.

- The biggest impact of the paradigm shifts described above will be felt by small and medium-sized airports, which will find themselves in a much stronger position to attract traffic due to the emergence of the new regional and long-range jets.

- Over the next 15 to 20 years, the airline industry will become much more diversified in terms of its approach to business models, and travelers will get a far richer and more diversified service offering than the one they are receiving today.

Automation and Human-Machine Symbiosis

- The aviation industry, compared with other industries, is somewhat of a laggard when it comes to implementing or embracing new technologies. Nevertheless, over the next 15 to 20 years, the global aviation industry will be transformed as three technologies will begin to re-shape the industry in the areas of transportation, logistics, and telecommunications.

- Rapid strides are currently being made in robotics and actuators powered by "intelligence on the edge" devices and ultrafast communications, which will revolutionize airport management by enabling remote and virtual operations. This will lead to new economic efficiencies that will transform the way in which airport operations are structured and managed.

- The Internet of Things (IoT) is revolutionizing the way in which aircraft operational data are collected and processed by airlines, which will significantly reduce costs and enhance safety by using specialized software analytics that will predict when a component is likely to fail. This will mean that repairs or replacements will only be done as-needed.

- At airports, many routine tasks such as runway inspections, foreign object detection (FOD), and physical plant repairs will be radically changed as IoT-generated data will impact many departments; personnel will be freed up from routine tasks and reassigned to more value-added tasks.

- Regulation and enforcement will be much more effective and far less costly under IoT as the digitization of data means that they can be shared and supervised by external regulatory bodies in real time.

- IoT will greatly enhance the quantity and quality of the data collected, which in turn will help airport operators manage their facilities much more dynamically and pro-actively than they can today.

- The implementation of IoT at airports will mean that many employees will require new skill sets to program and manage the new technology, while other staff will be required on the frontline, dealing with customers, in order to implement the programs.

- IoT will make single checkpoints at airports a thing of the past because sensors can be placed in many locations and will monitor travelers throughout the curb-to-air-craft-door journey. This will also make it much easier to handle the unpredictable nature of multiple unique passenger circumstances.

- Security inspections will be greatly streamlined using IoT technology, as large, costly, and space-hungry inline inspection machines and stations will be replaced with much smaller, more numerous, and relatively inexpensive IoT devices.

- Cargo handlers at airports will be slower to adopt and benefit from IoT technology because numerous independent intermediaries, over which the airport has no direct control, are still involved in the pickup, delivery, and handling of cargo; current systems are not digitized and are largely still paper-bound.

- For IoT technologies to work as they should, it is imperative that people trust the technology and have confidence in it. This is probably the biggest challenge facing the technology today because people are bombarded daily with media stories about yet another massive security breach.

- Information and communications technology (ICT) has produced the answers to resolve IoT security issues, and blockchain and hashgraph technologies are expected to transform the way in which data are exchanged and will have a profound impact on the international aviation industry over the next 15 to 20 years.

- The ground handling business will be transformed over the next 15 to 20 years because IoT sensors can communicate with ground handling before a flight arrives, transmitting operational data to ground-based devices so that ground services will be fully prepared when the flight arrives, improving turnaround time and reducing costs.

- IoT and ICT technologies have been used to create RTCs (remote tower controls), which currently operate in a number of countries. Using the same idea, smaller airports can hire a smaller number of generalist personnel, backed up by specialists based in central locations that can cater remotely to several airports through technology.

- A recent trend that is expected to grow in the coming decades is the use of remote management technology by large multinational groups that develop, manage, and operate networks of airports across the globe (e.g., VINCI, Fraport). This model uses a disciplined management approach that allows standardized operations and results in effective management and cost savings.

The Data Revolution: Big Data and AI

- In the coming decades, airports in particular will see their role redefined as they become the focal point for most of these technological changes. Using artificial intelligence capabilities (AI), they will become crucial data and decision-making nodes, and this transformation will impact the entire air transport system.

- The ubiquity of data will facilitate the extensive use of artificial intelligence, and this in turn will impact decision-making at both the operational and the strategic levels of the aviation industry and will affect travel decisions and regulations as a whole.

- The "millennial generation" is known to place user experience (UX) at the top of their priorities list. The notion of "experience" will be at the heart of the transformation of travel over the next 15 to 20 years as the balance of power shifts towards travelers.

- Airlines already know that over 50% of millennials are willing to pay additional fees to upgrade parts of their journey experience. Data ubiquity will be able to drive the creation of value-added services to enhance the customer experience (UX).

- To successfully deal with the UX approach in the future, aviation service companies will need to revisit and redesign their entire value chain to provide the specific experience(s) that their customers will be looking for by providing unique service experiences at different price points.

- In the future, airports will need to invest in real-time data systems that will allow them to take a much more proactive role in controlling the entire value chain of services and will facilitate the necessary close collaboration with governments, airlines, and other service providers.

- Air traffic control currently involves managing a large portion of airspace using the same tools and techniques as 25 years ago. Over the next 15 to 20 years, these older systems will become more unified and streamlined to handle traffic growth and congested airspace. Technologies already exist that can manage and run far more complex systems than ATCs.

- Some "islands" of AI exist within the airlines that analyze everything from fuel consumption and staff allocations to aircraft routing. There is, however, no single larger umbrella AI system that spans all an airline's functions. Without a doubt, this will happen during the next 15 to 20 years.

- The biggest change brought about by full implementation of AI will occur on the ground at the airport, where the air travel experience starts and ends. AI will allow airports to open up their terminal areas and provide new experiences as spare time will be freed up and traveler stress levels reduced by eliminating choke points.

- AI will also bring about major changes to the passenger experience in the sky as airlines will move towards ever more customized in-flight experiences that will be designed around the users' known interests.

- Both low-cost carriers (LCCs) and full-service carriers (FSCs) will continue to experiment with experience-centric pricing bundles based on data analytics of passenger behavior and purchasing habits. In the future, AI algorithms will continue to churn out a plethora of pricing bundles for their various market segments.

- New AI airfare models will combine customer preferences with yield management theory in order to maximize airline revenues. Both airlines and airports will need to provide better and differentiated services, as well as changing the physical layout of airports because each passenger's curb-to aircraft-door journey will potentially be different.

- AI will also help solve the growing logistical challenges generated by the new user experience (UX) business models by speeding up the allocation and decision-making process for day-to-day operations.

- To fully leverage the benefits of AI technology in the future, the various players in the industry, from airlines to airports, as well as other service providers and ground

- handlers, will need to cooperate and work together much more closely than they have in the past.

- Possibly one of the biggest data-related changes that will come about in the next 15 to 20 years will be the convergence of all these systems into a new data-centric model in which data will be shared and pooled by all parties in real time.

- In the next 15 to 20 years, airports or their DSPs (data service providers) will make significant investments in ICT and communications backbones to be able to provide their customers with a wide range of services. Airport operators will reap the benefits of these investments because they will be able to pool expertise across many locations and minimize costs as they roll out these platforms across various locations.

- Airlines, especially LCCs, will be particularly attracted to this data-centric model because airport groups will be able to propose identical and predictable services across many locations.

Cybersecurity

- One of the biggest challenges in the next two decades will be protecting individuals and corporations alike from the inherent risks of all these technological changes and innovations through enhanced cybersecurity measures. Because of its global and high-profile nature, the international aviation industry is a prime target for cyber-attacks.

- It is imperative that players in the aviation industry examine how and why these threats have emerged and how they can be dealt with using the industry's traditional regulatory approach, in addition to what practical solutions can be immediately put in place. Ways must be found by airlines, airports, and other aviation players to stop or minimize these attacks when they occur.

- Airlines and airports need to engage cybersecurity specialists to advise them on how to plan for cyber-attacks in advance and how to react to them most effectively when they do occur. It is important to be aware of what tools are (or are not) at the disposal of airlines, airports, and others before such attacks happen.

- Because of their data-centric position, airports will be uniquely placed in the coming decades to become the guarantors and protectors of data and operations. This will undoubtedly provide those airports that embrace this shift with enormous opportunities, which they will be able to monetize and use to their advantage. This will be an enormous challenge because the vast majority of airports are not ready for this transformation.

- As convergence and integration accelerate, airlines, airports, and other stakeholders will become more intertwined and therefore much more susceptible to cyber-attacks.

- The threat of "cyber terrorism" is often exaggerated, and in reality, ICT systems are becoming much safer, and cyber-attacks are becoming less frequent overall. Nevertheless, airlines, airports, and air navigation service providers need to be vigilant in protecting against such attacks because when they do occur, they can be devastating.

- Regulation in the field of ICT (information and communications technologies) will become a major trend over the next 15 to 20 years and will no doubt create many fundamental challenges because aviation industry regulators are currently poorly equipped and may not even be aware of what lies ahead. Developing and implementing new regulations in the aeronautical field will take time and patience.

- There is a worldwide paucity of technical expertise in ICTs in aviation, and it will take years before ICAO and the national regulatory bodies of ICAO Member States will be able to recruit properly qualified experts. When it comes to developing and adopting new cybersecurity regulations, the aeronautical industry will need to take a different approach than they have in the past.

- Since regulation is often an after-the-fact solution, industry players must seize the initiative themselves, come up with their own solutions, and adapt to the new reality of possible cyber-attacks that could occur anytime, anywhere, 24/7, worldwide.

- Over the next 20 years or more, the global aviation industry needs to make serious efforts to standardize its ICT systems, which are severely fragmented, with many different technologies, standards, and protocols coexisting; a significant portion of these are obsolete due to outdated regulations or technologies.

- In the next decade, airports will need to move toward a more data-centric model in which they will become the service and data provider for all their stakeholders. They will then need to provide ICT services and become data hubs that align with the ICT systems of their main business customers, the airlines.

- Although the aviation industry has been slow to move its operations to cloud-based technologies for a number of practical reasons, a more unified and collaborative approach needs to be developed by both the aviation industry and cloud solution providers because ICT development costs will only spiral upwards as traffic grows.

- Over the next decade or more, the aviation industry needs to deliberately and methodically embrace and implement AI-based business systems because it is well understood by all parties that this will lead to truly smart airports and systems, operating as part of a fully integrated air transportation system worldwide.

Managing Change

- Technological development will radically transform the aviation industry and its business models over the next 20 years. However, for these changes to have positive and successful outcomes, the human element in managing change is just as important as the new technologies being introduced.

- The four main elements that managers must deal with to successfully implement change are planning, competent teams, methodology, and technology.

    - Planning needs to incorporate a wider array of disciplines than it does today. This should start with a technology transformation roadmap and a much higher level of inclusion of and collaboration with clients and stakeholders.

    - Competent teams must be assembled, adding ICT and UX design specialists to already highly professional existing teams. Teams must also embrace and integrate in their *modus operandi* the new user-experience-based culture. This will not only ensure satisfied passengers, but will also align with the culture of the new generations and make the aviation workplace much more attractive to them.

    - Methodology is already well ingrained in the aviation industry, thanks to a solid tradition of solid regulations and best practices such as ICAO's SARPs. This is further reinforced by high levels of technical proficiency and a culture of training and sharing.

    - Technology is the fourth element and has been discussed in detail throughout this chapter.

REFERENCES

[1]   Christensen, C. M. (1997). *The innovator's dilemma.* Boston, MA: Harvard Business Review Press.

[2]   Jonathan Betts-Lacroix is an American medical scientist and entrepreneur. He adapted the Gartner Hype Cycle and Geoffrey Moore's Technology Adoption Life Cycle to explain why up-and-coming technologies failed or slowed down despite growing adoption. Moore, G. (1991). *Crossing the chasm.* HarperBusiness. Fenn, J., Raskino, M., & Burton, B. (2013). *Understanding Gartner's hype cycles.* Gartner. ID: G00251964.

[3]   Bergen, Oslo, Stockholm, and LAX (2018). *Sustainable aviation fuel in flight.* Aviationbenefits.org.

[4]   Pawlyk, O. (2017). *Drone milestone: More RPA jobs than any other pilot position.* Military.com.

[5]   Wikipedia article: https://en.wikipedia.org/wiki/ETOPS.

[6]   (2018, 10 July). "Airbus and Boeing are tightening their hold on the sky". *The Economist.*

[7]   GDPR portal at https://www.eugdpr.org/.

[8]   Shead, S. (2017, January). "Amazon now has 45,000 robots in its warehouses". *Business Insider..*

[9]   Moravec, H. (1998). *Mind children.* Harvard University Press.

[10]   Turnbull, G. (2015, October). "Remote tower technology: A new era in air traffic control?" *Airport Technology.*

[11]   (2017, 1 February). *Remote tower revolutionizes air traffic management.* SAAB Group.

[12]   Castells, M. (2000). "The rise of the network society: The information age". *Economy, society, and culture, Volume I,* Wiley-Blackwell.

[13]   Marsan, C. D. (2010). "Web sites must support IPv6 by 2012, expert warns". *Networkworld,* January 2010, and progress reports issued by RIPE NCC, 2018.

[14]   Tafoya, W. F. (2011, November). *Cyberterror.* FBI Law Enforcement Bulletin.

[15]   Denning, D. E. (2003, May). [Georgetown University]. *Cyberterrorism.* Testimony given to the US House of Representatives.

[16]   Valero, J. (2016, July). "Hackers bombard aviation sector with over 1,000 attacks a month". *Euractiv.*

[17]   GDPR portal at https://www.eugdpr.org/.

[18]   (2015). "Solution stack". *Computer Desktop Encyclopedia,* Computer Language Company.

[19]   Whittaker, Z. (2015, 16 November). "A 23-year-old Windows 3.1 system failure crashed Paris airport". *Zero Day.*

[20]   Webster, V., and Webster, M. (Eds.) (2018). *Successful change management,* Leadership Thoughts; Kotter, J. (2002). *The heart of change.* Harvard Business Review Press; Jurevicius, O. (2013, December 20). "*McKinsey 7s Model*". www.strategicmanagementinsight.com.

7

GLOBAL
CONNECTEDNESS

INTRODUCTION

In recent years, numerous authors have addressed the growing trend towards increased connectedness on a global scale. In fact, there is a certain amount of confusion that exists between the terms "connectedness" and "connectivity", and their extended versions "global connectedness" and "global connectivity". For example, some prominent authors and researchers have used the term "global connectedness" to define and describe the depth and breadth of a country's integration with the rest of the world, exclusively in the context of international flows of goods and services among countries (i.e., international trade). A prime example of this is DHL's highly publicized Global Connectedness Index.[1]

However, this Megatrends book defines and discusses "global connectedness" in a somewhat different way. So, in order to clear up any possible terminology misunderstandings from the beginning, let's take a quick look at the actual meanings of the two terms "connectivity" and "connectedness". Both terms are nouns. "Connectivity" refers to "the ability" (or not) of things/entities to connect with others, whereas "connectedness" refers to "the degree or extent" to which things/entities are actually connected to one another.

Accordingly, this book defines the "global connectedness" megatrend as the degree and extent to which the world is connected via networks of every type. In a general sense, connectivity enables connectedness through innovative technology. Essentially, it is about the way in which humans are connected to data and communication networks on a worldwide basis. From an aviation perspective, connectivity through airline networks refers to meeting the needs of the people of the world for efficient and economical air transport. In many ways these two are intertwined; both are concerned with the speed, accuracy, quality, quantity, control, and distribution of people, information, goods, and services through their respective networks. The four sub-trends in particular that need to be considered in the context of global connectedness and aviation are access to information, network proliferation, quality of information, and connectedness and aviation impacts.

In his seminal book "*Future Smart*", James Canton defines connectivity as, "...the super-glue that binds all transactions, technologies, relationships, and businesses." He goes on to explain how connectivity will define how people interact with the world and how they will interact with other people, nations, markets, and businesses.[2] The term "connectedness" on the other hand, can be defined as the extent to which the world is connected. In other words, connectivity is a means or a way (i.e., a tool), whereas connectedness is a state of being. According to Canton, "The most important impact on the world of the

Connected Planet Trend will be universal access to all human knowledge by everyone on the planet."[3] So, a fully connected planet will be one in which all humanity will have access to any and all information on demand, at any time desired.

A current example of global connectedness in action is in the field of medical research. Through global network connectivity technology, that activity now extends far beyond the individual laboratory and is often conducted through online networks connecting other scientists around the world. Another example is in the field of music, where concerts are now being played via the Internet with musicians located in different locations all around the globe. In medicine, surgeons can now direct the conduct of complex surgical procedures performed by others from remote locations. In the field of transportation and tourism, providers of travel experiences can now connect to potential individual passengers from all over the world, and passengers have direct network access to any travel and tour offer from just about anywhere in the world.

Many of us are already experiencing these new connected inter-relationships without noticing them. For example, products from around the world are available almost instantly anywhere we want them. At the tip of our fingers, we can access literally any information, reach anyone we want to communicate with, or learn from the most learned individuals, who may even be part of our social network.

As mentioned above, in the context of the international aviation industry, the global connectedness megatrend can be broken down into four key sub-trends as follows:

Access to Information: This sub-trend is all about the speed at which information is becoming available and the massive quantities of it that are now available to virtually anyone in the world. How can people, and aviation managers in particular, deal with this onslaught?

Network Proliferation: The discussion of this sub-trend will examine how it is becoming easier to establish connections with similar sites of interest or with people who hold common values or interests. To what degree should we restrict access to certain networks and ensure that the appropriate people and/or organizations have access to the appropriate networks? To which networks do aviation managers need access, and to what degree?

Quality and Quantity of Information: This sub-trend deals with the following questions: How can we ensure that the information that we are getting is accurate? How can we validate the information coming to us? How do we handle information overload? What steps should aviation managers take to ensure that the quality of information they use is acceptable?

Connectedness Technology - Impacts on Aviation: The discussion of this sub-trend documents the various ways in which the degree of connectedness worldwide and advances in related technology will impact aviation over the next 15 to 20 years and beyond. As the level of connectedness increases, it will impact almost every aspect of the international aviation industry.

This chapter discusses each of these sub-trends in terms of what they mean and how they are likely to influence the future of aviation and hence impact the role of aviation managers. The aviation industry will be increasingly concerned with the impact of these three sub-trends because they are fundamental to its ability to deliver its primary product, air transport, to its customers. The discussion will end with a section titled *"Connectedness and Aviation"*, which will look specifically at all the ways that global connectedness is expected to influence the direction that aviation will take, and how aviation managers might shape the industry so that it will stay relevant and play a significant role in the new interconnected world. As Canton puts it, "Connected networks of people, capital, data, and smart products—Always Aware and Always Online—will create a new Global Digital Culture that will expand global prosperity well beyond what we have seen today."[4]

ACCESS TO INFORMATION

Access to information today happens at the speed of light compared with the Internet access of the 1990s, when connections were only possible by landline, data transmission speeds were very slow, and there was too much static on the line. Today, one can access almost any information by typing on a simple keyboard (or tapping a touch screen) and within microseconds get a reply with dozens of possible options. One can then select the one that looks the most promising and investigate the answers from there. The amount of data available online these days is truly mind-boggling. Not long ago, *Science Focus Magazine* quantified this mass of data as, "... the sum total of data held by all the big online storage and service companies like Google, Amazon, Microsoft, and Facebook. Estimates are that the Big Four store at least 1,200 petabytes among them. That is 1.2 million terabytes (one terabyte is 1,000 gigabytes). And that figure excludes other big providers like Microsoft, Amazon, Google, IBM, Alibaba, and Tencent, to say nothing of massive servers in industry and academia."[5]

That estimate was made a couple of years ago. Since then, the amount of information created and available has grown exponentially and is expected to continue to do so as the future unfolds. According to the experts at Infineon Technology, by 2030, the information available to everyone connected to the World Wide Web and the way they will be able to access it will be beyond what we can imagine even today, and that's only a decade or so away.[6]

Apparently, by 2030, life will be much easier. Everything will be electronically connected. According to Gartner Research and Consulting, there were eight billion connected devices in 2017. IBM has estimated that there will be 50 billion devices by 2020. Today, there are few if any electronic devices that are not connected through the Internet. This saves a lot of time because information is automatically passed on from device to device. Strictly speaking, data automatically know where to go to be processed.[7]

In fact, Gartner's predictions could even be too conservative. Considering that 5G mobile communications already bring 100 times faster transmission at a fraction of the time required today and 1,000 times greater capacity, leading to 50 billion connected devices by 2020, the future will be exponentially greater than this. We are looking at the future from the small end of a cone. The vision gets bigger as we move forward.

In his book "*Future Minds*", Richard Watson states that "...knowledge is becoming instantly available to almost everyone. One skill that people will need to acquire is.... *knowing how things relate to one another*."[8] Indeed, the knowledge might be there, but we will have to learn how to select the applicable knowledge and how it relates to what we already know or don't know.

In a recent article in *Forbes Magazine*, Bernard Marr presented some enlightening facts and statistics about activity levels on the World Wide Web:

- More than half of Web searches are now conducted via mobile phone.

- By 2018, more than *3.7 billion* humans were using the Internet (7.5% more than in 2016).

- On average, Google processes more than 40,000 searches EVERY second (3.5 billion searches per day).

- Although 77% of searches are conducted on Google, other search engines are also contributing to daily data generation. (Worldwide, there are 5 billion searches per day).[9]

With so much information at our fingertips, we're adding to the data stockpile every time we turn to our search engines for answers. These statistics listed above are as of May 2018, and the progression is more than exponential. Figure 7-1 presents some additional statistics from 2017.

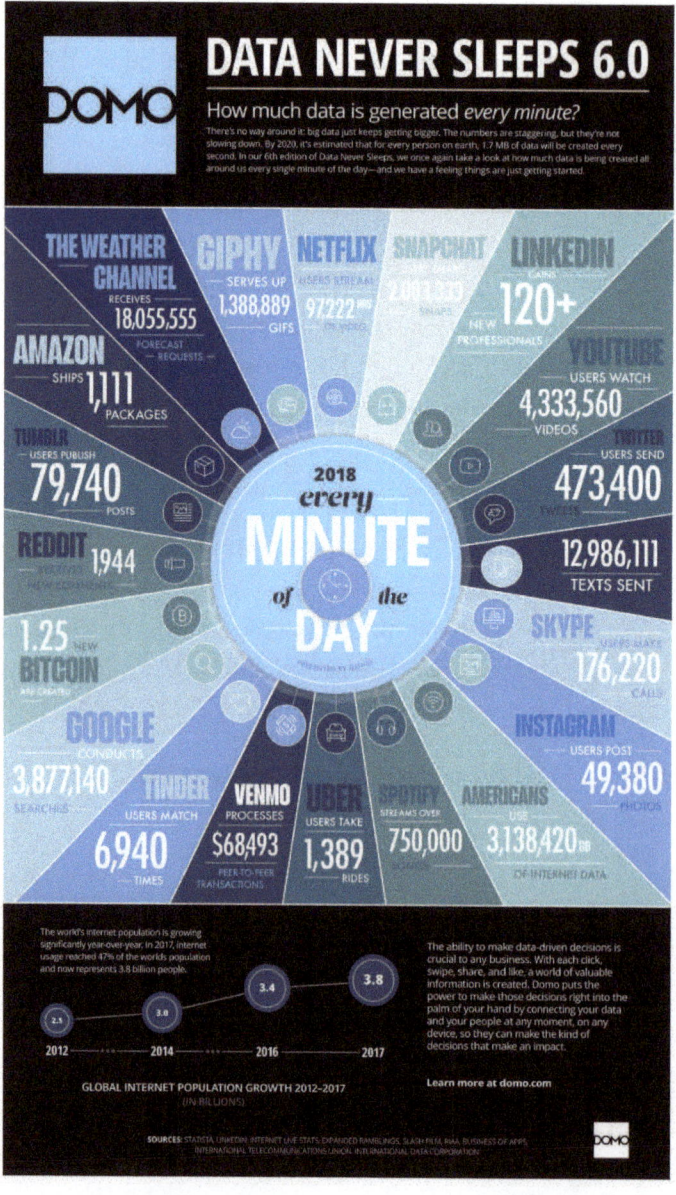

Figure 7-1   Data Never Sleeps (domo.com).

The biggest problem with this massive creation and availability of data of course is, and will continue to be, information overload. How does one deal with all this information and learn to take advantage of the possible benefits of having such knowledge available at one's fingertips? It will be challenging to decipher what is appropriate information and what is not. Access to information will become like a huge buffet and unless we control ourselves, we might get a case of indigestion from bad information, or even get poisoned.

The problem is overwhelming and still growing, and it's so big that humans just can't begin to deal with it in a meaningful way. Fortunately, modern technology, coupled with network connectivity, has presented a powerful solution for dealing with this avalanche of information—artificial intelligence (AI). The main goal of AI is to sort and sift through massive data to provide clarity for decision-making and/or make autonomous decisions. In the field of aviation, in the near future (or now in some cases), we will have autonomous solutions that are capable of running many complex tasks such as air traffic control, aircraft maintenance and checks, and systems and runway inspections much better than humans.

Everyone is Getting Connected

The idea behind the Internet of Things (IoT) is to connect everything to everything else and eventually to connect every person to every other person on Earth. (See Chapter 6, *Innovative Technological Change*, for a detailed discussion of IoT). The concept of "six degrees of separation" between everyone will soon be replaced by "two degrees (or two connections) of separation". Through major search engines like Google and Bing, people can now connect almost instantaneously to any person, anywhere in the world, as long as the other person is also online. People are now connected to just about anyone with no more than two or three degrees of separation at the very most. The same is true with products and services; we can now connect to any product or service with two or three clicks of a mouse via the Internet.

The following scene is a daily occurrence these days. Three young adults are sitting in an airport departure lounge, and all three are texting without talking to each other. Suddenly, two of them start laughing simultaneously and look at each other while holding up their mobile phones to show the third one the exchange they just had. A poll conducted by a UK mobile phone company revealed that phones are no longer used simply as telephones; they have become connectivity devices. In fact, of all the numerous functions provided by a mobile phone today, the survey found that the actual telephone function was the eleventh most used function, far behind texting and taking photos.[10]

Today, members of the younger generations are connected to the point where their ongoing interactions with other people are based primarily on system connectivity rather than on physical relationships. Their relationships are often contingent on whether they are connected to someone through the same social media platform. They first meet online, and eventually they might meet in person. The exchange of information is somewhat limited to certain parameters that are common only to a certain group of individuals (even though there could be millions of these).

Online gaming has become so popular that even the International Olympic Committee is considering introducing eSports at the Tokyo Olympic Games in 2020. The Asian Games in Jakarta in 2018 are showcasing eSports as one of the competitions. Fans already have their favorite stars, and new online teams are created every day.

This degree of connectedness among young people will only increase in the future. The millennial generation is the first fully connected generation, and the generations that come afterwards will only be exposed to a fully connected world. (See Chapter 5, *Demographic Changes and Trends*, for a more in-depth discussion of the millennial generation).

Information Access and Aviation

More air travel trips are sold directly through the Internet today than through traditional bricks-and-mortar travel agencies. This situation would have been unthinkable even at the end of the last millennium. Nowadays, everything a person needs to know about their means of travel, their accommodation at their destination, and what to do when they get there is available online with a few clicks of a mouse. Some people still use travel agencies today to plan their trips, but these are mostly people in the older generation who are not as comfortable arranging things online. Most trips these days are arranged without the client and the provider ever meeting in person. As they see it, what more could they say in person that cannot be communicated online?

This ease of information access via the Internet is also changing the relationship between airlines and their passengers. Compared with a decade ago, there is much less need for air travelers to interact directly with airline personnel, either by telephone or in person. This person-to-person disconnect is only expected to increase in the future as more information becomes directly available to passengers and more services are automated. This is not necessarily a bad thing, but airline and airport staff will need to be aware of the reality of this changing dynamic with their customers. It won't be long before passengers on board aircraft will casually interact with one another or be subjected to a series of new and innovative activities during their flight via their mobile phones.

For example, when one books a flight directly online, one has to acknowledge having read and understood the conditions of the purchase. In the past, if a traveler had questions, an airline agent would explain the conditions to them. Online, they are given the option of reading a very long and complicated document written in legalese, as an option. However, in the name of time and efficiency, most people skip reading the detailed conditions and click on a link to a page confirming their commitment to thousands of dollars of unknown obligations or exclusions on their part as customers.

As already discussed, there is no doubt that commercial air travel will be more accessible in the future. The forecast shorter travel times to reach a destination will allow providers to increase the number of operations, thus giving travelers more choices. Imagine being able to travel by air to attend a concert in Europe or Asia. Imagine being able to visit relatives that you have not seen for years simply because they live abroad. Then imagine doing these things at the last minute, not suffering from jet lag, and returning home the same day or the next. This is the future of personal transport by commercial airlines.

As mentioned above, this evolution in direct and rapid access to information and how it affects human relationships is certainly impacting the way business is conducted, including the aviation business. It definitely impacts the ways in which companies and individuals organize their business decisions and personal travel. Today, more people travel for personal reasons than ever before. For many air travelers, this means residing in a private home at their destination, rather than a hotel or resort. The largest accommodation company in the world, Airbnb, has zero accommodation assets, but offers more than 4.5 million spaces worldwide[11]. This not only makes it easier for people to travel, but it often connects them with real people at their destination. Albeit briefly at times, travelers get to meet the owners of the space they have rented and sometimes make friends with them. Such friendships are now possible on all continents. These friendships are then facilitated by connectivity tools such as email, social media, and Skype. Thus, the sharing of information via connectivity leads to sharing of experiences, values, and friendships. Without the ubiquitous accommodation information and global connectedness that exists today, a company like Airbnb would not be able to operate. One could say that company's service is a prime example of connectedness that is a direct product of connectivity.

In cases of disputes with airlines, disgruntled customers are now more empowered than ever before through the leverage of social media. There have been numerous highly publicized instances in which individual unhappy customers have "shamed" large airlines into settling with them. All it takes is for one horror-story Tweet or one Facebook post to go viral to make an airline look bad to hundreds of thousands, if not millions, of prospective customers. And these days, it doesn't seem to matter whether the shaming post is true or not. Once it has gone viral, it is too late to undo the damage.

NETWORK PROLIFERATION

As of 2017, 70% of the world's youth were online. This represents 830 million individuals. The number of Internet users globally went from 1.9 billion in 2009 to 3.4 billion in 2016. And these users had access to over 1.8 billion Websites.[12]

The World Wide Web today is an online place where everyone can meet and share information. In addition, there are other webs that are not totally accessible to everyone: SIPRNet, Dark Web, Deep Web, and Dark Internet, among other such networks. As the amount of information keeps increasing, some of those could become even less public or available to anyone than they are today. These types of ultra-private networks are expected to increase and grow and will only be accessible to those with proper credentials.

The Internet of Things (IoT) is already penetrating all segments of aviation. This network technology is being used to perform such tasks at airports as tracking ground equipment and reporting on the status and location of moving vehicles. Airlines and maintenance companies are using it to monitor the performance of aircraft engines. The link to immediate information via the Internet is changing the nature of airport and airline management. Airlines now have "connected aircraft". As aircraft become "smart", fully connected machines, new services can be introduced to benefit the passenger experience, grow revenues for the airlines, and improve safety. To function properly, the "connected aircraft" needs reliable and seamless connectivity, from the cabin to the cockpit.[13]

As general access to all types of information is facilitated through instant communication, networks are now created without moving the hardware infrastructure to the same location. Previously, the computer servers were almost always located in the same location as the users. Today, it is believed to be preferable to have various components located in different locations, thus spreading out the risk and reaping the benefits of a distributed presence. Increasingly, companies and organizations are moving some or all of their computer and communications applications to "the cloud", where their software runs on the servers of a Web services company such as Amazon World Services. In these cases, the companies (and their customers) access all the company's services via the Internet, but the servers could be located in a safe/secure place almost anywhere in the world. (See Chapter 6, *Innovative Technological Change*, for an in-depth discussion of cloud computing).

Shane Wall, CTO of Hewlett-Packard and Global Head of HP Labs, said at a conference in 2016 that the future will be quite different. We are becoming hyper-global while also becoming hyper-local. He stated that by 2020, there will be 80 billion connected devices, which for a population of 8 billion, is quite significant. He said that this is all about 'people' connecting people to people.[14]

As James Canton puts it, "The Fourth Internet Wave will be a collaborative web that will have at its root the dynamic intimate cooperation and deep learning between business, organizations, markets, and people, and machines for work, learning, essential social services, and entertainment will mature."[15] The globalization of markets and resources, the cyber world of Facebook, LinkedIn, Twitter, and other such borderless activities all aim to form new community networks.

In aviation, the growth and evolution of network technology has now made it possible to automatically collect and share all kinds of information about the aircraft with other components of the system: equipment to staff, staff to staff, equipment to equipment, equipment to maintenance, equipment to regulator, etc. Using today's network technology, all these functions are now in constant contact and can quickly check on each other's status. (See Chapter 6, *Innovative Technological Change*, for a more in-depth discussion of this type of technology).

Again, the dependability of connections among networks will become even more important, and if that is maintained, acceptance by the world will follow.

Networks and People

When we talk about network connectivity, we are not just referring to technology. In fact, modern network technology has enabled the creation of many new human networks that connect millions of people globally.

For the last 1,500 years or more, societies on Planet Earth have tried to protect their citizens, their means of production, and their market interests. Since borders between countries mean very little to technology and communication networks, perhaps it is time to move on and join forces with previous competitors to better utilize the resources available and strengthen exchanges and codes of conduct (legal codes). In the age of network proliferation, it no longer makes sense to act only on behalf of local people; it is time to also consider the needs of people globally. This is exactly what has been happening since the advent of the Internet with the creation of online community networks.

Modern-day networks span multiple sovereign borders and are forcing into existence a new world order that benefits all members of the connected communities. In fact, currently there are hundreds, if not thousands of online communities that connect millions of people based on common interests and beliefs. The list includes Facebook, Twitter, Pinterest, Instagram, and LinkedIn, and the list goes on and on.[16] A list of virtual communities (i.e., networks) with more than one million members is maintained on the Wikipedia.org Website.[17]

Figure 7-2   Internet and social media penetration (Hootsuite, 2018).

As can be seen in the previous illustration, social media have become ubiquitous to the point that half the world's population *virtually* lives there. The impact for the aviation industry, similar to that on all industries, is that social media are now part and parcel of the daily experience of its main customers, the passengers. In this light, social media fulfill different roles that have different impacts on many aspects of aviation as an industry. Four main use cases are summarized in the following few paragraphs.

Brand Creation and Marketing

This is probably the oldest use, and it was pioneered mainly by airlines as an extension of their brand marketing, although airports and many other aviation players have stepped in. Initially, information was merely pushed out by the various marketing departments, and the messaging was carefully controlled by them. In a recent study, Sherpa Marketing found that more people follow brands on social media than follow celebrities[18].

However, social media are about much more than controlled messaging; they are inherently interactive. Hence, most of the communications are not generated by marketing departments, but by users themselves, and users determine whether an entity's overall role and presence is positive or negative. As a result, businesses, and especially airlines, have turned to social media influencers to send positive messages. For instance, Qantas Airlines has turned to Nicole Warne, aka Gary Pepper Girl, one of Australia's top influencers with 1.7 million followers, to promote the airline on her Websites, as well as creating original content for the airline. Nicole also works closely with major cosmetic brands, Chanel and Dior, thereby increasing the upscale media presence and cross-marketing Qantas to desirable consumer groups worldwide.

Lead and Sales Generation

Businesses were quick to seize upon the power of social media to increase their reach and multiply their audience, as well as to increase their efficiency. Before the age of the Internet, marketing, and business development, the main activities devoted to lead and sales generation were expensive and imprecise endeavors. Marketing campaigns seldom reached their intended audiences because paper, radio, or TV ads could only cover wide audiences without much precision, and business development usually involved expensive in-person visits or presentations that often were poorly timed or ended in low sales conversions because the wrong person was targeted. Online tools, on the other hand, allow for very precise targeting, accurate needs prediction, and greatly improved sales conversion ratios. Paradoxically, social media have increased the need for business travel as well as targeted and proactive business visits, and have greatly increased the effectiveness and ROI of business development trips and campaigns.

User Experience

If social media have increased the reach of savvy marketers and companies, they have also fueled the growth of consumer-oriented content based on user experience. At the most basic level, consumer reviews have now become ubiquitous; for anything but basic consumables, shoppers now research and make their purchasing decisions based on reviews, mostly ones external to the vendor's Website. For airlines and airports, a plethora of specialized sites and vlogs (video blogs) are available to show and compare what to expect from a particular terminal or airplane seat. Beyond influencers, savvy consumers understand and assess ahead of time what to expect on their journey. This is a unique tool for the aviation travel industry to hone and promote the various services that it wishes to offer, and demand for additional paying services beyond basic travel represents a fast-growing income source.

Incident Handling

The flip side of the previous point is that social media also greatly accelerate and clarify the perception and consequences when things go wrong. Airports and airlines have discovered the hard way that incidents and mishaps circulate far faster in social media than through their own management and information systems, perpetually putting them in a reactive position. This, however, can be turned to their advantage, as Figure 7-3 shows. Quick and targeted action using social media actually improves future sales and perceptions, even after a negative incident or experience.

A study of tweets to airlines shows that when a tweet is answered in five minutes or less, the customer will pay almost $20 more for a ticket on that airline in the future.

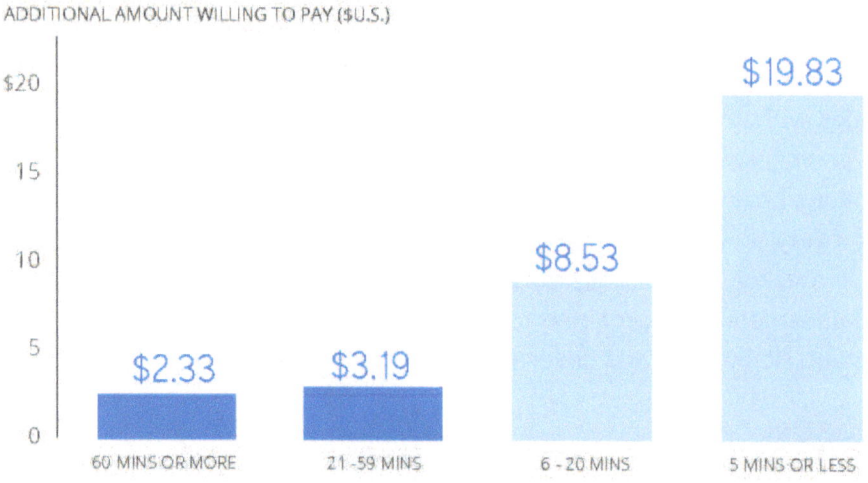

ADDITIONAL AMOUNT WILLING TO PAY ($U.S.)

Figure 7-3   Relationship: social media response time and future sales (Harvard Business Review, 2018.) [19]

Networks and Aviation

Networking technology has already resulted in the creation of numerous online communities that deal with almost every aspect imaginable of aviation-related work and recreational interests and activities.[20] There is no doubt that this type of network creation will continue in the aviation community in the future. Clearly, these types of aviation-related networks improve the professional and personal lives of the people who make up the worldwide aviation community, in its broadest sense.

The aviation industry actually pioneered some of the world first global networks in the form of airline reservation systems. As the demand for air travel increased in the 1950s, it became more and more difficult to reserve and issue airplane tickets using manual systems primarily based on human operators using telephone lines in centralized locations. The SABER system (semi-automatic business reservation system), developed by American Airlines, was one of the very first global network-based data systems. It enabled for the first time the global coordination of reservations without duplications, as well as the rationalization and optimization of flights and frequencies. SABER, along with the current market leader, Amadeus, which was developed by the European airlines, were and are at the forefront of many of the tools used by current social media platforms.

Over the last twenty years, increasing congestion on the ground and in the air has led to the creation of public networks and platforms designed to increase the efficiency, safety, and security of global travel. Most national air traffic control systems routinely share data automatically to ensure smooth and safe navigation of aircraft. Europe, because of its congested skies, has mandated Eurocontrol, a shared trans-national agency, to coordinate flights and movements even before airplanes take off. Similarly, growing security concerns have also led to automatic transfer of passenger information between States so that recipient States have all the data about inbound passengers before they arrive at their border control facilities.

The near future will see even more integration and sharing of information as passenger volumes grow, for two main reasons beyond safety and security, one being efficiency and cost savings and the other facilitation.

As more and more people travel, States are footing an ever-increasing bill for receiving and processing all these new travelers in a safe and secure way. Greater networking and predictive intelligence will prove to be invaluable in predicting and managing these flows. Just as importantly, these technologies are already lifting the decision-making burden from slow and inefficient customs and immigration officers to intelligent border control stations, thus allowing for cost-effective processing and the targeting of key human services to questionable or dangerous individuals. Expect to see much more automation at the borders, a trend that is welcomed by the vast majority of passengers.

Beyond cost savings, these new networks and algorithms are having, and will have, an even greater impact on facilitation, one of ICAO's main goals related to the travel experience. Facilitation refers to the goal and obligation of the signatories of the Chicago Convention to facilitate air travel for all civil aviation users. This applies obviously to the physical processing of travelers at borders, where ICAO and the main industry representative bodies such as IATA and ACI have issued formal service level targets. Beyond these, connectivity is also transforming to which countries travelers choose to travel. Thanks to automated processing, more and more visa applications are now made online, thereby accelerating and simplifying the application process. Looking ahead, current voluntary application processes will be supplanted by even more automation in which the purchase of a plane ticket will someday automatically trigger the visa application and authorization process.

Likewise, data sharing will also lead to faster and more reliable security checks, which are probably the biggest hindrance to air travel today. Traveler backgrounds and past behavior will be used to classify and assess security risks for individual passengers, thereby streamlining physical security checks, as discussed in more detail in Chapter 6, *Innovative Technological Change.*

This is where user experience and travel experience will meet and converge as the tourism industry continues to grow. As traditional tourist centers become congested or even start limiting the number of tourists, new destinations are attracting and will attract more visitors by ensuring a smooth, safe, and obstacle-free travel experience. Those destinations that can use connectivity to offer these types of experiences will, in turn, be rated highly in social media, thus creating a virtuous cycle that will spawn further growth.

By definition, the aviation activity itself facilitates and enhances the degree of global connectedness among people and communities. For example, as the cost of aviation fuel decreases and airplanes become more fuel-efficient, air transport becomes an increasingly accessible commodity. It allows families to reunite more often, even though they may be located on different continents. It also allows manufacturers of products to connect with a much larger market than their traditional territory, with the added benefit of higher volumes reducing production costs. Better connectivity allows the involvement of a much wider supply chain of service providers and workers. As the aviation industry moves gradually towards aircraft that will be flown by fewer pilots, production costs will continue to decrease, thus making air travel more affordable for almost everyone. Even short three- to four-day holidays on the beach will become routine given that they will be no more expensive than a weekend in New York City. Travel time will no longer be a major constraint since it will often be a matter of just a few hours, instead of a day or more, for holiday travel to go anywhere today. The increasing connectedness of aviation will empower millions of people worldwide in the coming decades.

The benefits of better network technology in the aviation industry in general will make the dreaded jet lag a condition of the past. Less travel time, coupled with new technology that will provide a better in-flight environment with improved air quality and lower noise levels, will make flying a more pleasant and comfortable experience than it is today. Less stress traveling by air will translate into a more enjoyable time at destination. Thus, both improved network technology and the increased connectivity of aviation will continue to result in tangible benefits for the traveling public.

Improvements in network technology will also drive air cargo activity upward. In 2016, UPS shipped nearly 5 billion parcels and documents. This is expected to increase exponentially as well, until we find another way to transmit parcels. Remote 3D printing and teleportation of objects cannot be that far away.

On the air navigation services (ANS) side of aviation, new network technology and related equipment will change the way in which airspace is managed. In the years to come, air navigation services will be provided from a facility located somewhere remote from the airport or not even in the country where the services are used. This is already the case at London City Airport in the UK, which is in the process of launching a new virtual control tower that will be housed in a facility 80 miles from the airport. It is quite possible that similar technology will be developed for remote piloting of aircraft in the not too distant future.[21]

On the African continent, l'Agence pour la sécurité de la navigation aérienne en Afrique et à Madagascar (ASECNA)[22] has been providing air navigation services to 17 African countries since 1959. ASECNA is one of the leaders in the development of satellite navigation and air traffic management (CNS/ATM). Its program of new technologies and equipment will allow it to perform quite differently from today. Africa is indeed a fertile ground for expansion of remote networked services, given the difficulties in recruiting qualified human resources and obtaining funding for equipment. From its current base of 17 countries, ASECNA might expand beyond French Africa and start partnering with Eastern African countries like Mozambique and Zimbabwe. It is already in Madagascar off the southeast coast of Africa, so filling in the geographical gap would be a natural progression. Again, connecting more countries together could lead to greater inclusion of trade and economic development in a region, if not a continent—new communication and trade networks through aviation.

Greater Availability of Networks: Impacts

As mentioned earlier, alternative sources of energy and new methods of propulsion (solar, electric, ionization, etc.) in the air transport industry will reduce costs and prices and make passenger transport by air more affordable over the next couple of decades and beyond. They will also increase the number of service offerings available. These factors will enable more people around the world to start visiting each other. The more people that go out and visit others, the more return visits will take place.

More connectedness through improved networks is also empowering the millennial generation to travel and connect more than ever before. According to the International Monetary Fund, the current millennials tend to work more for themselves than for an employer. This trend towards increasingly working as independent contractors is expected to continue into the foreseeable future.[23] This kind of work, with the help of the widespread availability of network technology, can be done remotely, from just about anywhere. This, coupled with their desire to see the world and meet everyone, means that the millennials and their children will be the "frequent flyers" of tomorrow, but in a different sense than those of today. (See Chapter 5, *Demographic Changes and Trends*, for more discussion on the characteristics and impact of the millennial generation).

The proliferation of networks has also opened up access to education to the whole world. Large numbers of foreign students are now entering the education systems of other countries. Universities promote their programs abroad in the hope that they will attract foreign students. The main reason for this is financial because foreign students regularly pay two, three, or even four times the tuition that local students contribute. As this trend continues into the future, it could have a direct impact on the type and quality of education being offered as educational institutions customize their curricula to meet the needs of the higher-paying foreign students.

Using Canada as an example, there has been steady growth in the number of international students going to Canada to study. As an example, the University of Toronto enrolled 17,452 foreign students in 2017, making up 20% of its student body compared with only 10% in 2007[24]. If the trend continues, by 2040, that institution will have more foreign students than Canadian resident students, making it truly an international university. In line with this trend, there has been a similar increase in the number of foreign professors in Canadian universities and colleges. Naturally, as these foreign students and faculty members interact with each other and with the locals, both academically and socially, they become the seeds for expanded international networks. It is believed that this example is representative of what is going on with international students and faculty around the world. Clearly, the opening up of communication channels in international education has created a breeding ground for global networking on an international scale. (See Chapter 5, *Demographic Changes and Trends*, for more discussion on the characteristics and impact of foreign students).

In the air navigation world, greater access to networks will see a major growth in the number of flights, with airlines exchanging not only passengers, but also their aircraft and crew. There will probably be fewer employees because aircraft will communicate with each other through satellites. The likely scenario will be larger airplanes with smaller crews on board. Safety will be handled in-flight, with less staff needed as automation will take the lead role in all aspects of the flight.

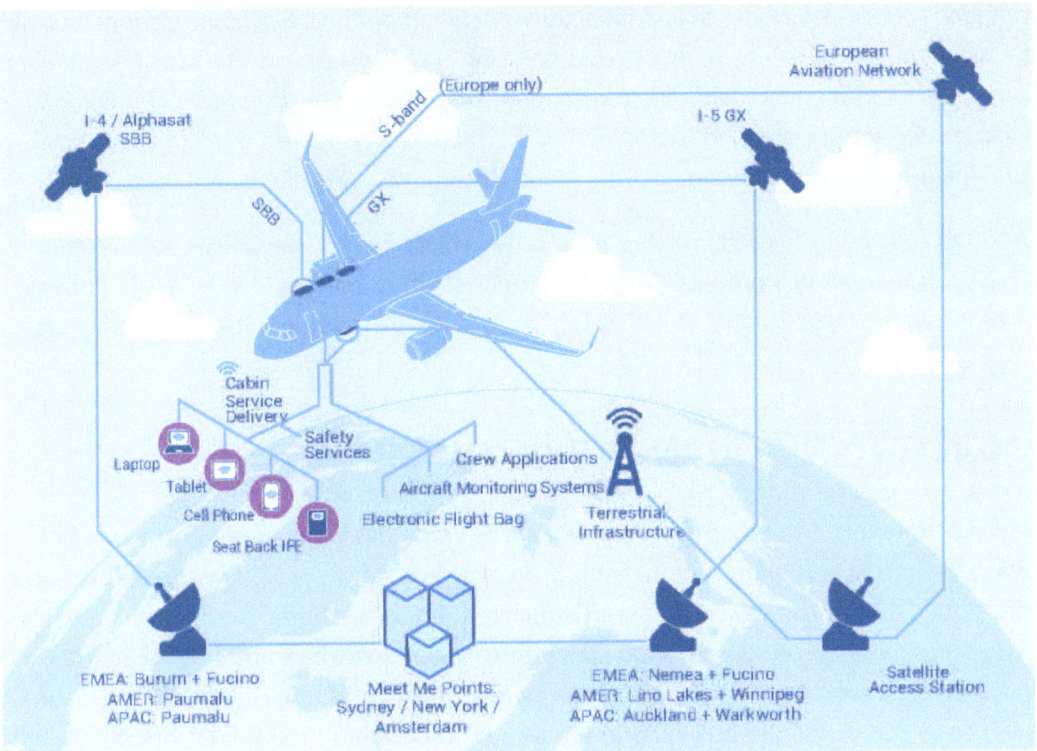

Figure 7-4   The aviation connectivity revolution (adapted from inmarsat.com).

Airports, too, are being impacted by their users who have increased network access. Many of them are already seeing a reduction in the amount of space used by airport tenants to provide various services because passengers have greater access to services and products through online networks. For example, with many passengers doing pre-flight check-in online, there is less need for check-in counters in the terminal building. Soon, baggage will be checked at remote locations and will not require as many baggage drop-off counters. Security checks will also become transparent or invisible because passengers and baggage will be checked as they move through the airport, without having to stop at any control points. Duty-free shopping will be done online through the airport Website or the airlines. Purchases will be delivered either at destination or at home. Boarding will no longer require another stop and another identification stage because passengers moving through the airport and the boarding area will be identified through facial recognition and other biometric validations. All these contact points will be connected to all participants involved in the entire trip, from origin to destination. As travelers arrive at their destination, they will be given the baggage carousel number on their mobile phones, and a map of the airport will appear showing them where to go for luggage pickup and where to find local transportation options. Eventually, airports might become merely transfer points between ground transportation and aircraft, with few if any true contact points with the passenger. (See Chapter 6, *Innovative Technological Change*, for a more detailed discussion of the technology that enables these new ways to track and process travelers as they move through the pre-flight process).

Another innovation directly related to improved network connectivity could be that by 2030, passengers will probably be paying online with a bitcoin type of cyber currency. Airlines already use Special Drawing Rights (SDRs)[25] to calculate the price of tickets.

QUALITY AND QUANTITY OF INFORMATION

In its 2018 report, *Country Readiness for Future Production*, the World Economic Forum warned that, "... growing nationalism, protectionism, and parochialism, coupled with developed countries seeking to reindustrialize or upgrade their manufacturing sectors, raises questions around reshoring. Therefore, the Fourth Industrial Revolution could potentially coincide with a slowdown or even reversal of international collaboration. It also says that it has the potential to lead to unprecedented gains in productivity, efficiency, and quality."[26]

To reap the full benefits of this "Fourth Industrial Revolution"[27], which is a technological revolution, we will need to find ways to harness and leverage the massive amounts of information becoming more and more available in ways that are understandable and can be trusted. We will also need to make sure that we do not lose control of the information that inundates us every day. The faster the information comes to us, the faster we tend to react and respond, thus leading to possible over-reactions and incorrect perceptions. Already, the speed of distribution of messages is so rapid that it often leads to the distribution of "fake news", which then gets redistributed without validation so rapidly that people actually believe the false news.

Companies and organizations now make more rapid-fire decisions with what seems like more and better information. However, that information may in reality be incorrect or misleading because it has not been validated. Somehow, managers will need to develop their own filters to be able to discern what information is right and what is wrong in order to separate the meaningful from the irrelevant, the appropriate from the extreme. This will apply to aviation managers as much as those in any other field. In fact, it may be more critical for aviation managers due to the ongoing concerns about the safety and security of passengers as they transit from ground transportation to the aircraft and back again.

The importance of using search results that are verified and cross-checked cannot be over-stressed.

In the article, *"How to Validate Results from a Google Web Search"*, author Harold Davis offers the following advice:

"When you validate research results from a Google Web search, your goal is to determine the credibility of the information you've discovered. Evaluating the credibility of a Web page, like any complex skill, is part art and part science. The most important thing you can do when assessing credibility of information is to start with a skeptical frame of mind."[28]

The challenge for all managers in the future will be how to most effectively assess the credibility of information coming to them when such information has been networked through multiple stakeholders and sometimes prepared uniquely for their own use. Canton refers to "crowdsourcing" to describe the fact that information is already connected to everything and everyone. Using multiple networks and making them all available instantly goes even beyond the "Internet of Things" of the 2010s.

As mentioned earlier in the *Access to Information* section of this chapter, information overload is a massive challenge faced by managers in all fields, including aviation. In recent years, it has gone beyond managers' ability to cope. Trying to sort through massive mountains of data on a daily basis, trying to separate fact from fiction, real news from fake news, has become impossible for anyone. Fortuitously for everyone faced with this problem, we have now entered the age of artificial intelligence (AI). Something that AI is very good at doing is sifting through complex volumes of information and breaking it down to provide clarity that will assist managers in their decision-making process. In the aviation industry, AI will be very useful in providing solutions to complex tasks such as air traffic control, aircraft maintenance and checks, and systems and runway inspections that are much better than human-generated solutions. These are still the early days of AI, so this area of technology is expected to continue improving on an ongoing basis well into the future. (See Chapter 6, *Innovative Technological Change*, for a detailed discussion of AI).

Global Connectedness and Personal Information

Safeguards will be required as the Web moves from passive to very active and gets to know each one of us individually. Yes, the Web is learning about each of us individually. Each interaction we have online is recorded and stored for future reference by whichever Web services we are dealing with. Controlling completely how much information is collected about one online will be very difficult, if not impossible. In a sense, it will increasingly become a "cost of doing business" online.

Concerns have arisen about the quality of information that comes with increased network connectedness. A case in point is a phenomenon known as "medical tourism". For various reasons, many people are choosing these days to go abroad for specialized medical treatment and/or surgery. For example, in 2017, some 63,000 Canadians traveled to countries like India, Romania, or the USA, among others, to receive medical treatments.[29] In such cases, an interesting challenge is how to validate the information found online that triggers such travel. In other words, when people travel around the world for treatment, how can they confirm the quality of the surgeon, the quality of the medication, and the level of health standards of the hospital? Beyond this medical tourism example, these same types of questions essentially apply to the provision of any product or service for which the information is found through online networks. How can one trust that a product or service that "appears" to be excellent in another country will in fact deliver on its promise? In the future, it is quite possible that some sort of international ISO type of validator will be created to assess and regulate the publicity claims made by all providers around the globe.

As touched on earlier, the degree of global connectedness through increased connectivity will give lead to the formation of new communities where members will share their experiences, perceptions, and values with other members. The members of these communities will rely on each other to validate their selections and decisions and to confirm (or not) the accuracy of information shared through their network. Similarly to how people trust their families and friends to recommend products, services, or suppliers, the communities of tomorrow will become the reference point for their members. Such networks already exist, but it is expected that many more will be created as the degree of worldwide network connectedness increases.

In the field of aviation, the parsing and validation of the huge amount of information that will be available by 2030 will surely be critical for aviation decision-makers. The new era of flight will be affected in more ways than are anticipated today.

Figure 7-5   Information overload is real (telegraph.co.uk).

The unprecedented amount of information available about the entire world through the Internet these days has become a game-changer for tourism. Through information distribution via the Internet, the world has in a few short years become a much smaller place. Tomorrow's tourists will want to travel to and discover many new destinations on their own; they will visit new resorts more often. The wide diversity of travel information now posted and readily available online has led to new "experiential travel trends". These are expected to become the norm in the not-so-distant future. For example, these types of specialized travel experiences include such excursions as food tours to France, cooking classes in Italy, flower observations in Ecuador, fishing on the Amazon, and many more. In 2017, historical and heritage tours had grown by 125% over the previous year. Similar growth occurred with various specialty tours, including sunset cruises, private day trips, snorkeling, kayaking, and canoeing, sailing trips, catamaran trips, food tours, cooking classes, and museum tickets and passes.

With access to information leveling the playing field for everyone connected online, a fast-growing trend in recent years has been the "skip-the-line" ticket. With all the information they need empowering them, people are no longer ready to wait in line like sheep; they want to live it now, without waiting. If many people no longer want to wait for an attraction and are ready to pay to move ahead of the line, what will happen to the price of regular tickets? This skip-the-line phenomenon could have the effect of pushing ticket costs upwards, thus reducing the overall demand for those types of specialized tours. Soon, augmented reality will be standard on these types of tours. As Elon Musk once said, "The only possible path is the merger of machines and men".

As discussed earlier, the ongoing development of the Internet and related technologies has significantly increased the ability of humans to communicate and will continue to do so. It will also increase the business and operational potential of passenger airlines globally. As airline operators build reliability into advanced IT systems, they will be able to start considering the possibility of creating subsidiaries around the world—not just franchises, but true subsidiaries. Whether the result is a subsidiary or a franchise operation, the aircraft operator will have greater access to information on its operations instantly and will quickly understand the impact of distant situations on the overall network. As this situation evolves, regulations will be changed to allow international ownership of airlines and facilitate the use of foreign air crew to travel around the world. Air industry decision-makers will have to adapt and modify their criteria of profitability. Bottom-line financial results will not always be the only important factor. Broader issues like environmental protection, people care, and local community contributions might also become important factors because they will all directly impact the viability of the global air transport system.

In summary, an increasing quantity and quality of information is empowering the air transport industry and is allowing the industry to become a driver of the development of communities around the world. In turn, these communities will also support the ongoing development of the air transport system. More information will lead to more transparency, which may lead to better information.

Personal Data in Exchange for Personalized Services

These days, people appear to be more willing to give up their personal information through online channels in order to get something in return instantly. The typical online shopper does not like to delay gratification and wants his/her product or service to be delivered as soon as possible. It is becoming ever more common for people to pay for products and services over the phone, with fingerprint or facial recognition as confirmation. The more people use these new technologies, the more they seem to trust them. This seems to be the case with most innovations. The "curve of acceptance" is more or less pronounced, but it is always going upward over time.

As already mentioned, advanced technology, coupled with the vast amounts of personal data collected through online interactions, enables the customization of services down to the level of the individual person. This is true up and down the spectrum as automation allows the flexibility to group market segments and to cater to the specific needs of each market. Automated distribution of products and services, as pioneered by Amazon.com, might someday be the example for the air transport industry, at least insofar as the number of human interventions needed to provide a product or service will be reduced to a minimum. Using automated distribution technology, the speed of delivery will be increased, costs will be reduced, and the possibility of offering/shipping diverse portfolios of products will be increased exponentially. Although it started exclusively with books, Amazon now offers a wide range of products, from clothing, to groceries, to motorcycle helmets, to garburators, among millions of other items. Amazon Web Services is now the biggest supplier of online cloud services as well. Amazon's cargo airline, Amazon Air, has a fleet of almost 40 large jets that it uses to deliver customers purchases, and it is building a huge cargo facility.[30]

Large amounts of voluntarily supplied personal information allow suppliers to provide highly customized personalized services. For example, in Dubai, when passengers travel First Class, they are picked up at home by a chauffeur-driven luxury car. Upon arrival, they are taken directly from the plane to access a personal control room where their paperwork will be expedited, so as not to delay them. This paperwork can even be done while in flight. On arrival, the passenger only needs to prove that he/she is the actual person identified in the documents. This is similar to the Nexus pass in Canada for expedited pre-cleared immigration, or APEC in Asia, or Privium in the Netherlands. Soon travelers will be able to just walk through checkpoints, and the validation process will be done via face recognition and other such biometric identification technology. There is even talk of implanting electronic chips in people's bodies (i.e., wrist or shoulder) in order to facilitate their travel even more.

Ubiquitous network connectivity means that personal handwritten signatures will no longer be required when one makes a payment by credit card. Today, in some countries, when a customer uses their PIN with their credit card, no signature is required, although in many countries, the PIN is still not recognized as valid, and one must sign the slip. It's only a matter of time before no signature will be required anywhere. New technologies and opportunities do not mean that businesses automatically change their processes accordingly and that the regulator will recognize them instantly. There is always a phased waiting period before these new technologies are accepted everywhere, but they are invariably accepted everywhere eventually.

Sometimes, different parts of the same organization can complicate things and make the adoption of a new technology difficult. For example, a credit card company may say that signatures are no longer required when using a PIN as identification. However, a hotel clerk at a major hotel insists that their finance department needs the PIN plus a signature to validate the transaction. The hotel's finance department, on the other hand, would like to eliminate the need for a signature, but the hotel's bank insists that the PIN is not yet recognized by the Central Bank. The Central Bank has not changed its regulations because the law of the country still does not recognize electronic validation as an acceptable means. This lack of connectivity between the different layers of the same community can be an impediment to progress.

The same situation certainly exists in the air transport industry, where so many things related to information requirements still need to be changed. For example: Why do travelers still need to be informed of the legal conditions of travel when very few ever read them, nor have they ever worried about what those conditions are all about? Beyond aviation, how many people have ever read the detailed "terms of service" statements that are presented before signing up for an online service or downloading and installing a program on their computer or an app on their smartphone? Regulators will have to find new ways of protecting users than expecting them to read and understand long and complex documents.

Information and Aviation Regulation

With the ability to monitor everything through technology, it is technically possible that aviation industry regulators could install Internet of Things (IoT) chips to monitor such situations as safety infractions, near-occurrences, and regulatory transgressions and then automatically take action. Some car insurers use this approach to assess the risk of drivers. By monitoring how a car is used, the insurer will include fast accelerations after a stop, quick stops, and so on in risk assessment, and the premiums will reflect that. Certain parameters have been inserted into a tracking device, and extremes are immediately reported to the insurer and premiums adjusted accordingly. Of course, this system also works in favor of the insured if their driving is within the set parameters; the premium would then be lowered.

With respect to worldwide civil aviation, it will be interesting to see how this enhanced information collection and monitoring ability via increased connectedness will be used by civil aviation authorities. For example, the International Civil Aviation Organization (ICAO), the UN agency responsible for international air transport, develops and adopts Standards and Recommended Practices (SARPs) with which Member States promise to comply. Through their membership in ICAO, the 192 Member States promise to comply with the standards adopted by the organization. They also promise to notify the organization in case they choose not to comply or cannot comply with one or more of these standards.

To do so, States need to monitor the status of the operators within their territory. For example, a State has to ensure that all airlines comply with applicable regulations, which are, for the most part, modeled on ICAO's SARPs. The same applies with airports and air navigation service providers (ANSPs). This monitoring is basically done by conducting audits and inspections of various players and/or parts of their operations. Because this monitoring requires a lot of resources, ICAO has moved to a more risk-based approach whereby States that generally comply are trusted a bit more than others. ICAO's Continuous Monitoring Approach (CMA) is an extension of the previous Universal Safety Oversight Audits that previously took place approximately every two years.

Aircraft maintenance has evolved rapidly now that engines are monitored while the aircraft is in flight. By sending a "ping" on a regular basis, the engine allows the maintenance department of the airline to assess its performance and to plan corrective actions or adjustments upon the next landing. What used to be fixed periodic reviews and examinations is now a continuous process, thus reducing greatly the interruption required for specific mandatory inspections of critical components on the aircraft. Not only does this reduce overall maintenance costs, but it also enhances safety when problems are detected and rectified right away before they become more serious. (See Chapter 6, *Innovative Technological Change*, for a more detailed explanation of this technology).

A similar process now applies to airports and ANSPs. Operators must implement a Safety Management System (SMS). This SMS will lead to the certification of the operator by the State, in line with ICAO SARPs. The SMS is intended to create a "safety culture" within which everyone in the organization, and also its stakeholders, views safety as a means of ensuring continuity and reducing the potential for accidents. In order to benefit from such a system and enhance monitoring for safety reasons, regulators will need to identify Key Performance Indicators (KPIs) that will indicate the safety fitness of the operator in a truly globally connected environment. States will monitor operators on a continuous basis, just as airlines monitor their aircraft.

Figure 7-6   Information and aviation regulation (beaconiamps.com).

Being able to follow 10 to 100 times more equipment with less manpower through enhanced connectivity should lead to automated auditing and inspecting of aircraft, airports, and ANSPs. Given that information about equipment, people, and processes will be instantly available, this might jeopardize personal privacy somewhat since complete privacy will no longer be possible. At the same time, for the same reason, because everything will be more transparent, this might lead to greater trust and more ethical business practices.

Regulators in the various Member States need to join forces by standardizing and harmonizing their regulations as issued by ICAO. The aviation industry as a whole must regulate the areas that will have the greatest impact on the mission of the industry, in such a way that this becomes more important than financial profit. Environmental concerns must become a major aspect of regulations, almost before safety, if the aviation industry wants to sustain the development of air transport for the benefit of the people of the world.

In the age of global connectedness, how will regulators continue to regulate truly international assets like aircraft that are owned by international consortia? Obviously, the current model will need to change. Maybe the role of the ICAO will change. Maybe its Member States will agree to have ICAO actually manage and deliver services instead of just issuing standards. Imagine an ICAO that would actually become a true regulator. The question will soon become: how to regulate flights that go from New York to Sydney operated by a remote pilot based in Mumbai with an aircraft from China? Today, the status of the aircraft is the responsibility of the State of registration, operations are pretty much the responsibility of the State of occurrence, and so on. No entity is really responsible for everything.

The idea of ICAO having an expanded role makes some sense. ICAO already gets involved in "managing" a process rather than just expressing ideas submitted and sometimes supported by States. In the case of the Private Key Directory[31] that supports the exchange of information pertaining to the validity of passports presented at border control, ICAO actually manages the process and is the middle point of information exchange between the States. ICAO is currently paid a small amount for its role. This first instance where ICAO actually "manages" could easily be expanded into other areas. For example, ICAO could become THE global authority in terms of air navigation services and function as a "contractor" responsible for providing all navigation services on behalf of States. This would make it much easier to truly harmonize all rules and procedures worldwide. Such an approach would offer numerous benefits, including that States would still receive overflight revenues within their airspace, employees would be better coordinated, and operators would save time and gain efficiency, just to name a few. In a truly globally connected world, aviation regulations need to reflect all this.

ICAO could start operating the entire global airspace on behalf of its member States (for a fee of course), which would allow much more efficient use of airspace than occurs today. This would greatly improve connectivity and connectedness on a global level. Airlines could operate truly globally in the future, like trucking in North America or Europe, where one truck delivers for one company and picks up for another client. Perhaps commercial aircraft do not always need to go back to their home base. Sea containers keep traveling around the world and seldom return home. However, the aviation case is more complex because people do need to return home, although equipment does not.

Programs like ICAO's Universal Safety Oversight Audit Programme (USOAP-CMA)[32] could be franchised. After all, if IATA was able to franchise its Operational Safety Audit program (IOSA) to private companies, why couldn't ICAO do it on behalf of its Member States? Most States already contract out many of their operations (airports, air navigation services, and others) to private organizations like ASECNA in Africa and NATS in the UK. Contracting out additional aviation support services to ICAO would seem to be a logical extension of this.

In summary, the future will not happen without States around the world taking a more united, global connectedness approach to their aviation operations. ICAO is the logical choice to lead the way in this effort.

CONNECTEDNESS TECHNOLOGY – IMPACTS ON AVIATION

From its very beginning, aviation passenger travel has been a "connector" of people and places, at first locally, and later around the entire world. Nevertheless, in spite of its role as a unifying and connecting force, aviation has also enabled the spread of diseases. In previous centuries, if people didn't die on board their ship while traveling across an ocean for weeks, they would often carry diseases to their destination port. Today, aviation can transport diseased individuals overnight to have them end up infecting an entire continent. In recent years, this was the case with such outbreaks as the Asian flu, Mad Cow disease, Ebola, and others.

New Connectivity Technology

As the quarter-century mark in the 21st Century approaches, new aviation-related equipment has come to the fore, both to help us and haunt us. This is particularly the case with unmanned aerial vehicles (UAVs), commonly known as "drones" (see Figure 7-7). These vehicles have been around for a while, but have grown in popularity as they have become accessible to everyone. Of different shapes and sizes, they are widely available for purchase at relatively low price points. At first regarded as largely a backyard recreational item, they have since become important military and business tools, with new practical applications being announced on a regular basis. They are now in wide use as military equipment, both for reconnaissance and weaponry. Practical applications to date include package delivery, surveying, crop dusting, business/home security, construction supervision, law enforcement, and safety inspections, just to name a few. By mid-2018, the FAA in the US had issued some 73,000 Remote Pilot Certifications.[33] This shows how attractive and somewhat useful this new type of vehicle is and why it is already widely used and popular. It is already a $6 billion business and is expected to grow to $22 billion by 2020.[34]

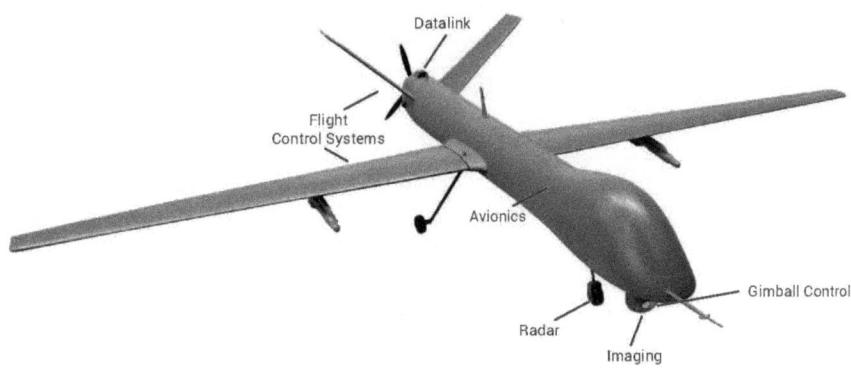

Datalink

Flight
Control Systems

Avionics

Gimball Control

Radar

Imaging

Figure 7-7   Unmanned aerial vehicle (drone) (ASI Institute).

There is no doubt that drone technology will be developed specifically for applications directly related to civil aviation. For example, drone shuttle taxis have already been proposed in Dubai. In the foreseeable future, small remotely piloted aircraft may be flying domestically, with remotely-piloted short international flights not far behind. (See Chapter 6, *Innovative Technological Change*, for more information on drone technology).

As the extent of global connectedness increases and more and more systems connect to each other, we can anticipate the day when a passenger makes a reservation with an airline and their degree of assessed security risk may affect the price of the ticket. It is certainly possible that before the passenger arrives at the destination, the ground services and concessionaires at the airport might already know such things about the incoming passenger as passenger name, baggage that he/she is carrying, and ground transportation preferences.

Connectivity through Space

As more and better information becomes available in the global airline industry and all the stakeholders start truly complementing one another, the rewards will be lower prices, higher frequency, and better profitability. As traditional airspace becomes more congested, airlines will be looking to near space as an option. The graph shown in Figure 7-8 was published by the FAA in 2017; it gives the forecast for commercial space flights in current years until 2020. One can easily see the significant increase over a few years. Projected out to 2045, the numbers could easily increase by a multiple of 10 and include commercial air transport with passengers, thus making Planet Earth truly accessible to almost everyone.

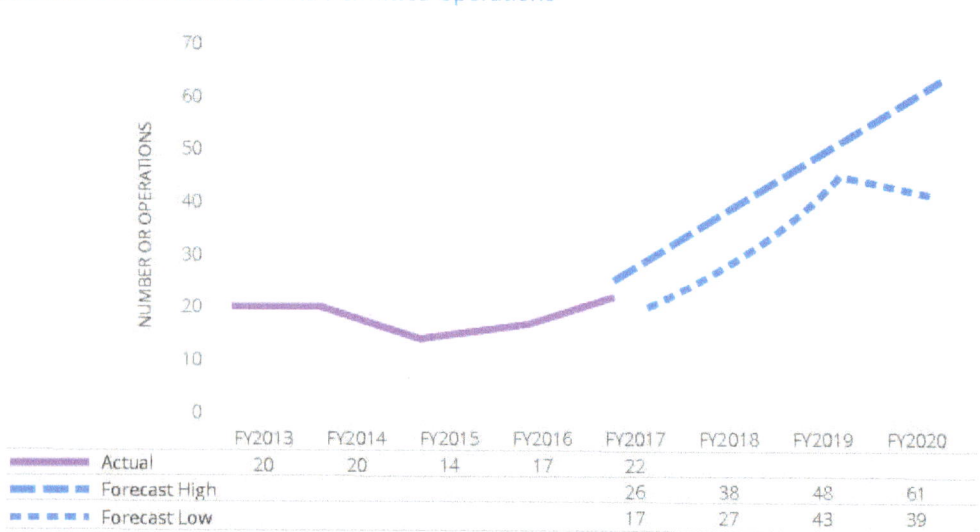

Note: FY2017 forecast finalized secon quarter FY2017. FY2018-20 forecast finalized second quarter FY2018.

Figure 7-8   Commercial space flights, actual and forecast, 2013–2020 (FAA).

In late 2018, the company SpaceX announced that it plans to take civilian passengers around the moon and back in 2023. Once that happens, it won't be long before such flights become a common occurrence.[35] However, given the reduction in operating costs of such operations with reusable rockets, as demonstrated by SpaceX and Blue Origin[36], it is possible that even the most optimistic forecast might be lower than what reality will bring.

Since the signing of the Convention on International Civil Aviation, aviation activity forecasts have almost always been surpassed by actual levels, to the point where today almost all airports have a shortage of capacity to handle demand, particularly in terminal buildings. Aviation activity levels are currently forecast to more than double by 2030. Aviation managers and planners are going to be seriously challenged over the next couple of decades to provide facilities and services to meet these forecasts. Imagine now if visionary business leaders, inventors, and disruptors like Jeff Bezos, founder of Amazon and Blue Origin, and Elon Musk, founder of Tesla and SpaceX, were to start working together to find solutions for the aviation passenger model? And what if Richard Branson of Virgin Airlines and Virgin Group and Tony Fernandes of AirAsia and the Tune Group joined them? Surely, commercial passenger flights would surpass anything ever known before in air transportation development, just as the Chicago Convention intended.

The Connected Traveler

Increasing global connectedness will make travel in the future a very different experience from what it has been until now. Dubai will probably launch the first drone airport-city taxis, good for two passengers and baggage. Many will find it fantastic that they can call for a taxi to the airport and not worry about traffic! Airports will need fewer parking lots, and access roads might become a thing of the past as this business grows. By 2045, drones might become the main mode of transportation to and from airports, and possibly for intercity transport as well.

It is expected that before 2050, major cities will have fewer personal cars. Rather, residents will use community car-share vehicles that they can call for when needed. These cars will be autonomous, drive on their own, and be used as public transport. Aviation isn't likely to be far behind this concept. Perhaps drones, or some combination of trains and drones, will replace intercity flights in the future. It is expected that drone routes will be regulated as highways are; drones will not exceed the speed limit since they will simply embark on the route assigned, and follow traffic. When they arrive at destination, they will just pull out to the parking area and then move on to their waiting station for the next call. Passengers of drones will not be concerned with going faster because their productivity will continue during the transport. They will be connected via network technology and the Internet from the start to the end of their brief trip. At all times throughout their trip, they will be connected to family, work colleagues, friends, and services at their destination.

For the connected traveler, there will be no more hassles of vehicle ownership, insurance, maintenance, licensing, and so on. Transport will become a commodity like electricity and other public services. At some point in the future, almost everyone will have access to personal connected transport.

In aviation, in addition to drones, with the application of Internet of things (IoT) technology, numerous ancillary services will emerge that will simplify the monitoring of activities and allow for greater access to air transport and a greater degree of connectedness. Examples of such services already mentioned in this chapter include home/hotel baggage pick-up and delivery, duty-free purchases from home and delivered to home, passenger and baggage check-in from home, and access to destination services while in transit. A similar array of services will also be available for air cargo shipments.

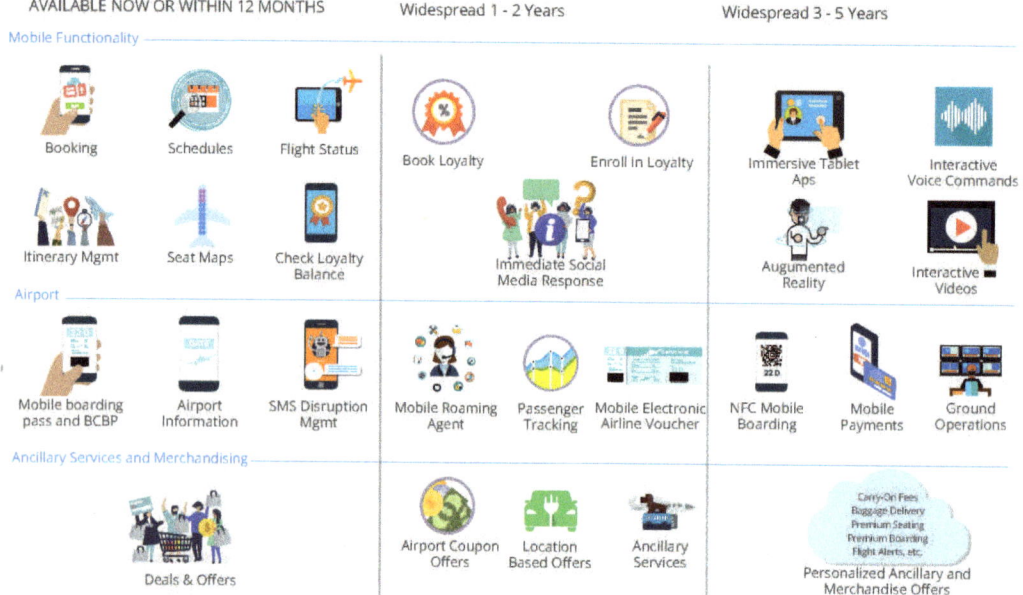

Figure 7-9 The connected air traveler (ASI).

In 2017, SITA (Société internationale de télécommunications aéronautiques) reported that, "...80% of airports will be investing in IoT initiatives that smooth the passenger journey through the airport by beacons and sensors powering wayfinding solutions, using passenger location to advise time and route to the gate, and tailor messages about airport facilities or offers."[37]

The Hospitality Industry Model

This kind of thinking is prevalent throughout all sectors of the hospitality industry. Hilton Hotels is using IoT to introduce the "connected room", in which everything requiring control will be available through an app installed on the customer's smartphone. IoT technology is also very useful for controlling operating costs at hotels and resorts, controlling such things as water usage to match the demand, electricity, heating and cooling, kitchens, laundry, and much more. Both Hilton and Marriott are considering smart rooms as people bring more technology into their smart homes. It is only normal that consumers will start to expect the same capabilities at destination as they have at home.

Starwood Hotels and Resorts already use a technique called "daylight harvesting" to control the LED lights depending on the amount of natural light coming into the room[38].

This is just one more example of savings that are now possible because of IoT technology. Other areas of service improvement and/or cost reduction are: predictive maintenance, mobile engagement, hyper-personalization, and location-based interactions. These are just a few of the applications that the hospitality industry is investing in.

Hospitality Technology magazine was already reporting in 2016 that 54% of hotels were spending more on technology to meet escalating guest expectations: payment security, guest room technology, bandwidth, and mobile engagement.[39] With the advantages brought by these new technologies, a small resort can now cater to a refined clientele originating from anywhere in the world. It is now possible to provide unique high-end services at a fraction of the cost of yesterday. For example, in December 2017, Tata Communications of India and Ooredoo, Maldives joined forces to bring IoT to the Maldives[40] thus enabling operators of hundreds of resorts to benefit from all that technology had to offer. It is now possible to be staying on an island in the middle of the ocean, sitting by one's own private pool, working on a contract for one's employer via the Internet cloud, while also communicating by Facetime or Skype with one's loved ones at the other end of the world.

There is no reason why many of the solutions and innovations already adopted by the hospitality industry cannot also be adapted by the various players in the aviation industry, particularly airlines and airports.

The Connected Air Travel Experience

The evolution of electronic data has already had a great impact on the flow of goods, allowing for immediate release once at destination. The regulated agent concept, defined in the ICAO Security Manual as, "*... an agent, freight forwarder, or any other entity who conducts business with an operator and provides security controls that are accepted or required by the appropriate authority in respect of cargo or mail,...*", is one example of processes that are now possible, given that these agents have access to security equipment commensurate with the volumes they handle. The natural expansion of those services might possibly apply as well to moving people.

Airports will have to adapt to such new processes, which will also mean a review of the design and construction of terminal buildings. Figure 7-10 presents a sample timeline of what a typical connected business trip might look like for someone named "Pat" in 2035.

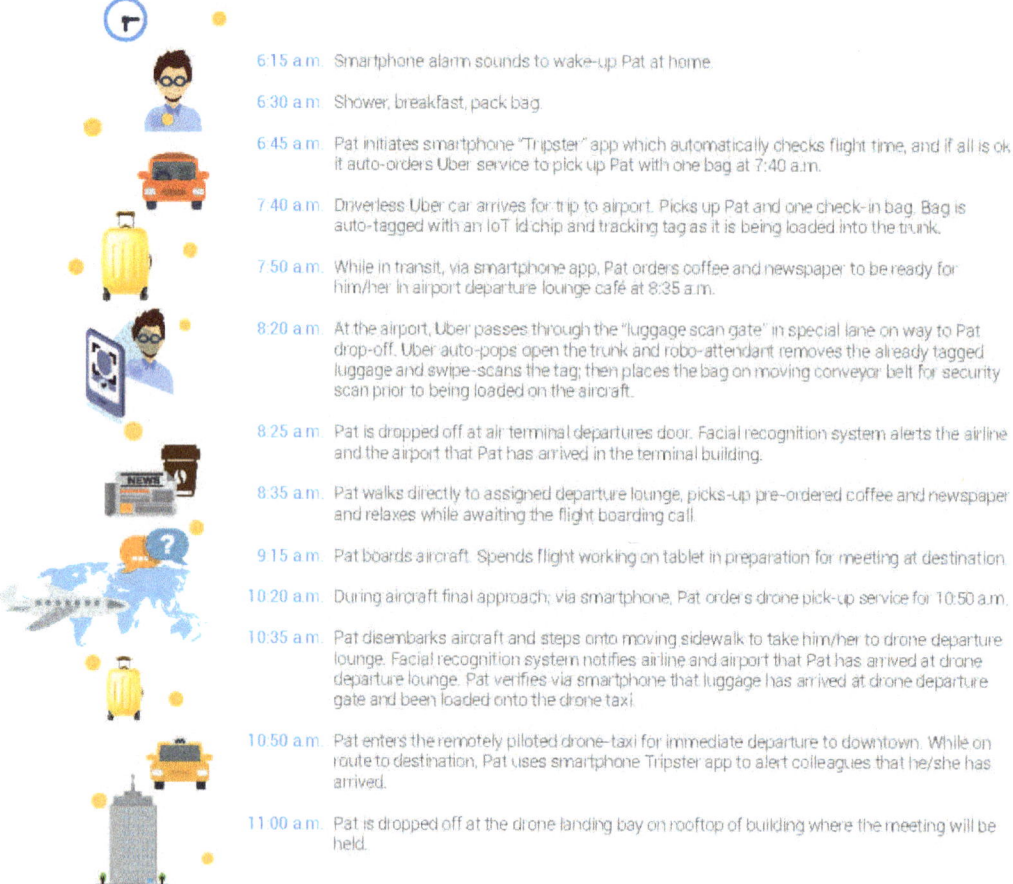

6:15 a.m.　Smartphone alarm sounds to wake-up Pat at home.

6:30 a.m.　Shower, breakfast, pack bag.

6:45 a.m.　Pat initiates smartphone "Tripster" app which automatically checks flight time, and if all is ok it auto-orders Uber service to pick up Pat with one bag at 7:40 a.m.

7:40 a.m.　Driverless Uber car arrives for trip to airport. Picks up Pat and one check-in bag. Bag is auto-tagged with an IoT id chip and tracking tag as it is being loaded into the trunk.

7:50 a.m.　While in transit, via smartphone app, Pat orders coffee and newspaper to be ready for him/her in airport departure lounge café at 8:35 a.m.

8:20 a.m.　At the airport, Uber passes through the "luggage scan gate" in special lane on way to Pat drop-off. Uber auto-pops open the trunk and robo-attendant removes the already tagged luggage and swipe-scans the tag; then places the bag on moving conveyor belt for security scan prior to being loaded on the aircraft.

8:25 a.m.　Pat is dropped off at air terminal departures door. Facial recognition system alerts the airline and the airport that Pat has arrived in the terminal building.

8:35 a.m.　Pat walks directly to assigned departure lounge, picks-up pre-ordered coffee and newspaper and relaxes while awaiting the flight boarding call.

9:15 a.m.　Pat boards aircraft. Spends flight working on tablet in preparation for meeting at destination.

10:20 a.m.　During aircraft final approach; via smartphone, Pat orders drone pick-up service for 10:50 a.m.

10:35 a.m.　Pat disembarks aircraft and steps onto moving sidewalk to take him/her to drone departure lounge. Facial recognition system notifies airline and airport that Pat has arrived at drone departure lounge. Pat verifies via smartphone that luggage has arrived at drone departure gate and been loaded onto the drone taxi.

10:50 a.m.　Pat enters the remotely piloted drone-taxi for immediate departure to downtown. While on route to destination, Pat uses smartphone Tripster app to alert colleagues that he/she has arrived.

11:00 a.m.　Pat is dropped off at the drone landing bay on rooftop of building where the meeting will be held.

Figure 7-10　Sample business trip timeline for the connected air traveler circa 2035 (ASI Institute).

Of course, Figure 7-10 is just an example of what such a trip might look like 15 to 20 years in the future. Nevertheless, when conceived, the example was based on existing technology, or technology known to be under development at the time, so it is probably not far off the mark. The important point to note about this example is that it is entirely enabled by a high level of device connectedness. Without full network and device connectivity, it would not work.

Another example of expedited processing through IoT technology could be with airline and airport supplies used for the flight itself or for airport operations. The current "regulated supplier" concept will grow to include most suppliers to the aviation industry. As trust grows, facilitation will also improve, and regulations will have to adapt.

As already mentioned, drone taxis could become the norm at large airports sometime in the next decade or two. Under this scenario, it will be interesting to see what will happen to individual transport near short-haul destinations. Today, one-hour flights have become almost impossible in that timeframe because security controls take too long. The way things are currently going in this area, by 2045–2050, one-hour travel time for short commercial flights could possibly become two to three hours given the time that will be spent in controls, waiting in line, and moving on the ground (to-from gate to runway), etc. For example, on a recent 11-hour flight from Frankfurt to Singapore experienced by this author, one hour and 20 minutes was spent on board the aircraft, moving to and from the runway and the gate, at both airports. It seems that the bigger and busier the airport, the longer the transition. Munich Airport in Germany has found creative ways of making these processes more efficient and is now the airport with the shortest average connection time in Europe, at less than 50 minutes. The secret? Good planning, appropriate equipment, qualified staff, detailed procedures, and good governance. This is how Munich has become the best in class and a benchmark for many of its competitors.

As the international aviation industry moves towards total connectedness on a global basis, there will be good reasons for all major airports (and smaller ones as well) to harness IoT and related technologies to significantly streamline all aspects of the air passenger journey from arrival on the airport property to on board the departing aircraft.

CONCLUSION AND SUMMARY

The first part of this closing section is a brief Conclusion containing some overall general remarks that summarize the essence of the foregoing discussion of the *Global Connectedness* megatrend and offer some general advice to managers about how best to cope with it. The second part of this section is a Management Summary that recaps in point form all the major subjects discussed earlier during the detailed analysis and discussion of the *Global Connectedness* megatrend. The points are presented with the perspective of aviation professionals and managers in mind. Essentially, each point in the Management Summary represents a key observation or conclusion that was made during the detailed analysis and discussion.

Conclusion

As discussed throughout this chapter, connectedness will largely influence the way we live and the way we travel in the future. The millennials of today and the millennials of tomorrow, the Gen Z group (those less than 30 years of age today), do not know the world without technology. They adopt new technology quite easily and expect service and product providers to connect with them using technology.

The number of connected devices has increased by 4,000% between 2003 and today. The new IPv6 Internet protocol allows for a massive number of connections that is believed to be sufficient for the foreseeable future (i.e., 340,282,366,920,938,463,463,374,607,431,768,211,456).[41] (See Chapter 6, *Innovative Technological Change*, for more on the IPv6 Internet protocol). It is becoming easier to use connected devices than it is to watch HD television. By 2045, there will be 20,000 times more digital information than there is today.[42] Aviation will be an important user of such digital information.

In light of such statistics, one could be worried about finding work. Obviously, machines are likely to take over certain jobs from people, with developments in artificial intelligence ultimately meaning that education could focus on those (few) areas of human thought and activity that machines are unable to deliver efficiently. This means that education will play an important role in enhancing people's ability to develop new ideas, to interact empathetically with other people, and to take responsibility—all things that it is difficult to envisage machines doing by 2045.[43]

Even more global than the millennials, the Generation Z teens will create a brand-new world because they already consider themselves citizens of the world more than of any local place. For the Gen Z'ers, the "Internet of Things" will become the "Internet of Everyone". The Internet will be seen as a way to communicate, to educate, to socialize, and to interact with everyone, independently of their actual physical location.

Since Gen Z'ers will be shaping the aviation industry of the future, there is no doubt that the industry will, in many ways, be significantly different than it is early in the 21st Century. This will apply both to the management and regulation of the global industry and the travel experience itself.

According to SITA[44] in its *2015 Airline IT Trends Survey*, 86% of airline companies believe that IoT will provide "clear benefits over the next three years."[45]

In 1980, airlines worried about the advent of new technology and its impact on the demand for business travel. That new technology was the fax machine. Airlines wondered why anyone would travel on business when one could fax a document and have it signed and returned the same day. After that, they worried about the emergence of teleconferencing replacing the business trip. In the 1990s, the same questions were asked about the new technology of the day, the Internet.

One could now ask the same questions with respect to the development of increased global connectedness to the point where everyone will be connected to everyone else, anywhere, 24/7.

It can now be said that the easier communications are, the more reasons there are to travel. In fact, it could be said that Communication with a capital "C" is at the heart of air transport. As has been said many times, air travel is about much more than buying an airline seat; it is more about helping people to go places to meet people. In other words, it's all about connecting people all over the world. Isn't this one of the key messages contained in the preamble of the Chicago Convention?

> "WHEREAS the future development of international civil aviation can greatly help **to create and preserve friendship and understanding among the nations and peoples of the world**, yet its abuse can become a threat to the general security; and

> WHEREAS it is desirable to avoid friction and to **promote that cooperation between nations and peoples upon which the peace of the world depends;**

THEREFORE, the undersigned governments having agreed on certain principles and arrangements in order that international civil aviation may be developed in a safe and orderly manner and that international air transport services may be **established on the basis of equality of opportunity and operated soundly and economically;"**

Many leaders in aviation have ignored this preamble as they were planning the development of their businesses while continually protecting, or trying to protect, their existing operations rather than improving the overall connectedness of the air transport system for the benefit of the peoples of the world. The Convention is all about "Connectedness", and the more the people involved in shaping the international industry, the better the world will be.

The world is definitely getting smaller as global communications become faster and cheaper and are always available. This of course is changing the way we see the world and the way people move around the world. As populations move, this is having an impact on the choice of destinations and the routes that airlines are considering as part of their network.

Management Summary

Based on the foregoing discussion, there is no doubt that the *Global Connectedness* megatrend will have major impacts on the international aviation industry over the next 15 to 20 years and beyond. In many ways, adapting to this megatrend and implementing mitigation measures will have considerable impact on the way in which airlines, airports, and air navigation services will develop and operate their businesses, particularly during the next decade, as they continue to adjust to this new reality. Numerous significant conclusions and observations have been made during the course of the detailed analysis contained earlier in this chapter. The following are the important information highlights that aviation managers at all levels will need to take into account when determining how best to deal with the *Global Connectedness* megatrend when preparing for the future.

Access to Information

- The amount of data available online these days is hard to even visualize. Experts estimate that the amount of data available online is at least 1,200 petabytes, which is the equivalent of 1.2 million terabytes (one terabyte is 1,000 gigabytes).

- It is estimated that there were eight billion connected devices in 2017. IBM has estimated that there will be 50 billion such devices by 2020.

- More than 75% of searches are conducted on Google, and it processes more than 40,000 searches EVERY second (3.5 billion searches per day)!

- The biggest problem about this massive creation and availability of data of course is information overload.

- Members of the younger generation are "connected" to the point where their ongoing interactions with other people are based primarily on system connectivity rather than on actual human relationships, and this trend will intensify in the future. The millennial generation is the first fully connected generation, and the generations that come after will only be exposed to a fully connected world.

- More air travel trips are sold directly through the Internet today than through traditional bricks-and-mortar travel agencies. Most trips these days are arranged without the client and the provider ever meeting in person.

- Forecast shorter travel times to reach destinations by air will allow airlines to increase the number of operations, thus giving travelers more choices.

- The largest accommodation company in the world, Airbnb, has zero accommodation assets, but offers more than 4.5 million spaces worldwide. It is a direct product of global connectivity capabilities. Without the access to information and degree of global connectedness that exists, it would not be able to operate.

Network Proliferation

- The number of Internet users globally went from 1.9 billion in 2009 to 3.4 billion in 2016, with access to over 1.8 billion Websites. By 2017, 70% of the world's youth, or 830 million individuals, were online.

- The Internet of Things (IoT) is already beginning to penetrate all segments of aviation. IoT-based technology is performing such tasks at airports as tracking ground equipment and reporting on status and location of moving vehicles. Airlines and maintenance companies are using it to monitor the performance of aircraft engines.

- It is estimated that by 2020 there will be 50 billion network-connected devices, which for a population of 8 billion, is quite significant.

- The growth and evolution of network technology has made it possible to automatically collect and share reams of information about aviation operations using communication modes such as: equipment-to-staff, staff-to-staff, equipment-to-equipment, equipment-to-maintenance, and equipment-to-regulator. With today's network technology, all these functions are now in constant contact and can quickly check on each other's status.

- Modern-day networks span multiple sovereign borders and are forcing into existence a new world order that benefits all members of the connected communities. There are thousands of online communities that connect millions of people based on common interests and beliefs (e.g., Facebook, Twitter, Pinterest, Instagram, and LinkedIn).

- Networking technology has already resulted in the creation of numerous online communities that deal with almost every aspect imaginable of aviation-related work as well as recreational interests and activities.

- The aviation activity itself facilitates and enhances the extent of connectedness among people and communities globally. As fuel costs decrease, making airplanes more fuel-efficient, air transport becomes increasingly accessible, allowing families and friends to reunite more often, even when living far apart.

- The benefits of better network technology in the aviation industry will result in less travel time, and new in-cabin technology will provide a better in-flight experience with improved air quality and lower noise levels, thus making flying a more pleasant and comfortable experience that it is today.

- New air navigation services (ANS) network technology and related equipment will change the way in which airspace is managed. In the years to come, air navigation services will be provided from a facility located somewhere remote from the airport or not even in the country where the services are used.

- Better connectivity through more and improved networks is empowering the millennial generation to travel and connect more than any generation before. The widespread availability of network technology will allow them to work remotely, making them and their children the "frequent flyers" of the future.

- The proliferation of networks has also opened up access to education to the whole world. Large numbers of foreign students are now entering the education systems of other countries. Universities are promoting their programs abroad in the hope that they will attract foreign students.

- Greater access to networks will see major growth in the number of flights, with airlines exchanging not only passengers, but someday also their aircraft and crew. There will probably be fewer air navigation services employees required since aircraft will communicate with each other through satellites.

- Many airports are already seeing a reduction in the amount of terminal space used by airport tenants to provide various services because passengers have greater access to services and products through online networks.

Quality and Quantity of Information

- Aviation managers will need to find ways to harness and effectively leverage the massive amounts of information becoming more and more available in ways that are understandable and can be trusted. They also need to make sure they do not lose control of the information that inundates them.

- Managers will need to develop filters and use artificial intelligence (AI) tools to discern what information is right and what is wrong in order to separate the meaningful from the irrelevant, the appropriate from the extreme. This may apply to aviation managers more than those in other fields due to ongoing critical concerns about passenger safety and security.

- The challenge for all managers in the future will be how to most effectively assess the credibility of information coming to them when such information is networked through multiple stakeholders. Ai tools will be very useful for this.

- Global connectedness will give rise to the formation of new communities in which members will share their experiences, perceptions, and values with other members. Members of those communities will rely on each other to validate their selections and decisions and confirm (or not) the accuracy of information shared through their network.

- In the field of aviation, the parsing and validation of the huge amount of information that will be available by 2030 will surely be critical for aviation decision-makers. Artificial intelligence tools will be ideal for this.

- As airline operators build reliability into advanced IT systems, they will likely start creating subsidiaries around the world. These branch operators will have greater access to operational information instantly and will quickly understand the impact of distant situations on the overall network.

- These days, people appear to be more willing to give up their personal information through online channels in order to get something in return instantly. The typical online shopper does not like to delay gratification and wants his/her product or service to be delivered as soon as possible.

- Large amounts of voluntarily supplied personal information allow suppliers to provide highly customized personalized services.

- Advanced connectivity technology coupled with the vast amounts of personal data being collected through online interactions enables the customization of services down to the level of the individual. It allows the flexibility to group market segments and to cater to the specific needs of each market.

- Connectivity technology will make it possible for aviation industry regulators to install Internet of Things (IoT) chips to monitor such situations as safety infractions, near-occurrences, and regulatory transgressions and then automatically take action.

- It will be interesting to see how this enhanced information collection and monitoring ability through increased connectedness will be used by civil aviation authorities. For example, to what degree will ICAO use it to monitor Member State compliance with its Standards and Recommended Practices (SARPs)?

- Through modern connectivity technology, aircraft maintenance has evolved to allow remote ongoing assessment of aircraft engine performance and to plan corrective actions/adjustments upon the next landing. This has almost eliminated the need for expensive periodic reviews, thus reducing costs related to interruptions that were previously required for mandatory inspections of critical aircraft components.

- Enhanced connectivity technology will allow airports and ANSP operators to implement Safety Management Systems that will lead to the certification of operators by States, in line with ICAO SARPs. This is expected to create a "safety culture" within the organization aiming to reduce the potential for accidents.

- Once there is a true globally connected environment, ICAO Member states will be able to monitor the operators on a continuous basis, just as airlines monitor their aircraft.

- ICAO could become THE global authority in terms of air navigation services and function as a "contractor" responsible for providing all navigation services on behalf of States. This would make it much easier to truly harmonize all rules and procedures worldwide.

- ICAO could start operating the entire global airspace on behalf of its member States (for a fee), which would allow much more efficient use of airspace than occurs today. This would greatly improve connectivity and connectedness on a global level.

- Airlines could operate truly globally in the future like trucking in North America or Europe, where one truck delivers for one company and picks up for another client.

Connectedness Technology – Impacts On Aviation

- Unmanned aerial vehicles, commonly known as "drones", will become a serious factor in aviation operations of the future. By mid-2018, the FAA in the US had issued some 73,000 Remote Pilot Certifications, which shows how popular and somewhat useful this new type of vehicle has become. This is already a $6 billion business and is expected to grow to $22 billion by 2020.

- As the extent of global connectedness increases and more people and networks connect to each other, it is possible to anticipate the day when a passenger makes a reservation with an airline and their degree of assessed security risk may affect the price of their ticket.

- As more and better information becomes available to the global airline industry through enhanced levels of connectedness, the rewards will be lower prices, higher frequency, and better profitability.

- As traditional airspace becomes more congested, airlines will be looking to near space as an option. The company SpaceX has already announced that it plans to take civilian passengers around the moon and back in 2023. Once that happens, it won't be long before such flights become common.

- Increasing the degree of global connectedness will make traveling by air in the future a very different experience for passengers from what it has been up until now.

- In aviation, through the application of Internet of things (IoT) technology, numerous ancillary services will emerge that will simplify the monitoring of activities and allow for greater access to air transport and a greater degree of connectedness.

- The way in which the hospitality industry is already using IoT technology and enhanced connectivity to better serve its customers is a model that that the aviation industry should follow closely.

- Very soon, tour operators will be able to assemble their tour passengers in a hotel lobby and screen people and baggage before transporting them in a secure bus (or high-speed train car) to the airport, bypassing check-in counters and baggage drops at the airport, and then dropping them off at the departure gate.

- As the international aviation industry moves towards total connectedness on a global scale, there will be good reasons for all major airports (and smaller ones as well) to harness IoT and related technologies to significantly streamline all aspects of the air passenger journey from arrival on the airport property to on board the departing aircraft.

382 GLOBAL MEGATRENDS AND AVIATION

REFERENCES

[1]   Ghemawat, P., & Altman, S. A. (2016). *DHL global connectedness index 2016*. https://www.logistics.dhl/content/dam/dhl/global/core/documents/pdf/glo-core-gci-2016-full-study.pdf.

[2]   Canton, J. (2015). *Future smart: Managing the game-changing trends that will transform your world* (p. 16). Kindle Edition. Boston, MA: Da Capo Press.

[3]   Canton, J. *Future smart*.

[4]   Canton, J. *Future smart* (p. 17).

[5]   Mitchell, G. (2018). *How much data is on the Internet?* https://www.sciencefocus.com/future-technology/how-much-data-is-on-the-internet/.

[6]   *The Internet of Things in the year 2030*. https://www.infineon.com/cms/en/discoveries/internet-of-things-2030/.

[7]   Panetta, K. (2017, October 3). *Gartner top strategic predictions for 2018 and beyond*. https://www.gartner.com/smarterwithgartner/gartner-top-strategic-predictions-for-2018-and-beyond/.

[8]   Watson, R. (2010). *Future minds: How the digital age is changing our minds, why this matters, and what we can do about it*. London, UK: Nicholas Brealey.

[9]   Marr, B. (2018, May 3). "How much data do we create every day? The mind-blowing stats everyone should read". *Forbes Magazine*, https://www.forbes.com/sites/bernardmarr/2018/05/21/how-much-data-do-we-create-every-day-the-mind-blowing-stats-everyone-should-read/.

[10]   (2017, March, 13). "REVEALED: Top uses of our smartphones - and calling doesn't even make the list". *The Daily Express*, https://www.express.co.uk/life-style/science-technology/778572/Smartphone-phone-common-reason-use-call.

[11]   https://press.airbnb.com/airbnb-unveils-roadmap-to-bring-magical-travel-to-everyone/ (2018).

[12]   Fowler, D. (2018). *How many websites are there in the world?* https://tekeye.uk/computing/how-many-Websites-are-there.

[13]   *The complete connected aircraft*. https://www.inmarsat.com/aviation/complete-connected-aircraft/.

[14]   Hewlett-Packard (2016, October 6). *CTO Welcome & Overview of Megatrends, Global Reinvention Week*. https://www.youtube.com/watch?v=MqvCNPMlIn0.

[15]   Canton, J. *Future smart*. p. 138.

[16]   Aelieve (2018). *Most popular online community sites: Website rankings 2018*. https://insights.aelieve.com/Website-rankings/online-communities/best-online-communities/.

[17]   Wikipedia (2019). *List of virtual communities with more than 1 million users*. https://en.wikipedia.org/wiki/List_of_virtual_communities_with_more_than_1_million_users.

[18]   Newbury, C. (2018, 2 May). "23 benefits of social media for business". *Hootsuite*..

[19]   Huang, W., Mitchell, J., Dibner, C., Ruttenberg, A., and Tripp, A. (2018, 16 January). *How customer service can turn angry customers into loyal ones*. Harvard Business Review.

[20]   Thirty Thousand Feet (2018, July 3). *Thirty thousand feet aviation directory: Aviation communities*. http://thirtythousandfeet.com/message.htm.

21   (2017, May 19). "London City Airport's new digital air traffic control tower 'safe from cyber-attack'". *The Telegraph*, https://www.telegraph.co.uk/news/2017/05/19/london-city-airports-new-digital-air-traffic-control-tower-safe/.

22   L'Agence pour la Sécurité de la Navigation Aérienne en Afrique et à Madagascar. https://www.asecna.aero/index.php/en/.

23   Sundararajan, A. (2017, June). "The future of work". *Finance & Development (IMF)*, 54,2.

24   Harris, K. (2017, September 3). *Foreign students flock to Canada as government struggles to get grads to stay*. https://www.cbc.ca/news/politics/international-students-jump-1.4268786.

25   International Monetary Fund (IMF) (2018, April 19). *Special Drawing Right (SDR)*. https://www.imf.org/en/About/Factsheets/Sheets/2016/08/01/14/51/Special-Drawing-Right-SDR.

26   Kearney, A. T. (2018). "Readiness for the future of production: Report 2018". *World Economic Forum*, http://www3.weforum.org/docs/FOP_Readiness_Report_2018.pdf.

27   Schwab, K. (2017). *The fourth industrial revolution*. New York: Crown Publishing Group.

28   Davis, H. (2005) *How to validate results from a Google Web search*. https://www.dummies.com/education/internet-basics/how-to-validate-results-from-a-google-Web-search/.

29   Fraser Institute (2017, July 3). *63,000 Canadians left the country for medical treatment last year*. https://www.ctvnews.ca/health/63-000-canadians-left-the-country-for-medical-treatment-last-year-fraser-institute-1.3486635.

30   Del Rey, J. (2017, January 31). *Amazon is building a $1.5 billion hub for its own cargo airline*. https://www.recode.net/2017/1/31/14462256/amazon-air-cargo-hub-kentucky-airport-prime-air.

31   International Civil Aviation Organization (ICAO) (2013). *Public key directory*. https://www.icao.int/Security/FAL/PKD/Pages/default.aspx.

32   International Civil Aviation Organization (ICAO) (2016, September). *Universal Safety Oversight Audit Programme (USOAP): Continuous Monitoring Approach (CMA)*. https://www.icao.int/safety/CMAForum/Documents/USOAP%20TRIFOLDaug29%20view.pdf.

33   Federal Aviation Administration (FAA) (). *FAA Aerospace Forecast FY 2018-2038*. https://www.faa.gov/data_research/aviation/aerospace_forecasts/media/FY2018-38_FAA_Aerospace_Forecast.pdf.

34   Joshi, D. (2017, July 18). "Here are the world's largest drone companies and manufacturers to watch and invest in" *Business Insider*, http://www.businessinsider.com/top-drone-manufacturers-companies-invest-stocks-2017-07.

35   Malik, T. (2018, September 18). *SpaceX to unveil 1st passenger for private BFR moon trip tonight!* https://www.space.com/41853-spacex-bfr-moon-passenger-flight-reveal-Webcast.html.

36   Berger, E. (2017, April 7). *Blue Origin has built three new rockets, may begin flying again this summer*. https://arstechnica.com/science/2017/04/blue-origin-may-begin-second-round-of-new-shepard-tests-by-late-summer/.

37   Société internationale de télécommunications aéronautiques (SITA) (2016). *Air transport IT trends insights 2017*. https://www.sita.aero/resources/type/surveys-reports/it-trends-insights-2017.

38   DePinto, J. (2016, June 14). *7 trends for the Internet of Things in hospitality*. https://www.linkedin.com/pulse/7-trends-internet-things-hospitality-jesse-depinto.

[39]   Terry, L. (2016, April 11). *6 mega-trends in hotel technology*. https://hospitalitytech. com/6-mega-trends-hotel-technology.

[40]   https://www.pr.com/press-release/739716.

[41]   Ministry of Defence, United Kingdom, Strategic Trends Programme (2014). *Global strategic trends out to 2045*. p. 57.

[42]   Ministry of Defence, United Kingdom, Strategic Trends Programme (2014). *Global strategic trends out to 2045*. p. 56.

[43]   Ministry of Defence, United Kingdom, Strategic Trends Programme (2014). *Global Strategic Trends out to 2045*. p. 64.

[44]   SITA is the world's leading air transport IT and communications specialist. www.sita.aero.

[45]   Société internationale de télécommunications aéronautiques (SITA) (2015, June 18). *Airline IT Trends Survey 2015*. https://www.sita.aero/resources/type/surveys-reports/ airline-it-trends-survey-2015.

8

THE FUTURE-WISE
AVIATION ORGANIZATION

INTRODUCTION

This book is about global megatrends and their impact on the air transportation system and the macro business environment in which it operates as an industry. It brings to light several drivers of these trends as well as many potential implications going forward to the middle of this century. It also raises many questions and discusses several possible outcomes. However, the fact remains that the future is relatively unpredictable with any accuracy. Our world is convoluted and turbulent, and early warning signs point to more complexity and systemic shifts ahead that will affect global outcomes within which air transportation will evolve.

Clearly, doing nothing is not an option. For aviation, there will no doubt be critical systemic impacts related to the evolution of megatrends. This eventuality, combined with the accelerating pace of change, means that a significant transformation is needed in how we manage air transportation. We need to shift our organizations to a future-ready stance.

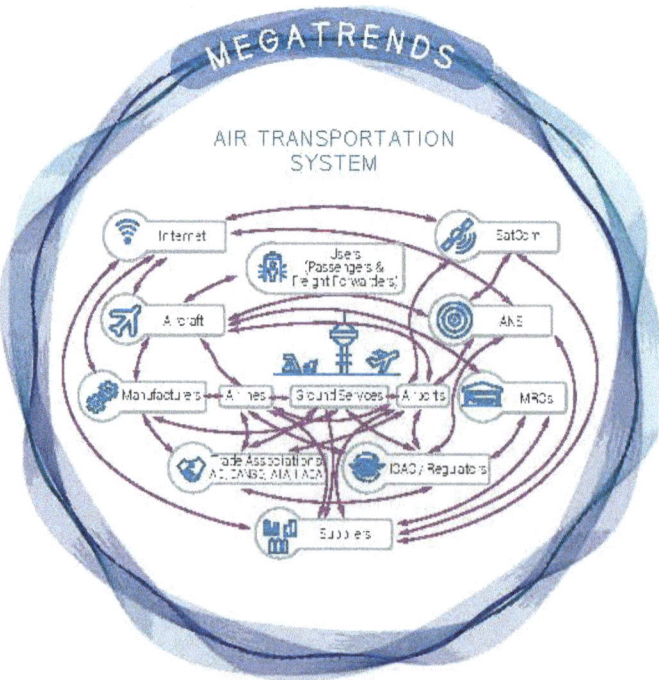

Figure 8-1   Megatrends and the air transportation system (ASI Institute).

As explained in the *Introduction* chapter of this book, ultimately the impacts of global megatrends on aviation have a critical influence on the performance of the industry and the benefits accrued by its stakeholders, including investors and citizens in general. This will translate into changes in demand, levels of service, and regulations, and these changes will be reflected in significant adjustments to "PASS" considerations (i.e., People-Assets-Systems-Structure). However, anticipating the future and determining related potential impacts is highly challenging, as confirmed in a 2010 European Union study on megatrends, which indicated that "The complexity of interlinkages and the manifold uncertainties inherent in megatrends require an exploratory, qualitative approach..."[1]. Clearly, the focus needs to be on overall performance, resilience, and agility. We don't know exactly how things will unfold, but we need to have a robust, albeit flexible, stance that allows rapid changes to respond to megatrend impacts.

In recent years, the co-authors of this book had the opportunity to lead or participate in workshops related to the future of aviation. Invariably, industry leaders in attendance acknowledged the crucial importance of global megatrends and the profound impact that they will have on air transportation over the next 15 to 20 years. Still, when pressed on how these megatrends, taken together, could impact the air transport system in specific terms, and over what likely timeframe, most of these senior executives acknowledged the challenges in articulating comprehensive practical responses. This was not all that surprising. Actually, the way our world might evolve and the growing ambiguity surrounding its future have prompted the writing of many books over the years by a number of well-known authors. These include: "Future Shock" (Tofler, 1970), "Megatrends" (Naisbitt, 1982), "The Art of the Long View" (Schwartz, 1991), "The Next 100 Years" (Friedman, 2010), "Future Files" (Watson, 2010), and "The Future of Everything" (Orrell, 2007). In one way or another, all these authors emphasize the complexity and relative unpredictability of the future.

When doing research leading to the publishing of "Future Smart" (2015), Canton concluded that many business leaders, "don't know how to get to the future" and "ask how to manage the speed and complexity of change". He found that situation somewhat worrisome because (even) the "next 10 years will be mind-blowing", and he said he had the impression that "no one is ready".[2] These views have been shared by many others for some time. Haines, in "The Systems Thinking Approach to Strategic Planning and Management" (2000), cautioned that, "...while it is important not to surrender to the complexity, chaos, and speed of life, it is necessary to understand that without thought and careful planning, anyone is subject to a crash landing."[3]

This is actually why this final chapter is about *how to manage towards the future*, a notion that Peter Drucker promoted in his best-selling book, "Managing For The Future" (1992), which he wrote to help executives "understand the rapidly changing world...and to stimulate them into action".[4] It is obviously not about "managing" megatrends, which by definition cannot be done, but rather, it is about enhancing the odds of successfully leading organizations through the ongoing rollercoaster of unpredictability and turbulence created by the impact of megatrends on the air transportation business.

Future-wise aviation organizations will have to prepare differently than they have in the past to remain relevant, sustainable, and successful. They will have to apply and exploit systemic ways of thinking. They will have to approach strategic planning innovatively and with more energy. Scenario planning will need to become one of their top areas of excellence, supported by predictive analytics and risk mitigation. They will need to adjust and calibrate their human capital development against a set of new competencies and to position themselves as a "learning" entity. They will learn to value partnerships. Above all, they will need to optimize their governance framework and learn to be truly agile.

The Paradox of Dealing with the Future

In this context, one observable phenomenon is that, in spite of all the talk about the need to get ready for the future, there seems to be very little discussion among industry leaders on "exactly how" to evolve the way we traditionally manage into a way to manage differently. There appears to be relatively limited insight available, be it in aviation or other industries, on how to adapt managerial business models as well as related strategies so as to factor in the uncertainties and likely disruptions engendered by megatrends.

Furthermore, sometimes one gets the impression of a lack of balance in many establishments, corporations, or sectors of activity between the focus placed on the short-term versus the medium-to-long-term future, despite the high stakes and inherent strategic risks. This tendency has been noted by several academics specialized in strategic planning and also by a number of futurologists. For example, Rolf Kreibich, the Director of the Institute for Future Studies and Technology Assessment (Berlin), said in his article titled "All Tomorrow's Crises" that, "Although megatrends and the core problems of global change are even now deeply affecting all areas of life, and although we already have a great deal of knowledge about the future, very little is being done. There is a huge gap between the challenges—even crises—that we know lie ahead and the practical responses offered on the global, national, and regional levels."[5] Along the same lines, Canton (already cited) remarked that, "Most people are not prepared for the drastic changes on the horizon...

they have not run the scenarios, evaluated the risks, thought about the possibilities, or fully understood the drivers of change". In Dixon's book, "The future of <Almost> Everything", the author bluntly declared that, "Short-termism will destroy corporations".[6]

A second phenomenon worth noting is that the evolution and impacts of global megatrends and especially those treated in this book (i.e., *Power Shift Eastward, Rapid Urbanization, Demographic Change, Innovative Technology, Climate Change*, and *Global Connectedness*), are widely considered to be accelerating exponentially. John Naisbitt, the author of "Megatrends: Ten New Directions Transforming Our Lives", the widely acclaimed book published in 1982, recently said that in the last 30 plus years, the manifestations of the trends that he had originally described "became more obvious and the speed of implementation accelerated ("Mastering Megatrends").[7] Ramirez & Wilkinson, in their book, "Strategic Reframing", stated that, "While the experience of increasing change is not a new phenomenon, there is today a common perception of a quickening pace of more disruptive, large-scale changes..."[8]

Change is happening exponentially on a global scale. Geopolitical transformation is materializing more rapidly than ever; the degradation of the environment is accelerating, and technology is evolving more quickly that most of us can comprehend. Uschi Schrieber, the Ernst & Young Global Vice-Chair of Markets, in the introduction to a 2015 paper on *Megatrends*, astutely remarked that in our current world, "the ever-increasing acceleration of change is one of the few constants". Also, according to Kurzweil's "The Law of Accelerating Returns" (2001): "We won't experience 100 years of progress in the 21st Century—it will be more like 20,000 years of progress"[9] based on the pace of progress to which we were previously accustomed. One striking example of this is the rapid expansion of information repositories. In his book, "The Data Revolution", Rob Kitchin observed that, "90% of the data in the world has been created in the last two years alone".[10] Of course, the rate of change is quite perceptible in other broad dimensions of the world macro-environment, including the reshaping of world socio-political forces, the swift evolution of global connectedness, and the rapid degradation of the environment, which is visible through the increasing occurrence and severity of natural disasters. For organizations, there will be no such thing as "more of the same" going forward.

The combination of the two phenomena described above, i.e., the fact that the unfolding megatrends and their converging impacts have been so far mostly ignored in many industries, coupled with the noticeably accelerating pace of their incidence, both militate in favor of a much more proactive leadership approach to facing the challenges of a turbulent future. Given the pervasiveness of megatrends and the pace at which they are evolving and interacting, it becomes increasingly more difficult for countries, industries, and organizations to argue that there are more important issues to deal with in terms of future implications.

Although there is a general consensus among experts and some leaders about the significant expected socio-economic, technological, and political impacts of megatrends, there is little evidence of widespread and systemic efforts to face this phenomenon and strategically prepare for the future by systematically using anticipatory management methods such as scenario planning. One often-mentioned cause for the lack of interest in these methods is the perceived growing complexity and unpredictability of the future. This is somewhat illogical since the very purpose of scenario planning is to provide a foundation for attempting to manage for an ambiguous future while maximizing the chances of success and mitigating the critical risks. Surely the high level of uncertainty should not be a pretext for retreating to purely short-term concerns. In essence, it is in situations of great ambiguity and uncertainty that scenario-based planning brings about the greatest benefits.

However, as mentioned before, factoring in megatrends and their impacts on aviation and many other sectors does not seem to get the level of attention that it urgently deserves. There are a number of reasons that can explain this situation. Some executives possibly feel that any attempt to deal with the extreme uncertainty of the future is a waste of time and therefore favor a "wait and see" strategy. Some more pervasive considerations possibly have to do with the typical private-sector executive compensation system, whereby performance rewards are given out for the achievement of short-term financial P&L results. Quite often, the performance bonuses of senior managers exceed their base salary. This obviously discourages them from focusing meaningful professional energies on medium- or long-term corporate strategy. According to Financial Times and CNN business and economic analyst Rana Foroohar in her book, "Makers and Takers", "80% of CEOs responded in a recent survey that they would pass up making an investment that would fuel a decade of innovation if it meant missing a quarter of earning results".[1]

In some industries, the problem is considered so serious that regulatory solutions are now being contemplated to compel organizations to implement "deferred" compensation for performance-related pay and bonuses. Similarly, in the public/parastatal sector, if there is no meaningful shielding of organizations from partisan agendas, short-term considerations of a political nature can prevent effective consideration of best courses of action for the long-term.

A new mindset is required for facing the future.

FUTURE-WISE ORGANIZATIONS: EIGHT PRIMARY AREAS OF EXCELLENCE

The background research conducted for this book led to the identification of eight primary areas in which organizations need to excel in order to optimize their future-wise posture. These targeted areas of excellence are: systems thinking, future-wise strategic management, scenario planning, data analytics, risk analysis, competency-based human capital management, agile organization culture, and partnership building organization. These are schematically presented in Figure 8-2, and each one is discussed in detail in the paragraphs that follow.

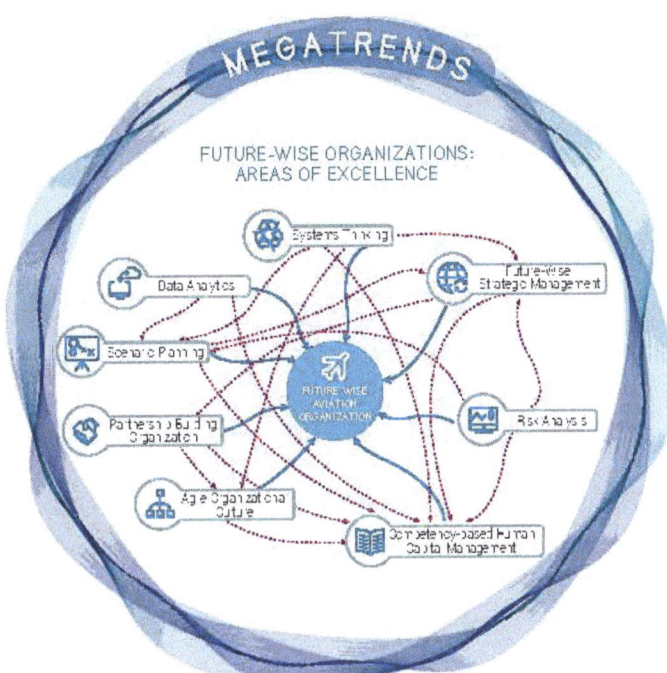

Figure 8-2 Future-wise organizations: Areas of excellence (ASI Institute).

Systems Thinking

A "system" is a collection of interrelated parts forming a structure, with elements usually interfacing in a complex arrangement and interacting for a purpose. Systems have inputs and outputs. They also have feedback loops that allow the whole to continuously strive for balance. Most complex systems incorporate sub-systems as well as unique elements, and they also tend to be part of bigger systems.

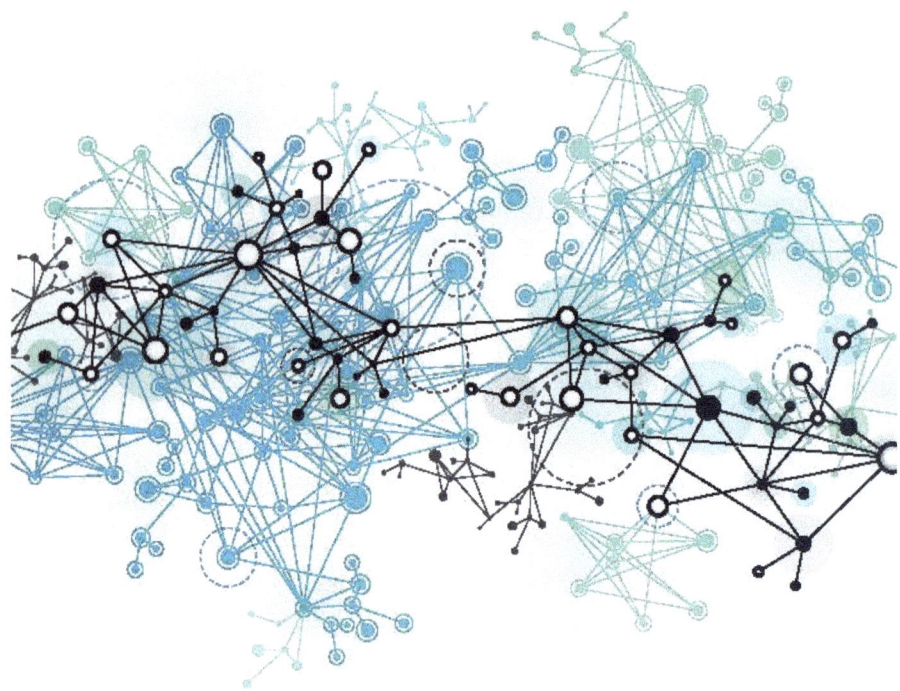

Figure 8-3   Conceptual representation of a system (ASI Institute).

Air transportation is a global dynamic system made up of many sub-systems, including the air transport industry, the airport industry, the air navigation services industry, and the aircraft manufacturing industry. Within these individual industry sub-systems are other systems in themselves, such as airlines, airports, air navigation services providers, equipment manufacturers, regulators, and users. These are all constantly interacting with technologies, rules, and procedures. Global aviation can also be described as incorporating many other distinct forms of organized sub-structures, such as airline alliances, airport enterprises operating several aerodromes, and air navigation services providers such as Eurocontrol, which supports air traffic control throughout Europe in coordination with country-specific agencies.

The aftershocks of critical incidents in the history of civilian air transportation have had far-reaching ripple effects and have led to major readjustments over the years. Unfortunately, one of the most common problems encountered in the strategic management of aviation organizations is the lack of a systemic or holistic perspective. There is a tendency to view problems or analyze situations from the narrow viewpoint of one's own organization or even one's individual work responsibilities. Part of this is probably due to the inherent structure of the air transportation sector. It can be argued that, generally speaking, all executives in the system deal with only a segment of the industry. The only exceptions to this are the Council Members and the Secretary General of the International Civil Aviation Organization (ICAO) (the United Nations agency established by States in 1944 to manage the administration and governance of the Convention on International Civil Aviation). They are in essence the only individuals that are formally mandated to consider aviation from a systemic perspective on an ongoing basis.

It is not unusual to observe industry leaders and managers addressing problems and challenges, as well as the future, from a relatively narrow perspective, which they genuinely believe is enough to do their job. This type of limited approach is no longer tenable because it has become clear that the development and performance of the international air transportation system and its components are profoundly impacted by the evolution of global megatrends.

Impact of Air Transportation Systemic Breakdowns

Any breakdown of a key segment of the air transportation system adversely affects the aviation industry as a whole.

Arguably, the most compelling example of a systems failure occurred with 9/11. Following the events of September 11, 2001, the international insurance industry gave notice that, effective immediately, third-party war risk liability insurance, covering airline operators and other service providers against losses and damages resulting from war, hijacking and other perils, would be cancelled. This brought the entire worldwide air transport industry to a halt for some days.

One instance of systemic failure in the regions was the Ryanair crisis. In September 2017, Ryanair—the largest airline in Europe in terms of number of passengers carried—announced that from November 2017 to March 2018, it would be cancelling 18,000 of its scheduled flights, affecting 34 routes and grounding 25 of its 400 aircraft. This decision impacted 315,000 bookings. The reason given by the airline for this cancellation was the lack of availability of its pilots because the leave rosters had not allowed a number of pilots to work during the time in question, and that they therefore had to go on mandatory leave according to international requirements.

Another case was when ground services and terminal services failed to cope with heavy snow and ice that pounded Europe for a week or so in December 2010, grounding air travel across the continent and leaving thousands of passengers stranded as airports struggled to clear a backlog of flights that had been canceled or delayed by snowfalls. Frankfurt Airport, Germany's biggest, was clear of snow and ice, but officials canceled about 300 of 1,340 flights because of problems elsewhere in Europe. During the period of crisis, French civil aviation authorities requested airlines to reduce their flights at the two main Paris airports by 30 percent. Thousands of travelers were stranded after about 400 flights in and out of Roissy-Charles de Gaulle were scrapped, with some 30,000 travelers disrupted by the cancellations and delays. Eurocontrol, Europe's air traffic supervisory body which supports its member States to achieve safe, efficient and environmentally-friendly air traffic operations across the whole of the European region, reported that approximately 3,000 flights had been canceled across Europe in a single day on 21 December. The airline industry and the traveling public suffered greatly because of inadequate infrastructure and lack of corporate foresight in one key area of the System.

There are many other examples of systemic failures of the air transportation system, including those caused by natural or human-made disasters such as volcanic ash eruptions (i.e., the 2010 eruptions of the Eyjafjallajökull volcano in Iceland) and major nuclear accidents (e.g., the catastrophic 1986 Chernobyl accident, which lofted plumes of fission products into the atmosphere, seriously affecting air navigation throughout Europe).

According to author O.A.J. Mascarenhas, systems thinking can be defined as, "a discipline for seeing the 'structures' that underlie complex situations, and for discerning high from low leverage points."[12]

The challenges that the air transportation system faces are growing in step with the exponentially increasing demand for aviation services. This is compounded by the fast-paced evolution of future trends and technologies and the intensification of their interaction, as shown in Figure 8-4.

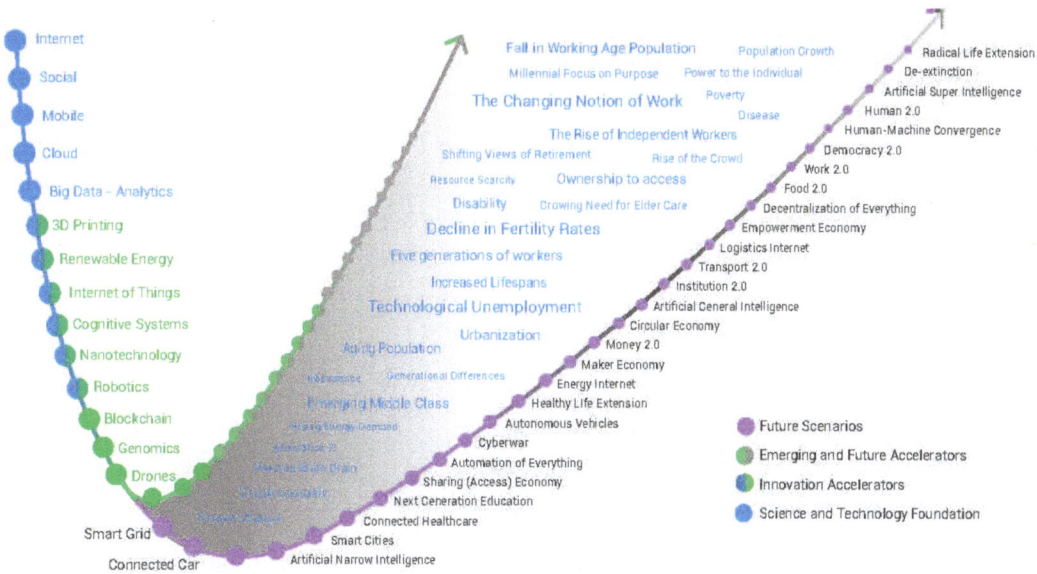

Figure 8-4 Reimagining the future (Frank Diana, Tata Consultancy Services).

Responses to these challenges cannot come from one specific individual, group of experts, or a given organization alone. Effective strategies or solutions can only be developed through "higher-order" thinking and cross-functional collaborative frameworks. There is no doubt that in order to manage effectively towards the future, visionary leaders and organizations need to see their situation in context. P.M. Senge also stated his belief that "systems thinking" is the cornerstone of a "learning organization".[13] Future-wise aviation organizations must facilitate the learning of their members and continuously transform themselves.

Systems thinking is a fundamental pre-requisite for developing plausible scenarios for the future, which are needed to facilitate the formulation of organizational strategy, as well as meaningful and actionable vision and mission statements.

Systems thinking is the first building block of future-wise organizations.

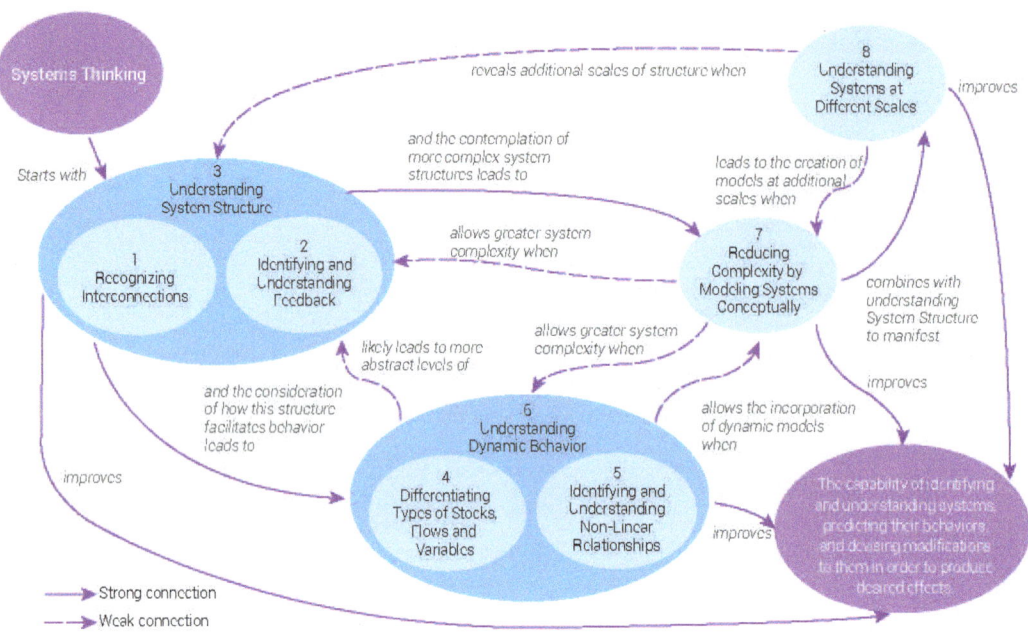

Figure 8-5   Systems thinking—Structure and dynamics (Arnold, R.D. & Wade, J.P. "A definition of systems thinking: A systems approach", Procedia Computer Science, December 2015).

Future-Wise Strategic Management

Strategy and a Changing World

The science of business strategy focuses on ways and means of keeping organizations targeted, relevant, and performing. The Balanced Scorecard Institute (2017) defines strategic planning as: "...an organizational management activity that is used to set priorities, focus energy and resources, strengthen operations, ensure that employees and other stakeholders are working toward common goals, establish agreement around intended outcomes/ results, and assess and adjust the organization's direction in response to a changing environment. It is a disciplined effort that produces fundamental decisions and actions that shape and guide what an organization is, who it serves, what it does, and why it does it, with a focus on the future."[14]

The concept of strategy has historically been tied to military contexts from ancient Greece to modern times. In the business world, strategic management as a science found its roots at Harvard University Business School, where the Harvard Policy Model was first conceived in the 1920s, although it wasn't articulated as such until the late 1950s by Igor

Ansoff, who is often referred to as the father of this field of study. Interestingly in the context of this aviation-related book, Ansoff did this work while he was employed as a senior planner for Lockheed Aircraft Corporation. His book, "Corporate Strategy", first published in 1965, had a significant impact on the business world at the time.[15]

In essence, the justification of "strategic management" as a branch of the administrative sciences is the fundamental recognition that the contextual environment of an enterprise, a public entity, or even an entire industry is in a constant state of evolution. As early as 1982, John Naisbitt (cited earlier) discussed the need to acknowledge many of the profound changes that were expected to occur on the global stage. At around that time, "environmental scanning" became a formal step in the strategic planning process. Since then, we have learned that the success of managerial action plans is largely a function of the quality of the analysis and interpretation of relevant external contextual situations and their potential impacts.

The linkage between the future and strategy is the object of interesting observations by Haines (cited earlier), who makes the point that many enterprises are stuck in managing from past experiences and that there is a lack of systematic consideration of major trends and their implications for the sustainability of public and corporate enterprises. Interestingly, after reviewing work done by the World Future Society, the Deutsche Bank (Germany), MITI (Japan), and others, Haines noted that civil aviation was identified as one of ten industries that would emerge or would undergo major transformation in the 21st Century. He also observed that most strategic planning models embody an analytical approach to systemic problems, and he challenged readers to embrace a more qualitative approach. Einstein is reported to have said, "...problems that are created by our current level of thinking can't be solved by the same level of thinking". There is a growing consensus in the academic literature that one has to learn to manage the present *from* the future, and this requires a shift in the contemporary way of devising organizational strategy. In fact, a major shift is required in the way that industry leaders factor the future into their visions and plans.

Over the years, the approach to business strategy has been expanded and refined. Numerous concepts have been developed by a score of academics and specialized consultants, including systems thinking, management by objectives, key performance indicators, balanced scorecard, SWOT analysis, performance-based management, emerging strategy, the five forces model, environmental scanning, PESTE analysis, areas of excellence, benchmarking, competition assessment, and many others. Each one of these explored and expanded on new theoretical perspectives and enriched the practice in the field. Critical reviews emphasized the benefits and limitations of each approach and pushed the research envelope outward.

The Issue with Contemporary Strategic Management

Generally speaking, the commonly used approach to strategy formulation is a rational sequential process made up of the steps shown in Figure 8-6.

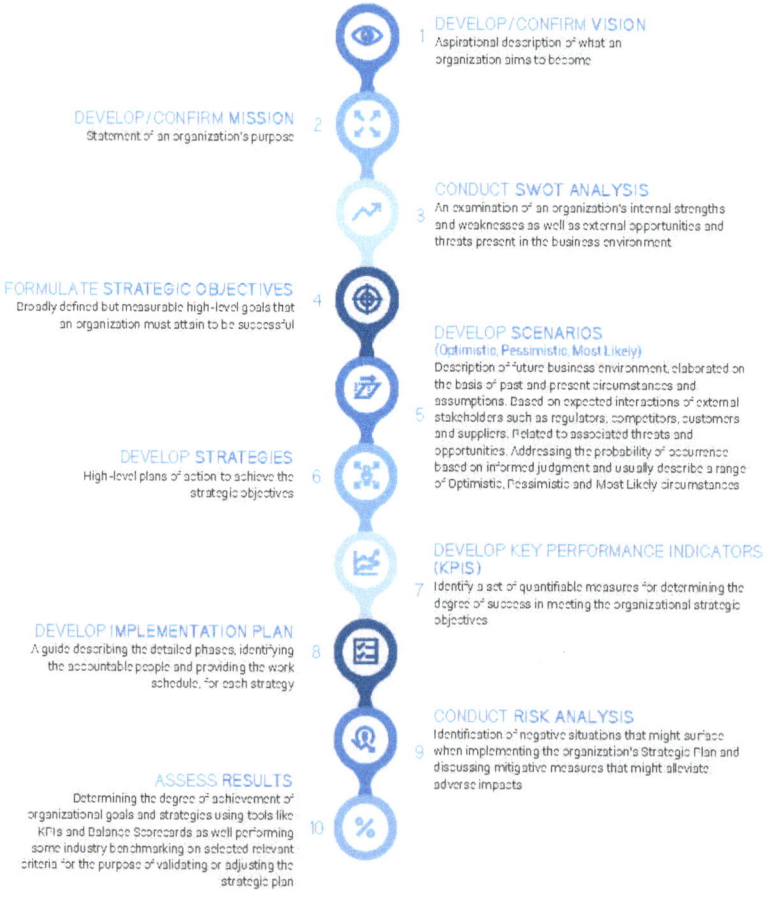

DEVELOP/CONFIRM VISION
1 Aspirational description of what an organization aims to become

DEVELOP/CONFIRM MISSION
2 Statement of an organization's purpose

CONDUCT SWOT ANALYSIS
3 An examination of an organization's internal strengths and weaknesses as well as external opportunities and threats present in the business environment

FORMULATE STRATEGIC OBJECTIVES
4 Broadly defined but measurable high-level goals that an organization must attain to be successful

DEVELOP SCENARIOS
(Optimistic, Pessimistic, Most Likely)
5 Description of future business environment, elaborated on the basis of past and present circumstances and assumptions. Based on expected interactions of external stakeholders such as regulators, competitors, customers and suppliers. Related to associated threats and opportunities. Addressing the probability of occurrence based on informed judgment and usually describe a range of Optimistic, Pessimistic and Most Likely circumstances

DEVELOP STRATEGIES
6 High-level plans of action to achieve the strategic objectives

DEVELOP KEY PERFORMANCE INDICATORS (KPIS)
7 Identify a set of quantifiable measures for determining the degree of success in meeting the organizational strategic objectives

DEVELOP IMPLEMENTATION PLAN
8 A guide describing the detailed phases, identifying the accountable people and providing the work schedule, for each strategy

CONDUCT RISK ANALYSIS
9 Identification of negative situations that might surface when implementing the organization's Strategic Plan and discussing mitigative measures that might alleviate adverse impacts

ASSESS RESULTS
10 Determining the degree of achievement of organizational goals and strategies using tools like KPIs and Balance Scorecards as well performing some industry benchmarking on selected relevant criteria for the purpose of validating or adjusting the strategic plan

Figure 8-6   Typical strategic formulation and implementation process (ASI Institute).

In the typical approach to strategy development and implementation (Figure 8-6), there are often variations in terms of the sequencing of some of the steps—for example, dealing with *Mission* before *Vision,* or developing *Strategic Objectives* before embarking on the *SWOT Analysis.* What is striking, however, in many commonly used organizational strategy development processes is the lack of substantial emphasis on the examination of the macro-environment within which the enterprise or entity being considered exists. Logically, this should be the starting point of any such process. Unfortunately, many existing frameworks for strategic planning processes propose a sequential approach in which the analysis of the external business environment is only considered after the formulation of vision and mission statements, and often only at the stage of discussing the opportunities available or the threats that could materialize. This therefore prevents a thorough challenge to the roles and purposes of organizations in the context of an ambiguous future.

Considering the anticipated tidal wave of global megatrends effects, choosing not to base strategic planning and management on an initial thorough scanning and assessment of plausible futures and their implications is equivalent to attempting to erect a major infrastructure on quicksand. Therefore, the traditional approach to strategic management illustrated above is considered sub-optimal.

A better approach is depicted in Figure 8-7, which shows how the "strategic planning cycle" should ideally be initiated, i.e., starting with an "understanding of the global environment and emerging trends".

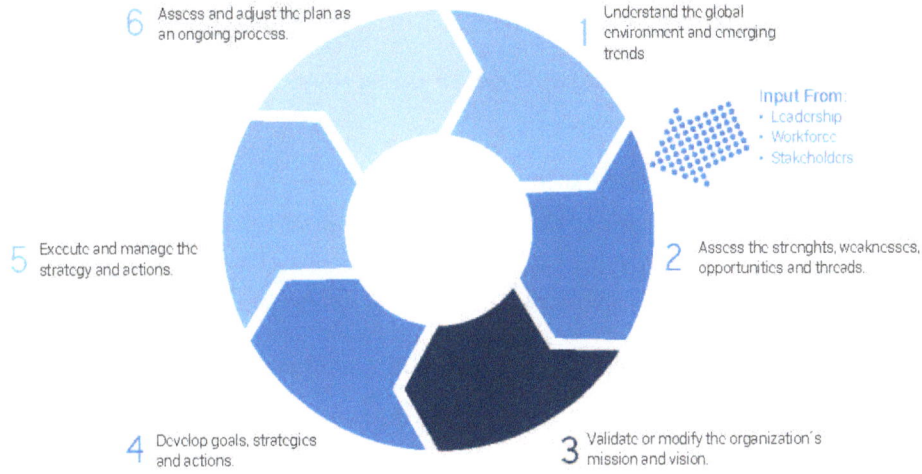

Figure 8-7   Strategic planning cycle (Lynn Carbone & Associates, "Strategic Planning").

The future is uncertain. The practical risks are high. There is an urgent need to be more conscious of these realities that impact all individuals, organizations, and entire industries worldwide, including air transportation, which is the focus of this book.

Megatrends and their accelerating impacts pose new challenges to the way that strategic planning and management are approached. This is part of the normal evolution of managerial science. What is called for now are more sophisticated ways to manage proactively "into" the future.

Scenario Planning

Definition

Schwartz (cited earlier) explains that scenarios are in fact "stories" about possible futures. They are developed to describe "pathways" that might exist going forward. They are meaningful because they allow organizations to develop contingency plans to be ready for a variety of plausible forthcoming business contexts.

There are many definitions of scenario planning, with dozens of books and more than 2000 peer-reviewed academic articles written on the subject. For the purposes of this chapter, the discussion will rely on the definition and the framework adopted and promoted by the Oxford Scenario Planning Approach (OSPA) of the Oxford University Said Business School, a leading center of excellence on the matter.[16]

According to Ramirez and Wilkinson in their book, "Strategic Reframing" (Oxford University Press, 2016), scenario planning "...is a methodology that uses the inherent human capacity for imagining futures to better understand the present situation and to identify possibilities for new strategy"[17].

Conceptually, the OSPA places the formulation of scenarios of the future in the "context of a context". In other words, it considers that an organization operates within a given "transactional" environment that is itself framed within a global "contextual" environment, or more specifically at the intersection of the two, as illustrated in Figure 8-8.

This conceptual approach has proven to be very robust. It clearly connects global megatrends, contexts, scenario planning, and strategy.

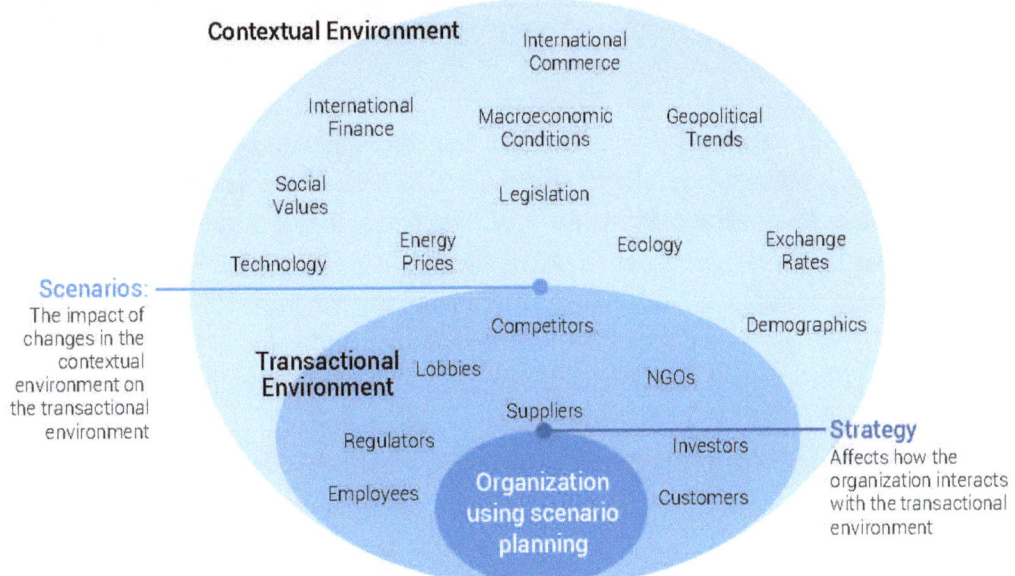

Figure 8-8   Using scenario planning to reshape strategy (Ramirez, R., Churchhouse, S, Palermo, A., Hoffman, J., "Using scenario planning to reshape strategy", MIT Sloan Management Review, Summer, 2017).

Pertinent History

From the outset, the science of strategic planning has primarily focused on optimizing the processes for formulating organizational strategy (i.e., elaborating vision and mission statements, setting strategic objectives, conducting SWOT analyses, devising implementation schemes, allocating responsibilities, and measuring impacts). However, one dimension that was arguably given relatively less attention until much later is environmental scanning for the purpose of scenario planning. Research in that area was initiated in the 1960s by Herman Kahn, who worked at RAND Corporation and subsequently became of one of the founders of the Hudson Institute. However, the major player since the 1970s for applying scenarios to a comprehensive business environment has been Dutch Royal Shell, which has continued to use that approach even up until today. As a lead strategist within that enterprise, Pierre Wack led the development of the practical use of scenarios in support of strategy formulation. Along with his team, he was able to foresee three oil crises (i.e., 1973, 1979, and 1986), the fall of the Soviet Union, and the emergence of radicalism in the Muslim world. The body of research on scenarios also grew through the work performed by the Stanford

Research Institute (now SRI International) and the SEMA Metra Consulting Group from France.

Irrespective of its initial recognition in many circles, scenario planning subsequently lost some of its popularity as several organizations that were early adopters of the technique eventually found it difficult to develop scenario narratives for effective real-world decisions. There seemed to be several reasons for this. First, meaningful scenarios are complex to develop; they require serious research, multidisciplinary perspectives, thorough discussions, several iterations, and careful formulation. Furthermore, they need ongoing maintenance because the contextual and transactional environments of organizations are in constant evolution. In addition, today, many governance structures tend to reward short-term thinking, particularly in the private sector where the profit motive is paramount. Unfortunately, in such a short-term horizon context where the need to maximize shareholders' quick return on investment is the priority, scenario planning is of very limited value.

Lately, however, the growing interest in megatrends and their impact on global society, industries, and their various actors has placed renewed significance on the crucial importance of systematically posturing for a highly uncertain and surely disruptive future.

Scenario Thinking and Plausible Future States

Scenario thinking has been described as "a structured process of thinking about and anticipating the unknown future with no pretense of being able to predict the future or being able to influence the environment in a major way. The objective is to examine possible future developments that could impact on individuals, organizations, or societies to find directions for decisions that would be the most beneficial in any future environment. The philosophy is to proactively think and plan for future developments instead of being a passive victim of change".

In contemporary times, not attempting to get ready for the future is unthinkable. Clearly, 30 or 40 years ago, the world was evolving at a much slower pace than it does today, but now the cycle time for major changes has been cut drastically. Executives can expect to live through seismic-type changes in their industries a number of times in the course of their careers. The ability to lead and manage in constant consideration of a long-term outlook is now a critical essential aptitude. This is now true in spite of the fact that the future is characterized by what the OSPA describes as "TUNA" conditions. TUNA conditions are characterized by turbulence, unpredictability, novelty, and ambiguity. One thing for sure is that the future will not be like the past, yet many executives insist on trying to predict the future "from the past" by relying largely on trend analysis techniques.

There is an abundance of "plausible" futures under these TUNA conditions. In her book, "The Future: A Very Short Introduction", Jennifer Gidley summarized some global alternative futures[18] (see Figure 8-9).

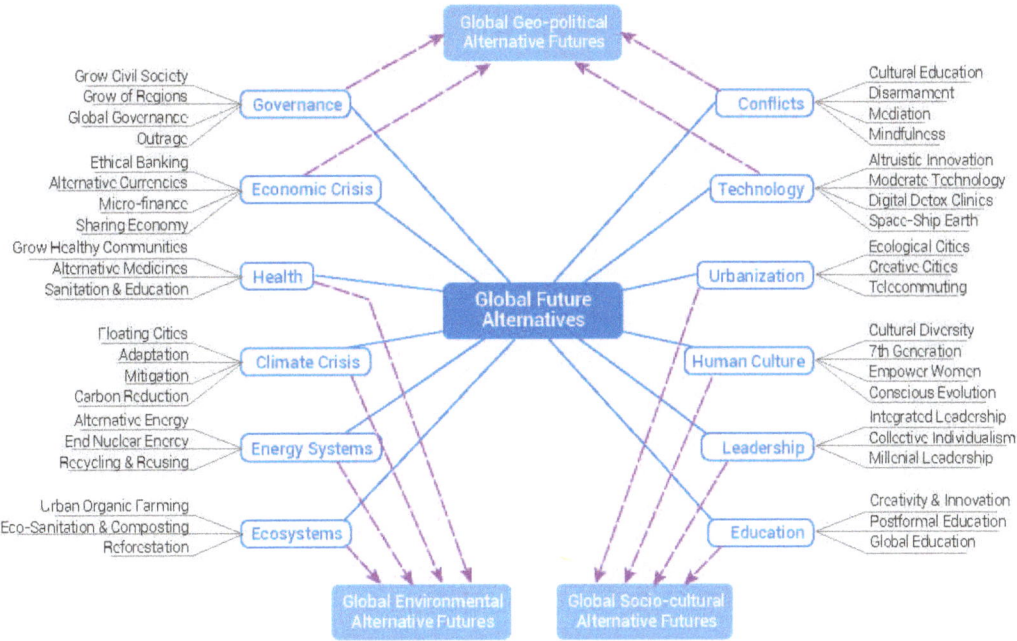

Figure 8-9   Global geo-political alternative futures (Gidley, J. M., "The Future: A Very Short Introduction", Oxford University Press, 2017).

Scenario thinking is a rich and broad domain. It has to do with attempting to visualize the future to determine how to best prepare for it. Van der Heijden explained that the strength of scenarios and scenario planning is based on the six following positive features: "(1) they respect differences and encourage multiple perspectives; (2) they combine quantitative and qualitative knowledge; (3) they combine different fields of knowledge and ways of knowing; (4) they reframe questions across disciplines; (5) they project the future as 'full of possibilities'; and (6) they are based on collaborative conversation".[19]

However, as noted by Dawson, "One of the challenges is that many people talk about 'scenario planning', often meaning very different things, and not infrequently degrading the term by applying it to unsophisticated approaches to dealing with uncertain futures".[20] Unless scenario planning is applied through a rigorous process it: will not succeed, will waste resources, and will actually add risk.

Key Success Factors for Scenario Planning Users

Purpose and Timeframe

Scenarios must be developed with a clearly enunciated purpose and timeframe in mind. In their book, "Scenario-based Strategic Planning", Schwenker and Wulf described the "definition of scope" as the first step of scenario planning[21]. Ramirez and Wilkinson (cited earlier) explained that "defining the purpose in scenario planning includes appreciating why the scenario learner (or client) has decided to consider scenario planning, that is, why, why now, and what for". In terms of time frame, scenarios usually deal with the medium term (15 to 25 years) or the long term (beyond 25 years); the short term usually falls into the domain of trend analysis.

Backcasting

A number of underlying factors create the foundation for what today are considered the "best practices" of scenario planning. First, scenarios should be unencumbered visualizations of the future. They are not the result of trend analysis. The fundamental premise here is that, under TUNA conditions, the "past" is a very poor indicator of what the future might be, and one should adopt the principle of managing "from" the future. This concept is referred to as *"backcasting"* or *"downframing"* in the Oxford Scenario Planning Approach, and it is "a process that starts by identifying a vision of the future and then working backwards from that future to the present to identify what would have to happen—i.e., policies and programs—to make progress along the direction of change implied to achieve the vision" (cited earlier).

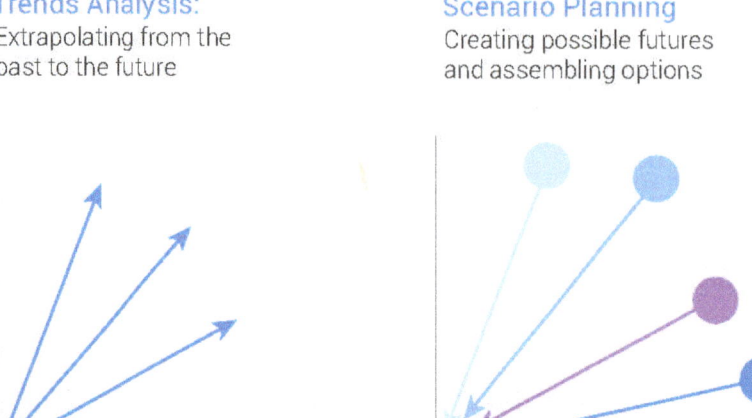

Trends Analysis:
Extrapolating from the
past to the future

Scenario Planning
Creating possible futures
and assembling options

Figure 8-10 Trend analysis vs. scenario planning (The Management Centre, "Tips and Tools", 2012).

Plausibility vs. Probability

A corollary to this is that "best practice" calls for the formulation of *plausible rather than probable* scenarios of the future. The notion of probability is excluded from the OSPA as inappropriate when building scenarios that deal with longer-term horizons; they must stretch the imagination and purposely avoid considering the future based on the past. In addition, as explained by Ramirez and Selin, "plausibility invites further inquiry, whereas probability closes it down".[22] Logically, the notion of probability only makes sense when addressing the short-term future through "forecasts", as illustrated in Figure 8-11.

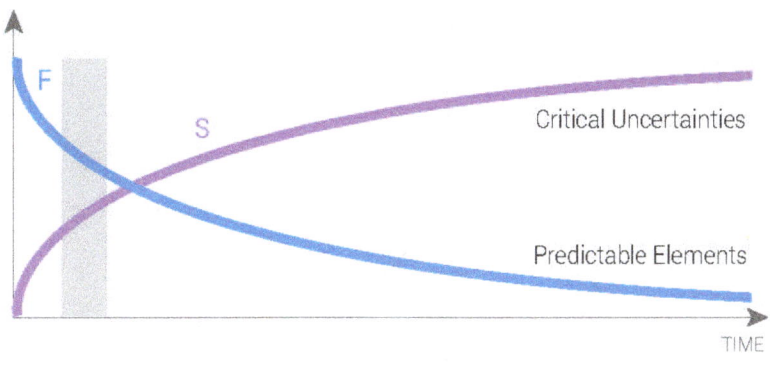

F - Forecasting most useful
S - Scenarios most useful

Figure 8-11   Forecasting versus scenario planning (Dawson, R.C., "Why Is Scenario Thinking—More than Scenario Planning—Critical for Executives Today").

Multidisciplinary Groups

All serious scenario planning methods developed by academics and supported by empirical research emphasize the need to have scenarios developed by multidisciplinary groups of individuals that include both end-users of the scenarios and other stakeholders or subject matter experts. This, of course, is to ensure that scenarios will be as comprehensive as possible and stretch the imagination by considering a large number of drivers as well as taking into account "weak signals" (i.e., indicators of surfacing transformations and concealed possibilities).

Multiple Scenarios

Since scenario planning is not about accurately predicting the future, but instead about investigating what the future might be like, it is necessary to develop a series of scenarios that depict various plausible and sometimes conflicting visions of the future. "Scenarios come in sets, reflecting the fundamental uncertainty in the situation. They show how different interpretations of the driving forces of change can lead to different possible futures. By setting up several scenarios, a *possibility space* is created, and it is within this space that the future is likely to unfold. Scenarios also overlap in aspects of the future that are likely to persist" (van der Heijden, cited earlier). Figure 8-12 illustrates the context of multiple scenarios.

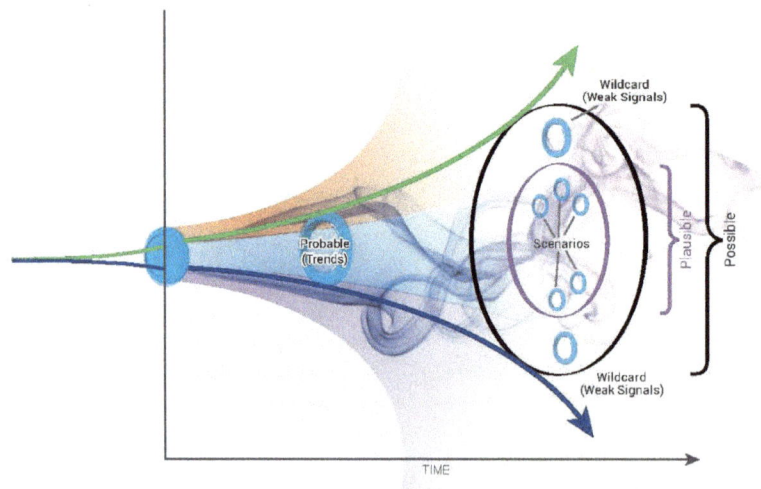

Figure 8-12 Multiple possible future scenarios (ASI Institute, adapted from: Voros, J., "A generic foresight process framework", Foresight, 5(3), 2003).

Reframing Cycles

In the Oxford methodology, the development of scenarios is an ongoing process where learning from their elaboration is the objective rather than the end-product scenarios in themselves. This thinking is based on the fact that scenarios need to be constantly updated through a series of "reframing" and "re-perception" cycles that take into account the constant evolution of both the contextual and transactional environments and therefore the need to engage in environmental scanning on a continuous basis, as shown in

Figure 8-13. This is also why, in the OSPA model, the primary users/developers of scenarios are also considered as "learners".

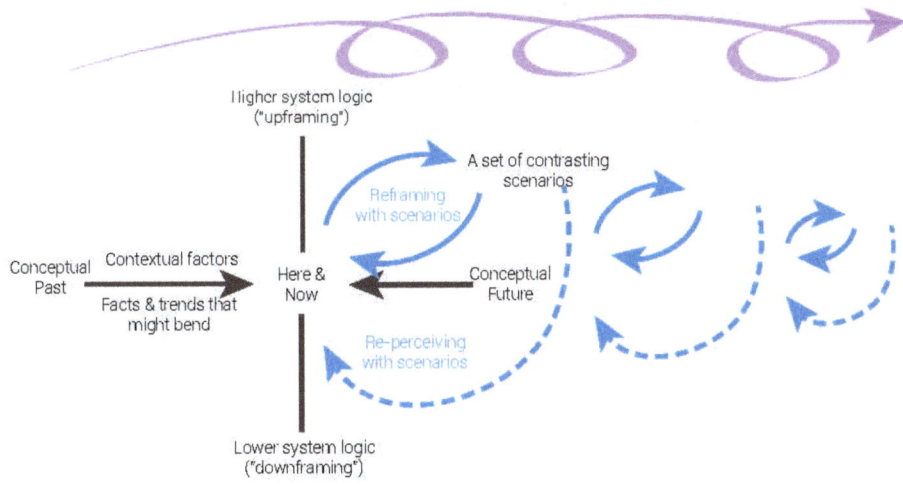

Figure 8-13 Scenario development through reframing (Ramirez, A., and Wilkinson, A, "Strategic Reframing", Oxford University Press, 2016).

Actionable

The main challenge of scenario planning is that the scenarios developed must be "actionable" in the context of why and for whom they are being elaborated. Each of the scenario narratives must clearly segment the vison of the future that they propose and provide some basis for determining elements and plans for the devising and/or adapting of organizational strategies going forward. This requires that special attention be given to how the scenarios are written and also how they are communicated. This shows the importance of having clearly stipulated purposes for developing a set of scenarios and also for involving users in the process.

One element in the pursuit of actionable scenarios is the assessment of how much an organization would have to depart from its current *modus operandi* to meet the requirements and characteristics underpinning some of the plausible future scenarios. In their book, "Scenario Planning", Lindgren and Bandhold observed that in a project they conducted in Sweden, one of the four scenarios they developed did not require new organizational strategies, although "the other three scenarios showed that the stakeholders had to start working on completely new strategies if they were to succeed".[23]

They stressed the importance of this initial gap analysis when contemplating possible future circumstances. Mind mapping, which is leveraging the collective intelligence of scenario development teams, is highly useful for elaborating scenarios that facilitate the discussion of feasible strategies, making visions of the future more actionable by future-wise organizations. Above all, to be actionable, scenarios need a proper strategy implementation "enabler" or "champion" to be accountable for results.

Example of Scenario Planning in the Aviation Sector

One of the best ways of illustrating what a solid scenario planning effort looks like is to consider an actual case. A very interesting example is a series of four scenarios of the future that a multi-modal team in the US Department of Transport developed with the support of the Futures Group of Deloitte Consulting. The working group considered 250 factors (i.e., "drivers") likely to affect the world over a horizon of 30 years. The FAA then convened its own group of aerospace experts to consider the four scenarios and describe their potential impacts on the aviation industry. The four scenarios were published as an appendix to the *FAA Aerospace Forecasts Report* issued in March 2000.[24] The theme and the main characteristics of each scenario are presented in the insert below.

Aviation Scenarios of The Future: A Special Report (March 2000)

(Note: Points below are summarized and/or quoted from the source document)

Global Prosperity

- Giant multinational corporations solve many problems.
- Decentralized government facilitates commerce.
- Europe to become a strong trade block competing with the US.
- The US pulls back from a global orientation.
- Strong US economic vitality.
- Restrained role of government.
- Low unemployment.
- World working 24 hours a day.
- Development of space transportation.

- Increase in leisure travel.

- Business travel tempered by e-commerce.

- Shortage of pilots and systems engineers.

- Increased airline competition mainly amongst mega-carriers.

- Air cargo booming.

- New types of airlines to serve the leisure market.

- Increased popularity of smaller aircraft to serve point-to-point markets.

- Air traffic control might get privatized.

- Airport and airspace infrastructure likely to be a constraint.

Western Hemisphere

- Advent of three major trading blocks: the Americas, Europe, and Asia.

- Trade issues leading to more trade barriers.

- US expanding NAFTA to South America.

- EU takes the lead in setting standards.

- More leisure time.

- Education is highly valued.

- Quality over quantity.

- More power to regional and local governments.

- Communities push back regarding new or expanding airports.

- Space travel expanding and blurred lines between the use of airspace and near space as airports serve both.

- Increased passenger traffic with 60 to 40 split between business and travel.

- Fully automated cargo flights by 2028.

- Security a major issue for aerospace industry.

- Business aviation operating more from larger airports.

- Pilots becoming system monitors.

- Major airports likely to expand.

- New airports to be located far from city centers.

- City centers to be served by vertical flights.

- Possible adoption of the Eurocontrol model for airspace management in all the Americas combined (high altitude vs. low altitude).

- Sustained importance of safety and security oversight mechanism.

Aging America

- Weak US economic vitality.

- Decreasing globalization.

- Interventionist government.

- Prolonged economic stagnation.

- US industry losing its competitive edge to the benefit of Europe.

- Investment going abroad.

- Baby boomers well off at the expense of the bulk of taxpayers.

- Education collapsing.

- Dual-income families are a necessity.

- Aerospace industry doing better worldwide than in US.

- US airlines shrinking.

- Decrease in general aviation.

- Space travel not living up to its potential.

- Air cargo demand is flat other than for small packages linked to online shopping.

- Airbus surpasses Boeing, which will no longer be purely a US manufacturer.

- Main markets for new aircraft are China and Europe.

- Limited growth for pilotless aircraft.

- High demand for pilots, but no shortage.

- Senior citizens representing a sizeable portion of the commercial passenger market and related activity at destination airports.

- Cyberterrorism is a major concern.

- Commercial aircraft, air traffic control, and especially air cargo might be increasingly vulnerable to unlawful interference.

- Airport and air traffic control deteriorating significantly over the 30-year horizon, but capacity should be adequate due to an overall decline in demand.

- Air navigation services likely to be provided by a performance-based organization (PBO) under an FAA contract; however, if the business case does not hold because of low traffic volumes, the PBO may be dissolved by the end of the planning horizon (30 years).

- Decrease in number of air traffic controllers to be expected due to increased automation and low demand.

- The role of ICAO and Europe in setting new standards will increase.

Global Climate Change

- Weak economic vitality.

- Increasing globalization.

- Interventionist government.

- By the end of the planning period, there has been 30 years of increasingly severe weather.

- The entire world understands the need to reverse negative environmental degradation as a paramount priority.

- The 70% of the world population that live in coastal areas are greatly affected by rising sea levels and landslides.

- Addressing the causes and effects of global warming, including violent storms and flooding, tops the world's agenda.

- Patterns of housing, work, and travel all become more emissions-efficient.

- People live near their workplace.

- Using vehicles for individual trips is a scarce luxury.

- Space and satellites become critical for environmental monitoring.

- Space and commercial transportation keep growing, but not at the expense of the need to improve the environment.

- Commercial travel faces challenges: load factors are high, fares are high, seating densities are high, and schedule frequencies are low, making air travel unpleasant, yet considered a luxury.

- Environmental disaster recovery is a big driver of aviation activity.

- Air cargo business declines in this scenario because cost becomes a bigger factor than time.

- Flight schedule reliability is greatly up because of the need to reduce environmental problems.

- Lighter-than-air possibly reappearing as an emissions-efficient way of moving air cargo.

- Many smaller communities lose air service as people move to megacities.

- There is an overall drive for efficiency across the air transportation system driven by environmental impact targets.

Interestingly, the highlights of these FAA scenarios demonstrate that, in essence, they meet most of the scenario planning key success factors presented and explained earlier.

Data Analytics

Another area where future-wise aviation organizations will need to possess expertise will be in the field of data analytics. This is the science of making sense of the ever-growing abundance of data in order to evaluate performance, explore hypothetical situations, and support systems thinking in aid of decision-making.

Data Explosion and Interpretation

According to IBM, about 2.5 exabytes (EB) of data are generated everyday (one EB is 10^{18}, i.e., 1 followed by eighteen zeros, or a million terabytes), and as discussed earlier, this is growing exponentially.[25] Of course, massive amounts of facts and figures are only of interest if *useful* information can be extracted from them. This presents a practical challenge when time and resource limitations are of concern. Data scientists are a new breed of professionals that work on producing "curated data" using artificial intelligence and other means to generate meaningful actionable information.

This "data explosion" correlates with all megatrends discussed in this book and most of their impacts, but it is mainly evidenced in conjunction with the *Innovative Technological Change* and *Global Connectedness megatrends*, as discussed in Chapters 6 and 7 of this book.

Scope of Data Analytics

Data analytics covers many subjects. It can be used to systematically monitor and measure organizational performance, both in real time and after the fact, and to support decision-making by creating options and analyzing the impact of "what-if scenarios". A relatively comprehensive taxonomy of the field of data analytics has been compiled by the American Institutes for Research and is shown in Figure 8-14.

Figure 8-14 The multiple elements of data analytics (American Institute for Research).

With reference to Figure 8-14, the elements *Data Integration & Visualization*, *Policy Analytics & Decision Support*, and *Social Media & Digital Outreach* are of special interest to the aviation industry, particularly for airlines and airports in conjunction with the design of advanced command centers (as referenced later in this chapter).

A model developed by Gartner, Inc., for value-based data analytics[26] focuses on answering four questions:

- What happened? (i.e., "descriptive analytics").

- Why did it happen? (i.e., "diagnostic analytics").

- What will happen? (i.e., "predictive analytics").

- How can we make it happen? (i.e., "prescriptive analytics").

The notion here is that the level of complexity grows as one goes from collecting to using the data, and so does the value of the output. Description and categorization of the information is useful, but not as much as the ability to predict situations or to recommend courses of action arising from data analysis.

Predictive Analytics

In the context of global megatrends and their impacts on aviation, which is the main subject of this book, the most relevant aspect of data analytics is currently the predictive analytics part. As explained by Abbott in his book, "Applied Predictive Analytics", the term is relatively new and "stands on the shoulder of other analytic-centric fields such as data mining, machine learning, statistics, and pattern recognition".[27] Among others, it supports the optimization of operations, investment decision-making, and the acquisition and retention of customers. Global enterprises such as Amazon have already positioned themselves as leaders in the use of the technique (i.e., in the form of "customer analytics"), with huge impacts on profitability and efficiency.

In the earlier discussion of scenario planning, it was established that foresight is not an exact science and that TUNA conditions (i.e., turbulence, uncertainty, novelty, and ambiguity) render the use of trend analysis and probabilities of outcomes rather meaningless for the medium to long term. However, predictive analytics can complement scenario planning by focusing on the shorter-term horizon, where the likelihood of situations occurring and the assignment of probabilities make more sense. This would be an intermediate step towards the more distant future and would flag issues that need to be factored into the development of long-term future scenarios, including components of outlier scenarios such as "weak signals". Finally, when "managing from the future", predictive analytics can help validate certain assumptions used for scenario formulation or related action planning, as well as shedding light on some of the main associated risks.

Human-Computer Collaboration

Robert Watson, a respected futurist, predicted in one of his books that by around 2030, the point will be reached where computers will eventually become more intelligent than people.[28] However, he later admitted in another book that the *general intelligence* of computers was probably further away.[29] In this respect, Thomas Malone, in his recently published book, "Superminds: The Surprising Power of People and Computers Thinking Together"[30], points out that many experts have predicted that general AI was 15 to 20 years away, but that they have said so for the last 60 years! In his opinion, long before the development of artificial intelligence will lead to computers overtaking humans, there will be a prolonged and impactful period of brain-machine cooperation, and he mentions several examples of this, including:

- Using semi-automated tools to generate and evaluate possibilities.
- Using machine learning to recognize patterns.
- Using smarter sensing (e.g., to detect potential terrorist attacks).
- Fostering enhanced collaboration by coordinating interdependencies among tasks.

It should be noted that most of the applications that foresee human-machine collaboration will be related to improving the speed and quality of decision-making.

Data Analytics and Aviation

A number of interesting examples already exist involving the use of data analytics in aviation. Leading airports are evolving their traditional Airport Operations Control Centers (AOCCs), which were originally designed to enhance the real-time coordination of airport activities, into much more sophisticated Airport Enterprise Management Centers (AEMCs) (ASI Institute, IAP-COP Community of Practice - Industry Working Group)[31]. This new type of center will cover the performance optimization of the full spectrum of airport functions, and in addition, it will integrate AI-supported predictive capabilities for the purpose of looking into "what-if" scenarios related to airport development decision-making. These new-generation facilities will be especially helpful in dealing with the potential impact of unusual operating conditions requiring contingency planning and analysis of risks.

Figure 8-15 Typical airport enterprise management center (stock photo).

Figure 8-16 Cebu Pacific recently opened its Customer Command Center (courtesy of Cebu Pacific).

Airlines are also developing new generations of command centers that incorporate predictive analytics. Interestingly, many of the most recent facilities incorporate dedicated social media monitoring functions that make use of various data analytics tools to facilitate customer service management, benchmarking, real-time marketing, and crisis management.

Cebu Pacific recently opened its Customer Command Center, "the first of its kind in the airline industry with an integrated facility and technology for social intelligence and customer engagement".[32]

Risk Analysis

Definitions

In general terms, "risk" can be defined as the possibility of a hazardous condition happening. According to B. Fischhoff and J. Kadvany, "Risks involve threats to outcomes that we value. Defining risk means specifying those valued outcomes clearly enough to make choices about them"[33]. Along these lines, ISO 31000 describes "risk" as "the effect of uncertainty on objectives".[34]

"Risk management" is a decision-making support function that aims to identify risks against organizational or project objectives, as well as to reduce potential adverse impacts on the achievement of desired outcomes and/or to maximize opportunities. It integrates the identification, analysis, prioritization, control, mitigation, and monitoring of risks.

Figure 8-17 Risk management components (ASI Institute).

"Risk analysis" is the essential component of risk management. It is the process leading to the determination of issues that are likely to impact the realization of desired organizational outcomes. It includes the assessment of the likelihood and severity of impacts through a variety of techniques. It aims at providing management with actionable intelligence. Figure 8-18 shows the interaction of likelihood versus consequences when analyzing risks.

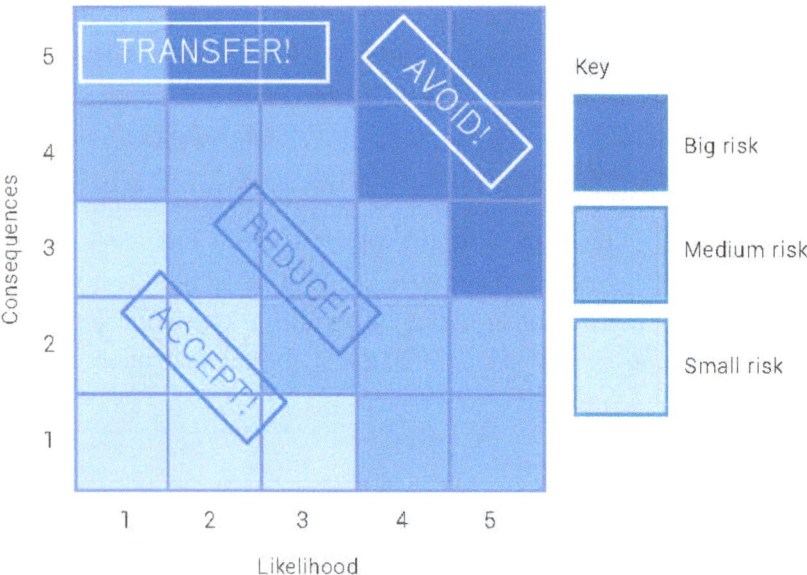

Figure 8-18   The 5 x 5 risk matrix (Evans, V., "Key strategy tools", Financial Times Publishing, 2013).

Relevance

Risk analysis is a required core domain of expertise for future-wise aviation organizations. Of all the various ways to analyze the future and its implications, risk analysis has a special place in the spectrum of useful techniques. Since it is based on assessing the probabilities of issues looking forward, it is most beneficial to managers when they are trying to forecast horizons where critical uncertainties are relatively low and predictable elements of the business environment are relatively high. On an organizational timeline, it belongs in the short-term zone alongside trend analysis tools.

Because it involves determining the assignment of probabilities, traditional risk analysis is relatively incompatible with the best-practice OSPA methodology for the formulation of longer-term scenarios of the future, which should be based on plausibility rather than "likelihood of occurrence" (i.e., probabilities). However, the qualitative assessment of risks can, for example, quite usefully inform the exercise of foresight by flagging considerations related to wildcard situations and outlier conditions that must be factored into scenario planning. Moreover, and conversely, the study of megatrends provides invaluable information as input for the identification of risks and the likelihood of their occurrence.

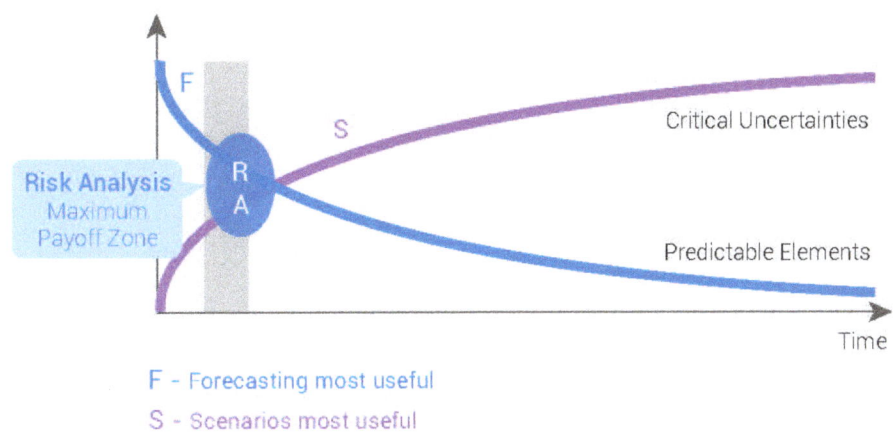

F - Forecasting most useful
S - Scenarios most useful

Figure 8-19   Risk analysis payoff zone (adapted from Dawson, R.C., "Why Is Scenario Thinking—More Than Scenario Planning—Critical for Executives Today").

The notions of risk and megatrends are intertwined in many ways, as illustrated in Figure 8-20, which was adapted from the *World Economic Forum Global Risks 2017 Report*.[35]

As another example of the risk-foresight interface, Willis Towers Watson PLC recently surveyed more than 1,500 business leaders around the world and devised an index consisting of five global "risk megatrends." Their underlying hypothesis was that, "Few businesses today have the luxury of operating within a geographic or industry bubble. Around the world, interconnected political, economic, and commercial factors influence the direction and destiny of companies, both large and small, across a range of sectors. As a result, risks that once could be understood and managed locally have become ever more challenging and global, while new risks seem to appear almost daily."[36]

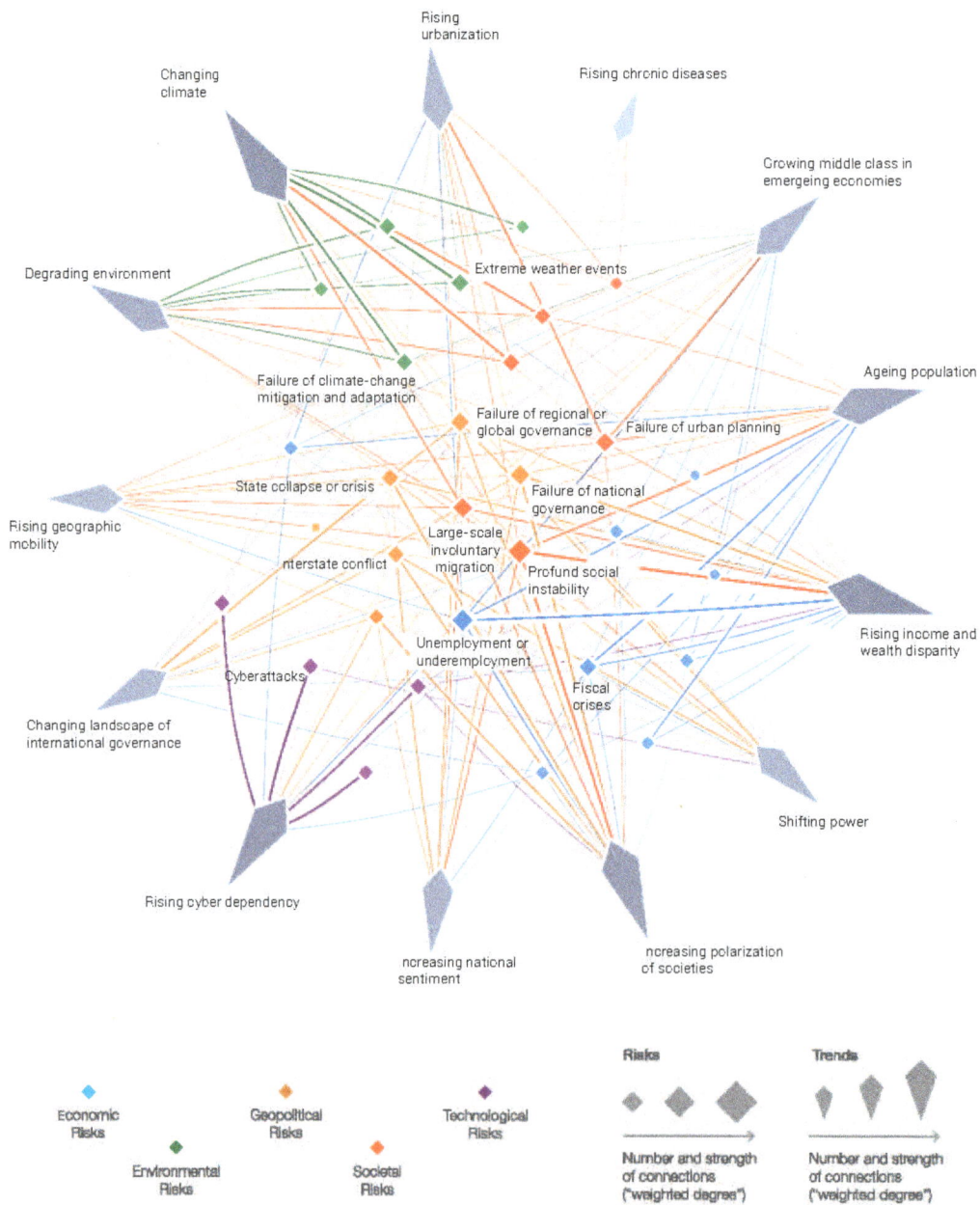

Figure 8-20 Risk-trend interconnections map (World Economic Forum, 2017).

Of course, risk megatrends are different from the global megatrends described in this book, but as mentioned earlier, they intersect with each other, and this intersection is mainly visible in the area of scenario planning. The five risk megatrends identified by the

WTW survey (cited above) and their relative rankings (composite of *Severity* and *Ease of Management*) are:

1   Regulatory/Geopolitical Uncertainty

2   New Technology Strategy

3   Challenges

4   Talent Optimization

5   Operating Models.

It is important to note that global risks are not static; they actually evolve relatively rapidly, so much so that the World Economic Forum has been recording the changes on a yearly basis since 2007. Figure 8-21 shows the changes from 2007 to 2017 in terms of risks, their likelihood, and the anticipated severity of their impact.

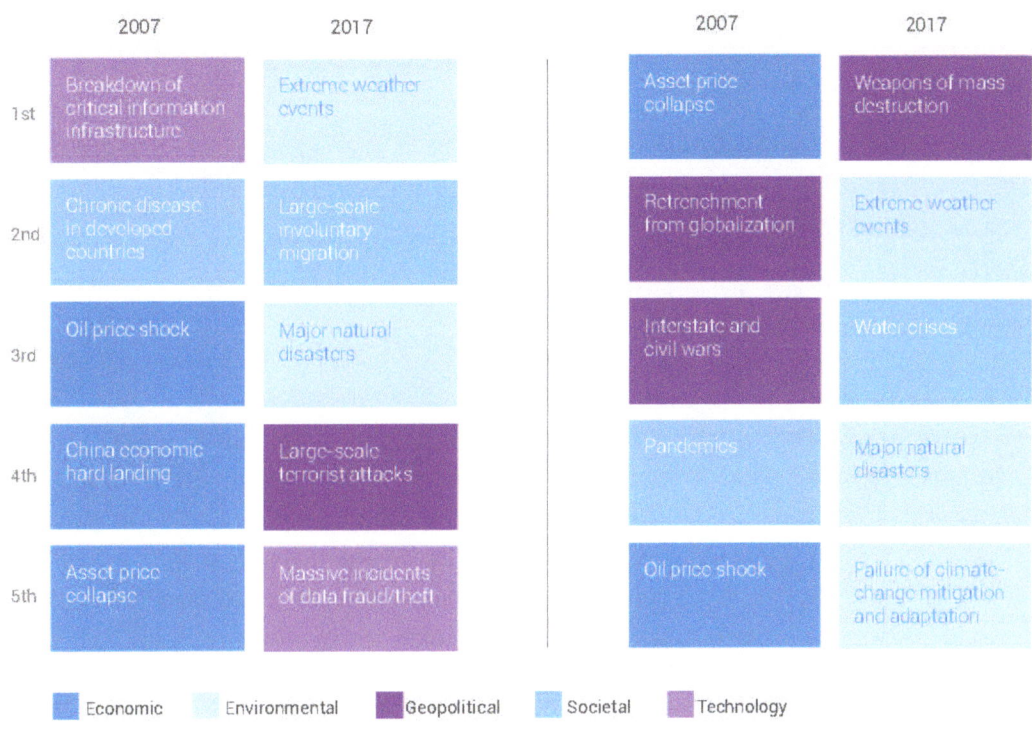

Figure 8-21   Top 5 global risks—Likelihood and impact, 2007-2017 (World Economic Forum, 2017).

Risk and Aviation

The use of risk analysis is engrained in the aviation sector. It is at the heart of all ICAO guidance that pertains to safety and security. For example, it is the cornerstone of safety management systems, aircraft design, airspace management, airport construction and operation, aviation security programs, and personnel licensing. For a number of years already, the European Aviation Safety Agency (EASA) has been advocating a scenario-based approach for assessing future risks. As Masson and Morier stated in their book, "Methodology to Assess Future Risks", "One major difficulty with the assessment of future risks is to predict the future system with enough certainty and provide a good, complete and trustable description of the future...Methodologies for assessing risks should, <among other things>, have sufficient 'power of anticipation', consider a range of possible futures, consider the multiple dimensions of the system(s), have the ability to model dynamic phenomena, and aid in identification of unanticipated uses of technology."[37] Risk analysis is also fully integrated into strategic business planning for aviation enterprises. For instance:

Airlines devote a lot of effort to studying the risks associated with the price of fuel and currency exchange rates.

Airports have to constantly monitor the evolution of airline business models and the ongoing restructuring of the market (e.g., new entrants, mergers and acquisitions), as well as competition (mainly for transfer traffic).

Air navigation service providers need to focus on uncertainties regarding the introduction of new technologies and standardization issues.

Risks also tie into the "sustainability" of aviation organizations. Flouris and Yilmaz have extensively discussed the matter in their book, "Risk Management and Corporate Sustainability in Aviation", in which they propose an "Enterprise Sustainability Risk Management Model (ESRM)" and explain that "economic, social, and environmental issues are creating both risks and opportunities for businesses".[38] In a segment of their model related to corporate sustainability for airlines, they emphasize, as a first step, the need to analyze the external and internal factors in the business environment, a *de facto* reference to megatrend considerations.

In 2016, WTW studied the risks in the transportation sector from data, coupled with insights gained from interviews with 350 corporate-suite executives. Their work makes it possible to isolate findings for the aviation sector, and these can be summarized as follows for the most important risks (i.e., in terms of the combination of anticipated severity of impact and ease of management):

Digital Vulnerability and Rapid Technological Advancement

- Failure of critical IT systems.
- Inability to keep up with pace of change and technological advancement.
- Increased security threat from cyber and data privacy breaches.

Geopolitical Instability and Regulatory Uncertainty

- Antitrust scrutiny associated with merger and acquisitions.
- Social unrest, involuntary immigration, and terrorist threats.
- Increased complexity of regulation.

Talent Management and the Complexities of a Global Workforce

- Lack of potential leaders.
- Escalating duty-of-care costs.
- Cost of maintaining competitive compensation.

It is interesting to note that current aviation sector leaders seem worried about the human capital risk going forward, including leadership as a top concern. Considering this matter in the context of some of the global megatrends should lead to even stronger cause for alarm. As an example, the West to East economic power shift (i.e., isolationism) and the emerging challenges to free trade should trouble multinational enterprises, including airlines and global airport operators, because the mobility of personnel could be seriously affected. Another consideration will be the impact of robotics on workforce requirements.

Again, new thinking is needed.

Competency-based Human Capital Management

Background

This section deals with two issues: the new set of competencies that future-wise aviation organizations need to nurture, and competency-building master plans (CBMPs), the emerging best-practice frameworks for structuring human capital requirements.

People are an organization's greatest asset. Although it sounds like a cliché, it is a fundamental truth. Therefore, it goes without saying that developing people needs to be a key and explicit part of any organization's strategy. Among the many reasons why an organization should prioritize investing in its people, perhaps the most compelling is the fact that when done strategically, spending money on developing human capital boosts productivity more than any other expenditure.

Knowing this, it is concerning that recent research from PricewaterhouseCoopers found that fewer than half of human resources leaders indicated that they are "very confident" that they will have access to the right talent to execute their business strategy in the foreseeable future.[39] To meet the growing challenges of the future, it is imperative that organizations be able to attract, select, develop, reward, and retain the best talent possible. Although the first step is attracting and selecting the best people, a key component is to develop these individuals through a robust competency-building process that ensures the best return on an organization's human capital investment.

In the context of global megatrends and their impact on the air transportation industry, this requires a thorough identification of competencies required for the future, evaluation of gaps, and development and implementation of strategies to address them. Competent employees are more productive, and when their accomplishments are recognized and rewarded, they tend to stay with the organization that develops and values them.

More than ever, organizations must focus on competencies to build an effective and resilient posture to tackle the future. Defining human capital requirements in terms of comprehensive sets of competencies is a strategic task. The notion of job-related competency is far-reaching. It obviously includes expertise in *Knowledge* and also the mastery of directly relevant *Aptitudes*, but of paramount importance is the ability to demonstrate the capacity to perform "in context". This can be referred to as *"Situational Judgment"*.

The effective development of human capital resources within high-performance work organizations (HPWOs) should be focused on three competency-building activities:

- Development of competency profiles.
- Systematic assessment of competency gaps.
- Development of pragmatic strategies to close these gaps.

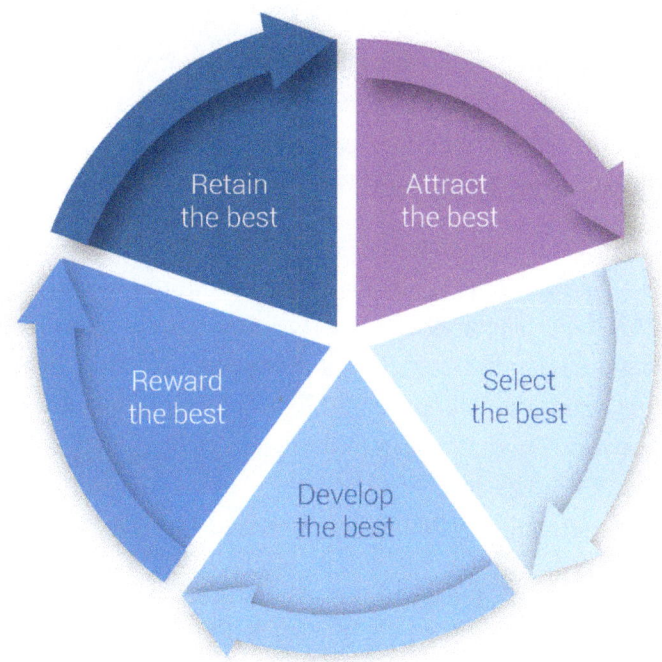

Figure 8-22 Human capital management cycle (ASI)

DEFINITION OF COMPETENCY

Competence is a combination of knowledge, attributes and situational judgment that are required to perform a job.

To achieve competence in a particular job, a person should be able to apply knowledge and aptitudes in context to perform various tasks or skills at a target proficiency level.

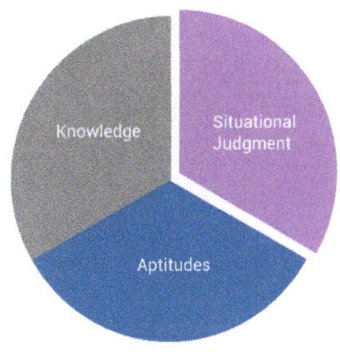

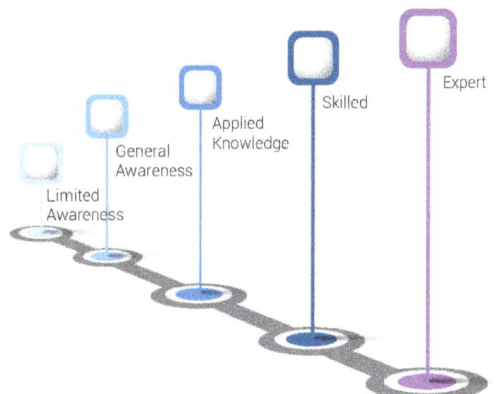

Figure 8-23 Definition of competency (ASI Institute).

Competencies of the Future Needed Now

In essence, global megatrends are bringing about an environment of radical and accelerated change, where organizational competencies that will be required in the future are remarkably different from those that have been sought in recent years. This is especially the case because many jobs will be significantly different.

A recent report by Deloitte indicated that 47% of today's jobs would not exist in 10 years.[40] Common wisdom relates this issue mainly to the impact of robotics, but actually the main undercurrent is the replacement of "goods production jobs" by "service jobs". Most informed observers actually do not see a major reduction in the level of employment, but rather a form of structural change in the nature of the required competencies. For example, one of the fundamental theories of Malone (already cited) is that long before computers will replace humans, there will be extended periods of humans and machines working together to accomplish new tasks and meet competency requirements.

A large amount of material has been published about what the competencies of the future will be. One of the best inventories of these new requirements has been developed by the Institute for the Future (IFTF) and is depicted in Figure 8-24.[41]

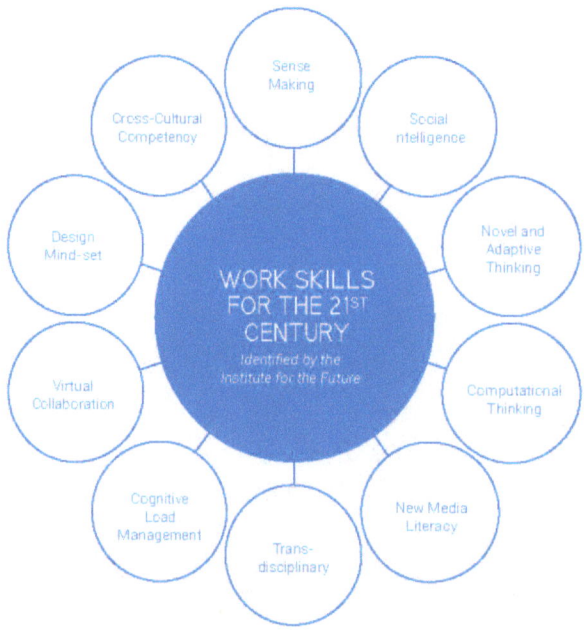

Figure 8-24 Work skills/competencies for the twenty-first century (IFTF).

Of the skills identified by the IFTF, some warrant special attention in the context of this book:

- *Sense Making:* distinguishes humans from computers and is essential in support of quality decision-making.

- *Social Intelligence:* is essential to quality team cooperation in different settings.

- *Trans-disciplinarity:* the ability to recognize the value of working across disciplines to develop richness of perspectives.

- *Cognitive Load Management:* the ability to focus when inundated by data.

- *Cross-Cultural Competency:* the aptitude to work efficiently with people of different origins and values.

When considering the nature of air transportation and its likely evolution under the influence of global megatrends, some specific competencies are of special relevance and should be cultivated as *domains of expertise* within future-wise aviation enterprises:

- Systems thinking.

- Foresight, mind mapping, and scenario planning.

- Visionary leadership.

- Performance-based management (across the board).

- Predictive analytics and decision support systems, including the development and use of simulations.

- Robotics.

- Human-machine interface.

- Passenger experience management, including knowing your future customers (Canton and Haines, previously cited).

- Distributed management systems.

- Business Intelligence.

- Risk management.

- Competency-building master planning (as a strategic endeavor and the core function of human capital management).

- Upgrading of multi-cultural teamwork.

- Project management (including multidisciplinary resourcing as an organizational practice).

- Knowledge transfer management (or *knowledge exchange* as per the World Bank), including the establishment of communities of practice.

URGENCY

According to the World Economic Forum, by 2022:

"no less than 54% of all employees [worldwide] will require significant re- and upskilling. Of these, about 35% are expected to require additional training of up to six months, 9% will require reskilling lasting six to 12 months, while 10% will require additional skills training of more than a year. Skills continuing to grow in prominence by 2022 include analytical thinking and innovation as well as active learning and learning strategies".

(WEF, "The Future of Jobs Report, 2018". Insight Report, Center for the New Economy and Society, 2018)

Acquiring Competencies of the Future: The Learning Organization

The consideration of the competencies of the future as discussed above raises the question of how one acquires such skills and expertise. Unfortunately, the verdict of the majority of experts in foresight and futurology is that the global education system is grossly inadequate. In the report, "Future of Skills: Employment in 2030", the authors highlight the "divergence between the pace of change and the inertia of our institutions"[42], as well as "a forty-year gap between experts who are exploring where the world of work and where the state of learning will need to be in fifteen years' time"[43]. Canton (cited earlier) summarized the situation by indicating that the education system and the curriculum today are out-of-sync with the real world. In his opinion, we should focus more on "critical thinking, reasoning, collaboration, problem solving, and logic".

One thing is sure: future-wise organizations must be "learning organizations". The concept was best described by Peter Senge in his book, "The Fifth Discipline: The Art and Practice of the Learning Organization". In it he refers to an organization that is in constant search of improvement and is led by inspiring visionaries that value systemic thinking, learning, and teamwork.[44]

As Sadler (cited earlier) explained, "One competency is common to all competency models for the future: LEARNING". Actually, this is the whole thesis of this book. Megatrends and their impacts require organizations to be "agile" if they are to succeed and thrive, and *Agility* requires constant *Learning.*

Competency-Building Master Plans

In aviation, the approach to a competency framework can best be implemented through the development of *competency-building master plans* (CBMPs) that should be formulated at the global, state, industry sub-sector, and enterprise levels. Typically, in air transportation, performance gaps, which are frequently identified through mandated audits, pertain largely to human capital issues and often relate to managerial competency concerns. The elements of a CBMP for a national civil aviation sector can be illustrated as shown in Figure 8-25.

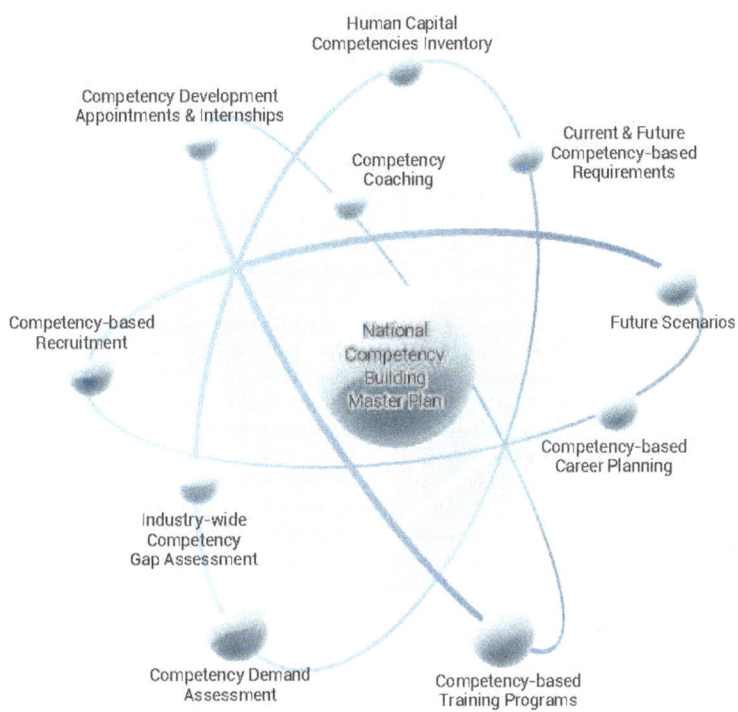

Figure 8-25 National competency-building master plan—aviation sector: Airlines, airports, air navigation service providers, regulators, policy-makers (ASI Institute).

CBMPs constitute an emerging best practice and an improvement over traditional, often poorly justified training plans. A key distinctive feature of CBMPs is that the training activities that they incorporate relate directly to organizational performance targets where corresponding returns on investment (ROI) must be justified. As a policy, under a CBMP framework, no training activity can be undertaken if it does not directly contribute to meeting fully rationalized competency requirements.

Developing a competency-building master plan involves a number of steps that can be grouped into four main activity categories:

Guiding Principles	Performance Needs Assessment
• Link to corporate vision	• Determination of competency requirements
• Clearly articulated outcomes	• Formal competency assessment
• Inherent organizational values	• Gap analysis
• Learning organization	• Background and data analysis
	• Forecast analysis
	• Processes and procedures analysis
	• Task analysis
	• Benchmarking

Implementation	Impact Measurement
• Competency-based training	• Impact on mission and bottom line
• Competency-based coaching	• Organizational performance
• Assignments and internships	• Customer satisfaction
• Design and development plan	• Employee satisfaction
• Competency development resourcing plan	• Return on investment
• Time frame	

Competency-building master plans constitute a fundamental element of a performance-based organizational culture, and as such they should:

- Address all levels of an organization, namely, frontline, middle, and executive management, in an interrelated manner.

- Integrate targeted management and technical competencies.

- Incorporate a structured plan for both internal and external training activities that provides access to relevant managerial best practices, whether from the target industrial sector or from pertinent areas of excellence in other industries.

- Focus on achieving organizational performance with reference to contextually meaningful and recognized best practices.

- Feature a "coaching" dimension in all key functional areas to ensure that concepts and tools get implemented to the fullest possible extent.

- Link formally and transparently to succession planning programs.

- Identify anticipated returns on investment (ROI) clearly for each competency-building activity that is included in the Plan with a realistic, meaningful measure of its success.

- Promote systems thinking and the elimination of functional-silo perspectives.

- Include a competency assessment system (CAS) that integrates a battery of work-related situational simulations and psychometric tests that aim to identify the development requirements of learners, determine their progress, and support the mapping of their career paths within the organization.

One of the key consequences for organizations that use a competency-based framework to develop and manage their human resources is the effective positioning of human capital as a strategic asset. CBMPs have the advantage of allowing the treatment of the human element as a critical organizational resource on the same footing as financial assets and infrastructure, including equipment and systems.

The methodical and transparent rationalization of human resources investments matched with competencies that are a direct function of organizational strategic objectives has a beneficial effect. It positions the HR function at the senior executive (CXO) table. As a result, backward thinking that often leads to systematic cuts in training, hiring freezes, pay restrictions, and layoffs during a downturn period becomes highly questionable as a tactical response. In some cases, mitigating measures might even require new investments in human resources.

Competency Assessment Systems

There are three competency-building activities that organizations must deal with: elaboration of competency profiles, assessment of competency gaps, and development of strategies to close these gaps. Of these three, there is no doubt that the main challenge pertains to the systematic determination of competency gaps.

Most organizations rely on annual performance appraisals, which can be optimized by adopting a well-structured process, using comprehensive criteria and rating scales, and including review committees. However, this approach still incorporates a high degree of subjectivity. One way to mitigate this situation is to supplement the performance appraisal process with the use of a wide-ranging validated competency assessment system.

Figure 8-26 Airport Management Competency Assessment Test (ASI Institute).

One such system was developed by the ASI Institute. It was the result of two years of research into the specifics of functional performance requirements, testing, and proto-typing by a team of subject matter experts and industrial psychologists. Through that process, the Institute developed a validated instrument as a tool for assessing the compe-tencies of senior-level airport management personnel for the purpose of recommending related human capital developmental strategies.

The "Airport Management Competency Assessment Test" (AMCAT) measures knowl-edge, aptitudes and situational judgment and allows for individual or group testing as well as benchmarking. Interestingly, it also assesses the degree of "silo thinking" that is present at the individual and team level. Although it is administered online, it is a fairly sophisticated, statistically validated tool that requires expert interpretation of the results. From a systems perspective, it would be useful if similar instruments could also be developed for the managerial staff of airlines, air navigation services, and regulatory agencies.

Agile Organizational Culture

Background Perspective

It goes without saying that the relative unpredictability of new business environments on the horizon, especially for the medium to long term, are characterized by TUNA con-ditions as defined earlier. Accordingly, organizations will have to be very flexible as they prepare for the future. They need to be able to adapt quickly or face dire consequences. At the same time, this does not mean that everything has to be in a constant state of flux or chaos. What is required is a combination of being constantly aware of plausible future scenarios coupled with understanding their implications, to which they must respond to with constant agility.

Agility

Agility is essentially the ability of an organization to quickly transform itself and adjust in response to changes in the business environment. A strong agility posture will help enterprises or governmental entities to react successfully to the emergence of sudden and even radical shifts in overall contextual conditions.

In many instances, traditionally successful organizations have not yet adopted agility as a full-fledged practice. They frequently operate in silos and are entrenched in linear planning. They have not yet made the "agility shift", which has been defined by Pamela Meyer as "the intentional development of the competence, capacity, and confidence to learn, adapt, and innovate in changing contexts for sustainable success"; organizations that adapt are typically "responsive, resilient, resourceful, reflective and relevant".[45] Empirical research already indicates that truly agile organizations consistently display results that are superior to the norm. Some of the benefits of this agility were compiled as a result of an extensive survey of more than 1000 organizations conducted by the Project Management Institute (see Figure 8-27).

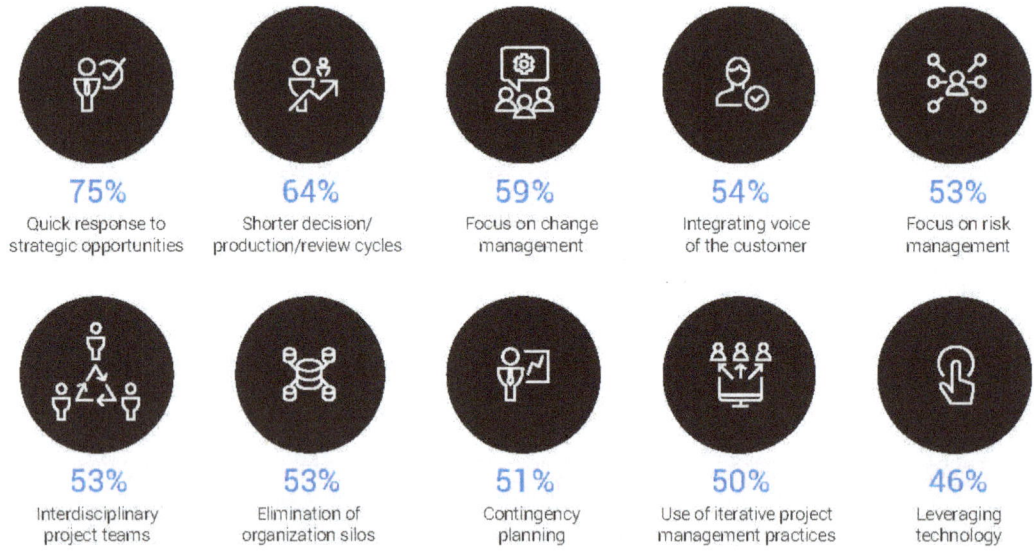

Figure 8-27 Benefits to organizations that operate as agile organizations (Project Management Institute, 2012).

Fundamentally, organizational agility is implemented by abandoning traditional organizational structures in favor of a managerial approach based on a "project team" *modus operandi*. The rapid response capability to changing environmental conditions is based on establishing a structure made up of a multitude of small multidisciplinary special-purpose teams. According to Price and Toye, such properly empowered teams are the engines of the organization and become critical to the delivery of high-performance results.[46]

As shown in Figure 8-28, McKinsey & Company have graphically illustrated the intent of the shift in managerial approach needed to move to an agile organization.

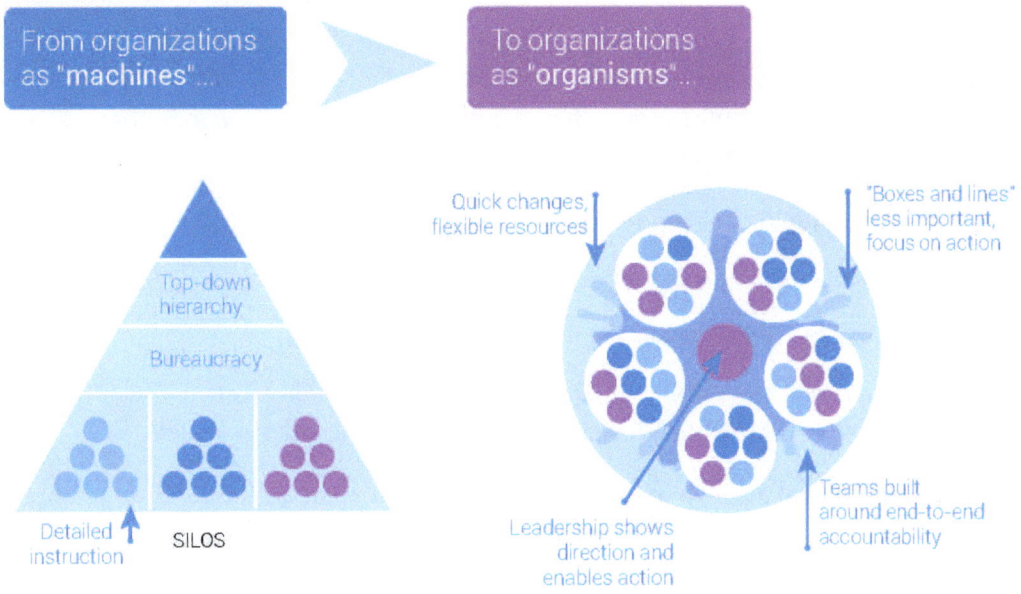

Figure 8-28 "The McKinsey agile tribe—Organizations as machines to organizations as organisms", McKinsey & Company, 2017).

Interestingly, in the context of this book, of 19 Industries surveyed by McKinsey in the *Travel, Transport, and Logistics* sector on the subject matter of agility shift, respondents perceived the instability of their business environment as relatively low, with only about 24% of them reporting that organization-wide agile transformations were underway; the lowest level of agility shift among the groups surveyed.[47] In another study, Deloitte found that, based on a sample of over ten thousand business executives and human resources professionals, a very large proportion of interviewees considered "agility and collaboration" critical to their organization's success, but only 6% were of the opinion that their entities were currently "highly agile."[48]

Still, in spite of some degree of denial about the future and the major, albeit ill-defined, impact of global megatrends, there is an abundance of literature on how to achieve organizational agility by applying the following: clarity of purpose, performance focus, autonomous teams, operational simplicity, rapid response, ongoing learning, relentless innovation, technology road-mapping, empowerment of young leaders, cross-functional collaboration, and culture-promoting partnerships.

Agility and Aviation

There are specific challenges ahead in the aviation sector that will involve global megatrends, including exponential urban change and climate change, among others. These challenges will require aviation organizations to shift to an agility posture where they can:

- Be capable of rapid decision-making.

- Have ready access to capital as needed.

- Be self-financing to the maximum extent feasible.

- Have the ability to take some types of investment risk, whether it is on Design-at-Risk for assets or on commercial decisions on a return-on-investment basis.

The shift in the global aviation industry over the past 20 years towards full, meaningful commercialization and privatization needs to continue. Aviation executives in government entities will need to educate political leaders on the accelerating pace of change and its potential significance with regard to performance.

Agility For Airports As An Example

The future-ready organization will have assets that are agile, resilient and flexible. Some high-performance airlines are already positioned for this. For airports and air navigation services providers, however, the challenges are much greater. Because of their long design, acquisition, and construction cycles, meeting these three criteria involves:

- Future-ready master planning;

- Design-at-risk;

- Intelligent phasing; and

- Land banking.

Future-Ready Master Planning

Infrastructure planning for airports and ANS organizations is already a well-structured process. A future-ready approach, however, will draw on the systems and processes of the future-ready organization to improve its planning of facilities. Scenario planning will drive its forecasts, including consideration of megatrend impacts, and predictive analytics will allow refined assessment of impacts.

Typical facility master plans look forward 25 to 30 years. Within that window, for example, sea levels are forecast to rise 40 to 70 cm. For coastal areas, this can potentially mean that 100-year storm events will now be 20- or 25-year events (and in some areas, as frequent as annually) [15]. There are many airports around the world in coastal areas, including some of the busiest. The impact of this on airports in the coastal zones can be expected to be dramatic. As was pointed out in Chapter 2, there are 64 airports in coastal areas less than 120 cm above sea level. A future-ready planning approach will consider megatrends, develop scenarios, extract meaningful potential impacts, develop risk assessments, and plan for mitigation and protective actions.

Design-at-Risk

One of the most frequent failures of infrastructure-based aviation enterprises is the inability to provide sufficient capacity under conditions of rapid growth. The reasons for this are both structural and planning weaknesses. The structural constraints are discussed in more detail in the section on Structure. The planning failures involve poor forecasting and a linkage of expansion decisions to time frames, not activity levels. An agile organization will have:

- Effective scenario-based demand forecasts;

- Trigger points based on planning activity levels;

- The ability and willingness to move to design at an early stage to have "shovel-ready" expansion plans;

- Processes and authorities that enable pre-qualification and rapid tendering for construction.

The early move to design requires the authority to spend significant investment funds on design, with the knowledge that some changes may need to be made before construction.

Intelligent Phasing

Intelligent phasing goes hand in hand with design-at-risk. It requires facility designs that consider phasing from the outset and for a planned approach to phasing that addresses the minimum acceptable time between phases. Obviously, no enterprise wants to undergo the disruption of continuous construction, but the more phases of development that can be planned and the smaller the interval in between, the more agile and flexible the infrastructure will be. For airports that have used this approach, a typical phasing can look like 3 years of construction, followed by 5 to 7 years of use, followed by another construction phase.

Land Banking

Clearly, one of the largest single challenges for airports facing the systemic pressures of megatrends will be the availability and cost of land for expansion of new airports. Land banking can provide a way forward, although like design-at-risk, it requires the authority and willingness to commit potentially large sums of capital well in advance of possible need. With the reluctance of users to fund far into the future, this points to a role for governments in creating these land banks. The exclusive right of governments to the rights of expropriation or eminent domain also point to government participation. This does not automatically imply a permanent taxpayer commitment. At the appropriate time, as demand warrants, the banked land can be sold to the airport.

Not all locations have this potential, but some do. Sydney and Toronto provide useful illustrations. In Sydney, a second airport has been planned since the 1940s and the land banked for this second airport at Badgerys Creek, but the decision on development has been continuously postponed until recently. In 1985, traffic at SYD was only 9.2 million enplaned/deplaned passengers. By 2016, traffic had increased to 41.6 million passengers. Only in 2018 did development work start on this second airport.

In Toronto, land for a second airport east of the city was banked at Pickering in 1972 and remains banked until traffic levels will support development.

Partnership-Building Organization

In today's context, a major component of organizational sustainability is known as the *"Ability to Partner"*. The notion here is twofold: just as a team of people will outperform any individual effort, complementary organizations working together should achieve superior results, even more so if the environment in which they operate is uncertain and the level of risk can be reduced through cooperative arrangements.

With the risks confronting organizations and the opportunities that become available to them, and with an ever-accelerating future unfolding, it is increasingly difficult for organizations to successfully move forward. It is clear that success in going forward requires partnerships with others, be it through cooperation with firms offering complementary services or products, suppliers, customers, or even with competitors in certain instances.

As discussed in Chapter 7, which focused on the *Global Connectedness* megatrend, the world is moving towards a future where information, people, things, and systems will all be fully interconnected. This backdrop makes it easy to understand that leading organizations will be defined by their relationships and mainly by their partnerships or alliances. Agile organizations will also want to further excel by sharing expertise, intelligence, risks, and opportunities.

Some of the key criteria for successful partnerships have been identified by Altreya Consulting and are graphically presented in Figure 8-29.

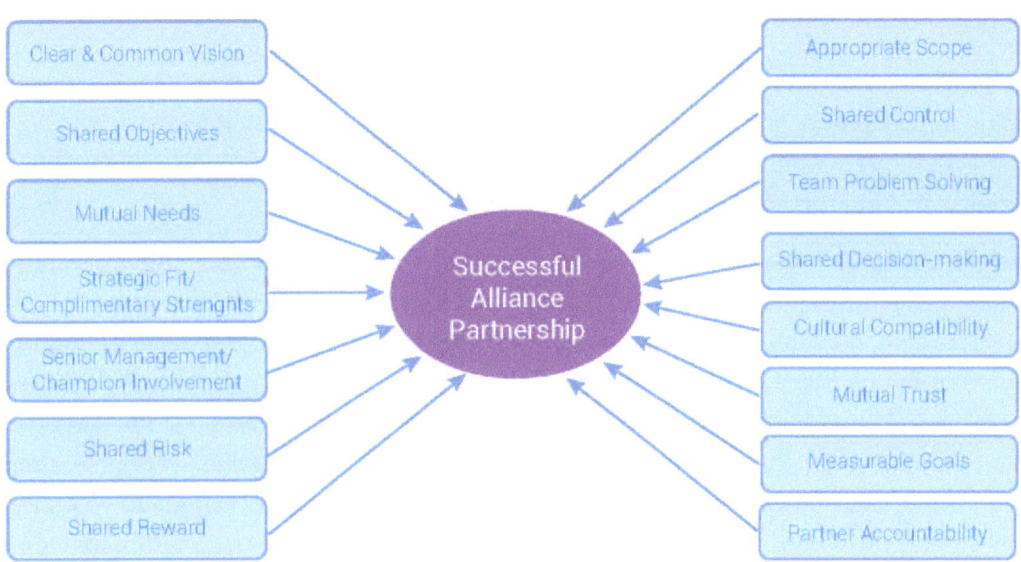

Figure 8-29 Critical success factors for successful partnerships and alliances (adapted from Altreya Consulting).

Collaborative partnerships build value by designing and delivering services, products, and solutions that benefit the entities involved in a formal relationship. Ramirez and Mannervik have written about the importance of value co-creation in their book, "Strategy for A Networked World". In it, they place strategy design in the context of an ever more "interconnected and uncertain world". They present the role of strategists as one of "... designers of interactions and of the value-creating systems (VCSs) that these interactions entail and bring forth".[49] They explain that a properly designed system of relationships enables those involved to come together and create value. This ties together the notions of megatrends, scenario planning, uncertainty, partnerships, and value creation, as elements of strategic endeavor.

Agile organizations also emphasize partnerships with the recipients of their services or the customers of their products. The special nature of this type of relationship is described at length by Ray McKenzie in his book "The Relationship-Based Enterprise"[50]. Quality relationships with customers are nurtured to evolve from a *Vendor/Supplier* interaction to a *Trusted Advisor* situation and eventually into a *Trusted Partner* role. Under TUNA conditions, agile organizations that entertain a close collaborative rapport with their customers will be in a better position to read "early warning signs" of the direction in which the business environment might be moving, thereby enhancing the development of plausible and informative scenarios of the future.

In summary, well-founded and well-designed organizational partnerships ensure more value for customers and reduce the level of risk for all parties involved.

Agility and Partnerships in Aviation—The Case of AirAsia

As discussed earlier in this chapter, the three fundamental parameters that define an *"Agile Organization"* are the ability to adapt quickly to critical changes in the business environment, dedication to ongoing learning across the board, and a belief in the high value of partnerships. These characteristics are all present in the fascinating success story of AirAsia as a contemporary example of a future-wise organization; one that operates in terms of agility and stresses ongoing learning as a core value. Of course, there are always risks associated with being on the edge of the future, but for 10 years in a row now, AirAsia has been named the world's best low-cost carrier by Skytrax, including its latest award for 2018.[51] This has put it ahead of other successful carriers in the same category such as Norwegian, easyJet, and Southwest Airlines.

AirAsia Berhad is headquartered near Kuala Lumpur, Malaysia. It is the largest airline in Malaysia by fleet, size, and destinations. AirAsia Group operates scheduled domestic and international flights to more than 165 destinations spanning 25 countries. Its main hub is klia2, the low-cost carrier terminal at Kuala Lumpur International Airport (KLIA). Its affiliate airlines Thai AirAsia, Indonesia AirAsia, Philippines AirAsia, and AirAsia India have hubs in Don Mueang International Airport (Bangkok), Soekarno-Hatta International Airport (Jakarta), Ninoy Aquino International Airport (Manila), and Kempegowda International Airport (Bangalore) respectively, while its sister airline, AirAsia X, focuses on long-haul routes.

AirAsia operates with the world's lowest unit cost of US$0.023 per available seat-kilometer (ASK) and a passenger breakeven load factor of 52%. It has hedged 100% of its fuel requirements for the next three years, achieves an aircraft turnaround time of 25 minutes, has a crew productivity level that is better than that of Malaysia Airlines, and has an average aircraft utilization rate of 13 hours a day. In 2007, The New York Times described the airline as a "pioneer" of low-cost travel in Asia. AirAsia is the sponsor of Malaysia national football, the Singapore national football team, and Queens Park Rangers (Australia), as well as a former sponsor of Manchester United.

(Source: *https://en.wikipedia.org/wiki/AirAsia*, retrieved October 22, 2018)

AirAsia exhibits all the characteristics of a *"Partnership-Based Agile Enterprise".* The airline is anchored by the leadership of Tan Sri Anthony Francis Fernandes, who founded it as the first budget no-frills airline in Malaysia. His vision that *"Now everyone can fly"* became the mainstay of its initial promotional campaign. AirAsia promotes the use of small teams to run its business. It assembles small, highly skilled, empowered groups of employees to tackle priority tasks, and it promotes creativity. The new AirAsia Headquarters, "RedQ", is designed to facilitate human interaction and teamwork.

The airline is highly innovative, as exemplified by several initiatives such as:

- Partnership with Google - to become a "data-first" business and is executing a five-year plan to become a digital airline.[52]

- Partnership with Airbus - AirAsia Group has confirmed that its existing and future A320 and A330 fleet will be powered by Airbus' Skywise Predictive Maintenance Services. According to Airbus, AirAsia currently has around 230 aircraft in service, as well as 66 A330neos and more than 400 A320/A321neos yet to be delivered, and all of them will be maintained by Airbus Skywise.[53]

Figure 8-30 AirAsia headquarters (courtesy of AirAsia).

- OURSHOP – AirAsia recently announced the launch of OURSHOP, a new digital marketplace designed to connect international travelers with airport, high-end, and local specialist retailers. This pioneering initiative seeks to turn the digital and e-commerce challenge into opportunity, linking the consumer with multiple marketing and shopping touchpoints throughout the travel journey.[54]

All in all, leadership plays a major role in the success of AirAsia. The culture implemented by Tony Fernandes has inspired his staff, and his hands-on approach, including in difficult times, has earned the admiration of many within and outside the company. A case in point was his direct involvement in the hours following the QZ8501 tragedy, when he flew to Surabaya, Indonesia, immediately after the incident to speak to the families, his employees, and the media. In his recent book, *"Flying High – My Story to QPR"*, he said, "From great tragedy to smaller annoyances, the only way to gain trust and enhance your reputation and to get better is to be open and truthful. Apparently, our handling of the loss of flight QZ8501 and the 167 passengers and crew has been the subject of some academic papers on 'Crisis Management.' In such tragic circumstances, you can only hope that some good will come of it. If AirAsia's reaction to the terrible, terrible loss of life is helpful to others, then maybe that's a contribution."[55]

HOW IT WORKS?

An online retail store that focuses on exclusive items, anchored on best value.
Product offerings are dynamic to the flown routes.

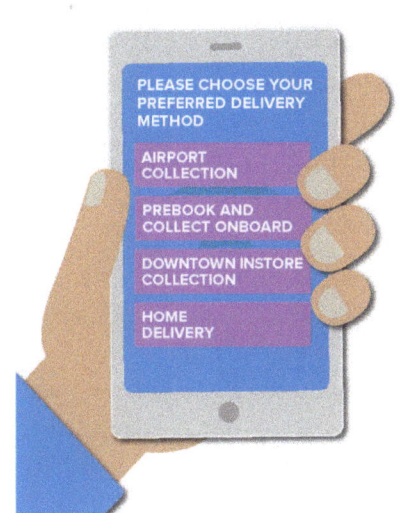

AIRPORT COLLECTION

Taking advantage of airport retailers
This enables guest to shop inflight
and collect their items upon landing.

PREBOOK & COLLECT ONBOARD

Special travel retail items
Currently available on
selected routes.

DOWNTOWN INSTORE COLLECTION

Taking advantage of local retailers
This enables guest to collect
downtown instore; thus creating
extra foot fall to the stores.

HOME DELIVERY

Partnerships with external
merchants to support home
delivery.

Figure 8-31   AirAsia OURSHOP (courtesy of AirAsia).

FUTURE-WISE AVIATION ORGANIZATIONS: READINESS ASSESSMENT

Managing smartly towards the future is a major challenge. As discussed earlier, in order to be *"future-wise"*, organizations need to be proactive and excel in eight areas: systems thinking, future-wise strategic management, scenario planning, data analytics, risk analysis, competency-based human capital management, organizational agility, and partnership building.

Often, organizations tend to tackle one or more of these issues on an *ad-hoc* basis, but they rarely address the full set of performance factors together. Following is a set of "assessment checklists" organized by target areas of excellence that were developed to allow an organization to evaluate its degree of "readiness" as a future-wise organization. The assessment criteria range from 1 (very poor) to 5 (excellent), and the corresponding performance levels are described for each area.

Future-Wise Readiness Assessment Checklists

✓	⊛ Systems Thinking	*(1=Poor, 5=Excellent)*
☐	1	*The organization operates on the basis of specialized areas of functional expertise. It suffers from a "silo" mentality. It is difficult for employees and the management team to see the "big picture". Only the CEO understands the multitude of variables that come into play for achieving the best results.*
☐	2	*A relatively large group of managers within the organization are aware that a "silo" mentality exists and that this is detrimental to the achievement of optimal results. There is no formal overall action plan to correct the situation.*
☐	3	*Action plans have been developed to break down pure functional perspectives and instill more systems thinking within the organization. There is a marked increase in the number of multi-disciplinary committees and the number of projects they work on.*
☐	4	*Managers are able to map out the organizational processes required, across functional areas of expertise, to achieve desired corporate outcomes. Employees understand what they need to contribute to the success of the organization, even though ongoing efforts are required to prioritize common goals over divisional objectives.*
☐	5	*The management team understands the broad context within which the organization operates. Megatrends are monitored together with their potential implications for the specific vision and mission as well as the overall challenges and opportunities that they might bring about for the organization. The management team is able to explain these considerations to employees. All involved see the value of cooperating across functional areas to achieve organizational objectives.*

| ✔ | 🌐 **Future-Wise Strategic Management** | *(1=Poor, 5=Excellent)* |

1. *The Strategic Plan needs to be updated. The latest version is at least five years old; many things have changed in the business environment, and there are many new members of the management team. The organization is looking at retaining an external consultant to draft a new Plan for consideration.*

2. *An external consultant produced/updated the Strategic Plan. Numerous meetings were conducted to discuss many aspects of the plan, including strengths, weaknesses, opportunities, and threats (SWOTs). Issues regarding the implementation of strategic objectives were identified. Things are moving too slowly, and it is felt that many managers show disinterest regarding the strategic management initiatives. Consideration of creating a dedicated Strategic Planning Unit within the organization is required.*

3. *In an effort led by the CEO, a full Strategic Review was conducted. Working groups on key topics were established, and there is a strong focus on how to best achieve the Mission and Vision. An external consultant was used to assist in the review process. SWOTs were re-examined as well as the relationships with customers/stakeholders. Implementation and accountability have proven to be a struggle as the need for strategy review is evolving and ongoing.*

4. *A new Strategic Business Plan exists. The review effort was led by the CEO, but the Plan is a product of an organization-wide effort. A more efficient implementation management system is now in place. Accountabilities for results are clear, and resources are delegated accordingly. The challenges now reside in better ongoing reading of the external environment and becoming more proactive about making necessary adjustments quickly when required. Much more emphasis is put on developing scenarios of the future and analyzing potential implications.*

5. *The approach to Strategic Management is the result of an organization-wide effort. Management and staff contribute fully to the formulation/updating of the Strategic Business Plan. Strategy formulation/management is not delegated to a special-purpose unit; it is everyone's business. The approach is based on a continuous monitoring of megatrends and how they might affect the contextual and transactional environments. Plausible scenarios of the future are developed which are updated on a regular basis. These scenarios serve as the foundation of the entire strategy development process. They allow for regular review of the organizational mission and vision. The strategy drives the formulation of action plans and the assignment of responsibilities and accountabilities for results. There is a need to manage for performance and use key performance indicators wisely. All that is done gets coordinated through the strategic business planning process, which incorporates inputs and contributions from across the organization. The strategy is well thought through, but it is flexible because the organization strives to be "agile". There is a need to generate sustainable "value" for all customers/stakeholders, directly, or in partnership.*

✓	🖵 Scenario Planning	(1=Poor, 5=Excellent)

☐	1	*Scenarios are not developed for the future. Instead there is a need to concentrate on monitoring the market and the wishes of customers/stakeholders. Organizational priorities are established accordingly.*
☐	2	*The organization has been refining its approach to strategic management and now incorporates some scenarios related to how it anticipates the business environment to be evolving. A consultant has been retained to help with this process and advise the newly created strategic planning unit. The organization believes that it will now be able to react more rapidly to changing conditions.*
☐	3	*Scenario planning has been used for a while as part of the organizational strategic management process. The strategic planning department develops scenarios in conjunction with the regular review of strengths, weaknesses, opportunities, and threats (SWOT analysis). Narrative descriptions are produced of what are deemed as optimistic, pessimistic, and most likely scenarios resulting from reading the market/ framework within which the organization operates, and probabilities are assigned to these. Organizational action plans are developed accordingly.*
☐	4	*Contemporary best practices in scenario planning have been researched, and the organization has started to modify its approach in this area. The concept of "plausible" scenarios is replacing the notion of "probable" scenarios. More key people are involved in the development of scenarios (i.e., the formulation of scenarios is not solely restricted to the Strategy Planning department). Variables are considered in both the transactional and contextual environments to produce the scenarios.*
☐	5	*Properly researched and formulated scenarios are of paramount importance to sustainable success of the organization. Therefore, the rapid acquisition of strong expertise in the development of plausible scenarios of the future under TUNA conditions (i.e., turbulence, uncertainty, novelty, and ambiguity) is required. Scenarios are developed by multidisciplinary teams from staff in various departments supplemented by outside subject-matter experts (SMEs) as needed. Scenarios are linked to the anticipated evolution of the macro environment and factor in relevant aspects of global megatrends. They are reframed and revised on a regular basis because they are critical to the formulation of organizational strategy, including the mission and vision. The scenarios make use of some inputs from the risk assessment and predictive analytics undertakings. People within the organization are conscious of the importance of scenario planning as an area of excellence and of the related benefits.*

✓	📦 **Data Analytics**	*(1=Poor, 5=Excellent)*
☐	1	*There is no good understanding of what data analytics is about in practical terms. Too much data can be perceived as confusing and as slowing down the decision-making process. There is no belief or "buy-in" in the value of costly management information systems.*
☐	2	*There is a belief that the data currently accessible is of poor quality or simply irrelevant. Better information is required relative to the business environment and evolving trends. The development of relevant key performance indicators (KPIs) and getting timely information on how things are functioning are critical. The data used also need to be cleaned.*
☐	3	*There is currently no data analytics strategy beyond limited and sketchy ideas. Systems "use-cases" are developed for data analytics with the help of external subject-matter experts. There is consideration of hiring data specialists. The organization is looking at which applications could generate short-term benefits based on feasibility and impact.*
☐	4	*A strategic framework has been developed defining how the organization can optimize the way it uses data as part of its decision-making processes. The hiring of data specialists is required. The analysis of use-cases specific to the enterprise has been completed, and the organization is already leveraging data in a number of priority areas. The organization intends to rapidly develop its competency in predictive analytics. Unfortunately, analytics expertise is not yet fully in sync with the business operations, but the organization is working to correct the situation.*
☐	5	*Data is considered a strategic asset. A Chief Data Officer (CDO) position has been established, and data specialists are employed to develop tools to monitor the key performance indicators, analyze trends, and elaborate what-if scenarios. Predictive analytics is an area of excellence for the organization. High importance is placed on effective data visualization. The organization is accelerating the use of artificial intelligence in areas such as customer /stakeholder experience and operations.*

| ✓ | Risk Analysis | (1=Poor, 5=Excellent) |

1. *Within the organization, risk analysis work is mainly related to the implementation of safety standards and related best practices. There is some thinking about expanding risk management practices into other areas of the business, but management is not yet fully aware of all key risk factors that might impact the organization; more research in this area needs to be conducted.*

2. *The organization adheres to the regulated safety requirements and the related incident reporting and management procedures. Risk assessments are also conducted in conjunction with the financial management process, especially at the time of budget formulation (i.e., Capital and O&M). There is a need to better utilize the risk assessments for determination and especially for implementation of mitigation measures.*

3. *The organization is expanding the risk assessment process outside the financial management and safety management streams. Risk assessments apply at various stages such as the introduction of a new process or significant changes to an existing process. These apply to changes such as major changes in the use of physical plant and equipment as well as for new infrastructure at the conception, planning and design, construction, commissioning, handover, and use phases.*

4. *Risk management is important for the organization. It is progressively becoming an integral part of managerial processes. The management team is trained in the area of risk management in order to expand the awareness of all types of risks and their implications. Work is progressing with insurance brokers to further define the organization's operational risks; however, risk management is not yet formally applied to the formulation of the organizational strategy and related action plans. A risk assessment unit has recently been created and has been tasked with the development of risk management policies. Risk assessment techniques are being introduced such as "sensitivity analysis", "suns & clouds charts", and "composite risk index".*

5. *Risk Analysis is considered as one of the strong areas of excellence of the organization. The practice is embedded in all activities and deals with all types of risks, including those of an operational, financial, and reputational nature. In-house risk management SMEs exist to provide support to management and project teams. All investment decisions undergo a go/no-go risk assessment and consider mitigation measures. The approach to risk always considers "potential impact" and "manageability". Risk analysis has been linked with the assignment of probabilities to short-term scenarios.*

✓ 📖 Competency-Based Human Capital Management *(1=Poor, 5=Excellent)*

1   *The Human Resources function reports to the VP Finance and/or Administration. A Training Plan exists which is updated annually based on requests from the various departments of the organization and/or organizational priorities.*

2   *Job descriptions/associated qualification requirements for all key positions in the organization have been revised and are used to make the annual training plans more relevant. The Finance Department is analyzing the ROI of all training programs.*

3   *Training plans are quite comprehensive and take job requirements into account, but complaints are received from functional units that they are not responsive enough to operational needs. Moreover, from time to time, training programs need to be cut when the organization faces budget constraints. When this happens, it is often difficult to determine which programs should be cut or reduced in scope. The organization is studying how it could introduce a competency-based approach to the management of human resources, looking into industry best practices in place at similar organizations.*

4   *Work has commenced on defining the competencies currently required for each job in the organization. This work is performed by the HR department in cooperation with all functional units of the organization. Employee performance appraisals are also analyzed annually. Appraisal results serve as the basis of training and succession plans that are reviewed and approved by the Board of Management as submitted by the Senior VP of HR, who reports directly to the CEO.*

5   *The entire organization has been defined in terms of competency requirements taking into account industry best practices as well as the specific business environment. There is an assessment of the relevant impacts of megatrends on future competency requirements. The organization strives to hire, develop, and retain the best people against its competency framework. Human capital is an organization's most important asset. A comprehensive competency-building master plan (CBMP) has been developed; competency assessment tools are used together with employee performance appraisals as inputs to the plan. Extensive use of problem-based learning is implemented in training programs to make them highly relevant to real-life situations. Competency-building activities are customized to a specific context. Teamwork is prioritized as an organizational value.*

✓	🔲 Agile Organizational Culture	(1=Poor, 5=Excellent)

🔲	1	*The organization is highly structured and based on functional areas of expertise. Detailed delineation of functional responsibilities is in place. The mission and vision have remained the same for five years or more. Staff turnover is high. A relatively slow decision-making process exists. The organization often suffers from insufficient capacity or low levels of service because investment in assets or infrastructure involves a complex and/or slow approval process. Staff members know their roles well, but are not fully aware of the responsibilities of other organizational units. The organization operates too much in silos and lacks proper coordination on many issues.*
🔲	2	*The organization seems to suffer from a lack of responsiveness in view of the changing business environment. There is a need to make adjustments. The decision-making cycle is too long, and decisions are made on the basis of limited information. There are long-term investment plans, but decision-making on these investments is cumbersome.*
🔲	3	*Major adjustments are required to the way the organization operates. Too many opportunities are missed, and the organization is running into issues with its various stakeholders. The organization is studying the concept of "agile organizations" and examining best practices in this area.*
🔲	4	*The organization is actively pursuing a shift in its organizational culture, going from a traditional multi-level to a more flat-type structure. A detailed work plan is being implemented to help the organization evolve into an "agile" posture. An external consultant has been retained to provide guidance through the change process and assist with the buy-in from staff.*
🔲	5	*The organization has a clear common purpose. People are the most important asset. Work is carried out on a project basis. The organizational structure is defined by a network of teams that are empowered and accountable for achieving their mandates. Project teams are multi-disciplinary and incorporate pertinent functional expertise. Results are emphasized over structure. The changing business environment is actively monitored. The organization learns constantly and makes decisions quickly. It incorporates scenario-based thinking into asset and infrastructure planning and can move quickly to provide additional capacity, new services, and new technologies. Excellent technology-enabled decision-support systems exist. The organization is good at anticipating and innovating. Staff turnover is relatively low.*

✓	⊗ Partnership Building Organization	(1=Poor, 5=Excellent)
☐	1	*The organization operates in a tough business environment. Competitors and stakeholders are constantly challenging the organization in the achievement of its mission. Strong expertise exists in-house, and it is believed that there is little value in pursuing time-consuming and complex partnerships. The organization's policy is to hire all the expertise required and rely on the core strengths of the company to ensure success.*
☐	2	*The organization has a good reputation, but it cannot seem to capture all the opportunities that come its way. Sub-contracting more non-core activities may be needed. Some competitors or stakeholders are closing or merging. The organization is considering abandoning a number of activities that are either becoming obsolete or less sustainable.*
☐	3	*The organization has been closely monitoring the evolution of the business environment and has found that many similar organizations are embarking on partnerships. Best practices are being researched into the establishment of various forms of organizational partnerships, and the associated advantages and disadvantages are being studied. The organization faces issues in meeting the demands of its clients and stakeholders and is currently investigating to what extent some specific partnerships could be of benefit to the organization.*
☐	4	*The organization has experimented with a few partnerships to extend its reach and range of services and products. A thorough approach was taken to identify compatible partners. The organization now plans to examine other types of partnerships and possibly to evolve this into a strategic initiative.*
☐	5	*Several partnerships are in place that resulted from a strategy to strengthen the organization within its business environment. The organization is constantly looking for strategic partnership opportunities to complement its areas of expertise and to benefit from external knowledge and new networks. The organization also views partnerships as a way to reduce financial, operational, and reputational risks in the face of a turbulent and uncertain future. A policy exists to engage customers and/or stakeholders as partners in the achievement of the organizational mission. Co-creating value with all partners is paramount. Scenario planning activity takes potential partnerships into consideration.*

Once an organization performs its *Readiness Assessment* using the criteria described above, the results can be translated from a 1 to 5 scale to a percentage scale and plotted on a spider diagram, as illustrated in Figure 8-32.

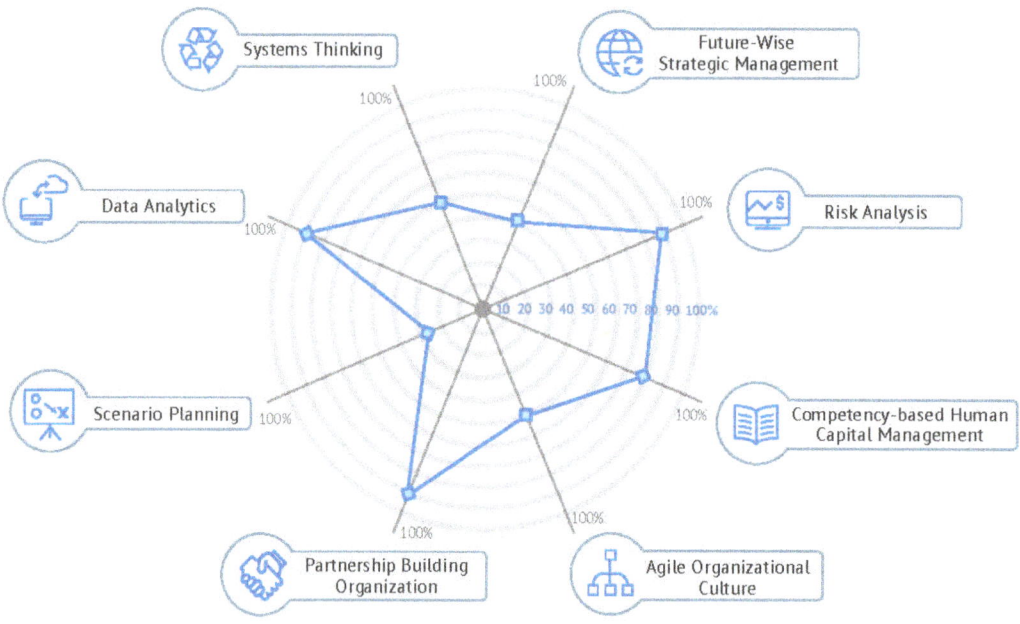

Figure 8-32 Sample future-wise readiness assessment results (ASI Institute).

IN THE END: IT IS ALL ABOUT PERFORMANCE

In the end, the ultimate purpose of organizations becoming future-wise is to sustain or improve their performance in the face of turbulence and uncertainty. Being future-wise is about *resiliency*. Focusing on key strategic drivers (i.e., the PASS elements: People, Assets, Systems, and Structure) is all about *performance excellence*.

Being future-wise is a deliberate posture and an indispensable building block for moving forward robustly. However, organizations need to leverage their future-wise state within their specific contextual environment to maximize their performance. The future-wise areas of excellence must exert impact on the PASS dimensions defined in the *Introduction* of this book in order to enable an organization to reach the "high-performance work organization" (HPWO) level.

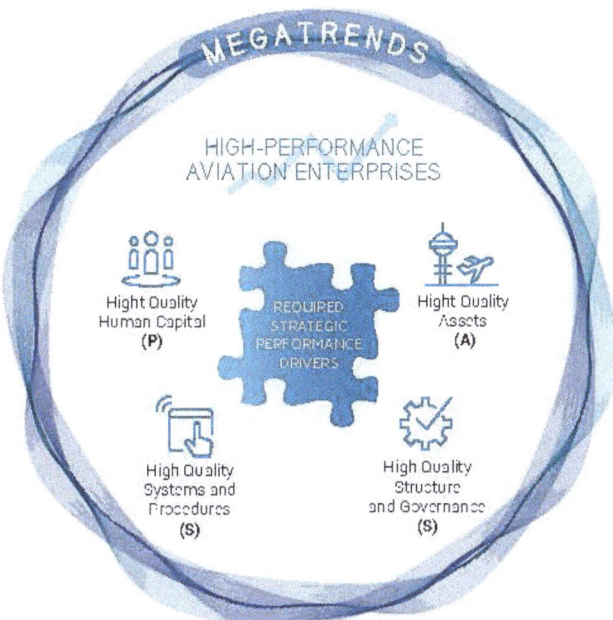

Figure 8-33 Megatrends and high-performance aviation enterprises PASS elements (ASI Institute).

According to Holbeche, in her book, "The High-Performance Organization: Creating Dynamic Stability and Sustainable Success", the future-wise state is characterized by the "ability to recognize the need to adapt to the surroundings that the organization operates in. High-performance organizations can quickly and efficiently change their operating structure and practices to meet needs...these organizations focus on long-term success while delivering on actionable short-term goals."[56]

The interaction between the future-wise areas of excellence and the pursuit of high performance by leading organizations is depicted in Figure 8-34.

The primary motivation behind this chapter was to make the case for the main require-ments for organizations to be best prepared to navigate the future successfully. In other words, future-ready organizations must excel in systems thinking, strategic management, scenario planning, data analytics, risk management, human competency building, agility, and partnerships. However, this has real meaning only in the context of the four PASS dimensions because it was already well known that, for an aviation industry organization, real success can only be achieved through the outstanding contributions of its human capital, its assets, its operating processes, and its governance system.

In essence, this is the main message that we mean to convey through this book.

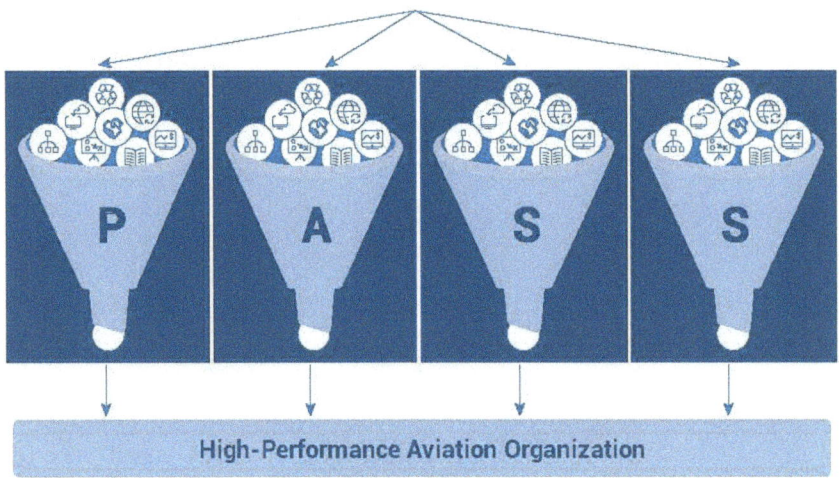

Figure 8-34 The PASS factors and high-performance aviation organizations (ASI Institute).

REFERENCES

[1]   European Environment Agency (EEA) (2010). The European environment—State and outlook. 2010. https://www.eea.europa.eu/soer/synthesis/synthesis.

[2]   Canton, J. (2015). *Future smart: Trends that will transform your world*. Philadelphia, PA: Da Capo Press.

[3]   Haines, S. G. (2000). *The systems thinking approach to strategic planning and management*. Boca Raton, FL: CRC Press.

[4]   Drucker, P. H. (1992). *Managing for the future*. New York, NY: Butterworth-Heinemann.

[5]   Kreibich, R. (2007). *All Tomorrow's Crises*. In: IP - Global Edition, Nr. Spring, "Limits to Growth", S. 11-15. http://www.ub.uni-koeln.de/ssg-bwl/archiv1/2009/67818_all_tomorrows_crisis.pdf

[6]   Dixon, P. (2015). *The future of almost everything: The global changes that will affect every business and all our lives*. London, UK: Profile Books.

[7]   Naisbitt, J., & Naisbitt, D. (2017). *Mastering megatrends: Understanding and leveraging the evolving new* world. World Scientific.

[8]   Ramirez, R., & Wilkinson, A. (2016). *Strategic reframing—The Oxford scenario planning approach*. Oxford, UK: Oxford University Press.

[9]   Kurzweil, R. (2000). *The age of spiritual machines: When computers exceed human intelligence*. Penguin Books.

[10]   Kitchin, R. (2014). The data revolution—Big *Data*, Open *Data, data* infrastructures and their consequences. London, UK: Sage.

[11]   Foroohar, R. (2017). *Makers and takers: How Wall Street destroyed Main Street*. New York, NY: Crown Business.

[12]   Mascarenhas, O. A. J. (2011). *Business transformation strategies: The strategic leader as innovation manager*. New Delhi, India: Sage.

[13]   Senge, P. (1990). *The fifth discipline: The art and practice of the learning organization*. Crown.

[14]   The Balanced Scorecard Institute, https://www.balancedscorecard.org/.

[15]   Ansoff, I. (1979, 2007). *Strategic management: Classic edition*. New York, NY: Palgrave MacMillan.

[16]   Oxford University, Said Business School. https://www.sbs.ox.ac.uk/.

[17]   Ramirez, R., & Wilkinson, A. (2016). *Strategic reframing—The Oxford scenario planning approach*. Oxford, UK: Oxford University Press.

[18]   Gidley, J. M. (2017). *The future: A very short introduction".* Oxford University Press.

[19]   van der Heijden, K. (2005). *The art of strategic conversation*. 2nd edition, Wiley.

[20]   Dawson, R. C., (2018). Why scenario thinking (more than scenario planning) is critical for executives today. Retrieved August 26, 2018, *https://rossdawson.com/blog/why_scenario_th/.*

[21]   Schwenker, B., & Wulf, T. (2017). *Scenario-based strategic planning*. Springer Gabler.

[22]   Ramirez, R., & Selin, C. (2014). Plausibility and probability in scenario planning. *Foresight, 16*(1), 54-74).

[23]   Lindgren M., & Bandhold, H. (2009). *Scenario planning: The link between future and strategy.* London, UK: Palgrave MacMillan).

[24]   Federal Aviation Agency (FAA) (2000, March). FAA aerospace forecasts. FAA-APO-00-1, Appendix A, March 2000. Retrieved August 27, 2018, from U.S. Department of Transport, Federal Aviation Administration, Office of Aviation Policies and Plans. https://www.faa.gov/data_research/aviation/aerospace_forecasts/2000-2011/.

[25]   Jacobson, R. (2013, April 24). 2.5 quintillion bytes of data created every day. How does CPG & Retail manage it? https://www.ibm.com/blogs/insights-on-business/consumer-products/2-5-quintillion-bytes-of-data-created-every-day-how-does-cpg-retail-manage-it/.

[26]   (2019). Gartner IT Glossary. *https://www.gartner.com/it-glossary*, retrieved February 3, 2019.

[27]   Abbott, D. (2014). *Applied predictive analytics.* Indianapolis, IN: Wiley.

[28]   Watson, R. (2008). *Future files—A brief history of the next 50 years.* Nicholas Brealey.

[29]   Watson, R. (2010). *Future minds.* Nicholas Brealey.

[30]   Malone, T. (2018). *Superminds: The surprising power of people and computers thinking together.* New York, NY: Little, Brown, and Company.

[31]   ASI Institute (2018). Airport Enterprise Management Centre: A step towards an industry standard. https://aviationstrategies.aero/?__hstc=36464127.05ac769c176dd0e33980f37b7a0eb92a.1547154594526.1547154594526.1547154594526.1&__hssc=36464127.65.1547493410634&__hsfp=1162517767.

[32]   Adobotech (2017, October 16). Cebu Pacific unveiled its customer command center. *http://www.adobotech.net/cebu-pacific-unveiled-its-customer-command-center*, retrieved on September 20, 2018.

[33]   Fischhoff, B., & Kadvany, J. (2011). *Risk: A very short introduction.* Oxford University Press.

[34]   Fischhoff, B., & Kadvany, J. (2011). *Risk: A very short introduction.* Oxford University Press.

[35]   World Economic Forum (2017). The global risks report 2017, 12th edition. Retrieved September 24, 2019, *http://www3.weforum.org/docs/GRR17_Report_web.pdf.*

[36]   Watson, W. T. (2016). Navigating risk in the transportation sector: Transportation risk index 2016. *https://www.ahcusa.org/uploads/2/1/9/8/21985670/ transportation_risk_index_ willis_tower_watson.pdf.*

[37]   Masson, M., & Morier, Y. (2012). Methodology to assess future risks: European Aviation Safety Plan (EASp)". *https://www.easa.europa.eu/sites/default/files/dfu/sms-docs-EASp-EME1.1-Methodology-to-Assess-Future-Risks---11-Dec-2012.pdf*, retrieved September 25, 2018.

[38]   Flouris, T. G., & Yilmaz, A. K. (2011). *Risk management and corporate sustainability in aviation.* Routledge; Watson, W. T. (2016). Navigating risk in the transportation sector: Transportation risk index 2016. *https://www.ahcusa.org/uploads/2/1/9/8/21985670/ transportation_risk_index_ willis_tower_watson.pdf, retrieved September 24, 2018.*

[39]   PwC Hungary (2018, January 22). CEO optimism booms despite increasing anxiety over threats to growth. https://www.pwc.com/hu/en/pressroom/2018/ceo_survey.html.

[40]   Deloitte (2018). Global human capital trends. https://www2.deloitte.com/insights/us/en/multimedia/videos/human-capital-trends-2018.html.

[41]   Institute for the Future (2011). The re-working of "work": Future work skills 2020. http://www.iftf.org/futureworkskills/

42   Schneider, P., and Bakhshi, H. (2017, September 27). The future of skills: Employment in 2030. https://www.nesta.org.uk/report/the-future-of-skills-employment-in-2030/.

43   Bakhshi, H., Downing, J. M., Osborne, M. A., and Schneider, P. (2017). *The future of skills: Employment in 2030*. University of Oxford, Oxford Martin Programme on Technology and Employment, London.

44   Senge, P. (1990). *The fifth discipline: The Art and Practice of the Learning Organization*. Bantam Doubleday Dell.

45   Meyer, P. (2015). *The agility shift: Creating AGILE and effective leaders, teams, and organizations*. Routledge.

46   Price, C., & Toye, S. (2017). *Accelerating performance: How organizations can mobilize, execute, and transform with agility*. Hoboken, New Jersey: John Wiley.

47   Aghina, W., De Smet, A., Lackey, G., Lurie, M., & Murarka, M. (2018). The five trademarks of agile organizations. https://www.mckinsey.com/business-functions/organization/our-insights/the-five-trademarks-of-agile-organizations.

48   Deloitte (2018). Global human capital trends. https://www2.deloitte.com/insights/us/en/multimedia/videos/human-capital-trends-2018.html.

49   Ramirez, R., & Mannervik, U. (2016). *Strategy for a networked world*. Imperial College Press.

50   McKenzie, R. (2001). *The relationship-based enterprise—powering business through customer relationship management*. McGraw-Hill, Ryerson.

51   https://www.worldairlineawards.com/worlds-best-low-cost-airlines-2018/

52   AirAsia and Google: *https://cloud.google.com/customers/airasia*

53   AirAsia and Airbus: *http://newsinflight.com/2018/02/13/airasias-entire-a320-and-a330-fleets-will-be-powered-by-skywise-predictive-maintenance-services*

54   AirAsia "OURSHOP": *https://www.moodiedavittreport.com/this-changes-everything-airasia-unveils-ourshop-digital-marketplace*.

55   Fernandes, T. (2017). *Flying High—My Story to QPR*. Portfolio Penguin.

56   Holbeche, L. (2005). *The high-performance organization: Creating dynamic stability and sustainable success*. Oxford, UK: Butterworth-Heinemann.

9

CONCLUSION

The driving force behind the creation of this "Global Megatrends and Aviation" book was a genuine belief by the collaborators that the future is quickly closing in on aviation organizations worldwide—a rapidly approaching future for which most of us in the industry are simply not prepared. In deciding to write this book, the co-authors believed that if they could shed significant light on what is coming and then couple that information with some practical tools for analyzing the future-preparedness of organizations, this would be a valuable step toward a better level of readiness among aviation industry organizations. The co-authors are steadfast in their belief that this book will help to lay the groundwork for the development of realistic forward-looking plans and strategies for the future.

At the beginning of this exercise, it was not at all clear whether this goal could actually be achieved. A couple of big questions loomed. The first was whether global megatrends affecting aviation could be defined clearly and be interpreted specifically in the aviation context and whether their impact on the international aviation industry could be clearly isolated. The second question, which was even more challenging, was whether it would be possible to develop a practical approach that aviation organizations could apply to analyze these megatrends and then use them to develop strategic plans for the future. Tremendous effort was required to answer these two questions, involving more than a year of applied teamwork: multiple brainstorming discussions, detailed subject-matter research, methodology development, more in-depth discussions, and drafting and re-drafting of texts. Now that all is said and done, the project team collaborators believe that the guidance that they have produced is valuable and will be helpful to aviation managers in preparing for the future.

Nevertheless, there is still a great deal to be done in this area. Global megatrends and their impact on worldwide aviation must be monitored consistently and on an ongoing basis. The methodologies and guidelines described in Chapter 8 of this book, which discusses how to develop a "future-wise aviation organization", must therefore be enhanced further and adapted over time. Additional research and development will be required to improve on these approaches, as well as to create innovative new tools and methods. This work should be carried out in a concerted and deliberate fashion in an effort to keep up with the rapidly approaching and ever-changing future that is already facing the aviation industry. At the speed that the world is moving on all fronts, organizations that do not keep pace risk quickly falling behind, and recovery will more than likely be very difficult. We believe that any aviation organization that wants to remain relevant and at the forefront of its sector in the industry must embrace and act on the information and tools documented in this volume.

As the creator and publisher of this book, the ASI Institute plans to remain proactive and relevant on this subject and will work to collaborate with other organizations involved in various facets of the international aviation industry.

In summary, the work documented in this book is far from over, and the Institute's contribution should be regarded as a modest first step in the ongoing challenge of developing realistic and responsive industry-wide methodologies that will hopefully aid aviation organizations to become future-wise. We believe that the need is there to continue monitoring and updating the impact of global megatrends on international aviation.

INDEX

smaller airports
    decreasing number of 300
small island developing states (SIDS) 124
small lightweight electric motors
    potential for aircraft design 278
small multidisciplinary special-purpose teams
    to provide agility 434
social benefits of air travel 190
social capital of airlines 154
social enterprise
    management philosophy 154
social media
    ubiquity of 348
    various roles of 348
southwestern United States
    flight cancelations due to excessive heat 2
Southwest Florida International Airport (RSW) 248
SpaceX 368
Special Drawing Rights (SDRs) 356
spread of diseases
    facilitated by air travel 366
spread of Western culture
    after Second World War 96
Standards and Recommended Practices
        (SARPs) 59, 61, 363
state-backed vs. alternative currencies 197
state capitalism 94
state-owned flag carriers 232
statistics about Web activity levels 341
strategic management
    developed at Harvard University 396
strategic planning
    definition 396
strategic planning cycle 399
strategy formulation
    common approach 398
subsidies to small airports 300
sustainable alternative fuels
    for aviation 29
sustainable aviation fuels (SAF) 57
sustainable consumption and production
    components of 31
Sustainable Energy for All (SE4ALL) initiative 29

sustainable fuels on commercial flights 57
sustainable patterns of production and
        consumption 28
sustaining technologies 271
Swissair 233
systems thinking 394

T

technology
    as component of change management 323
The Innovator's Dilemma 271
The Population Bomb, Paul and Anne Ehrlich 222
thin point-to-point routes 285
thirty-minute city 180
time-based separation (TBS) 52
tipping point
    50% middle-class or rich households 226
Toffler, Alvin, The Third Wave 94
Toronto Pearson Airport
    case study 205
tourism
    impact of Internet on 359
Transportation as a Service (TaaS). See Mobility
        as a Service (MaaS)
transport infrastructure
    to support high-density population growth 187
tube-and-wings design 274
TUNA conditions 402, 414, 433
turbofan engine
    data generation by 292

U

Uber car service
    example of UX-based operation 304
UK Civil Aviation Authority (CAA)
    guidelines respecting autistic travelers 258
ultra-private networks 346
UN Conference on the Environment (Rio de
        Janeiro (Brazil), 1992) 31
under-utilized airports
    use to spread capacity 239
Union of Concerned Scientists (UCS) 31

CPSIA information can be obtained
at www.ICGtesting.com
Printed in the USA
LVHW082126040619
620162LV00001B/2/P